Isak Dinesen

Isak Dinesen

The Life of a Storyteller

JUDITH THURMAN

ST. MARTIN'S PRESS
New York

Grateful acknowledgment is made for permission to reprint from the following: *Letters from Africa: 1914–1931* by Isak Dinesen, ed. by Frans Lasson, trans. by Anne Born, copyright © 1981 by the University of Chicago Press; *Out of Africa* by Isak Dinesen, copyright 1938 by Random House, Inc.; *Seven Gothic Tales* by Isak Dinesen, copyright 1934 by Harrison Smith and Robert Haas, Inc.; *Winter's Tales* by Isak Dinesen, copyright 1942 by Random House, Inc.; *Tanne, Min Søster Karen Blixen* by Thomas Dinesen, copyright © 1974 by Gyldendal; *My Sister, Isak Dinesen* by Thomas Dinesen, trans. by Joan Tate, copyright © 1975 by Michael Joseph, Ltd.; *Titania: The Biography of Isak Dinesen* by Parmenia Migel, copyright © 1967 by Random House, Inc.; *Notater om Karen Blixen* by Clara Selborn, copyright © 1974 by Gyldendal; *Romance for Valdhorn* by Ole Wivel, copyright © 1972 by Gyldendal; *Pagten* by Thorkild Bjørnvig, copyright © 1974 by Gyldendal; *The Gayety of Vision: A Study of Isak Dinesen's Art* by Robert Langbaum, copyright © 1964 by Random House, Inc. Gyldendal has granted permission to quote from letters by Mrs. Westenholz, Wilhelm Dinesen, Ingeborg Dinesen, Mary Bess Westenholz, and Ea Neergaard. Torben Dahl has granted permission to quote from letters written by Ellen Dahl and Knud Dahl. The estate of Robert Haas and Random House, Inc., provide permission to quote from letters written by Robert Haas.

Design by Dennis J. Grastorf

Library of Congress Cataloging in Publication Data

Thurman, Judith, 1946–
   Isak Dinesen: the life of a storyteller.

   Bibliography: p. 467
   Includes index.
   1. Dinesen, Isak, 1885–1962—Biography.
2. Authors, Danish—20th century—Biography.
I. Title.
PT8175.B545Z89   839.8'1372 [B]   82–5573
ISBN 0-312-43738-2   AACR2

for my parents,
Alice Meisner Thurman
and
William A. Thurman

Contents

CONTENTS

BOOK THREE: ISAK DINESEN

BOOK FOUR: PELLEGRINA

Contents

List of Illustrations

[ix]

Acknowledgments

THIS IS THE FIRST BIOGRAPHY of Isak Dinesen to make use of the large number of letters, unpublished manuscripts, and family documents in her archives, and while it is not in any way an "authorized" biography, I am inestimably grateful to the Rungstedlund Foundation and the Dinesen family for their permission to quote from this material. Without the particular and generous help of Mr. and Mrs. Thomas Dinesen, Clara Selborn, Ingeborg Michelsen, and Ole Wivel this book would not have been possible.

I can never adequately thank the people who have helped me in the course of the past seven years: who have talked to me about art, life, and Isak Dinesen; who have given me books, letters, and photographs; who have done research; read my manuscript; offered me hospitality; and kept up my courage. I hope that they will understand if I simply list their names in alphabetical order, and express my deepest gratitude.

Lady Altrincham; Hans Andersen; Christopher Aschan; Ulf Aschan; Birthe Andrup; Ann Barret; Peter Beard; Thorkild Bjørnvig; Doria and Jack Block; Anne Born; Hans Henrik Bruun; Suzanne Brøgger; Rose Cartwright; Beatrice Cazac; Charlotte Christensen; Meghan Collins; Merwyn Cowie; Michael Denneny; Paul Dinas; Deborah Emin; Anna Falck; Nina and Bill Finkelstein; Dr. Mogens Fog; Mr. Hans Folsach; Dr. Vibeke Funch; Kamante Gatura; Winston Guest; Robert Hamburger; Esther Henius; Cockie Hoogterp; Elspeth Huxley; Bjarne Jørnæs; Carl Kähler; Nathaniel Kivoi; Gustav Kleen; Anne Kopp; Erik Kopp; Robert Langbaum; Frans Lasson; Ingrid Lindström; Ernst Lohse; Kaare Olsen; Dr. Duncan MacDonald; Nieves Mathews de Madariaga; David Mairowitz; Beryl Markham; Sir Charles Markham; Esmond and Chrysee Bradley Martin; Remy Martin; Eve Merriam; Charlotte Meisner; Bent Mohn; the late Cynthia Nolan; Bert Phillips; Morris Philipson; Judith Rascoe; Anita Rasmussen; Steen Eiler Rasmussen; Lilian Moore Reavin; Count Christian Reventlow; Countess Sybille Reventlow; Michael Roloff; Martha Saxton; Robert Seidman; Betty Sih; Ruth Sullivan; Alice Thurman; Eva Thurman; Errol Trzebinski; Finn Ulrich; Diana Wylie.

I would like to thank two generous institutions, the National Endowment for the Humanities and the MacDowell Colony, for their support of my work. And I would like to thank the staffs of the Royal Library in Copenhagen and of St. Martin's Press.

Finally, I would like to thank my husband, Jonathan David—who has never known me or a married life without Isak Dinesen—for his all-enabling love.

JUDITH THURMAN
New York City
February 11, 1982

Note on Citations

KAREN BLIXEN'S ARCHIVES, which contain her manuscripts, correspondence, and other personal papers, are abbreviated throughout the citations as KBA. They are housed in the Royal Library, Copenhagen, and permission from the Rungstedlund Foundation is necessary to consult them. When citing material from the archives, I have used the archives' own master index numbers and numerals. There are 105 file envelopes of letters by, to, and about Karen Blixen. Her manuscripts begin, with her earliest childhood notebooks, in file 106. There are 52 folders of manuscripts and notebooks, numbered 106–157, and another 40 folders containing typescripts, reviews, articles, interviews, drawings, diary notes, speeches, pertinent manuscripts by other authors and family members, *dubia,* and miscellany. They are numbered 158–197.

The only major collection of papers that does not belong to the archives is Karen Blixen's correspondence with Robert Haas, which is on file at Random House, her American publishers, and a copy of which Mr. Morris Philipson, publisher of the University of Chicago Press, has most kindly made available to me.

I have used the following abbreviations for Isak Dinesen's major published works. All references are to their American editions:

SGT *Seven Gothic Tales*
OA *Out of Africa*
WT *Winter's Tales*
LT *Last Tales*
AD *Anecdotes of Destiny*
SG *Shadows on the Grass*

In quoting from unpublished correspondence and from interviews, I have used the following abbreviations:

For the family:
KB Karen Blixen
Ea Ea de Neergaard

ED	Ellen Dahl
MrsD	Ingeborg Dinesen
TD	Thomas Dinesen
WD	Wilhelm Dinesen
IM	Ingeborg Michelsen (Thomas Dinesen's younger daughter)
MrsW	Mary Westenholz ("Mama")
MBW	Mary Bess Westenholz ("Aunt Bess")

Other:

TB	Thorkild Bjørnvig
RH	Robert Haas
DFH	Denys Finch Hatton
IL	Ingrid Lindström
SER	Steen Eiler Rasmussen
CS	Clara Svendsen
OW	Ole Wivel

Certain people who granted me interviews requested anonymity. In these few cases I have supplied the date and place of the interview.

Most of my own research and writing was completed by the time Isak Dinesen's *Letters from Africa, 1914–1931* was published in Anne Born's excellent English translation. In most cases I have substituted her translations for my own, but in some cases I have kept my own translations from the Danish original, and then I have given the page numbers in both editions. This has also been done where I have used my own translations from Thomas Dinesen's memoir, *Tanne, Min Søster Karen Blixen,* rather than the English translation by Joan Tate, *My Sister, Isak Dinesen.* All other translations from the Danish, the French, and so forth are my own, where they are not otherwise credited.

ISAK DINESEN'S PATERNAL FAMILY AND RELATIONS

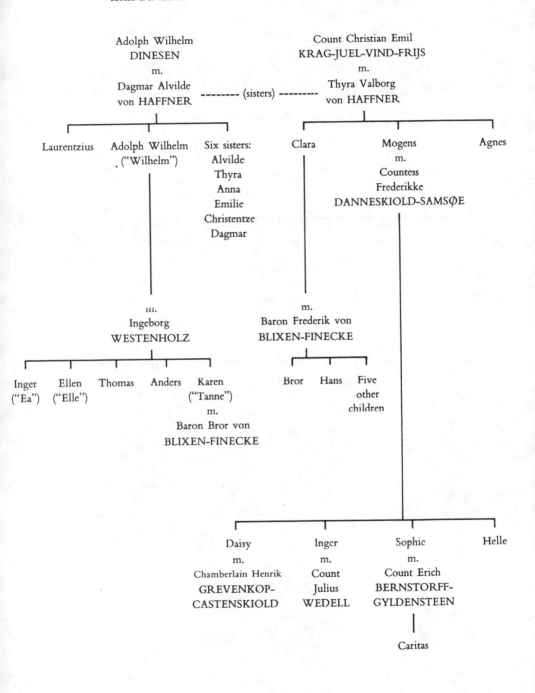

Adolph Wilhelm **DINESEN**
m.
Dagmar Alvilde **von HAFFNER**

-------- (sisters) ---------

Count Christian Emil **KRAG-JUEL-VIND-FRIJS**
m.
Thyra Valborg **von HAFFNER**

Laurentzius

Adolph Wilhelm ("Wilhelm")

Six sisters:
Alvilde
Thyra
Anna
Emilie
Christentze
Dagmar

Clara

Mogens
m.
Countess
Frederikke
DANNESKIOLD-SAMSØE

Agnes

III.
Ingeborg **WESTENHOLZ**

m.
Baron Frederik von **BLIXEN-FINECKE**

Inger ("Ea")

Ellen ("Elle")

Thomas

Anders

Karen ("Tanne")
m.
Baron Bror von **BLIXEN-FINECKE**

Bror

Hans

Five other children

Daisy
m.
Chamberlain Henrik **GREVENKOP-CASTENSKIOLD**

Inger
m.
Count Julius **WEDELL**

Sophie
m.
Count Erich **BERNSTORFF-GYLDENSTEEN**

Helle

Caritas

[xv]

ISAK DINESEN'S MATERNAL FAMILY AND RELATIONS

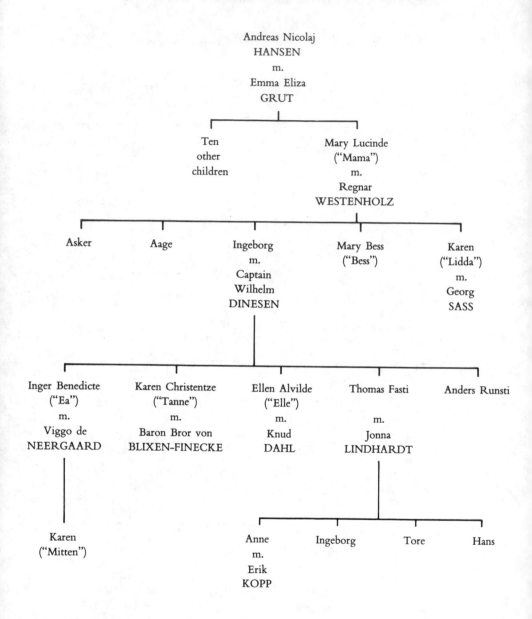

Andreas Nicolaj
HANSEN
m.
Emma Eliza
GRUT

Ten other children

Mary Lucinde
("Mama")
m.
Regnar
WESTENHOLZ

Asker   Aage   Ingeborg
m.
Captain
Wilhelm
DINESEN   Mary Bess
("Bess")   Karen
("Lidda")
m.
Georg
SASS

Inger Benedicte
("Ea")
m.
Viggo de
NEERGAARD   Karen Christentze
("Tanne")
m.
Baron Bror von
BLIXEN-FINECKE   Ellen Alvilde
("Elle")
m.
Knud
DAHL   Thomas Fasti
m.
Jonna
LINDHARDT   Anders Runsti

Karen
("Mitten")

Anne
m.
Erik
KOPP   Ingeborg   Tore   Hans

Book One

TANNE

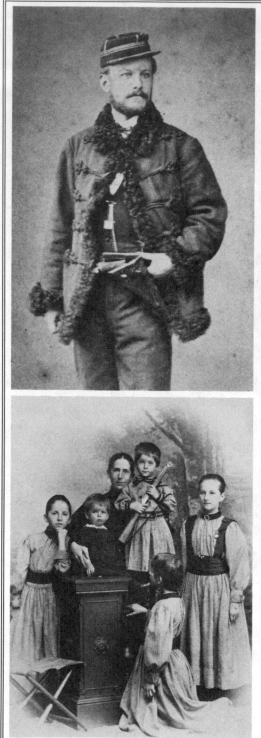

Above left: Wilhelm Dinesen as a young lieutenant at the time of the Dano–Prussian War (1864). *Above right:* Ingeborg Westenholz and Captain Wilhelm Dinesen at the time of their engagement (1880). *Left:* Ingeborg Dinesen and her children in a photograph taken shortly after Wilhelm's death (1896). Tanne is at the far left. Thomas holds his first gun.

Right: Tanne Dinesen (left) and her cousin, Daisy Frijs (Countess Anne Margrethe Krag-Juel-Vind-Frijs) *c.* 1910. *Below:* "Mama" (seated, center, in the cap) surrounded by her children and grandchildren on her seventieth birthday, July 24, 1904. Aunt Bess sits on Mama's left. Next to her is Ea Dinesen. Ingeborg and Aunt Lidda sit on Mama's right. Seated, bottom, left to right: Thomas and Elsebet Westenholz; Anders and Thomas Dinesen. Standing, left to right: Elle Dinesen; George Sass ("Uncle Gex"); Ulla and Aage Westenholz; Asker Westenholz; Tanne Dinesen; the housekeeper; Sanne the Westenholz nanny.

One must pay dearly for immortality:
one has to die several times while still alive.
                                    —FRIEDRICH NIETZSCHE
                                    Ecce Homo

It is to a poet a thing of awe
to find that his story is true.
                                    —ISAK DINESEN
                                    "The Diver"

Introduction

SHE WAS BORN Dinesen on April 17, 1885, and christened Karen Christentze. Her family called her "Tanne," which was her own mispronunciation of Karen and a nickname—forever diminutive—that she disliked. She subsequently took or acquired other names: Osceola, her first pseudonym; Baroness von Blixen-Finecke, by her marriage to a Swedish cousin; Tania and Jerie to her white and black African familiars, respectively; Isak, "the one who" —with a certain noble perversity—"laughs." Her admirers often called her after her own characters or imaginary incarnations. To a childhood playmate she was "Lord Byron." To her secretary she was the old battle horse, Khamar. To various literary disciples she was Pellegrina, Amiane, or Scheherazade. In Denmark, when she was elderly, she was spoken of and to almost universally as *Baronessen,* the Baroness, in the third person, according to feudal usage. The name on her tombstone is Karen Blixen.

These names had their own etiquette, logic, and geography. They were separate entrances to her presence, varying in grandeur and accessibility. But the name "Dinesen," unmodified either by a sexual or a Christian identity, was that idea of herself and her origins which the child carried with her into old age. It expressed what she considered essential in her life: the relation to her father, to his family, to a sense that they were a tribe—a *stamme,* in Danish—a rootstock. When she reclaimed the name Dinesen in middle age to sign her fiction with it, it was a gesture typical of her spiritual economy. It was also the storyteller's love of fate.

I

Either/Or

Morality is three-quarters of life, and sex is one-half of morality.[1]

I

ISAK DINESEN was born to two people who embodied very different attitudes to life. The Westenholzes, her mother's family, were exemplary bourgeois. The men of the family were traders, self-made millionaires; rich by their own adroitness, hard work, and frugality. The women were high-minded and accomplished. They were also—which was rarer—passionate feminists and noncomformists, converts to the Unitarian Church. But while it was an immensely vigorous family, it was not a vital one. Their energies went into practical or abstract projects, and mostly toward their own moral excellence. Life was like a long and costly mortgage to them; they were debtors in relation to existence, slowly paying off their souls.

The symmetry is not perfect, for her father's people were by no means a band of decadents or esthetes, nor were they titled. But where the Westenholzes were urban, literate, and squeamish, the Dinesens were country people —affable and lavish—and cousins to the greatest noblemen in the kingdom. The men tended to be virile and opinionated, the women elegant and pretty, and by Westenholz standards somewhat "frivolous and shallow."[2] They did not feel bound to leave a mark upon the world but had an aristocratic confidence of their place in it: a sense that "existence itself was obviously inherited"[3]—with no moral liens. Their hands were free. Isak Dinesen remembered them to have, and felt she had inherited, "a great, wild joy at being alive."[4]

From her childhood Isak Dinesen saw the two families as antitheses, one infinitely alluring, the other infinitely problematic. She steadfastly claimed that she was "not like"[5] her mother's family and that they disliked her. She rebelled at their contempt and fear of the erotic, and at the relentless surveillance that had enforced it, depriving her childhood of its rightful charge. In this revolt, the central drama of her life, her father was an ally and an

[6]

inspiration. While he lived, which was not long, he rescued her from the Westenholzes physically, and after his death he continued to act as the emissary of life's dangerous powers. Indeed, where Isak Dinesen uses the word "life" it is often synonymous with the word "father."

But she also inherited many qualities from her mother's family, and in particular she had their sometimes oppressive self-demand. The Westenholzes had implicit faith in the virtue of self-making, and even Christ's example was to them, as devout Unitarians, one of unique moral greatness, achieved rather than innate. Life seemed immoral without some calling and the tireless effort necessary to bring it to fruition. All of the children tried to find such a calling. Isak Dinesen's brother, Thomas, sought it in battle, volunteering in the First World War and emerging from it with the Victoria Cross. Her younger sister, Elle, sought it through marriage and social work, and wrote several books of high-toned parables. Her older sister, Ea, devoted her life to classical music, then to motherhood, and died young. Anders, the youngest, slower than the others, less articulate, was a kind of casualty. He lived quietly on a family farm and was treated by the others as something of a bumpkin. Tanne was probably the most ambitious, the most self-critical of the siblings. Her life had a series of great aims and tasks, and the tales she began to write at the age of forty-six "redeemed"—in her grandmother's sense—a promise that had long been outstanding. But as much as this ambition was native to her, she also recoiled from it, concealed it behind pseudonyms and nonchalance, envied and desired to belong to that miraculously static world where there were no panting arrivals, no personal triumphs or inadequacies. To the "nobleman" as she described him, "individual talents and characteristics were supposed to be concerns of human beings outside his sphere. . . ."[6]

This was not precisely the "sphere" of the Dinesens, and if you look closely, the image of a symbolic antithesis between the families dissolves into a multitude of distracting details. But if you stand back, far enough so that they become silhouettes, it is possible to see the two sides as Dinesen herself did, against the background of a great cultural conflict—and then they are face to face. This is the conflict that had emerged in the nineteenth century with the rise of the bourgeoisie, and which Kierkegaard reflected upon in *Either/Or* (1843), opposing the "ethical" to the "sensuous-esthetic," the instinctual to the moral life. It was this dialectic, much elaborated, that would dominate Danish culture for the rest of the century, and which Isak Dinesen encountered in the literature and philosophy she read as a young woman, in the plays and lectures she attended, in the public debates on sexual freedom and women's rights, and in the political struggles between the conservative aristocracy and the liberal middle class (and later the rising socialist coalition of small farmers and urban laborers). The intellectual schema she got from her times fit her own primary experience with unlikely precision. And when she shows herself, in her tales, such an excellent historian of the Romantic "split," it is because she had a kind of carnal knowledge of her material.

The poles Isak Dinesen knew as Dinesen/Westenholz, freedom/taboo, aristocrat/bourgeois organized her ways of feeling and her stock of images like a magnetic field, sorting its contents, giving them the beauty of a pattern. In an earlier age such a pattern would unabashedly have been called Destiny. The modern biographer more cautiously says that hers is a "readable" life. Events seem to fall into place, and even small details are conserved, to appear later at some dramatic moment. They are like those birthmarks by which, in the old tales, one recognized the lost royal child.

By the time Isak Dinesen began to write, she believed there was an absolute sense, a divine Intention to life. In such a scheme, if you can be faithful to it, the losses will seem inevitable. And it is this confidence that gives her fiction its immense authority to console.

2

The great bourgeois fortune that staked Isak Dinesen to her African farm began to accumulate at the turn of the nineteenth century. Her great-grandfather was a man named Andreas Nicolaj Hansen who owned ships and made a killing during the Napoleonic Wars. He continued to expand his fleet, and it made him one of the richest men in Copenhagen. During the 1820s he married a minister's daughter from the Isle of Guernsey and built her a great house on the Bredgade. This was the capital's finest street, lined with the rococo palaces of the nobility. The Hansens' austere neoclassic mansion went up on a corner, and in that neighborhood their name, too, struck a defiantly plain and solid note—the cock's crow of a new age.

*Oldefader** Hansen was an abusive husband who gave his wife a diamond for every child, eleven in all. She lost the jewels, and the children grew up quarrelsome and unhappy. Some of them, resenting the way their father had used their mother, took her name: Grut. The family had its saint, its black sheep, and its beauty—this was Mary, the second eldest daughter. Her long face had a picturesque severity that might almost have been Sienese or Spanish, an interesting face to a painter of madonnas. The slight arch of the nose, the pallor, the narrowness of brow and lip were inherited by her own daughter, Ingeborg Westenholz, and by her granddaughter, Isak Dinesen.

The Hansen children lived in the shadow of their father's "violence, peevishness and pessimism,"[7] unprotected by their mother, who was weak. They all clung to their reason and feared their senses with great tenacity. It was said of them by a contemporary that they resembled the English Puritans: their spirits were undoubtedly great, but they enjoyed no horizontal mobility; they were forced either up or down.

Mary Hansen, who was to play such a bleak role in her granddaughter's

---

*Great-grandfather.

life, was a spiritually ambitious woman. She aspired to be a perfect wife; a
perfectly good woman; an exemplary mother, Christian, and patriot. As she
was demanding of herself, she was militant toward the imperfections of
others. Her vehemence was nourished by the moment in history when she
had come of age: the revolution of 1848, the war against Prussia, and the
period of Liberal rule that followed the victory. It was a stirring moment
to be conscientious and bourgeois, allied with the forces that had brought
the king to accept Denmark's first democratic constitution and to abolish
many of the old privileges and abuses of the aristocracy.

The "moral and ethical laws"[8] Mary Hansen lived by were imposed
strictly, and with a kind of coercive warmth, upon her children and grandchildren. Her sense of "good and evil" was overdeveloped, even for her
times; she believed her judgment on the subject was irrefutable;[9] and she
would paint the dangers of sexuality, in particular, in the "blackest" and
"most dreadful" colors.[10] It seems that she had had one poignant experience
with this side of life that had confirmed its danger for her. Isak Dinesen knew
the story and was perhaps thinking of it when she wrote about Emilie
Vandamm and Charlie Dreyer in "The Dreaming Child." There are in her
tales any number of fierce, withered old ladies who once felt a spark of
passion and were terrified by it. Mary's spark was ignited by her music
teacher, "a long-haired and poor man, who cut something of the *romanfigur*
in the sober milieu of the Bredgade."[11] Her father somehow learned of the
attachment and suppressed it with his usual brutality, kicking the young man
down the stairs. Whatever he did or said to Mary so humiliated her that she
"henceforth considered it a terrible disgrace for a young girl to encourage
a fruitless proposal."[12] When the original feelings had receded a little they
left—etched in a stubborn and proud character—an indelible mistrust of
erotic love.

Mary Hansen married a man of her father's world, a "self-made" man,
someone the old shipowner could and did admire. She was twenty-one and
he, Regnar Westenholz, was thirty-eight, a widower with a son. His origins
were modest; he was the son of a town clerk from Skagen, in the north of
Jutland, and the scion of Hanoverian parsons. After his own father's death
he became an apprentice to an Aalborg merchant, and later a partner in a
commodities firm that traded corn. He had an almost awesome touch for
making money. On the day the English Parliament repealed the corn laws
Westenholz had ships, laden with corn, riding at anchor in the Thames
estuary. His main office was in London, where he had met his future bride,
then still a maiden of seventeen, on a visit to her mother's family. It was
important to him that she spoke English beautifully and shared his ideals of
a pious, quiet, and disciplined family life.

Regnar and Mary rather quickly had five children. In 1852 he retired from
trade to an estate in Jutland—Matrup—near the town of Horsens and de-

voted himself to the pastimes of a country gentleman: speculating in railroads, improving his stock, experimenting with farming techniques, and collecting books. His library of nineteenth-century Danish classics, bound in morocco, found its way to Africa with his granddaughter. He also found time to stand for Parliament. After one term in the lower house he became a financial counselor to the king and, for a year, minister of finance. His Majesty once honored Matrup with a visit, bringing his mistress. This controversial figure, the Countess Danner, had been a ballet dancer and a milliner in her youth. Now she had six double chins, smoked a pipe, and laughed heartily at her lover's somewhat familiar jokes. The young Mrs. Westenholz endured this trial with aplomb.

Daguerreotypes of Regnar Westenholz show a slight, grizzled man with rather untidy whiskers, a pompadour, and a judicious air. According to his daughter Bess, he was "an individualist and a liberal, with an outstanding sense of practicality."[13] His family revered him, and his grandson Thomas called him "a warm-hearted and indulgent papa to his children"[14]—except in sexual matters, for which he, like his wife, had much high-minded disgust. An interesting story survives in the family archives. Once Regnar Westenholz summoned his eldest son into the study to question him about a "suspicious" sickliness. "Have you," he began, "been smitten in a loathesome and abominable manner by a disease which means that no honorable person will ever again have anything to do with you?"[15] Fortunately for his honor, the young man had an ulcer.

Regnar's own death, in 1864, was due to strictly decorous natural causes. His widow, at thirty-four, was devastated by the loss. The family had little social life beyond its own confines and had lived with unusual intensity and interdependence within them. Now Mary Westenholz gathered her children even more closely around her, never put off her mourning, decided that to have a Christmas tree at any point in the future would be unseemly, and undertook to administer her tremendous fortune and the estate herself. She became increasingly formidable as a parent; in an "affectionate but firm way [she] directed her children's minds and thoughts . . . for the rest of their lives."[16] Of the six children, three were daughters: Ingeborg, born in 1856; Mary Bess, born in 1857; and Karen, who was called Lidda, born in 1861. Ingeborg was a sweet-natured and obliging child, and her mother's pet. This makes it the more interesting that she would, at the age of twenty-five, marry Wilhelm Dinesen. For it was a union uncongenial to both families.

3

The Dinesens also lived in Jutland, and Isak Dinesen's two grandfathers, both major landowners in the same province, had corresponded about farming and politics. The Dinesens' lands, which lay to the south of Grenaa, were rather bleak and windswept, and their manor, Katholm, was a red-brick castle built in the sixteenth century. The estate had come into the family in 1839, but the Dinesens themselves were part of that steep, vertical world that still had its roots in feudalism. Dinessøns, "sons of Denis," had risen up through village politics and the trades to become at first modest and then considerable landowners. Before the seventeenth century, however, their ancestors had been peasants.

Isak Dinesen's grandfather, Adolph Wilhelm, was originally a soldier, "the first Dinesen in uniform"[17]—a tradition that has been carried on by every subsequent generation. He fought in the 1848 war against the Prussians and commanded a valiant "Dinesen Battery." But as a young lieutenant, with nothing much to do, he had traveled through Italy for a while, joining up with his compatriot Hans Christian Andersen between Milan and Rome. Andersen, not yet famous, was large-nosed, effusive, virginal, and greedy to be loved. Dinesen, a little younger, was peremptory, dogmatic, self-centered, and good-looking. He got fed up with the sensitive *artiste* and soon went his own way. "How very much," sniffled Andersen to his journal, "I have learned from this young, determined person, who has so often hurt me in my affection for him. If only I had his character, even with its flaws. Adieu, D!"[18]

Eager to see action, Adolph Wilhelm enlisted with the French army for a tour of duty in Algeria. Colonial warfare was disillusioning. "Wherever the French turned up in Africa," he would remember, "the trees disappeared, the wells dried up, the inhabitants fled, and all that remained was the desert."[19] The misuse of real estate made him indignant, and after his return to Denmark he bought Katholm and its extensive, challenging terrain at public auction. The lands were neglected, the landscape poetically wild, and Dinesen systematically made them into a "gold mine,"[20] draining fields, planting forests, investing his capital in farm machinery, and bullying his workers into greater productivity.

After acquiring his estate, Adolph Wilhelm married, fathered eight children, and continued his career as a bully on a domestic scale. A daughter remembered that for some principle, obscure even then, the children were obliged to gather around the dining table in the evening to share a reading light, while Adolph Wilhelm sat alone in splendor, burning lamps on every side. His wife, Dagmar Alvilde von Haffner, was the daughter of a general. Her mother had lived as the general's mistress for years before their relationship was legitimized, but this did not affect the social position of her two daughters. The younger, Thyra, married Count Krag-Juel-Vind-Frijs, the greatest landowner and premier nobleman in Denmark. The Frijs and Dinesen cousins would be closely tied for several generations.

Of the Dinesens' eight children, six were daughters and two were sons. Christentze, the youngest but one, was the godmother and the idol of her niece, Tanne. Two of the sisters never married and became the models for the spinsters in "A Supper at Elsinore." One of these, "Aunt Emy" (Emilie Augusta), left her niece a small inheritance. Tanne once called her "God's chosen snob," adding that she herself was His chosen snob as well. "If I cannot be with the aristocracy or the intelligentsia I must go down among the proletariat . . . the real aristocrats . . . for the proletariat have nothing to risk. But the middle class always has something to risk, and the Devil is there among them in his worst, that is to say, his very pettiest, form."[21]

Family annals are rather more informative about the two sons. Laurentzius Dinesen, the elder, joined the army but never had any serious ambition for advancement. He led an easy and somewhat careless life, was vain of his good looks, and Isak Dinesen describes, in *Daguerreotypes,* how he made a career of them. Lacking his father's "determination" and his younger brother's passion and depth, he became a "blusterer"[22] in later years and liked to exaggerate his youthful triumphs. He could not administer the complicated estate; it began to decay, and, after his death and the premature death of his son, Katholm passed out of the family.

The younger son, Adolph Wilhelm, was born in 1845 but dropped the "Adolph" and vigorously resisted all further resemblance to his reactionary father. He inherited, as the cadet, a status defined by what it was not: the not-heir. There was a certain casualness inherent to this condition, a lightness that was itself potentially a burden. Many younger sons were blown like milkweed to the colonies, or dissipated by other forms of casualness, and they often marked a space rather than occupied a position in their families.

From their fantasies about him, we gather that Wilhelm was a romantic figure to his younger sisters. His son Thomas describes him as the *enfant terrible* of the family, both its darling and its troublemaker. He was an immensely restive and vital man, and if he was not at war, he was hunting or in love —all three "affair[s] of the heart." Isak Dinesen was perhaps thinking of him when she wrote: "Eroticism runs through the entire existence of the great wanderers."[23]

After the adventurous part of his life was over, he wrote several books. One, a highly personal and yet stylized epistolary memoir, *Letters from the Hunt,* has become a minor classic of Danish literature. His daughter was surprised that the work was still so well read in her own day but complained that the "lightness" of his style misled people, who perceived him—and tended to dismiss him—as superficial *("un élégant").* He was, she felt, "serious in a way that was different from other people."[24]

2

The Captain

There are free, impudent spirits who would like to deny that at bottom they are broken, incurable hearts.

—Nietzsche[1]

I

WILHELM DINESEN was a supremely distracted *(adspredt)* man: that is the word his friend, Georg Brandes, chooses for him.[2] It is Brandes who provides the best literary portrait of Wilhelm—in a survey of his work, written in 1889, and in an obituary, written in 1895, shortly after he had committed suicide. Brandes is no longer widely known outside Scandinavia, but he was the greatest critic of his age: the man who championed Ibsen and "discovered" Nietzsche, who wrote a sweeping intellectual history of Romanticism that is still exciting to read today, and who was responsible for the fifty years of intellectual foment that the Danes call their "modern breakthrough" period. Brandes would have enormous influence on nearly all of Scandinavia's major writers, including Isak Dinesen, whose attraction to him was enhanced by the fact that he had known her father.

Brandes describes Wilhelm as an elusive, passionate, and rather troubled man, always in search of "a more intense experience of his being."[3] He found this intensity first in war, and whenever it eluded him later in his life, his impulse was to re-enlist. He loved war "for its own sake . . . with an artist's love"[4] and could write of it: "Bayonettes like diamonds have their *beaux jours* . . . It is young blood which enchants them both."[5] War has another sort of charm for those who are deeply malcontent: it can annihilate the personal at the same time that it sharpens the will to live.

Wilhelm's first experience in battle came during the Dano-Prussian War of 1864. Thomas Dinesen gives us a glimpse of his father as a young second lieutenant, stepping forth, after a cease-fire, to speak over the dead. The bodies were arranged in rows, waiting for a priest. Wilhelm seized the moment to give his own tumultuous feelings a voice. "The right word simply came from him at that instant . . . and he spoke in verse, something to affect both the enemy and the friend."[6]

Denmark was defeated by the Prussians and forced to cede the south Jutland border duchies of Schleswig and Holstein. This was not only a humiliation for the army, but a devastating economic and demographic loss, as the two provinces represented a third of Denmark's territory and two-fifths of its population. After the war there was a period of paralysis, a common sense of "being left behind in a small, weak kingdom without any prospects."[7] Brandes believed the generation that fought the war suffered collectively from a feeling of failure, made particularly bitter in relation to their fathers' victory over the Prussians in 1848. Many of them, he observed, turned "inward," attempted to "bury themselves" in domestic and even selfish pursuits. Like the romantics of a previous generation in France and Germany, Wilhelm Dinesen sought his private peace by "surrendering his being to Nature, spirit, fantasy . . . to the love of freedom and the pursuit of Eros."[8] He became a man who gave the impression, both in his conversation and his writing, that he was "elsewhere"—inaccessible, wrapped up with some private joy or sadness. Brandes describes him as looking, despite having been an "officer with life and soul," like "a dreamer in broad daylight," and as being "an eccentric and an original whose being was a little loosely knit."[9]

After the war Wilhelm returned to the capital and cut that nonchalant but melancholy figure Isak Dinesen describes as Ib Angel in "Copenhagen Season." He learned to balance his sword and cap in one hand and his teacup in the other; he made the rounds of the game preserves and the boudoirs of high society, and toward the end of the decade, when he was twenty-five, he fell in love with his eighteen-year-old cousin, Countess Agnes Frijs. Agnes had an angelic little face, made to seem even smaller by the turret of braids she wore. She had been his childhood playmate, and her mother was Wilhelm's aunt. But they were by no means social equals, and he could have no realistic hopes to marry her. Two years later she died a nineteenth-century angel's death—catching typhoid on a trip to Rome. Wilhelm's sisters, and particularly Christentze, romanticized his attachment and grief for Agnes and went so far as to suggest that it drove him to suicide twenty-five years later. We do not know what he really felt beyond the single line he entered in his diary in April of 1871: "Letter from Bardenfleth, *Agnes død.*"[10] But later he wrote about "great passion" with a certain lofty reticence. He claimed that the deepest loves were aroused by what could not love you in return. This idealism appealed enormously to his daughter, who echoed his words: "A great passion, such as does really and truly devour your heart and soul, you cannot feel for individual beings. Perhaps you cannot feel it for anything which is capable of loving you in return. Those officers who have loved their armies, those lords who have loved their soil, they can talk about passion."[11]

When the Prussians declared war on France in 1870, Wilhelm, eager for a second go at them, resigned his commission in the Danish army to accept one in the French, as a captain of the eighteenth brigade. Throughout the winter his troops suffered one defeat after another, and in his journal he recorded that after the battle of Villargent "everyone burned a small candle to the Virgin, except me!"* By March the war was definitively lost. Wilhelm was briefly interned in Switzerland but managed to escape and made his way to Paris, arriving on the eve of the Commune. He was unprepared for the horror of the succeeding days—not, evidently, the horror of death and mutilation, but of what seemed to him the most mercenary and ignoble fratricide. His sympathies were with the Communards, and he wandered among the barricades, pausing to add a symbolic stone to each one. Later he irritated his father with the remark that he would have enjoyed seeing the red flag flying over the kaiser's palace in Berlin. But when the government's acts of repression provoked atrocities of spite from the citizens, Wilhelm's enthusiasm for their cause began to wane. "Soul-sick . . . dull and limp . . . nauseated by both sides,"[12] he returned to Katholm, with a feeling that he himself would never achieve anything. That summer he mourned Agnes "in silence, with his rifle around his neck,"[13] and five months later he sailed for North America.

2

The voyage to America was a traditional Romantic pilgrimage, and by the 1870s even something of a cliché.† Chateaubriand had undertaken it fifty years before, and *Atala* and *René* anticipate certain aspects of Wilhelm's sensibility. Like their author, Wilhelm was of the tribe of officers and younger sons, excitable and melancholy, prone to suffering from "repressed and therefore overpoweringly fatal loves."[14] They all sought serenity in the wilderness, inspiration from the courage and simplicity of its natives, and redemption through the trials of hardship and solitude. Their underlying assumption about Nature as the great moral force and their sense of Western culture as "the betrayal of the original distinction of mankind"[15] Isak Dinesen would take up in *Out of Africa*.

Wilhelm arrived in Quebec and made his way south to Chicago, where he looked up a banker cousin who introduced him to a coterie of Danish émigrés—hard-living, good-natured, and independent spirits whom he

---

*On the subject of religion, Wilhelm wrote to his fiancée, Ingeborg Westenholz: "I myself am . . . perhaps many times more a free-thinker in religious matters than you are. I have seen so many and such strange religious performances that nearly all religion seems to me to be mad, absurd, idiotic, sometimes abominable . . ." But he ended the letter by saying that where his own future children were concerned, their baptism and religious education would be "left to their mother to decide." See Thomas Dinesen, *Boganis: Min Fader, Hans Slægt, Hans Liv og Hans Tid*, p. 57.
†Frédéric Moreau, the hero of Flaubert's *Education Sentimentale*, typically yearns to become *"un trappeur en Amérique."*

would commemorate in a little article called "Three Friends." They in turn helped him to find work: as a corn merchant, in a land office, as a postmaster. He made hunting and fishing expeditions into the Nebraska Territory, and he "got to know the Indians very well, apparently hunting with them—and making love to them. The somewhat cryptic notation of his diary suggests that he did not discriminate but bestowed his favors on Sioux and Pawnee in an unpartisan fashion, though they were at war with one another."[16]

With a Danish doctor, a nobleman who had chosen to live out his life practicing medicine on the frontier, Dinesen traveled into the wilderness around Oshkosh, fishing for sturgeon and shooting ducks. Eventually he returned to live there, buying a cabin near a place called Swamp Creek, which runs into the Wolf River. He called it Frydenlund, after one of the houses of the Frijs family. It was built of pine logs and had two small rooms, one with a stove and a loft, the other with a fireplace. He made a bed in the loft, stuffed a mattress with bracken, and slept under the skins he had trapped. The house stood on a little bluff with its back to the forest. "He who seeks peace in the world cannot do better than to set up his domicile in the Wisconsin woods,"[17] Wilhelm wrote. He remained alone at Frydenlund for months at a stretch, baking his bread in the "excellent" stove and hunting for his provisions. The Chippewa, who camped near him in the spring, gave him the name "Boganis"—hazelnut[18]—which he would take as his *nom de plume,* and he observed them sympathetically and intelligently. In his long essay on America, he compares the families and the economics of the plains tribes, who hunted buffalo, to the forest and mountain tribes, who trapped and fished. The essay is lucid and bitter about the genocide casually practiced by the American government and its agents. The government, he wrote, "sometimes finds it necessary to decimate [them] with the help of soldiers, but usually liquor, smallpox, venereal disease and other maladies will do the trick, in concert with the extermination of their vital necessity—game. . . . In a short time they sell their land to the government in exchange for a Reservation, a miserable little tract which they cannot leave without permission of an agent. Here, for a few years, they lead an abominable, idle existence until . . . the whites get tired of having these wretched beggars in their backyard and send them further west. . . ."[19]

Dinesen felt a deep affinity with the Indians: their code of honor, their elegance and bravery, their knowledge of animals and the wild. Perhaps he romanticized their wisdom: "Their eyes see more than ours," he would tell his daughter, "[they] are better than our civilized people of Europe."[20] But there is no presumption in his admiration. He acknowledged their otherness —an integrity that defied even his own friendly intrusion and that precisely which the whites had set about to destroy.

Toward the end of 1874, Wilhelm was recalled to Denmark by the news that his mother was about to die, and he remained at Katholm for the next two years, a period spent in conflict with his father and his milieu.

The conservatives had returned to power, or rather had wrested it from the liberals. They amended the constitution so that they could rule despite the majority their opposition possessed in the lower house. The king had shown himself a blatant partisan of the old ruling class, and Wilhelm, writing sarcastically in the *Morgenbladet,* called him "Christian by the grace of God, King of the Conservatives."[21] Adolph Wilhelm, the elder, was a staunch supporter of the most reactionary new legislation and looked upon his son as a traitor to his class, an opinion shared with varying degrees of disapproval or indulgence by a large number of his relatives and friends. They continued to seek him out as a hunting companion and dinner guest—his prowess and charm compensated for his transgressions—but he always stood out from them in some way as an oddball, a black sheep. Isak Dinesen never knew her grandfather and got to know her aunts and uncle well only after Wilhelm's death, when they were her last link with him. She tended to overlook his "contempt for their bigotry and narrowmindedness."[22]

Adolph Wilhelm *père* survived his wife by only two years, leaving his prodigal son a large sum of cash. After the estate was settled, Wilhelm embarked upon yet another restless tour of Europe. When the Crimean War started he went to Turkey, hoping to fight against the Russians, but never actually engaged in battle. He lingered in Constantinople, keeping his intelligence of the war fresh and absorbing the local color.

In one of the *Letters from the Hunt* there is a vignette from this period. Wilhelm had made friends with a Turkish carpet dealer who had adopted a young Bulgarian girl, orphaned by the fighting. Wilhelm admired the beauty of her "fair hair and dark eyes" and accepted the merchant's offer to sell her for a day. He took his slave to a French dressmaker and let her choose "the costume of a modern lady." Then he asked the saleswoman to accompany her to the baths and to a coiffeur. When she emerged, transformed, he trotted her out in a landau for a tour of the city. "I have never promenaded with a more beautiful or elegant lady," he boasted. "We could not speak, she understood only Bulgarian. But . . . when she walked on her little spiked heels—ladies then wore little spiked heels—she moved like a dancer. The things she bought, she chose with taste. She ate charmingly, and cast glances full of grace upon the beggars who ran alongside our carriage, calling to us. When the excursion was over, I delivered her to the marketplace with her old and new clothes."[23]

Other erotic adventures are evoked discreetly but thrillingly in *Letters from the Hunt.* A sly Turquoise, attended by her eunuchs, winks at the narrator from under her baldachin. A lovely Communard, spine taut, hair billowing, stands poised at her barricade, and she is the only woman Wilhelm will allow ever "looked good" with a rifle.[24] He admits us to the dressing room of a great diva after her triumph as Zerlina at the Paris Opera. She whispers to her lover (who must be the narrator, for he reports it), *"Je ne chante que pour toi."** But elsewhere he suggests that the greatest treat for a connoisseur is *"l'amour d'une laide."*†

In considering Wilhelm's spiritual affinities, Georg Brandes was tempted to call his friend "an aristocratic radical," which was the epithet he had coined for Nietzsche and also used for himself, and he hesitated only because Dinesen was so passionate a democrat.[25] Intellectually he was a rebel, even—in his own words—a "Red."[26] But by temperament he was an epicure and an esthete. He might have said, with Stendhal, "I love the people and hate the oppressors, but it would be torture for me always to have to live with the people."[27] It is worth remarking that at a moment in history when women like Mary Westenholz, the liberal prudes, were calling for sexual equality and militating for the vote, aristocratic radicals like Brandes and Dinesen, the intellectual warriors, were still claiming Woman as their reward. Wilhelm is proprietary about "woman's secret power: the intimated."[28] His daughter ultimately sympathized with his views—though not without a period of dissent. Her perspective was in any case that of an insider, and she would define the "secret power" as that nerve it takes to sit on a powder keg and threaten to ignite it, while all the time you know that it is empty.[29]

In 1879 Wilhelm returned to Denmark, and with his widowed sister Alvilde bought a large parcel of land on the coast, fifteen miles north of Copenhagen. It was an investment he hoped would increase greatly in value once a railroad was built out to it, and it also contained some of the most beautiful property in northern Zealand. There were great tracts of forest, moor, and beach, and the estate had several principal houses: Rungstedgaard, which Alvilde chose; the manor of Folehave, near the village of Hørsholm; Sømandshvile and Rungstedlund, on the Strandvej (the coast road). Rungstedlund was a low, rambling building with a thatched roof and an ancient lilac bush by the back door. Its stables and outbuildings formed a courtyard with the main house, which was first licensed as an inn in the sixteenth century and had been a local meeting place and the way station between Elsinore and Copenhagen. In the eighteenth century the great lyric poet Johannes Ewald had briefly lodged and written there, drunk ale in his linen shirtsleeves, courted the innkeeper's daughter, and received the Muse on a hill behind the house that Wilhelm christened Ewald's Hill.

For an inveterate wanderer, this was a considerable financial and geographic commitment, and it suggested to his friends that Wilhelm, at thirty-five, was planning to settle down. Almost at once he began to court his future wife. She was not a woman of his own circle or temperament, but someone who would be a kind of ballast for him. She herself would find his choice

---

*"I sing only for you" (Wilhelm Dinesen, *Jagtbreve og Nye Jagtbreve*, p. 33).
†"The love of an ugly woman" (ibid., p. 139).

of her, and the fact he could show her such love and understanding, "a riddle . . . it must have been something in him that needed another side of life . . . more peace and quiet after a stormy spell."[30] His daughter Tanne would spend much of her life searching for the "lightness," for the "wings" he had cast off.

3

The first impression Ingeborg Westenholz had of Wilhelm Dinesen was from the balcony of the Royal Theatre, while he, standing in the *parterre*, "conversed with the Misses Treschow."[31] He wore his hair cropped to a point, like a medieval visor, which gave his handsome figure, correct in its evening clothes, a touch of erotic mockery.

They met a few days later at a skating party on the frozen moat of the Citadel. Ingeborg urged Wilhelm to take her younger sisters, Lidda and Bess, for a turn on the ice, and he obliged. A sympathy was struck, but when Mrs. Westenholz took her daughters home to Jutland in the spring, Ingeborg "did not yet feel anything special" for the Captain.[32]

He, however, had made up his mind, and he pursued her to the country, appearing at Matrup one morning on horseback, uninvited. Mrs. Westenholz asked him to stay for lunch and on that occasion was much taken with him. He enthralled the family with his tales of war and of life among the Indians, and this was how he would woo Ingeborg: like an Othello. Compared to his strange and rich experience of the world and the wisdom he seemed to have drawn from it, her own life, she feared, "must seem so strangely meaningless."[33]

Ingeborg was twenty-four when she met Captain Dinesen. She was cultivated, fluent in several languages, and described herself as a "free-thinker" and a "bookworm of the most gluttonous sort."[34] She had seen something of the world, for after her father's death the family had embarked upon a program of educational travel. At the outbreak of the Dano-Prussian War, Mrs. Westenholz decided it was time for the girls to improve their French and had dragged them with a nanny, a governess, and "Uncle Harald, as protector," across the ice and through a Germany swarming with troops to live *en pension* at Lausanne. Here they saw part of the French army Wilhelm was fighting with and offered them chocolate and cigarettes. Ingeborg was distraught that she could do nothing to help "the poor horses."[35]

To improve their English they had lived in London, in a rented villa near the Crystal Palace. For unspecified improvements they had gone to Rome and spent the winter in an apartment overlooking the Spanish Steps. A tutor was engaged to take them around the churches and museums, but he caught typhoid and died. Then Ingeborg had it too and was dangerously ill for a long time. She also outraged her mother and incurred her undying mistrust for having "encouraged a fruitless proposal." The young man was her "best friend," and she had simply not noticed the shift in his feelings from affection to love. "Mama," however, made a scene so terrible and righteous that it left Ingeborg "completely cowed" for a long time to come. She remained reticent with strangers. "I am never myself outside the home," she confessed to Wilhelm. "But I am someone quite other within it."[36]

That reticence blurs her figure somewhat, particularly since Wilhelm's is so vivid in comparison. In a photograph taken at the time of their engagement he fingers the statuette of a cupid and stares boldly at the camera with his heavy-lidded and voluptuously tired eyes. She poses formally and inexpressively, holding a book. She is sheathed to the neck in black silk; her hair is pulled back from her forehead and plaited into a bun; she has her mother's features, but reduced and set in a softer face, with the eyes too close together. Everything about her seems gentle and unassuming, and this was how her family preferred and even insisted upon seeing her: as its own "clever ... pious ... pleasant ... obliging" and naive little *"Mohder"**—the madonna of them all.[37]

When Captain Dinesen appeared, Mrs. Westenholz had not yet been called upon to sacrifice a child to love, and the prospect alarmed her. She perceived Wilhelm as a menace, in part because he succeeded in charming her and she didn't like the feeling. After Rome, she had had no confidence in Ingeborg's judgment and imagined her committing all kinds of follies, leading inevitably to perdition. As soon as Wilhelm's courtly letters began to arrive, she intercepted them and dictated Ingeborg's responses—though she also frequently wrote her own, cast in the editorial "we." "You will find us 'slow,' " she says, "but you must try to take it gracefully." Or: "I do not think we are so far as a visit to Katholm." Or: "Please be so kind as to solve a riddle which has puzzled us."[38]

The riddle was a riding hat from a fashionable milliner in Paris, which Wilhelm hoped Ingeborg would wear when "you exercise your horse."[39] But Mrs. Westenholz disliked the idea of a strange man imagining her daughter on a horse; the very chic of the hat was an impertinence, and Ingeborg was forced to return it with the excuse that it was "too pretty to be used in the country."[40]

From then on the romance was full of tension, rumor, and opposition. Mrs. Westenholz went so far as to talk down her daughter like an inferior piece of merchandise. "You will find Ingeborg . . . dependent, immature and vulnerable," she writes. She warns him that her child has "few qualities which can win or capture a man's heart."[41]

---

* *Mohder* is the old-fashioned spelling of the word "mother" *(moder)*, which Ingeborg's sisters, mother, and husband, as well as her children, used affectionately when they referred to her, and which they pronounced with their characteristic "old Copenhagen" drawl. Normally the word would be pronounced *môr*. They drew it out a little, so that it became two syllables.

Wilhelm evidently disagreed. And despite the bullying she endured, Ingeborg was able to hold up her own end of the romance with a great deal of maiden wit. An interesting voice comes through her letters, playfully ironic. "My family, I hope you know, are as bourgeois as possible. I hope it will not bother you. . . . My uncle is our greatest advertisement where physical beauty is concerned . . . he is my guardian, but you certainly know I am an old maid. Next Spring I come of age, and can do what I want. I think it will be something terrible."[42]

The proposal was made at Matrup. Wilhelm had spent the night and the next day, and when he and Ingeborg stood alone he asked her, as she put it, "the decisive question."[43] She felt her knees give way and could not answer. But later she wrote to him that "I am almost afraid for myself when, after what you have said to me, I find it so easy to say that your person and your letters are so profoundly welcome."[44]

"Mama," whatever her misgivings, behaved like a sportswoman in defeat. "How shall we reckon with an erotic element among us?" she asked the Captain. "None of my children has known, thus far, such a feeling, and I have always been afraid of it. Now it terrifies me that it comes so near. But it is narrow-minded to feel this way."[45]

They were married in the spring of 1881. The occasion was somewhat stilted, as the two families barely knew each other and upon closer acquaintance found little to say. After a honeymoon, the Dinesens moved into the old Rungsted inn. Wilhelm slipped with apparent ease into his new life. His figure thickened; he became a country squire with his guns and his dogs, his real estate deals and his hunting trips, his politics and his memoirs. But he found it difficult ever to make peace with peace. "He had to be experiencing something," his wife would explain, "whether it were joy or sorrow, anything but stagnation, 'respectability.' "[46]

"Love and peace," he himself would write, "hate, persecute, and annihilate one another."[47]

3

A Family Romance

The soul of a child demands these mighty passions, opposition and adversity.
—Isak Dinesen[1]

I

A FTER THE NEWLYWEDS had lived in Wilhelm's "bachelor apartment" at Rungstedlund for a few months, they abandoned the idea of moving to the larger and more comfortable manor house on their property, a mile inland. They could not "bear to part with the Sound,"[2] which lay just beyond their courtyard across the Strandvej. Here a little to the south there was a smooth beach and a jetty, where the steamer moored to take on passengers for the short trip down the coast to town. At the end of the century a hotel was erected in wood; it had a bathing establishment attached to it, with rows of little cabins and striped umbrellas. In the summer the air was soft and the channel full of sails. Tanne Dinesen's two brothers would later have a boat and take her up and back in it, between Copenhagen and Elsinore. In winter the east wind, chilled by the water, penetrated the rooms of the old inn and made them uncomfortable to live in. But it was the freedom of the view and the "poetry" of the old house that attracted the Dinesens and kept them loyal to Rungstedlund despite its inconveniences. As an old woman, Isak Dinesen suggested that living only a hundred meters from the sea had made it "a natural thing" for her, as a girl, "to view my enterprise in life in terms of seafaring," and to choose an admiral's motto for it: *"Navigare necesse est vivere non necesse!"**

Mrs. Westenholz had planned to move from Jutland to the neighborhood of Rungstedlund as soon as her daughter's honeymoon was over. With the nearby manor of Folehave now vacant, she settled there with her two unmarried daughters and a staff of four. For Lidda and Bess the move was

---

*Isak Dinesen, *Daguerreotypes*, p. 5. The Latin quote is Pompey's exhortation to his crew: "It is necessary to sail, it is not necessary to live."

dramatic. They missed Matrup acutely and felt isolated in the new house. Lidda would eventually brave her mother's phobia toward sons-in-law; seven years later she became engaged to an old family friend, George Sass—"Uncle Gex"—who owned an estate in Jutland and took her back there. Bess, however, spent the next sixty years at Folehave.

Describing the period of her adjustment, Bess varnished her own feelings with the heartiness typical of her. But through that varnish one may read her resentment at being subordinated and in a way sacrificed—still very young—to her mother's obsession with Ingeborg. For "Ingeborg's welfare" now became Mrs. Westenholz's "main interest in life." It was the family joke —how "barefaced partial" she was.[3] That partiality was a dubious blessing, for her mother used it as an excuse to oversee Ingeborg's domestic life as she had meddled in her courtship. She was the epitome of the critical mother-in-law. Although she professed to be "charmed" by Wilhelm, to admire his writing and his "un-Philistine" views of life, she also continued to look upon him as a spiritual menace. He was never "good enough to and for" her daughter. Under pressure, she confessed that "being a mother-in-law was an insoluble problem."[4]

Wilhelm had a world of masculine pleasures to retreat to—a political career, his writing, hunting trips with friends—and he always managed to "behave beautifully" to Mrs. Westenholz. He felt "genuine affection"[5] for her and perhaps even saw, in this frank and intelligent old tyrant, a worthy adversary. Ingeborg's feelings remain obscure. But Bess was stranded in the predicament of so many Victorian spinsters and maiden aunts who were expected to accept their lowly status without complaint and sacrifice themselves for the children of others. Bess was a woman of uncommon vigor and determination, a prominent member of Denmark's Unitarian Church, and an outspoken feminist. But after all her decisive forays into the world she was reabsorbed, consumed, and in a sense diminished by the demands of family life.

Of all Ingeborg's children, Tanne Dinesen had the most difficult and tempestuous relationship with this aunt—*Moster**—Bess. They were well matched in stubbornness, they loved each other deeply, and Bess had always encouraged Tanne's artistic talents. But she also felt that Tanne owed a loyalty to her family greater than any to herself. This was the sacrifice she had made, willingly and virtuously as she saw it, and she was all the more vigilant for any signs of "betrayal" or "ingratitude." Suspicious of men and opposed to Tanne's marriage to Bror Blixen, Bess was cast as the old aunt in "The Pearls" who discourages her niece's engagement to a nobleman:

She had an energetic nature and had long ago made up her mind to live for others, and she had established herself as the conscience of the family. But in

---

*Moster, maternal aunt. Literally, *moders s\$ster*, mother's sister.

reality she was, with no hopes and fears of her own, a vigorous old moral parasite on the whole clan, and particularly on the younger members of it.[6]

2

When the Dinesen children were born, Mrs. Westenholz "could never get enough of them."[7] The first to come was Inger (called Ea), in April of 1883. Her grandmother, aunts, and cousins crowded so possessively around the cradle that the child's father, feeling completely "useless and shunted aside,"[8] went out with his rifle and promised himself that the next one would be "his."

The next one was a second daughter, Karen Christentze (Tanne), born on April 17, 1885. Ellen (Elle) followed a year later. There was a space of six years until Thomas arrived, and then Anders, in 1894. For the early part of her childhood, Tanne was one of a triptych of sisters, extremely close in age, with the same fine Westenholz features and always—or at least in all their photographs—identically dressed. They pose in the snow by their mother's sleigh, in hooded capelets with fox scarves. They stand in a row, hands clasped, lips pursed, in pinafores and polka dots. They sit on the steps of a garden in fine smocking, and on a blanket with an infant brother, wearing shifts and straw boaters. They all receive the same little strand of pearls, the same gamin bob, the same pompom hat. And even at the ages of seventeen, fifteen, and fourteen respectively, they face the camera wearing the same dark Sunday frock of dotted swiss with a high white collar. Tanne, in the middle, is the one with a wry smile.

Later in her life, Isak Dinesen hated to be told that she resembled anyone, particularly anyone in her family. She became famous for her chic, her love of dramatic costumes, the way she wore hats and scarves, and for shooting her own fur coats. That originality was perhaps partly inspired by the memory of a childhood in uniform.

Ea, Tanne, and Elle were referred to as a unit—*Pigerne,* the girls—and shepherded about as one. They were all equally well educated and encouraged to become "accomplished," but there was very little recognition for individual superiorities. Competition, except in the abstract—as "spiritual struggle"[9] —was forbidden. Praise was meted out generously but somewhat indiscriminately. Even a half century later, when Isak Dinesen published *Seven Gothic Tales,* she "had the impression" her family expected her to "play down" its success because a book of Elle's, published previously, had not done very well.[10] "Little Tanne" found the scrupulous equality of the nursery inane and infuriating. She had a precocious confidence in her own singularity.

3

There are certain irreducibles in the character of Isak Dinesen, as in the character of each of us. Some children have a depth to their nature from birth

—a passionate curiosity—while others are cautious, passive, or serene. While almost anything can happen to those original qualities—in particular they can easily be discouraged—they also define a mysterious ground of one's being that defies analysis. Tanne was a proud, deeply feeling, touchy and vital child. She was a dreamer from the beginning, and it was her fate to have that quality within her recognized and nourished by her father, who took his second-born as his favorite and gave her time the others did not share. In a sense she led a double life as a child—as one of three, and as herself, only.

No one has ever really been privy to Isak Dinesen's intimacy with her father. She believed that if you talked too much about the "good things" that happened to you, they lost their savor. She has referred only sparingly to Wilhelm, and then in sentences that, for their clarity and longing, always seem to leap up from the page. She would say of him that he had understood her as she was, even though she was only a small child, and loved her that way. She would also say that, since he had abandoned her, it was his "responsibility"[11] that she had such a hard time in life; had he lived, things would certainly have been very different.

There is in Dinesen's work and thinking a frontier—more of a fixed circle, like an embroidery hoop—that separates the wild from the domestic. Within it there is firelight and women's voices, the steam of kettles, the clockwork of women's lives. Beyond it there are passions, spaces, grandeurs; there lie the wildernesses and battlefields. Wilhelm led his daughter out of the domestic limbo and into the "wild." He took her for long walks in the woods or by the Sound; he willed her his great love of nature; he taught her to become observant, to distinguish among the wild flowers and the bird songs, to watch for the new moon, to name the grasses. He exercised her senses, made her conscious of them the way a hunter is, in imitation of his prey. This was a kind of second literacy that she says she acquired at about the same time she learned to read, and its discipline and pleasure were at least as important in her life as those of books.

Reminiscing to Parmenia Migel, her first biographer, about her childhood, Isak Dinesen described what she thought was her first memory: being led by the hand up a high hill and shown a "spectacular" view. There is such a scene in "Alkmene": "When the sun was just above the horizon we came out in the fields. Here there was an exceeding high hill. We walked to the top of it, and from there had a great view to all sides over the golden plains and moors, and the glory of them. Alkmene stood quite still and gazed at it all. Her face was as clear and radiant as the air."[12]

Alkmene and her friend Vilhelm share a secret life together, a "companionship . . . of the woods and the fields" which "became suspended or latent when we were back in the house. . . . It began when she begged leave to go with me when I was out shooting or fishing. She was so swift of eye and movement that it was like having a small cute dog with you. Here I learned that the fearless girl was scared in the face of death. The first time that I picked up a dead bird, still warm in my hands, she was sick with horror and disgust. But she would catch snakes and carry them in her hand. And she had a fancy for all wild birds, and learned to know of their nests and eggs. Then it was pleasant to hear her, in summer, imitate and answer the ringdove and the cuckoo in the woods.

"We did thus become friends in a way, I believe, unusual with a big boy and a small girl . . . we seemed, both of us, to be aware that we were, amongst the people of our surroundings, the only two persons of noble blood. . . ."[13]

Tanne, too, defined herself by opposition to the plebeians of her surroundings. She and her father made an aristocracy of two, and her greatest pride was that she was his and not "theirs." Mrs. Westenholz apparently tried to balance the scales, throwing her own formidable weight onto the other side, and this contributed to Tanne's belief that "my grandmother did not like me. She liked my sisters better."[14] But while Wilhelm was alive, it didn't matter. He redeemed her from the nursery and its competitions. He ransomed her from the authority of her grandmother and Aunt Bess. He gave her a taste of a man's life, uninhibited and sensual, which was an alternative to the limited world of the women, with its ethical perils and self-denial. Above all, he gave her a sense of her own erotic power that was, from the outset, exaggerated. For of all the women in the household—before her sisters and even before her mother—Wilhelm had chosen her, or so she construed it. This was the decisive privilege of her life, and also perhaps its fatal distortion, the grain around which the pearl would form. Alone in the woods with her father, they might just as well have been alone in the world. It was her time before the Fall.

4

The excursions with Wilhelm were by no means regular. When he was at home they perhaps went out daily, but he was not at home much. He still traveled a great deal, revisited his "beloved Paris," returned to America for several months with a group of former fellow officers. He was often invited to hunt on the great estates. In 1892, when he was elected to Parliament, he lived in Copenhagen during the week in a flat he kept there. Tanne could not depend upon or anticipate seeing him. Their moments alone were snatched from the routines of her schoolwork and sisterhood.

Isak Dinesen would fall into or create a similar pattern with both of the men she lived with. Her husband Bror Blixen was restless and independent and even in the better days of their marriage came and went on the African farm as he pleased. Her friend Denys Finch Hatton visited her between his safaris, perhaps only for a week at a time between absences of many months. Later, in her writing and her remembering, Isak Dinesen would idealize what had, in fact, been a great deprivation, claiming that the best marriage was a sailor's: the bond between a rooted and civilizing woman and a free man.

As she grew older, Wilhelm talked to Tanne rather freely about his life. His exploits as a soldier stirred her fantasies and made her fierce. His stories about the Indians also affected her deeply. She went on to read Fenimore Cooper and idolized Natty Bumppo, and when she went to Africa she was extremely proud to enjoy that relationship of mutual respect with the Africans she imagined Wilhelm had had among the Chippewa and Pawnee.

But apart from one little scribble on the flyleaf of a book—"from Papuska to Babuska in her belligerent mood"[15]—there are no documents, no letters from Wilhelm to his daughter.* For a more detailed perspective of his enormous and pervasive influence we must turn to his *Letters from the Hunt,* which he was working on between 1886 and 1892, the early years of Tanne's childhood. When Robert Langbaum, one of Isak Dinesen's best critics, describes how she "rediscovered in Africa the validity of all the romantic myths, myths which locate the spirit in the elemental—in nature, in the life of primitive people, instinct and passion, in aristocratic, feudal and tribal societies which have their roots in nature,"[16] he gives us an index of Wilhelm's themes and Tanne's lessons.

Letters from the Hunt is a personal book, meditative, loosely woven together of anecdote and image. Like all pastorals, it presents itself as a sensuous surface and feigns timelessness. It is a bell jar, and its intensity comes from the pressure, which it resists, of everything it has excluded.

While the narrator tracks his prey or lies in wait for it, he discourses on the unique challenge and pleasure that each species affords him. This leads to digressions about love and woman and the relations between the sexes, which are framed in the same terms. Hunting and loving are both "mortal" struggles and both forms of play. The gallantry of the two parties and their mutual respect for the ritual of the pursuit are more important than its outcome. This playfulness finds its purest form as the "great gesture." Great gestures recur over and over in Boganis's work: something impossible is yearned for; it is realized in symbolic form. A task is set, involving enormous risk; it is performed as if no effort were involved. A great price is demanded. An even greater one is casually paid. The essence of all great gestures is to mock necessity—economic, biological, or narrative. The gesture defies the bourgeois impulse to appraise an experience in practical terms, in terms of its market value. Survival itself, the most basic of necessities, has the highest price, and therefore the greatest gestures have to do with that "exquisite

---

*Clara Svendsen, now Clara Selborn, suggests that Tanne had "evidently been in a rage about something. [Wilhelm] also goes on to threaten her with a dark hole where belligerent little girls are sent." (Letter from Clara Selborn, 1982.)

savoir-mourir"[17] that Isak Dinesen also admired so deeply. One is forced by life to pay the price for one's existence, and this is pain, loss, and death. But one is also free to laugh at the price and at oneself for caring about it. This disdain for the common-sense view of experience, this noble "perversity of the mind"[18] as Nietzsche called it, was one of Wilhelm's most impressive lessons to his daughter. It contained a great germ of self-destructiveness. It was also the ideal that she believed was so often mistaken for lightness and frivolity in the work of both.

5

In 1892 the Dinesens' first son, Thomas, was born. The same year, Wilhelm was elected to the Danish Parliament as an independent with sympathies for the Liberals *(Venstre)*. He had been writing letters to the newspapers and political pamphlets for several years, hoping to gain support for his strong but somewhat quixotic views on national defense. But he had overestimated the impact he could have from inside the government, and he quickly—and rather unrealistically—became disillusioned. "A man full of bitter criticism for the party he is in greatest agreement with," wrote Thomas Dinesen of his father, "can never acquire any real influence."[19]

The same year, he published a second volume of *Letters from the Hunt,* which was generally considered inferior to the first. Frustrations accumulated; he seems to have had a relapse of that old "soul-sickness"—the numbness, the restlessness, the anxiety which he felt in Paris and which had driven him to America. Sometime around 1893 or 1894 he sounded out Ingeborg on the prospect of taking a year to go around the world. She would not uproot herself or the children, but she told him she was prepared to let him go.

At the same time, we are told that his talks with Tanne "seemed to gather momentum." "Allusions to people he had known, to an unnamed woman he had loved, reminiscences, warnings, advice all poured out in a sort of accelerating monologue. . . . He seemed to urge Tanne beyond her age and comprehension."[20] These confidences confused and frightened her and later left her with a great burden of guilt—a feeling that she ought to have comforted and deterred him.

In March of 1895, a month before Tanne's tenth birthday, Wilhelm made the long trip to Jutland to visit Katholm but stayed only for a day. The following night the children's nanny, Malla, heard him pacing the library, muttering something which she later claimed was, "I'll have to do it, I'll have to do it."[21] On the twenty-seventh he attended the session of Parliament but left early, returned to his apartment, and hanged himself from its rafters.

Thomas Dinesen hinted but would not confirm that a doctor had told Wilhelm he was suffering from a disease "which could only conclude in a dark, helpless future."[22] When Thomas was twelve he asked his mother if

Wilhelm had killed himself, and Ingeborg admitted that he had. "You must understand," she told him, that "a man like Father, a soldier and an outdoorsman, could not live with the thought that he would have to continue to exist, throughout many years, as a wreck, a helpless relic of what he once was."[23] Thomas later believed it was "likely" the disease was syphilis.

Hanging was not an honorable death for an officer. It was a method by which the army executed its deserters. Wilhelm was a connoisseur of gestures, and this final one suggests he felt he had betrayed some deep principle of his own—not, perhaps, by contracting a venereal infection but by abandoning his wife, five children, and a political commitment.

At the time, the children were told only that their father had been ill and then that he had suddenly died. Even when they learned of his suicide, they were ignorant or misled as to its motives—which, in fact, are not known. When they were living in Africa, Thomas shared his conclusions about Wilhelm's suicide with his sister, and she accepted them as logical and even probable. By that time she herself was suffering from syphilis. It was one of the many details that led her to remark: "My father's destiny has, curiously enough, to a great extent, been repeated in my own."[24]

4

"Alkmene"

I have had so many qualms of conscience because I allowed Folehave to bear down on you with its loving but heavy weight.

—INGEBORG to THOMAS DINESEN[1]

I

THE CHILDREN were at Folehave with their grandmother on the afternoon they learned of Wilhelm's death. The news was broken to them in stages: first that he was ill. One of their aunts came into the drawing room, and Tanne asked her, "How is Father?" She was then told that he had died. "After a while her sister Ea said to one of the grown-ups, 'Tanne is trembling so.' "[2]

Her grief was lonelier and her loss more dramatic than the others'. She had lost the father himself, the genial man, the privilege of "talks on Ewald's Hill." But she had also suddenly been deprived of that source of self-esteem, that enabling self-love Wilhelm had sanctioned for her. "It was," she would say without exaggeration, "as if part of oneself had also died,"[3] and that part was an ability to love spontaneously and trustingly. Isak Dinesen lived for the rest of her life with a fear which "approached real horror . . . of putting one's life into, and abandoning one's soul to something that one might come to lose again."[4]

Mrs. Westenholz had a heart condition, and the shock of Wilhelm's suicide triggered a stroke. For a period of four years she couldn't move and spoke with difficulty. Only with the greatest effort did she finally recover her faculties. The rest of the family naturally tried to spare her any further chagrin, but in the process the natural outpouring of grief was cut short. It was an extremely tense and grim period. Ingeborg was lost in mourning, and many of the day-to-day decisions now fell to Moster Bess. She decided that the best thing for the children was to keep them to their routine and to speak as little of their father as possible. They were admonished, however, that "a widow's children must behave better than other children."[5]

[30]

Tanne felt that she had suddenly been stranded among strangers. "My mother's family, among whom I grew up after Father's death," she told a friend in words that imply she had not lived with them before, "didn't like him except that they certainly acknowledged the worth of *Letters from the Hunt.* I have a feeling that much further back . . . in regard to them, I constantly thought: I know better."[6]

It was always "my mother's family" and never "my mother" for whom Tanne reserved her deepest resentment. Ingeborg was the only one whose loss was as enormous as her own, and they became allies and even conspirators in their devotion to Wilhelm's memory. Ingeborg had accepted him above her family's deep misgivings, loved him with a passion that was the greater for being opposed and misunderstood, and his suicide was not only a loss of the greatest personal dimensions for her, but a kind of shameful defeat. If Ingeborg felt her mother and sisters "did not like" Wilhelm, she never reproached them for it; she did not have a heart capable of revolt. But she became "passive . . . melancholy . . . inhospitable."[7] Like Madam Ross, the sea captain's widow in "Tempests," "no one got to know what she felt about it."[8]

2

We know what Tanne's feelings were, for forty years later she put them in the tale "Alkmene," one of the most purely tragic and transparently autobiographical stories she ever wrote.

Alkmene is a little girl of six, an orphan uprooted from her rightful milieu and delivered into the hands of strangers. She is, we are told, so "singularly and tragically situated in life . . . that indeed she might be named Perdita after the heroine of Shakespeare's tragedy."[9]

Her story is narrated by a young man named Vilhelm, the son of an extremely ill-tempered and egotistical country squire not unlike Adolph Wilhelm Dinesen. Vilhelm studies with the local parson on his father's remote Jutland estate; it is into this parson's austere and righteous care that Alkmene is delivered.

The parson, however, has a past. He once studied in Copenhagen, wrote poetry in the classical mode, frequented an artistic circle, and had the ambition to make some great mark upon the world. But he forsook that life— fled from it in terror—because he perceived the signs of megalomania in himself. Instead, he accepts a meager living from Vilhelm's father and marries a country girl, someone who is used to hardship and loss. Gertrud has a plain face but, as we learn, a "divine body." An old friend of the parson's, a "professor" at the Royal Ballet, visits the parsonage and immediately recognizes what the provincials have overlooked: that Gertrud is a "living, breathing Venus." He confides this to Vilhelm, who suddenly understands why he has felt so comfortable in Gertrud's presence. For Vilhelm, like Alkmene, is an alien in his own milieu—a pagan. Gertrud, however, is unconscious of her own beauty and has no use for it. Her husband has deliberately severed his connections to the world of myth and poetry, and she—who might have taken the role of a goddess in the hearts of men—longs only to become a mother.

This, however, is not to be; the parson and his wife cannot have a child. He is resigned, but Gertrud rages against her fate. One day they receive a letter from the old professor, soliciting a home for a little orphan whose nativity is a terrible secret. He hints, however, that she is a child of some great and illicit passion. "I know of no human being who does more completely and pathetically answer to the proverbial saying of the brand to be snatched from the fire."[10]

The parson senses that his friend is manipulating him with this romantic "tale out of a book" and that the little girl is probably the child of some actress or ballerina. Even her name, he tells Vilhelm, is a clever invention of the old professor's to play upon his own weakness for Greek poetry. She is called Alkmene, like the heroine of one of his own epics. "Yes," he concludes, "the old fox . . . means to call me back to Olympus," and perhaps to call Gertrud, the unconscious Venus, back with him.

Alkmene comes well equipped to seduce two resolutely ethical beings back to Olympus, to the mythical roles and mythical aspects of their natures from which they have turned away. She is a child of "strange, striking noble beauty"; she has a rare lightness of movement, and Vilhelm, a connoisseur of the ballet, declares her to be more graceful than any dancer. She is "altogether without fear" and pointedly without sexual fear: "Neither the bull nor the gander frightened her; she liked them best of all the farm animals." She is extravagant with or indifferent to material things and gives away her own clothes and possessions. And she does not discriminate between truth and fantasy, "but things to her looked different from what they did to other people, often in the most surprising way."[11]

This classical figure delights her Christian parents, but she also deeply troubles them. For at heart she is without the feeling that is the cornerstone of their own lives: guilt. Gertrud, who "could never have minded" Alkmene's fantasies "for she had the peasants' love of fables and inventions," feels obliged, in her role as the parson's wife, to "teach her fear." And the parson, although he teaches her Greek, forbids her to dance, an activity he associates with her early life and the sinful milieu—"the fire"—he has snatched her from.

The one person with whom Alkmene has a natural affinity is Vilhelm. He admires precisely those qualities in her, the esthetic qualities, that frighten her parents. He takes a brotherly but erotic role in her life. Once he gives her a ball gown of his dead mother's, which she hides from her parents but wears for him, on walks in the woods. As she matures, he contemplates both marriage and seduction but rejects the former as unworthy of his own station and the latter as unworthy of his respect for Alkmene. "The chief feature of our relations," he explains to the reader, "was a deep, silent understanding of which the others could not know. We seemed, both of us, to be aware that we were like one another in a world different from us. Later on I have explained the matter to myself by the assumption that we were, amongst the people of our surroundings, the only two persons of noble blood, and hers was, possibly, even by far, the noblest."[12]

Alkmene is unable to waken her parents to their mythical natures, and she tries to escape from them. The first time, at nine, she refuses to admit any remorse for the "great grief" she has caused them. The second time, at eleven, she follows a band of gypsies who are suspected of having killed a man. Vilhelm rides after her and finds her struggling along on the moors. She asks for his horse so that she can make better time. "You frighten your people, you fool, when you run away," he chides her ". . . your folks love you, and think you a glorious girl, if you will only agree to stay with them." Alkmene answers: "What about the children, Vilhelm, who do not want to be loved?"[13]

A problem arises over Alkmene's birth and real identity when the time comes for her confirmation. The parson wants to tell her she is not their daughter, but Gertrud is afraid this knowledge will alienate her irretrievably. She is mistaken. When Alkmene learns she is an orphan, that the parson and his wife are not her real parents, her attitude of "distrust, revolt and hostility" toward them dissolves. A secret conviction of her own otherness is confirmed.

But the tale ends dismally. When she is sixteen Alkmene inherits a great fortune, presumably from her real father. The parson and Gertrud debate whether to accept the money on her behalf. The fortune seems to corroborate the veiled suggestions about Alkmene's high birth. Now the old squire, Vilhelm's father, presses him to propose. Vilhelm refuses. It is beneath his dignity to pounce on his old playmate, to exploit their intimacy now that she is rich.

Time passes, and the old parson dies. While Gertrud is on a visit to her sister, Alkmene asks Vilhelm for a favor: to take her to Copenhagen. Long ago he promised to do so and now he makes arrangements to arrive in the capital on a day she has specified. They travel overland, passing as brother and sister, although Vilhelm is awakening to the knowledge that he loves Alkmene and wants to make her his wife. When they reach the city Alkmene reveals the purpose of her visit: to see a notorious murderer beheaded. They make their way to the square where the execution will take place, and the crowd stares at Alkmene. Even the murderer seems to seek out her eyes. She is gravely moved by the awful spectacle and quotes a poem her father once read to her about a girl who was also beheaded:

> *Now over each head has quivered*
> *the blade that is quivering over mine.*[14]

She implies the execution contains a warning for her.

Before they return to Jutland, Vilhelm wants to show Alkmene a little of the town and takes her to see the king's palace. Outside its gates they pass an old man with his arms full of roses, whom Vilhelm recognizes as the professor. He stares at Alkmene and seems to know her, but he is on his way somewhere and does not speak to them. They travel home by sea, and once on board the ship Vilhelm proposes to Alkmene, but she refuses him. "You, you speak about my life now. But before, when it was time, you did not try to save it. . . . They all loved Alkmene. You did not try to help her. Did you not know, now all the time, that they were all against her, all?" Vilhelm replies that "it never occurred to me but that you were the stronger." "Yes, but it was not so," she says. "They were the strongest."[15]

"They" had refused to recognize Alkmene, to "save" her life by permitting her to fulfill the destiny she was born for. Vilhelm, her friend, might have awakened her to sexual love. The old professor might have spoken about the identities of her real parents and given her access to their world. Even at the last moment, outside the palace gates, he might have opened them to her. Gertrud, with her "peasants' love of fables and inventions," might have sanctioned Alkmene's rich imagination. The parson, her adopted father who taught her Greek, might have carried her "back to Olympus" with him and returned her to her rightful place. But he abandoned Alkmene as he had once abandoned the old gods.

Alkmene's strange request—to watch a man die for his sins on a scaffold —is her gesture of surrender, of resignation to the parson's world. In one stroke she accepts that "fear of God" which until now she has so "strangely" lacked. When she realizes that no one will really "save" her—save her in the deepest psychological sense—she accepts the other "salvation": Christian guilt and repentance.

Years later Vilhelm has the chance to revisit his old friend. She is living with Gertrud on a remote and desolate sheep farm and has become a miser, hoarding the great patrimony of her real father. Her gold, like her beauty, her grace, her fearlessness, her "destiny," are useless to her.

3

Rungstedlund was Tanne's "parsonage," and after Wilhelm's death her own childhood became a battle—waged mostly in her own imagination— to be recognized as what she felt and wanted to believe but like Alkmene could not prove she was: a changeling with the blood of kings, courtesans, or poets in her veins. She knew her family loved her greatly and in their own way meant her only well, but they denied her nature. "It seems to me [they]

... have a frightful capacity for making life difficult,"[16] Tanne would write.

Wilhelm, like Alkmene's real father, represented "Olympus," that reign of the old pagan gods, that lost order under which, in both a practical and symbolic way, the erotic and the spiritual had been a unity.

Isak Dinesen turned her own childhood into myth in "Alkmene." The child is her double, her self-ideal. But the resemblance would seem to end with Alkmene's "fall." If we are to believe *Out of Africa* and the tales, Dinesen did not succumb to the "tyranny," as she called it, of her mother's family. She escaped to the highlands, reclaimed the patrimony of her father, discovered that "God and the Devil are one."[17]

It is possible that the tale is simply the tragic alternative ending to her own story. But it is also possible that it shows us the way in which appearance or even biographical facts diverge from or even belie feeling, psychological truth. Dinesen cultivated in her work and her persona precisely those qualities of spirit and those emblems of strangeness that she gave Alkmene, and the young Alkmene is resurrected in the old Dinesen. But she also seems to acknowledge in the tale—with a penetrating honesty—how much the guilt and conflict of her childhood had really thwarted her. Tanne, in fact, did want to be loved, was not indifferent to the "grief" she caused, and felt that her family had a "strange power" to make her feel she was wrong to rebel against them.

5

Three Sisters

I

ALTHOUGH INGEBORG WAS "not really very hospitable"[1] to strangers after Wilhelm's death, there was always a considerable bustle of relatives between Rungstedlund and Folehave. Ingeborg's brothers had married and were fathers, and they brought their children to see Mama and to play with their cousins. Mrs. Westenholz's eleven brothers and sisters had proliferated energetically, and there were Gruts, Ræders, Sasses, Hoskiærs, Plums, and Berrys who came to visit. For the Berrys, the Scottish branch of the family, the descendants of Aunt Emily Hansen, "one always had to be on one's best behavior."[2] There was at least one family tradition Isak Dinesen loved: her grandmother's birthday party in July. The fruit was ripening, the roses were in bloom, and it was warm enough to bathe in the Sound. The whole clan would gather at Folehave around a table set under the great elm tree and dine on roasted chicken and white strawberries.

Mrs. Westenholz was a pillar of Hørsholm society, and Tanne and her sisters were often invited to pour the tea for the likes of Countess Ahlefelt and her daughter, Ulla; for Fru Funch, the wife of the Rungsted physician; and for other excellent ladies whose conversation even Ingeborg had to admit was completely bourgeois and stagnant.

Tanne much preferred the company of the servants. Clara Svendsen* recounts how she liked to have her breakfast downstairs with them, where she could drink coffee instead of tea and listen to the gossip of the fisherwomen, the dairymaids, and the grooms. The currency of these stories was lust, revenge, foolishness, deceit, drunkenness, strokes of good and bad luck. Thomas Dinesen remarked that "Tanne maintained all her life that she had a special relationship with 'lower-class people' (her own words) . . . and this understanding stemmed from her close friendship with the kindly helpers of her childhood home."[3] Among the "kindly helpers," speech was frank, humor broad, and feelings stripped of genteel disguises.

---

*Clara Svendsen was Isak Dinesen's secretary and companion for twenty years.

2

Tanne had practically no opportunity to meet people on her own, outside the family circle and the "pleasant [local] backwaters." The closest friends of her childhood were the children of Ingeborg's own girlhood friends. Else Bardenfleth, daughter of Ida Meldal Bardenfleth, was a shy, beautifully bred young girl who had, according to Tanne, "a steady Orthodox nature" [4] and who stood a little in awe of her friend's daring. They took bicycle excursions together, and Else lived in Switzerland with the Dinesen sisters in 1899. In 1909 Else became engaged to Count Eduard Reventlow, a young diplomat from a great Danish family who was then stationed in Paris. Count Reventlow was a worldly man "with much more of the Devil in him" [5] than his fiancée, and quite independently of her he would play an interesting minor role in Tanne's life.

A second and more intimate friend was Ellen Wanscher. Tanne admired Ellen's mother for cultivating interests outside her family—the theater, literature—and she wished that Ingeborg, who was single-mindedly absorbed in motherhood, could be more like her.[6]

Ellen Wanscher enjoyed a degree of confidence that Tanne shared with only two other people in her life, both men: her brother Thomas and her African servant Farah.* Tanne could unburden her heart to Ellen, knowing that what she told her would never be judged or betrayed. This was precious because the Westenholz family was so judgmental and intrusive; they lived, spiritually, in each other's pockets. Once, at a moment of crisis, Tanne had told an important secret to her Aunt Lidda, who broadcast it at the dinner table the same evening. They were so clannish, so nosy, so arrogant about their moral superiority that living among them must have been an endless indignity to a naturally private person. But at the same time, such a passionate interest taken in a child's existence must also have been nourishing. Isak Dinesen would eventually come to appreciate it and to understand the moral "toughness," not to say the truculence, with which it had endowed her.

Besides her gratitude for Ellen Wanscher's "unshakeable" loyalty, Tanne admired a more elusive quality. Without having any particular glamour, beauty, wealth, or even talent, Ellen was a compelling figure to her friends, someone whom they were always happy to see and whom they felt honored to know. She had a simple confidence in her own "worthiness" that Tanne, since her father's death, could not feel about herself.

Tanne spent most of her childhood in the company of her two sisters, and her affection for them, while deep, also suffered from this inescapable com-

---

*In her *Letters from Africa*, Isak Dinesen spells her servant's name *Fara*, while in *Out of Africa* and *Shadows on the Grass* it is Farah. I have used the latter spelling.

munity. Her letters to them from Africa are warm, chatty, and at times effusive, but not self-revealing. She seems to have guarded her privacy—as she guarded her distinction—fiercely.

She and Ea "squabbled"[7] with each other as little girls, although Ea later became a mother figure to the others, dispensing sympathy and, at times, reproach. Ea had a lovely voice, often sang *lieder* for the family, and hoped to have a musical career. Her sweet soprano added to the impression she gave of yielding and somewhat melancholy femininity. But it is difficult to render a fair likeness of Ea for she died in her thirties, after the birth of her second child, and the family kept her saintlier qualities as their mementos. Tanne wrote to Elle that with Ea's death they had lost their unifying spirit.

Elle and Tanne shared a room, were only a year apart in age, and had a secret language called *pirogets*.[8] They were both strong and intense though very different characters. Elle inherited much of Aunt Bess's idealism, and something of her stolidity. As a young woman she was troubled and restless, in search of some ideal or cause deserving of her life's devotion—first socialism, then the recovery of South Jutland from the Germans. She would later make a success of her unlikely marriage in the same spirit of commitment, and as a rich matron she took up social work, providing shelter and meals for the unemployed. There was something tragic in Elle's temperament, something repressed. She envied the impunity with which Tanne could "rage at fate,"[9] and she often criticized her frivolity, her "showing off," to which Tanne replied that showing off was a "necessity of life. . . . Both Elle and Thomas can thrive on mere prose," she told their mother. "I think that what is most indispensable to me is a certain kind of poetry."[10]

Tanne did not enjoy herself with Elle as she did later with her cousin, Daisy Frijs; nor did she confide in Elle as she did in Ellen Wanscher. But there was a deep mutual respect between the two sisters. Elle was Tanne's captive audience for her first stories; she would try them out in the darkened nursery, usually droning on for so long that Elle begged her to go to sleep. But she also must have proved herself a discerning critic, for she was Tanne's sounding board for the tales of her twenties and a first-line critic for Isak Dinesen's mature work.

3

In 1888, the year Tanne Dinesen learned to read in the day nursery, Georg Brandes was concluding a series of lectures on Friedrich Nietzsche.* Nietzsche was still unknown, and Brandes, who was himself a great rebel and iconoclast, was the first major critic to champion his work and to introduce it to a large public. The audience jammed the hall at the University of

---

*The lectures, titled "On Aristocratic Radicalism," were republished with the Brandes-Nietzsche correspondence in 1900.

Copenhagen, perched on the window ledges and spilled out into the court-yard. With wild enthusiasm they heard Brandes lecture on Nietzsche's ideal of the "true teacher," someone who educates the young in opposition to their age, who instructs them to struggle against "all forms of obedience. . . . Only he who has learnt to know life and is equipped for action has a use for history . . . only he who feels that in his inmost being he cannot be compared with others, will be his own law-giver. For one thing is needful: to give style to one's character."[11]

This liberating advice helped to shape the sensibilities of an entire genera-tion of Danish artists and intellectuals, and when Brandes reported to Nie-tzsche on the reception of the lectures, he felt that it could be summed up in the remark of the young painter who came up to him afterward and said: "What makes this so interesting is that it has not to do with books, *but with life.*"[12] It is precisely this vitality that was missing from the education of Tanne Dinesen and of which she would feel so desperately deprived. And she would, as an old storyteller, attempt to embody the Brandesian and Nietzschean ideal of a "true teacher" to the next generation.

The three sisters were "educated privately," an expression that has a certain undeserved patrician glamour. Tanne lamented the fact that she was permit-ted to grow up "totally ignorant of many things that are common knowledge to other people"[13]—mathematics, for instance, for which she felt she had a flair. Like most women of their class, the Dinesen sisters were not prepared to earn a living—it was assumed that they would marry—although Tanne was indignant that they were not even taught about housekeeping or enter-taining. Later she would express a fine, feminist indignation at a system that could allow "practically all my abilities to lie fallow and [that] passed me on to charity or prostitution in some shape or other. . . ."[14] In Africa, living among English public school alumni, she came to look upon their strenuous, aristocratic colleges as an ideal. "If I had a son," she told her brother, "I would send him to Eton."[15]

Her own brothers had left for boarding school—not so illustrious a one as Eton—at the ages of eight and six respectively. Their older sister, who was then begging to be sent to the Royal Academy of Art, watched them go with a deep and justified envy. The boys were given guns, soldiers' uniforms, boats, permitted to wander through the park at night, or to fish on the ice when the Sound froze. Thomas marveled as an old man at the indulgence Ingeborg had shown them. Overprotective of her daughters, she was committed to raise her sons as "their dead father would have wished."[16] Tanne secretly believed that Wilhelm would have wished a richer scope for her, as well. But there was no way she could prove it.

The schoolroom at Rungstedlund was presided over by a series of young and old women. A retired schoolmistress from the village taught the girls to read. She was succeeded by a governess, Miss Maria Zøylner, who shared the major burden of the girls' education with Mrs. Westenholz. Mama taught them English and French, chastity and selflessness. Miss Zøylner filled in the rest. She may have been ignorant of mathematics, but she was a stickler for good writing. Some of the girls' homework has survived, corrected in red. They outlined their themes fastidiously, learned to marshal facts and support opinions, and to revise. They also memorized great quantities of poetry and translated such writers as Scott and Racine into Danish.

Even as a girl, Tanne's prose had a well-honed, rhetorical edge. From eight to fourteen she was an amusing and persuasive essayist on such subjects as "Women in the Folk Ballad"; "Our Danish Proverbs"; "It's the Will that Counts"; "Women in the French Revolution"; "Matter and Spirit"; and "Christine Oehlenschläger."[17] Christine was the wife of the Danish romantic poet, Adam Oehlenschläger. "She had a rich, warm and gifted nature, but was not meant for happiness," Tanne wrote. "It is often an envied destiny to be the wife of a genius. It is, however, rare that geniuses are happy, or capable of making others happy, to whom their fates are bound."[18]

We are indebted for the survival of that insight to some member of the Dinesen family who made a large bundle of Tanne's copybooks and stored them in the attic, presumably to preserve the plays and poetry they contained. But also scattered among the pages of the square booklets, the size and color of American college blue books, there is a wealth of doodles, mirror writing, coded messages, letters to friends, lists of mottoes, diary entries—a haphazard, often cryptic, but voluminous record of the future writer's imaginative life.

The earliest of these notebooks is dated 1893. It contains, in the bold, round handwriting that would grow spidery with time, "The Poetry of Karen Dinesen": "Lovely Spring!" "Lovely Summer!"[19] There is also the first collection of Dinesen tales, each a page or two in length and connected, in the oriental fashion, by a figure who recurs in all of them: a little elf. This *nisse* stumbles upon a troll's lair, loses his hat to a muskrat, is soundly teased. Elsewhere, he surprises a girl named Henrietta Bruun. Her servant has been teasing her that if she fails to send porridge to the elves, she will have a calamitous new year. "To tell the truth," Tanne wrote about her heroine, "Henrietta believed in elves, although she denied it shamelessly."[20]

Teasing is a prominent source of dramatic conflict in the *nisse* stories, as it was among the Dinesen children, who were fiercely competitive, hot-tempered, even rowdy. Ingeborg tried to civilize them on the same principle one housebreaks puppies: she forbade them to scream, cry, tussle, argue, tease or fight in any of the principal rooms of the house—where they were not to enter or remain without her permission. But in their own playroom, the *legestue,* "everything is permitted which does not draw blood or inflict injury. No one, however, may cry for help from the grownups for what goes on in the playroom."[21]

The restiveness was natural, given the isolation of their country life, the clannish character of their family, and the enforced cheerfulness that held them so tightly together. "All spiritual conflict is permitted," Ingeborg had written, "but no anger. Whoever is angry must absent himself from the public spaces, and from the stairs and corridors, so long as the anger lasts."[22] But it was inevitable that the forbidden feelings would seek other channels.

4

The Dinesen sisters did not have an opportunity to see much of *den store verden*—the great world—a phrase that recurs wistfully in Tanne's writing. Their uneventful lives revolved around Rungstedlund and Folehave, the beech woods and the sound. In summer they made the journey to Jutland, by train and coach, for peaceful vacations with their cousins at Matrup or Katholm. On Sundays, prettily dressed, they were driven the little distance south along the Strandvej to the Deer Park,* where they strolled with their governess and baby brothers in the shade of the great hawthorn trees. There were occasional trips to town, to the museums, to a matinée at the ballet, to shop for shoes or notebooks, to walk on the Langelinie† or to drink tea with their great-aunts. But for them, as for most Danish children, the most exquisite of treats was a visit to the Tivoli Gardens.[23] The gates opened at four with a cannonade, and the crowds streamed in. Every class and age of Dane was represented. There were willowy young merchant seamen; bankers wearing homburgs; servant girls on their half-days off, walking arm in arm, flirting with the drunken students who came to meet them. There were rich Americans; decorated naval officers; lords and ladies visiting from the country, trailed by their children in pinafores and sailor suits and the children's nannies. The trees were strung with lights; thousands of Chinese lanterns illuminated the lake; and here a full-rigged frigate lay at anchor, a replica of King Christian IV's battleship, *Trefoldigheden*. Rowboats ferried people back and forth to it, and in its main cabin there was a variety show.

Paths lined with flower beds led from the lake to the shooting galleries and the carousel, the games of chance and the refreshment booths. There was a great Moorish palace, a wooden building with minarets and a dome, that accommodated several restaurants, and on its terrace you could eat the finest *smørrebrød* and ices. One orchestra played classical music, another popular songs and waltzes, and at the heart of Tivoli was a great open lawn where, as in the market square at Port Said, there were jugglers, acrobats, clowns,

---

*The *Dyrehaven,* or Deer Park, lies just to the south of Rungsted on the coast. It surrounds the royal hunting lodge (the Hermitage), and small herds of deer still roam freely there. The landscape is open and gently undulating, the trees are very old and therefore tall and spreading, and the neatly kept dirt paths are a very popular promenade for the citizens of Copenhagen.
†The promenade alongside part of the port.

rope dancers, trapeze artists, trained animals, and from time to time the launching of a hot-air balloon.

But probably the most famous of Tivoli's attractions, and the one that seems to have made the deepest impression on Tanne Dinesen, was the pantomime. The *commedia dell'arte* was kept alive in Denmark long after it had disappeared from the rest of Europe, and today Pierrot and Harlequin are still fighting over Columbine on a replica of the original carved and gilded "Chinese" stage.* The tradition of virtuoso improvisation would help form Dinesen's sense of what it meant to be an artist, and the masquerade —the drawing of character in broad, mythic strokes—was an important element of her own art.

Tivoli itself is a great northern fantasy about southern life and love of pleasure, about Italian brilliance and temper, about Eastern luxury—a civic expression of the Either/Or. The gardens were laid out, interestingly, the same year that Kierkegaard's book was published (1843), and by a Dane named Carstensen who was born and raised in Algeria, and who rightly calculated that to his sober countrymen such a fantasy would be irresistible. "A susceptibility to the Southern countries and races," Dinesen would also write, ". . . is a Nordic quality."[24]

5

Mingling incestuously in Tanne's copybooks with the well-outlined and liberal-minded essays were dramatic writings in quite a different vein.[25] Their background was not the Bastille but the Petit Trianon. Their characters were not the sturdy Valkyries of the folk songs, the oppressed wives of geniuses, or the proto-feminist, bloodstained heroines of the people. They were slender figures in corselets and silk pantaloons with names like Ganymede and Galatea, Blancheflor and Knight Orlando, Pierrot and Columbine. At the age of ten or eleven, Tanne began writing plays—most of them heady pastoral romances—that the children and friends staged for the family. Next to one cast list there are the names of the actors who will play them, and it sets the precedent. Ea is always Columbine; Elle is Harlequin; and Tanne, Pierrot. The Pierrot is foolish and proud. He has a minor and a comic part. Tanne never took the romantic leads in her own plays; the real romance was being their author.

In the *legestue,* at Sunday dinner, on glee club outings, for their lessons and in their photographs, Tanne Dinesen remained one of the triptych of sisters. There is always Ea to the left, a little stodgier, a little bigger; and Elle to the right, a little prettier, a little grimmer. But when she began to write her "great dramas," as she playfully called them, she created a new and distin-

---

*The original pantomime theater in Tivoli was burned by the Nazis in 1944 as an act of reprisal for sabotage carried out by the Resistance.

guished position for herself among the children: their impresario. Or, to use one of her own favorite expressions, their *maître de plaisir.* In addition to making life generally gayer and introducing subjects generally forbidden, one must suppose that writing the plays restored some of Tanne's lost prestige.

One early teenage work, *Cassandra's Journey,* is fairly typical. The characters are Cassandra and her maid Jacinthe, her daughter Columbine, Columbine's suitors Pierrot and Harlequin. A little later in the notebook there is a new cast list, and a familiar Dinesen transformation has taken place. Cassandra has become Cassander, "a rich man." In this version he is a widower and a miser. Jacinthe tries to marry him. Pierrot adores Jacinthe. The dialogue is done in stiff, broad strokes, like that of a marionnette comedy, but sometimes it takes an unexpectedly earnest turn:

HARLEQUIN *(On the verge of eloping with Columbine):* My sweet bride, think well before you follow me. I am flighty and untrue, with no sound common sense as ballast. Think well before you come aboard my ship, before perhaps it tosses you up and down. O Columbine, what am I doing now? Oh that I were dumb and blind and a hunchback so that I could not corrupt you by deception.
COLUMBINE: Oh my sweet bridegroom. I would rather be storm-tossed with you than sail in peace with anyone else on earth.
HARLEQUIN: You frighten me.
COLUMBINE: Yes, yes, I frighten—Destiny. . . . Everybody's destiny is contradictory, and what you think will happen, never does.[26]

Here Columbine certainly speaks for her thirteen-year-old author, who was just biding her time until she could forsake all prudence and cast herself passionately upon life's uncertain waters.

6

The plays were only one aspect of Tanne's extremely luxuriant fantasy life. The notebooks are full of doodles that grow progressively more daring and accomplished. There are sinuous mermaids, ballerinas in transparent gauze, athletically muscled cavaliers, leering villains, winged nymphs. Next to the draft of "Damon and Phyllis, a Comedy" is a series of nudes: a headless woman with voluptuous breasts and thighs, a naked demon crushing a sinner under his foot.

Tanne had a kind of private serial with Ellen Wanscher that they made up as they went along and whose central characters were Lord Byron and Lady Arabella.[27] Tanne was Byron, and even as an elderly woman, Ellen signed letters to her old friend, "Arabella." One does not have to look too far to discover Byron's charm for Tanne. He was a male Alkmene: "The proud and lonely hero marked by destiny who refuses society's moral claims upon him . . . in [whose] past there is a secret, an awful sin. . . . He is rough and wild but of high descent; his features are hard and impenetrable but noble and beautiful; a peculiar charm emanates from him which no woman can resist."[28]

These ironic captions are from a description of Byron as the prototypical demonic hero, the "fallen angel" of Romanticism. Such characters would always attract and fascinate Isak Dinesen, who would later claim a close, personal relationship with Lucifer himself.

On July 14, 1898, a fire broke out in the long, straw-thatched farm building which lay parallel to the house and enclosed the courtyard from the Strandvej. Ingeborg was the first to discover it; she raised the alarm and rushed out in her nightdress to save the horses. One of them, in his wild terror, kicked her to the ground, and she was temporarily paralyzed. But she managed to crawl to safety just as the stable roof collapsed.

The children threw on their clothes and tried to carry some of the more precious family possessions out of the main house. The sparks rained down on them, igniting the thatch of a tenant's cottage, and a farmhand was killed by the blazing straw. The dairyman managed to save the cows, but the pigs and chickens were roasted to death, and Thomas lost his beloved Icelandic hound, Geyser. After Ingeborg had recovered from the ordeal, she made plans to leave Denmark for a while. She "just *couldn't* bear going round the old places any longer."[29]

Their departure was postponed for six months while plans for the restoration were drawn up and the workmen engaged. In the interval the girls were sent to confirmation classes in Søllerød with a Pastor Vedel. Isak Dinesen later used "the parson's house in Søllerød" as the setting for "Peter and Rosa." From her description it has much in common with Alkmene's parsonage and its prototype, Folehave: a place "where death was zealously kept in view and lectured upon"; where "daily life was run with a view to the world hereafter"; and where "the idea of mortality filled the rooms. To grow up in the house was to the young people a problem and a struggle, as if fatal influences were dragging them the other way, into the earth, and admonishing them to give up the vain and dangerous task of living."[30]

After the New Year 1899, the Dinesen family and Else Bardenfleth departed for Switzerland. It was a strictly female party, as Thomas and Anders had been left with their nanny. They settled at a pension in Lausanne, where Ingeborg had come twenty-eight years earlier for the same purpose: to improve her French. For the first time in their lives the sisters were sent to a "real school," the École Benet. There was still no mathematics on the curriculum, but in addition to French they studied drawing and painting. Tanne showed real promise, and her sketchbooks are filled with delicate pencil landscapes from around Lake Geneva. It was the beginning of her long and inconclusive training as an artist.

When summer came they traveled south and spent August on the shores of Lago Maggiore. Tanne did some sketches of Isola Bella, its white peacocks, its palace and terraced gardens. She began a diary there but neglected it. For the whole nine months abroad we have only a single line: "Tanne, Isola Bella. *Qui est mon meilleur ami? Celui qui deigne le moins.*"*

---

*"Who is my best friend? He who cares the least" (KBA 196, VI I, drawings).

6

The Road to Katholm

The essence of his nature was longing.
—Isak Dinesen[1]

I

WHEN ISAK DINESEN created the character of Rosa in "Peter and Rosa," she drew heavily upon the feelings and scenes of her own life at the turn of the century. Her heroine, the moody, imaginative Rosa, youngest of three sisters, the "spoilt child of the house," was a girl very like herself at fifteen, whose "despair itself had vigor in it." Rosa is another changeling, another pagan, a proud and resentful introvert who has, as she emerges from childhood, "come into possession of a world of her own, inaccessible to the others. . . . They would never understand her, were she to tell them that it was both infinite and secluded, playful and very grave, safe and dangerous. She could not explain, either, how she herself was one with it, so that through the loveliness and power of her dreamworld she was now—in her old frock and botched shoes, very likely the loveliest, mightiest, and most dangerous person on earth."[2]

Something of that secret life is visible, hinted at, in photographs of the three sisters. Tanne is often posed in the middle, a small, delicate young girl with thick chestnut hair and the suggestion of her mature face. While Ea and Elle acquiesce passively to the camera with puffy cheeks and unconscious stares, Tanne offers a playful resistance. Her face has lost some of its childish roundness, and her fine bones are emerging. The smile is sweet, but it already tilts slightly in irony. The eyes are quizzical, deep, and bright.

The nine months abroad were a natural intermission between childhood and adolescence, and when Tanne entered the Danish scene again some imaginary observer—let us say some old friend of her father's—might have smiled at her new gestures of sophistication: the little refinements and expressions; the "charm" that was still tentative and external, not yet quite a part of her, like a borrowed costume or a plaything. She had spoken French with

[46]

strangers and ordered dinner in hotel restaurants. She had observed the human comedy on Italian trains and joined in the exalted debates on life that take place in their compartments. She had studied landscapes and faces with a painter's concentration and had begun to feel the first rapture of talent, before it encounters its own limits and inhibitions. The world had clearly announced to her: "You are to live."[3] But even as she unpacked her foreign books, her new clothes, her sketches of Ingeborg and of Lake Geneva, this imperative was contradicted by her surroundings; they refused to take change into account. Children in the Westenholz family did not grow up, just older; meals were served with the same order of courses at the same time every day; individuals behaved in a manner consistent with the idea others had of them. Georg Brandes maintained about the Danes in general—and it was perhaps even more true of the Westenholzes in particular—that they suffered from a too keen sense of the ridiculous, which destroyed the possibility for any "originality of manners, any free play of the imagination . . . all natural expression of feeling."[4]

There was a very pleasant side to this static and claustrophobic life: it was extremely secure. That security would comfort Isak Dinesen enormously when, for example, she was visiting from Africa and wanted most of all to do nothing, think nothing, and be taken care of. But the price was vitality. Depression was always waiting for her when she came home. We may assume she felt it at fifteen; those were the "fatal influences . . . dragging [Rosa] the other way, into the earth and admonishing [her] to give up the vain and dangerous task of living."[5]

2

The year 1900 was a turning point for Tanne. It began with the return to a strange house. The fire had leveled the old farm buildings and opened the view of the Sound; in the main house the rooms had an unexpected airiness, and they had also been completely renovated and refurbished. But it was no longer her "childhood" home, which would always be—whenever she reached back for it in her memory—the Rungstedlund before the restoration: darker, more rambling and rickety, with its steep old stairs down to the kitchen and up to the garret, and the door in the north wall that led to the nursery.

Early in the new year Tanne, Elle, and Ellen Wanscher were packed off to Folehave to stay with Mrs. Westenholz while Ea, who had fallen ill in Jutland, recovered at Aunt Lidda's house. Tanne's comment on that experience is laconic and was only set down several years later, for "Mama's amusement." "1900: . . . lived for a while at Folehave, where to all of us are some of the most *hyggelige* things we have ever known."[6] The peculiar contortion of the sentence is itself interesting. It was unlike her—she took pains with her prose—and it suggests that she was self-conscious about the clever little hypocrisy she had perpetrated. The word *hyggelig* was a compliment to Mrs. Westenholz and anyone else likely to read it. But it summed up what Tanne considered were the most mediocre and contemptible aspects of life at Folehave: heavy meals and platitudinous discussions, homely gatherings, sentimental effusions. The word actually means "cozy" or "comfortable,"* and *hygge* as an antidote to a cold climate is a concept the Danes are very fond of. But Isak Dinesen would always mock them with it, turning it into the proof of an impossible leadenness. "The Danish character," she wrote to a friend as an old woman, "is like dough without leavening. All the ingredients which supply the taste and nourishment are there, but the element which makes the dough able to change, to rise, has been left out."7

When she became the mistress of her own house, there would be boundless hospitality but little *hygge*. She preferred the beautiful to the convenient and the formal to the cozy—to the extent that she would live at Rungstedlund for thirty years, well past the middle of the twentieth century, before installing modern plumbing or central heat. One of the pleasures of life in Africa was, precisely, the hardness of its edges, the uncertainty at its center and the extravagance of human energy that was its "leavening."

3

Rosa, Isak Dinesen wrote, "had often been so weary of, so angry with her surroundings that in order to escape and punish them she had wished to die. But as the weather changed she too had changed her mind. It was better, she thought, that the others should all die. Free of them and alone, she would walk over the green earth, pick violets, and watch the plovers flitting over the low fields."8 Writing in *Out of Africa* about the fawn Lulu, a wild orphan adopted by her house, raised on milk out of a saucer, petted and spoiled, she attributes the same adolescent frustration, the same death wish for her well-meaning captors: "You are furious with us now, and you wish that we were all dead. But the trouble is not as you think now, that we have put up obstacles too high for you to jump, how could we do that, you great leaper? It is that we have put up no obstacles at all. The great strength is in you, Lulu, and the obstacles are within you as well, and the thing is, that the fullness of time has not yet come."9

Tanne's state of conflict, like Rosa's and Lulu's, was that of many young women of her class and epoch. From their ranks Freud recruited his early

---

*It is worth noting briefly, in regard to the author of *Seven Gothic Tales,* that the opposite of *hyggelig* is *uhyggelig,* not only "unhomely," "uncomfortable," but also "uncanny." There is a similar relationship between the German words *heimlich* and *unheimlich,* and Freud has written an admirable essay on the subject. His conclusion is that an uncanny feeling or experience occurs to civilized people when a repressed childhood fear or desire is revived, or when "the primitive [animalistic] beliefs we have surmounted seem once more to be confirmed" (Freud, "The Uncanny," *On Creativity and the Unconscious,* pp. 122–161).

patients and made his observations about hysteria and repression. They were often the "spoilt children" of their houses, fed out of saucers, petted, but sheltered from experience and taught fear and shame for their own instincts. Like Tanne, they often fell in love with animals and masculinity, dreamed of surrender and perdition, and were drawn to the wilderness in all its forms —but trapped inside the circle of firelight. It was not even that they were tied down there, but rather restrained by the power of their tacit privilege to remain. Those young girls, worshiped for their innocence and virtue for so many centuries, had the greatest difficulty rejecting what amounted to a spiritual privilege. To do so they not only had to become "unnatural" but also "ungrateful," and ingratitude is the most awkward of double binds. Tanne would explain to her brother that she felt it was impossible to rebel against the family, to reject their goodness—for the "strange" reason that her own conscience made her feel unworthy when she tried.

4

From the moment she returned from Switzerland, Tanne would complain, her schooling had abruptly stopped: she didn't learn another thing from Miss Zøylner; the family made no further effort either to prepare her for some career or for the responsibilities of marriage and domestic life. They saw to it that she was literate, that she spoke foreign languages, and they sent her to a "cookery school" for a few months in 1901—there is still a recipe for chocolate brittle among her papers. But that was as much finishing as she would get.

The real privation was not of cultural opportunities or raw materials, but that someone of her intelligence and depth should have no community of her peers and no older person of distinction to help her make something of herself. Georg Brandes sets forth her predicament beautifully in his essay on Friedrich Nietzsche. "On entering life," he wrote, "young people meet with various collective opinions, more or less narrow-minded. The more the individual has it in him to become a real personality, the more he will resist following a herd. But even if an inner voice says to him, 'Become thyself! Be thyself!' he hears it with despondency. Has he a self? He does not know; he is not yet aware of it. He therefore looks about for a teacher, an educator, one who will teach him not something foreign—but how to become his own individual self."*

Tanne had no such teacher until she met her friend and lover, Denys Finch Hatton. She would try to approach Brandes himself, but the family, in an excess of moral outrage and prudish zeal, stopped her. And in that long interval she did what so many richly gifted and determined young people

---

*Brandes, *An Essay on Aristocratic Radicalism*, pp. 9–10. This is also the essence of the point Ibsen was making, and it was the great theme of the Scandinavian counterculture of that epoch.

have done, whether they are stranded in parsonages or suburbs, in ghettos or among rich philistines. She found her teachers in the library and communed with them in her imagination. She let a "real self," a secret and inviolate self, live in their works and their company, while a "false self," vague and compliant, met the demands of a humdrum existence. This is a surprisingly common but also desperate resort. For once divided, it is almost impossible to reunite those separate selves. Fantastic hopes and daydreams grow up around the secret self to protect it, becoming so intense and satisfying, and so sacred, that the intimacies and achievements of real human life seem mediocre and even vulgar by comparison. In only the rarest cases are those who "hold out" for their dreamworlds vindicated—as Isak Dinesen would be—though at a price, through a forfeit, of which she would make an exceptionally astute appraisal.

5

There is no proof that Tanne read Brandes's lecture on Nietzsche when it was reprinted in 1900, although some evidence suggests she did. She told her Aunt Bess in a letter from Africa that by the time she tried to see Brandes at nineteen, she had been "immersed" in his books for years and that "it was he who had revealed literature to me. My first *personal* enthusiasm for books —for Shakespeare, Shelley, Heine—came to me through him."[10] There is no mention of Nietzsche, although perhaps she did not wish to offend Aunt Bess unnecessarily. Thorkild Bjørnvig, the young Danish poet who became Dinesen's protégé, tells us that she had "loved the Zarathustra books since her early youth."[11] She took a line from Zarathustra as the epigraph for *Out of Africa,* * and Nietzsche's philosophy, sometimes even his words, echo throughout her work. Brandes's essay suggests the scope of Dinesen's debt to Nietzsche, or at least their kinship. He discusses Nietzsche's contempt for the Christian heritage of dualism, which Dinesen felt had poisoned her own early life and which she took as the subject for a number of tales.† He explains Nietzsche's belief that fate, rather than guilt or sin, is the cause of suffering, and that fate should be courageously embraced—a lesson taken from the book of Job, to which Dinesen refers again and again. In a particularly interesting passage, Brandes reiterates Nietzsche's call for "a new nobility" —a class of people who have learned to know life through action and who therefore have a "use" for history. It was this "class" Dinesen invariably admired when she came across it in real life, which supplied the heroes for *Out of Africa* and her tales, and which she lamented, as an old woman, had so sadly declined in modern Denmark. Finally, Brandes gives Nietzsche's

---

Equitare, arcem tendere, veritatem dicere: To ride, to shoot with a bow, to tell the truth. *See* Nietzsche, "On the Thousand and One Goals," *Thus Spake Zarathustra, The Portable Nietzsche,* p. 171.
†"Alkmene," "The Cardinal's Third Tale," and "Babette's Feast," to name a few.

definition of "the real nobility in man," which is identical with Isak Dinesen's, as "man's capacity for answering for himself, and undertaking a responsibility."[12] This, in the form of the Finch Hatton family motto, *Je responderay,* was the ideal of Dinesen's personal morality, the model she held up in her tales and even the basis of her method as a writer. For by stepping into a role, by taking action and the responsibility for that action, by embracing their fates, her characters become "themselves."

Georg Brandes's book on Shakespeare had also guided Tanne's first reading of his plays. Dinesen told Ms. Migel that her discovery of Shakespeare at fifteen was "one of the really great events of my life."[13] Her own dramatic writing passed through its Shakespearean phases—historical, tragical, and pastoral—as did her doodling. But perhaps his greatest influence was that his standards for the human spirit would set her own: the princes for nobility of character, the melancholics for ironic wit, the bastards for wickedness and caprice. She was extremely drawn to the epicene sexuality in the comedies without knowing why; she longed for the freedom to dress as a boy and in such a guise to demonstrate her gifts as a courtier, which she secretly began to cultivate. Her "favorite female character in all of literature" was Viola. But when she tried to hold the real world to these standards, and in particular her own little Danish world, it let her down.

It is a shame we do not know more specifically what impression Heine and Shelley made.* Perhaps Heine gave to Tanne something of what he gave to Nietzsche: "The highest conception of the lyric poet. . . . He possessed that divine sarcasm without which I cannot conceive the perfect. I estimate the value of human beings, of races, according to the necessity with which they cannot understand the god apart from the satyr."[14]

Tanne herself was a lyric poet at fifteen. She writes about "holy sorrow, mother of all happiness," surrenders herself to the "silence of the night," and addresses the elements as her friends. The ocean's great voice calls to her, and the "wild wind" is her brother.[15] While there is no divine sarcasm in her poetry, it is full of pantheism and sensuality, and indeed Tanne "called [her] self a pantheist" from an early age.[16] This must have been part of Shelley's great appeal. He, too, was in revolt against Paradise, and perhaps his glamorous transgressions inspired plans for her own.

She had other early masters and teachers, including many Danes whose work will be unfamiliar to an English-speaking audience. But among the most influential of them was the urbane, ironic novelist Meïr Aron Goldschmidt (1819–87). Tanne "lived" in his books as a young girl, absorbed his

---

*She refers to both Heine and Shelley in *Out of Africa.* Lulu, the bushbuck fawn, looks like a "minutely painted illustration to Heine's song of the wise and gentle gazelles" (p. 71). She takes a line from Shelley's *Prometheus Unbound* to describe Kamante (p. 26) and had Denys Finch Hatton quote from his song, "Rarely, rarely comest thou, Spirit of Delight!" (stanza four) at the end, to ward off any slump in her morale (p. 344). Shelley was also one of Denys's favorites, and they often read his work aloud.

ideas about Nemesis, and particularly loved *Homeless: A Poet's Inner Life.*
Goldschmidt founded *The Corsair,* a liberal and satiric literary review, whose
"shafts of wit . . . pierced the philistines of art and letters and the absolutists
of politics."[17] He wrote about his sense of foreignness and estrangement from
the Danes in a novel called *The Jew* (which prompted the Jewish Brandes
to remark that it was tiresome to be "perpetually serving up one's grandmother with a *sauce piquante*"[18]). Isak Dinesen would also feel like an outsider
in the Danish literary milieu, disliked and misunderstood, and on this and
other grounds she had a great affinity with Goldschmidt.

Denmark's greatest lyric poet, Johannes Ewald (1743–81) was a kind of
household genius for Tanne Dinesen, as he had lived at Rungstedlund when
it was an inn. He consecrated his brief life to passion and left a memoir
written "in an intricate and sensitive style learnt from [Lawrence] Sterne,"[19]
who was in turn one of Tanne's favorite English writers. Ewald is the
protagonist of Dinesen's tale, "Converse at Night in Copenhagen."

Her letters and notebooks also contain many admiring references to Steen
Steensen Blicher (1742–1848), Holger Drachmann (1846–1908), Hans Christian Andersen (1805–1875)—whose translators and editors have not served
his genius well—and to J. L. Heiberg (1791–1860), who was one of Kierkegaard's models for the esthete. Heiberg was an enormously influential play-
wright, critic, wit, and director of the Royal Theater, who introduced
vaudeville* to the Danish stage and wrote marionette comedies in a satirical
and fantastic vein—works Tanne knew and loved and could still quote from
as an old woman. Her own most ambitious early work was a marionette
comedy, *The Revenge of Truth.* †

Perhaps what is most important to observe about Tanne's literary heroes
at this stage is that they shared something "festive and poetic" in their
makeup: an unusual charm, a fascination for people, an ability to "make a
myth" of themselves.[20] They were artists remembered and beloved for their
transgressions and their bravura, and around whom cults and tales grew up.
Dinesen sought the same charisma in her friends, believed her father had had

---

*As Michael Meyer points out on p. 91 of his biography of Ibsen, vaudeville in the Danish sense was
not music hall, but musical comedy.

†There was a genre of romantic fairy-tale comedy called the *märchenlustspiel,* which Meyer discusses in
relation to Ibsen and which is worth a footnote in the discussion of Isak Dinesen's literary heritage. Meyer
writes, citing a German critic called Herman Hettner: "The most important thing about this genre
. . . was the fact that it dealt with two opposite worlds, that of everyday reality and that of fantasy;
in the best plays of this kind, these two worlds are constantly being juxtaposed in such a way that the
world of dreams is shown as a source of truth and wisdom, while that of everyday reality is made to
seem comic and unrealistic. As a prime example of this type of play, Hettner instances Shakespeare's
A Midsummer Night's Dream. It is a genre that has always seemed to hold an especial appeal for
Scandinavians—Oehlenschläger, Heiberg and Hostrup had all experimented in it, and so . . . had Hans
Andersen" (Meyer, *Ibsen,* pp. 95–96). Tanne's own marionette comedy, *The Revenge of Truth,* is also,
consciously or not, a *märchenlustspiel.*

it, and her cousin, Daisy Frijs. It was, she said, a quality one found in the old Norse heroes and in the Prince of Wales, the future Duke of Windsor, who would dine with her in Africa. She made it the subject of the last tale she would ever write. One book, says Pipistrello, the marionette master, to his double, Lord Byron, "one book will be written and revised" long after all the others have been neglected. "Which book is that?" Lord Byron asks. *"The Life of Lord Byron,"* says Pipistrello.[21]

6

Before he died, Wilhelm Dinesen had written to his wife about their children. "Ea and Elle will be able to fend for themselves," he told her, "but my heart aches for little Tanne."[22] It is not clear what the context was, but it is possible he wrote this in a suicide note. He must have known, or guessed, what his death would mean to her. Indeed, as she entered adolescence, Tanne thought "constantly" about her father and felt his absence from her life as an intolerable tragedy. She cries out to him in a passionate letter written about 1900, apparently as part of some tale but also unmistakably filled with her own feelings:

My dear and beloved friend, my wise and gentle brother:

If you had been on earth still, I should have come to you and you would have taught me to love and to approach thine [*sic*] light, but you are gone away to high worlds, I know not where you dwell, spirit that I love. But do not leave me alone, if your spirit dwells still sometimes on earth, where you loved and suffered, let it dwell within me, who love you. And give me only once a token that you live and are the same, and that my spirit could reach thine, and if you give it me, I shall follow your footsteps and be your disciple, today and always. Perhaps I shall be it in all cases, but you know, my brother, how hard it is to be alone, be with me, and give me your bless [*sic*] dear beloved brother, my master and teacher, my dearest friend.[23]

Parmenia Migel tells us something that indirectly sheds light on the letter. At fifteen, she says, Tanne "became obsessed by the idea that her father lived on in her and that only through her could his ideals survive." In the letter, the human depends upon the spirit for her survival; in the "obsession," it is the other way around. But both describe a covenant joining the living and the dead in an intimate and dependent relation. Whether she is the protected or the protector, Tanne's fantasy of union with her father—so full of both erotic and religious feeling—gives her a powerful, if imaginary, ally against despair.*

---

*That sense of union would outlast her adolescence. Writing to her mother from Africa at a moment when her farm and her marriage were both foundering, Tanne said: "If I can . . . make something of

There is something extraordinary about this letter besides its moving directness and deep sincerity. It is the only piece of prose from her early life written in English, and this cannot be a coincidence. The foreign language both distances and protects the passionate feelings. It was, of course, in a foreign language and behind a pseudonym that Isak Dinesen would find the freedom to write her tales.

In the course of her obsession with Wilhelm, Tanne turned to his family with immense interst and curiosity, and sometime in the course of 1900 she apparently made arrangements to visit them alone at Katholm.

As so many of the emotions of this period in her life were heightened, it is not surprising that when Isak Dinesen reminisced about them it was in the manner of a storyteller, unifying and simplifying events that were in fact ambiguous, and condensing impressions gathered over a period of time into dramatic vignettes. She claimed, to Parmenia Migel, that she had waited five years before going to see the Dinesens, afraid the sight of them would renew a sorrow still too fresh.[24] Ms. Migel in turn recounts the journey in a cinematic style: Ingeborg waves from the doorway as Tanne's carriage pulls out into the Strandvej, and she sees her child's eyes mysteriously "fill with tears"; Katholm itself becomes the castle of initiations in a Gothic tale, approached through a "tortuous forest road" and across a moat. This romantic isolation is made responsible for having shaped the singular characters of its inhabitants, who feel "different" and "set apart" from the more mundane aristocrats of Copenhagen.

Once inside the magically evoked citadel, the young kinswoman admires the "almost legendary" beauty of her aunts and uncle; spends late nights submerged in their "insouciant and whimsical talk"; absorbs a sense of family history on nocturnal rambles through the armory; rides out alone onto "bleached and brindled" moors, deserted save for the wild geese, "to ponder" these new impressions; and gradually begins to see her dead father "smile at her through the eyes of" his surviving brother, Laurentzius, who resembles him "like sunlight and shadow of the same day." (Wilhelm was dark, Laurentzius blond.) In the course of "a few weeks" all of Tanne's "unasked questions answer themselves," and she beholds her own Dinesen reflection in the looking glass held up to her by the family. She has "imperceptibly"— which can mean only from one frame to another in a short sequence— become "one of them."[25]

If such a visit took place, Tanne had not waited five years to make it, nor were the Dinesens romantic strangers to her. Ingeborg took her children and

myself again, and can look at life calmly and clearly one day—then it is Father who has done it for me. It is his blood and his mind that will bring me through it. Often I get the feeling that he is beside me, helping me, many times by saying: 'Don't give a damn about it.'" *See* Dinesen, *Letters from Africa,* p. 110.

their nanny, Malla, to Katholm every summer for a month. Thomas remembered that there were "eight course meals with two bottles of wine apiece,"[26] and that the assembled cousins made up large, boisterous hunting and riding parties and went swimming in the moonlight. In her own recollection of Uncle Laurentzius, Isak Dinesen portrayed him as an old bear, prejudiced and tender-hearted, someone "a pretty woman or a clever old retainer could wrap around their little finger."[27] And Katholm, in the same memoir, was described as a welcoming Victorian household, filled all summer with sundry guests. Among these there might always be several unmarried aunts, old governesses, and retired army officers. On the light nights *(lyse nætter)* of July, the company would sit up after dinner with the doors of the drawing room open to the avenue of linden trees, the scent of roses on the air, while one group argued with Uncle Laurentzius about the propriety of ladies riding bicycles and another counted the falling stars.

What undoubtedly gave these visits their immense glamour for Tanne was the greater gaiety of life at Katholm, the observance of social rituals thought frivolous at Rungstedlund, and the presence of so many gentlemen. All her life Isak Dinesen would have a weakness for that species of upper-class war-horse like her uncle and his friends, the "old chevaliers" of her father's generation who had fought the Prussians, wintered in St. Petersburg, dined at the Café Anglais with their mistresses, and were pleasant talkers on "theology, the opera, moral right and wrong, and other unprofitable pursuits."[28] They were also likely to appreciate a young lady's pains with her toilette and her tact as a listener—refinements superfluous at Folehave. It was probably at Katholm that Tanne first had a chance to test her own power to attract, the charm she had been cultivating in a vacuum, and her claim that "one's real worth lies with the opposite sex."[29]

7

It is not clear whether Tanne Dinesen actually went to Katholm alone in 1900 in search of her identity as a Dinesen, or whether the trip as she remembered it was the dramatic focus of many visits. It is a fact in her own retelling of her life, in the official version. In her talks with Ms. Migel, in "Copenhagen Season," and in interviews over the years she portrays the Dinesens, and herself among them, as a race physically apart: they have senses as keen as wild animals, inhuman stamina, a rapturous joy in pleasure and beauty. Even among high-born friends they prove to be the true aristocrats.

This is the language of myth, and particularly of those childhood myths that make of a dead parent, or a distant role model, a divinity. It is also the image retailed by a canny old storyteller, at home in the castles of fairyland and conscious of her own "mythos." But in the middle years of her life, Dinesen could appraise her father's family with greater candor. She could see them as the Westenholzes did: snobbish, hardhearted, and shallow. She could admit that even with these defects they still attracted her. Worldly egotists often have that charm for those who have been raised by loving martyrs and smotherers. One does not feel guilty showing off, preening a little; they always hold up their own end of a conversation or an affair. Among the Dinesens Tanne relaxed and thrived for the simple reason that they gave her room to feel more like "herself."

Of all the Dinesen relatives, Tanne was closest to her Aunt Christentze, who was her godmother. Christentze was forty-six in 1900, a still charming and lovely woman with the aura of a romantic past. She was two years younger than Agnes Frijs, her best friend, and nine years younger than her brother Wilhelm, whom she had adored. Christentze liked to talk to Tanne about Wilhelm's early life, their childhood at Katholm, the family myths, and she had a fertile imagination.

One of Christentze's poetic tales, offered to Tanne as hidden truth, was that Wilhelm had killed himself because he had never come to terms with his grief for Agnes.[30] Tanne believed it at the time, despite its wild improbability. Agnes died in 1870, Wilhelm in 1895, and he had had any number of excellent suicidal opportunities in that long interval.

Even if one makes allowance for Christentze's romantic sensibility, it was a particularly stupid and even somewhat malicious remark to make to a young girl who idolized her father and who was, like all fifteen-year-olds, struggling with her own sexual identity. Its message was: your father never loved your mother; she had no power to keep him; his erotic loyalty was to another woman, and it was so compelling that he killed himself. Effectively, it took Wilhelm away from both Ingeborg and Tanne and shifted the center of gravity in his life to the time before his marriage. Perhaps this was Christentze's unthinking intention, her revenge, for she had never liked her brother's wife or his pompous in-laws. She had never understood how Wilhelm could prefer such a timid, bourgeois girl to the dazzling young beauties of her own set—to Agnes, or perhaps ultimately to herself.

After the trip—or trips—to Katholm and after Christentze's revelations, Tanne's hostility toward Folehave was more pointedly expressed. She became haughtier and more demanding; she referred cuttingly to the way things were done "at my father's house";[31] she was secretive, moody, vain. Part of this display was, in fact, that teenage bravado which tries to conceal its yearning for dependence and safety under a mask of surliness, daring, or high spirits. It was Tanne who could not let go of her mother, as much as Ingeborg or the family that clung to her. The strength was within her, but the obstacles were within her, as well.

Mrs. Dinesen had never met a teenager in the modern sense before, but she weathered Tanne's storms, moods, and provocations with calm grace.

Aunt Bess, however, bore down like an avenging angel. She fought for her own investment of love and hope in Tanne. And twenty-five years later, when her niece was a woman of almost forty, Bess would still speak about the younger generation's "ingratitude," their "betrayal."[32]

7

Aunt Bess

Bene vixit bene latuit[1]

I

WHEN TANNE CAME HOME from visiting her Dinesen aunts, beguiled by their doll-like figures, their easy laughter, and their idle lives, she apparently flaunted her admiration at Folehave. Bess reacted like a rival. She made scenes that have, at least in the retelling, a distinctly jealous tone. Isak Dinesen remembered one of these vividly enough to pass it on, fifty years later, to her secretary Clara Svendsen. Bess, she said, had shown her a motto in a book and asked if she didn't think it would suit her. The motto was *bene vixit bene latuit;** the good life is the hidden life. Tanne was enchanted by it, and by her aunt's unexpected sympathy. But then Bess took the book away and told her sternly, "You could never live up to such a motto because you are far too frivolous for it, just like your father's sisters."[2]

It is not difficult to imagine how Bess understood *bene vixit bene latuit*. What was proudly hidden in her own life, hidden because she was good? What, precisely, did the Dinesen sisters and their set advertise with the frivolity of their lives? The motto was a trial of purity, a warning about sex, a crude test of loyalty.

Tanne never forgave her aunt and took revenge sixty years later, when she reminisced about her childhood to Parmenia Migel. The result is a portrait of Aunt Bess as unflattering as it is distorted. She is painted in *Titania* as a dowdy, predatory creature, both ominous and laughable. The adjectives "crusading," "humorless," and "meddlesome" rumble in her wake like box-cars attached to a steam engine. "One of my main reasons for going to

---

*The motto was inscribed on the tombstone of Descartes, and, interestingly, Nietzsche quotes it to Brandes in one of the letters published in the 1900 Danish edition of their correspondence. "A philosophy like mine is like a grave. It takes one from among the living. *Bene vixit bene latuit* was inscribed on the tombstone of Descartes. What an epitaph, to be sure!"

Africa," Isak Dinesen confessed melodramatically, "was to escape from the tyranny of this aunt."[3]

The African letters themselves tell a fuller story: of a relationship that was plainspoken and tempestuous, trying at times for both parties, but also rich in mutual affection and respect. Tanne called her aunt "the true patron of my art,"[4] and Aunt Bess wanted to publish her niece's letters. Writing them did a great deal to discipline Karen Blixen's prose, her powers of logic and perhaps also her confidence as a cultural critic. The two women argued about marriage; about feminism and sexuality; about art, literature, and morality; and about the enormous changes that were, in the years between the two wars, taking place in society and human relations. These were the extensions of the arguments they had once had on the terrace at Folehave when they had worked up "a good heat,"[5] and it is clear that they were salutary for Tanne. Where Ingeborg had been fragile, almost childlike in the way she exacted solicitude from her family, Bess was indestructible, a wall for Tanne to batter, to tone her strength and will against.

The incident of the motto, even the years of disagreement, are not substantial enough to bear the weight of Isak Dinesen's later betrayal of Bess Westenholz. We may attribute it in part to her extreme frailty and the unremitting pain she suffered, which could at times make her malicious. She drew a caricature not only of Bess but of Bror Blixen and other figures in her past. By the end of her life, she was also looking back and down from a distance and height that gave things an allegorical simplicity. Bess as a *symbol* was indeed powerfully negative. Her vehement denial of sexuality had been both frightening and impressive to Tanne as a child and became frankly "repulsive" to her as a young woman. Bess acquired a charge in Tanne's psyche that was the opposite of Wilhelm's, and together they made what Dinesen would later call a "unity":[6] they were the perfect spiritual foils. It was primarily in her symbolic role that Aunt Bess was—or came to seem— a tyrant. Perhaps the real tyranny was less the overbearing behavior of the woman herself than an image Tanne had internalized. "My sister was so terrified," said Thomas Dinesen, "of coming to resemble her."[7]

The work of Isak Dinesen is full of men, women, and especially adolescents who hide their real lives and selves, all the while refusing to be shamed or withered. The lives "well lived" in the tales are those with some kind of hidden charge or secret passion, which the "forces inimical to life" cannot find to extinguish. Her holdouts have in common an imaginative heroism that was also that of Tanne Dinesen as a young girl: the heroism of the dreamer. "You know, Tembu," says Mira Jama, in "The Dreamers," "that if, in planting a coffee tree, you bend the taproot, that tree will start, after a little time, to put out a multitude of small delicate roots near the surface. That tree will never thrive, nor bear fruit, but it will flower more richly than the others."[8] Isak Dinesen would succeed, with one of those bold strokes of irony for which she is famous, in subverting the motto Aunt Bess had denied her and setting it above her works: *Bene vixit bene latuit,* indeed.

2

The adolescent showdown between Tanne and Aunt Bess did the former a great service: it mobilized her resistance and her sense of irony. She now began to define herself as a rebel and a Jacobin, and her notebooks swell with demonic characters—suicides, fallen women, romantic poets. She also began to write essays on the French Revolution, including a discourse of fifty pages devoted to its forgotten heroines. Robespierre was a new and unlikely idol, and she wondered if, through suffering and hunger, "I could become a person like [him]."[9]

It was now that she found sanctuary in the writings of that great Scandinavian Lucifer, Georg Brandes, whom her family so energetically detested. Cultural life in Denmark at the turn of the century was polarized and combative, and Brandes and the Westenholzes were natural enemies. "In our day a new ideal is in the process of formation," Brandes told the students at the University of Copenhagen with contempt, "which sees suffering as a condition of life, a condition of happiness, and which, in the name of culture, combats all that we have hitherto called culture."[10] He could have been describing the Westenholz family and all that they held dear.

It is difficult to do justice to Brandes's charisma or his importance; he was not an original thinker or a creative artist, but he was a synthesizer of genius. His 1871 lectures on "The Main Currents of Nineteenth Century Literature" electrified the younger generation of Danish artists and writers and introduced them to the most interesting radical ideas of Europe—the philosophy of Renan, Taine, John Stuart Mill, and Schopenhauer, the poetry of the romantic satanists, and the novels of George Sand. Brandes urged the young to defy the smug pieties of their age, to transcend their narrow Scandinavian biases and to "think big" (as Ibsen put it). Above all, they should strive to "become themselves."[11]

When the lectures were published in 1872, Ibsen told Brandes that "it is one of those books which set a yawning gulf between yesterday and today."[12] But it was execrated in every Danish newspaper, and Brandes was denounced as the corrupter of Scandinavian youth, a promoter of atheism, suicide, and free love. His own irregular life came under scrutiny—his mistress at the time of the lectures was a married woman with six children. And Brandes himself was a flamboyant character, an impatient, sensual man who had tried, in his youth, "to play the roles of Faust and Don Juan rolled into one."[13] He looked conspicuously foreign, was something of a dandy, and continued to be a vigorous and indiscreet adulterer. All of this made him that much broader a target for his enemies and critics—who seemed to include nearly every respectable woman or man in Denmark. Edmund Gosse, who knew Brandes, found it "difficult to account for the repulsion and even terror . . . which I heard expressed around me whenever his name came up in the course of general conversation. . . . The tone of Copenhagen was graceful, romantic, orthodox; there was a wide appreciation of literary speculation of a certain kind, kept within the bounds of good taste, reverently attached to the tradition of their elders. This . . . was part of the political isolation of Denmark, of the pride which her two European wars had fostered, to be intellectually self-sufficient. It was orthodox to believe that the poetry and philosophy and science of the national writers was all that Danes needed to know of a modern kind. Here, then, was an angry Jew, with something of the swashbuckler about him, shouting that mental salvation was impossible without a knowledge of 'foreign devils.' . . . There was something exasperating, too, in the lofty tone which Brandes adopted. . . . He belonged to the race of iconoclasts, like Heine before him, like Nietzsche after him, and he was expected to disturb all the convictions of his contemporaries. In religion a deist, in politics a republican, in ethics an extreme individualist, Brandes seemed at that time prepared to upset every part of the settled and convenient order of things."[14]

If this were not sufficient to earn the undying enmity of the patriotic, orthodox, and liberal Westenholz family, Brandes became embroiled in a particular quarrel with the feminists of the 1880s that is worth looking at a little more closely. Within its provincial compass lie many of the conflicts that shaped Isak Dinesen's view of things.

3

The first wave of Danish interest in women's rights followed the publication of John Stuart Mill's *The Subjection of Women,* translated by Georg Brandes. In the same year, 1869, the Danish Women's Society *(Dansk Kvindesamfund)* was founded and began to publish a newspaper. Its objective as an organization was "to develop and qualify women for the functions and responsibilities of fully mature citizens."[15]

Mrs. Westenholz and her daughters were, Bess wrote, "passionately interested in women's liberation, and were warm supporters of co-education, of the 'self-supporting' woman, that is to say we believed then that women's equality with men would reform the moral outlook of the world and make the relations between the sexes more natural; we believed that 'liberation' would make women happier."*

---

*Bess's views became much more conservative as she aged. In her seventies she would look upon herself as a failure because she never married. See Mary Bess Westenholz, "Erindringer om Mama og hendes Slægt," *Blixeniana 1979,* p. 196.

Mrs. Westenholz had considered sending Ingeborg to England to be trained as a nurse, although her engagement forestalled the plan. Bess, however, did make a career outside her family, in the Unitarian Church. She became a member of its governing board, traveled, lectured at international conferences, and for a while was the editor of the church newspaper. Like her coreligionists in New England, she was a militant for social justice and would have felt at home with the elite of abolitionist Boston or transcendental Concord. She was also an outspoken suffragist.

In the 1880s the political aspects of women's subjection were eclipsed by the more enthralling sexual aspects. There were public debates on marriage, divorce, chastity, prostitution, conjugal fidelity, venereal disease, and "sexual parasitism" several generations before such subjects could even be broached in the rest of genteel Europe. The eminent critic Elias Bredsdorff calls this period of debate "the great Scandinavian war over sexual morality," and his book of the same title describes the manner in which it "left its particular stamp . . . on almost all of the North's most important writers."[16]

The key work on the subject was Bjørnstjerne Bjørnson's play *The Gauntlet,* in which a young woman named Svava discovers her fiancé is not a virgin and refuses to marry him. He is unremorseful and tells her that "a woman owes her husband both her past and her future; a husband owes his wife only his future."[17] Their families become involved. The young man's father exposes the infidelities of the young woman's father, her mother confesses how unhappily and hypocritically she has endured them, and the girl's ideals are brutally shattered.

Svava became the heroine of thousands of Danish women, and Bjørnson became the spokesman—with "male virginity" as his rallying cry—of a sexual reform movement that was a mixture of radical feminism and puritan metaphysics. Aunt Bess alludes to it when she speaks of her hope that sexual equality would reform the "moral outlook" of the world.

Both the intellectual left and the conservative Protestant clergy attacked *The Gauntlet.* The clerics grasped the subversive nature of Svava's demands, which were not simply for young men to save themselves for their brides but for the burden of moral responsiblity in the family and society to be shared equally. A Lutheran bishop's response was typical of many: "Woman's duty is to set her husband an ethical ideal."[18]

The intellectual left attacked the prudery and obfuscation of the reformers. Brandes published a series of scathing articles in *Politiken*—signed "Lucifer" —in which he humiliated, with an excess of wit, three of the feminists' leading metaphysicians.

Bjørnson's resentment of Brandes had been long-simmering, despite an old friendship, and he entered the lists on the reformers' behalf. The crowd parted to watch the great moralist and the infamous immoralist slug it out. What Bredsdorff calls "the three-months' war" ensued, its cannonades reverberating in every Danish drawing room, leaving a lurid afterglow. Brandes emerged with his reputation as a monster of depravity greatly enhanced. With a certain melancholy pride he wrote to Nietzsche: "I am the most detested man in Scandinavia."[19] Ten years later, when Ingeborg Dinesen was setting down the house rules about horseplay and spiritual struggle, she added—perhaps playfully—a clause that forbade the children to mention Brandes's name at the dinner table.

Sexual morality was discussed at great length and in enormous detail at Folehave, and Tanne later noted that it was strange how much the subject fascinated her old aunts, who disclaimed any interest in sex itself. Aunt Bess was a member of the Women Citizens' Society and a supporter of the feminist point of view, to which she tried to convert her young nieces. But they resisted, and Tanne perceived even then that the feminist movement had a long way to go before it offered her generation any real freedom. So long as women were either idealized or degraded as sexual objects, so long as chastity was the central issue in the debate, an essential element of their freedom—the erotic—was denied them. When she advanced this point of view, Aunt Bess responded with a long polemic about the ingratitude and "corruption" of the younger generation and her own "loss of faith" in their integrity. Walking through the snow to Folehave one Christmas Eve with her sister Elle, Tanne complained that nothing and no one could possibly corrupt them, not even Brandes, for they were "already . . . mummies."[20]

In the autumn of 1900, while Tanne and Elle were living at Folehave, Bess enrolled them in a course of lectures given at the folk high school in Hillerød. The folk high school is an indigenous Danish institution. The original one was founded in the 1840s by the great theologian, pedagogue, and poet N. F. S. Grundtvig. His object was to give young farmers an education that would make them more informed and therefore more independent citizens and workers, and also better Christians. The folk high schools were the backbone of the *Venstre* (Liberal) party and of the agricultural cooperative movement. With his democratic humanism, his faith in the common people, his Romantic theology and his progressive influence on Danish life, Grundtvig became a culture hero and a kind of saint. He commanded the ethical bulwark of the dialectic the way Brandes commanded the demonic bulwark. One of the three feminists whom "Lucifer" savaged in *Politiken* was, ironically, Grundtvig's granddaughter, Elisabeth.

The lectures at Hillerød made a deep impression on Tanne Dinesen, although at the time she did not understand why. But fifty years later she spoke of the experience to a young friend. He was going through a religious crisis; his poetry was growing opaque with abstractions, and he had joined a Christian revival movement that was reinterpreting the philosophy of the folk high schools in the light of existentialism. The Baroness was distressed by this, and after dinner she described her own first encounter with the Grundtvigian spirit:

I had only one brush with the folk high schools, which I understand you are now so very much enamored by. It was at Hillerød, when as a young girl I and one of my sisters attended an autumn session, where Holger Begtrup and Jakob Knudsen spoke. I felt repelled without knowing why, but now I know. The two men, powerful and articulate, and not a little self-centered, lectured in complete contradiction to their own personal radiance about mankind's frailty and impotence. They swindled their large, rapt audience, they worked them up into a state of musical possession, as you would certainly put it, but then repudiated the musical. They drew a distinction and boundary between the flesh and spirit, and I felt repelled. Now I know what I did not know then, that one spoke and thought this way in Denmark, even among poets, and that the heritage of symbolism was too heavy, and beauty too unwieldy for these brave teachers of youth.[21]

The adolescent Tanne had no doubt in whose camp she belonged or to what tradition in Danish culture. "To be thyself" is as much the battle cry of her mature work as it was of Ibsen's plays or Brandes's essays. Yet the heritage of the feminists also left its mark upon her. "There is hardly any other sphere in which prejudice and superstition of the most horrific kind have been retained so long as in that of women," Tanne told her sister Elle in 1923, "and I think it will be truly glorious when women become real people and have the whole world open before them . . . I will never cease to be grateful to the old warriors [of the women's movement]—from Camilla Collett to Aunt Ellen, because they worked might and main for it."[22]

The most compelling heroines in Dinesen's tales are the idealists, those who mistrust men and subjection, who make a sacrifice of sexual love for some more challenging spiritual project—self-sovereignty, knowledge, worldly power—which also enables them to be themselves. They are the Valkyries like Athena; the eccentric virgins like Miss Malin; the epicenes like Malli or the bold and easygoing Agnese, riding off to Pisa to learn astronomy. Despite the relish with which Isak Dinesen undresses her *grisettes,* and despite the passion and vitality with which she defends the erotic life, she also makes a case for what Aunt Bess called "a more natural relation between the sexes," which is to say an ideal of comradeship. "All my life," Tanne told her sister Elle in 1928, "I have cared more for Diana than Venus; I am both more attracted to her type of beauty . . . and would myself prefer Diana's life to that of Venus, however many rose gardens and dove-drawn coaches she might have. . . ."[23]

8

Art and Life

THE MOUNTING TENSION between Tanne and the family broke into open conflict when she announced her desire to study art in Copenhagen at the Royal Academy. It is difficult to understand why they balked as they did unless it was to punish her—they were supposed to be "warm supporters" of the independent woman. But she held out, exercising what her brother called "a stubborn and miraculous ability to get her own way,"[1] and in the autumn she was permitted to enroll in the private drawing school of Charlotte Sode and Julie Meldahl, which was housed in a mansion on the Bredgade.*

Every morning Alfred Pedersen, the coachman, drove Tanne to the station at Klampenborg, where she took the train into town. It was a short and pretty ride, mostly along the coast; five minutes to the south she passed the Deer Park; further into town the villas and summerhouses of the rich clustered along the water's edge. The city was rapidly expanding northward, country becoming suburbs. Wilhelm's property had, as he had hoped, increased stupendously in value when the railroad was built, and Ingeborg had begun to sell some of it. She did so with a twinge of guilt and regret, for the parcels of forest and tracts of rolling farmland were destined for development.

The ride gave Tanne an opportunity to throw her lunch out the window. In the evening she would only pick at her dinner, complaining that she had eaten too much lunch. This was the first of many fasts, undertaken in an effort "to achieve greatness" through "hunger and suffering."[2] There is a picture of Tanne from that year, suddenly gaunt, her face a narrow wedge with a huge bow pinned to the top and her eyes great and doleful beneath it. All

---

*Classes with the Misses Sode and Meldahl were required for all women students hoping to enter the Royal Academy, as women were excluded from the academy's own required preparatory classes. In 1904, women applicants had to show: "A completely shaded sketch of a head, or a modelled head; a shaded sketch of a detail of the human body; an outline of an entire body, approximately two feet high; (these provisions are to be carried out outside the Academy)." They also had to draw a twelve-inch sketch of a body "without guidance" at the academy itself and produce a portfolio of their classwork in the preparatory school and of their independent drawings. See F. Meldahl and P. Johansen, eds., *Det Kongelige Akademi for de Skjønne Kunster: 1700–1904* [The Royal Academy of the Fine Arts: 1700–1904] (Copenhagen: Hagerups, 1904), pp. xci–xcviii, 501–503.

her life she would struggle to be thin, for more than the esthetic satisfaction it undoubtedly gave her. "As the years go by," she told her sister Elle in 1928, "one learns to sort out the minor phenomena of life, that are necessary to enable one to be oneself. For instance, I know that I must not get fat; it is preferable for me to suffer the pangs of hunger, because being overweight *cramps my style.*" [3]

Thinness was a badge of her defiance to the *hyggelig,* a lightness not only of the flesh: it contradicted Westenholz solidity. Fasting became and remained for her, even when she was an old woman dying of emaciation, an ironic, powerful, and essentially feminine act of heroism.

2

Toward the end of 1903 Tanne took the entrance examination for the Royal Academy of Fine Arts and was accepted. She began attending night classes in January, living in Copenhagen with her great-aunt Ellen Plum, the youngest of Mrs. Westenholz's sisters and, according to Aunt Bess, the family "saint." The Plums' house was so like Folehave in its routine and tone that Tanne would call it an "offshoot of Paradise." [4]

The Royal Academy was and still is housed in the great baroque Charlottenborg Palace. Male and female students were then strictly segregated, the girls' school relegated to an annex of the main building. The girls' quarters, like their instruction, were in all respects inferior to the boys', and their "morals" more attentively supervised than their drafting. Isak Dinesen recalled that when they wanted to visit the studio where the academy's collection of plaster casts was housed,* a facility shared with the young men, the porter's wife, a Mrs. Grauballe, was obliged to go with them as a chaperone. She grumbled at the chore: "God knows," she told them, "cold plaster can't do you any harm." [5]

Tanne had never attended a school in her own country and school life was a novelty for her, as was the contact with a little society of her own contemporaries, and she remembered that "we young girls had a lovely time together." [6] Originally she had been shy with them; her "deep respect for artists" [7] convinced her they must be cleverer than she, and she didn't initiate any conversations. Yet this reticence could not have lasted long, for in her first year she was elected the vice-president of the student union, a popular office with many social responsibilities and one a shy, self-conscious girl could not have won. (Indeed, one former classmate remembered her as "arrogant and prepossessing.") [8] The union sponsored dances, and to one of these, a carnival ball, Tanne went as a "Watteau-esque Pierrot," [9] that character she had so often played in her own dramas. As the hostess ex officio of the

---

*Before the students graduated to live models, they had to show their proficiency at sketching classical forms from the academy's large collection of plaster casts.

evening, she had the guest speaker sitting next to her at dinner. The "great old man" was Harald Høffding, the philosopher and theologian. "I cannot remember feeling the least pressure because of my prominent position; I think that Høffding's mild, wise benevolence quickly made me feel at home beside him."[10]

After a month at the night school, Tanne graduated to the regular classes, where she began to receive a thorough, if conventional, academic education. She recalled of her first year that learning the laws of perspective "exposed a new and beautiful side of the world to me," which apparently she alone among her classmates could appreciate. While they found the exercises drudgery, she was "enchanted by the unshakeable justice and regularity in the laws of perspective. If I myself acted correctly the outcome could not fail to be correct—but if I permitted myself the least negligence it invariably, and with frightening power, took revenge at the conclusion of the assignment."[11] She would use almost the same words a few years later to describe the workings of destiny, "who is the most inventive of us all in her caprices ... and follows her own laws with great exactitude. ... This is, moreover, a great kindness, for it gives people what they strive for."[12]

Tanne remained at the Royal Academy for five semesters. Some of her drawings and paintings from that period have been reproduced in a lovely sketchbook, edited by Frans Lasson and published in Denmark in 1969. It contains portraits of her sisters, the delicate pencil illustrations she did for *A Midsummer Night's Dream,* and some of the work from her second year at the academy, when she had graduated from sketching the classical forms of the "cold plaster" and from exercises in perspective to life drawing. The students were provided with a series of models, and Isak Dinesen remembered an old woman who told stories from her "peaceful and uneventful life"; an old man who had done "a little of everything" in his time; and a young girl who had enchanted her with an absolute absence of expression, a blankness like that of a piece of writing paper.[13] There is finesse, skill, and feeling in all of the portraits, although it is difficult to judge how much real talent they show. Her teachers did not encourage her to be ambitious, which was more the expression of their general indifference to their female students than any personal lack of admiration for Tanne. It struck her, she wrote, when she began to get to know the young men from "Zahrtmann's School" (the men's division), that they "worked with an enthusiasm which we did not know in our school, and I understood that the responsibility of the true teacher is not first and foremost to 'instruct' but to inspire."[14]

3

In assessing her own debt to the art of painting, Isak Dinesen thanked it for, as she put it, "revealing the nature of reality to me. I have always had difficulty seeing how a landscape looked, if I had not first got the key to it from a great painter. I have experienced and recognized a land's particular character where a painter has interpreted it to me. Constable, Gainsborough and Turner showed me England. When I travelled to Holland as a young girl, I understood all that the landscape and the cities said because the old Dutch painters did me the kind service of interpreting it; and in the Umbrian blueness around Perugia I was, by the hands of Giotto and Fra Angelico, quietly blessed."[15]

But in her tales Isak Dinesen suggests that the great painters can be "interpreters" in a different sense, and particularly to young, unworldly people living in isolation, who have no way of recognizing their own real character or beauty from within. Frederick Lamond, the young theologian in "The Heroine," is one of these. He has lived a "seclusive life amongst books,"[16] but in the gallery of Das Altes, among the pastorals, another world is revealed to him. The young Countess Calypso, in "The Deluge at Norderney," is the most striking case. She has been raised by her guardian as a boy, for the Count Seraphina is a fanatical admirer of young masculine beauty and a misogynist. When her own budding female body can no longer be disguised, the count "annihilates" her—she ceases to exist for him and wanders through his castle like a ghost, disinherited from real life. One night, however, she resolves to escape from this unhappy limbo by cutting off her long hair and chopping off her breasts "so as to be like her acquaintances."[17] Stripping her clothes down to the waist in front of a mirror, she looks at her body for the first time, but her attention is distracted by a figure behind her in the glass, and she turns to find an "indecent" old painting, "a scene out of the life of the nymphs, fauns and satyrs"; in short, a pastoral.[18]

Calypso examines it by the light of the candle; in her loneliness she has developed a great tenderness for animals, and it attracts her to find that certain humans share "so many of their characteristics. . . . But what surprised and overwhelmed her was the fact that these strong and lovely beings were obviously concentrating their attention upon following, adoring, and embracing young girls of her own age, and of her own figure and face, that the whole thing was done in their honor and inspired by their charms."[19]

The erotic art of an earlier age awakens Calypso to her own beauty and sex, and to the terrible perversion of reality of which she has been the victim. She has been prepared to mutilate herself in the name of this perversion— but is stayed from the act by "friends" she did not know existed:

She knew now that she had friends in the world. By right of her looks she might step into the mellow golden light, the pale blue sky and grey clouds, and the deep brown shadows of these plains and olive groves. Her heart swelled with gratitude and pride, for here they all looked at her as their own. The god Dionysius himself, who was present, looked her, laughingly, straight into the eyes.[20]

The sixteen-year-old Calypso, incarcerated among woman haters, is not so unlike the sixteen-year-old Tanne, incarcerated among man haters—who would also feel "annihilated" when she showed the first stirrings of her sexual nature. It is a rather opulent and dramatic metaphor, but Dinesen herself admits that "correct or not [it] was to the heroine herself a symbol, a dressed-up image of what she had in reality gone through."[21]

4

A young, passionate, and needy person like Tanne Dinesen will often be overwhelmed by gratitude for the generosity and understanding that a work of genius seem to lavish upon her and which seem to be so sadly lacking in the older people of her own milieu. Perhaps Tanne's sense that she had "friends" among the great emboldened her to approach that great man who had revealed literature to her: Georg Brandes. While he was in the hospital in 1904, she sent him a bouquet of flowers with a note of deeply felt homage and respect. Brandes would have known from her name and address that she was related to Captain Wilhelm Dinesen—Boganis; perhaps she told him. In any case, he was evidently much touched by the message, for he later called at Rungstedlund to thank the sender in person. Mrs. Dinesen received him —graciously, we must presume, for he had been a friend of her husband's. But she told him that her daughter was not at home. After he had gone, Tanne was called down and lectured indignantly by the family council. She had "betrayed" them, committed a gravely improper and disrespectful act. She had even courted ruin by approaching Brandes, a famous seducer. Their approach stung and humiliated her, despite the conviction she had acted only out of "the fervent enthusiasm of a young heart for . . . [its] first revelation of intellectual genius."[22] Writing to Aunt Bess from Africa in 1924, she lamented the great lost opportunity for his friendship and encouragement: "Brandes might have made a writer or an artist of me, as he did with so many people . . . not one of Denmark's artists or writers in the last fifty years has not in some way become so through him. . . . Had I realised at the time how much was at stake . . . I would probably have had the strength to deceive you, and I wish I had done that. . . ."[23]

Yet in a general way, Brandes did help to make a writer of Isak Dinesen. He fired her love of literature and informed it. In his essays on the nineteenth century she would find that very large and complex perspective of the romantic tradition which is the framework of her own tales. Brandes was a great psychologist and contextualizer of romanticism, and the same could be said of Dinesen herself. As Robert Langbaum lucidly observes, her "coherence derives from her fidelity to the romantic idea. . . . It is because she shows herself such an excellent critic of this tradition, because she sums it up and carries it a step forward, that she is in the main stream of modern literature."[24]

9

Countess Daisy

I

Tanne was starved for fun and liveliness at her Aunt Ellen's house. There were only two other drawing rooms in Copenhagen where she could spend an evening: those of Mrs. Ida Bardenfleth and her Aunt Ellinor Knudzton, neither precisely a lion's den. She made friends on her own, at the academy, and even managed to meet some of the young men from "Zahrtmann's School." But she confessed years later that she felt "insecure and guilty" at the balls and parties when she should have been enjoying herself.[1]

It is difficult to say precisely when things began to look up, but they did. Drafts of letters in her notebooks give us a glimpse of her budding friendships and flirtations. These drafts are rarely dated and are usually pretty rough; they provide an altogether tantalizing, unsatisfactory, and allusive record.[2]

Tanne had one friend named "Etienne." From the pert, familiar tone she takes with him, he seems also to have been her confidant. She calls him *kamerat,* so perhaps he was also a fellow student. One of her letters accompanies the return of a "mystic and frightful apparatus" that he has loaned her. She goes on to tease him about his forthcoming trip to Munich with "the ravishing Kirstine B"; alludes to a "more saucy" outing they had hoped to make together but which fell through; and she tells him she will think of him with envy, turning up his nose at everything in Germany. The letter ends "with many regards and a kiss from your ever-devoted pal, *Poca animata.*"

Very much in the same spirit is her friendship with a certain Vidur, with whom she had also hoped to travel. Vidur was apparently a family friend; the proposed excursion included Tanne's cousins, the Countesses Sophie and Daisy Frijs. When the Frijs sisters couldn't go, Tanne didn't get permission either. "It is very bitter to think that you are having a wonderful time, while I sit here with two ancient ladies who are visiting us."

Then there was a "most lovely and beloved Cecil." Tanne makes a casual appointment to see him in town and then launches into a sarcastic little tirade about their mutual friend, a certain "T." "As for T," she writes, "although we used to be such chums, I should like him to know I am not quite as much in love with him as he imagines. . . . He seems to me to be a mixture of

a rather spoiled urchin and a roguish knave, rather more of the latter.
. . . Apropos, don't I owe you a hundred?* With much love and ever yours,
etc., etc., as time is very short, Tanne."

2

In 1906, while Tanne was living at the Plums' in St. Annæ's Square, she
began keeping a diary. It was little more than a weather report, a record of
family visits, of what she wore to dinner and whom she sat beside. There are
no intimate thoughts or feelings in it; for the undercurrents we must turn to
her prose. But it gives us a sense of the surface texture of her life, the rather
undistinguished background upon which her rich fantasies were embroidered.[3]

Tuesday, the thirteenth of February, is a typical day. Tanne notes that the
weather was excellent, that Ingeborg was ill and that Uncle Asker Westenholz stayed for lunch. In the afternoon she goes to the hairdresser, where she
spends twenty-five kroner. Aunt Ellinor stays for supper; she has Uncle
Thorkild as a dinner partner, and the meal is interrupted by a porter with
a message about his "unfortunate expedition to the agricultural college." Ea
is there. The two sisters both wear their black dresses.

A few days later there is a break in her routine. Tanne goes home to
Rungstedlund after school. Aunt Bess comes for a visit and takes her to
Hørsholm, where they have a picnic. "It was lovely in the country." They
dine at Folehave, and Ea spends the evening assiduously nodding agreement
to the banalities of an old aunt, rather like the elder sister in a Jane Austen
novel. Tanne allows that it "certainly must have been very tiresome." They
return to Copenhagen after supper "with extraordinary trouble," for the city
was full of foreign officers and dignitaries who had come to attend the funeral
of King Christian IX.

The following day Tanne spends the afternoon at her window, watching
the funeral cortège on its way to Roskilde. "Saw the whole world going to
the burial. . . . The foreign officers were very dashing. In the afternoon wished
Mother and I had gone to the [Church service]"—presumably to be able to
ogle the officers at closer range—"but instead went to the Langelinie." Two
cousins come for tea, and Tanne tries to press one of them, Christian, into
"acting comedy" with her.

Early the next week the morning is filled with consecutive visits from the
Frijses, Mrs. Bech and her daughter Grethe, and Aunt Bess. Tanne and her
mother pay calls all afternoon; Ea dines out on her own; and Ingeborg and
Tanne attend the opera, arriving half an hour late. It is *The Marriage of Figaro*.
"Very amusing," is Tanne's judgment.

---

*In 1900 a hundred kroner were worth about twenty-six dollars.

The brief mention of the Frijses suggests that it was not unusual for Tanne to see them in Copenhagen. She gives no special emphasis to the meeting, and they reappear just as casually: "Visit from the Frijses . . ." "The Frijses to lunch—very amusing . . ." "To the Frijses."[4]

The Frijses—or the Krag-Juel-Vind-Frijses—were the most exalted of Tanne's seemingly inexhaustible store of relations. Count Mogens Frijs, son of Thyra Dinesen, was Wilhelm's first cousin, hunting companion, brother-at-arms, and best friend. He had married the Countess Frederikke Danneskiold-Samsøe, whom Tanne called Aunt Fritze. They had four daughters: Sophie (Agnes Louise), Helle, Inger, and Daisy (Anne Margrethe). Daisy Frijs, three years younger than her cousin Tanne, would become "the best friend she ever had."[5]

It is difficult to say when this friendship was singled out and invested with its great intensity. Among the notebooks from 1900 there is the scrap of a letter addressed to "my best-of-all and sweetest cousin [*kusine*]" in which Tanne asks Daisy to be "your accounts' keeper."[6] Daisy would then have been a girl of fourteen. By 1906 she and Tanne met often in town and had begun a correspondence, of which, unfortunately, only the barest fragments remain. One of these fragments gives us a glimpse of Tanne's clandestine social life. She had come to town to meet a friend and convinced the porter at the Frijses's mansion on the Ny Kongensgade to admit her when no one was at home. Countess Frijs found out and made a scene.* Tanne wrote to Daisy, asking her to intercede. "It was *not* either to steal or to have an assignation," she assured her cousin, "but in all virtue and honesty to see Tolhetzer" (perhaps the mysterious "T"). But then Tanne crosses out this explanation in the draft and continues: "I was namely in town to get some sketchbooks, and it was impossible to stay in the streets because of the [February street carnival]. I hope Aunt Fritze isn't angry. If she is, I am terribly sorry. *Many* thanks for your letter. I shall certainly serve you up *une chronique scandaleuse* when I get the material for it. Yes, I think it is a brilliant plan for us to travel abroad together, although we shouldn't make it a public touring society. . . . Forgive this hasty letter, a more amusing one, hopefully, shall follow."[7]

Daisy Frijs was a lithe, elegant, and wild girl, flawed by a deep streak of carelessness. She was ready for any gaiety or adventure, but also ready to risk her future or reputation on a whim. She had a gambler's contempt for or thrill at the possibilities for total ruin, and she seemed to be taking revenge with her very exuberance for some wound she was too proud or too angry to dress. Once she decided to elope with a lover, but laid her plans so clumsily that Count Frijs discovered them and swore to kill the man. Daisy's marriage was also contracted in a kind of tantrum, apparently to mock the universe

---

*The incident is echoed in "Copenhagen Season," where Adelaide gives Ib a rendezvous at her aunt's empty house.

and herself. She became engaged to a balding, middle-aged nobleman in the foreign service whom her family could not object to, but a man with no fire, no real interest for her. She lived a formal and unhappy life with him— constrained by the protocol of his profession—and an increasingly ruinous secret life of her own.

Daisy's bravado, so glamorously inexplicable, fascinated Tanne. She envied it, mistook it for fearlessness, thought it noble and poetic. It reminded her of Wilhelm; his niece had the same charisma. Servants, strangers, casual acquaintances fell under her spell, and she was one of those who "made a myth" of themselves. But Daisy also suffered from Wilhelm's restlessness. She could not be held down, anchored to one place or by any relationship. By the end of her short life, Tanne believed, Daisy yearned for such an anchor. In retrospect, she, like Wilhelm, seemed to have been doomed.

There are several portraits of Tanne and Daisy as young girls in the tales of Isak Dinesen. They resembled the two proud sisters in "The Invincible Slave Owners," changing roles, keeping the world at arm's distance, playing out a drama with intrigue and danger, silliness, and pathos. They were also like the friends in "Carnival," modern in their abandon, "bringing out the worst in each other,"[8] sharing an erotic complicity tinged with despair. Perhaps the best likeness comes from "A Supper at Elsinore," the portrait of the De Coninck sisters in their youth:

> . . . within their own rooms, they would walk up and down the floor and weep, or . . . lie in bed at night and cry bitterly, for no reason in the world. They would talk, then, of life with the black bitterness of two Timons of Athens. . . . Then again the girls would get up, dry their tears, try on their new bonnets before the glass, plan their theatricals and sleighing parties, shock and gladden the hearts of their friends, and have the whole thing over again. They seemed as unable to keep from one extremity as from the other. In short, they were born melancholics, such as make others happy and are themselves helplessly unhappy, creatures of playfulness, charm and salt tears, of fine fun and everlasting loneliness.[9]

Yet it was not an equal friendship. For Tanne it was an opportunity and a challenge. It called upon the reserves of wit and charm she had cultivated for so long, without an audience. Like art school, it was "hard work";[10] she evidently felt the pressure to make herself interesting and desirable by "serving up" entertainments: *chroniques scandaleuses,* plays, stories, theatricals. She became a kind of superior and elegant handmaiden to her cousin: Viola to Orsino. The persona of the storyteller as the confidante of a capricious king —Mira Jama, Scheherazade, the wise thrall in "The Fish"—was born here.

For her part, Daisy Frijs seems to have loved and admired Tanne, but she had three sisters of her own and remained close to them. Their world, that of the highest aristocracy, was a closed and incestuous one, and although Tanne was their second cousin, she was an outsider. The other Frijs sisters, daredevils and sportswomen, found Tanne somewhat "affected."[11] She was "more intellectual than a girl of the nobility,"[12] they thought, which was not a compliment. They also remarked on her curious habit of "opening wide her abnormally large, dark eyes."[13] Her own family had similar complaints. They felt Tanne "acted" to them in a strange way, although they had a different adjective for that unnatural effort. The Frijses thought her "affected," her own family "insincere." One is, we may note, an esthetic, the other a moral judgment.

When Tanne began to frequent the society of the noble Frijs sisters, to dine with them in town, to go to their balls, to spend weekends at Frijsenborg, she suffered keenly from a sense of her social disadvantage and perhaps acted —put on a special show of brilliance—to distract from it. She was invariably the only guest at the castle without a personal servant. This was a particular humiliation for her, and perhaps it informed her notion that it is the loyalty of the servant which defines the aristocracy of the master. With what pleasure she would write casually, sixty years later, that in Africa "you always bring your own servant with you when staying in the houses of your friends."[14]

Aunt Fritze and other noble ladies, whom Tanne also called "Aunt,"* nevertheless found subtle ways of condescending to her. She would be paired at dinner with some young cousin of the house with no title or some older man already married. They reserved the most eligible young noblemen for their female counterparts and constrained Tanne with little checks, glances, and slights to know her place.

Tanne's own family, and in particular Aunt Bess, looked "with despair" upon her friendship with Daisy Frijs, who was considered to have a "casual moral attitude."[15] From the days of her own engagement Ingeborg Dinesen remembered a voluptuous, "oriental" dinner at Frijsenborg. The guests had been seated on cushions and the general air of negligence and freedom had made her uneasy. A great deal had been written in the eighties and nineties about the "sexual parasitism" of the aristocracy, the way great lords preyed upon their servant girls and countesses dallied with their coachmen. Much of this was undoubtedly romance, but the family feared, with Tanne's capricious nature, for the worst. In one sense their fears were grounded. What attracted Tanne to the aristocracy was precisely this: her sense that their emotional life, their instinctual life, was freer. No one lectured the Countess Daisy about "the dangers . . . of becoming worldly and vain"[16] or about self-sacrifice.

Tanne was the only one of the three Dinesen sisters who was infatuated

---

Aunt was used in that circle as a title of affectionate respect for female relatives or family friends of one's parents' generation.

with the Frijses. Ea was assiduously studying music in Copenhagen and Berlin, and had begun to give concerts. She was ambitious for a singing career, but also totally without social pretensions or any taste for grandeur. As Tanne would remark: "I am so much more demanding than she is."[17]

Elle, in the meantime, was studying secretarial skills, Russian, and Esperanto ("in the hopes universal brotherhood would prevail")[18] and had become a socialist. She wanted very much to visit Russia and live in a commune of young nihilists, and she made the trip just before the revolution. Tanne was critical and somewhat contemptuous of her younger sister's political idealism, which had been strongly influenced by their Aunt Bess. In one of her notebooks there is a little passage in mirror writing which asserts that "in my view, the Radicals are scarcely human."[19]

In effect, Tanne's friendship with Daisy was a divorce from her own sisters, their values and their style. She passed out of the world they had shared and into the brilliance of life at Frijsenborg as through a prism that separated the Westenholz from the Dinesen. With Daisy she was not one of three, but unique; free to pretend she was a child of great or unknown parentage like Alkmene, or the offspring of a spiritual love affair like Jens in "The Dreaming Child."

"*1908: Sacrificed myself to high society in the winter. Was bridesmaid at Frijsenborg in a snowstorm.*"[20] In that image—the intricacy, lightness, and fury of the falling snow; the splendor of the great palace; the social and erotic expectations of the marriage; and the irony that turns this experience into a "sacrifice"—there are most of the elements of Daisy's irresistible allure.

First Tales

And pearls are like poets' tales: disease turned into loveliness, at the same time transparent and opaque, secrets of the depths brought to light to please young women, who will recognize in them the deeper secrets of their own bosoms.
                                                    —Isak Dinesen[1]

I

THE FAMILY THEATRICAL was a beloved institution of the leisure classes in the nineteenth century. It was also one of the few channels and sources of approval for the creative ambitions of young girls, and it is striking how many women writers of the last century began as the dramatists or impresarios of their family circles.

Tanne had played this role at Rungstedlund for years, and at Christmas in 1904 she wrote one of her last plays for the family. Thomas, thirteen, was unwillingly cast as the heroine, and it took great bullying and cajoling to make him deliver his crucial line, "I love you, Jan Bravida."[2] Tanne as usual took a minor but pivotal role. She was a witch, an old gypsy woman who appears in the first act and interrupts a squabble between the villain, a miserly innkeeper, and his helper, Mopsus, while they are plotting to rob and murder a young soldier of fortune.

Destiny, she warns them, is cleverer than they, and she sets a curse upon the inn: all the lies told under its roof that night will be revealed as truth by the morning light. The curse provides for the comic reversals of the plot: it beggars the miser, saves the hero, turns deception into love, and gives the little play its name: *The Revenge of Truth*.

If we compare the revenge of truth to the revenge of perspective, which Tanne was just discovering at the academy, they bear a notable resemblance. Betray destiny, and it will turn the tables on you. Make an error in your drafting, and perspective will ". . . invariably and with a frightening power, [take] revenge at the conclusion of an assignment."[3] Far from intimidating the young artist, these inexorable laws reassured her. She felt herself to be in the hands of an "Artist" infinitely more capable than herself.

The Revenge of Truth is a distillation of Tanne's nineteen-year-old wisdom. She would recast it again in 1912, and in 1925, then as a marionette comedy. While the materials of the piece don't change noticeably over the years, its irony grows mellower. Eventually the little play would be produced on the stage of the Royal Theater in Copenhagen and on Danish television. For one of its last performances, in 1960, the author gave instructions that Amiane, the witch, should look like "Isak Dinesen."

2

By the end of 1904 Tanne had also started work on a series of tales to which she would devote serious attention for the next four years. She wrote them in longhand in the blue exercise books, grouping them together under the title, "Likely Stories." That was ironic, for they are mostly in the "gothic" mode and full of ghosts, visions, and cases of possession.

In one of the earliest "Likely Stories," "The Lawyer of Bergen," a respectable man is persecuted by a spirit. "Two periods follow such a discovery as a rule; the first frightfully disturbed, confused, in doubt, when one feels as if one will be the plaything of a power whose intentions one doesn't know, and the period which comes next, when one understands the intentions of one's lord or persecutor, and as one gradually acquires more interest in and understanding of the persecutor, one learns to reckon with him."[4]

In a second tale, "Sebastian di Sandeval," a Spanish nobleman of that name is bored with a soul that inhibits his indulgence in worldly pleasure. He pawns it off on the Devil, who is reluctant to accept it. Some years later he has a change of heart and asks the Devil to give it back. The Devil doesn't refuse outright but hedges, betting the nobleman he cannot live for a year without committing some immoral deed—seducing his neighbor's wife or stealing his land.

In a third tale, "The Devil's Opponent," which, like the others, is incomplete, a young English nobleman falls into the hands of two adventurers in London who have an unlimited "passion for amusement." "There was something sensitive and fine [in the nobleman's] being, which aroused a wicked impulse in the eldest [of the adventurers], who was sometimes up, sometimes deep down, and who felt at ease in both places."[5]

As a rule, the tales are brilliantly sketched out for the first few pages and then trail off. Developing her characters interests Tanne less now than the mechanics of narrative structure. Once she finds the key to a tale, its central conflict, she lets it wind down again unattended.

These little keys also happen to fit her own situation in 1904 as she begins to go out in society, meet men for the first time, experience their desire for her and hers for them. Like the lawyer of Bergen, she is confused, in doubt, and frightened about being "possessed," becoming the "plaything" of a spirit she cannot control, but she is also hopeful that once the initial strangeness has worn off she will grow to like it. Like Sebastian di Sandeval, she is growing "bored" with her inhibitions and eager to experiment with "worldly pleasures." But she has not outgrown the fear of eternal regret, of losing herself irreparably. And like the fine, sensitive young English nobleman, she has fallen in with friends—and one friend in particular—whose example of dissolution both tantalizes and alarms her. For Daisy, like the elder of the adventurers in the tale, has a "passion for amusement" and a spirit equally at home on the heights or in the depths.

3

While she was studying at the academy, Tanne made the acquaintance of a young man who was to give her literary career its first real guidance and encouragement. His name was Mario Krohn; he was four years her elder and the scion of a distinguished intellectual family. His father was the curator of the Museum of Applied Arts (Kunstindustrimuseet); Mario would become curator of the Throvaldsen Museum and, by his early twenties, he was already a respected and largely self-taught connoisseur of art, an expert in the painting of the eighteenth century and the relations between French and Danish artists of that era. His photograph shows a pale young man with a high forehead, a beautiful profile, a soft and refined expression, and the hint —in a fastidiously knotted tie—of the taste for which he was so noted.

Tanne's own references to Krohn are sparse and date mostly from her diary of a trip to Paris in 1910, when she saw a great deal of him. She told Parmenia Migel that he proposed to her but made very little of it. She seems to have maintained with him that delicate tension between flirtation and friendship she had engaged in with her "chums" Cecil, Vidur, and Etienne.* We may only speculate on the degree of his influence; how much, for example, his own love of the eighteenth century informed her own. He arrived on the scene at an age when Tanne, like Calypso, was suggestible, and he was a handsome and willing mentor. In Paris he would take her around the museums and the private galleries, lecture her on the Impressionists, try to convince her of the merits of Millais and speak about that "mobility of the soul"[6] that he found far more interesting in a woman than mere beauty. "He took great pains," she would write ". . . to guide a beginner."[7]

Krohn was Tanne Dinesen's first reader outside the family. (She had "tried out" the "Likely Stories" on her sister Elle as they were dressing for dinner

---

*But this is not certain, for in a letter to her brother about sexual desire and jealousy, Karen Blixen wrote: "I have emerged from any love affairs that I have had as the very best friends with my partner. What has captivated or infatuated me, or however you like to put it, has been a human personality or some kind of mutual interest that we have shared—or else the whole relationship has been . . . like a game or a dance. I don't think I am capable of treating a sexual relationship in itself with any great seriousness." See Dinesen's *Letters from Africa,* p. 321.

in the evening.) He was a good audience, one of those skillful appreciators able to discern raw talent and imagine its possibilities. He urged her to take herself seriously as a writer, and so that she might, he arranged to have some of the tales read by Valdemar Vedel, the editor of *Tilskueren,* Denmark's most distinguished literary journal.

Vedel responded promptly with a letter full of solid criticism and careful praise. He rejected one of the pieces, a long, idealistic story about the French Revolution that he called a "lecture." "It was," he told her, "too broad and a little too artistically contrived, and the whole tone too hearty and sim-pleminded. It is also too long." He found a second tale, "The Hermits," also too long, but this one was "so original . . . and so well made that I would like to take it for *Tilskueren.*" With a few other "Likely Stories" it could well make a book, he thought. "There is certainly talent in the author."[8]

"The Hermits" appeared in *Tilskueren* in August 1907, under the name of Osceola. Tanne would publish two more tales using this pseudonym: "The Ploughman," which appeared in *Gads Dansk Magasin* in 1907; and "The de Cats Family," in *Tilskueren* in 1909, by which time Mario Krohn had become its editor. In 1962, Clara Svendsen edited a special edition of Osceola's work.[9] In addition to the three previously published tales, Ms. Svendsen added several poems from the same general period and the unfinished tale, "Grjot-gard Ålvesøn and Aud."

4

The original Osceola (1804–38) was a leader of the Seminoles, born to an English father and a Creek mother. When the American government pres-sured the tribe into signing a treaty that forced its emigration from Florida to Arkansas, Osceola mounted an armed insurrection and swore that any chief who led his people into exile would be killed. He defeated the American troops in a series of battles, eluding every effort to take him captive. This was finally accomplished, through bribery and betrayals. He died in prison shortly afterward.

Wilhelm Dinesen had naturally admired Osceola and had himself written under an Indian pseudonym, Boganis. If we consider Osceola as a literary, rather than a historical, figure, a number of Romantic and Wilhelmine ideals converge in him. He is the noble "natural man," making a final and impossi-ble stand against his extinction. Like so many of Dinesen's own heroes and like her own persona in old age, he combined great moral strength with a stubborn denial of the modern world. He was a quixotic figure, brought to ruin by the purity or obsessiveness of his idealism.

Osceola was also the name of Wilhelm's German shepherd, the faithful creature who had accompanied father and daughter on their walks, and so the pseudonym had a private meaning and was, perhaps, a private joke. Osceola the lesser also predisposed Tanne toward his kind. Dogs held a special place in her life and her affections. In 1908, at the height of the Osceola period, she was given a shepherd dog whom she named, to keep things in the same literary family, Natty Bumppo.

In 1934, when the author of *Seven Gothic Tales* had, after much research by Danish journalists, been unmasked, Karen Blixen explained her reasons for taking a pseudonym. She told an interviewer from *Politiken* that she had done it "on the same grounds my father hid behind the pseudonym Boganis . . . so he could express himself freely, give his imagination a free rein. He didn't want people to ask, 'Do you really mean that? Or have you, yourself, experienced that?' . . . I moved my own tales back a hundred years to a truly Romantic time when people and their relations were different from now. Only in that way did I become completely free. In many things I resemble my father."[10]

The richly symbolic and dreamlike tales of Osceola are full of Wilhelm's presence and influence, and also full of the yearning, seen in the English letter to "my beloved friend," to make contact with the dead. Dead fathers counsel their troubled children; dead officers woo human maidens; demons beg for redemption at the feet of gallows; and ghosts speak with poignant and seductive voices.

5

"Grjotgard Ålvesøn and Aud" takes us back to the old Denmark, to a semimythic period of transition between paganism and Christianity. It was inspired by the saga of King Olav the Holy, who had baptized the Vikings. The Dinesen children all knew this story well, as Ingeborg loved the sagas and used to read them aloud with great feeling. Tanne and Thomas, in particular, shared a lifelong enthusiasm for the sagas' barbaric (and also Nietzschean) ideals of heroism and honor.

One of Olav's liegemen, Ålve of Egge, refused to accept the new God and continued to sacrifice to the old ones. Olav had him killed and was in turn killed by Ålve's kinsmen. Grjotgard was Ålve's son, and Osceola invents a destiny for him. He falls in love with his brother's wife, Aud, whom he identifies with a female spirit of the woods. She encourages him ambiguously. Watching him wrestle with another warrior, she tells him he is the strongest of men and adds: "If I were you I would let no man be my equal."* Confused by this incestuous desire and troubled by its corollary—his secret wish for his brother's death—Grjotgard seeks the wisdom of his dead father. Ålve emerges from his burial mound and tells his son to honor his race and his family above all. The tale has a nobly tragic ending. Grjotgard learns his

*Karen Blixen, *Osceola*, p. 22. It is interesting to compare this to Brandes's remark in his essay on Nietzsche: "He who feels that in his inmost being he cannot be compared with others, will be his own lawgiver."

brother has been murdered, avenges his death without a moment's further hesitation, and is killed in turn. Aud mourns both of them with queenly stoicism: "Shall we, who have seen them, forget them?"[11]

Those epic passions are a little too remote from Tanne, and her prose has an artificially rough-hewn solemnity. But "Grjotgard" shows us where her ambitions lie; she attempts a feat that Isak Dinesen will later carry off with such virtuosity—"to talk at once," as Robert Langbaum puts it, "about psychology and culture."[12]

Grjotgard is also one of those noble atavisms we shall meet often in Dinesen's tales, their greatness obsolete in changing times. His thrall, Finn, who narrates the story, is another original: the proud servant. He is inscrutable in his wisdom, maternal in his tenderness, belligerent in his fidelity to the hierarchic idea. "The hierarchy of the world of created things," writes Walter Benjamin in his wonderful essay on the Storyteller, "which has its apex in the righteous man, reaches down into the abyss of the inanimate by many gradations. . . . This whole created world speaks not so much with the human voice as with what could be called 'the voice of Nature.' "[13] It is this voice that speaks through Finn to Grjotgard, as it will speak through Farah, through Kamante, and through Africa itself to Isak Dinesen.

6

"The Hermits," which Vedel chose for *Tilskueren,* is by far the finest of Osceola's tales. It is set at the end of the eighteenth century, and the hermits of the title are a young married couple, Lucie and Eugene Vandamm. Like the author, Lucie is a girl of twenty, lovely, high-spirited, eager for life but deprived of it. She has been brought up in yet another of those "parsonages" by yet another of those frustrated, somber, and repressed parents, a scholarly father who cares only for the "driest facts" and has a "deep contempt for women." Eugene is his disciple, a young idealist enamored of Rousseau and at work on a book he is convinced will "reform the world." There is an echo in Tanne's gentle scorn for him of her attitude toward the politics of her sister Elle and her Aunt Bess.

For their honeymoon, Eugene takes Lucie away to a remote and uninhabited island, where he ignores her for his work. She is extremely lonely, but after a while a ghost appears to keep her company. He is a young naval officer whose ship was wrecked on the island a hundred years before, and he, too, is lonely. They strike up a sympathy; he tells her about his life, the girl he loved, and how unwillingly he was wrenched from them. She talks a little of herself and sings for him. When her husband comes into the room she stops abruptly—for he cannot see the ghost. When Lucie tries to explain about him, she realizes she cannot. "She knew that he would never believe what she told him was true, and more so, that according to his conception of truth, it could not, indeed, have been so."[14] Lucie's relationship to her gallant, ghostly friend is much like Tanne's romance with her dead father. The others at Rungstedlund could not "see" him, never spoke of him, and Tanne could not have explained her feelings had she wanted to.

Gradually this dead man who is so passionate for life woos Lucy away from the living man who is so indifferent to it. "Can you, who has aroused them, guess what feelings . . . you have given back to me?" he asks her. "Give me your sorrows," she replies, as Tanne said to Wilhelm, "let me take part in your pain." After a terrible tempest, she will join him forever.[15]

Osceola tactfully leaves us in doubt as to the authenticity of the ghost, and even Lucie herself wonders at the last moment, "Is it I who shrieks?" It is impressive how clearly Tanne grasped, even at nineteen, the relationship between the supernatural and the unconscious. It is also impressive that she could render so subtly a portrait of her own dangerous attachment to the dead.

7

"The Ploughman" is a much less controlled piece, bursting with violent feelings the plot is too fragile to contain. It begins with an apostrophe to the primeval forest. Tanne lavishly describes the world when it was new and untamed by man. She imagines elephants roaming through the virgin wilds and the awe the forest inspired in those uncivilized human beings who contemplated its forbidden depths. Finally she laments its "death," its "murder" by civilization. Then a tale begins that will also glorify an archaic and demonic grandeur: that of a soul.

We are led from this dream forest into a patch of the deep woods that once lay inland from the Strandvej, south of Elsinore, and thus not far from where Tanne and her father took their walks. A young girl comes to this eerie place on the way home from market as night is falling. There is an old gallows in the middle of the woods. She sees a man spread-eagled on the ground at its base; her horse, not normally skittish, bolts, and at first she thinks the man is a spirit. When he demands flour from her wagon, she recognizes him as a desperado of a more common sort and threatens to kill him if he comes near her. But raising her arm to strike, she finds it paralyzed. He tells her she cannot harm him—nor can any human being.

His name is Anders Ostrel, and he is half-human and half-demon. His father was a rich merchant who married a witch, mistreated her, and died. He and his mother lived alone, shunned by society, until he was eighteen. Then he fell in love with a merchant's daughter and proposed to her. But she spurned him because of his demon blood, and he—in a tantrum of rage —cursed his mother and the day he was born. "You who cursed your birth for the sake of an unfulfilled desire, shall have all your desires fulfilled," she tells him. And adds the fatal twist: "You shall have other reasons to wish yourself unborn."[16]

Anders proceeds to take advantage of his magic invulnerability to "try everything" in life: "arrogance, power, happiness without bounds, wealth, omnipotence . . ."[17] But eventually his omnipotence begins to oppress him. There is no one able to set limits to it, and like a Frankenstein he becomes destructive, commits heinous crimes, seeks out evil and misery as relentlessly as he has amassed wealth and indulged in pleasure. His soul fills with bitterness toward humanity, and that bitterness has drawn him to the forest.

His parents' miscegenation is the origin of Anders's torment, for demon and human impulses contend within him. "You are not worthy to live on the earth," he tells the girl, as a representative of humanity. "You are slaves of your free will. . . . We, the wood's wild animals, despise you, who have felled the forests . . . given things a name . . . and built gallows. . . . But your blood in me is so strong that it has vanquished me; I care nothing for your laws, your gallows are a disgrace, but now they have drawn me to them."[18]

The gallows are for Anders, as they will be for Alkmene, the symbol of guilt: the civilizing force internalized. Alkmene also despises them and is drawn to them. Anders calls civilized people "slaves of their free will," which means of their free acceptance of the doctrine of sin and redemption; Christianity has made them slaves. These are the terms in which Tanne formalized her own conflict with "Paradise," with the morality of her family, their denial of the instincts. If she, like Anders, fancies herself "a child of the free wind," she also has the blood of "rich merchants" in her veins, and through them of all the lawmakers and gallows builders.

After he has told her about the excesses of his life, Anders implores the young girl—rather unreasonably—to sentence him for his crimes, to pronounce his doom and thus to set him free. She is a human being, he tells her, and she will therefore be able to judge him according to the standards of human justice. Overcome with trembling, weeping, rage, and confusion, she refuses and rides away. The tale then shifts to her.

Her name is Lea; she is a farmer's daughter, and we recognize her immediately as one of Dinesen's Valkyries: all strength and innocence. When she reaches home she goes straight to bed. Her world is shaken, "everything is changed." The worst of it is that for the first time in her life "it was necessary for her to mull over her feelings, something she had always considered the most complete waste of time." In other words, Lea has had a Fall; she can no longer remain unconscious. "A man has confessed his crimes to her, a heavy burden."[19]

This is the last moment the tale has any psychological authenticity, for Lea subsequently "redeems" Anders by putting him to work plowing the earth. They kiss, fall in love, and the nightmare turns into a daydream. But before that happens we might recall an experience in Tanne's life, very similar to Lea's, which conceivably she wanted to relive and to give a different ending.

[83]

Just before his death, Wilhelm Dinesen unburdened himself to his child about many episodes in his past which "seemed to urge Tanne beyond her age and comprehension. She listened wide-eyed, at times almost frightened, and remembered what he told her without having understood it."[20] But she had understood its essence: that her beloved father was tormented by a violent and mysterious unhappiness. In her childish imagination it began to acquire dreadful proportions, and at the same time it also merged with that "torrent" of reminiscence, much like Anders's, about a career of sensuality and transgression. While Lea manages to save Anders, Tanne could not deter her father from making use of a "gallows." He had reached out to her, and she had failed him. "The Ploughman" is apparently her attempt to retell that traumatic story and to alter its fatal course.

There is another refrain in this dream tale, that of the child with tragically divided loyalties. Not only does the blood of Anders's parents contend in his veins, the real father and mother contend for his identity. Anders describes to Lea how, after his father's marriage, he had spurned his wife, treated her like a servant, and how he was filled with loathing when she came near him. Anders, too, curses her, rejects her, desires to have one parent only: a father.

We glimpse, in Tanne's sympathetic portrait of the witch, her very painful impression of Ingeborg as a woman scorned by her husband who, if she was to believe her Aunt Christentze, had always loved another woman and killed himself for that love. We glimpse Ingeborg as the mother doubly betrayed, scorned by her own child as well. Tanne had wished for one parent only and had had that classic wish briefly fulfilled. It was inevitable that this "omnipotence" should frighten her, as Anders's boundless power frightened him, and that it should generate a devastating sense of guilt.

II

Love, Humble and Audacious

I

THE TALES OF Osceola bracket a period in the author's life when fear, struggling with desire, produced what Isak Dinesen later called "the mystic melancholy of adolescence."[1] Tanne gave those forces the names that her own upbringing and a romantically religious age provided for her: God and the Devil, virtue and sin, Christianity and paganism. In a sense she experienced a religious crisis with its vicissitudes of conscience, its sexual tension and morbidity, its philosophical groping. Her asceticism was one phase of this crisis —throwing her lunch out of the window in order, "through hunger and suffering," to know the heroic. So, too, was her yearning for "ecstasy," for the overpowering, for a fate she could surrender to. Thomas Dinesen tells of an afternoon in the spring of 1906 when he was fourteen and his sister twenty-one. They went for a walk together in the woods around Folehave, and, stopping to rest, they sat down at the edge of a small pit of gravel. Tanne, who had a book with her, Hans Kaarberg's *Big Game,* opened it and read a passage aloud to Thomas. It was the story of a young boy named Svend, who asks his father to explain what God is. The father replies that "if he only once meets the greatest thing a man can perceive, then he has also met God." As an old man, Svend is hunting bear on the coast of Greenland and finally shoots his quarry. But the shot cracks the glacier and precipitates an avalanche. At the sound of this great break, "a superhuman joy came over [Svend]," Tanne read, "his heart trembled with ecstasy. Secure and happy as an outlaw who . . . lays his grey head to rest on the pillow of his childhood's cradle, he lay down on the heaving ice-floe near the fallen bear. 'God is watching over me, my father's God' it sang in his soul as the sea took him—the heathen."

Tanne closed the book and admonished her brother always to remember that "it is . . . feelings like that which make life worth living."[2]

The living and the surrendering, we should note, are simultaneous here. Death and sex were inextricable to Tanne at this age. When she felt herself imprisoned at Rungstedlund, her vitality stifled or depressed, she imagined a fate—an ecstatic or heroic death, an apotheosis—that would rescue her. Thirty-five years later, she adapted Kaarberg's little story for the ending of her own tale, "Peter and Rosa."

[85]

Ecstasy is rarely gratuitous in the work of Isak Dinesen. There is always a price to pay—generally loss or death. Dinesen's heroes and heroines pay it willingly and even gaily, and that is the definition of their heroism.

2

Darkest adolescence gradually passed, and a reflection of the distance between Tanne at twenty-four and Tanne at twenty is the story she published in 1909, "The de Cats Family," her last work as Osceola. The earlier tales are raw and unguarded; "too hearty and earnest," was Vedel's criticism. "The de Cats Family" is playful, full of charm, light in the Wilhelmine sense of the word: its true seriousness is elusive. In this tale of a race of upright burghers, modeled on the Hansens, Osceola treats virtue and sin as part of a comedy of manners.

In August of 1905 Tanne accepted the invitation of her Scottish relations, the Berrys, to visit them at Glenstriven, their house near Edinburgh. She kept a diary of the trip that catalogs her activities in detail but unfortunately offers no comment upon them. Crossing the North Sea, she saw three dolphins and forbade the captain to shoot them. It rains and blusters; she makes excursions to medieval castles and browses in village bookshops; she tramps the moors in a tweed skirt and a straw boater, with her sketch pad. In large parties of pale cousins she shoots grouse, gathers mussels, scavenges for raw emeralds in the burns, and at a picnic accidentally sets fire to her favorite red cape. There are endless tea parties, and she reports on their chatter exhaustively to her mother. Only once does the writer rouse herself from a holiday daze to make a crisp observation, of a couple who arrive for luncheon one afternoon, a young lord and lady: "What pure, beautiful, stupid, noble English."[3]

The Scottish trip was a prototype for the kind of wholesome family vacation Tanne took and seems to have enjoyed in the next few summers. In 1906 she went to "fetch Elle in England," stayed with a Professor Carlyle and his wife in Oxford to study English and lived in London for a while —a period about which we have no information except that she was "shown around Parliament by [a] John Burns." The following year she made a trip with Thomas to the peninsula of Kullen in southern Sweden. They boarded with a sea captain named Helgeson who taught them to sail. "Tommy" was almost sixteen, a tall, handsome athletic boy who was studying sciences and engineering. He was extremely proud that his older sister confided in him "as if I were an equal."[4] This trip consolidated their friendship—and a special affinity for one another among the siblings—which would prove very precious to Tanne in her hard years in Africa.

The next summer she went north again, with her sisters, and they toured the fjords—"a wonderful tour."[5] They might well have crossed paths there —on one of the steamers that plied the jagged coast, on the terrace of an inn overlooking some mountain vista, or climbing a steep path in the crystalline morning air—with a handsome English family. The Viscount Maidstone (Maisie), the Lady Gladys Finch Hatton (Topsy), the Honourable Denys Finch Hatton (Tiny) and their mother, Nan, Countess of Winchilsea, spent part of every summer in Norway.[6]

3

Once Tanne dropped out of the Royal Academy, her life had very little formal structure. From 1907 until she left for Africa six years later she continued to draw for her own pleasure and to write, but her literary output was modest, even if one includes the unfinished manuscripts. Thomas supposes that "after a while some criticism arose over her slightly empty life,"[7] probably from Aunt Bess, who, according to Ms. Migel, wanted Tanne to "work for the Church."[8] But the pressure did not amount to much, and Isak Dinesen would complain—unfairly under the circumstances—that it was scandalous how her family had permitted her to grow up without acquiring any lucrative worldly knowledge.

Clara Svendsen suggests an image for Tanne's state of mind as she embarked upon these formless years. It is that of a little boat she writes of in two poems, "Fair Wind" and "Rowing Song," both of which date from around 1906, the year Thomas was given his first dinghy, the *Basia,* and began taking his sisters out for "cruises." "The light boat swept along by the currents is seen as an image of the irresolute mind set adrift by 'imagination and fantasy, old tales and thoughts at twilight, words and moods and dreams.' "[9]

The early part of this idle period held some of the most purely happy, carefree, and voluptuous moments of her youth. She became a regular of the sport-loving and aristocratic "smart set," which included the Frijs sisters and her Swedish cousins, the twin barons Bror and Hans von Blixen-Finecke. Their pastimes were not much different from those of their counterparts elsewhere at the turn of the century. They raced horses, played bridge and golf, drank whiskey, danced to the gramophone, gave costume balls, shot large flocks of small game birds, acquired airplanes and motor cars with all their accoutrements, and made love with a cynicism and a poise that would have astonished their Victorian parents had they been aware of it. In Denmark, however, there was a great deal less of the glamorous decadence that has made Edwardian London and belle époque Paris such irresistible subjects for social research. The flamboyant characters from the theater world, the symbolist poets, the homosexual pianists, the great eccentrics and demimondaines were missing.

"There is hardly any other closed society in the world that can exhibit such a collection of fine figures as the Swedish aristocracy," wrote Boganis,[10] and Tanne took note of it.

Bror and Hans Blixen were born in 1886 and were part of a large family. Their father, the Baron Frederik of Näsbyholm, in Skåne, had married the Danish Countess Clara Frijs, sister of Agnes, first cousin of Wilhelm, and aunt of Daisy. There was an older brother, heir to the estate, and four sisters. Hans was the elder of the twins and, as often happens in such cases, had the edge in relation to Bror, both dynastically and psychologically.

They were raised in the country in a great house, in proximity to animals, servants, and royalty, though not to books. There were few inhibitions strong enough and few ideas or necessities serious enough to give their characters any shape different from the tribal one. They were robust, confident, and irrepressible. Conquest in all its forms, though particularly of large mammals, was the central passion in both their lives. Hans was a great horseman and later became a flyer. Bror, a man of legendary stamina, was supposedly the original of Hemingway's great white hunter, Robert Wilson, in "The Short, Happy Life of Francis Macomber." To his tent, in the finest Hollywood tradition, trooped the wives and daughters of his clients in a lascivious procession.

As children, Hans and Bror went to school in Lund, where they became "a constant worry to their teachers and parents, never taking work seriously, and always up to pranks and tricks." They accounted for their allowance as follows: "Received, 100 kroner. Spent, for exercise books, pens, erasers, 1.85 kroner; for this and that, 98.15 kroner."[11] Once they invited their father to a grand dinner at the Hotel Angleterre in Copenhagen to make amends for their bad behavior. But when the bill was presented, Hans had to pledge his father's fur coat to pay for it.

It was the custom in noble families for the second son to become an officer, and Hans eagerly entered the cavalry. He was the best rider in Sweden and acquired an international reputation. One of his most often cited and admired feats was to have ridden and won a race in Malmø, then to have flown his plane to Denmark, where he rode in and won a second race later the same afternoon.

Bror was less conspicuous in early youth. He enrolled in an agricultural school in Alnarp but, according to an old friend, "spent most of his time pursuing studies of a different nature, mostly in Copenhagen."[12] After he graduated, he was made the manager of a small family estate, a dairy farm at Stjärneholm, but was a failure at it. Bror's extravagance with money and irresponsibility with credit would become legendary on three continents and amounted, by all descriptions, to a kind of fiscal imbecility. As a farmer he always had "large holes in all his pockets."[13]

The twins were short, powerfully built, fair, with strong features and fierce, heavy-lidded blue eyes. Hans was slimmer, and in his full-dress uniform at a dinner party or spattered with mud after a victory at the track, he was an almost official symbol of masculine glamour. Isak Dinesen's Swedish friend, Ingrid Lindström, who knew the brothers in Sweden before she emigrated to Kenya, described Hans as "slightly better-looking" and suggested that he "stole most of the thunder." The old baron preferred him to Bror, whom he treated "cavalierly."[14] But if the scales of paternal and popular favor were unbalanced, there is nothing to suggest that Bror suffered very deeply from that deficit. In fact, he appears to have been almost maddeningly without moods. He was, by the descriptions of his friends, particularly those in Africa, one of the most durable, congenial, promiscuous, and prodigal creatures who ever lived.

<h4 style="text-align:center">4</h4>

Tanne fell madly in love with Hans.

He did not return her passion.

"More than anything else, a deep, unrequited love left its mark on my early youth," Isak Dinesen told Clara Svendsen.[15]

We know very little else about the romance. But in "The Old Chevalier," a tale of reminiscence about first love, Isak Dinesen evokes that experience in detail. If we reverse the sex—a procedure she so often uses herself—the image comes into focus: a castle, an admired rider, a smitten outsider:

> I had met her and had fallen in love with her in the autumn, at the chateau of a friend where we were both staying, together with a large party of other gay young people who are now, if they are alive, faded and crooked and deaf. We were there to hunt, and I think that I shall be able to remember to the last of my days how she used to look on a big bay horse that she had, and that autumn air, just touched with frost, when we came home in the evenings, warm in cold clothes, tired, riding side by side over an old stone bridge. My love was both humble and audacious, like that of a page for his lady, for she was so much admired, and her beauty had in itself a sort of disdain which might well give sad dreams to a boy of twenty, poor and a stranger in her set. So that every hour of our rides, dances and *tableaux vivants* was exuberant with ecstasy and pain, the sort of thing you will know yourself: a whole orchestra in the heart. . . .
>
> Love, with very young people, is a heartless business. We drink at that age from thirst or to get drunk; it is only later in life that we occupy ourselves with the individuality of our wine. A young man in love is essentially enraptured by the forces within himself.[16]

Tanne persisted in loving Hans Blixen despite his indifference, at least until her marriage to his brother. There were, she claimed, other men who courted her and proposed, but she kept them at a distance. She preferred the idea, with its infinite possibilities, to the compromise of reality.

Human love of the lasting kind, the daily kind, with its abrasions and disappointments, cannot compete in the short run with those great imaginary passions that the lover can recharge at will. No matter how much Tanne yearned for the "light and warmth" of a normal and secure relationship, she would inevitably, she confessed to Thomas, manage to escape when the "crunch" came; she equated her fantasy with her freedom.[17] But she also understood, and "unconditionally" accepted, what she thereby stood to forfeit: how marginal, solitary, detached, and even mad a fantasist's existence could become. It is a theme that runs throughout her tales from the earliest, "The Hermits," to the last, "Tempests," in which, with the wisdom of a lifetime, she sums it up.

5

The first rapturous period of Tanne's love had ended by the beginning of 1910, when she left for Paris in an extremely depressed state of mind, convinced that "I shall never again have the happiness to feel as if I stood high and looked out over the whole, great beautiful world."[18]

Daisy Frijs had been married that February to Chamberlain Henrik Grevenkop-Castenskiold. It was a subdued wedding, particularly compared to the way Frijsenborg had blazed with splendor for the marriage of Inger Frijs to Count Julius Wedell two years before. Daisy was apparently not in love with her groom, the Danish ambassador to Vienna and Rome, a man twenty-six years her senior. Tanne and Inger, her bridesmaids, got drunk on her behalf the night before.

The role of bridesmaid casts a woman's own success or failure with love into relief, and Daisy's gesture moved Tanne to reflect on her own recent self-deceptions. "Is it not wonderful how easily we betray ourselves," she wrote in her notebook, "and turn aside from the path we have ourselves chosen, and wander off? . . . What frail timber are people made of."[19]

She left for France with her sister Ea almost immediately after the wedding. The journey was in some sense an effort to repair that lapse in vigilance. Tanne had decided she would find an art school and take up painting again seriously; that she would live on her own, seek out new people, recover some of that momentum and courage she had felt so keenly at seventeen and which, at twenty-four, she had lost.

12

Rue Boccador

I

TANNE AND EA LEFT Denmark on the twenty-third of March, 1910, almost fifteen years to the day that Wilhelm committed suicide. Anders brought Natty Bumppo to the garden gate, and Elle rode into Copenhagen with them. Ellen Wanscher and Else Bardenfleth met them on the platform of the central station, where they also ran into Sophie Frijs, who was on her way to Jutland. Tanne was in a filthy mood, "a truly horrendous melancholy, the kind in which one hopes both that one will die and kill everyone else at the same time."[1]

There was time enough before their departure to take in the pictures at a mediocre exhibition, "an idiotic thing to do," Tanne thought afterward, as it reminded her how "detestable, trivial and meaningless" life was. Nor did she have any confidence in the power of the trip to restore her faith; she was at that moment sorry to be going away. "It was really a kind of madness."

The train crossed Zealand; they boarded a ferry and resumed the journey south, through Jutland. There was a thick fog at the border with Germany, where Wilhelm had fought at the age of seventeen, and Tanne was disappointed that she couldn't see it. At Hamburg they stretched and drank tea in the station café. A Norwegian gentleman helped them with their baggage at Bremen, where they spent the night at a hotel. The next day they struggled back to the train through a downpour and rode south through a seemingly endless industrial landscape. Tanne almost missed her long-anticipated glimpse of the cathedral at Cologne. In the dining car they sat next to two "simple Swedes," but once back in their compartment they drew the shades and the journey began to acquire "an eternal character. We fall asleep and wake up and read and fall asleep and wake up," she wrote. She had broken in a new diary for this trip, and as a kind of motto, a caveat against self-delusion, she had inscribed the words *"Aerlig, Aerlig"* on the cover: Honest, Honest.

It was the night of the twenty-fifth when they reached Paris. A hansom piled with their luggage carried them through the dark streets to the crowded Hôtel de Malte, where they could get only a "tiny" room. Tanne was at that moment so "disgusted" with life that she felt no surge of pleasure or anticipation at her first sight of Wilhelm's "beloved Paris."

It was the beginning of spring, and the city was still wrapped in a chill. The light was watery after a winter of inundations, and the great chestnut trees that lined the avenues were spiky with tight green shoots. Easter Sunday was, suddenly, a day of brilliant sunshine and warmth, and Ea, in an exalted mood, took her sister to Nôtre Dame. They were part of an immense crowd, and the priests and choirboys were only indistinct white figures, far away, swaying in a cloud of incense. Tanne was only grudgingly impressed by the grandeur of the architecture and the beauty of the music. "Ea," she noted, "was very moved. I could not, with my best will, feel anything."

Their first week was naturally taken up with sightseeing—the Luxembourg Gardens, the Panthéon—and with finding a place to stay. This proved difficult for Tanne. Ea was going to study singing while her sister studied art, and she wanted to live near her music teacher in Neuilly; without trouble she found herself a simple room there. But Tanne inspected and rejected a number of lodgings, one as "too horrible" and another as "too depressing," before she finally settled into a pension, rue Boccador, recommended by Count Eduard Reventlow. This she found "too stuffy" and would have moved had it not been for the charm of the clientele—a changing stream of young foreign officers, who were to provide her with a supply of escorts and intrigues. When she finally made the trip across town to visit her sister, she confided to the diary: "Saw Ea's room. I am so much more demanding than she is, who is not so at all."

This observation touches a central nerve of their relationship. Ea had Ingeborg's sweet and uncomplaining nature and took things as she found them. She worked extremely hard at her music, yet when her hopes for a career were disappointed—her voice was not powerful enough—she made a quiet marriage and settled down on an estate in Jutland. Ea was a comforting figure to her younger sister, but not a friend. Tanne could not confide in her about her own great seesaws of emotion; not because Ea lacked compassion, but because they were incomprehensible to her. "I couldn't do anything better to restrain my frustration and hopelessness," Tanne wrote at the beginning of the diary, "than to complain to Ea how idiotic and meaningless I thought the trip was. Without in the least being able to understand me, she was very sympathetic."

In one of her early diary entries Tanne draws a sharp little picture of life in the rue Boccador:

Monday, April 4. How tired, tired, tired I am. How trivial it all is. Perhaps I should have moved to another place, here it is so stuffy. I shall certainly go to art school, although one has the feeling that it is not any use. . . .

At lunch Madame [the proprietress] sat me beside an idiotic French schoolmistress. The company otherwise was: a divorced French lady who, a month ago, wanted to kill herself and now entertains everybody with it; a Rumanian officer, rather affected; a pleasant, simple young Count Wedell; a German officer; a French couple; a handsome young Englishman; a German gentleman, learning to paint, with his wife!

. . . The meal was better; the divorced Frenchwoman spoke about Life with the Rumanian; I with Count Wedell, who promised to take me to the *concours hippique*. After dinner we chatted in Madame's sitting room. She gave us good advice about getting married. Made a bridge party. To bed early. My birds had grown tame.

The following morning she received a letter from Aunt Bess, and after reading it she rushed out to visit Venus de Milo. She spent the day at the Louvre, mostly in the eighteenth-century collections—"Corot, Watteau and Chardin." But the museum and, in fact, all museums were "loathesome" to her. "The Louvre is embalmed. The King ought to live there." She took the metro home and missed lunch, but later Count Reventlow came for a visit, and she ran out to buy flowers and tea cakes for him. It was the first of many calls from this young gentleman.

2

Eduard Reventlow had been engaged to Else Bardenfleth for a month and was the first friend from home the sisters looked up. He was then twenty-seven and stationed at the Paris embassy, the first post of a long and distinguished diplomatic career.

Eduard was a slight, elegant man with an excellent sense of humor and that capacity for "intellectual playfulness"[2] Isak Dinesen prized so highly. He and Tanne immediately struck up a friendship that would develop unexpected, but also unexpressed, depths of feeling on both sides. The count escorted Tanne to the opera, to the grand cafés to drink champagne, to the boulevards to see *apache* dancing. They stayed out late and walked home across the deserted Champs Élysées in the small hours of the morning. Once Eduard stayed a little behind Tanne to see how many men would accost her, and once, furious at him over what she considered a lack of generosity, she scornfully threw a handful of gold coins at his feet.[3] But he had what the Danish critic Aage Kabell calls "spiritual flexibility."[4] Like other of Isak Dinesen's girlhood friends, and unlike many of the adorers of her old age, he knew when to laugh at her.

However serious it was on both sides, this attraction was treated lightly. Tanne and Eduard dispatched postcards together to Else; Eduard teased Tanne about getting married, and they talked about what kinds of hats her husband would wear. He gave her, as a parting gift, a book entitled *Une Jeune Fille à Marier*. For him it was the last taste of freedom before his own marriage, and the fact that Tanne was Else's friend perhaps gave it a certain poignance but also imposed more rigorous limits. If strict propriety was stretched a little so they could have a good time, it was never rent.

The proof, or at least the very convincing evidence, is that Tanne engaged in half a dozen flirtations with other young men, most of them guests at the pension. There was a redheaded American with dandruff, who invited her to the theater and procured seats in the front row. She found him "decent enough, but unappetising." There was a nobleman named Hohenemser, who left the pension but then came back "for my sake," Tanne believed. He was the friend of a somewhat overbearing German, Dürang, with whom she ate lobster at the Café de la Paix. Count Wedell attracted her a great deal, took her to the Eiffel Tower and to the steeplechase, and taught her an important lesson: always to cast her heart over the hurdle first, so that her body would be obliged to follow.

When Wedell left the rue Boccador, Tanne was "very sorry for it," but he was soon replaced by a dashing and somewhat fickle Russian named Raffaelovich, "to whom people said I should become engaged." Tanne herself was not averse to the idea: "Yes, I wish it, to God," she wrote, although she barely knew him. She dressed up for this Russian and one evening "made an experiment of flirting with him on the stairs . . . but nothing came of it."

The study of painting—Tanne's ostensible motive for the trip—played a very minor role in her Parisian life. She narrowed her choice of academies down to two and decided upon Simon et Menard, in the rue de la Chaussée. The directors waived their standard criterion, that the applicant show a piece of work, perhaps because they were impressed by the fact that Tanne had attended the Royal Danish Academy. But her attendance at their own establishment was erratic, to put it kindly. She went, one afternoon, "to get rid of Dürang," and another time to avoid the necessity of "spending time with people for whom I have no feeling," and a third time in hopes of speaking with a "nice French painter" she had met there the week before but who never reappeared.

There was in any case not much time for art, as Tanne and Ea had managed to excavate an astonishing number of acquaintances. Two ladies who apparently were friends of the family, Aagot and Cæcilie Sunde, were almost constant visitors at the rue Boccador. They came for tea; to fetch Tanne for drives through the Bois; to eat pastries; to buy corsets at the Galeries Lafayettes. Cæcilie tinted her hair and was a dreadful gossip, and Tanne begged God "to preserve me from becoming like her."

Another faithful attendant was Emil Hoskier, a former Danish vice-consul who had settled in Paris and become a banker. He was a widower with a grown daughter, Rosalie, who became a friend of Ea and Tanne's, but this did not prevent him from taking a rather amorous interest in both of the

Dinesen sisters. They enjoyed it, permitted him to kiss their cheeks in the vestibule, and teased one another about his shifting preferences. Hoskier was generous and rich, promenaded them in his carriage, offered them "monstrously ugly bouquets," dined them at excellent restaurants. At the end of their stay he wanted to give each of them a lavish present, and Tanne suggested that an evening dress would be suitable. She admitted to her diary that this was, in fact, rather scandalous but chose "a ravishing pale blue chiffon" with no further qualms. Mrs. Westenholz, who had objected to Wilhelm's gift of a riding hat, would no doubt have considered her granddaughters completely fallen.

3

Parmenia Migel and Aage Kabell place Tanne Dinesen in the audience at Diaghilev's *Ballets Russes,* which was having its second season in 1910, and at Sarah Bernhardt's *Hamlet,* but during the period Tanne was in Paris neither was playing. She does on one occasion record having gone to "the ballet: very amusing," and one of her major interests and greatest extravagances was the opera, both grand and comique, although in the diary she devotes more notice to the elegance of the ladies in the boxes than to the efforts of the artists on the stage.

Although she spent a great number of her evenings with Ea in the company of various respectable family friends, Tanne was possessive about those more interesting new friendships with young men, which she wanted to enjoy unchaperoned. Once she invited Ea to come with her and Wedell to the opera but then pretended she had not worked out any plan with him. Ea went home to Neuilly disappointed, and Tanne spent the evening with Wedell. "It was rather naughty of me," she confessed. They saw *Samson and Delilah* and afterward ate fruit and drank champagne at the Café de Paris.

If Ea was deceived that time, she watched with particular resentment and disapproval as Tanne flirted with Eduard Reventlow, whom she was meeting practically every day. She stopped by the consulate for lunch; he came to the pension to play bridge or dominoes and drink whiskey; he loaned her money, dropped by for tea, invited her to dine at Rumpelmayer's. Ea was often included, but even in a large party Tanne and Eduard made their complicity, their pleasure in each other's company, obvious.

That pleasure was curtailed when Admiral and Mrs. Bardenfleth arrived with Else for a week. Tanne went to their hotel to greet them and immediately felt "depressed" by the "homely spirit they brought with them." The whole time they were in Paris, Tanne became forgetful. She buys Else a basket of chocolates but forgets it at Malmaison. She forgets what happens and forgets to write in her diary. There is a dinner in honor of the engagement at which Else, according to her old friend, "looked her worst" and Eduard "was in a bad mood."

When the Bardenfleths finally returned to Denmark, Ea had it out with her sister in an "expensive tea-salon" and warned Tanne that she was "spoiling something between Eduard and Else. I got really furious."

The reproach, however, stung. It must have forced Tanne to examine her ambiguous intentions and perhaps the illusion that this was what she was really looking for—that it was "truly life." The next day the exuberance disappears from her diary. "Sad, sad, sad," she writes, "everything is disgusting and trivial as before. How little grasp I have of anything in the world."

4

For the two months Tanne lived at the rue Boccador, she was by turns numb and furious, passive and impatient, amused and hopeful, and then suddenly, on a drive along the Seine, "lighthearted, strong for the first time . . . able to laugh at myself." But no sooner had the laughter ceased than she was plunged again into a "lethargy," a "stupor." The diary documents the almost daily fluctuation of Tanne's moods, which was not just a temporary Parisian phenomenon but a fact of her life until the end of it. She had, as she would write shortly about a girl named Rosa, "a spirit balanced on the edge, where to one side it could tumble into sorrow, or sooner anger, and to the other into great joy."[5]

Tanne passed her twenty-fifth birthday at the pension. Early in the morning of April 17 a card came from Ellen Wanscher and a letter from Aunt Bess. She drove out to see Ea in Neuilly and brought roses. Together with Cæcilie and Aagot, they took the tram to Saint-Cloud, found a little restaurant near the barracks, and ate outdoors. It was "a little cold, it rained while we ate, but suddenly it got beautifully clear." That evening they dined with friends, and Tanne "got champagne in my honor." At home she found a photograph from Daisy.

In the first week of May, Mario Krohn arrived in Paris. His timing was propitious, for he was able to distract Tanne from the Bardenfleths. He took her to the "bois sacré, in the Variétés" on their first evening. They went home on foot, stopping to drink tea in a sidewalk café, where they spoke of the divine right of kings, and later stood at the front door of the pension for such a long time, talking and laughing, that one of the guests, a Miss Humphreys, rapped on her window.

During the week he spent in Paris, Mario Krohn saw Tanne frequently, although she did not sacrifice any other amusements to spend time with him. They made the rounds of the museums and the private collections, to which his influence as an art historian procured them entrée. Tanne was delighted by his gallantry, his knowledge, his eminence, but she was also elusive with him. One afternoon she abruptly canceled an appointment to meet him at the Musée des Beaux Arts, and he responded with a large bouquet of roses. She was also elusive when he pressed her about new work, about her literary ambitions, her plans for life—which he hoped might include himself. She told him firmly then, and with a hint of disdain, that she wanted "all things in life more than to be a writer—travel, dancing, living, the freedom to paint."[6]

Mario Krohn disappears from Tanne's diary as casually as he enters it. He returned to Denmark and within a year had married a widow ten years his senior. His own career continued to flourish. He edited *Tilskueren,* assumed the curatorship of the Thorvaldsen Museum, and left a permanent mark on the study of art history in Denmark. But his friendship with Tanne Dinesen waned as she was absorbed by ambitions and relations outside his sphere. In 1922, while she was in Africa, he died of tuberculosis.

That jaunty, proud, and somewhat naive resolution, to renounce Art for Life, was more difficult to carry out than, in her moments of strength and lightheartedness, Tanne imagined it to be. Suddenly, and for no apparent reason, she changed her mind about staying in Paris. Ea had announced that she would return, and perhaps Tanne was afraid of being on her own. Perhaps, too, her friendship with Eduard was becoming too frustrating for her. The morning after a particularly lovely evening with him she decided, "as I lay in bed, that I would go home with Ea."

The little circle was gallant and sorry to see her leave. The morning of her departure Hoskier came with a bunch of "posies" and a basket of chocolates. Eduard arrived that evening to take her to dine. Afterward they drank coffee in Bullier's, where they talked about "born instincts," and hired a hansom cab to drive them slowly around all of Paris. "Stood on the bank of the Seine, ended up at Maxim's; it was almost light when we drove home for the last time." A light rain was falling, and Tanne recorded that she unpinned her hair.

Fifty years later, when she was on the brink of death, Karen Blixen wrote a Christmas letter to Eduard and Else Reventlow, with whom she had remained friends all her life. Eduard responded: "Above all," he said, "your letter has made me think so much of being together with you half a century ago. It was a moving time of my life for me. I never forgot the sorrow of your leaving, or of missing you when you were away. I have never been very communicative when it concerned something very close to me, but you could not have been completely with out knowledge of my feelings."[7]

13

"La Valse Mauve"

I F TANNE HAD BEEN DEPRESSED by the "homely spirit" the Bardenfleths brought with them from Denmark, as if from their open luggage an unpleasantly astringent and familiar scent had risen up, how much more depressing was the homeliness of Rungstedlund itself. An image from her notebook suggests that she had, entering its precincts once again, "something of the same feeling, moral and intellectual, that one encounters physically in a crowded compartment or waiting room, where the windows are kept closed: the air has been consumed."[1]

With Thomas and Anders away at school and the three unmarried sisters all entering their late twenties, there was, in that chaste household of matrons and spinsters, the aura of a comfortable lay convent. Tanne, who had announced her plans for "living" with such determination to Mario Krohn, once again subsided into a state of boredom and depression. She began to outline a tale about "a young French nobleman who returns from Paris to settle down on his estate. . . . He was one of that tribe who can find no satisfaction in life . . . and spent his days and nights without knowing what he should do with his body and soul, and so grew more and more melancholy."[2]

That melancholy suffuses the fiction she continued to write, and she conceives a series of heroes and heroines who, without exception, suffer from it. A famous French poet is obsessed about Destiny and dreams of suicide; a famous Spanish poet survives his "unreasonably" unhappy childhood, having envied everyone's existence and ability to feel joy; a young girl named Rosa finds release from her troubled feelings through love and death. "Rosa," the tale, was an early version of "Peter and Rosa," which Isak Dinesen would finish in 1940 and include in *Winter's Tales.* The mood, characters, and scenes of the early story are similar to those of the mature work and offer us only one of many examples of Isak Dinesen's astonishing economy with her materials.[3] As early as 1911 she was contemplating a collection of short fiction to be called "Seven Tales"; its table of contents includes the titles of other works she would come back to, some as much as forty years later: "The Fish" ("Fra det Gamle Danmark"); "The Revenge of Truth"; and "Carnival," which was then called "La Valse Mauve." "Carnival" was drafted again in 1926, revised in the early thirties, and Isak Dinesen planned to include it in *Seven Gothic Tales*. But she decided that its modernity would jar with the historical settings of the other tales, and it was not published until after her death.

The 1911 version is evocative of her own experiences at Frijsenborg. It has a voluptuous surface, nonchalant dialogue and beneath it an erotic tension that seems to have been her own:

> The year when this story really took place, the mauve waltz was in fashion. . . . A waltz that is called blue had been the rage some years before, but this one . . . was more suited to a generation which both pretended to know and really did know—but in a different way—that nothing had any worth. Two servants carried whiskey and sodawater into a little vestibule which opened into the ballroom. . . . Only five or six couples were dancing to the gramophone, the other houseguests played cards upstairs. The women were all beautiful except for the governess, and none over five and twenty. Four of them were married, but did not have their husbands with them. . . .⁴

2

Tanne had continued to visit Frijsenborg when she returned from Paris, and particularly to make her appearance at those occasions where she could meet Hans Blixen. Her account books show that she paid a hundred kroner for a length of white crêpe de chine for a "racing costume," and in a photograph we see her wearing it, probably during the summer of 1911, at the Klampenborg track. The elegant dress has been trimmed with a sash in which Tanne wears a gardenia. She has a long white boa and a large hat with a drooping brim, laden with tulle and feathers. Although she is barely recognizable beneath it, we make out her eyes, half-closed, and her blissful smile. Her figure seems once again to have been starved into fineness, and it is being frankly admired by a young blade in a straw hat.

Tanne's friends, according to one of them, noticed that she had changed after her trip to Paris. She had become "prettier" but also more "artificial, witty, sharp-tongued—a *raffinée* young lady who frightened men."⁵ She smoked cigarettes and pronounced her name with a slight Russian twist now: "Tania."* It is possible that Raffaelovich was responsible for this piquant alteration which, however, never took with her old friends.

---

*In Africa, Karen Blixen was *Tania* to all her English friends, and Ms. Migel claims that Denys was the first to use this nickname. But old Danish friends were sure that *Tania* dated from 1910. The Scandinavians in Africa, like Ingrid Lindström, continued to call her *Tanne*, as did her husband and her family. In later life only her closest, oldest Danish friends and relatives still used *Tanne*, and to the rest of the world, or that part of it on first-name terms with her, she was *Tania Blixen*. That is how her name appears on the German editions of her work.

If we imagine "Tania's" high-strung charm, her deepening voice with its slightly affected accent, the extraordinary vigor and even menace of that "spirit balanced on a sharp edge" between anger and joy, it is no wonder that the blunt, stable young sportsmen of her set were afraid of her. The old friend claims it was her "intellectuality" that unnerved them, but it was certainly also an intensity that may well have seemed a little mad to them.

It was always these men, the Hans Blixens, the Wedells, the Raffaeloviches, whom she sought out. Someone like the tender and civilized Mario Krohn, who was able to appreciate her, who might have offered her a more compatible and intimate relationship, was perhaps not "a real man" enough for her. Erotically, she responded to conspicuous virility, to Nietzsche's "man for war and woman for the warrior's delight."[6] And she seems, at least as a young woman, to have been quite prepared to sacrifice a more delicate complicity with a lover. Her maxim, often repeated, was that the final word as to what you are really worth lies with the opposite sex. Given her outrageous flirting and her romantic failures, Tanne must have suffered, in her late twenties, from a grave doubt about her final worth.

She also, however, had confidence in her power, in her "star," which no amount of rejection or failure seems to have shaken. In Paris, passing an old man selling lottery tickets for which the grand prize was a million francs, she had bought one, recording in her diary: "Perhaps Destiny will see its way to making good its debts to me."[7] And in relation to Hans Blixen, she seems to have clung to the same kind of optimism.

Fragments of notes and letters, some of them dated, suggest what elaborate intrigues Tanne carried out: intrigues to meet Hans, to avoid him, to arrange meetings at such times and in such places as would be propitious. "I will not go to Frijsenborg," she writes, apparently to herself in July of 1911. "The circumstances will be too little in harmony with my feelings for [Hans]. What I experienced the last time I was with him . . . I shall never go through again." She runs through the possible excuses she can give to Countess Frijs and rules out guests or illness, for she wants to be able to appear at the races that Sunday. She decides that she will claim she has hurt her foot and will therefore pretend to limp.[8]

This sterile expense of energy and imagination—on her clothes, her figure, her social strategies—exacerbated her nervous momentum, those swings between elation and depression. By the end of the year Tanne was suffering from what was then called sentimental exhaustion. Thomas, home on vacation from the polytechnic institute, proved himself very sensitive to his sister's needs and "persuaded" her to make a trip with him to Finse, in the mountains of Norway. Here, he remembered, "she must have experienced some of the beauty of the countryside she had always thirsted for. She had never previously worn skis, but on the very first morning, as we looked out toward the huge Hardanger glacier, she cried out ecstatically, 'We must go up there, even if it kills us!' " And she turned "one somersault after another on her way down the icy mountain slope."[9]

Suicide in some guise was frequently on Tanne's mind, although as an imaginative rather than as a practical solution. One of her heroes decides he will put an end to his "miserable existence," but this resolution brings him such relief that he has no need to go through with it. Jules Bertillon, the "famous French poet," recounts to a company of lords and ladies at a manor house that when he was younger he had been deceived by a girl he adored and rejected by publishers, and had "made plans for suicide without really thinking about carrying them through." He stood, he tells them, by a quay in Paris, looking down at the water with a longing for peace ". . . and made an epitaph for myself: When I love no one and no one loves me, when I feel no joy and nothing gladdens me, when I am good for nothing, and nothing is of use to me, then Farewell, world. But," he goes on, "one has thoughts and hesitations one has not suspected. . . . It came to me with the sharpest consciousness that I couldn't do it for God's sake, that I owed it to Him or to His world because I was an artist. I don't know how I got this conviction for I had not previously believed in any God. I also realized that the sins of the human being, Jules Bertillon, continued to desolate him for the sake of the poet, Jules Bertillon."[10]

As much as she romanticized death and suicide, Tanne had, like her hero, an extraordinary and, we may even say, heroic will to survive. That resource of faith, unsuspected until she was challenged by the hopelessness of neurosis, was one expression of it. Another was that inner loyalty to her talent, a sense of indebtedness to "God or His world," a conviction that she possessed within her a quality too precious to destroy. She could not always count upon this strength, as we have seen from the frequency of her depressions. But it did not fail her at the worst moments of her life—and particularly the most critical of them all, the period when she returned, bereft, from Africa. Her first book, *Seven Gothic Tales,* is the fruit of it. The human being, Karen Blixen, was desolated by her "sins"—her desires, errors, and sorrows—and wanted to die. But the artist, Karen Blixen, found the courage to turn them into tales.

3

In 1912 Tanne once again hoped that studying art abroad might rally her talent and her morale, and this time she decided to try Rome or Florence, where she could be near her cousin Daisy, who was the Danish ambassadress to Rome and Vienna. Daisy seemed eager for Tanne to come. She herself was deeply troubled, restless in her marriage and with the conventions of her life, and Tanne had received "a sad missive" from her that spring, to which she had replied: "Ak, dearest D . . . one must simply try to bear up . . . with firmness and steadiness, and hope for better times."[11] It was subsequently arranged that she should travel south in May.

If there was a diary from this trip, unfortunately it has not survived, and most of our information has come from Karen Blixen's description fifty years later, in various interviews. To the American writer, Eugene Walter, she reminisced with relish about visiting the Casino Valadier, driving in the Borghese gardens and ogling the famous beauties of the day.[12] To Parmenia Migel she recalled the diplomatic receptions and balls, the young bachelors paraded before her by her cousin, who hoped to ignite some spark of a "sentimental response."[13] At one of these functions, she told Clara Svendsen, an old man came up to her and whispered that the ribbons on her petticoats were showing. She almost "sank to her knees in embarrassment," which the old gentleman, perhaps with a certain malicious thrill, observed. *"Cela n'a pas d'importance, mademoiselle,"* he reassured her, *"car je suis un homme marié."**

Daisy was a wonderful cicerone who was able, as Karen Blixen would write, "to lift life up out of the mundane . . . and give it poetry."[14] She showed Tanne the Rome she loved and took her for long gallops in the Campagna. Tanne was "struck by the grand and simple way the peasants would invite them into their houses for a drink of water."[15] They drove into Umbria and as far as Tuscany in an open carriage with a dignified old coachman. When Tanne asked the name of a distant hill town, he answered her with the "solemnity of a cardinal, 'That, signorina, is Assisi.' "[16] Tanne would always remember Daisy against the background of that medieval city, with its stone towers and its stone streets and the "Umbrian blueness" around it. She found it strange and wonderful that "such a modern person could step right into that world and belong there, as she did."[17]

Their moving reunion had only really begun when Tanne and Daisy received a piece of news that signified it was over. Henrik Castenskiold was summoned to Vienna to receive the members of the Danish royal family, who were making an impromptu visit. Daisy was, of course, obliged to accompany him. Distraught at the prospect of losing one another, they "drove around on an afternoon, bathed in fog, from one beloved place in the city to another, and agreed that it would be impossible—unless Destiny gave us the power to fulfill our plan—to come up with something that would really permit us to remain in Rome."[18] That night, however, the Castenskiolds received a telegram informing them that the King of Denmark, Frederik VIII, had died suddenly in Hamburg and that Henrik was recalled to Copenhagen. Daisy and Tanne were vouchsafed at least two more months together,

---

*"It doesn't matter, young lady. I'm a married man." From an inteview with Clara Svendsen, Dragør, July 1976.

and Karen Blixen would claim years later and only partly in jest, "I have often felt that it was I who killed [the King]."[19]

Rome was theirs, and without the paternal and inhibiting company of Daisy's husband. They were both, Isak Dinesen remembered, "almost perfectly happy together."[20] But when they were not happy, they rediscovered the consolation of their old complicity, and each one confided a disturbing secret to the other. Daisy was involved in potentially compromising negotiations to finance her gambling debts. Tanne was drawn into this drama—which could have been written by Ibsen or Flaubert—as a go-between. She in turn told her cousin she was contemplating marriage: not to the man Daisy knew she had loved for several years, but to his twin. Apparently neither revelation diminished their gaiety and may, on the contrary, have enhanced it. Rome was a grand and picturesque backdrop for living in the moment, while preparing to throw themselves away.

14

Noble Prospects

I N THE DIARY that he kept fastidiously all his life, Thomas Dinesen recorded that his sister arrived from Italy on the twenty-third of July, shut herself up without speaking to the family, and seemed more depressed than he had ever seen her.[1] He attributed this state of mind to the fact that she had no plans for the rest of the summer, although, in fact, it was a symptom that would recur throughout her life whenever she returned from abroad to her mother's house, to the rage, the numbness of spirit, and the frustration that overwhelmed her there.

Actually, she did have definite plans for the future: she was going to marry Bror Blixen. For a while, at least, she prudently kept this decision a secret from her family, though without much help from Bror, who was staying at Frijsenborg and dashing off sultry love notes to Rungstedlund, not always enclosed in envelopes. After the first of such, Tanne fired back: "My one and only Bror. In the future do not send me such compromising *open* postcards. Regards, Tanne."[2]

We know rather little about their courtship. In the 1950s Karen Blixen told the Danish art historian and literary critic, Christian Elling, that she and Bror had been good friends *(kammerater)* for several years, and in the course of 1912 they had begun to speak about getting married. But she had resisted, telling Bror that she could never settle down in Skåne where he managed a family dairy farm—"in some respects the most provincial spot on earth."[3] It was not until the chance to emigrate arose that she accepted his proposal. Errol Trzebinski, the biographer of Denys Finch Hatton, adds that Bror courted Tanne with much persistence, and that "ironically it was her barely concealed admiration for his brother which provoked [his] tenacity and brought about her final acquiescence after his third proposal."[4] And Clara Svendsen offers a little vignette that illustrates the kind of rough charm and spontaneity that captivated Tanne. At a summer house party on the Frijs estate the young people decided to go crayfishing at midnight, still wearing their evening clothes. Tanne lost her net, which drifted out into the middle of the muddy pond, and Bror waded in to retrieve it.[5]

When Tanne finally did tell the family, they were appalled. They knew

Bror well and were fond of him in a general way. But as a future son-in-law, "their respect for [him] was not great."[6] He had all the erotic impertinence of Wilhelm without his finesse, intelligence or integrity. Aunt Bess, in particular, found Bror antipathetic to all her principles, and especially her feminist ones. This strenuous and affable hedonist had no goal in life nobler than a good time. He looked down benevolently and lasciviously upon womankind and had been raised to believe the entire world existed, as did the fish in his streams and the game in his woods, for his pleasure. Bess declared that the only good she could see in the engagement was the fact that Bror was poor.[7]

Ingeborg's opposition was less theoretical. "Her intuition told her," writes Ms. Migel, "that Tanne didn't love him."[8] She was also afraid that her daughter, who "rapidly abandoned her most optimistic plans,"[9] was acting on impulse and was in for a bitter disillusionment. She opposed the marriage with all the arguments and, finally, all the fury she could summon. Their struggle was the model for that terrible battle of wills between Madam Ross and her daughter in "Tempests," when Malli announces that she has decided to become an actress:

> In her present conflict with her daughter she became as if deranged with horror and grief, while on her side Malli was completely unbending. It came to a couple of great, wild scenes between the two, and it might have ended with one or the other of them walking into the fjord.[10]

In the end, Aunt Bess would write, "Mutt [Ingeborg] was taken by storm."[11] The engagement was announced on December 21, 1912, and Ingeborg and Tanne left for the official visit to Näsbyholm.

Tanne had often been a guest on the Blixens' great estate for hunting weekends, and she would recall in Africa, with mixed outrage and amusement, how her "Aunt Clara" (Baroness Blixen) organized the household around its "menfolk," and how they were adored, deferred to, and spoiled as religiously as oriental idols. The role of Woman at Näsbyholm was of complete subservience: she existed to charm the heroes at dinner after a strenuous day of shooting; to admire their knowledge of wine, politics, and cigars; and to take the blame for any of their failings or lapses. Tanne had always been refreshed by the boldness with which Inger and Sophie Frijs defied convention to go shooting with the men and to come back as disheveled and dirty as they were, and glowing with the same mysterious emotion.[12] After her marriage, her own relations with "Aunt Clara" were strained by the Baroness's fanatic "partiality" toward Bror[13] and the stream of exhortative and critical letters from Näsbyholm to Africa.

There was much skepticism about the engagement when it was made public. Many of the couple's friends saw only how incompatible they seemed: Bror, the rough, extroverted nobleman and remorseless prankster; Tanne, the moody and artistic bourgeoise with her prudish upbringing, literary accomplishments, and longing for grandeur. Perhaps some of these friends went so far as to question Tanne about the depth of her feelings or her integrity in the matter, for all her life she maintained a special contempt toward people who presumed to judge a marriage or a love affair from the outside.

2

Bror Blixen conjectured that he might have spent his life living in Skåne and become a "well-to-do farmer" if he had not become engaged to "the girl I called Tanne but whom the world was to know many years later as Isak Dinesen. . . . The human imagination is a curious thing. If it is properly fertilized it can shoot up like a fakir's tree in the twinkling of an eye. Tanne knew the trick and between us we built a future in our imagination in which everything but the impossible had a place."[14]

It was clear to Tanne that their future lay as far as possible from Rungstedlund and Skåne, in "some distant country with prospects not yet realized," but it was ironically her uncle Aage Westenholz who first gave substance to the fantasy. "What would you say," he asked Bror, "to exchanging Stjärneholm [the dairy farm] for my rubber plantation in Malaya?"[15] This, Bror replied, was like asking a horse if it wanted oats, and he "accepted without a moment's reflection."[16] But not long afterward, Bror's uncle, Count Mogens Frijs, came back to Denmark from a safari in British East Africa and told the engaged couple: "Go to Kenya, you two."[17] He spoke so glowingly about the country's beauty and its fantastic economic potential that on the strength of his description they changed their minds. "For Penang we read Nairobi, for Malay, East Africa. We would milk cows and grow coffee . . . and the only anxiety was how I should be able to put all the money in the bank."[18] But as Karen Blixen pointed out to Mr. Elling, other members of the family were less enthusiastic. Bror's father was extremely unwilling to lose his youngest son and *"maître de plaisir,* and all our acquaintances in Skåne called us madmen."[19]

In this adventure—their marriage and departure for parts unknown—they became partners. A bond of dependence and anticipation grew up around it, heightened by the skepticism of outsiders. They conspired the way two prisoners, thrown into the same cell by chance, might have conspired to escape, unromantically sizing up each other's potential assets and liabilities, but with no choice than to make the best of them when the sign should be given and the moment come to risk their lives together. It was Tanne, older and cleverer, who logically supplied the form and imaginative energy for their plans, and Bror, fearless and hardy, who supplied the readiness for action. There was certainly another important trade-off: Bror's title and connections with the highest nobility, including the Swedish royal family, and Tanne's access to the Westenholz fortune, which would underwrite their farm. But there is also no question that—despite their differences, Tanne's love for Hans, an element of *dépit*** and mutual exploitation—there was real affection on both sides. Isak Dinesen would later protest that she had put her "soul" into this marriage, and long after its failure she could still speak of its early days as one of the happiest periods of her life.[20]

3

Their plans to emigrate were laid, as Thomas Dinesen would say, "without any petty attention to detail."[21] Aage Westenholz and Ingeborg Dinesen each committed one hundred fifty thousand kroner to buy land, a sum equivalent to about eighty thousand (1912) dollars. After a "voluminous correspondence with Africa a farm of seven hundred acres was bought. The gold mine was ours. All we had to do was extract the rich ore."[22] Bror left promptly for Africa to settle the deal, furnish a house, and establish himself before sending for Tanne. It was planned that they would marry on the day of her arrival at Mombasa, at the beginning of the new year.

In the meantime he became an exuberant correspondent. In September of 1913 he sent Tanne a thirty-page safari journal, full of photographs, bloodstains, and misspellings. The family was not reassured to hear that he had abandoned his original intention, which was to raise dairy cows and breed cattle, and had sold the farm they had negotiated in order to buy a much larger coffee plantation. "Gold meant coffee," he rationalized in his memoirs. "Coffee growing was the only thing that had any future; the world was crying out for coffee from Kenya. I . . . sold my seven hundred acres and bought instead from Mr. Sjögren the Swedo-African Coffee Company, owning 4500 acres near Nairobi and about the same near Eldoret."[23]

This acreage seemed to be at an ideal altitude for coffee, which was already under successful plantation in the highlands at even greater heights. But it was impossible for Bror to have known that his soil would be too acidic and the rainfall insufficient ever to grow coffee successfully on his farm. Ironically, the land would have been better suited to stock breeding, or to a "mixed farm," with only the lower acres planted with coffee trees.[24] That deal with Sjögren for the Swedo-African Coffee Company, enthusiastically entered upon, expensively subscribed to, and hastily concluded, was the seed of Isak Dinesen's tragedy in Africa.

---

*Writing about Emilie Vandamm's marriage of convenience to her cousin Jakob in "The Dreaming Child" (*Winter Tales*, p. 163), Isak Dinesen remarked: "Many young girls of Copenhagen married in the same way—*par dépit*—and then, to save their self-respect, denied their first love and made the excellency of their husbands their one point of honour. . . . Emilie was saved from their fate by the intervention of . . . her forefathers, and by the principle of sound merchantship which they had passed on into the blood of their daughter. The staunch and resolute old traders had not winked when they made out their balance-sheet; in hard times they had sternly looked bankruptcy and ruin in the face; they were the loyal, unswerving servants of fact. So did Emilie now take stock of her profit and loss."

Tanne, in the meantime, packed her trousseau. She had, even before she left Denmark, the ambition to make her house an oasis of civilization. She took a set of flat silver, crystal goblets, china, furniture, linens, paintings, jewelry, carpets, a French clock, photographs in ornate frames, an exercise machine, her notebooks, her grandfather Westenholz's library, and her favorite wedding present, a Scottish deerhound she called Dusk.

Early in December, when the days in Copenhagen are only seven hours long and it is dark by three, she made her formal farewell calls, sitting with each old "aunt" for a little while in a drawing room or a boudoir scented with beech smoke and oleander. Dozens of flaccid cheeks were presented for her to kiss, and each matron offered the young bride some advice. On the second of December there was a great emotional send-off at the central station. Ingeborg and Elle journeyed south with her to Naples, where they spent two weeks before the ship sailed on the sixteenth. The chaos, crumbling magnificence, and vivacity of the Italian port made it a spiritual as much as a geographical way station.

One of her fellow passengers, the Swedish Count Gustaf Lewenhaupt, lord-in-waiting to Prince Wilhelm of Sweden, who was traveling out to Africa for a safari, remembered how sweet, girlish, and radiant "little Tanne" looked as she stood with her family amid her luggage on the quay.[25] At the last moment, from the deck of the S.S. *Admiral,* she felt an "unbearable tenderness" for her mother.[26]

Book Two

TANIA

Opposite page, top to bottom: Bror and Tania Blixen on their first safari (1914). Tania Blixen and her staff outside Mbogani House in 1917. Farah is seated, second to left. Thomas Dinesen on safari, c. 1925. *Above:* Tania Blixen at her desk, 1918. *Below left:* Isak Dinesen holding Farah's son Saufe one year before she left the farm in 1930. Farah is on the left. *Below right:* Denys Finch Hatton in the 1920s.

Under the flag of my first motto I sailed
into a Vita Nuova, into what became my real
life.
                        —ISAK DINESEN
                         Mottoes of My Life

Navigation delivers man to the uncertainty
of fate; on water, each of us is in the
hands of his own destiny.
                        —MICHEL FOUCAULT
                         Madness and Civilization

15

Sea Change

THE PASSAGE TO East Africa in 1913 took nineteen days. The *Admiral* steamed through the Mediterranean and the Suez Canal into the Red Sea, then east through the Gulf of Aden to the Indian Ocean, following the smooth crescent of the Somalian coast south to Mombasa. At Port Said, the mouth of Suez, Tanne Dinesen went ashore on African soil for the first time. The marketplace had not changed much since the time of Sinbad. Beggars displayed their sores; the blades of the sword swallowers flashed in the burning sun; the smells of dung and mint mixed with the dust; and "everything was for sale: silks and scimitars, opium, whisky and small children."[1]

By New Year's Eve the ship was halfway to its destination, and there was a party in first class. South Africans who had farmed the country for many generations discussed crops and stock breeding with the more recent emigrants to the East Coast; sportsmen retold their exploits, whetting the appetites of the newcomers; a German scientist, making his twenty-third trip to Tanganyika (German East Africa), held forth on the character of the natives. There was dancing in the salon and games of bridge. Briton and German were united by the bonds of class and an imperial self-confidence. At midnight they raised their glasses to toast a year that would later find them chasing one another through the *bundu*.

The man who was to lead that chase, emerging as a legend to both sides, fetched Miss Dinesen her champagne and drank to her health. His name was Paul von Lettow Vorbeck; he was then forty-four and on his way to take command of the German forces at Dar es Salaam. A brilliant career in colonial warfare was already behind him. He had fought with von Trotha in Southwest Africa, where he had been wounded in the eye by an Herrero warrior, an experience that helped to confirm his high opinion of the African soldier. He had also served with Botha and the Afrikaners, and alongside the English during the Boxer Rebellion. All this had molded him into a ruthless, slippery, and resourceful guerrilla strategist.

An overexposed photograph, taken at Moshi that February, shows von Lettow seated on a veranda wearing a white uniform and an eye patch, drinking gin and smiling at the camera. He has an almost perfectly round, cropped head, a beaked nose enclosed in the inverted commas of his eye-brows, and the smudge of a mustache. Charles Miller, an historian of the war in Africa, claims that von Lettow had a personal charm and sense of humor rare among Prussian officers of his generation: "He was capable of unbend-ing."[2] He unbent sufficiently for Tanne to inform her mother, with a girlish pride of conquest, that "he has been such a friend to me."[3] As the nights grew increasingly sultry they sat on the deck, watching the equatorial stars and speculating about their African destinies. His family had fought opposite hers in three European wars, and they may well have spoken of the old campaigns. "He belonged to the olden days," she would write, "and I have never met another German who has given me so strong an impression of what Imperial Germany was and stood for."[4]

It was a chaste flirtation. Colonel von Lettow gave Miss Dinesen his photograph on a horse, but she would wait forty years to give him a kiss, teasing him about it by letter in the interval. Before they parted in Mombasa, they arranged to make a safari together that coming August, and in the meantime he commissioned her to find ten breeding mares for his cavalry. She accepted with a certain reclaimed Amazonian confidence—this same young woman who, eighteen months before, at a Roman soirée, "sank to her knees in embarrassment" when an elderly gentleman told her a ribbon of her petticoat was showing.

2

Isak Dinesen has written little and unsuggestively about this momentous journey, perhaps because she was seasick, nervous, and "depressed"[5] for a good part of it. A German stewardess named Martha took motherly charge of her and also agreed to come ashore at Mombasa, promising to spend at least six weeks helping her settle into her new house. At last Tanne had acquired that vital appendage to her dignity and her person, a lady's maid. But at Aden, on the Somali coast, a much more significant and poetic figure was waiting to enter her service. Bror Blixen gave her a title, but Farah Aden made her an aristocrat, and she must have recognized him from the outset as a figure she herself had imagined. It was at that moment her *"Vita Nuova"* truly began.[6]

Farah was Bror's steward and had been sent ahead to meet the ship and to help Tanne with her baggage. He was dressed in a long white *kanzu,* an embroidered waistcoat, and a red turban, and he made his mistress a deep salaam. Unfamiliar with the variety of African physiognomies, she first mistook him for an Indian, but he was a Somali of the Habr Yunis tribe, a member of a fierce, handsome, and shrewd East African trading and cattle-raising people. She would grow to feel a deep affinity for the fatalism of his Moslem faith, its code of honor, its eroticism. In *Shadows on the Grass* she describes the Somalis as aristocrats among the Africans, "superior in culture and intelligence." They were also well matched in *hauteur* with the Europeans they chose to serve, whom she calls the "Mayflower" people of the colony. "Here were Lord Delamere and Hassan, Berkeley Cole and Jama, Denys Finch Hatton and Bilea, and I myself and Farah. We were the people who, wherever we went, were followed, at a distance of five feet, by those noble, vigilant and mysterious shadows."[7]

Farah's shadow was, in fact, unusually short for a Somali; he was the same height as his mistress, and also about her age. He was slight, fine-featured, and courtly, but with a share of his tribe's rich gift for contempt. When they met at Aden, Farah spoke English badly, with the guttural Somali accent. Even when he became more fluent, his speech retained a peculiar biblical emphasis, as if part of it were always in italics. He was the vizier of Karen Blixen's house and farm ("our house"); he kept her cash and paid out her accounts and wages, drove her car, ran her stables and her kitchen. This naturally gave him enormous clout among local suppliers, and in time he set up his own *dukka* (grocery shop) at Ngong and did a flourishing business on the side. Karen Blixen sometimes suspected that their interests were in conflict, even that Farah cheated her at times, and their eighteen-year relationship was not without its *shauries*. * Like all the men closest to her in life, he was a wanderer and would leave the farm for months at a time to run Bror's safaris or to make his own. From the early days of their marriage, the Blixens competed for his loyalty and his service.

If Karen Blixen was possessive of Farah, it was because her dependence upon him was so complex. He shared her daily life, mediated her relations with the Africans, relieved her of a great many practical burdens. But he also became her confidant. He was someone in whom she had an almost mystical trust, which she would call a covenant. "I talked to him about my worries as about my successes, and he knew of all that I did or thought." The English thought this intimacy with a servant and a black man strange and even suspect; they could imagine only a lewd motive for it. But Karen Blixen herself called it a "creative unity." The servant's pride and fidelity defined the master's honor and prestige, and the master's need for him gave the servant an identity. Both partners needed the relation to become "themselves."[8]

The terms of this unity bear a striking resemblance to that other creative unity, the Victorian marriage, with the servant playing the wife's role. They might also be compared to the unity between a mother and a small child. The devotion of its servants enabled the ruling class to enjoy the physical dependence of early childhood throughout their lives, and helplessness was the ironic standard of their power. But one important difference between a servant such as Farah and a mother such as Ingeborg was that Farah never

---

Shaurie is the Swahili word for business, dealing, affair—and also trouble, intrigue.

circumscribed Tanne with concern. He simply followed her at a respectful distance, with a cashmere shawl and a loaded rifle.

3

The ship docked at Kilindini harbor on a humid morning, the thirteenth of January, and Bror came aboard to fetch his bride. There was as yet no quay, and the last hundred yards to shore were navigated in a rowboat. The heat was already searing, and the cliffs shimmered beneath its glaze. Beyond the inlet the breakers of the Indian Ocean drew "a thin, crooked white line" and gave out "a low thunder."9

Mombasa is a very old port. It reached the height of its prosperity in the fifteenth century when it was a kind of African Venice, the center of a rich Swahili culture and a flourishing trade in gold, ivory, cotton, and, later, slaves. Then the Portuguese arrived, plundered the local population, ruined the coastal commerce with their taxes and their corruption, and built an impregnable-looking fortress, Fort Jesus, that still dominates the harbor.

The narrow streets of the town wind down to the sea, and along the cliffs grow palms and old gnarled baobabs. The houses have thick walls cut from the pastel coral rock; acacias bloom in their inner courtyards, and many of the doorways are carved in the graceful old Swahili style. In 1914 the steamers of the Hamburg and Southhampton Lines docked beside the dhows of Lamu. The city was the terminus of the Uganda Railroad, the port from which the crops of the highlands—flax, coffee, pyrethrum, and timber—were shipped to Europe. It was also a great local market. Under the shade of mango trees veiled women with kohl-rimmed eyes bargained for chickens and honeydew. Merchants of cloth and silver stood in their doorways spitting betel juice into the gutter, and everywhere the smell of fish and freshly roasting coffee hung on the thick air.

That evening Bror Blixen and Tanne Dinesen dined with von Lettow and spent the night at the Mombasa Club. Tanne had told her family, for propriety's sake, that they were married the morning of her arrival, but, in fact, the ceremony took place the next day. The district commissioner officiated, and Bror's witness was Prince Wilhelm of Sweden. When pressed for details by Ingeborg, Tanne reported that she had worn a shantung suit, a blouse she had bought in Naples, and a "helmet," and that the ceremony was "easy and simple and only took ten minutes."10 The prince gives a slightly more obliging account in his memoirs:

The rite was performed by a thin, chalk-faced civil servant with glasses who looked sickly, and whose clothes were too large. . . . He sat behind an unpainted wooden table on which lay a law book, a sheet of greasy paper and a rusty fountain pen. The walls were whitewashed. On one of them hung a leopard's head.

'And now I ask you . . . sorry, what's the name? . . . if you will take this.
. . .' They help him graciously. The bridegroom with broad shoulders, blue
eyed, sunburned, confident and composed in his white clothes, which have not
been pressed in a long while. She is slim, shapely, with deep-set and intelligent
eyes and regular features under the abundance of chestnut hair. The simple but
well-cut morning dress betrays the handiwork of a first-class fashion house. A
lovely and elegant young woman now far away from all that. She has come
alone to join her destiny to the man at her side. No family, nor any friends
besides those gathered on the way.[11]

At four that afternoon the wedding party and the royal entourage en-
trained for Nairobi. The Governor of the Protectorate, Sir Henry Belfield,
had put his personal dining car at their disposal, and Sir Northrup Macmillan,
the American millionaire, sent his cook. "The wedding supper," wrote His
Royal Highness, "was consumed to the accompaniment of the rattling wheels
and their hard bumps against the rails. We made our toasts in champagne
and felt our pores contract with drink in the intense heat, despite the fact
that the entire company sat about in pyjamas, excellent formal wear for the
tropics. . . ."[12]

Along the coastal strip the train passed little villages where, at dusk, people
sat talking around their fires. It crossed the tropical lowlands with their cover
of palms and banana trees, climbing up toward the Taru desert. Here the
world was as flat as a pie crust, rounded at the edges, with the hills rising
in irregularly shaped scallops around the rim. The air cooled and the night
fell abruptly. The moon rose, and the stars—the planet Venus was exceptionally bright that year—and the plains swarmed with the sinewy purple shadows of the game.

There were no sleeping compartments on the train, and that coincidence
of luxury with roughness, of a royal wedding guest and a wedding night
spent on a banquette, was to be typical of Karen Blixen's Africa. Bror had
the foresight to bring sheets and a blanket.

16

A Still Country

THE TRAIN THAT CARRIED the Blixens toward their farm ascended a narrow gauge toward a vast plateau of fertile, temperate, and spectacularly beautiful farm and grazing land. The rail line bisected the country. To the east lay the humid lowlands of the coast, and to the west the land drew itself up into a jagged escarpment that then fell away, almost vertically, into the Rift Valley. Here was a moon landscape strewn with lava, soda lakes, and thorn and furrowed by stony rivers.

The highlands lay at altitudes of between five and eight thousand feet, rimmed by a range of ancient mountains and extinct volcanoes, and dominated by the snowcapped peak of Mount Kenya. The air was exceptionally clear and pure, and it was said, then, to produce "euphoria" in white people, who were therefore not held strictly accountable for their behavior. B.E.A. (British East Africa) had a highly erotic atmosphere; it was a place where, with the sanction of Nature, civilized inhibitions were let go. Serial monogamy was athletically practiced, and in the bars of steamers that carried settlers out to their farms or hunters to their adventures, women were accosted with the famous question, "Are you married, or do you live in Kenya?"

Lushness alternated with spareness in the highlands. On the plains "the colours were dry and burnt, like the colours in pottery."[1] But the undulating hills were covered with the dark green of great coffee plantations, with a patchwork of fields and foliage, and further up on the slopes grew rain forests of camphor trees, yellowwood, and giant bamboo.

Besides coffee, maize and sisal grew very profitably. There was excellent pasturage for stock, for much of the country was an immense parkland of high grass. Game abounded, fantastic in its variety. Millions of flamingos nested in the mountain lakes; buffalo, eland, and rhino roamed the hills; elephants flourished in the dry bush country; giraffes grazed the spreading thorn trees; monkeys chattered in the forest; the savannahs were dark as far as the horizon with herds of zebra, wildebeest, gazelle, who in turn fed their feline predators. Nowhere on earth did life offer such a spectacle of vigor, beauty, harmony, and, above all, scale. It evoked a feeling of religious awe, a sense of gratitude in many of those who beheld it for the first time. "This was," as Carl Jung wrote of the Athi Plains, "the stillness of the eternal beginning, the world as it had always been."[2] Looking back on her life in Africa, Karen Blixen felt "that it might altogether be described as the existence of a person who had come from a rushed and noisy world, into a still country."[3]

2

The Blixens were traveling on the main trunk line of the Uganda Railroad, which ran from Mombasa to Kisumu on the shores of Lake Victoria. This railroad had opened the interior to white settlement. Before its completion in 1901, the only Europeans who had lived in the highlands were missionaries, traders, and a few colonial officers. Even the imperialists who had argued so vigorously for a rail line had not foreseen the richness it would unlock. Their motive was to clear a strategic passage to Uganda and the headwaters of the Nile, and their fear was that an enemy might invade that colony from the south, dam the river at its source, dry up the Nile delta three thousand miles away, and thus control the Suez Canal. It was certainly one of the more elaborate paranoias in the history of geopolitics.[4]

The terrain was surveyed in 1894, and an army of Indian laborers imported to lay the tracks. These heroic coolies dragged six hundred miles of iron through malarial swamps and across deserts, throwing viaducts over ravines, climbing up escarpments and descending into torrid valleys. They also succumbed by the hundreds to fever and parasites, and to the man-eating lions who stalked their encampments. The job took five years and cost the British six million pounds.

Once it was made, the investment had to be recuperated, and "white farming settlement appeared the only route to solvency, if not prosperity."[5] In 1902 the East African Syndicate sold five hundred square miles of prime highland real estate at low prices and as if it had been vacant. By 1915 over four and a half million acres had been alienated to about one thousand white farmers, a ratio that would not change substantially until the 1950s.

It must be remembered that although it was possible to acquire a vast barony of virgin territory at a relatively modest cost, the risks and uncertainties in developing it were enormous. This fact determined the class, and in a sense the temperament, of the early pioneers. They were well capitalized and influential, drawn from the upper strata of society and nostalgic for "the world of dependency and obligation which their ancestors had lost to the Industrial Revolution."[6] They were also individuals who, for the most part, had a compelling enough reason to leave their comfortable situations in Europe and the independence, the ambition, the prowess, and the sheer stubbornness to master life on a frontier.

Before examining the aristocratic profile of those farmers, we should pause to consider the people from whom their land was expropriated.

The native African population of Kenya in 1913 was about three million. The majority were the Bantu-speaking Kamba and Kikuyu, who farmed the central highlands; and the Luo, who lived in the district west of Lake Nyanza. The priests of the Luo had encouraged them to welcome the British, whom they mistook for a race of benevolent "red strangers" promised by their ancestors. This perception was not shared by their nearest neighbors, the Nandi, who had to be "pacified" by a series of punitive expeditions. The British used African troops to do the fighting and pillaging, recruiting them from the friendly Luo and warlike Masai and Somali tribes.

The Masai, a Sudanic people, had originally come to Kenya from the north, migrating toward the central highlands in search of pastures for their cattle and raiding villages as they went along. They were wildly brave in battle, hunted lion with their long spears, and groomed their young warriors on a diet of milk and blood. This tribe had a kind of Nietzschean allure for the early settlers, or at least some of them. Lord Delamere smiled with benign indulgence when they stole his sheep and cows; Berkeley Cole studied their language and organized them as scouts during the war; Karen Blixen painted their lithe and storklike figures and admired "that particular form of intelligence which we call *chic:*—daring, and wildly fantastical as they seem, they are still unswervingly true to their own nature, and to an immanent ideal."[7]

The Somali, their brothers-in-arms, were also a tribe of proud and touchy warrior herdsmen, who had crossed into Kenya from Somalia and settled— if that is the word—in the blistering desert country of the northeast. They were a people of "The Book," devout Muslims who looked down upon the pagan tribes. Unlike the Masai, they did occasionally enter the service of the Europeans but maintained an aloofness the whites distrusted and considered impudent.

There were many smaller tribes: among them the Dorobo, famed for their skill at hunting elephant; the Turkana, naked and braceleted, who lived in the wild country around Lake Rudolf; the Baluyia (Kavirondo). Finally, there were the Swahili of the coast. For years they had been a buffer between the tribes of the interior and the various invaders, and their own vital urban culture had managed to survive repeated devastations. They, too, were Muslims, descended from the Arab traders of the Golden Age* and their Bantu wives. They had an architecture, a written language, a rich poetry. KiSwahili was the lingua franca for East Africa then, as it is today.

In view of the attitude popularly taken by the settlers toward the Africans —that they were "creatures," or "children," or that they were "emerging from the Stone Age," or that they should be grateful to be civilized and given work—it is worth quoting an insight of the eminent historian Basil David-

---

*The period of Arab exploration and the spread of Islamic culture, roughly between the ninth and fourteenth centuries.

son. While the indigenous civilization of Kenya "remained simple in most of its material things, in tools and weapons, in means of transport, in housing, in lack of reading and writing, in methods of producing goods, its everyday life became rich and complex in certain other ways. It became a civilization of dignity and value in its spiritual beliefs, in methods of self-rule, in arts such as dancing and singing, in skills that were needed for the solving of problems of everyday life.

"It was also, for the most part, a peaceful civilization, generally far more so than that of Europe. . . . They lived at peace among themselves, thanks to methods of self-rule that were often powerfully democratic; and they lived at peace with their neighbors because there was usually enough land for all. . . ."8

Almost from the beginning, Karen Blixen had a similar appreciation of the Africans. This is not to deny that her relations with them were feudal, that her knowledge of their customs and history was circumstantial, or that her vantage point was both romantic and paternalistic. Yet she saw, without any urging, the "dignity and value" of their arts. She grasped, without any study deeper than her own observations, that wisdom which could create a moral order so much more functional than that of her own race. She deplored, at least privately in her letters home, the vicious smugness of a ruling class that could believe and declare: "We have in East Africa, the rare experience of dealing with a *tabula rasa,* an almost untouched . . . country where we can do as we will."9

17

The Clear Darkness

I

A S A SEAT OF GOVERNMENT and a gateway to the splendors of the highlands, Nairobi was a singularly rough, mousy, and ramshackle little town. It had grown up around the railhead, on a flat piece of terrain, and looked as if its street map had first been etched in the dirt with a rifle barrel. The wooden sidewalks were shaded with rows of eucalpytus trees and lined with *dukkas,* offices and bungalows roofed in corrugated tin. The prominence of this material led Bror Blixen to compare Nairobi to a can of anchovies. Its thoroughfares were paved with red dust that turned to mud the color of oxblood when it rained. Afterward there were enormous potholes. In 1911 a group of irate but witty settlers had used them to plant banana saplings.[1]

There was a large Indian community in Nairobi, for the most part crowded into the poor quarters of the bazaar. There was an equally flimsy Somali ghetto outside the town, on the road to Limuru. It "lay exposed to all winds and was shadeless and dusty, it must have recalled to the Somali their native deserts."[2] But for the settlers there were quite a few amenities: a fine government house with a ballroom and a "pretty garden"; a racetrack; two good hotels, The Norfolk and The New Stanley, on whose terraces one could take in the gossip of the country over glasses of tepid whiskey. The Muthaiga Club, founded by Berkeley Cole, opened the week Karen Blixen arrived. It was housed in a mansion of pink stucco and had a golf course, tennis courts, a croquet lawn, stabling for polo ponies, two limousines with drivers, and a chef from Goa. The roster of members read like a sampler of Debrett's Peerage, and Baron Blixen immediately put down his name. Such a place in a raw country glowed literally and figuratively in the night, stirring the imagination of outsiders.

During the twenties Muthaiga came to be called "The Moulin Rouge of Africa," and it had a number of famous romances and even a shooting or two associated with its name. A handful of titled adulterers, like the Earl of Erroll, the Countess de Janzé, and Lady Idina Sackville, who had five husbands, did much to promote its reputation, which amused most of the other settlers. "We were," as one of them assured me, "a hard-working solid lot, who led solitary lives on our farms, and liked our bubbly when we got to town."[3] The speaker also laughed at the reports of orgies. Muthiaga was always replacing its chandelier, and parties tended to degenerate toward dawn, but into steeplechases. Lord Delamere liked to shoot golf balls onto the roof, then climb out to retrieve them. Algy Cartwright shinnied up the pillars. Denys Finch Hatton would butt over armchairs like a bull and end up sitting in them, and Tania Blixen practiced, envied, but never mastered the technique. Those who were still afoot by nine o'clock, when Emile Jardine opened his wineshop on Government Road, might repair there for a last bottle of champagne and afterward drive off for a mud bath at the Blue Post Hotel.

Nairobi had its "rag," *The Leader,* which reported on local politics, land transactions, fauna, shipping, and weather, and had a lively social column. The week Tanne arrived, her name was mentioned in two separate places. In the shipping section she was listed among the passengers on the *Admiral,* a "Frau Karen Dinesen." On the society page she was featured as one of the guests at the governor's reception for Prince Wilhelm: "Baroness von Blixen-Finecke."[4] She herself was a little dazzled by that promotion. The governor, she reported, sat her at his right and called her Baroness "every other word."[5]

2

The spacious landscape around Nairobi, once you get a little outside the town, is dominated by the Ngong hills. There are four peaks along the ridge, which look, from certain angles, like the knuckles of a clenched fist, unevenly rounded. During the cool parts of the day they turn a darker blue than the sky, and Karen Blixen compared them to "immovable waves" against it.[6] But they change constantly with the light, almost like a face, affecting the mood and scale of everything around them. After a rain they stand out with such dramatic clarity that both the Masai and Kikuyu have a name for the effect, "the clear darkness," a phrase that suggests a quality of Isak Dinesen's prose.

Her enterprise, the Swedo-African Coffee Company, owned forty-five hundred acres at the foot of the hills, and after the luncheon for the prince, Bror drove his bride out to survey them. It was a brilliant day; the fields on either side of the road were blooming with wild flowers whose scent, rising up to the open car, reminded Tanne of a Danish bog myrtle. Twelve miles from Nairobi and several hundred feet higher up, they turned into a graveled drive, and she saw her house for the first time. It was not the handsome stone manor where *Out of Africa* is set, which the Blixens bought in 1917 when they also acquired another fifteen hundred acres, but a relatively modest brick bungalow with four square rooms and a small porch. Surrounding it, however, was a great sweep of lawn, and all her twelve hundred field hands had assembled to greet her. They gave out a "roar" of welcome, crowded forward, laughed and tried to touch the couple. Bror was annoyed, but Tanne ravished. After she had walked through the woods that would be cleared for coffee and taken tea with the six European managers, she stood on the steps to promise the Africans some meat and to make them a speech of thanks. No young queen could have been more gratified by such a "magnificent enlargement" of her horizon,[7] could have risen to it with more ease, and perhaps none had ever felt it was so long overdue.

Karen Blixen's affinity for the Africans had been immediate and sensuous. "They came into my life," she wrote at the end of it, "as a kind of answer to some call in my own nature, to dreams of childhood perhaps, or to poetry read and cherished long ago, or to emotions and instincts deep down in the mind. . . ."[8] She felt she shared a kind of "covenant" with them. This idea recurs in her life and in her vocabulary when she wishes to describe the most charged and intimate of her relationships. At fifteen she had had the fantasy of a "covenant" with her dead father, full of mystical and erotic feeling, which made Wilhelm her ally against the despair of adolescence. Much later she spoke of a "covenant" with her friend Thorkild Bjørnvig, the young Danish poet she thought of as her protégé and spiritual heir. That relationship, too, came at a moment when feelings of loss and despair—those of old age—threatened to overwhelm her. As a young woman in Africa she would face harrowing periods of illness and insecurity, and the feeling of a "covenant" with the Africans—a deep, mutual and unchanging bond—saw her through them. Most of the time she viewed herself as the parental figure. But "there was a time," she told Bjørnvig, "when Farah and my other people and all things in Africa and Africa itself said one and the same thing to me: 'Trust in us and we shall protect you.' "[9]

About that other charged and intimate relationship, her marriage, Karen Blixen has been much more reticent. It started out, at least, as an idyll. She played the chatelaine to Bror's rough lord and boasted to her family that he was the most considerate and practical human being ever to have lived—and the most admired farmer in the country. He, in turn, extolled her charm, her courage, and her resourcefulness as a housekeeper who had done wonders "with a staff of raw niggers."[10] Before they settled down in Mbagathi House they had a short honeymoon, a trip to the beautiful country around Lake Naivasha. Here they hunted at night and slept during the day in a small lodge with an earthen floor and a stone fireplace. Around them on all sides was a spare, undulating landscape of high grass, stretching to the edge of distant mountains. Game abounded and lions roared through the night, a sound as penetrating as "the thunder of guns in the darkness." Writing from bed one morning, with a runner waiting to take her letter, Tanne tried to describe her feelings and her surroundings but was too overwhelmed to be precise. "So you must take it as it is," she told Ingeborg, "and despite the muddled style try to get an idea of this great new life and all that has happened [to me] out here."[11]

Tanne's first project was an ambitious renovation of the bungalow, which took almost a year and turned it into something rather more like a villa. She had the porch enclosed and made into a pretty garden room where she hung her pictures and laid her Persian rugs; she built a pillared verandah and a wing of offices and workrooms, laid out a kitchen garden, landscaped the lawn, excavated a little duck pond, and planted creeping vines that eventually grew up over the ugly brick. The house still exists today, as part of a hotel in the suburb of Karen.*

Bror was equally energetic in his role as the country's "most admired" coffee planter. It would actually take the trees some years to mature, so the fact that he knew nothing about coffee was not yet an inhibition. He rode around the farm in an enormous hat with a *kiboko*† and a pair of superb English riding boots, supervising the clearing of the forest and the vaccination of the oxen against rinderpest. In his leisure moments he sat up scheming with his cronies over shots of excellent whiskey, and his office was an informal club for the local Swedes. Tanne described it, with affectionate condescension, as a place redolent of "menfolk" and their cigars. Kenya's shady characters recognized a soulmate in Bror, bringing him their mining stocks and their railroad speculations, and he invariably subscribed to them. He made safaris with his friends, camped at Uasin Gishu, where they had land, or inspected some acreage at Eldoret that he might want to acquire; and he often spent nights in Nairobi at the Muthaiga Club, when "business" kept him there. Tanne apparently did not complain and could not have kept up with him had she been invited, for she caught malaria at the end of February. It was a bad case that stranded her in bed for weeks, and she suffered from a depression after the fevers. "It is a little tedious as Bror is naturally out a lot," she told Aunt Bess with considerable understatement. Farah took up the slack, nursed her through the fevers "better than a white lady's maid,"[12] kept her current with farm gossip, taught her Swahili, and, when he saw her spirits fail, spoke confidently about God's will.

To some degree, however, the young Baroness Blixen also courted her own isolation. She was conscious of her rank and kept her distance from settlers not equal to it. For its part, the English aristocracy was slow to admit unanointed newcomers. Lady Belfield, the governor's wife, did drive out for tea at the farm (or at least her car got stuck on the Ngong Road and was pulled out by Tanne's Kavirondo laborers). When she spoke about the dreadfully provincial tone of Nairobi parties, Tanne commiserated into her ladyship's ear trumpet. To her mother, she prayed that God would continue to preserve her from such festivities. There were a few poetic souls, a few of her neighbors who had charm: Mr. Grieve, a gallant old pioneer; Ture

---

*When Karen Blixen's farm was sold to a developer in 1931, he named the district Karen in her honor.
†A whip made of cured hippopotamus hide.

Rundgren, a melancholy Swede whom Tanne likened to a "kind of Hamlet";[13] but these were the exceptions. Her letters to Denmark seethe with contempt for the banality of the white settlers and the English in particular, which should surprise the readers of *Out of Africa*. Their racial prejudice offended her most of all. Regarding the Africans as subhuman, they required their field hands to work through the daily rainstorms and their Somali servants to interrupt their prayers. When Tanne tried to discuss the difference between the races as if there might possibly be some basis for comparison, the English ladies laughed at her "originality." White moral superiority, she concluded, was an illusion, and by all the important standards—honor, for example, or humor—the Africans were far more civilized.

Violent antipathies are generally reciprocated, and the English did not at first take warmly to Tania Blixen. They looked with suspicion upon a clever foreign woman with somewhat affected manners and a clumsy accent, who thought herself too good for their society and advanced views about the moral beauty of the natives. They found her, said a contemporary, "a queer bird," "a cold fish," "a frightful snob."[14] During the war they believed she was a German spy. This was absurd and hurt her deeply, although she had confessed to Elle that she found the German spirit more congenial than the English and consoled herself, even at a distance, with von Lettow's friendship. Bror was judged on his own merits and generally much better liked and understood. No one thought him too intellectual or suspected his racial loyalties. He was gregarious with men, a great rough wit, a good storyteller and buyer of drinks, and charming to women, who found the Baron "all but irresistible."[15] This may have inspired Tanne's passionate caricature of a typical predatory English flirt: short skirt, bleached hair, shrill laugh, high-heeled boots and a hip revolver that she didn't know how to fire. There were, she assured Elle, not ten "decent" women in the country.[16]

Early in April, the chief of the Kikuyus appeared to pay Baroness Blixen his respects. Kinanjui was an impassive, birdlike man with half-closed eyes and an extremely refined profile. It so resembled that of Isak Dinesen in old age that they might have been the two sides of a medallion. Most of the time he wore a net over his bald skull, a silver bell in his right ear, a tartan blanket, and, on ceremonial occasions, a cape of blue monkey skins. When he arrived that afternoon he was attended by some of his sons. Tanne was entertaining Åke Sjögren, the Swedish settler* who had sold Bror the farm and loaned him a considerable sum of money. Sjögren greeted Kinanjui with loud guffaws, making a joke of his "civility" to a native. This was a pity, Tanne observed, as Kinanjui was by far the greater gentleman and someone who also happened to command the goodwill of Sjögren's field hands. She chatted with the chief; he was gracious and promised her that her own farm would

---

*Also the Swedish consul.

never be short of manpower. It was the beginning of a cordial friendship.

Tanne's response to her alienation was then—and would be in the future —to root her life among the Africans. She made the rounds of their *shambas* in a rickshaw Bror gave her for her birthday, with Farah as her interpreter, learning their names and listening to their woes. She carried sugar and pennies in her pockets for the children and snuff for the old women, which, needless to say, made her extremely popular. But her reputation was not based solely on her charity. The people on the farm, said her cook Kamante Gatura, reciprocated her love, and strangers came to her for refuge when they had been mistreated elsewhere. She would write with awe about the natives' absolute trust in her judgment and of what she learned about submission to higher powers from this experience. The old women gave her the name *Jerie,* * a feminine Kikuyu honorific which means, among other things, "the one who pays attention."[17] An old Kikuyu whom I met, still living in Ngong, remembered Karen Blixen as the only white person he had ever seen who "picked up an African child and carried him in her arms. We children," he said, "called her our mother."[18]

When she was feeling fit, she saddled her mare, Aimable, and went for long solitary gallops on the Masai Reserve, across the river to the west of the farm. The Masai impressed her with their proud bearing and the candid manner with which they met her eyes when she spoke to them. She and Farah started a rather profitable sheep-trading business with them. They bought the animals for five or six rupees apiece and resold them in Nairobi for seven-fifty. With a capital of three thousand rupees, Tanne could clear five hundred a month profit. She liked doing business, certainly had it in her blood, and claimed that it suited her much better than writing books.

Tanne had, to her undying joy, a superfluity of household help, which proved to her the aptness of Voltaire's saying, *Le superflu, chose si nécessaire.* Her Somali cook, Ismail, was "an old man of much sense and a gentle disposition,"[19] but he had a limited and vulgar repertoire, particularly of desserts—the fault of his previous English mistress. Tanne taught him to make flans, meringues, soufflés, and several kinds of cake, and asked her mother to send her a cookbook from the 1830s, a period compatible with the resources of her kitchen. Ismail's helper was a young Kikuyu named Ferasi, who had an "angelic" disposition. There were also two impeccable

---

*The Africans generally displayed both a fine sense of sarcasm and justice in their names for the Europeans. Bror was called *Wahoga,* which he thought meant "wild duck" but which, in fact, meant "Waddler." Denys was called *Bêdar,* which means "the Balding One." He was also called *Makanyaga,* which roughly translates to "Master of the Put-Down." "Bwana Finch Hatton," the argument ran, "can tread upon inferior men with his tongue. He can punish with a word . . ." (Errol Trzebinski, *Silence Will Speak,* p. 210). Ingrid Lindström's husband Gillis was called *Samaki* because he was so fond of fish, and Erik Otter, the Blixens' friend, was known as *Risase Moja*—One Shot.

Somalis who did the housework under Farah's supervision, and a groom *(syce)* who kept the stables.

In addition to its formal staff, the household also included a large number of hangers-on, visiting relatives, and *totos,* small boys who helped in the kitchen or looked after the dogs. These were the children of the farm's "squatters." Swedo was, like the other great plantations of the Protectorate, a vast fiefdom. Some of the field hands were the same Kikuyu farmers who had lived on the land before it was sold and who, as Karen Blixen wrote, "very likely regarded me as a sort of superior squatter on their estates."[20] About a sixth of the acreage was given over to their family plots of sweet potato, maize, and beans; to grazing land for their stock; and to their villages of conical mud huts. In exchange they worked for their landlords a specified number of days each year.

The workers who were not tenant farmers were wage laborers, many of them migrants from elsewhere in the country. These young men lived in communal huts, ten or twelve to each. Tanne was impressed, when she made her rounds, by the order and friendliness that seemed to reign among them, and doubted that Europeans could live so amicably under the same conditions. With their meager salaries—a few shillings a month—they bought manufactured goods, tobacco, or blankets and paid their hut taxes to the British. As the colony expanded, a policy of de facto forced labor, highly controversial in England, was instituted, with the hut tax used as a means of controlling the supply of workers for construction projects and white farms.* As the tax was raised, the Africans had to work for longer and longer periods every year, until they owed almost 50 percent of their wages to the government. This system destroyed their independence, undermined their tribal life, and made them poor. Karen Blixen was from the beginning appalled to see so proud a people beggared, and she attempted to "plead the Natives' cause" to each successive governor, to a number of influential settlers who became her friends, and finally to the Prince of Wales, who dined with her on the farm. Her own situation, as one of the greatest feudal overlords in the country, was a paradox, as was the fact that her own *noblesse oblige* in the role gave her such pleasure.

Writing from her bed the week of Kinanjui's visit while she was recovering from malaria, Tanne sent a chatty letter to each member of her family. To Aunt Bess she discoursed on social questions, racial injustice, the relations

---

*"There are two points to consider," Sir Edward Northey, Governor of the Protectorate, wrote in 1919 on the subject of compulsory labor for the Africans. "Firstly, that native labour is required for the proper development of the country; and secondly, that we must educate the native to come and work for his own sake, because nothing is worse for a young native than to remain idle in the reserve. . . ." Elspeth Huxley, *White Man's Country: Lord Delamere and the Making of Kenya,* vol. 2, p. 62.

In the first few months of her life in Africa, Karen Blixen also subscribed to this view, but her feelings changed rapidly.

between the sexes. To Thomas she described the rapture the highland landscape inspired in her and her sense of mystical union with the Africans and
the game. To Ea and Elle she wrote about her housekeeping, in mock despair
at her incompetence. Never marry, she warned them, without first learning
how to cook. To Ingeborg she extolled her husband, her servants, and her
domestic happiness and promised secretly to let her know if she got pregnant.
But, she added, this was unlikely, for it would not be desirable to have a baby
right away. Africa was too rough and wild, and the married women in the
neighborhood were "always wailing about the *awful nuisance* it was to have
a child."[21]

The letters are also filled with exotic and, at times, rather lurid vignettes:
how Bror came home from safari with chiggers under his nails, which had
to be plucked out with a tweezer; how a litter of kittens was devoured alive
by red ants; how she soaked through her silk lingerie when she had a fever;
or how she mediated a drunken quarrel among the "boys." But there is also
a common theme, which is stated with greatest economy in *Out of Africa:*
"Here I am where I ought to be."[22] The letters also share a common
undertone of pride, even vindication. For this was the scope, the freedom,
the eroticism, the raw grandeur she had dreamed about in Denmark and of
which she had felt so long deprived. "Life is more brutal," she told Aunt
Bess, "and would probably upset you more than the worst revelations from
life at home; I for one, prefer it like that. . . . There is one choice possible,
and the test of whether one has chosen rightly can never be made by
considering what is best, only by whether one has rightly judged what made
one happy. . . ."[23]

18

Safari Life

I

THERE WAS ABUNDANT RAIN that spring* for the first planting. Six hundred acres had been cleared and rows of deep holes dug in the wet earth. Tanne herself, "young and hopeful," carried boxes of black-green coffee seedlings from the nursery and watched as the field hands set them tenderly in the ground. They would not bear fruit for three to five years. "Coffee-growing," she would write in *Out of Africa*, with typical understatement, "is a long job. It does not all come out as you imagine."[1]

By the time the work was done, Bror and Tanne longed for a holiday. She was pale and thin after months of fever, and the doctor had recommended a change of air. Bror was eager to go hunting and suggested that, instead of going to a health resort in the hills, they make a month-long shooting safari on the Masai Reserve, southwest of the farm. This was to be Tanne's first prolonged experience of the wild and her initiation to the rigors of safari life. She had never slept in a tent, sat up in a *boma*,† handled a big gun, or taken a life, and before they left Bror gave her a rifle with a telescopic sight and some instruction. There is a photograph of her doing target practice outside the house, dressed in a very smart tweed suit, black pumps, and a felt

---

*The seasons in Kenya do not correspond climatically to the seasons in Europe and America, although to keep things simple I still refer to "spring," "summer," etc. There are two rainy seasons in the highlands: a period of "long rains" between April and June, and the short rains between October and December. January is generally a dry month, and there is also a long dry spell between July and September. Rainfall varies from place to place, depends upon altitude, and can be capricious, as we shall see, although it is, for the highlands as a whole, abundant (forty-two to one hundred inches a year, on the average).

The weather is pleasant and rather bracing, with strong sunlight and cool breezes, although there can be thick, wet fogs in the dry season. On a hot day in Nairobi the temperature averages 80° Fahrenheit, and on a cool night, 56°. At Ngong, which is several thousand feet higher up, it is cooler; the days average 60° to 70° and the nights 54° to 63°. There is, however, considerable variation. At midday, in the burning sun, it can reach 90°, and at three in the morning, which was an hour people set off on their safaris, it can drop to 40°. The climate at Mombasa, on the coast, is tropical, hot and extremely humid, without much variation. February, March, and April are the hottest months (82°, mean), and May is the wettest. In Karen Blixen's day the coast was considered unlivable by Europeans—or those who had never spent a summer in New York City.

†An enclosure to protect domestic animals from wild predators or an improvised shelter, usually made of thorn branches, where hunters sat vigil. Just outside the *boma*, hopefully upwind and within shooting range, some kind of bait was laid.

hat. She was, in fact, quite unprepared for her own blood lust. A week into the safari, drunk with it, she offered her apologies to all hunters for any prior skepticism toward their "ecstasy."[2]

They left Ngong in the middle of June with three mule wagons and nine servants, a party scaled down for mobility. For four days they followed an extremely crooked and rocky path over the escarpment, descending through dense thorn bush where there was no game. Then suddenly they emerged onto the savannah. The plains were blooming with violets after the rains and ringed by a majestic panorama of blue mountains. Here they camped and proceeded to shoot their fill of "all the usual kinds of deer, zebra, wildebeest, eland, dik-dik, marabou, jackal, wild boar . . . and a large number of birds." Tanne missed the chance to bag a particularly splendid leopard, which "rankled" her for weeks afterward. "If I hadn't been the biggest fool on earth, I would have had it," she told her brother. The carnage was astounding.[3]

After a while they began to concentrate upon lion. A hunter returning from his own safari gave them directions to a place where he and his partner had stalked a large pride. The Blixens found it—a fetid campsite near a riverbed—but they had no luck here and were eaten alive by flies. Tanne was also almost eaten alive by one of the elusive lions, who left his spoor outside her tent; and from then on, while Bror was in the *boma,* Farah kept vigil with her through the night, passing the time by telling Somali folktales.

Breaking camp, they moved east, taking a young Masai *moran* as their guide. He led them to a beautiful and remote piece of country between the mountains and the plains where Tanne believed no white people had ever camped. The animals seemed almost tame; the great herds of zebra and eland looked up from their grazing but didn't flee, and here, after a few nights, they found their prey.

Tanne and Bror had been out to shoot some dinner when their *syce* came running after them in great excitement. He had seen a tremendous male lion in the high grass by the river crossing. They followed him back, spotted the lion, and Bror, quickly changing guns, shot. The lion was resting when he took the bullet and died as he lay, with his great head between his paws. Tanne ran up to him, and there was an instant before the others reached her. The lion's eyes were open, and the life seemed to drain out of them as she watched. As the servants began to flay him, peeling back the bloodied golden skin, she saw that his muscles and sinews did not have a "particle of superfluous fat"; he was arrogantly perfect in death, elegant to the bone, "all through what [he] ought to be."[4] That economy was a quality she would strive for in her own works of art, her own figure, and her fate.

Bror had a camera, and they both posed with some of their trophies. In one snapshot he leans on his rifle with a fierce grimace, his legs bowed slightly and a lioness at his feet. In another she sits with a leopard cradled tenderly in her lap. There are shots of the open plains, the dusty campsites, and one of Tanne and Bror together, with two more lions. They stand close to each other but not touching, two lean brown figures with an almost tangible sexual current flowing between them. Their happiness was certainly never again to be so simple and untroubled. At the end of the hot days they bathed in the rocky river; at dark their servants roasted game on spits over the fire. Farah poured their wine, and Ismail, the gunbearer, told them Somali hunting stories, "the love tales of another age."[5] Thirty years later, when she had many reasons to remember the moment differently, Karen Blixen told a friend, "If I should wish anything back of my life, it would be to go on safari once again with Bror Blixen."[6]

2

The Blixens returned home in the middle of July, after a few days of luxury at the Kijabe hill station. Tanne had not yet found von Lettow's horses, and toward the end of the month she went to Naivasha to look for some. Her timing was imprudent, for there were already rumors of war. On the third of August the British began to delay cable messages for Tanganyika. On the morning of the fourth a large fleet of Arab dhows, flying the American colors, docked at Kilindini harbor in Mombasa, carrying British, French, and Belgian refugees from the German colony. In Nairobi someone spotted a German aircraft—which turned out to be the planet Venus. The same day, war was declared.

Almost at once a group of Swedes met at Mbagathi House to decide what action they should take in the event Sweden sided with Germany. Their position was extremely awkward. As settlers in a British protectorate, their loyalties were with the British. As subjects of the Swedish king, they could not honorably fight for an enemy. At this meeting, there were, besides Bror, the Baron Erik von Otter; Emil Holmberg, one of the founders of a famous safari firm; and the farmers Helge Fägerskiöld, Nils Fjæstad, and Ture Rundgren. After much debate they resolved to offer their services to "our adopted country"[7] but to excuse themselves from active duty should Sweden side outright with the kaiser.

On August 5 two of the men, the Barons Blixen and Otter, bicycled into Nairobi to report to the recruiting office. They found the town in a state of high excitement, and in the streets an almost "carnival atmosphere. . . . Bands of settlers," wrote Charles Miller, "cantered into Nairobi on horses and mules and formed themselves into mini-regiments of irregular cavalry. Their weapons were fowling pieces and elephant guns, their uniforms tattered bush jackets and broad-brimmed tera hats with fish-eagle feathers protruding from leopard-skin puggarees. They went by such names as Bowker's Horse and Wessel's Scouts, after the fellow-colonists who more or less commanded them. One called itself the Lancer Squadron . . . and galloped through the streets of Nairobi brandishing steel-tipped bamboo spears that had been hastily fashioned by a local blacksmith."[8]

Erik Otter joined the East African mounted rifles. Bror, after some uncertainty about the best place to serve, volunteered as a noncombatant intelligence officer with Lord Delamere's border patrol. His duty was to arrange communications between the head intelligence officer in Nairobi and Delamere, who was somewhere along the two hundred miles of frontier with the German territory. Rundgren and Fjæstad were dispatched to the southwest with him. They were to use motorcycles where there were roads, native runners through the denser bush, and carrier pigeons where the terrain was impassable. An assistant from the farm was sent to the railhead at Kijabe to receive their messages and dispatch supplies. Tanne decided she could not wait at home, possibly to be interned in protective custody with the other white women. (It was not yet known how the edifying spectacle of whites killing one another would affect the Africans.) So she went to Kijabe, too, bringing Farah and some of her "boys," riding her horse Aimable and trailed by her deerhound Dusk. They made camp near the station among the stacks of firewood for the engines.

Karen Blixen describes her subsequent experience in *Out of Africa:* how she made friends with the Goan telegraph operator and began to teach him Danish; how her husband asked her to send an ox train with supplies and to find a white man to go with it; how she engaged a young South African by the name of Klaproot, who was promptly interned as a spy; and how, lacking any other appropriate male, she led the supply train herself and spent three months on the Masai Reserve with twenty-one young Kikuyus and three Somalis. It was the time when she felt most keenly, without distraction, one with Africa: "The grass was me, and the air, the distant visible mountains were me, the tired oxen were me. I breathed with the slight night-wind in the thorn-trees."[9]

That version is a poetic condensation of the real events. The safari was, in fact, a series of short expeditions, leaving from and returning to base at Kijabe, and other details have been left out or embellished. But it does justice to the experience, from a reader's point of view, as perhaps no factual description could. Karen Blixen would say of the Africans that "They were never reliable, but in a grand manner sincere."[10] And that is true of her own autobiography.

During this period Bror visited his wife's camp when he could find it, which speaks well for his ardor. Once he showed up on a brief leave, suffering from dysentery and having walked eighty-six miles in two days. Along the way he had run out of food and water and slept in a Masai *manyatta.* The next morning, while the servants were breaking camp, he picked up a bottle which he thought was soda but which turned out to contain concentrated lysol. His mouth and tongue were badly burned, and Tanne, who thought he would surely die, sent frantically to the district commissioner for some milk. But this was one of the many occasions when Bror survived against all odds. He had a Rasputinlike constitution, which not poison, disease, malaria, war, breaks and gashes of all kinds nor the most violent general wear seemed able to dent. The next day he had improved enough to travel for ten miles in an ox cart, and the following morning he cheerfully waved good-bye, stuffed a sandwich into his pocket, and set off for his post on foot, as he had come.

3

At the beginning of October, Tanne was ordered home. The other irregulars had also begun to return to their farms as the army was organized into properly outfitted companies of real soldiers. After the first heroic rush for the recruitment office, many of the settlers had begun to have second thoughts about the war. Their farms reverted to bush if left untended, and there could be little strategic impact on the outcome of the war in Europe from a campaign in Africa. There was also a mood of complacence about a British victory, which was considered a foregone conclusion. It irritated Tanne who, in spite of her "ancient hatred for the Germans,"[11] found it unbearable to hear the English boast about their strategy and pretend that the enemy were imbeciles. At least one ranking English officer shared her perception: Colonel Richard Meinertzhagen. From a long career in Africa, he had learned to respect the skill and courage of Germany's African *askaris* and the resources of von Lettow. It alarmed him to hear his fellow officers speak with such false confidence. In the end, both his and Tanne's judgment were proved sound. Von Lettow managed to outmaneuver the British for four years, with a much smaller force that was cut off completely from resupply. "It was entirely in keeping with the aggressiveness of von Lettow's army," wrote Miller, "that it should learn of its own defeat [in 1918] by capturing the news."[12]

When Tanne reached her house, she found it in complete disorder. It had been chosen as a headquarters for the white farms in the neighborhood should there be a native uprising, and she wrote to her mother that she could well understand why, as it was impossible to get into. The brickwork on the new verandah had been stopped halfway, the walls built up but no stairs or floor laid. The painters had left in the middle of their job, taking with them a door and window. Her kitchen garden was a "sahara," and her first duty as a "housemother" was to order a whipping (twenty lashes with a *kiboko*) for some *totos* who had gotten drunk and almost murdered three other little boys.[13] At this moment Farah announced that he would like to take three months' leave to visit his family in Somaliland. Tanne made him promise to come back but expressed sympathy for his nomadic urges. She consoled herself by hiring a new cook and teaching him to make Swedish pancakes and stuffed cabbage, which became specialties of the house and a particular surprise and treat for the local Scandinavians.

Bror came home the first week in November, gaunt and sunburned. The same week, the British suffered a terrible defeat at the battle of Tanga. Von Lettow captured enough ammunition and supplies for three companies and humiliated their command. This initiated what was known as "the black year" in the country. Morale plummeted, the army resented the settlers' lack of patriotism and the settlers blamed the army for its incompetence. Everyone blamed the Swedes, and Tanne told her mother that they were looked upon virtually as traitors or at least potential traitors, and she admitted that, in fact, most of them did sympathize with the Germans. Some of her neighbors contributed to a collection for the Belgian refugees and presented it to the governor as a gesture of goodwill from the "Swedes and Danes at Ngong." But Tanne thought this was rather pointless, especially as it was, "God knows, hard enough to raise money in such times." It was such a shame, she wrote in her last letter before the mails were censored, that Sweden or Denmark didn't have a colony: "One always feels a foreigner—now the English are particularly foreign to me, so it is lucky that I feel for the Somalis and natives like brothers."[14]

19

Lucifer's Child

I

T HE WAR NEARLY RUINED the Swedo-African Coffee Company. The British commandeered Bror's wagons, and his oxen died of a fever. Many
of the field hands were drafted into the Carrier Corps, and despite Kinanjui's
promise the farm was seriously short of manpower. At Christmas, Bror and
Tanne had planned to make a short safari to cheer themselves up, but things
on the farm were too unsettled. Tanne herself was ill with an unidentified,
recurrent malady which at first she thought was malaria. She had been losing
weight, was unable to sleep, and Bror, thinking she was "pretty sick," had
written a "sad" letter to Ingeborg about her. Tanne found it and in a rage
tore it up.[1]

Her symptoms did not improve, and toward the end of February she wrote
home herself, describing a very strange, distressing, and, in retrospect, ambiguous incident.[2] According to the letter, she had been suffering from insomnia
for several nights, had grown impatient with it, and, after taking two
powders of Veronal one night with no effect, she had taken four the next
night. It was nearly a lethal dose. Bror had come into her bedroom by chance
in the afternoon, found her lying there in a stupor, and had done his best
to revive her. She vomited steadily for the next two days, and after that he
made her go to a doctor in Nairobi. In the letter Tanne claims that at the
end of a thorough examination the doctor told her he had never seen such
a robust constitution. In fact, he declared that she had a case of syphilis as
"bad as a trooper's"[3] and prescribed the only remedy he had at hand: mercury
tablets.

There are conflicting accounts about the background to this tragic revelation, Tanne's response to it, and its effect upon her marriage. The story Isak
Dinesen told Parmenia Migel in 1960 does not fit the other facts, descriptions,
and informed speculations from a variety of reliable sources. According to
Ms. Migel, Tanne discovered some time "after the first year or so" that Bror
was having "several affairs" in Nairobi and lying to her "clumsily" about
them. One was with the wife of a good friend, a man who had loaned them
money, and this made her particularly indignant. At the same time her own
health had begun to "suffer," and she was finally forced to see a physician.

He told her how serious her condition had become and advised her to leave at once for Europe. Tanne, according to this account, determined she would go without telling her husband why, presumably leaving his own case of syphilis untreated, and would let him assume she had left in a fit of jealousy. But when he demanded that she leave Farah behind, she confronted him "bluntly, in a cold white rage, [with] why she had to go and how grave her illness was. . . . Bror stared at her incredulously for a moment, struck silent by her unaccustomed outburst, and then turned and left the room."[4]

Karen Blixen's Danish physician, Mogens Fog, has stated that she first learned she had syphilis in 1914,[5] and the scattered references in the letters suggest she began to suffer from the disease toward the end of the year, when she was losing her appetite and her ability to sleep. Malaise, fever, headaches, and pains in the joints, particularly severe at night, are the symptoms of secondary syphilis, which generally appear from four to eight weeks after the primary infection. This would place it, although without certainty, during the period of her supply mission on the Masai Reserve, when Bror appeared at her camp having spent the night in a Masai *manyatta*. Syphilis was almost epidemic among the Masai, the cause of widespread sterility among Masai women. One wartime friend of Baron Blixen's remembers that "it was a scandal to everyone that Blixen never hid the fact of his relations with Negro women."[6] It seems possible that these relations were the source of his infection.*

By February, when she took the Veronal, Tanne would have been suffering a variety of miseries that could well have prevented her from sleeping. Yet the recklessness with which she used the drug suggests that she may have had a more desperate motive. Severe depression is also a symptom of secondary syphilis; it may have been aggravated in Tanne's case by the revelation, or the suspicion, of Bror's infidelity with his friend's wife, other Europeans, or a series of African women. Confiding in Thorkild Bjørnvig about her own unhappiness in love and the experience of jealousy, she said, "It is as if a claw had grabbed your heart, as if you had been shaken and tumbled by a wild animal. How I remember it. How I knew it."[7]

Whatever her immediate response, Tanne did not leave Africa until May of 1915 and, in fact, went off for a two-month safari arranged by Bror, in the care of two of his Swedish assistants, for another "change of air." If there was a bitter confrontation, there is no reverberation of it in any of her

---

*All the available information on Bror Blixen's medical history comes from indirect references in Karen Blixen's *Letters from Africa*. He was apparently treated by her Danish venereologist, Dr. Rasch. He does not, however, seem to have suffered much or at all in the early stages of the disease. His second wife refused to believe that he had ever been ill. But when he was living in Tanganyika in the twenties, he apparently had at least one severe attack that he believed was due to the disease. The course syphilis takes is different for each individual, and some people are almost completely free of symptoms. Bror, with his extraordinary constitution, may well have been such a case.

subsequent letters or in what exists of her correspondence with Bror. Many years later she would tell her secretary Clara Svendsen: "There are two things you can do in such a situation: shoot the man, or accept it."[8] And writing about the disease to her brother Thomas, she confessed that it shocked her much less than other people; it wasn't really so alien to her being.[9] That nonchalance, rather than the moral outrage Ms. Migel describes, corresponds better to Karen Blixen's friends' and family's perception of her attitude. Even after the diagnosis, she wanted to remain married to Bror. Years later they would still give the impression of a couple with great and sound affection for one another. It had been a practical rather than a wildly romantic union from the beginning, and they subsequently gave one another a surprising amount of latitude. Tanne would tolerate Bror's affairs, and he in turn would smile upon her friendships with Erik Otter and Denys Finch Hatton. Ultimately it was Bror, not Tanne, who instigated their divorce.

2

From the beginning of 1915, "the black year," all letters sent to Europe from British East Africa were censored, and the Blixens began, for the convenience of the censor, to write in English. Bror's was ungrammatical, although he spoke it more fluently than his wife. Hers was stilted; she claimed that living almost exclusively among the Africans had made her sound "like Friday in Robinson."[10]

On March 3 Bror wrote to Ingeborg to say that Tanne was better after alarming everyone with a spell of bad health, and he hoped that her safari would restore her strength. She left for two months in the beautiful Aberdaire mountains, where the air was cool and there were herds of buffalo and elephant. "Bror," she told her mother, "has arranged everything so excellent, [sic] he is splendid at that, he makes everything so easy for me."[11] Whatever she truly felt, whatever hurt, rage, or betrayal, she was determined to let no one at home suspect it.

The safari naturally did not solve her problem, and when she returned she was very ill with a high fever. The doctor now advised her to return to Europe to seek treatment, and only with great determination could she secure passage on a steamer bound for Marseilles. She took Farah with her, partly, perhaps, as a small gesture to deprive Bror of his services while she was gone, but mostly because she was simply too ill to be alone. She sent him back when they reached France; he "seemed too much out of his natural environment."[12]

When she reached Paris at the end of May, she took a room in the pension where she had lived in 1910 and dashed off a letter to Ingeborg, which she was able to send with a Swede on his way to Copenhagen. In it she attempted to prepare her mother for the consequences of the disease, without revealing its true nature. She described it as a very serious tropical fever, a kind of malaria that, if not treated promptly, might cause sterility.

The French doctors she did consult, specialists in the treatment of venereal disease, told her honestly that she would need long and painful treatment if she was ever to be cured permanently, and there was no assurance that she could be. This treatment was impossible to undertake alone in a foreign country during the war, and so she set off for Denmark by train, stopping in Switzerland to break the ride. From her Zurich hotel room she could see the clock tower of the town hall, and she told herself that it was certainly ticking off the last hours of her life. She reached Copenhagen with her sense of doom undiminished and entered the National Hospital, under the care of two of Denmark's leading venereologists, Drs. Rasch and Lumboldt. In order to keep her real condition a secret from the family she was given a bed in a general ward, rather than one in Dr. Rasch's special wing. There she underwent a course of therapy that lasted for three months. Its main ingredient was Salvarsan, Dr. Erlich's "magic bullet," an arsenic-based medication invented in 1909. Salvarsan had been an important advance over mercury in the treatment of syphilis, although it was itself extremely dangerous. "Toxic reactions were frequent and severe, and death sometimes resulted."[13] It was customary to give repeated courses of weekly injections lasting ten to twelve weeks, alternating between courses of intramuscular bismuth, for periods of up to two years or more. Karen Blixen complained during her treatments of pains in the mouth and neck, which her doctors later attributed to mercury poisoning from the tablets prescribed in Nairobi. The Salvarsan seemed to be effective. A Wassermann test administered to her in December 1915 was negative. Two spinal fluid taps taken in September and December showed a steady decrease in the number of white blood cells. But Mogens Fog has written that "the early normalizing of the Wassermann reaction in the blood simply meant that 'active' syphilis, and with it the risk of infection, had been arrested in the secondary stage."[14] The disease was by no means cured, or even under control. Only the symptoms had retreated.

3

On the seventh of September Mrs. Westenholz died at Folehave. She was eighty-three, blind, senile, and had acquired an ethereal quality in extreme old age. Her sister called her a "moonbeam."[15] On the same date forty-seven years later, in similar mild autumnal weather, Karen Blixen was to die at Rungstedlund.

Tanne, still in the hospital, thought her own death was much more imminent, although she spoke cheerfully about it. Thomas, who kept her company and became her confidant, was both impressed and puzzled by this fatalism. She even seemed to look upon her illness as a rare spiritual opportunity. "It could easily have brought her to the edge of despair," he wrote, "but she took her sufferings in quite a different way, as if thinking, 'Now I've endured that too, now I'm even nearer to experiencing really great things.' "[16] Later in her life she would explain that she had taken her affliction much more lightly than other people and that she reckoned it as part of the bargain she had struck in marrying a man like Bror. "If it didn't sound so beastly I might say that, the world being as it is, it was worth while having syphilis in order to become a Baroness."[17]

Isak Dinesen alludes to the disease several times in her writing.* In *Shadows on the Grass* she mentions trying to medicate the Africans with Salvarsan, and once being poisoned with an overdose of arsenic, administered accidentally by a servant. In "The Cardinal's Third Tale" she makes the disease, innocently contracted, a remedy for her heroine's implacable frigidity of spirit. It corrects Lady Flora's horror of the flesh, her contempt for humanity, the deficiency—a sexual deficiency—of experience. Perhaps it is not outrageous to suggest that for the sufferer herself there was an element of pride in having syphilis. Later in her life she looked back upon it as the price exacted not only for her title, but for her art. She would claim, indeed, that she had promised her soul to the Devil, so that everything she experienced might be turned into tales. That promise had been sealed, she would say, at the moment she discovered her disease and could no longer hope for a normal sexual existence.[18]

If Karen Blixen was not afraid to die, she was afraid of being stuck in Denmark. "As I lay in the hospital in Copenhagen I yearned for Africa and was afraid that the difficulties of a journey out would be so great that I could never get back."[19] That yearning inspired her to write a poem, "Ex Africa," which would be published in *Tilskueren* ten years later. It is a lyrical evocation of a lost paradise, and specifically of the landscape and sensations of her first safari with Bror. Addressing the moon, the poet thinks how it looked in the sky over the Masai Reserve, reflected in the waves of the Guaso Nyeri river, behind the hills of Kijabe, "over Suswa and Ngong, in my free land, in my wide land, my heart's land."[20]

Tanne apparently wrote nothing else that winter. She convalesced, had long talks with Thomas about philosophy and literature, and waited for news from Bror about the farm. He wrote rambling, affectionate, trivial letters, always addressing her as "my beloved."

---

*Also among Isak Dinesen's unpublished manuscripts is an unfinished tale called "Cornelia" (KBA 147, III), for which she did extensive research on prostitution and the spread of venereal disease in the nineteenth century. It is the story of a virtuous woman who defies convention to do charity work among the lowliest prostitutes, and it was apparently intended to air some of society's (and men's) hypocrisies and paradoxes where women and sex are concerned. "A man who takes pains to hide his sins [visits to a house of ill fame] from his mother and sister might freely confide to them that he had committed a murder," Dinesen writes. And of the good woman who visits the prostitutes, her complacent male narrator says: "As a tale it is good, even moving, like a legend of those ancient saints who debased their humanity for the glory of God. But transferred . . . to real life your Christian heroine becomes abhorrent . . . scandalous, like a lunatic or a witch. Neither you nor I could bear to look her in the face, to speak with a woman of whom we knew these things to be true."

The other Dinesen children felt just as restless and on edge as Tanne. Elle was suffering from the "unbearable emptiness" of an inactive life and soon after the outbreak of the war had gone to England to volunteer as a nurse, hoping to be sent to the French front. She was rejected, returned to Rungstedlund "bitterly disappointed"[21] and in that frustrated state of mind began listening to the proposals of a man who had been courting her for a long time, a rich lawyer named Knud Dahl. They were married in 1916, Elle without great enthusiasm, although she "grew to love her husband and made her marriage into a great success."[22] Tanne never reconciled herself to Dahl. She found him brittle, bigoted—he was a notable anti-Semite—and affected. His fortune was bourgeois and his politics ultrareactionary. Although he was to publish the first Danish edition of *Seven Gothic Tales,* he and Tanne quarreled bitterly shortly afterward and were not reconciled until the winter before his death.

Ea also married in 1916, having given up her hopes for a musical career. Her husband, Viggo de Neergaard, was a hearty, rather provincial country squire, and she left to live on his estate in Jutland. Thomas, who was now twenty-three, was studying engineering, bursting with patriotic feeling, and longing to join the fighting. He saw the war as his opportunity to help Denmark win back North Schleswig and to carry on the family tradition of courageous service in foreign armies. "But more than anything else," he explained, "my feelings were the same as Tanne's. These were circumstances in which one had to offer one's life."[23] He waited until he was sure Denmark was not in any immediate danger of an invasion, took his examination for the Polytechnic Institute, and then put his decision before his mother. She was furious, terrified, appalled, as she had been when Tanne announced her decision to marry Bror. Tanne interceded, arguing that Thomas needed and deserved the freedom to pursue his destiny, and that Wilhelm would have approved. In the end Ingeborg gave her blessing, and Thomas enlisted in the Black Watch Regiment of the Canadian Army. He was sent to France, showed outstanding valor on the battlefield, and in 1918 received both the British Victoria Cross—an extraordinary distinction—and the French Croix de Guerre.

Bror came home that summer full of optimism about the farm. War shortages of coffee had driven the price up, and Swedo now looked, even to so shrewd a businessman as Aage Westenholz, like an excellent investment. Uncle Aage incorporated the farm as The Karen Coffee Company, with himself as chairman of the board. Shares were sold to family and friends, and a bank loan of a million kroner was raised. The total capitalization now amounted to half a million (1916) dollars.

Elated about their future, and grateful to all those who had subscribed to it, Tanne and Bror made a round of visits to their families to offer thanks and say good-bye. They were particularly effusive to their Uncle Mogens

Frijs, who had given them such good advice about East Africa. That November they left for London, staying at the Carlton Hotel for a few weeks of sophisticated recreation before journeying south to Marseilles. Tanne was overjoyed to find herself in a great town again. She shopped for riding boots and lingerie and had an audience with the Danish-born Queen Mother, Alexandra, who was "exceptionally gracious and kind" to her.[24] The Blixens also visited Henrik Castenskiold—Daisy apparently was not there—and the Reventlows, who were all stationed at the Danish embassy. These old friends warned them that the Mediterranean route was too dangerous, and that they risked being torpedoed. So they booked passage on an English ship, the *Balmoral Castle,* sailing south through the Atlantic and around the Cape.

Reflecting upon the war, the sight of soldiers in the streets, the risks that forced them to change their own plans, Tanne told her mother that she understood Tommy's desire to be part of it, to offer his life, to test his courage. The terrible scale and gravity of the events put her own "small sorrows" into perspective.

4

It was a long, tedious journey to Durban, enlivened by a troop of extremely pretty young English actresses who kept the older women scandalized and the men titillated. Bror, she wrote, had found a group of emigrant farmers and spent most of his time discussing the future of Africa with them. There was also a large party of English officers on board who had seen action at the front. But Tanne found it disturbing that their experiences seemed to have made so little impression upon them and that, like the rest of their compatriots, they plunged cheerfully into the endless games of shuffleboard and bridge and kept up a stream of trivial chatter. "I have the feeling," she said, "that it must be because they don't dare to be serious; they cannot do it and are afraid of the vacuity of their own character."[25]

They reached South Africa the second week in December, where there was a two-week holdover until the boat for Mombasa picked them up. In that interval they lodged at the best hotel, swam on a beach that reminded Tanne of Trouville, and bought a car, a two-seater. Tanne was learning to drive and thought it would be "tremendous fun" to have an auto on the farm.[26]

The Swedish consul entertained them while they were in Durban and gave them letters of introduction to prominent local people whose plantations, long established, might offer them some useful models. Bror wanted to see a great variety of farms, for he had extremely ambitious plans to diversify his own. He would breed pigs, chickens, and cattle, brew beer, grow flowers, manufacture bricks, start a nursery of coconut trees on some land along the coast, and plant a thousand acres with sugarcane.

One of the farmers they went to see was a rich and well-born Englishman named Joseph Baynes, who owned an immense barony in Maritzburg called

Nels Rust. His family had been there for generations, and the Africans on the farm had, Tanne wrote, a feudal loyalty toward them. The Honourable Mr. Baynes was himself a "great original," entertained them handsomely, proved to be a scholar of Shakespeare and the Bible, knew the best people in England, and had been the houseguest of kings. But what impressed Tanne the most about him was an anecdote told by a retainer, illustrating the great love Baynes commanded among the Africans. Once, the story went, he had fallen very ill and was forced to return to England to see a doctor. He had very little hope of surviving, and he had bade the people on his farm a last farewell. But once abroad his health improved; when he left the hospital he went to a London record company and recorded a long message in Kaffir for the servants and field hands. The record was sent out, the gramophone set up on the verandah, and the Africans summoned to hear their master's voice. "Never," said the retainer with great reverence, "had he seen people as moved as [the] Natives had been then."[27]

Aboard the Mombasa steamer Tanne set up her easel on the deck. She had bought some watercolors in London and was determined to take up painting seriously again. Her first piece of work was a portrait of Bror's brother-in-law, Gustaf Hamilton, an officer in the Swedish cavalry who would be a somewhat burdensome houseguest at Mbagathi for the next few months. Bror also had his creative pastime; he was writing a book about Africa. Tanne promised it would certainly be "first class."[28]

The ship stopped at Zanzibar, and the Blixens had their car off-loaded to tour the island. In the marketplace of the old burning white city stood an auction block upon which slaves had been sold. The English had induced the sultan to stop the slave trade by paying him a compensatory yearly fee and supplying him with Kikuyu labor to replace his slaves. But since that time, Tanne reported, his life had lost its "savor," and he had gone to live in Paris.

They were then only a day out of Mombasa, and it was almost "unimaginable" to her that within a week she would be home. On the twenty-sixth she cabled Ingeborg to say that they had reached the farm, and on February 1 she wrote that it was "like a dream to . . . see everything again. One of you at home must come out someday and connect the world at home with this one; now it seems far too much like two separate existences."[29]

20

The Wing of Death

I

Nineteen seventeen was a year of loss and disaster. It began with unseasonable rains, the heaviest anyone remembered, and then a ruinous prolonged drought. The coffee bloomed spectacularly but withered on the boughs, and there was practically no harvest. The Blixens' financial agreement with Karen Coffee was to receive a 10 percent royalty of any profits. When there were none, they discovered they could not subsist on their salary alone, fifty pounds a month. Uncle Aage was not sympathetic, and Tanne appealed to Ingeborg, asking her to convince her brother they deserved a raise.

Almost as soon as they returned from Europe their manager, Åke Bursell, left the farm, saying he didn't want to see it come to ruin. Actually, he had the opportunity to buy some land of his own. Bursell had been virtually indispensable to the Blixens; he had the prudence and the practical experience Bror lacked. Tanne was bitter about this defection after all the "help" they had given him, and when Bursell made a success of his own farm, it was "hard" for her.[1]

That spring the news came from Sweden that Hans Blixen had died in the crash of his small plane. His widow, temporarily deranged with grief, wrote to Bror asking him to marry her. There is no record of Tanne's response, either to Hans's death or to his widow's letter, but the loss must have been devastating, particularly as she could not share its private dimension.

While she was mourning Hans, she learned that the estate of Katholm had been sold. After the death of Laurentzius Dinesen's only son it had been offered to Thomas, but he was not prepared to accept the responsibility or expense of running it. Tanne feigned indifference but in the same breath spoke of trying to buy it back. This news was followed by a letter from Else Reventlow in London, which broke the news that Daisy Castenskiold had committed suicide. Tanne told her mother:

> I feel that so much color and radiance has gone from life with her passing, and for me so much of my youth. Although I have seen so little of her in the recent years, there are few people I will miss more, and now that she is dead I realize

how much I have indeed thought about her. . . . I don't think that one can say that she was unhappy. She felt more joy in life than most people, she was always engaged in something and had so many interests, and she was loved as few people are. I would gladly exchange my life for Daisy's. . . . Poor Henrik, I feel so sorry for him. . . . He is the only one who was really good to Daisy, and although one can say that he is the only person she wronged in her life, still I think that she did him more good than harm. The time he spent with her is probably the only period when he was really alive, and he must realize that himself. There are so few people who can lift life up out of the mundane run and give it poetry, and in spite of everything I believe the thing one feels most for them is gratitude.[2]

2

Bror remained cheerful about the farm and full of confidence in his own abilities, despite the loss of Bursell. He was interested in planting flax, which was being grown with great success in the Protectorate and fetching high prices on the European market, and in March he took Tanne to visit some flax plantations in the magnificent high country around Gil-Gil. They were also invited to inspect a few of the large cattle ranches in the same neighborhood. One of these was owned by Galbraith Cole, son of the Earl of Enniskillen and brother-in-law of Lord Delamere. Tanne thought him "the nicest man" she had met in Africa; he typified the cattle farmers in general, whom she found to be a nobler and more independent sort than the coffee farmers around Nairobi.[3] She was suddenly seized by a regret that they had not started out with cattle, rather than coffee.

"Nice" was probably not the adjective for Galbraith Cole, who had been deported from the country before the war for murdering an African poacher. But he and his brother Berkeley, his brother-in-law Lord Delamere, and their friend Denys Finch Hatton all possessed what Karen Blixen called "the most important thing about a nobleman . . . un fond gaillard."[4]

At the end of the month the Blixens moved to a new house, one more in keeping with the scope of their plantation. It was a fieldstone manor originally built by Åke Sjögren, and it came with some of his fine Swedish furniture. He had also left behind a library of beautifully bound books, none of them ever opened. There were works by Kipling, Oscar Wilde, Bret Harte, Selma Lagerlöf, and Robert Louis Stevenson, among others. Tanne, who was generally starved for reading matter, was delighted.

Sjögren's house was a little closer to Nairobi and beautifully situated. Its six main rooms were spacious and cool; there were stone mantels, excellent plumbing, and fine mahogany paneling in the dining room. Once some trees were felled, it commanded a magnificent view over the lawn and the rolling foothills to the peaks of Ngong. The woods around the house were filled with storks, swallows, and nightingales, and Bror suggested they call it *Fuglsang* (Birdsong) in their honor. Tanne tactfully pointed out that the

English would never correctly pronounce *Fuglsang* and proposed *Frydenlund,* after Wilhelm's hermitage in Wisconsin. Then she learned that the Africans called the place Mbogani, "house in the woods." It was an almost perfect homonym for Boganis, and that settled it.

In the quiet of an April evening Tanne sat down to write to her mother from Bror's new office, sending her some photographs. A fire was burning in the hearth; Farah stood behind her chair, making conversation every time she put down her pen, and she remarked that her life was very like life "in Denmark about the year 1700."[5] The rains had closed the main road to Nairobi to all but mule or foot traffic. Bror walked or rode into town for business, but she was unable to make the trip. Mail came once a month; commodities were scarce; whatever they lacked they had to improvise; and they hunted most of their meat. Entertainments were also improvised, books precious, good talk highly prized. The roles of men and women were unambiguously defined, the men hunters and protectors and the women providers of civilized refuge and pleasure. This heightened the attraction between them. As in the eighteenth century, the great abundance of human energy made up for the privation, which suited her better than the modern system of appliances and equality. She loved contrasts and extremes and the manner in which their play, their interdependence, and their tension produced "harmonies."

In one of the photographs she sent her mother she poses with her staff on the lawn. She looks plump and radiant, is dressed head to toe in white with a rose in her belt and a long, heavy amber necklace, a gift from Farah. The eight servants seem noticeably less relaxed, although they were perhaps just not used to posing. They are handsome black men wearing shabby jackets over their *kanzus,* except for Farah in an embroidered waistcoat. There was Ali, the new cook; Juma, who would remain with Karen Blixen until she left Africa and raise his children on the farm; Esa, a new houseboy; Kebri and Kamao, who helped in the kitchen and looked after the dogs; and Abdullai, a young Somali boy who followed at Tanne's heels, looked after her like an "old nanny," and whom she petted and loved "as much as if he were my own son."[6]

3

There was a virtual cease-fire that spring because of the extraordinary rains, but the British army and, to a lesser extent, the settlers were depressed by their inability to subdue von Lettow. He had never once been defeated and had become something of a mythical demon, feared and idealized at the same time. Tanne was proud to have known him.

One of the greatest problems for the British army was the chain of supply, and that spring they acted to improve it. Instead of ox or mule power they would utilize porters, and by the summer the number of Africans in the

Carrier Corps had increased from 7,000 to more than 175,000. On the whole the Africans were simply press-ganged, and the servants on the farm were terrified of being taken. The British also decided to expand their African fighting forces, observing how successful von Lettow was with his. They had been reluctant to do so for several reasons: they were afraid to arm the natives with weapons that could be turned against them; and they were afraid that the Africans—who were soldiers of great prowess, stamina, and courage—would lose their respect for their white superiors.

This "arming of the natives," the strange weather, the elusiveness and ferocity of von Lettow all contributed to a general malaise in the country. People looked for an excuse and decided that there must be an enemy within. Feeling against the Swedish community was revived, and a series of articles in *The Leader,* written by a Mr. Bromhead, accused the Swedes of having German ties and "tainted" money. Members of the "best circles," Tanne wrote, believed this to be true, and it was even discussed heatedly among the Somalis.[7] The Blixens, having more of the "tainted" money than almost anyone else, were particularly suspected. Tanne had not concealed her prior friendship with von Lettow, and she had actually been buying horses for him at Naivasha when the war broke out. Now the British decided she was a spy, and she was cut dead everywhere she went. If she lunched on the terrace of The New Stanley, people at the next table moved away from her. If she walked into Mackinnon's grocery, the conversation stopped.[8] Isak Dinesen writes of this traumatic experience in *Out of Africa,* explaining that whenever she was ill or worried later in life it was vividly recalled. At such moments she "suffered from a special kind of compulsive idea. It seemed to me that in the midst of this disaster I myself was somehow on the wrong side, and therefore was regarded with distrust and fear by everybody."[9]

Bror was thicker-skinned, and Tanne marveled how he took everything "so calmly and never gets angry."[10] Instead, he went to see the acting governor, who was reassuring, and he also made an appointment with Mr. Bromhead, who, after a long conversation, agreed to publish a retraction of his articles. This duly appeared, but, as in all such cases, the damage was easier to inflict than to undo. Not until Thomas Dinesen won the Victoria Cross —the highest British military honor—were Tanne's innocence and good name reestablished.

She was out of touch with the world throughout that summer, as there was more than three months' delay in the mails from Denmark. When she wrote home about Bror, it was often to say that he was away and that she had some time to herself: an evening of quiet, a week in bed, a few days of solitude at Lake Naivasha. She made it sound desirable, and perhaps by then it was.

When Ingeborg's letters did reach Ngong, they were overwrought. She wrote that Ea was expecting a child but was afraid the news would be "hard" for Tanne, who had been unable to conceive. Tanne denied it; she had not yet given up hope for a child of her own, and what was hard was everyone's morbid sympathy. Ingeborg also tormented herself for having let Thomas leave for the war. She was voracious for reassurance, and Tanne, who worried about her brother constantly, worked hard to infuse some vitality and courage into her mother's panicked spirit. She exhorted her, verbally caressed her, and also offered some examples of vital wisdom which had been of use in her own moments of despair. One was the stoicism of the Somalis, Farah's "unwavering submission to Destiny." Another was the absolute self-confidence of the English aristocrats she had recently come to know, men like Delamere and Galbraith Cole, who "understood their own natures and acted fearlessly in accordance with them."[11]

Thomas Dinesen wrote to his sister from the front in France, full of ardor for battle and boundless idealism toward humanity, and sent her some poems. She poured out her love to him in letters addressed to "D'Artagnan" or to "Olav Trygveson," a hero of the sagas, promising him that through such trials and suffering he would find his destiny. "So much that I myself have dreamed but never achieved has been realized through you,"[12] she told him with more pride than envy. And in exchange for his poems she sent some old work she had revised and something new, which she warned him he would find "sad." There is indeed the draft of such a poem in a notebook from this period, scrawled in pencil and called "Harp Song":

> The years of my youth run out and disappear
> I have only two things left: my dead youth and
> the knowledge that you are dead
> Two fragments alone remain in my hands
> While all the rest, the rest flows on with no trace.[13]

In the isolation and sadness of that year with all its deaths, Tanne began to paint again. It was a way of collecting her energies, of taking the bearings of her spirit when she felt in danger of having them swept away. She remarked that she had a much finer sense of form and color than when she was younger and attributed it to her greater experience of life. The same maturity is also noticeable in her letters. Their voice has changed; they are more pensive and revealing. Sometimes, she confessed, her life seemed to be missing many things; she and Bror had such different tastes. He spoke, for example, of settling down in Denmark, of buying back one of his family's old estates and of ultimately leaving it to a nephew, Hans's son. She still hoped that she might "have my little Wilhelm to bring up—to take over our concern out here, and develop it further."[14] Africa, despite everything that wounded her and wore her down, had given her a glimpse of "life itself." She could no longer imagine a future apart from it.

21

Dramatis Personae

I

A NUMBER OF NEW PEOPLE entered Karen Blixen's life at the beginning of 1918, enlivening it considerably. Around Christmas she and Bror were invited to hunt buffalo in the Kedong Valley with Frank Greswolde-Williams, a cattle farmer, one of the country's early settlers. Greswolde-Williams had much of the rough grandeur, the blunt speech, the knowledge of animals, and the remoteness Isak Dinesen would later ascribe to Vitus Angel in "Copenhagen Season." Angel reminded the Danish nobles of their old grooms and keepers; Greswolde-Williams had been raised by the grooms and keepers of his father's great estate, whose manners he seemed to have adopted. When Tanne met him, he had recently blown out his eye in a hunting accident and lost his son to von Lettow in Tanganyika. He was one of that tribe of bearish, solitary old warriors for whom she had a special weakness.

From Kedong they went to stay with Sir Northrup and Lady Macmillan at their shooting farm in Juja. Sir Northrup had come to the country in 1904 and was a member of its Legislative Council. He was many times a millionaire and weighed four hundred pounds. But he had an unlikely grace of movement and a great courtliness of manner, and lent all these qualities to Isak Dinesen's Prince Potenziani in "The Roads Around Pisa." Tanne now also met the Macmillans' permanent houseguest, Mr. Charles Bulpett, who took her out in an automobile to shoot rhino. Bulpett was then sixty-seven and in retirement from his career as an explorer and *homme du monde*. He figures in *Out of Africa* as "Uncle Charles," the narrator's "great friend . . . and a kind of ideal to me. . . ."[1] He reminded Tanne of her own Uncle Laurentzius in his prime, a somewhat finer version. He was also one of the models for the courtly but impractical Baron von Brackel, who narrates "The Old Chevalier" and who "had travelled much and known many cities and men" but who had "shown very little skill in managing his own affairs."[2]

The Swedish Baron Erik von Otter was not a new acquaintance, but he now became a more intimate one. Otter returned to Nairobi that winter on leave from the King's African Rifles and was a frequent visitor at Mbogani House. He was a spare, handsome man of twenty-nine. The sun had bleached part of his face and browned the rest, and it had a strange blotched pattern of brown and white, repeated in his mustache. A friend remarked that "women were fascinated by it, but from the little I saw of him in Nairobi, he did not have much to do with the opposite sex."[3]

Erik had ridden into Nairobi with Bror during the first week of the war but had stayed to serve throughout its duration. He was a legendary figure in the K.A.R., to both the white and black soldiers. He chose to live with his African *askaris,* eating their rations, mastering their language, and, what was more difficult, their sense of humor. They called him *Risase Moja,* One Shot, for he was an amazing marksman with any kind of weapon. The Earl of Lytton writes with awe about Erik's "pistol shooting; the scattergun shooting at sandgrouse; the picking off of a distant buck with a 256; the cool destruction of lion after lion. . . . There was some rumour that he was dying; that he spoke Swahili and Sudanese and Turkana incomparably better than anyone else, white or native; that, having been crossed in love, he never looked again at a woman. Other friends spoke of a wife, with whom he was on such bad terms that he preferred the Turkana desert."[4] Such was the romantic grain to the hardness of Erik Otter.

When he met Tanne again she was gaunt and beautiful, full of restless energy and bright talk—a lightness that also seemed to be keeping much suffering at bay. He knew, as did most people, about Bror's infidelities* and no doubt admired Tanne for putting up so brave a face to them. Perhaps this struck him as a feminine version of his own heroism and austerity. In any case, he fell in love with her and made up his mind to rescue her from what he perceived as her sham marriage.

Tanne was initially drawn to Erik, too. He reminded her of Wilhelm, and she wrote to her brother about his love of war, his reverence for nature, his feeling of kinship with the Africans—all of which were so like her own. Erik was a disciple of Islam and knew the Koran by heart, and Tanne began reading it with him. She found it "very charitable, because unlike Christians [Muslims] have no concept of *sin,* and their moral code consists of hygiene and ideas of honor—for instance they put discretion among their first commandments."[5] That February, with her own notions of hygiene, honor, and discretion much enlightened, she and Erik left on a safari together to the Tana plains to shoot buffalo and rhino, to read *The Deerslayer* and *The Three Musketeers,* and, in all probability, to make love. ". . . There is something about safari life," she told her mother in a passage that suggests the nature of her own feelings, "which makes you forget all your sorrows, and feel the

---

*In a letter to Tania Blixen written on board a ship en route to Europe, her friend "Ginette" tells her: "There are several people on board who know you, and will insist on talking about Bror. . . . I simply can't tell you how I admire your pluck and perseverence—nearly as much as I do your eyes—& that's saying a lot—You *do* fight so well." (From "Ginette" to KB, undated, KBA 56.)

whole time as if you had drunk half a bottle of champagne—bubbling over with heartfelt gratitude for being alive."[6]

But out of his element—the wilderness—Erik Otter was "a rather difficult man to know . . . inclined to retire into his shell."[7] He came to visit Tanne when Bror was away and would often spend the evening staring at the fire. Once he proposed, or at least suggested she divorce her husband and marry him. She considered it seriously for a while, and his devotion "did much to restore [her] faltering self-esteem."[8] But there was finally something exasperating about Erik. The nobility of his spirit did not make up for its dead seriousness. There was nothing playful in him, nothing volatile or mischievous. Tanne would later speak of Erik in "unflattering" terms to her friend, Ingrid Lindström, and she told her sister that she had probably made him "very unhappy."[9]

2

If Bror was jealous of his friend Erik he made light of it, only complaining that there was to be no discussion of Muhammad between twelve and four.[10] When Otter went back to his regiment, Bror too left Tanne and Nairobi, for a month-long safari to Uasin-Gishu. Another period of solitude and boredom yawned before her, aggravated by a severe drought that would not abate for many months. The dryness of the air and the constant nervous expectation of rain wore her down and made her extremely homesick. She longed to see what new sculptures the Thorvaldsen Museum had acquired, and she missed music "terribly."

Toward the end of March she wrote a long letter to Ea, to congratulate her on the birth of a daughter, Karen. The letter gives a particularly lucid and beautiful picture of her suspension in that moment.

> When you write that you have run into Ellen Wanscher on the Vimmelskaft it is incredibly evocative and rich in meaning for me, but what in the world can it interest you to hear that I have been to the *Blue Post* Hotel with Lieutenant Cartwright? On the other hand it is a good thing that something of my existence—coffee and flax, Farah, Dusk, Lord Delamere, safaris and trading—enters your consciousness, and it is so lovely for me that you understand a little how I live here.
>
> Unfortunately there has been a drought here for some time, which surpasses anything one at home could imagine. If it goes on the whole country will die, and even as things are it is maddening enough. Now we are beginning to feel some of the shortages you have had at home for such a long time; butter, milk, cream, green vegetables, eggs—they exist practically only in memory. All the plants are withering; more of the plains burn every day and lie scorched and black, and when one drives into Nairobi and approaches the town it looks as if it were in the midst of a horrible conflagration—dust hangs over it day and night, and in these thick golden skies, with the wind from the Somali town

and bazaar, one has the feeling that plague and cholera bacillae gayly whirl about in it. There is also an unaccountable death-rate among small white children in Nairobi, and for adults the eternal scorching, dessicating wind gets on one's nerves, so that one must be extremely guarded in one's social intercourse. But . . . it must come to an end, and one must hold out long enough —*aber frage nur nicht wie. . . .*"11

On April 5 Tanne attended an intimate little dinner at Muthaiga, given by that same new English friend, Lieutenant Cartwright, who was going back to the front in Egypt. Algy Cartwright had only two other guests: Monica Belfield, the daughter of the former Governor; and Denys Finch Hatton, a fellow officer. Tanne had been curious to meet Finch Hatton, for she had heard so much admiring talk about him. He proved to be a tall, witty, lean, wry, balding, impossibly handsome aristocrat of thirty-two, who had just come back from Somaliland and who regaled the company with his adventures there. Their next recorded meeting took place a month later, just before Denys returned to Egypt, where he was supposed to enter flight school. The Blixens organized a hunt on their farm in honor of General E. H. Llewellyn and invited a small group of friends to join them. Denys came, as did Erik Otter; General Llewellyn's brother, Jack; their neighbor, Johnny van der Weyer; and several others. There was a light rain in the morning and afterward a cold lunch and a blazing fire in the dining room. Among them they killed thirty stags, two jackals, and a leopard. Denys stayed for dinner and then, as it was late, spent the night. The next morning Tanne drove him into Nairobi, and they lunched together. By then she was madly in love. "I think it is extremely rare . . . at my sorry age to meet one's Ideal personified,"12 she told her sister Elle. "It is seldom one meets someone one is immediately in sympathy with and gets along so well with, and what a marvelous thing talent and intelligence is,"13 she told her mother. Three days later she was planning a safari to Somaliland on the strength of Denys's enthusiasm for that country, and a visit to Cairo. Bror teased her about it. He was convinced, she admitted, that "the only thing in the world I care about is to see Finch-Hatton [*sic*] again."* He was right.

3

The Honourable Denys Finch Hatton† was so precious that he is mentioned sparingly in *Out of Africa*. He seems to appear from nowhere, at certain

---

*Isak Dinesen, *Letters from Africa*, p. 70. Isak Dinesen hyphenates Denys's surname in her letters and in *Out of Africa*. But the present Earl of Winchilsea, Denys's nephew, told Errol Trzebinski that the family prefers its name to be spelled without a hyphen.
†Denys's father was the thirteenth Earl of Winchilsea and Nottingham, his mother the former Nan Codrington, daughter of an admiral. He had an older brother, Toby, Viscount Maidstone, heir to the title, and a beautiful older sister, Gladys, widowed during the war.

moments of epiphany, in time to share them. His death, followed swiftly by the farm's collapse, rounds out "the stork's shape" and gives Isak Dinesen the feeling that she is not having "what people call a run of bad luck," but that grander persecutorial forces are at work: "some central principle. . . . If I could find it, it would save me."[14]

Denys first scouted East Africa in 1911, returning the following year to settle permanently. He owned a farm at Eldoret, where he grew flax, and interest in another at Naivasha, where he planned to breed cattle and grow pyrethrum. In 1913 he bought the former Macmillan mansion, Parklands, near Nairobi, for four thousand pounds.* When Prince Wilhelm of Sweden came to Africa in 1914 on the boat with Tanne Dinesen, Denys had put the mansion at his disposal. He was far from the roofless vagabond that Parmenia Migel—and Isak Dinesen herself—have made him out.

Trading, rather than hunting, which came later, was Denys's major source of income and pleasure in the early years. He set up a string of outposts on the Masai Reserve, owned a chain of *dukkas,* bought and sold property, and later managed several companies, one of which exported timber. He had a reputation for sharp dealing, and it was even rumored that he loaned money at high rates of interest. A trader's life suited his restless temperament, although it was an odd vocation for an earl's son and a graduate of Oxford.

Denys had left England, his friends said, to escape the conventional life of his class there and because he needed space. "There were too many people at home,"[15] as a friend put it, and most of them seemed unable to restrain themselves from adoring him. At Eton he had been, both to masters and boys, "an adored tyrant" who "dominated the school as few . . . can ever have dominated it before or since."[16] The catalog of his perfections, talents, and eccentricities could well be compacted into the word princely. As one who apparently had no peer, he was the elusive object of much fantasy, and his favor conferred immense prestige.

But if Denys found it hard not to be charming, his charm was not an offering. Since boyhood he had experienced a deference from the world, and from his family, which made him terrified of being bored, depended upon, exploited, or possessed. It was a deference to his physical prowess and beauty, to his intelligence and taste, but above all to a special and undefinable assurance which he possessed. As a result Denys, much like Wilhelm Dinesen, was looking for some kind of challenge—risk, pleasure, danger—great enough to engage him. Such a yearning may often express itself in caprice, create its own surprises when it cannot find any external ones. Denys was a great prankster. Once he flew to London simply to hear an opera, without

---

*Errol Trzebinski, *Silence Will Speak,* p. 83. Ms. Trzebinski's biography of Denys Finch Hatton, her letters to me, and our talks on the subject have been the major source of my information about Denys's childhood, finances, family, and general career.

calling anyone in his family, and flew back to Africa the next morning. Another time a friend sent him an urgent cable, which reached him via runner in the remote bush. "Do you know the address of so-and-so?" it asked. The reply went back by the same route: "Yes."[17]

Tania Blixen understood this aspect of her friend's character, found it lovable, and displayed the same appetite for surprise in her own old age. She was probably thinking of Denys when she wrote: "To love [God] truly you must love change, and you must love a joke, these being the true inclinations of his own heart."[18]

Early in the twenties, Denys would give up his other lodgings and move his things to Karen Blixen's house at Ngong. Here he stayed between safaris, generally for a week or two, between absences of many months. These brief and intense sessions with her lover kept Tania hungry and poised. Denys created an emergency in her life, and she rose to meet it. Her great love for him was partly a feeling that he demanded the best in her—all those spiritual resources she had cultivated so long in a vacuum. If Denys was her "living ideal,"[19] it meant that with him she became her own "living ideal."

Among the most stirring moments in the tales of Isak Dinesen are those when two great and equally matched partners do combat. They have generally lived in solitude until then, unable to gauge their own strength. In this class are Agnese della Gherardesci and Prince Nino of "The Roads Around Pisa"; Athena von Hopballehus and her cousin Boris of "The Monkey"; Kasparson and Malin Nat-og-Dag of "Deluge at Norderney"; Malli and Herr Soerenson of "Tempests." Wilhelm Dinesen had also spent his life searching for the lover/enemy worthy of his respect. It is the experience Dinesen describes when she writes about the lion hunt, which was "each single time . . . an affair of perfect harmony, of deep, burning, mutual desire and reverence between two truthful and undaunted creatures, on the same wavelength."[20]

She felt, with all the pride and gratitude of which she was capable, that in Denys she had met her match. It was probably the real *noblesse oblige* of her later years, when she believed her match no longer existed, that she made the experience possible for other young people: Thorkild Bjørnvig, Aage Henriksen, Jørgen Gustava Brandt, Viggo Kær Peterson, Clara Svendsen, and so many of her readers.

4

Denys Finch Hatton was a reluctant soldier—or "sodjer," as he contemptuously pronounced it—and once declared that "people in uniform were not human beings."[21] But at the outbreak of the war he joined his friend Berkeley Cole commanding a band of extremely fierce and proud Somali irregulars, known as Cole's Scouts.

Berkeley Cole had been an officer in the Ninth Lancers and had fought in the Boer War. In the early days of the Protectorate he had run a small, rowdy frontier hotel at Londiani in which he was a partner with Lord Cranworth. Later, he had a farm on the slopes of Mount Kenya. He was a slight, fine-boned young man with red hair, who reminded Tania Blixen of a cat, sensual and prejudiced. His tastes were fastidious, he had the cynicism of a fin-de-siècle dandy and, like Denys, he loved practical jokes. "Out of a kind of devilry," wrote Karen Blixen, "he was most charming to the people of whom he had the poorest opinion. When he really chalked his soles for the job he was an inimitable buffoon. But . . . where the jest was carried far in its daring and arrogance, sometimes it became pathetic. When Berkeley, a little heated, and as if translucent with wine, really got on his high horse, on the wall behind him the shadow of it began to grow and move . . . as if it came of a noble breed and its sire's name had been Rosinante."[22]

Berkeley's health was fragile. He suffered from arthritis, as did his brother Galbraith, and had a bad heart. He lived alone on his beloved farm, but it was rumored that he kept a beautiful Somali mistress outside Nairobi, "conveniently situated on the road to the Muthaiga Club."[23] Denys brought him frequently to Tania's house, and he became a familiar there, calling it his "Silvan Retreat."[24] With Denys, he helped fill its cellars and its humidor and arrived for visits laden with fruit and game from his own farm. Every morning at eleven he would drink a bottle of champagne in Tania's forest, poured for him by his Somali servant Jama into one of his friend's finest crystal glasses. Berkeley also had or feigned a certain romantic exaltation. He tried to make each moment a perfect little work of art.

Cole's Scouts fought bravely on the northern frontier, but they chafed under conventional military discipline, and eventually they mutinied.[25] Denys and Berkeley subsequently joined the East African Mounted Rifles. They were so much together with a third friend, the diminutive A. C. ("Tich") Miles, that they earned the nickname "Three Musketeers."[26] Denys spent his leaves at Galbraith Cole's thirty-thousand-acre sheep farm, Keep-kopey, on Lake Elementeita. It was a haven where one could hunt lion or sit around a fire and discuss philosophy. Denys began to teach himself the guitar while he was there and often sang to his own accompaniment. One of Cole's friends, Llewellyn Powys, remembered meeting Denys at Keep-kopey in 1916 and likened him to a "sinuous-limbed dog-puma indolently sunning himself under the palm-trees of the Amazon until such time as vigorous action is imperative. . . . He had the same quality of courage as Berkeley—but was far less reckless, combining the audacity of some old-time Elizabethan with the wisdom and foresight of the son of Laertes. . . . I liked the look of his scholarly appearance, which also had about it the suggestion of an adventurous wanderer, of a man who knew every hidden creek and broad reach of the Upper Nile. . . ."[27]

Denys went on to serve under Major General Hoskins, saving his life from ambush and earning a Military Cross. After a leave in England, he traveled out to Mesopotamia to be Hoskins's ADC and on the ship met a young American officer who became a lifelong friend. This was Kermit Roosevelt, Teddy's son. At Port Said the ship's stokers deserted, and Denys and Kermit, citing their "experience in the tropics," volunteered to replace them.[28] When the chance to attend the Royal Flight School presented itself, Denys seized it. He would one day have his own plane in Africa, take Tania up to see how the farm looked from the air, and give her the "most transporting pleasure" of her life.[29] But just before he was to start the course, his business partner died, and he was obliged to return to Nairobi. This was early in the spring of 1918, when he met Tania for the first time at Muthaiga.

5

The Blixens' marriage survived Tanne's love affair with Denys, as it had survived the diagnosis of syphilis, their frequent separations, and Bror's affairs with other women. They still lived together, attended parties as a couple, shared bedrooms when they stayed with friends, and generally gave the impression of two good old loving friends. Bror was not a hypocrite, and, if anything, he was proud that his wife's lover was of such high caliber.[30]

It was certainly not a solid marriage. Karen Blixen was a proud woman and Bror's behavior—passes at young American girls, scenes at the Muthaiga Club, unpaid bills and debts—must have humiliated her. Nor was it a compatible marriage; Tanne and Bror had very few tastes, passions, or enthusiasms in common. But she could tolerate that incompatibility in part because he fit her ideal of a "real man," which was a sort of *condottiere*, brutal, perhaps, but also sensual and lordly. On the whole, she took an eighteenth-century view of marriage. She had signed a contract, pledged allegiance to an idea, rather than just an individual, and she would keep her faith with it. Within the bounds of her formal compliance, she felt free to pursue her own pleasures. If she had not taken lovers before Denys (and presumably Erik), she had many admirers. One of them, General Polowtzoff, a courtly, older Russian diplomat, made a remark she herself quoted approvingly and that helps put this aspect of her character and experience into perspective. He told her that he had never known "<u>anybody so sensual and so little sexual</u>."[31]

It is tempting to see Bror and Denys as a unity in the Dinesen sense: spiritual foils. There is a photograph of them, taken in 1928 when they were both out on safari with the Prince of Wales, and it suggests such a relation. Bror is short, compact, robust, with a certain coarseness to his expression. Denys is languorous and refined, with an almost marbly elegance. Bror was the man of whom his wife remarked, "He didn't know if the Renaissance came before or after the Crusades."[32] Denys taught her Greek, acquainted her with the Symbolists, played Stravinsky for her, tried to inform her taste for modern art. The two men had their prowess, their extraordinary physicality, in common and were considered the two greatest white hunters of their time.[33] They liked each other, so said their friends, and for a while they actually shared a bedroom at Ngong, each having the use of it while the other was on safari. There is often some incestuous feeling between two friends who love the same woman, and perhaps this was part of their attraction. With his franker sexuality and his cruder charm, Bror might have been the first draft of his successor: that aspect of "Dionysius" Nietzsche calls the "billy goat." Denys, to all who knew him, was the God.[34]

6

There was another terrible drought in East Africa in 1918 that lasted into the winter of the next year. Many farmers laid off their field hands, for there were no crops to harvest, and then there was no maize to feed them. The Masai burned the plains each year to make way for the new grasses, but when the long rains failed, their lands lay "black and waste, striped with grey and white ashes."[35] The water holes dried up; the desperate animals came down from the hills to drink from the deep pond on the farm. All over the country the Africans were starving and dying by the tens of thousands, and plague followed the famine. The Blixens had themselves and their workers vaccinated against smallpox, and Tanne did what she could to feed the children. For a while she had a relief station on the farm and gave out *posho*, ground maize—the staple of the African diet. But as the *posho* became scarcer, the tradesman commissioned to provide it "ran away," and she had to give up her role as "Samaritan."[36]

The drought naturally did not spare the Blixens' coffee, and there was not a cent of profit for them in 1918. Tanne wrote about the "starving sharehold ers" at home, ready to devour her when she showed her face there. Bror had also invested heavily in dubious new improvements and new loans, and had begun to run up large private debts against the credit of the farm, giving it a bad name in Nairobi. Finally, he could not even pay his bills at the Muthaiga Club and the following winter was suspended until he did so. But he continued to go to parties there, giving, as one friend put it, "good value for the money."[37]

Aage Westenholz was alarmed and wrote critical letters about Bror's management, but Tanne defended him passionately. She complained that at a time when they might reasonably expect some understanding or even sympathy from those at home, they were persecuted with reproach and doubt. The drought was an act of God; Bror had done everything he could under the circumstances, and she called him a man of uncommon vision and tenacity. "You may laugh at me," she scolded Ingeborg, "but I feel now, in these hard times, like Khadijah, the Prophet's wife, and it is certain that I am married to a great man."[38] To dramatize her confidence in Bror, Africa, and the farm, she proposed that the other shareholders sell out to them. They would rent the farm for five years, paying generous interest on the capital until the principal was repaid. Uncle Aage refused, and Tanne noted with some grim satisfaction that now the shareholders would have to take the good times with the bad.[39]

That August, Tanne lost her beloved deerhound, Dusk. She had driven up to Nakuru to meet her husband, and they were planning to spend a weekend with the Delameres. En route she saved Dusk once, when he jumped out of the car at a level crossing. The train bore down, and she pulled him from the tracks at the last second, nearly getting killed herself. Lord Delamere watched the rescue from the sidelines and declared that it was the "pluckiest thing" he had ever seen.[40] But the pluck was in vain. Tanne later briefly entrusted Dusk to a Swedish friend, from whom he ran away. She left Lord Delamere's house to scour the wilderness desperately for the next week, questioning everyone she met. Farah finally found him in the mountains, emaciated and bleeding, standing vigil over a young zebra he had killed. He died the next afternoon. Tanne was bereft. She wrote about the incident in minute detail in several letters. "He was so faithful to me," she wailed, "I believe that when I die I will get to see him again, and then I will most fervently beg his forgiveness for leaving him. My wonderful faithful Dusk. I miss him so much, and if I live to be seventy I believe I will never think of him without weeping. . . ."[41]

She had another accident the same month, in nearly the same place. Bror had a commission to plow two thousand acres of land at Naivasha, and they returned there together for a working holiday. Tanne camped in a tent on top of a "great hill, with a view for miles around." She had two young Somali boys with her, and they roamed the mountains, sailed on the lake, and took Dusk's son, Banja, hunting with them. The change of air distracted Tanne from her grief, and her letters from the Naivasha "hermitage" were bright, full of gossip and a poetic delight in her surroundings. But she had a fall from a mule one afternoon and tore open her leg on a rock as she hit the ground. The wound became infected; she developed a fever, and Bror took her in an ox cart, almost unconscious with pain, to the nearest doctor, a charming but crazy Irishman by the name of Burkitt. There was some concern that she might lose her leg, but he cut out a chunk of *"dead flesh,"* gave her a little chloroform and sewed it up.[42] The gash opened twice and was twice restitched. Each time, Burkitt promised her there would be no scar. This, naturally, was gallant blarney; an ugly black ladder ran the length of her leg from knee to hip, didn't heal for five months, and never completely faded. Bror proved to be a tender and attentive nurse and became quite deft at wrapping bandages. "He hopes," she told her brother gamely, "that not many people will be allowed to see [the scar.]"[43]

7

When the news of the armistice reached Nairobi, a great bonfire was lit in the Ngong hills, and patriotic crowds flowed out from the town to see it. The next week the African soldiers paraded through the capital; balls and dinners were held at Government House and people danced in the streets. Early in December the news came from Denmark that Thomas Dinesen had won the Victoria Cross, an honor the East African *Leader* carried as a headline: "Baroness Blixen's Brother gets V.C."[44] Everyone stopped Tania on the street to congratulate her, and she wrote with pride that the English now treated her as one of them. "It . . . really puts a stop to the continuous gossip that some people were spreading with incredible persistence about our being pro-German."[45]

The troops were demobilized, the young men went back to their farms and the country's social life gathered momentum. A new governor arrived, Sir Edward Northey, and was welcomed with a series of elaborate parties. In February there was a week-long race meet in Nairobi. Now that the Blixens' patriotism had been so splendidly exonerated, they were much sought after. They lunched with Delamere at the racetrack and stayed over at Government House. Tanne had begun to entertain more frequently at Mbogani House and was delighted that her guests were so appreciative of her cuisine and decor. Denys was home from Egypt, and on February 26 she mentions to her mother that he was ill with fever and staying at the farm. "I am delighted to have him; I don't think I have ever met such an intelligent person. . . ."*

Denys's return coincided with the first real rain the country had in almost a year. There were four inches in three days, and with it the parched landscape revived, the *shambas* greened, the hills swelled with shadows. "Perhaps now the time of our tribulation is really over," Tanne wrote. "It . . . is beautiful here, a paradise on earth. . . . I have a feeling that wherever I may be in the future, I will be wondering whether there is rain at Ngong."[46]

Denys took her out alone for a safari "around Mount Kenya,"[47] and for a long while there are no letters. Tania Blixen withdrew into her paradise.

---

*Isak Dinesen, *Letters,* p. 98. Denys's "intelligence," his Oxford education, his love of art, music, and poetry were indeed rare among the settlers, who were an unbookish lot, most of them in the same mold as Bror. Denys never showed off his erudition and was supposedly modest, even diffident about it. But several old friends stressed that it set him—as it set Tania—"apart" and "above the heads" of their contemporaries.

22

Intermezzo

I

T HE BLIXENS SAILED for Europe together in August of 1919 for a little recreation in London and Paris, a long winter visit with their families, and the unpleasant prospect of facing the shareholders of Karen Coffee. They traveled first-class on the *S.S. Pundua,* and Tanne brought two little Somali pages to help her pack and unpack her trunks. The grave, beautifully dressed *totos* followed their mistress through the blue European dusk, carrying her parcels or her umbrella. At the Carlton Hotel they spent the night in her bathtub when there were no other quarters for them. Her African friends thought it amusing, although somewhat silly, and it was an item of gossip among them. In Denmark people stared at her on the streets, apparently offended by the flaunting of a decadent fantasy. It was not, in fact, a completely original decadent fantasy, for several well-known society *vedettes* of the era, notably the Princesse de Faucigny-Lucinge and the Marquesa Casati, also had their liveried Negro page boys. Years later Karen Blixen admitted to Bjørnvig that the gesture had "fallen flat."[1]

The coffee had been harvested before they left, and it had been a reasonably good year. Despite their debts and setbacks, both Tanne and Bror were completely confident about the farm's future, and they had no qualms about drawing upon their capital for a luxurious holiday. At Maxim's in Paris Bror ordered the best champagne, with the excuse that it was cheaper, per bottle, than his wife's perfume. At Baccarat they replenished their wedding crystal with an order for eight dozen wine and water glasses. Tanne gorged on music, opera, and plays, went to a first-class hairdresser and masseuse, and on a spree for new clothes. She had a mannequin made for her at Pacquin's,* chose several stylish hats at the Maison Lewis, and left her measurements with Madame Dupré, the celebrated corsetière of the Place Vendôme. Both she and Bror replaced their riding boots, and she had shoes made at Hellstern's, in Paris, from snakeskins she brought with her. "It is amazing how much clothes mean," she confessed to Thomas, "perhaps I value them too highly.

---

*Perhaps this house particularly appealed to her because its clients included the grandes dames of St. Germain *and* the great demimondaines, like Caroline (La Belle) Otéro.

But nothing—be it illness, poverty, or loneliness or other misfortunes, distresses me more than having nothing to wear. . . ."*

Denys was in England, staying at the Conservative Club in town and cutting a poetic figure in the drawing rooms of Mayfair. He had a collection of romantic clothes and peculiar hats (which concealed his baldness) and wore them with a suntan and a crooked smile. On weekends he went down to Haverholme Priory, his family's house in Lincolnshire, and let them feast upon him. None of them seemed able to get enough.

His older brother Toby, the Viscount Maidstone, had recently married an American heiress, Margaretta Drexel of Philadelphia, a beautiful woman whom, depending upon one's informant, Denys either loved madly or couldn't stand. But he did enjoy her parties with the "Anglo-American set," which included the Cunards, the Astors, Margot Asquith, the Kermit Roosevelts, the Duff Coopers, and the Ivan Moffats. Mrs. Moffat was Iris Tree, a poet, the daughter of Beerbohm Tree and a denizen of Bloomsbury, and she and Denys became close friends. He loved her work and had her book of poems with him when he died. Iris was an animated, restless beauty with golden hair and skin, and she was typical of the women Denys found attractive. They were adventurous or artistic, with a streak of what Karen Blixen would call *grandezza*. As a young man he had much admired his French cousin, Catherine (Kitty) Bechet de Balan, who had toured Morocco in native dress. Lady Winchilsea, an amateur photographer, had her pose at Haverholme in her veils and pantaloons, stretched out on a divan, and Errol Trzebinski has remarked that the portrait bears a striking resemblance to Tania Blixen.[2]

The Blixens held court separately while they were in England, and Tania presumably used her freedom to spend time with Denys. One evening Bror was invited to the theater by an African friend named Geoffrey Buxton. Buxton had a farm at Naivasha and had lived in British East Africa since 1906. He came from a Norfolk family of great distinction, had gone to school with Toby Maidstone, and his younger siblings, Rose and Guy, were Denys's good friends. It was at Geoffrey's urging that Denys had first gone to Africa.

The play, for which Buxton had some trouble getting seats, was the hit *Chu Chin Chow.* The other guests were his cousin, Ben Birkbeck, and Ben's young wife, Jacqueline—called Cockie by her friends, a nickname inspired by her resemblance to a plump, nimble, and vivacious robin. Buxton had touted Bror as a "splendid fellow" who was "always terrific fun," but for some reason the Baron barely said a word that evening. Mrs. Birkbeck was disappointed, for she liked to enjoy herself. When another host advertised Bror as the attraction for an evening, she turned him down. But they met

---

*Isak Dinesen, *Letters from Africa,* p. 97. Her bills, left unpaid when she left Africa in 1931, totaled more than 20,000 francs (KBA 75).

again, a year later, in Africa, and her second impression corrected the first.[3] After a long romance and two divorces, Cockie Birkbeck became Bror's second wife.

2

The Africans, Karen Blixen writes, "were adjusted for the unforeseen and accustomed to the unexpected,"[4] and she also had evolved an instinct, a kind of vigilance, with which she met the surprises and calamities of her life there. In Denmark she relaxed; there was a general slump in her character when she went home, the kind of spiritual fatigue an energetic person feels when she is suddenly discouraged from doing anything for herself.

She spent a sparsely documented year at Rungstedlund. Professor Rasch continued to treat her syphilis, and she was sick for five months with a combination of the Spanish flu and blood poisoning. The family circle closed around her, full of piety and advice. Her sisters came to visit with their rich, conventional Danish husbands, one who bored, another who vexed Tanne. Everyone spoiled and petted Ea's rosy little cherub, who was now two and nicknamed Mitten. Tanne later complained that she never should have come home and that she felt more than ever like a stranger there.

By 1919 the Dinesen family, or at least Ingeborg and Thomas, knew the truth about her illness, and that winter, in a moment of frailty or pique, Tanne told them something about Bror's ongoing infidelities, mentioning the possibility of a divorce. They would use this information to urge the divorce when she no longer wanted it. Then she tried to deny—if not the facts— the importance of her revelations. No outsider, she lectured Ingeborg, could truly understand the inner workings of a marriage, as Ingeborg should have learned from her own experience.

The family's original mistrust of Bror now turned into a frank and righteous abomination. Aage Westenholz wanted to see him out of the coffee business, for financial as much as moral reasons. When Bror left for Africa that March after a long visit to Sweden, his tenure as manager was almost over. Aage spoke about a sale, and he was supported by Countess Frijs, who owned a large block of shares. Bror, in the meantime, pawned Tanne's silver, had her furniture attached by creditors, and was ready to sign over the house and park to anyone who would negotiate a loan for them.

That November, Tanne sailed for London with her brother Anders on the first lap of her homeward journey. She was to meet Thomas there and wait for news from Africa before embarking. The cables crossed. She went to Marseilles and held up again, uncertain if it was really worth going back. When she finally booked passage on the *Garth Castle,* accompanied by Thomas, she was "in a state of acute despair."[5]

Bror, in the meantime, had been living a careless, hospitable, and, at times, dissolute life on the farm in Tanne's absence. An old friend spoke of "orgies with Masai women which were the scandal of the district."[6] A neighbor, Olga Holmberg, recalled that Tanne's best crystal was sometimes used for target practice. A former servant said Bror turned the house into a "hotel."[7]

Two old friends of Bror's, Ingrid and Gillis Lindström (not, however, of the dissolute set), had emigrated to Kenya in 1918, and while Tanne was away he saw much of them. They were both uncommonly warm and down-to-earth people. Gillis was a former officer in the Swedish cavalry, and Ingrid was an officer's daughter. She was a small, fair, round-cheeked woman full of liveliness and vigor, and had known both Blixen twins as a young girl in Skåne.

The Lindströms bought a house at Njoro from Algy Cartwright and planted flax there. Ingrid was as passionate as Tanne about her farm. When the market slumped badly the next year they could not meet their mortgage payments, and Ingrid tried to breed poultry and grow fancy vegetables for the Nairobi market as an alternative. Their household, with three small daughters, was, in Tanne's words, "the most happy-go-lucky thing you can imagine." Gillis made the furniture out of packing crates; there was an old legless sofa in the sitting room, and here Tanne and Ingrid would sit up late into the night, talking. Mealtimes were "chaotic," and generally the larder was missing such staples as sugar, butter, and milk. The children went around barelegged, dressed like gypsies, playing in the dirt with the animals and the chickens. "But in the midst of it all," Tanne would write, "it is the happiest family I have seen out here."[8] Ingrid adopted Tanne into it, shared her serenity and her health, teased her and laughed at her for her follies, and wept in her arms when times were hard for either of them.

Algy Cartwright pressed the Lindströms for his money in 1919 in an amicable sort of way. He even showed the house to some other friends who thought they might be interested in buying it. They were Ben and Cockie Birkbeck, who were staying with Geoffrey Buxton and talking seriously about emigrating. Cockie and Ingrid became good friends, and it was at Njoro that Cockie met Bror again.

Denys also turned up at the Lindströms. He came one day with Algy Cartwright but spent most of the morning fixing the car, and so Ingrid had assumed he was the chauffeur.[9] She took an immediate liking to him, as she would to Tanne the next year.

On at least one occasion, Cockie and the Lindströms visited Mbogani House together. Bror invited them all grandly to dinner, but they had to wait while Farah went into Nairobi and came back again with some food. On another occasion, Cockie met Denys there. Bror introduced him with a familiar slap on the back as "my good friend, and my wife's lover, Denys Finch Hatton." She could, therefore, never understand Tania's bitterness toward her own affair with Bror. "She felt she had been made a fool of. She never spoke to me again."[10]

23

Thomas

I

THOMAS DINESEN came to Africa to see if he couldn't settle there. As early as 1918 Tanne had given him the hope of buying Crescent Island on Lake Naivasha, where he could shoot ducks in the morning, bathe at sunset, and have a little harbor for a motorboat. On the *Garth Castle* they had talked of land the other side of Mount Kenya, where he would raise the finest dairy cattle in the country. But after his first rapturous impressions of the Colony,* its economic future began to discourage him. He sank the capital he had come with into Karen Coffee and stayed for two years, helping his sister run the plantation and engineering its coffee factory. This large, solid, practical younger brother was not, however, permitted to figure in the austere fabric of *Out of Africa*. He lived in his own cottage on the farm, retiring to it discreetly when Denys came, and sometimes left for long safaris on his own.

Shortly after Thomas arrived in Africa, Bror Blixen left the farm for good. There are differing versions of the events leading to his departure. Thomas perceived that the marriage was foundering as soon as Bror met them at Mombasa and delivered a jeremiad about the farm, almost, it seemed, as if he hoped they would take the next ship back to Denmark. Mrs. Hoogterp, the former Cockie Birkbeck Blixen, complained on Bror's behalf that he had been abandoned and mistreated by Tania's family and that they had literally "chucked him out to sleep on the veldt."[1] Bror actually did go to live on the Masai Reserve when he left the farm, but partly because he had no money and was a fugitive from his creditors, who were waiting to pounce on him if he showed up in Nairobi. Friends subsequently hid him out, including the governor and his wife, in whose house he was immune from prosecution. Later, they "bundled him off"[2] to Tanganyika on safari with some rich clients. He came back five thousand pounds richer, having done well with ivory, but he spent the entire sum gambling and drinking champagne while en route to Europe. "No one trusted Bror, but everyone tried to help him," said Mrs. Lindström. This precarious and undignified existence didn't seem to depress his spirits, diminish his charm, or curb his extravagance.

---

*In June of 1920, the Protectorate of British East Africa became a Crown Colony.

Tanne wrote about the scene she found at home—the broken glass, the furniture put up for sale—but then did not mention her husband again for seven months. When she finally did resign herself to filing for divorce in 1922, it was with tremendous sadness and reluctance. Bror was eager for it, Thomas and the Lindströms urged it, but she still looked upon it as an unmitigated tragedy. She would even have been willing, she confessed, to let Bror have his "freedom" while remaining nominally married to him so long as he avoided any scandal.

2

Denys was in England or on safari for most of the next two years, and Thomas Dinesen was his sister's only real companion. His presence was a great emotional luxury for her, for he was the one person in the family in whom she could confide. That confidence could at times be passionate and tyrannical. In later years, when Thomas had a family and could no longer devote "my whole life and fortune to my sister,"[3] she still tried to exercise a kind of *droit du seigneur,* which his children resented on their mother's behalf. After the Second World War, when she was surrounded by admirers, Karen Blixen called upon her brother less, argued with him more, and took a somewhat high-handed tone with him. But until then—in Africa and throughout the writing of her first three books—he was her sounding board, the person with whom she was able to rest from her own high "standard of gallantry" and to "speak about her troubles."[4]

The two were very different and saw nothing eye to eye. When Thomas first looked for the Southern Cross one evening on the deck of the *Garth Castle,* he was disappointed to find that "it wasn't a cross at all."[5] He was a democrat, an atheist, a partisan of Aunt Bess and the Westenholzes, and took the sensible and literal position in all of his and Tanne's debates on art and religion. There was some rivalry between them as to who more resembled Wilhelm. Thomas claimed to have inherited his father's talents as a hunter and a soldier, and his interest in "great issues." Tanne, he agreed, had inherited Wilhelm's talent as a writer, a "genius" he would urge her to develop. Writing, he believed—not farming or painting—was her one true calling. But he also regarded her "artistry" with a certain impiety and suspicion, and the "inaccuracies" in *Out of Africa* amused him. "Do you know the epigraph?" he asked me.* "Well, in fact, my sister couldn't ride or shoot an arrow, and she never told the truth. Her horse was unruly, and she couldn't mount it by herself. She would call her *boys* to help her, but when they couldn't hold him still, she would, on the spot, renounce riding forever, saying, 'Nobody helps me, nobody cares about me, I won't stay

---

Equitare, arcem tendere, veritatem dicere: To ride, to shoot with a bow, to speak the truth.

here. . . .' "[6] Tanne, he wrote more formally, "had a talent for depicting an attractive picture of everything she came across in life—people and country-side, ecstasy and despair. At times the artist can be so carried away by his picture that even his nearest friends may doubt its genuineness, the truth in its creation."[7]

Thomas Dinesen has been fastidiously loyal to his sister in everything he has published or said about her. If he describes her egotism, her caprice, her mercurial temper in one breath, he exalts her courage, her high ideals, her genius in the next. But she does emerge from his portrait as a trying soul to live with. She was extremely moody and could become furiously despairing, often over trivial matters. She took the shortcomings of her servants as a personal affront or rejection. "You want to get rid of me," she accused them when they let her favorite dog mate with a mongrel or when the housework was badly done. "You never helped me to become anything," she accused the family, and yet Thomas believed that "had they encouraged her in a profession she would have, on principle, refused."[8]

When Tanne wanted something, small or large, it was with a stubbornness and ferocity few people could resist. "One had to surrender to her," a niece said.[9] Even the Nairobi moneylenders, who turned down Thomas's countless requests for short-term loans, caved in to hers. "She had an astonishing ability to get her own way, to make all kinds of people bend to her wishes." It was, Thomas concluded, "a somewhat dangerous characteristic."[10] An African friend put it more bluntly: "People were afraid of Tania. She was likely to do anything. You had the feeling that she might suddenly shoot someone."[11]

3

Aage Westenholz arrived that spring for the purpose of getting rid of the plantation. He was a tall, thin man of sixty with a fine mustache who spoke what was on his mind in a plain and emphatic way. The Africans called him *Mzee*, "The Old Man," but by the end of his stay they were so impressed with his constitution that they began to call him "The Strong Old Man." He liked cold baths and long walks and was not interested in society. But he did try to be open-minded about the farm.

Thomas concealed his own misgivings and argued with his uncle that it was a venture well worth supporting with fresh capital. Tanne did not believe that the beauty of the country touched him in any way, but apparently her own determination did. When he left that June, they had worked out a highly conditional new agreement. She would assume all managerial responsibilities, in exchange for a salary of 80 pounds a month and a 10 percent royalty on all profits. Were the farm to be sold, she was to receive a third of any profits in excess of 100,000 pounds and could exercise an option to buy out the shareholders for 850,000 kroner, plus a second mortgage of 1,350,000.[12] But there were two draconian stipulations. Bror Blixen was never to set foot on the farm again, and Tanne, as a gesture of good faith, was to move out of Mbogani House and into a cottage with a thatched roof, which had formerly been occupied by her farm manager. The farm's unprofitability was thus treated by Uncle Aage as a sin, for which penitence must be done. Tanne refused to move, raged about Uncle Aage's "grass hut and office work"[13] for months to come, and never forgave him for suggesting it. It dramatized, once again, the gulf of temperament and values which divided her from her mother's family.

Tanne's determination to keep the farm and her determination not to divorce Bror consolidated, throughout 1921, into a tremendous battle for her autonomy. She fought the family then precisely as she had fought to keep her vitality, her secret self, intact from their intrusion as a young girl. Her house, her land, and her *totos* were, she declared, parts of her own being, and she had the feeling she had created all of them. When the family wrote concerned letters urging her to come home, stern warnings that they would have to sell, sermons about economy or selfishness, she told them that if they took her farm away they would never see her again. These exchanges became more acrimonious as the twenties passed and as her promises became discredited. To compensate, she had to keep asserting a high and even inflated valuation of her own competence and worth, her own way of doing things. She would, for example, insist *she* knew just how to manure the coffee trees or to treat the burns of her squatters, and she relied upon her instincts in administrative and financial matters. Perhaps she needed this degree of stubbornness to match Uncle Aage's and, much further back, to survive in a family of aggressively opinionated and strong-willed people.

4

When Tanne finally confessed to Mrs. Dinesen that she and Bror had separated, she begged her mother not to share the news with the family. She was desperate for some wisdom and a little simple consolation, not pity, not advice—the staples of the family's emotional larder. Rather than consult her siblings, she asked Ingeborg to "talk about me to Father. It is really he who is responsible for he deserted me, and must have seen that things were not going to be easy for me."[14] Ingeborg, however, discussed the problem at a shareholders' meeting, with the result that Tanne received a series of maudlin, righteous letters urging her to divorce. Her indignation may well be imagined. She threatened to cease all communications and send back all letters— even her beloved mother's—unread. She could not ever come home again, she wrote furiously, to live among pharisees. But even at the highest pitch of her fury, she was careful to reassure Ingeborg how much she still needed and loved her. Citing the words of a young friend, Lord Doune, that "when you ride you are holding onto a <u>mouth</u>," she told her mother: "Remember, when you write, that you are striking a heart."[15]

Divorce proceedings were at last started at the Swedish consulate in 1922. There were none of the "sordid aspects" Parmenia Migel refers to in *Titania*. [16] It was a civilized petition that stated the couple had been separated for a period of three years and had no children. The one piquant detail is that Tanne lied about her age, shaving off five years.* Thomas and the Lindströms were the witnesses, and everyone went out for a gay luncheon at The Norfolk. If Tanne "never forgave" Cockie Birkbeck, she did not—for a while, at least—seem to bear a grudge against her former husband. He, like Denys, stayed on the farm between safaris, brought clients for lunch to meet Tanne, and used the house when she was in Europe.

There was, however, one ongoing conflict between the Blixens, a sort of custody fight, and this was over Farah. He had been Bror's servant originally, and Bror continued to take him on his safaris, depriving Tanne of his services for months at a time. She resented this bitterly and they feuded—much as did Oberon and his wife over their fairy boy. Such a quarrel would have amused Denys greatly. It may have been the inspiration for the nickname he gave his mistress, which was Titania.

---

*In 1919, when she was thirty-four, she made Geoffrey Buxton guess her age, and he had said: "Twenty-seven" (Isak Dinesen, *Letters from Africa*, p. 96). So among her English friends, including Denys, she pretended to be seven years younger than she really was. (KBA 72, Karen Blixen's divorce petition and decree).

24

Kamante and Lulu

I

AT THE BEGINNING OF 1922, Ea de Neergaard gave birth to a stillborn child. She languished at home with a high fever for the next few months and died in June, only thirty-nine years old, leaving her daughter Karen to the care of Mrs. Dinesen. Tanne wrote at once, describing the distance between herself and Denmark as unbearable. But in subsequent letters, which much disturbed the family, she confessed that her sister's death lacked a certain reality for her and that her *shauries* with Bror were much more immediately painful. At least she and Ea had loved one another, had resolved old conflicts, and she had her happy memories. But of her marriage, nothing solid remained.

While Tanne often repeated that she had parted from her husband as his friend, the divorce proceedings, which took several years, depressed her enormously. She could not understand how Bror could renounce their partnership with such ease, with such casual disloyalty to a past in which there had been love, fun, and complicity and in which she, at least, had left behind "something of my soul." Bror, she said, "has been the person I was closest to in the world," and it felt as if she had lost a child.[1]

Thomas couldn't lift his sister's spirits. She wanted her mother and, sparing no sentimental flourish, she begged Ingeborg to come to Africa for the winter. But Mrs. Dinesen replied that she could not leave Ea's daughter, at least for now. To this Tanne countered that Mitten had more years than she did to enjoy Ingeborg's care and that the farm was like a grandchild, too, just as deserving of her blessing and solicitude. It is a measure of her unhappiness that she felt absolutely no shame in saying so.

That autumn the Kenya Colony got a new governor, Sir Robert Coryndon. Rumor had it that he was "pro-Indian" and "pro-native," and this suited Tanne very well. On the evening that Lady Northey gave her farewell party, Tanne was particularly depressed and had decided not to go. But after dinner she made an effort to shake free of her mood, ordered the *totos* to bring round her car and rig up a light, and she set off for Nairobi, driving herself. The party was only getting into high gear toward eleven, when she arrived. Denys was there. Lord Delamere introduced her to the new governor and murmured that he was a fine chap, had been a white hunter before he was a civil servant and understood the wilderness and the game. Everyone, Tanne noted, was particularly sweet to her, including Coryndon. He promised to visit the farm and did so, a month after he was installed. They had a long discussion about colonial politics, and she discovered that he shared her sympathies for the Africans and her ideas about their economic importance for the future of the country. Independent native production, she believed, would be increasingly vital. "These <u>tribes</u> could be taught to do many things. . . ."[2]

The epithet "pro-native" (though not "pro-Indian") was often attached to Karen Blixen's own name in the twenties. It refers to one of the most controversial issues of the decade. After the war there was an acute shortage of labor on the white farms. This was aggravated by a government program of new railway construction which employed thousands of African workers; by an influx of "soldier-settlers"—veterans chosen by lottery to receive three million acres of highland farmland; and by the series of famines and epidemics that had swept the country in 1918, killing thousands of Africans. The settlers wanted some form of compulsory labor for public works; they also wanted the government to bring strong pressure on the chiefs to make their young men work on the white farms. "In the old days," Governor Northey argued, "the young man was constantly on the warpath and led a healthy life of outdoor exercise; nowadays, unless he works, he has no compensation for the loss of the raids and fights of those old days."[3] (He was subsequently sacked for such opinions and replaced by the more "pro-native" Coryndon.) But unlike Karen Blixen and Coryndon, who favored independent native production, most settlers perceived that the Africans could not cultivate their own lands and those of the whites at the same time. They did not want the black men as "partners" in the Colony's development.

The "Indian question," which was as much racial as economic, also became a bitter controversy at this time. There were 23,000 Indians in Kenya in 1921 and 9,600 in the towns as clerks, stone masons, small shopkeepers, and shop assistants, and they lived in considerable misery and squalor. The whites wanted an end to unrestricted Indian immigration—a "brown wedge," as they called it, being driven between them and the Africans. They wanted segregation of schools and residential neighborhoods; and they wanted to prohibit the Indians from owning land in their own sacred white highlands, arguing that by constitution the Indians were fitted to live elsewhere, whereas the Europeans could tolerate only the temperate zones. But what was most essential, they opposed the demand of the Indian leaders for a voice in the government of the Colony and specifically for proportional representation on the Legislative Council. To give them a common voting roll was, in effect, to give them power.

The white settlers saw their farms, their livelihoods, their years of effort

and sacrifice threatened by these two issues; and, more than that, "civilization" itself, Kenya as a white man's country. They were "rather aggrieved,"
as Elspeth Huxley put it,[4] by the vehemence with which they were execrated
by reformers in the British Parliament and press, and among the missionaries
and civil servants in the colony itself. Their sense of embattlement increased
in 1923, when the British government published a Kenya white paper,
defining the interests of the Africans as "paramount" and the interests of the
immigrants, of whatever race, as necessarily subordinate, wherever they came
into conflict. But despite all the noble Foreign Office rhetoric, the whites
continued to hold their ground. They held onto their majority on the
Legislative Council and blocked unrestricted Indian immigration. While a
briefly implemented policy of forced labor (for public works) was abolished,
the number of Africans working on white farms continued to increase, due
largely to increments in the hut tax.

The whites in Kenya were prepared to resist any erosion of their position
by force, if necessary, and they went so far as to form a Vigilance Committee,
with Lord Delamere as the leading member, which met in secret and made
plans for an Ulster-like resistance. To be "pro-native" or "pro-Indian" in
such a climate was tantamount to class and racial treason. Within her own
small group of friends, Karen Blixen's views were tolerated, perhaps smiled
upon, for they did not have much effect. But she was talked about with
bitterness and resentment by many others. For her part, she wore her "pro-
native" label with defiant pride and even compared it to the way she had
borne her illness. "Many *shauries*," she told her brother, "that might seem
completely intolerable to some people, to me are quite stimulating. . . . In
the end it depends on whether they allow us to go on being ourselves. . . ."[5]

2

Denys subsequently came to spend a few days at the farm, and the alchemy
of his presence transmuted her depression into "pure joy." They played
Schubert's *Frühlingsglaube* * and agreed that "there was a distinct valley we
could see from the farm, the furthest and deepest valley, just after the rains
. . . ,"[6] and here they would be buried. On a longer visit, they would ride
up to explore it. But Denys had business in Nairobi; he left after three days
and went back to his pied-à-terre, which was a bungalow on the golf course
at Muthaiga. It was not until the following year that he moved his possessions
to Tania's farm and began to use it as his home base.

Thomas, in the meantime, had been away on a safari with the Lindströms
and came back in a restless and unhappy mood. His suffering as a young man

---

* *"Es bluht das fernste, tiefste Tal."* "The farthest, deepest valley is blooming." Ea had also sung this *lied,*
and it had many reverberations in Karen Blixen's life.

was much like his sister's. He, too, had the Westenholz exalted regard for great deeds and high principles and longed to be proved and tested. Though the war had done so, he could not now find another enterprise, calling, or passion great enough to absorb and reward his boundless idealism. Tanne could give him good advice in the matter. A few years later, when his yearning was giving way to despair, she told him to "hold out!" It was impossible that a man so upright and strong would not eventually find the means to action. It was also impossible that someone with his gift for love would not find a person worthy to receive it. He had envied her her love for Denys, and she promised him he would one day feel the same.

I don't think that . . . one gets a flash of happiness once, and never again; it is there within you, and it will come as certainly as death. I can speak from my own experience. When I was very young I fell very deeply in love—in 1909 it was—and really believed I would never feel that way again; then nine years later, in 1918, I did, and much, much more strongly and deeply than before. I once read the translation of a little Greek verse, which I so often think of in this regard:

> Eros struck out, like a smith with his hammer
> So that the sparks flew from my defiance.
> He cooled my heart in tears and lamentations,
> Like red-hot iron in a stream. [7]

This is my experience of it, and not at all as the yielding tenderness that one hears described. Just you wait; that hammer will certainly be raised for you again. [8]

But as much as Tanne loved her brother and missed him when he was gone, his vagueness and solemnity got on her nerves. They often quarreled, sitting up late after dinner or smoking a leisurely evening cigarette by the dam. Thomas was passionately interested in modern science and philosophy, and Tanne thought that Darwin, for one, ought to have been burned at the stake for his "depressing" view of life. [9] He called her a reactionary, and she countered that he was a Bolshevik. They disagreed about sexual morality— his point of view was wholesome and romantic; hers enlightened, in the eighteenth-century sense of the word—and about birth control, which Tanne thought was radically practical but not esthetic. Thomas told her that considering her general outlook she ought to become a Catholic, and she responded that without subscribing to any dogma she was a sort of Catholic, a Catholic priest at that, and she compared her work among the Africans, only partly in jest, to the mission of Bishop Absalon among the pagan Danes. Finally she turned up her nose at evolution, Kant, the perfect mate, "principles," and declared that she hoped she could "disappear with the old civilization." [10]

Actually, Karen Blixen's political and religious views were, like her moods, subject to erratic swings. (The one fixed point was her aversion to all things middle-class.) As a young girl she had revered the French Revolution and continued to speak of France as the "holy land" of freedom.[11] But she loved luxury and was a staunch defender of courtly manners, feudal privilege, and high culture. She lamented the decline of an "elite," the "social levelling" that blurred the old class distinctions,[12] but she passionately declared her love and affinity for the "lower classes." In 1910 she spoke of the Radicals as "scarcely human,"[13] but in 1919, when her Uncle Aage organized a highly controversial volunteer corps to fight against the Communists on the Finnish border, she expressed the opinion that "Bolshevism is the first attempt at realizing democracy, and may very well end in something good."[14]

Writing to Aunt Bess in the twenties, Karen Blixen called feminism the most important revolutionary movement of the nineteenth century,[15] and her analysis of sexism still reads brilliantly today. But in the fifties she repudiated any knowledge of the women's movement and claimed that "feminism is a matter which I do not understand, which I have never concerned myself with of my own volition."[16] Many of the same paradoxes charge her statements about religion. In 1914, again in a letter to Aunt Bess, she called herself an "atheist,"[17] and throughout her life she despised the "poisonous tradition of dualism"—of Christianity—that had divorced the sensual from the spiritual.[18] But God or gods (and devils) are ubiquitous in her work, and one of her most deeply held beliefs about art was that one wrote or painted because one "owed God an answer."[19]

Like her father, Karen Blixen was a born rebel and individualist—an intellectual *pétroleuse.* Her position on a given issue very much depended upon who was arguing it and, even more to the point, who was in authority. The impulse to defend her independence—to set herself apart from the herd, to be unique—remains constant, while her values change. When the consensus was conservative, prudish, and patriarchal, she was radical, liberated, and modern. As it became more liberal—then Marxist, in postwar Denmark—she took it upon herself to represent the *ancien régime,* made up "decadent" and fantastic stories about her past, and took great glee in shocking people with her "aristocratic pronouncements."[20] She loved provocation for its own sake, which was perhaps not as frivolous as it sounds. It was also for the sake of the erotic principle.

3

One evening in late October, after Thomas had retired to his cottage, he was awakened by Tanne's night watchman, who told him that the Memsabu wanted him right away at the house. Alarmed, he dressed quickly and followed the man back by lantern light. He found his sister leaning against the mantel in the sitting room, shaking from head to foot, crying uncontrollably and almost out of her mind with grief. He tried to calm her, and after a little while he learned what had happened. She had thought—and dearly hoped—that she had been pregnant with Denys's child, but that hope had been "disappointed." Mr. Dinesen did not, as an old man, care to elaborate, and the actual event remains somewhat mysterious. But she could not have been more than two months pregnant, and a miscarriage at that stage could well be confused with an overdue menstruation, or vice versa. (The chance of a miscarriage for a woman of thirty-seven, suffering from syphilis, is great.) This might account for the ambiguity in Thomas Dinesen's memory of the evening. He was unwilling to declare that his sister had actually been pregnant, partly out of delicacy and partly out of real uncertainty as to the facts.

Tanne never mentioned this disappointment to her mother or to anyone else, but on the twenty-ninth of October she wrote a particularly moving letter home. "I think so often about those words in the Bible: 'I will not let thee go before thou blessest me.' I think there is such deep meaning, something so glorious in them. I almost take it to be my 'motto' in this life. . . . The hardest thing for me has been that I have been unable to carry it through in my marriage—although it really was as good friends that Bror and I parted. But I also think that once one says these words, then one must agree and consent to let go of that which has given one its blessing."[21]

Esa, Karen Blixen's cook, died in December, poisoned by his young wife, Fatoma. Hassan Ismail temporarily took his place, and a strange and wild little Kikuyu boy was assigned to be his kitchen *toto,* washing the pots and sweeping the floor. "Mrs. Karen came every day and said my service was excellent,"[22] he remembered. His name was Kamante.

Kamante Gatura was about twelve years old when Karen Blixen met him. He was the son of a squatter who had lived on the farm since 1914. His father had been an elder of the Kikuyus, with six wives and many head of cattle, but he had quarreled with Kinanjui and lost his seat on the tribal council. After the armistice he died and the family broke apart, each wife and her children going their separate ways.

Kamante had a badly diseased leg when Karen Blixen noticed him on her lawn. This must have been early in 1921, for Bror and Thomas were both with her. He was "the most pitiful object that you could set eyes on,"[23] with an enormous head and absurdly spindly limbs, his legs covered with running sores. His face was blank and his great eyes cloudy and faraway. But when Karen Blixen asked him if he knew the names of her two dogs, he replied, with the stage presence he became famous for, "Dusk and Banja."[24] This pleased her enormously.

From the look of him, Kamante had only a short time to live. Tanne dressed and bandaged his sores, gave him some rice and sugar, and told him to come back. He did, faithfully, and endured her treatment of ointment and hot bandages with an utterly noble stoicism. When the leg showed no improvement she sent him to the Scottish Mission Hospital, where he became a convert to Presbyterianism. She came to fetch him home that Easter Sunday, and to surprise her he had bound up his leg in its old bandages. "All Natives," she wrote, "have a strong sense for dramatic effects."[25]

After that Kamante was made the dog *toto* (despite the fact that he "hated and feared" the dogs[26]) and later became a part-time medical assistant at Karen Blixen's clinics. It was there she "found out what good hands he had"[27] and promoted him to the kitchen. His first triumphs were cakes, which he learned to make from a volume called *The Sultan's Cake Book.* During the years of his apprenticeship* Karen Blixen sent him to the kitchens of The Norfolk, The New Stanley, and the Muthaiga Club to study with their chefs. But he was reluctant to take on these new responsibilities, "due," as he put it, "to childhood difficulties."[28] His mistress describes that reluctance some-what differently in *Out of Africa:* "In the kitchen, in the culinary world, Kamante had all the attributes of a genius—the individual's powerlessness in the face of his own powers."[29]

There was a second death on the farm that December. The coffee had been picked, the berries husked and graded at the factory, and then laden in sacks onto the ox carts that would carry them to the Nairobi railroad. One afternoon three little Kikuyu girls had—against all rules—hitched a ride on an ox cart. As it approached Mbogani House they leaped off, afraid, Kamante describes it, to be eaten by the deerhounds, but perhaps also of being seen by the Baroness. One of them, Wamboi, was carrying a little basket on a long string, and as she jumped, it caught in the frame of the wagon and pulled her under the great wheels. The driver was unaware of what had happened and probably could not have stopped anyway. Wamboi was crushed to death.

Her body lay on the road for three days, while Karen Blixen tried to determine who should bury her and the police tried to decide who was responsible. The Africans were extremely superstitious about corpses and would not touch the body. Even the parents of the little girl sent word that they would have nothing to do with her—and subsequently attempted to extort a settlement. This provoked one of Tanne's infrequent rages against the Africans. "The Kikuyus are really a base race," she said. "And yet there is something touching about them, and about the amazing faith they have in me . . . which disarms one's anger."[30]

It was Tanne and Mr. Dickens, her manager, assisted by Kamante, who finally buried the little girl. Kamante had "shown the strength of his reli-

---

*Hassan was the chief cook until 1926, when Kamante took over from him.

gion"[31] by volunteering for the job. After Wamboi's burial, he remembers, his mistress called the people together and remonstrated with them: "Mrs. Karen told us we should not fear death, because everybody is awaited by death."[32]

4

While Ingeborg Dinesen cared for Karen de Neergaard in Denmark, Karen's father arrived in Africa for a vacation, bringing Christmas presents from home and something of the Danish countryside itself. In his dress and speech there was a benevolent, homely, provincial quality that Tanne and Thomas both laughed at, but that also moved them. They made a traditional Christmas Eve: a tree decorated with candles, spruce on the mantel, a roasted turkey, a rice porridge, and some small almond cakes baked by Kamante.

That evening Tanne planned to attend the midnight mass at the French mission and a supper party afterward at Lady Northey's. She had promised Kamante she would take him with her, to show him the crêche and to allay the terrible fear, instilled by the Scottish missionaries, of the Virgin Mary —or, rather, of a fine, life-size pasteboard statue of which the French fathers were very proud. This was a period when Kamante began going everywhere with his mistress. When he first appears in her letters it is as a "little semi-idiot Kikuyu,"[33] a pathetic and amusing foundling, the subject of her experiments as a doctor. But when he had lived with her awhile she began to appreciate the real nature of his strangeness, to perceive him as a *destiné,* and this assured him a place in her mythology. Kamante was "the kind of stuff from which, in the olden days, they made court jesters."[34] He was "aware of this separateness of his, himself, with the arrogant greatness of soul of the real dwarf, who, when he finds himself at a difference with the whole world, holds the world to be crooked."[35] This is a quality found in many of Dinesen's heroes, and one she cultivated in herself. It is the heroism of the dreamer, the eccentric, and the pervert: all those who have been planted in life with their taproots bent and who never thrive, or bear fruit, but who seem to flower "more richly than the others."[36]

In January the factory burned to the ground, ignited by some burning embers in a pile of old coffee sacks. Thomas was more stunned by this catastrophe than his sister, for he had engineered the building and had virtually raised it by himself. But it was well insured, and Tanne, who was always able—and, indeed, compelled—to find the bright side of any tragedy, looked forward to collecting the premium and using part of it to offset the losses from another disappointing harvest.

It was not an auspicious ending for Thomas's stay in Africa, for he was to sail home at the end of March. He had used up the money he brought with him and had also exhausted his hopes and his patience with the farm.

In part because he refused to support her own optimistic view of things, to enter into her fantasies, his relationship with Tanne had grown strained.

In a series of letters to their mother full of elder-sisterly concern and an undertone of exasperation, Tanne described this tension from her own point of view. Africa didn't "suit" Tommy, despite his enthusiasm for safari life. He would never make a good farmer, for he was too intellectual. Those long discussions which she claimed to "detest" were the one thing he loved most of all. She sounded almost eager for him to go, although once he left she would miss him "desperately."

5

Nineteen twenty-three was to be a year of terrible loneliness and anxiety for Karen Blixen, when the threat of a sale hung over her head, and every reverse, however small, seemed to evoke a worried cable from the shareholders. There was not enough operating capital to see the farm through the first six months, and Tanne went so far as to sell her Paris gowns to a "Jewish lady" in Nairobi. In bitter letters to her mother, and to Thomas once he got home, she poured out her two perpetual woes: the lack of money and her insecurity. That spring she waited for the rains with the anxiety of one condemned and bound to the stake, the torch in the hand of the executioner. When they came—in great abundance—and the trees blossomed, and the farm looked "in brilliant condition," and an expert named Major Taylor gave her reassuring advice, she wanted to buy out the other shareholders and spoke of nothing but a loan for that purpose, from Thomas or Denys. But when the coffee cherries withered the next summer, the harvest was disappointing, the creditors pressed her for payments, and everyone told her it was hopeless, she begged for time, lectured the family about honor, accused them of loving money, and even made a veiled threat to kill herself if the farm were to be sold out from under her.

The shareholders were naturally resentful toward what were clearly attempts to blackmail them with her despair. "We were making an investment in Karen Coffee," said Countess Frijs, "and were not providing Tanne with a pleasant life."[37] They could not understand the magnitude of what she stood to lose. It was a business deal to them, and to her it was life itself. Perhaps, too, she looked upon the farm as just recompense for all the misunderstanding she had suffered at their hands as a young girl.

Ingrid Lindström saw Tanne's predicament with greater charity than anyone in her family. "She *loved* that beastly coffee," Mrs. Lindström said; "she didn't *want* to understand that it was hopeless, though her friends tried to tell her so."[38] And Remy Martin, the developer who finally bought the farm in 1931 to subdivide the land into suburban residential plots, believed that Karen Blixen failed as a manager because of her "stubborn devotion to the Africans. No one," he said, "made a success of coffee in Karen at six thousand feet. The soil increased in acidity with the altitude, and it was hopeless. But it would have made an ideal mixed farm—she could have well grown maize on a commercial scale and bred cattle at the same time; it was ideal for cattle. But to do that profitably she would have had to take back her squatters' land, and she wouldn't touch it. Her servants had the run of her place just because they were her servants, and she couldn't bear to interfere with them. Instead, she ran the coffee at a dead loss, and the Africans made the profit. There were three thousand head of squatter cattle on the farm when I took it over."[39]

With the violent and prolonged rains that spring, there were strange movements of the game. Lions ventured into Nairobi, and one visited the zoo night after night, looking for a mate. Another was shot by an adjutant just outside the door of Government House. Leopards prowled the farm, so that it was dangerous to walk at night unarmed. On the reserve the grasses had grown as high as a saddle pommel. Tanne still mounted the temperamental Rouge and rode out alone. Once, she said, the horse pitched her into a hole the size of a grave that had been hidden by the grass. By the time she managed to climb out, he had wandered off. Terrified that she would never catch him, that she would have to walk home through the lion-infested grasslands, she began to weep. Rouge apparently took pity and let her remount.

One of the wild animals came to stay—the bushbuck Lulu. Tanne had driven into Nairobi one morning to settle her insurance claim and on the Ngong Road passed a small group of children selling a fawn, which was trussed up by its ankles. She couldn't stop, and she didn't stop again that evening when she passed the children on the way home. But a terrible fright woke her in the middle of the night. "What, I thought, would become of the fawn in the hands of captors who had stood with it in the heat of the long day, and had held it up by its joined legs?"[40] She roused her servants and sent them out to find it, warning them they would be fired if they failed. The Africans were fairly used to such threats, as they had all been "fired" many times before. But the challenge still caused a stir; they fanned out in the moonlight, and the next morning Farah brought Lulu to his mistress with her tea. She was entrusted to the care of Kamante, who fed her from a bottle, and she would curl up like a kitten under Tanne's writing desk.

Lulu is another of Dinesen's noble foundlings, rescued from one cruel fate but perhaps condemned to a worse one: a tame existence. Lulu had the "devil" in her, like Alkmene, and when "her discontent with her surroundings reached a climax, she would perform, for the satisfaction of her own heart, on the lawn in front of the house, a war-dance, which looked like a brief zigzagged prayer to Satan."[41] Her portrait is one of the finest pieces of writing in *Out of Africa,* perhaps because so much personal feeling and remembrance is contained in it.

6

In the early twenties the children of Karen Blixen's servants had begun to grow up, and she had a tribe of dark-eyed "foster children" in her house for whom she felt a fierce, proprietary love. Juma had a daughter named Mannehawa (Mahu), born on Armistice Day, who grew into a lively and curious little girl. Mahu, Tanne thought, might eventually marry Abdullai, who had been her page in Europe, despite the fact that Mahu's grandmother's Masai blood made it a misalliance for him. Mahu had a brother, Tumbo, born in 1921. He was a sturdy, frog-faced, laughing child who wanted very much to go to school and to see the world. Karen Blixen paid for his education at a Somali boarding school (which Denys liked to call "Eton"), although she hated to let him go. When she was leaving Africa she asked Tumbo if he would like a heifer, which, to the cattle-loving Africans, was a lovely present. But he preferred a trip to Mombasa.

Juma also had a stepdaughter, his wife's child, whose name was Halima. She was Karen Blixen's special favorite and a kind of handmaiden to her. Halima was full of "fun" and "trickery" and did not fit well into the extremely quiet and respectable world of Somali women. Tanne called her a little gypsy and sometimes wondered what would become of her in life. She played the harmonica, sang in a reedy voice, and danced with a "quite astonishing lightness, and if I may say so—power, more than grace."[42] She was perhaps thinking of Halima when she wrote "Alkmene."

Farah Aden also had a family on the farm. He brought his brother Abdullai to East Africa after the war when, as Karen Blixen writes in *Shadows on the Grass,* he decided that her house needed a "page more consistent with its dignity."[43] Farah's first wife lived in Somaliland, where she had a child, but his second wife, Fathima, arrived in 1918, and they were married in a great celebration at Mombasa. His third wife, also Fathima, came to the farm in 1928 with her mother and sisters, and Karen Blixen built a house for them. This "young Fathima" gave birth to a little boy named Saufe, a beautiful acorn of a babe whom Tanne would adore.

Abdullai, Farah's brother, had very quickly shown signs of genius. Denys and Berkeley Cole liked to play chess in front of Tania's fire, and Abdullai stood behind their chairs and taught himself the game by watching. Denys was so impressed—especially when Abdullai beat him—that he urged Tania to teach him mathematics. She enrolled him at the Islamic school at Mombasa, where he did extremely well and, even as a young man, was sought out by his tribesmen for advice. In later life he returned to Somalia and became a judge. A Danish journalist met him there in the 1950s, told him Karen Blixen was still alive, and he sent back a message of respect and gratitude.[44]

Abdullai's achievements and Tumbo's ambitions gave Tanne the inspiration to start her own school on the farm, a night school, and she wrote to

Elle about finding a Montessori teacher who could work with both the children and the adults. Her friends told her she was crazy, and Denys made jokes about "keeping it the Dark Continent,"[45] but she argued that "civilization will take possession of them in one way or another, and so I think one should see that it happens in the best way."[46] Her more elaborate plans had to be abandoned, and she had to settle for a teacher from the Scottish mission, who taught reading and the Bible and led the Africans in singing psalms.

This sense of a "civilizing mission" may sound naive or even sinister to the modern reader, but in its own context—among the staunch imperialists at the Muthaiga Club—it had a rather subversive ring. Karen Blixen was willing to concede that the Africans were "educable," even that they were noble and highly moral people, and she was willing to do her part in preparing them for political "maturity," in the Western sense, however long that might take. The implication in her point of view, which was not lost upon her contemporaries, was that the Africans would one day be ready to take back their country. Throughout the twenties the white settlers agitated passionately against this same conviction, which was a cornerstone of Foreign Office policy. Their ideal was a state much like modern South Africa, and Lord Delamere spoke and thought for a majority of them when he outlined his own colonial policy to the British government in 1927. His first point was that "the extension of European civilization in Africa was in itself a desireable thing. A second was that the British race . . . was superior to heterogeneous African races only now emerging from centuries of relative barbarism. . . . A third was that the opening up of new areas by means of genuine colonisation was to the advantage of the world."[47]

7

There were two *ngomas* that June: one daytime affair in honor of Karen Blixen; and one at night, to honor little Betty Martin, a five-year-old white child who had never seen one of the big African dances. The daytime *ngoma* was larger, noisier and more monotonous; crowds of onlookers drove out from Nairobi, giving it the "character more of a fair than of a ball." But at night a number of small bonfires were lit along the drive, and the atmosphere was gala and intense, with dancers outnumbering the audience.

For these events the young unmarried girls on the farm freshly shaved their heads and put on greased leather tutus and as many beaded wire necklaces as could fit between their collarbones and their chins. The young men rubbed their bodies with pale red chalk and chalked their hair. Karen Blixen describes it as a "strangely *blond*" color, but it also gave them the look of dancers from an old Attic vase. The warriors brought their spears and shields and made up one or several circles, jumping up and down to the rhythm of flutes and drums. The old people sat around them on the grass, smoking, spitting, and gossiping. The district commissioner sometimes gave his permission to brew *tembu,* a powerful cane liquor. If not, Karen Blixen liked to offer some refreshment: snuff for the dancers and the old people and sugar for the children, which Kamante passed out on wooden spoons.[48]

Betty Martin, who was carried down to watch this spectacle, was the child of two of Tania's closest friends, Hugh and Flo Martin, who sometimes drove out to her farm to escape Nairobi. Flo ("careless Flo") was the daughter of Sir Edward and Lady Northey. Hugh was a director of the Land Department —a small, fat English mandarin; a brilliant talker; a man unshakable in his cynicism and aplomb. He called Tania "Candide" and "was himself a curious Doctor Pangloss of the farm, firmly and placidly rooted in his conviction of the meanness and contemptibleness of human nature and of the Universe."[49] At the end of Karen Blixen's life in Africa, Hugh would rally to her aid with great tenderness and concern; when Denys died his nonchalance suddenly disappeared, and he seemed to age and change. An ideal, Tania reflected, "is a strange thing, you would never have given Hugh credit for harboring the idea of one, neither would you have thought that the loss of it would have affected him like, somehow, the loss of a vital organ."[50]

8

Throughout the early part of 1923 Tanne suffered from a series of mysterious and sometimes severe symptoms no one could identify. Young Dr. Anderson in Nairobi, who succeeded the "crazy" Burkitt, thought she might have a bad case of malaria but wasn't sure. She thought it might be "lumbago" or an "inflammation of the spine." That July she felt so ill she entered the hospital, believing she would die. But they couldn't diagnose or treat her ailment, and when the danger passed they sent her home.

This was not the first time Karen Blixen had complained of mysterious and agonizing pains that her doctors in Nairobi had been unable either to diagnose or treat. She had a similar attack at Christmas in 1921 and periodic recurrences throughout the twenties. While they lasted, Tanne thought she was about to die and on several occasions wrote home to say that she had "not been well," that she really ought to consult a specialist, that she did not trust the skill or judgment of the doctors who were treating her. But she also speculated that there might be a psychological connection to her pains. The hospital stay in 1923 came at a moment of great frustration and boredom on the farm, when she badly needed a vacation and resented that she couldn't take one. Other attacks occurred when she was lonely or distraught, and she often lumped complaints about her health with complaints about her general state of being, or else fended off Ingeborg's alarm by making little of her problem. She went so far as to claim that she had actually enjoyed her hospital stay in 1915 and that she took her affliction much more lightly than everyone else in the family. If one reads the letters without knowledge of her medical history, they make her sound like a hypochondriac. But while her feelings may have contributed to her sufferings, it is certain that her syphilis, and not her psyche, caused most of them. The "lumbago" which she describes, the pain "like a toothache" in her limbs and ears, fit the clinical description of the "lightning pains" associated with *tabes dorsalis,* the spinal degeneration that was the form of syphilis from which she suffered.* Such pains often precede other symptoms by many years; they come and go abruptly and may frequently be confused with rheumatism (or "lumbago") or changes in the weather. While in some cases they cause only mild discomfort, they bring intense agony in others. There may be long periods of freedom between the bouts—as in Karen Blixen's case—and once the pains cease, the patient recovers rapidly. This aspect of the disease may have thrown Tanne's doctors in Nairobi off the scent, for at various times they diagnosed pneumonia, amoebic dysentery, and various tropical fevers. It confused Tanne herself, and she told her mother that it was perhaps too tempting to attribute everything to syphilis. Several of her African friends refused to believe that she could have had the disease and still lead so robust and active an outdoor life, and even in Denmark, when she was an old woman, more ill than not, there were people who insisted that she "made it up." She was undoubtedly capricious, but not more so than her syphilis, itself. "Few diseases cause such a wide variety of symptoms as *tabes dorsalis.*"51

9

Almost as soon as she got home, a runner brought her the news that Erik Otter had died of blackwater fever in Turkana. His commandant in the King's African Rifles wished to know if Tania could supply the address of Erik's wife. She couldn't—and in fact had not seen her old friend in many years. He had remained in the army after the war and continued to lead an ascetic life, aloof from white society and his old friends. His death caused her to reflect that the world of her early days in the country had almost completely vanished.

A second death notice arrived about this time. Count Mogens Frijs was dead at seventy-four. He had been Wilhelm's best friend, Daisy's father, lord of Frijsenborg and a central figure in Tanne's youth. With age, she reflected, she had come more and more to his outlook on the world, and only regretted she had not reached it sooner: "I could have avoided many difficulties."52

Those "difficulties" were the old, unresolved conflict between two sets of values and loyalties, Dinesen and Westenholz; and her unbounded admiration for the one, her unbounded dependence on the other. There were moments when she could speak fluently and firmly for herself in an authoritative voice that did not need violence or provocation to wrench itself free. But there were other moments when she would beg piteously for love and rage against

---

*See below, p. 256.

the family for having enslaved her to their morality, moments when her strength failed, her vision and insight vanished, and with them the *"klart overblik,"* the clear perspective of her life and circumstances. This conflict seems to have generated much of the depression she suffered. And for many years she would continue to blame her unhappiness on the family's influence and, alternately, to plead abjectly for their understanding.

25

A Love of Parallels

I

W HEN DENYS FINCH HATTON came back to Africa in May 1922 he turned his attention to neglected business* and didn't see much of Tania for a year. She speaks of running into him at the Muthaiga Club or at Lady Northey's parties, and on New Year's Eve he drove out to the farm with Lord Francis Scott, woke her up, and carried her off for a midnight supper. But at the end of August 1923 he decided to give up his bungalow and make the farm his pied-à-terre. "I am expecting Denys," Tanne told her brother on the nineteenth, "perhaps today, anyhow this week, and you will know that: Death is nothing, winter is nothing. . . ."†

Isak Dinesen was so reserved in her description of her friendship with Denys that it is never clear, in *Out of Africa,* what its real extent was. The book leads us to believe, by the convention of such reserve in other writers, that there was a great deal "more" than what she tells us and that the source of her discretion was gallantry, a noble diffidence, even the canniness of the old storyteller: *"A ce moment de sa narration, Scheherazade . . . se tut."*†† In the same spirit of reticence (and perhaps intimidation) she did not ever want Denys to know how adoringly she wrote of him to her family or how central he was to her happiness. A year later, when there was a chance that Thomas and Mrs. Dinesen might sail out to Africa on the same ship with Denys, Tanne warned her mother to pretend that she had never heard of him. And in a letter that betrays the strain of the deception, she begs Thomas that should she die and he meet Denys later, he must never let on how much he meant to her.

"He was happy on the farm; he came there only when he wanted to come," Isak Dinesen wrote of Denys,[1] and those were his terms—no commitments and no demands. She made a virtue of them, writing of their friendship as

---

*Denys still owned his *dukkas* on the Masai Reserve and was the director of two companies: Kiptiget, Ltd., which bought real estate for development; and the Anglo–Baltic Timber Company.
†Isak Dinesen, *Letters from Africa,* p. 167. The line comes from Sophus Claussen's poem "Røg" ("Smoke"). Frans Lasson supplies the remainder of the stanza in his notes to *Letters from Africa:* "For the flames, the fire/have reerected the fallen altars of my youth/in the grass by the spring" (p. 438).
††"At this point in her story, Scheherazade fell silent" (Isak Dinesen, *Seven Gothic Tales,* p. 79).

a "love of parallels,"* scorning those lovers who stared soulfully into one another's eyes, who took possession of each other's lives, who intersected. But like many women proud of their strength and superstitious about their mystery, she also suppressed a neediness that she wanted to disown. She could put her affairs in order before Denys came, and she could even, for the brief period he was with her, master all her sorrow or irritation. But the constraint, the instability, the fear of abandonment had to find some outlet, and apparently they did. She sometimes took to her bed for a fortnight after he left, sick or depressed or both. And some of her most furious and complaining letters home coincide with the moments when, after a wonderful visit, Denys has just departed.

Tania's love for Denys was a kind of rapture, kept fresh by his absences and her solitude and deprivation. "To poor mortals," she would write in *Seven Gothic Tales*, "the value of pleasure, surely, lies in its rarity. Did not the sage of old tell us: he is a fool who knows not the half to be more than the whole? Where pleasure goes on forever, we run the risk of becoming blasé, or . . . of dying."[2] There may be much of the sage's wisdom in this point of view, but there is also a certain austere, perhaps even puritanical, self-denial. While Isak Dinesen despised the "bookkeeping" approach to life, she kept her own spiritual accounts very strictly. If she would later claim her art was paid for by her syphilis, she believed, in Africa, that her brief moments of perfection with Denys were paid for by the droughts, the uncertainty, the loneliness and the endless *shauries* of the farm, and that this, indeed, was the secret formula, the bargain that entitled her to really live.

But what does it mean to believe that it is noble to pay so high a price for love, or that it is necessary to rise from the table hungry and the bed unsatisfied, because "where pleasure goes on forever we run the risk . . . of dying ? It suggests, perhaps, that the love is guilty, something to be atoned for, and the pleasure is, past a certain intensity, dangerous and even fatal. It also suggests a fear that those powerful needs and desires, once aroused, might not, in fact, be satisfied. In its most basic form many children know this fear —the anxiety over loss of a parent's love—and of the self-esteem, the happiness, the well-being which that love enables.[3]

2

Denys generally arrived without any notice, "starved for conversation." He and Tania sat up over their dinner on the first few nights so sunk in talk that they "then kept up the theory that the wild Masai tribe, in their manyatta

---

*It is a phrase used by Aldous Huxley in *Crome Yellow* to describe a rather sterile relationship. But as Karen Blixen pointed out to her brother, "I must surely be permitted to construe [it] as I like." She went on to say that in regard to Denys, "While one is oneself and striving for one's own distant aim one finds joy in the knowledge of being on parallel courses for all eternity." (Isak Dinesen, *Letters from Africa*, p. 271.)

under the hills, would see the house all afire, like a star in the night, as the peasants of Umbria saw the house wherein Saint Francis and Saint Clare were entertaining one another upon theology."[4] If he came from Europe, he brought her wine and records; and if she was out riding, he would play them with the volume up, the doors open to the terrace, so that as she approached the house it was Schubert or Stravinsky who announced his return. When she knew that he was coming she would have his favorite dish for him. This was "clear soup," Kamante's exquisite consommé. Perhaps the making of this soup taught Karen Blixen something about telling stories. The recipe calls for you to keep the spirit but to discard the substance of your rough ingredients: eggshells and raw bones, root vegetables and red meat. You then submit them, like a storyteller, to "fire and patience." And the clarity comes at the end, a magic trick.*

The two friends dressed for dinner, even when they dined alone. He had a favorite old velvet jacket and she a favorite taffeta dress, cut to show off her "dazzling white shoulders."[5] Farah served their coffee in the sitting room, which was lined with Denys's collection of rare books. He had shelves built for them, and after his death, when the house had been sold, she had two tiny brass plaques engraved with his initials and mounted unobtrusively. They are still there if you can find them, a lover's tattoo on the flesh of the old house.

It was a sensuous room, filled with small bouquets of roses and long-stemmed white madonna lilies in deep water. There was a leopard skin on the floor; a low divan with Persian pillows; and, concealing the door to the bedroom, an old French wooden screen, painted with fanciful oriental figures. This is the model for a screen Dinesen describes in her tale "The Monkey," as the backdrop for the seduction supper at Closter Seven. There was an exalted lewdness to that evening which was probably not unlike the late nights at Ngong. The old abbess in the tale administers a drug—a love potion—to her dinner guests, and their friends remember that Denys and Tania liked to experiment with the sensations hashish, opium, or miraa † could give them. Denys arranged the cushions on the floor before the fire and reclined there, playing his guitar. Tania sat "cross-legged like Scheherazade herself" and told him stories. Precisely how the evenings ended we are not

---

*I had the privilege of tasting Kamante's clear soup when I was in Africa and of watching him make it. After simmering the broth on a very low flame for twenty-four hours, he clarified it with eggshells.
†An indigenous African herb that has a mild hallucinogenic effect. Dinesen refers to it in "The Dreamers" by its other name, murungu, an herb whose dried leaves "keep you awake and in a pleasant mood" (Seven Gothic Tales, p. 272). The name Mira Jama itself seems to be a play on the word miraa. Lincoln Forsner, the other storyteller in the tale, also has the name of an intoxicant; the Africans call him Tembu, which is the Swahili word for alcohol.

privileged to know. But what Dinesen writes about sex to her brother—that she could not treat a sexual relationship with great "seriousness," that its real enjoyment was "purely spiritual"[6]—gives the impression that she preferred the imaginative foreplay, the anticipation, the spiritual complicity. Perhaps the power of her own fantasy was such that the act itself was something of a disappointment.

3

Isak Dinesen refers to herself in *Out of Africa* as Scheherazade, and that young woman was a heroine after her own heart. She was in love with risk, "versed in the wisdom of the poets and the legends of the ancient kings," and frustrated by a tame existence among women. When she offers herself to her father, the vizier, as the bride/sacrifice for the sultan, it is with a promptness he finds alarming and which suggests that the opportunity corresponds to some old ambition. "Nothing," she announces, "will shake my faith in the mission I am destined to fulfill."[7]

This mission is to disarm, through the erotic power of the narrative, an omnipotent male whose loss of faith in the ideal of Woman has made him murderous. Tanne had set out to create a figure like the sultan in her tale "The Ploughman," but he frightened her, and she took refuge in a romantic Christian ending. Anders Ostrel is subdued and redeemed by a virtuous young maiden and does his penance plowing the good earth. Scheherazade had more imagination and less taste for therapy. She did not attempt to convince the sultan that his view of human (and female) nature was faulty or his own actions reprehensible, but only that they were too small. Her "mission" was to show him a scheme of life so rich, a skein of fate so intricate, a perspective so sublime that his own betrayal figures as a tiny stitch—and he can laugh at it. The mature art of Isak Dinesen, which in its way is also an art of consolation, owes much to the methods, the intentions, and the audacity of her predecessor.

For Scheherazade, of course, the challenge of seduction was heightened by the perils of failure. Her life depended upon her powers of fascination, and, like any daredevil for whom triumph and survival are the same thing, she must have had her masochistic side. Isak Dinesen also associated the risk of death with pleasure; she was also compelled to test her power to enchant, to hold in thrall—and thereby to survive. Her girlhood friends noticed it when they described the frantic quality of her charm and her habit, when she spoke, of opening her eyes "unnaturally wide," as if to hypnotize the hearer. This testing would grow more urgent, and more theatrical, as she aged.

Denys played the sultan's role for Tania Blixen, and later she internalized him. The Sultan Shazrahad internalized yields a driven, perfectionistic artist. All the performing arts have a tradition of esthetic daredevilry, of the impossible feat*—and of the concealed agony and sacrifice necessary to achieve it. This type of sacrifice is common in the tales of Isak Dinesen, where the *virtuoso* is a prominent figure—and invariably a kind of priest. None of her many artists seems to escape some priestly or Faustian sacrifice, and generally a mutilation, willingly, even proudly, incurred. In the case of Mira Jama, who has had his nose cut off, and of Marelli, the "sublime" *castrato*, this mutilation is literal. In the case of Malli or Pellegrina or Cardinal Salviati, it is symbolic: the renunciation of normal human love. There are numerous mythical and religious precedents for this transaction; priests dedicate their celibacy to God as a means of entering into a protective union with him.† But it is also the form of many private neurotic bargains. Certain individuals take or seek inordinate pride in suffering, believe that it accounts for their greatness or their singularity and that without it their lives and work would be mediocre. Their hope is that their own vengeful deity will be appeased, perhaps will stand in loco parentis to them and will share his (or her) omnipotence and prestige.

4

There was a noticeable change in Karen Blixen's voice in the months that followed Denys's move to the farm. She became self-conscious about her intellect, or lack of it. Writing to Thomas (who was in England), she asked him to keep her abreast of the latest ideas and "trends," as she was afraid of reverting to idiocy in the bush.[8] In almost every letter she asks for some new book to be sent out or reflects upon some literary or philosophical question in lucid, elegant, and worked-over prose. One Sunday, after meeting an old friend in Nairobi, Tanne was struck by the fact that "age is the greatest test for everyone—just as with wine; it is only a really good vintage which can stand to be laid down. It is true not only with people but . . . with art. The lesser harvest one must drink right away, without illusions; it goes down well enough. But the really good ones—what charm and worth do they not acquire with maturity? As long as it is quite fresh, no one really can know its value; but after fifty, or even twenty years! When, for example, I read Oscar Wilde again, I think that it is all so thin and pathetic, most of it is to be spat out; but Oehlenschläger—the best of him—and Aarestrup—I

---

*It is possible that the pantomimes Tanne Dinesen saw at Tivoli had influenced her notion of the virtuoso, someone who could don a mask and step into a role. There is no evidence that she ever studied the *commedia dell'arte* formally, but there are a number of references to it in her work. The name itself means "a comedy of the profession, or of the skill." Actors were given a bare outline of the plot (a scenario) and had to improvise, testing their wit, nimbleness, and general mettle. But I think that Karen Blixen's conversations, for which she became famous, were really more in the tradition of the *commedia dell'arte* than her meticulously crafted tales.

† See "The Cardinal's First Tale," in Isak Dinesen's *Last Tales*, p. 21. "Pity him not [the artist, the priest]," says Cardinal Salviati. "Doomed he will be . . . and forever lonely. . . . Yet the Lord indemnifies his mouthpiece. If he is without potency, he has been given a small bit of omnipotence."

think that with the years they have acquired such depth and nobility, such a 'bouquet' that I don't believe their contemporaries could have felt, when they first read them. Finch Hatton, I believe, is—in contrast to Geoffrey Buxton—the kind of person whom the years will *improve,* so that he will, as Stevenson says about d'Artagnan, 'mellow into a man so witty, kind and upright—that the whole man rings true like a good Sovereign!' "[9]

The books she asked for were the favorites of her youth that she wanted to reread: Sophus Claussen's poetry, which she called her "Bible"; Mrs. Heiberg's memoirs; Cellini; Goldschmidt; an anthology of Danish love poems. Thomas sent her *Tilskueren,* but she found almost nothing of any interest in its pages, and Aunt Bess sent her a copy of the newly published *Kristin Lavransdatter,* by Sigrid Undset, with an elaborate eulogy. At first Tanne admired the work, but she ended with a feeling of repulsion for the uniform grimness of the characters. With her protest came a little credo: "What I am looking for in imaginative writing is an illumination of what Goldschmidt calls the magic of life—and that is not to be found in Sigrid Undset . . . [her vision] is like a great landscape under continual bad weather, devoid of color; the magic wand is missing, there is *kein Hexeri.* And I say with Otto Benzon [I think] that true art is always part magic."[10]

26

Nature and the Ideal

I

B Y LATE AUTUMN OF 1923 the sale of Karen Coffee seemed imminent.
There was an exchange of telegrams—critical ones from the shareholders
and bitter, proud replies from Tanne. She had, she told her brother, put her
youth and heart into the farm and felt now like Samson with his hair cut.

For a while she seemed to give up on Africa. "Hitherto I have regarded
my break with this place as an Armageddon. After that—nothing. But now
I am writing you to ask you to help me realize what is on the other side."
First, she wanted to know, would Thomas come to Africa and help her tie
up the loose ends of her affairs? And after that, would he, with a definite
sum of cash, help her to make "a new start in life?"[1] She had very little notion
of what she might do in her afterlife, although she was adamant that she could
not return to live among the "middle classes." She would like to travel, she
suggested, perhaps to China. She could study art in Rome or perhaps Munich.
She might run a small hotel for "coloured people" in Djibouti or Marseilles,
and it even occurred to her that she could "marry very well," although Denys
is explicitly not the candidate—she meant a marriage of convenience. There
is a desperate energy to this wild planning, this throwing herself at half a
dozen different careers, itineraries, fantasies of the future. Perhaps it was
necessary to counter the enormous pull of her desire to remain in Africa and
with Denys, with whom a single week "compensates for everything else on
earth, and other things mean nothing in themselves."[2]

When Denys left the farm at the end of October, a lonely calm settled
upon it. Tanne began to paint again, looking forward to her lover's return
when she could show him the finished work and have his criticisms. Her
model was a young Kikuyu who found it extremely unpleasant to keep still.
Once Tanne threatened him with a pistol, but this did not make an impression. The Kikuyus, she noted dryly, were less afraid of death than immobility.

Berkeley Cole arrived for a short visit on Armistice Day and coaxed Tania
forth from her solitude to a grand dinner at Muthaiga in honor of the
governor of Uganda. For the next few days he lived at the farm, sleeping
late and presumably drinking his bottle of champagne in the forest every
morning at eleven. "Berkeley," she told her mother, "is an exceptionally

amusing person, very quick and original—and completely, I believe, without moral scruples of any kind."[3] He was then serving on the Legislative Council and kept Tania current with—and amused by—the power struggles between the settlers and the Colonial Office.

There is in the "haughty and fantastical" person of the young Berkeley Cole an interesting presentiment of the haughty and fantastical old Isak Dinesen. He speaks, in *Out of Africa,* with the courtly irony that was a quality of her own voice as a storyteller and with the same indefinable but quaint accent, which gives the impression it has come from a grander and more corporeal language—the language of the past.

Berkeley had had an unhappy childhood, which helped to make him cynical. The family, he confessed, counted it a fortunate thing when his father, Lord Enniskillen, died. His mother had lived on her own for many years in a charming villa outside of Florence and held court there for a circle of poets and artists. Berkeley himself was an eccentric and solitary character, despite his amiability. His chronic arthritis left him "half an invalid" and made it, he claimed, "inadvisable to marry."[4] The volatility of his wit in such a slight and fragile body made Tania feel, as they sat by her fire and talked, that he might "at any moment go straight up through the chimney."[5] Dinesen's friends would later have the same impression of her.

Berkeley and Tania were perhaps too much alike to desire one another, although Berkeley, according to Tania, briefly thought that their marriage might be amusing. When she writes to her brother about a marriage of convenience, Berkeley was one of the three candidates. (The others were Geoffrey Buxton and Colonel Jack Llewellyn.) He was well-born, rich, and was about to receive 150,000 acres from the government, which "was always something." But in the next breath she violently repudiates the thought. It would be just as "meaningful" for her to marry her dog Banja. "I am," she reminded both Thomas and herself, "for all time and eternity bound to Denys, to love the ground he walks upon, to be happy beyond words when he is here, and to suffer worse than death many times when he leaves."[6]

The farm had been plagued with rats while Berkeley was there, and he cabled Tania to say that he was sending her a cat for Christmas. She spent the holidays alone, declining invitations, hoping that Denys might yet turn up, contriving a very quiet and private interlude for herself, which she used to work on an essay about sexual morality, love, and marriage in their changing historical contexts. She wrote in Danish, which she complained had become rusty as she had not spoken a word of it since Thomas left. Without reference books to quote from or a friend to volley her ideas with, the writing went very slowly; she was so frustrated with her own mental awkwardness that at one point she pushed her work aside in disgust and went off to teach Hassan how to make *croustades.* But the finished essay ran to seventy typewritten pages and had twelve carefully organized chapters. Its prose has an elegance, a dry formal intelligence for which there was little precedent, and it seems to reflect the voice, the style, the disciplined self she had begun to perfect for Denys.

The main contention of "On Nature and the Ideal"[7] is that love and marriage are two distinct and, in fact, dissimilar relations, each with its own function, pleasure, and meaning. She believed, with Shaw, whom she was reading at the time, that the middle classes of the nineteenth century had confused them, thus doing "more to destroy the conscience of the human race than any other single error." Marriage was best understood and undertaken by both partners as fidelity to an idea—of family, procreation, legitimacy, or God, rather than to an individual. By the same token, "free" love needed just that, freedom from domestic or dynastic responsibilities, which smoth-ered its mystery and its fire. This philosophy naturally reflected her own experience of both marriage and "free love." Bror, she thought, had misun-derstood the nature of the marriage contract and had wantonly destroyed an honorable and functional relationship. She attributed the perfection of her love for Denys to the fact that they made no real-life demands on one another but "ran parallel."

At the time that Tanne sat down to write, Bror Blixen happened to return from a long stay, which was really something of an exile, in Tanganyika, where he had been hunting elephant. When he met his wife again in Nairobi he was very friendly, and she felt no embarrassment or anger at seeing him. He was, however, evasive about going to the lawyers with her and behaved as if "one wished to lay a whole lot of worries quite irrelevant to him onto his already overburdened shoulders. . . ."[8] There was one change she particu-larly wanted to make in their divorce petition; she wanted some provision for alimony from Bror. On the surface this seemed absurd since he was so poor, but she had no intention of obliging him to pay. It was symbolic, and it was a small concession to appearances. Under English law a wife was considered to be the guilty party in a divorce if she were not given some form of maintenance. And it would still the voices in the Blixen family who insisted that Bror was a martyr, badly treated by the Westenholzes.

2

Tanne's work on her manuscript was interrupted early in February by the arrival of an unlikely visitor to the farm. He was an old Dane who had been a sailor and was now sick and blind. He begged her for a house where he could live and make the *kibokos* that were his livelihood. In *Out of Africa* he is called "Knudsen," but his real name was Aarup. He was a difficult old man who quarreled with the Africans, had a foul smell, and drank a great deal, becoming melancholy and embittered when he did so. Then he would repeat old stories about the swindlers he had known and about his horrible, shrewish wife, whose nagging had taken the joy out of his life. Still, Karen Blixen liked him and felt an almost patriotic tenderness for him. He had the compensating gift of "great, flaming inner visions to make up for his loss of sight," and he became ambitious for the farm, urging her to go into the charcoal business, to build a new fish pond, and to go into partnership with him for the purpose of extracting phosphate from Lake Naivasha. This scheme, he claimed, would make them millionaires, and Karen Blixen put it down to his vivid fantasy. But many years after his death she had a letter from an old African friend who wanted her to know that Aarup's scheme "was *not* wild. Some discovery has been made which verifies his theory."[9]

On the nineteenth of December, almost the anniversary of little Wamboi's death, a terrible shooting accident occurred on the farm—a misfortune described vividly in *Out of Africa*. Mr. Thaxton, the mill manager, had given his cook the night off, and his kitchen *toto,* Kabero, had invited a party of little boys to the house. As it grew rowdier, Kabero seized the rifle that Thaxton, who bred poultry, kept to shoot hawks and cerval-cats, and fired it into the throng of his playmates. That evening the gun happened to be loaded. By the time Karen Blixen reached the scene—summoned from her bath on a peaceful evening—one of the children was almost dead and died shortly after in her arms. The other, Wanyangerri, had been badly wounded, and part of his face was blown away. Karen Blixen bandaged him as best she could, and her presence and assurances seemed to calm him, for he stopped shrieking and lay still throughout the long ride into Nairobi. When she visited him there the next day and the following week, he had made much improvement. But the *toto* who had done the shooting disappeared afterward, and although his family searched the farm and the surrounding woods and plains, he was nowhere to be found. Some people speculated that he had gone over to the Masai, whose women suffered from sterility and who liked to adopt Kikuyu children. Indeed, one morning five years later Kabero returned, "a Masai from head to foot," having adopted their carriage and their coiffure and "the general rigid, passive and indolent bearing of the Moran, that makes of him an object for contemplation, such as a statue is, a figure which is to be seen, but which itself does not see."[10]

3

Thomas Dinesen had returned from Africa to live at Rungstedlund without a clear notion of what he would do with his life. Since the war he had spent very little time at home and perhaps did not realize himself how much Africa and the freedom of his sister's milieu, friends, and ideals had changed him. Ingeborg Dinesen soon began to write long, plaintive letters to her daughter about "Tommy's flirtations," which caused her great anxiety. He was apparently spending time with women whose class or manners she did not approve of, who were not "worthy" to be brought into the family, for she could only imagine that these flirtations would lead to marriage. The letters appealed to Tanne to intervene with her younger brother, which she naturally declined to do. He was a young man who had been so serious as a little boy that he was surely entitled to drink "all the Champagne he can get." Without any rancor but with considerable clarity, she reminded Ingeborg that her family lacked the ability to enjoy themselves, any feeling "for the wine of life," and the ability to imagine human happiness as anything but a diet of "milquetoast." The greater part of the human race, she asserted, longed for excitement, for a little intoxication, for pleasure and danger. "I think that if it were in my power to do something for humanity, whatever I could, I myself would *entertain them.*"[11]

Tanne also perceived Ingeborg's incomprehension of her son as a generational problem, and a particularly modern one. In a letter she later incorporated into her essay on marriage, she set forth her own experience of the changes that had taken place in the men and women who had fought the war. They had emerged as friends and equals, no longer two strange species which met for balls and summer holidays. They were now equal in their ambitions, in their education, and they had become equal in their erotic lives as well. Both sexes, at least in Africa, were satisfied with this development, without guilt in their love affairs, and the notion of a seducer had become passé. There was always the risk that one party would love more deeply and more dependently than the other, but there was that risk, she noted rather pointedly, even in an old-fashioned marriage.

Ideals changed as fashions changed, and perhaps with the same caprice. In the days when young women married at seventeen and were raised in convents, any girl who managed to have a love affair before her marriage must have had *"le diable au corps,"* and her suitor had every reason to be wary of her. But in the twentieth century, when young men and women played at the same sports, worked in the same offices, and breathed the same atmosphere of "freedom and eroticism," any girl who had not at least fallen in love once would give a potential suitor the same qualms.

"I have heard so many men speak with the greatest horror of marrying a *jeune fille,"* she concluded, which may or may not cast some light on her own premarital relations. Both General Polowtzoff and Erik von Otter had confided to her that they had married girls who were not only virginal but frightened of and revolted by sex, and whose inconceivable innocence had been a great hindrance to their happiness. Erik, in particular, so miserable with his wife, hoped that his own daughters would enjoy the freedom to experiment with sexual love and would consider it a natural part of life.[12]

4

By the end of January the coffee harvest was complete, a very mediocre seventy tons. Tanne was extremely restless. It was three years since she had been to Europe; she longed for a vacation and felt she should consult a specialist, perhaps in Paris, about her disease. She also saw her struggles and her privations with the farm in a heroic light and compared them to her brother's valor in the war. She, too, had "deserved a V.C. . . ."[13]

At the beginning of March Denys returned for what promised to be a long visit; he planned to remain with Tania until July, when he was to go elephant hunting in Tanganyika. She stopped virtually in midsentence of a long lament to tell her brother that she had never been so happy.

A close friend remembers visiting them that spring. Her name was Rose Cartwright; she was the sister of Geoffrey Buxton and had been a childhood playmate of Denys. Rose had first come to Africa for a visit in 1921 and, while she was there, had fallen in love with Algy Cartwright, whom she had married in Norfolk the following year. It was an incestuous little community. Algy had introduced Tania to Denys, Denys to the Lindströms, and Cockie to the Lindströms. Geoffrey had introduced Bror to Cockie, Cockie to Africa, and Denys to Africa.

Rose was then in her late twenties. She was a lanky and plainspoken young woman with marvelous blue eyes, who had been raised in a country house with brothers and was an admirable sportswoman. With the same sharp sight and steady hands that made her such a good shot, she did fine silk embroidery. Rose very much resembled those two Valkyries from the tales of Dinesen, Athena and Ehrengard, who were themselves spiritual descendants of Diana. After her separation from Algy Cartwright, she became a professional hunter and held a world record for bongo. When her daughter and only child was born, Rose was alone in a shack at Naivasha, and her one qualm was where to cut the cord.

"Some men are perfect friends, but hell if they happen to be your husband or father," she reminisced, as Diana might have. Both her own husband and Tania's fell into this category. Bror was her friend, but she "would have murdered him if he were my husband." Denys, however, was her idol, and he in turn felt a great brotherly tenderness toward her. He also still liked to play with her. While Tania was asleep, Rose and Denys would leave the house early in the morning to fish or ride or to shoot birds for lunch. Later, she helped both Denys and Bror with their safaris. Her manner with Tania precluded any jealousy, and her connection with Denys's past, his special feeling for her, made her a particularly welcome guest. "Denys liked me because I was unsociable and shy," she said, "but I was never so with them. Perhaps I was so comfortable because they didn't 'notice' me. You weren't an object of attention with them. Perhaps it was the easiness of their love for one another. In so many respects they were 'above my head.' And yet one never had to compete with them. You never felt a fool. You really were like a dog."[14]

Tania and Denys were relaxed enough with Rose to gossip in her presence. They had the habit of comparing all their friends to wine. Denys had been on safari with a certain American whom he referred to as "bad claret." Then there was a socialite who was "pink champagne." They also liked to match their friends with imaginary dinner partners: Madame de Pompadour or Genghis Khan, Shelley or King Tut. Perhaps it was the fact that Rose Cartwright was indeed so un-self-conscious around Tania and Denys—one of the rare people to respond that way—that she had the privilege of intimacy with them as a couple. They were not otherwise demonstrative. "Tanne shone for Denys," said Ingrid Lindström, "but there was no special intensity between them." Many other friends were of the same opinion. "She was cold"; "he was a sexless sort of person"; "the attraction was purely spiritual."[15] But Rose Cartwright made fun of the surprisingly common suggestion that the friendship was platonic. "I think," she said, "the reason that Tania and Denys were so happy was that their love was comprehensive. It had everything."

News that Denys was back traveled quickly. Hugh and Flo Martin came from Nairobi, as did Charles Gordon and his new wife, Honour. "Old Mr. Bulpett" motored up from Chiromo, the Macmillans' palatial new house east of Nairobi. He, in particular, appreciated the high standards of Tania's hospitality and could, like the old Baron von Brackel, entertain the younger guests with pleasant talk about the "opera, theology, moral right and wrong, and other unprofitable pursuits."[16] One evening Tania asked him if, after spending his patrimony on La Belle Otéro and his youth scaling the Matterhorn and swimming the Hellespont, he would care to do it over again, and without hesitation he replied, "Oh, every moment of it!" He was, she told her mother, "a virtuoso" at the art of living, and she hoped ardently that when she reached his age (seventy-three) she could be so joyful and alive.[17]

Karen Blixen was now almost thirty-nine. In pictures taken that spring, probably by Denys, she is a lovely and still youthful woman, her figure plump, her face thin and invariably pale under a large hat, and her expression warm and direct. During the day she dressed in shabby work clothes: a plain knitted cardigan and skirt, or a loose gingham dress, or the khaki chemise and divided skirt that were her "rainy season costume."* She had also bobbed her hair for practical reasons; it was short and thick, and she loved the sensation of the wind in it. But for her appearances at the Muthaiga Club or Government House, or even for evenings at home, she liked to create

---

*Tanne told her sister Elle that she would have loved to wear a trouser suit, or even shorts, as so many of the Englishwomen did, lamenting the fact that she had neither their coltish legs nor their moral fiber.

glamorous toilettes. "She painted terribly," said one friend with affection. She wore kohl under her eyes and belladonna in them to make them shine. She also used thick white powder to enhance her pallor. "Her elegance was a thing of her own invention," said Mrs. Cartwright. At a time when women were wearing the spare clothes of the twenties, "a few perpendicular lines cut off again before they had had the time to develop any sense,"[18] Tania Blixen had Pacquin make her an evening dress of white taffeta with a cinched waist, panniers, stiff petticoats, and an alluring décolletage. But she also might wear a skirt and blouse to a rather grand party, with a turban on her head and a Somali shawl around her shoulders.

Her clothes were ideas, metaphors, and as an old grande dame she would actually give them names. The Pacquin gown was a reference to those days when "woman was . . . a work of art, the product of centuries of civilization, and you talked of her figure as you talked of her salon, with the same admiration which one gives to the achievement of a skilled and untiring artist."[19] But if she liked to create a stir, there were also some practical considerations for her strange clothes and makeup. When she wrapped herself in a Somali shawl it was at times to hide the fact that she was stout. "Tanne wanted to be the thinnest person in the world," said Mrs. Lindström, who inherited a riding costume she had outgrown, only to be asked to give it back a few years later. "Fat made her miserable. It made me miserable as well. Once Tanne told me, 'If you really want to get thin, I can help you.' She gave me 'Marienbad pills.' It was a kind of laxative one took with every meal!"[20] The turban was affected at a period when, because of the arsenic she was taking, her hair had fallen out. And the powder was in part to conceal the subtle changes in pigmentation that were another side effect of her disease.

To her close friends these were all charming eccentricities, evidence of Tania's "originality." They accepted her moods, even her fits of "hysterical rage," because they were always balanced by her great warmth. "She was difficult, but she was lovely," said Mrs. Lindström simply.

There are three basic versions of Tania Blixen's character in the 1920s. With the friends she loved she was accessible most of the time and even earthy, someone who was up early to do the chores or who, after a lovely dinner, would sit on the floor playing records and telling stories. With people she was trying to impress she was worldly, gracious, charming, "although perhaps too self-conscious."[21] But with anyone she found prosaic—her less distinguished neighbors, civil servants, settlers without "poetry," "boring Scandinavians"—she could be "frigid," "witchlike," "rude," "an iceberg."[22] "Tanne had," Mrs. Lindström admitted, "an idiotic reverence for the aristocracy, and she could overdo the the role of grande dame. But at the same time, so much of what has been written about her gives the wrong impression. It makes her sound so snobbish and pathetic. She was *never* pathetic. It was often a miserable existence, but it was also a gay one. People laughed at their troubles then, and Tanne more than most."²³ Tanne herself put it succinctly when she criticized Sigrid Undset for her implacable grimness. "Reality is not like that," she told Aunt Bess. "There is certainly always some *gemütlich-keit* both during a plague, and among people who are going to the guillotine the next day."²⁴

5

Toward the end of March, Denys received a cable from England that his mother was extremely ill, and he left immediately for home. "Good-bye," he wrote from Mombasa on a piece of the cheapest yellow tissue, "and thank you for so many pleasant days when I was so bad-tempered."²⁵

The weather turned cold unexpectedly; a fierce wind began to blow from the Athi Plains; and old Aarup suddenly dropped dead on the road from his cottage to Mbogani House. Tanne and Kamante found him while they were out looking for mushrooms and brought his body to the house, noting that he was the third dead person they had carried together. He was buried in a violent rainstorm, which soaked Tanne to the skin and blew the open cart with the coffin from one side of the road to the other. Aarup, Tanne speculated, would have enjoyed the scene. When he was gone she began to miss him.

After the downpour the rains abruptly ceased. For weeks the air remained perfectly clear and the nights starry. All over the highlands, farmers walked out onto their lawns before they went to bed to check the sky for rain. Many believed that the brief-lived tempest was a bad sign and that the rains had failed.

On those almost wintry evenings Tanne spread her papers over the dining room table and worked on her long essay. She did not have much confidence in its worth; the problems of the farm distracted her, and she admitted that this was no excuse to a reader who could well ask why she had bothered with such a strenuous intellectual task under conditions so little congenial to it. But to Thomas she explained that it was a thing of great importance, a question of "moral commitment . . . to finish what I had started on, and to keep my thoughts clearly ranged. . . ."²⁶ In *Out of Africa* she put it more poetically: "I was young, and by instinct of self-preservation I had to collect my energy on something, if I were not to be whirled away with the dust on the farm roads, or the smoke on the plain." She says then that she began "to write stories, fairy-tales and romances, that would take my mind a long way off, to other countries and times."*

---

*Isak Dinesen, *Out of Africa,* p. 45. One of these pieces was a revision of her marionette comedy, *The Revenge of Truth.* By the end of May, two of the tales were done, and Tanne thought of sending them to *Tilskueren.* She had already sent off a batch of poems, most of them revisions of earlier work. Poul Levin, the editor, accepted one of these, "Ex Africa," which was published in 1926. All of her fiction was rejected.

Early drafts of those tales still exist in Karen Blixen's African notebooks. There are lists of titles, often much recopied, and short prose paragraphs, mostly in Danish, and they are, curiously, almost an index for Isak Dinesen's mature work. Here one may see what a conservative writer she was, conservative in the most literal sense. The same unfinished tales live on for decades, and she brings them with her from Denmark to Africa and back again to Denmark again.

One of the pieces Karen Blixen was writing was an essay about Africa called "Udenfor Tiden" ("From Time Immemorial"). "You see," she wrote, "a house or *manyatta* many hours before you reach it and it stirs your fantasies like the toys you were promised as a child; the question of who lives there and how they will receive you, and if you can get fresh butter or milk give substance to one's thoughts and conversations, especially with the blacks, with whom one speaks as repetitively and as simply as with small children."[27]

It is interesting, in passing, to compare this little fragment with the writing in *Out of Africa*. "Udenfor Tiden" is written with a traveler's pleasure in discovery and in sharing an exotic scene with a homebound reader; the strongest impression one gets is of the novelty—the setting still overpowers the experience. But in *Out of Africa* the novelty has been assimilated into something larger and more deeply felt, which is both personal and typical at the same time. And that is partly why it is so much more than a memoir or a "travel book."

The tales are in general too short and sketchy to make much of them. But in one called—even at that early stage—"The Roads Around Pisa," Tanne begins to develop some familiar characters. Two relationships are suggested in a brief paragraph of dialogue. The speakers are friends, one called Octavius (who will become Count von Schimmelmann in a later version), the other called Boris, and both are unhappy without understanding why. Octavius confesses that he cannot confide in his wife Lavinia; there is no sort of "sympathy" between them, no "answer" in one to the other's passions. Boris, in turn, describes his frustrating relationship with his mistress, a famous singer named Ernestine. "There is not a woman in the world I admire as I admire Ernestine; there is not one I respect more deeply either. She is a Queen . . . she keeps a court, and she feels toward her admirers the friendliness, the gratitude of a born Queen for her servants. . . . Yet what I want," Boris concludes, "is somebody with whom I can talk tomorrow of that which happened to me yesterday."[28]

If these early fragments give a clear sense of Isak Dinesen's subjects and direction as a writer, they are really unsuggestive about the quality of her finished work. They are small swatches of light, color, and texture, and it is not possible to imagine with what skill they will be cut or how finely finished. Walter Benjamin offers, in "The Storyteller," a way to understand what element is missing from them. "A man's knowledge or wisdom," he writes, "but above all his real life—and this is the stuff that stories are made of—first assumes transmissible form at the moment of his death. . . . This authority is the very source of the story. . . . The storyteller has borrowed his authority from death."[29]

Karen Blixen was still too close to her own life to see what things were meant to signify. She had not had that definitive experience of completion that would make her into a storyteller, which would come when she lost her farm, when Denys died and when she left Africa for good—all at once, the closing of a parenthesis.

6

Since 1914 Tanne had periodically begged her mother to come to Africa. The farm, she said, was like her child, and how could her mother not want to see it? When the trip had been proposed in 1922, Ea's death was still too recent and Mrs. Dinesen too busy caring for her granddaughter. Now it became possible. Thomas made the arrangements and decided to accompany his mother. They were scheduled to arrive that fall.

But as the time approached Tanne was suddenly overcome by fears and reservations. She had grown "distant" from the family, particularly in the last few years. Mrs. Dinesen had not given her the support she had hoped for during the bitter correspondence over her divorce, and this led Tanne to believe that with age Ingeborg had fallen more and more under the influence of her siblings. She was now afraid that her mother would find her dramatically altered—and that she could not live up to her expectations and fantasies.

But more specifically, Tanne was afraid that Mrs. Dinesen would view her relationship with Denys as a betrayal. "If Mother should get to know that I cared for another person who meant everything in the world to me, I believe that it would be incomprehensible to her, indeed, that it could cause her pain."[30] There is no evidence that Mrs. Dinesen actually thought or felt that way. She was, on the contrary, a great admirer of Denys. A few years later, when she was told what his real place in Tanne's life was, she accepted the fact gracefully, knowing it made her daughter happy. Letters to her other children reveal a deep understanding, a generous sympathy and acceptance of Tanne's "otherness," and of how she suffered for it in the family. Mrs. Dinesen also took the responsibility for her own role in that suffering, having let Folehave lay its "loving but heavy weight" on her.[31]

It was to the stalwart Aunt Bess, rather than to Ingeborg (whom Tanne needed to think of as fragile), that she vented some of these feelings. Bess had written her niece a long philosophical birthday letter, and Tanne used the occasion of her reply to revive some of their old quarrels. For the first time, she spoke of her anger and disappointment when the family had prevented her from seeing Brandes, and she remembered that Bess had then accused her of "deceiving" them. This was a favorite theme with Bess, who contended that the younger generation had, with its loose morals, lack of patriotism and respect, "deceived" or "betrayed the trust" or "disappointed the expectations" which their elders had placed in them. Point by point now, with great clarity and eloquence, Tanne rebutted the old charges, argued for her own good faith, described the family's misunderstanding of her and her own loneliness at being so misunderstood. The letter ends with a loving but also brazen declaration of her moral independence. "No doubt you will hear from Mother [*Mohder*] about what else is happening here; but I hope you are aware that I am breaking the ten commandments, and finding much happiness doing so. . . . Many, many greetings, beloved Aunt B., Your Tanne."[32]

Ingeborg and Thomas arrived on November 3 and stayed two months. Ingrid Lindström remembers Mrs. Dinesen as a "very nice old woman, not a bit like Tanne. She always dressed in black, in woolen socks and shoes, and impressed everyone with the fact that she never got hot." Isak Dinesen told Parmenia Migel that the African women and girls were fascinated by Mrs. Dinesen, who was the oldest white woman they had ever seen, and that once, to show them her still beautiful and very long hair, Tanne suddenly pulled the pins out of it while her mother stood on the verandah, surrounded by her admirers. "The hair," we are told, "had not lost its warm color."[33] This is an interesting little gesture. It is as if Tanne had suddenly exposed a surprising resource of youth, of sexual vitality, kept carefully bound and hidden.

Mrs. Dinesen sailed home alone on January 14, 1925, the day that would have been her daughter's wedding anniversary. Tanne was filled with the same "unbearable tenderness" for her mother that she had felt on the quay at Naples, eleven years before. "For everything, every word you spoke to me, every time you looked at me, I thank you more than I am capable of saying."

On the same day Tanne received a cable from her solicitors, informing her that the divorce had become final. Although most of their friends thought of it as a formality with little meaning for either party and believed that Tania ought to have been glad to get rid of Bror, she herself had other feelings. In a notebook, sandwiched between her laundry lists and the outline for "On Nature and the Ideal," is a poem entitled, "Au Revoir."

I have wept and said farewell
Thus justly ends our lovers' duel.
Both our honor was served well.
And to the honor of your soul
I shall remember each old place.
Friend, it was sweet, in any case.[34]

On March 5, Tanne, Thomas, and Farah set sail for Aden aboard the *Admiral Pierre*. Farah and Thomas continued to Somaliland for a safari. Unsure of her future, even of her name, Karen Blixen sailed home to Denmark, where she was to remain for the next eight months.

27

Holding Out

I

K AREN BLIXEN was a desperate woman when she returned to Rungsted-lund that April. Her future in Africa was extremely shaky, and now she faced it alone. She could count on Denys for no support, only occasionally for company, and was not even sure she would ever see him again. Her status as a divorcée troubled her, and she was sensitive to expectations from her friends and family that Denys ought to marry her. By setting her "free" the divorce compromised her real freedom, that which she had enjoyed within the formal boundaries of her marriage. She felt adrift in life. Looking back at forty over the preceding decade, she had a sudden retroactive fright, which she describes in *Seven Gothic Tales* as "dying of *malheurs passés.*"[1] Even the farm seemed forbidding; her daily life there trivial, harsh, a waste of her own talent and energy. She began to speak of "hating Africa" and of wanting to "chuck the whole thing."[2]

Part of it was the depression that always ambushed her at Rungstedlund when she came home. It was inevitable that she would feel like a stranger there; she always had. Elle and her girlhood friends were all settled into their lives and their middle age. They did not grope, as she continued to, toward some ideal of their own potential greatness, some fantasy of creating the perfect life or work of art, but took the days as they came, accepting a realistic degree of happiness. Tanne now envied that serenity (though not the conditions that produced it) and was contemptuous of her own "self-mortifica-tion."[3] She saw her life as an endeavor to scale a barren mountain when the real challenge, the "true religiosity,"[4] was to accept each moment as it came and not to wish it otherwise.

After a brief stay in the hospital,* Tanne settled into her mother's house and surrendered to its *hygge.* Ingeborg fed her the rye bread, the prawns,

---

*Dr. Rasch treated her syphilis with another course of Salvarsan. A lumbar puncture done toward the end of the year was normal, and he believed that the disease had been arrested. But as knowledge of the disease evolved, venereologists have come to realize that a patient with normal spinal fluid may have a marked case of the disease. Dr. Fog points out that Karen Blixen continued to exhibit symptoms of syphilis throughout the twenties; in the early thirties it reappeared dramatically, with its late symptoms, and by then was completely beyond arrest. (Mogens Fog, "Karen Blixens Sygdomshistorie," *Blixeniana 1978,* p. 142.)

the Norwegian goat cheese she had "dreamed about" in Africa. Downstairs in the kitchen, the servants shared their coffee and their gossip as of old, and if they now addressed her as *Baronessen* they still made her feel that she was a petted daughter of the house. On fine days she walked along the Sound or through the beech woods to Folehave, where she discussed marriage and Sigrid Undset with Aunt Bess. She took cooking lessons;* studied painting, as she had in 1920, with the well-known artist Bertha Dorph; and tried to get her poems and stories published in various reviews. The Danish literary critic, Aage Kabell, writing about Karen Blixen's attempts at a literary comeback, suggests that "it is worth considering . . . how helpless Karen Blixen, at forty years old, appeared . . . in a country and in a city where one literary miracle flashed brightly across the heavens every night."⁵

As one step toward ending her isolation as a writer, Karen Blixen arranged to meet Georg Brandes. He had helped make the reputation of nearly every significant young Danish artist, and she still felt bitter that the family had caused her to miss her own chance when, in 1904, they had turned him away at the door. Ironically, it was Aunt Bess who acted as the go-between, writing to Brandes to make the appointment. It is not clear how this happened. Perhaps Tanne was shy; perhaps it seemed more dignified for the older woman to make the overture. But Tanne's reproaches must have touched Bess deeply for her to take such a step. She thanked Brandes for setting aside a few minutes at five-thirty one afternoon so that her niece could "meet a man whose life work has meant so much to her . . . in the isolated African highlands."⁶

Brandes responded graciously, both to Bess and to Karen Blixen, and it is likely that they met more than once. In a letter of that December, Tanne thanks Brandes for the gift of his new book, *Hellas,* and expresses a desire to say good-bye to him before she leaves for Africa. In a letter from Ngong, a few months later, she yearns playfully to eat oysters with him at the Fiskehuset (a famous seafood restaurant in Copenhagen), and it is probable that they did dine or lunch there together. Aage Kabell imagines that the eighty-three-year-old Brandes was charmed by the attractive and worldly Karen Blixen.⁷ Although she has never alluded to the meeting, it was certainly a moving occasion for her—the climax of so much expectation and curiosity. There is a little of "the old Georg," as she called him privately, in every urbane erotic philosopher of her tales.

After her meeting or meetings with Brandes, Tanne resubmitted *The*

---

*Karen Blixen had the idea that she might actually get a job as a chef in a hotel if the farm failed, and while she was home she went into a famous restaurant on the Bredgade, the Rex, made friends with the proprietor/chef, a M. Perrochet, and apprenticed with him. M. Perrochet was supposedly so impressed that he offered her a partnership. That, at least, is a version of the "cooking lesson" story that Karen Blixen told to Danish interviewers in the forties and fifties.

Revenge of Truth to Poul Levin at *Tilskueren,* and he accepted it.* It was her latest version of the little play she had written for the family in 1904 at nineteen, recast in Rome at twenty-five, and worked on sporadically ever since. The 1910 draft had provoked an argument with Aunt Bess, who called it blasphemous. The final draft was a sophisticated little piece, overstocked with esthetic and dramatic ironies. Kabell writes aptly of its "nervous symbolism." The nervousness came, perhaps, from the author's dubious relation to her own philosophy of experience, which was to love fate, to "carry out the author's ideas," and "to speak those lines we have in us."[8] *The Revenge of Truth* was, in fact, written and rewritten at the moments of Karen Blixen's life that were the most uncertain, formless, anguished, and full of the blind hope that things would turn out.

2

The year that Tanne was at home, Thomas Dinesen announced his engagement to Jonna Lindhardt. Jonna was a radiant young girl whose father was a Lutheran dean in Aarhus. But she was somewhat shy of and out of place in the combative, intellectual Rungstedlund milieu. Tanne was secretly disappointed that her brother was about to make such a conventional marriage, and there was even a suggestion in what she later wrote to him that in doing so he had abandoned her and his own idealism.

From the heights of his bliss Thomas listened with alarm to his sister's tirades about her own life. When it looked as if she really intended to abandon Africa, he took her aside and told her "point blank" that she was crazy to do so. He saw, perhaps better than she did, that she did not have and could not procure the means to live alone in Europe in the luxury she was used to (and insisted that she deserved). He also felt, justifiably, that Tanne in Denmark would make demands that might jeopardize his marriage. "I could no longer concentrate my future years on helping my sister," he wrote.[9]

Toward the end of her stay, he took her on a three-day trip to Sweden so that they could "thrash things out" in private. Even if the farm were to fail, Thomas reasoned, Tanne had to see it through. She argued that she couldn't take any more. He countered that an absolute defeat was more congenial to her nature than a standoff. Once, when he had written to her

---

*Writing to Brandes from Africa early in 1926, Tanne asked him to use his influence with Levin to get *The Revenge of Truth* out of the editor's drawer and into print. (Levin had accepted it but gave no sign of wanting to run it.) Kabell speculates that the manuscript could only have been "alien" to Brandes, and that if he did intervene, it was "his last tribute to the literary ambitions of the fair sex." The piece appeared in the May 1926 issue, but Levin "still made his private opinion clear enough"—and perhaps his resentment at the pressure—"in that the priceless contribution of Karen Blixen-Finecke was printed in the smallest possible grade of type" (Aage Kabell, *Karen Blixen debuterer,* p. 87). He also made a last-minute and apparently spiteful change on the galleys. Tanne had requested that her pseudonym, Osceola, be used. Levin "impertinently" (Isak Dinesen, *Letters from Africa,* p. 265) substituted her real name.

in despair about finding the right path in his own life, she had counseled him with great passion and lucidity to "hold out." Now she must find the courage to do the same.

3

Karen Blixen wrenched herself from her family on Christmas Day and boarded a train for Antwerp, the departure timed, apparently, to dramatize the utter loneliness of her small figure setting off to face the world. Thomas gallantly went along to see her aboard the steamer. He tried to keep up her morale along the way with talk of destiny and greatness. "Even as early as this Tanne's future was beginning to dawn on me," he claimed. "It was defeat that would bring victory, it was despair that would create great art. Tanne was, understandably enough, in complete disagreement."[10]

The journey out was very rough through the northern seas. In the Bay of Biscay there was a gale, and as the ship pitched violently Tanne did not "dare" to become seasick. The memory of that storm came back to her often in the first months on the farm, when she felt scarcely less wretched or helpless and did not "dare" to be homesick for her family. She could not seem to shake her terrible cold, contracted on the ship, and she could not shake her almost year-long depression: her extreme fatigue, a general hopelessness about the future, an inability to work or concentrate. She tried to rouse herself enough to paint, to begin a book about Africa and a new marionette comedy, but she found it difficult to summon the energy to walk as far as her dam. In letters to Thomas, she complained that she could not hear her own voice, and so it was naturally impossible for her to write. This "mysterious disease,"[11] as she called it, lasted until early March.

There were no visits from Denys or Berkeley that winter to relieve the bleakness of her mood. Berkeley had died in 1925 of a heart attack on the doorstep of his farmhouse. Denys was on safari with a client; he had begun to hunt professionally the year Tania was away. There was a new administration at Government House, and after a year abroad she once again felt like an alien in the country. It infuriated her that at a time of famine the hut tax had been raised again; that the governor's wife gave an enormously expensive charity fête, with more money lavished on the festivities than on the charity; and that Lord Delamere invited two hundred guests to guzzle six hundred bottles of champagne at a reception. "If I start to preach," she told her brother helplessly, "I shall lose my power." Her only influence was as a good example, or as a "hostess and friend,"[12] and she was not feeling either friendly or hospitable.

To compound the misery of the famine there was an outbreak of pestilence in the highlands—blackwater fever. Karen Blixen's beloved Abdullai, her "page," succumbed and died on the eve of his wedding. She nursed the other victims on the farm, was on call for emergencies, and from this period her reputation as a great if quixotic doctor gained greater luster. There were other *shauries*. A tribe of vicious blue monkeys, protected by the game laws, took up residence on the farm and devastated the maize fields. The *totos* let a "revolting *shenzie* hound" mate with the noble Heather, and Tanne carried on as if her own daughter had been raped. Hassan left her service; Juma gambled away his patrimony; the rains came, but with them a kind of "inflammation" or "nervous lumbago" that no treatment seemed to affect. Finally, the May issue of *Tilskueren* arrived with *The Revenge of Truth* printed in an insultingly miniscule grade of type and signed with the wrong name.

Throughout this time Tanne remained, in her letters to Ingeborg, adamantly cheerful and forebearing. Mrs. Dinesen was having problems with Mitten, and Tanne lectured her on the blessings of adversity, from which she should not try to shield the child. One might wish to stop "the wind and the frost and . . . the onset of nightfall," she told her, "and yet one knows that it is a *good* thing that one cannot do so, for . . . [they] have a mission in the service of life."[13] But she found it difficult to bear up under her own adversities. Her letters to Thomas are filled with fury and despair.

4

When Denys came back in March it was only for two weeks; his passage to England was already booked, and he did not think of changing it. Tania tried to accept the gift of the moment, the feeling that there was nothing left in life to wish for, but her joy was spoiled by a morbid consciousness of the time passing, of the imminence of her loss. When they rode up into the hills to inspect their "graves," or watched the sunset from the millstone table, or listened to Schubert while the wind blew from the Athi Plains, Tania would remind herself ruthlessly that now she had only five more days left of the fortnight, or three more hours of the evening. She knew how perverse it was but couldn't stop it. What made her, she wailed, so incapable of accepting loss?

Out of Africa suggests one explanation. "When I was expecting Denys," she wrote, "and heard his car coming up the drive, I heard at the same time, the things of the farm all telling what they really were. . . . When he came back to the farm it gave out what was in it; it spoke. . . ."[14] She herself could "speak," could "give out what was in" her, when Denys was present to evoke it, and perhaps that was the personal dimension his family's motto had for her: *"Je responderay."* When he left she experienced a kind of panic at a loss, essentially, of self.

Karen Blixen was vulnerable to depression all her life, to violent swings of mood between despair and exaltation. The even, serene wisdom of her later voice and style, and its moral toughness, were ideals she never achieved for long in her real life but which she never renounced striving for. She was capable of great clarity, more than most people, about the causes of her depressions and of what she called "an uncommon resource of *joie de vivre*" that helped her "rise very slowly to the surface again."[15] If she often thought of death and sometimes planned it, she recoiled at the last moment because death was "emptiness and annihilation," and she wanted "so terribly to live."[16] She did not immediately know how she might regain the vitality she had lost, but she could at least figure out why she felt so dead. First, she explained to Thomas, she had made her love for Denys the center of her life, and it was clearly not enough to live on. Second, she was the victim of a morbid terror of abandonment and loss, and because of it could not stand on her own, with a firm conviction of her real worth. Third, and most important, she had never broken with her family, ended her dependence on them. She was still furious with them for holding fast to her, belittling her, making a child of her, and with herself for needing them too abjectly to rebel. She had recognized, as early as her adolescence, that "Lucifer was the angel who should have wings over me" and that her solution was, like his, to "fall into his own kingdom." This adolescent predicament in a woman of forty-one was pathetic, she thought, and she ought to "draw a straight line through the foolishness of the past, and go to hell, if that is where I ought to belong."[17] And yet she still felt incapable of doing so.

Karen Blixen had an answer to this outcry—not immediately from Thomas, to whom it was addressed and who was honeymooning in Paris—but from fate. She had, by May, all the signs that she was pregnant again and was convinced enough to cable Denys in England, letting him know. In the cable she used a code name for the child, one he must have recognized from some previous discussion. She called him Daniel.

Many years later Karen Blixen told her secretary that she had deeply wanted this child and had made plans to educate "him" in Africa, by founding a school for Somali boys of good family. "Not having a child was a great disappointment to her," said Ms. Svendsen. The plan to educate "Daniel" among the Africans, considering how much Tanne admired Eton, suggests that she expected him to be an outsider or an outcast in his father's milieu. Denys cabled back from London: "Strongly urge you cancel Daniel's visit."[18] Tania replied—that cable is missing—to which Denys countered: "Received your wire and my reply do as you like about Daniel as I should welcome him if I could offer partnership but this is impossible STOP You will I know consider your mother's views Denys." The tone of reasonable indifference barely conceals the outrage, and Tania was naturally offended by that tone. "Thanks cable," she replied proudly, "I never meant to ask assistance consent only Tania."[19]

Daniel was never born, and Karen Blixen never conceived another child. Given her age and medical history, it is likely she had a second miscarriage, although she herself was not positive she had been pregnant. By the end of

June a short, lame, consolatory letter from Denys reached Ngong. "Here are a few pictures," he scribbled. "I will write properly to you soon. I am rather depressed and could wish myself back at Ngong. I want your news. What of Daniel? I would have liked it, but I saw it being very difficult for you. Denys."[20]

Karen Blixen did not address another word to Denys for the remainder of the summer, and it is likely that this was a modest gesture of revenge. In September he wrote to her again, at some length, rather chagrined by her silence and perhaps inspired by it to an unusual poetic effusion. He would be coming out again in October, he informed her, and "I shall be glad to see Ngong and your charming self again. Those sunsets at Ngong have an atmosphere of rest and content about them which I never realized anywhere else. I believe I could die happily enough at sunset at Ngong looking up at the hills, with all their lovely colors fading out above the darkening belt of the near forest. Soon they will be velvet black against the silver fading sky —black as the buffaloes which come pushing softly out of the bush high up under the breasts of the hills to feed with sweet breath unafraid upon the open grass of the night. I am very much looking forward to seeing you again, Tania. You might have given me something of your news—nothing—no word even of Daniel. . . ."[21]

5

When Karen Blixen missed her period, she sat down to make a "reckoning" of her life in a blackly comic mood, feeling inclined to take the whole thing as a "great joke." She was forty-one and unmarried. She suffered from syphilis and had no fortune to compensate her child for the handicaps of his birth. (Of these she deemed poverty worse than congenital syphilis; it posed more obstacles to "being oneself.")[22] Furthermore, her lover was a confirmed bachelor, jealous of his independence, and her family could be expected to be horrified and, worse, full of pity.

These certainly were drawbacks to maternity, but they were not sufficiently daunting in themselves. What really appalled her, when she took stock of it, was the feeling that her own life was a failure, that she had squandered the passion and talent she had started out with and that she had unconsciously wanted a child to make up the deficit. This was precisely how her mother had "lived through" her, and how Mrs. Westenholz had lived through her own five children. It was a chain of dependence, well meaning but ignoble, which she had so despised and suffered from and now stood ready to perpetuate with the next generation. She was humbled, chastened, amused, and immensely enlightened by this revelation.

As she had so often done in the past, Tanne was able to generalize from her personal experience to the greater human one. In a long, searching philosophical letter to her Aunt Bess she concludes that her failure is in part the failure of a society that raises women to be useless and childish, lacking in confidence and dependent upon men's love and money. No one had prepared her to grow up emotionally. She had relied on a lover to give meaning to her life, had stood ready to "sacrifice" herself for a child when, in fact, she had not achieved anything on her own. This made her angry in a way that modern feminists will understand. The letter to her aunt does not, of course, mention a pregnancy or miscarriage, but it calls feminism the most "radical" and

most significant movement of the nineteenth century. . . .

If I were asked what this movement does consist of, I would reply that . . . women now—in direct contrast to what was previously the case—desire and are striving to be human beings with a direct relationship with life in the same way as men have done and do this.

. . . Although I do not agree with Karl Marx that all the phenomena of life are caused by the economic situation, I think that it explains many of them. . . . In my opinion "manliness" is a human concept; "womanliness" as a rule signifies those qualities in a woman or that aspect of her personality that is pleasing to men, or that they have need of. Men had no particular need for or pleasure from, and therefore no reason to encourage, women painters, sculptors or composers—but they did have for dancers, actresses, singers. . . . A man might well be attracted to and admire a woman who took a passionate interest in the stars, or who cultivated flowers with which to beautify his home; but she would be sinning against the idea of womanliness if she sought to establish a direct relationship with nature in these branches by taking up astronomy or botany. . . .

It is often said that chivalry will disappear from the world if women start to *live* by their own efforts. To this I can only say that . . . [a] chivalry in which one first binds fast the legs of the object of one's homage in order to serve her, seems to me of scant value, and that it would be more chivalrous to cut the bonds. . . . I think there ought to be—and I hope this will come—far more chivalry among people of the same sex, among friends and colleagues, than there is now. . . .

It is also often discussed how much influence the feminist movement exerts on women's morals, and these very discussions generally show to what a great extent women are regarded as sexual beings, and to what a small extent as human beings. A woman's "morals" are understood as something purely sexual just as a woman's "honor" always has to do purely with sex. An "honorable man" is in general thought to be a man who understands and follows such clear and simple human concepts as honesty, reliability, loyalty, fearlessness; an honest woman is . . . "a woman who can be had only through marriage," without regard for the moral value of that marriage. It is my opinion that the young women of today are more courageous, more truthful, less inclined to intrigue, more loyal than "the women of bygone days"; they are [better] *"gentlemen."* . . .

We have talked so much about sexual morality, you know—I think that
there should not be such a concept of sexual morality at all, any more than
political, diplomatic, or military "morals"; for I think that the same ideas of
decency should hold true for all the affairs of human beings.

Where the relationship between men and women is concerned, a French
author I have read says: To love a modern woman is homosexuality—and I
think he is right (apart, of course, from the physical unnaturalness which gives
the word an ugly connotation). But I believe . . . that such "homosexuality"
—sincere friendship, understanding, delight shared by two equal, parallel moving beings—has been a human ideal that conditions have prevented being
realized until now. . . .

Well, dearest Aunt Bess, I can almost believe that we have been sitting on
the veranda at Folehave having a really heated discussion . . . except, it's true
that my poor opponent has not had a chance to get a word in! If only I could
fly over there for an hour. . . .[23]

To stand in a direct relation to life. To accept fate without conditions. To
stop postponing life in the name of an ideal. To run parallel with her lover,
a friend, but not a possession or a sexual object. Those were the conclusions
of Karen Blixen's soul-searching. In the autumn she wrote a seventeen-page
letter to Thomas that closes this chapter of her life. In it she projects a serene
old age for herself, success on the farm, love for the Africans as a raison d'être,
Denys as her "trusted old friend," descendants of Banja and Heather at her
side and Farah's son as her butler. "There is probably nearly always one
moment in life when there is still a possibility for *two* courses, and another,
the next moment, when only one is possible. On that point I am also now
quite clear: this time I have burnt my boats. 'No retreat, no retreat; they must
conquer who have no retreat.' "[24]

There is a deep and moving sturdiness to this passage, in the letter to Aunt
Bess, and in Karen Blixen's reconciliation with loss. It could not be a
permanent achievement, and the "ups and downs" she had lived through
would afflict her again. But the balance, the self-acceptance, would be distilled into the voice which narrates her work.

28

A Release from Self

I

KAREN BLIXEN told her brother that she had found the peace of mind to begin writing again. This had been impossible until she had "heard my own voice, seen myself in the mirror, as another person to whom one is speaking—until I had rendered my accounts."[1] The work she turned to was a marionette comedy called "Carnival,"* begun the preceding winter in Danish. But at some slightly later point she decided the material would work better as a story and redrafted it, this time in English. The style is recognizably Isak Dinesen's, even if the tale as a whole is not up to her later standards. It seems significant that her voice came to her only when she had lived enough to make a "reckoning" with her losses, rather than through the continuous exercise of her craft. This is in keeping with Dinesen's own sense of her lineage as a storyteller, rather than as a writer. "The storyteller," Benjamin tells us—"he is the man who could let the wick of his life be consumed completely by the gentle flame of his story."[2]

The use of English for this tale was in part a practical decision. Her Danish was rusty from lack of exercise; English was the language of her daily life and of her primary audience and critic, Denys. But she also seems to have chosen it the way she chose to use a pseudonym, as a means to gain freedom through distance, a clearer *Overblik* (overview) and a kind of anonymity. To adopt a foreign language is to mask a prominent and essential feature of one's identity, and as Dinesen writes in "Carnival": "Your own mask would give you at least that release from self toward which all religions strive. A little piece of night, rightly placed for giving you its freedom without renunciation. Your center of gravity is moved from the ego to the object; through the true humility of self-denial you arrive at an all-comprehending unity with life, and only thus can great works of art be accomplished."[3] In their context these words are about the nature of erotic freedom, and the mask in question is worn by a lady with no clothes on. They apply equally well to the freedom—and the inhibitions—of speech and imagination.

The events in "Carnival" take place in February 1925, on the night of an

---

*The earlier (1910) version was called "La Valse Mauve."

opera carnival in Copenhagen, and it is only one of two Dinesen tales set in the modern age.* Eight *convives* gather in a villa outside the town for a midnight supper, coming directly from the ball and still in costume. They are all rich, good-looking, and disillusioned. Four of them are "very much in love with one another."[4] The tangled skeins of their fantasies and their affairs resemble the similar mess of relations the Nairobi "smart set" was famous for. The hostess is a young woman named Mimi, who is dressed as a "Watteau Pierrot" to dramatize, if only for herself, a permanent state of unrequited love. Tanne Dinesen played the same part in her own theatricals, and Mimi suggests the author in more than this respect. She is passionately but unhappily married to a "heartless," princely sort of fellow, who flies, races, hunts, is a connoisseur of art, and who wants her at all times "to run parallel with him in life." Mimi manages to do so, though only with much bravura and deceit. "God, Polly," she tells her sister before the others arrive, "how sorry one ought to feel for all the parallel lines which want to intersect as badly as I do."[5]

Julius, Mimi's elusive husband, has come to the party dressed as a Venetian lady. This is to suggest that he is like the heroine of a tale, around whom all the action broils while she herself remains unmoved—the prize and object of desire. Julius bears a remarkable likeness to Denys Finch Hatton, and the portrait suggests that in Tanne's case, as in Mimi's, a grain of resentment stimulated the pearl of her adoration. His life is "plain sailing"; he is indifferent to or even unconscious of what others think about him and does exactly, at all times, what he pleases. "Within the existence of his friends he held the place of an idol within the temple."[6]

The other guests have also used their costumes to express, in a stylized manner, a truth about their real natures—which is to say their sexual natures, for they have all come preoccupied with some sexual problem. Polly is the only virgin in the group, and she is tired of that honor. She wants to fall in love, a step her older sister strenuously disadvises. Charles, an English diplomat dressed as a magenta Domino, is in love with Polly, or rather with the fact that she is a virgin; he has a fetish for the untouchable. Annelise, a divorcée, is disguised as the young Søren Kierkegaard, or really as Johannes, the dandy of his "Seducer's Diary." Like Johannes, Annelise has chosen to pursue a career of ritual promiscuity—one night of passion for each lover and nothing more—and has offered such an opportunity on a "take it or leave it" basis to Tido. Tido, a "futuristic" Harlequin who has chosen his costume to outshine Polly, has also been divorced, and his wife has married Annelise's husband. He is tempted to accept her offer for he is attracted by her hardness, coldness, and contempt, which he finds heroic. Finally, there is Fritze, the "real beauty" of the party, who has come as a Camelia. She is promiscuous

*The other is a minor piece, written for publication in a magazine—"Ghost Horses."

by inclination rather than on principle, finds it difficult to keep her clothes on or to keep track of her paramours. She holds hands with Julius under the table for the simple reason, the narrator tells us, that they are both inexplicably happy. When they are not sunk in erotic reveries, these young people engage in clever banter about fucking, penises, syphilis, prostitution, fetishism, sado-masochism, divorce, adultery, the defloration of virgins, and *coitus interruptus*. Julius and Annelise keep up their end of the conversation in blank verse.

There is one guest who does not belong to this generation and who takes a different—and loftier—view of things. He is a great old painter by the name of Rosendaal, and he has chosen to wear the kimono of a eunuch at the Chinese court. Both a courtier and a celibate by disposition, he watches the "gambols of the less simplified human beings with sympathy and without prejudice," although there is a certain archness and an undercurrent of spite to his exalted talk, as one might expect from an old eunuch. "Rosie" surveys the pastel costumes and pleasant, superficial faces of his young friends, and complains about the absence of a "good true black" among them, by which he specifies the black of sin, of a bad conscience. He has a Nietzschean nostalgia for a nobler and more violent age, when there were "tragedies in high places, jealousy, red love and death," when the risk attendant upon life's excesses immeasurably enhanced their pleasure. Only the fanatic dieting of the young women meets his standard of idealism. It pleases him to watch them starve in the midst of abundance; "that undoubtedly has got charm, that furnishes us with a little bit of black." But modern love, so mechanical, so friendly, so contrived, seems utterly "insipid" to him. Its "working secret has been lost."[7]

Through a series of events—a lottery, the intrusion of a desperate stranger—the others come round to this point of view and recognize that the "working secret" is the risking of one's soul, the transgression of received ideas and norms of moderation. This is a dialogue implicit in many of Isak Dinesen's tales; between a figure who defends the inequities of the past with the charm and authority of the old painter, and a modern generation freed of old taboos but confused, bored, in need of wisdom—which is to say, her readers.

"Carnival" is striking because it treats the same themes—even in many of the same words—that Tanne took up in her letters of the summer to Bess and Thomas. But in her letters she *defended* the postwar generation for its courage, admired its sexual freedom and androgyny, and described her own oppression under the old standards. "Carnival" thus seems to short-circuit and even to betray her passionate personal conclusions. When she came to choose a persona, she set aside her feminism and her ambivalence, that very modern sensibility that comes as a shock when one reads the letters for the first time. The point of view in "Carnival," like the old painter's, like the imperial eunuch's before him, seems to have been artificially and almost surgically "simplified." It represents, as Dinesen herself acknowledges, a "shortcut to superiority and equilibrium."[8]

There is no simple explanation for this paradox, although several observations may be made. Karen Blixen had just lost her last chance for motherhood. She saw her future with Denys as nothing more than a "safe" friendship. She had regained her "voice" and a sense of integrity, but by making a fairly drastic reckoning with any "normal" happiness. That August, in a letter to Thomas, she explained her own understanding of the exchange:

> I cannot be possessed and have no desire to possess, and it can be empty and cold, God knows, but it is not cramped or close. I know, too, that I must accept this aspect of my life "unconditionally," for however much I may long for something more secure and intimate in my life, when the crunch comes I back out of it, and this recurs continually. You know that I have said that I would like to be a Catholic priest, and I still maintain this—and I am not far from being one—but he would have to be more than human if he did not sometimes heave a sigh on seeing the lights lit in the windows and the family circles gathered together.[9]

The role of Catholic priest, which is to say a wise, celibate, and lonely figure, is not unlike that of the old painter. And this, finally, would be Dinesen's view of her role and destiny as an artist. She would, as she saw it, renounce intimacy but be rewarded by the opportunity to perform a great spiritual service for humanity. The old painter is the prototype for other priestly, omniscient figures in the tales of Isak Dinesen, who speak for her own values. They are old cardinals and old maids, old abbesses and old lords, old witches and old impresarios. Like Rosendaal, they observe life from a safe distance, "with sympathy and without prejudice." But they have paid an exorbitant price for their exaltation.

There is, finally, a great irony in "Carnival," a twist to all this sacrifice and renunciation. Writing behind her mask, Karen Blixen was able to free her erotic energy. Perhaps the strongest impression of her that one takes away from the tale is of her insatiability, a metaphorical insatiability she is able to gratify precisely because she plays all the parts.

2

One afternoon in November, as Tanne sat at the millstone and reflected on the course her life had taken, she looked up and saw a stork standing on her lawn. He was a European stork, the kind of bird who might have flown out of a fairy tale by Andersen.[10] His wing was broken, and he stayed on the farm for several months, eating the rats and frogs the *totos* caught for him at threepence each. He followed Kamante about, "and it was impossible not to believe that he was deliberately imitating Kamante's stiff measured walk. Their legs were about the same thickness."[11] The *totos* laughed when they saw this pair. Farah believed that the stork might be the wandering caliph from the *Thousand and One Nights,* and Tanne boasted of her talent for taming creatures of the wild.

Throughout the autumn she had been urging her mother to make a second visit. It was a sort of diplomatic negotiation: the family posing all sorts of conditions; Tanne calling the visit off several times in sheer frustration; and Ingeborg, like some marriageable royal maiden, holding herself aloof. When Bess suggested that Tanne come home to Denmark instead of obliging her old mother to make the long journey out to Africa, she got testy: "I haven't been healthy since I came out . . . but I haven't thought of going home because of it, and would rather die out here if that should be, than lead an existence like a fly in a bottle. . . ."[12]

It was finally agreed that Mrs. Dinesen would embark after Christmas and that she would bring with her some very badly needed capital for the farm.

Denys Finch Hatton was, in the meantime, leading a sporting life on various country estates in England and Scotland, and writing to Tania that the atmosphere at home "depressed" him. He sought relief in Paris, where he ordered wine for the Muthaiga Club and explored some of the seedier night spots. Just before he left for Africa he bought an automobile—a Hudson—and told Tania that he wanted to drive up the coast and look at some property there. "I am determined to get a piece of land, of which I know, and to build a small bungalow, so that we can visit the sea from time to time. It is a nice place and will be right away from anyone else. Do not tell of this."[13]

The land he mentions was at Takaungu on the Indian Ocean, thirty miles north of Mombasa. It is still accessible from the same dirt highway, which turns into a rutted land and winds through a sisal plantation toward the coast. There was once a Swahili settlement here, and the ruins of its mosque are still visible amidst the mango trees, the baobabs, and the scrub. There is a minaret of "weathered stone" and some bleached, crumbling arches. The site has a resonance rare to find in Africa, where abandoned places are so cleanly and so swiftly reclaimed by wilderness.

Denys built his house on the cliff in the Arab style, from blocks of coral stone plastered and whitewashed. It had two rooms and a narrow, arched verandah that faced the sea. The thick low wall between the arches made a seat, and here Denys and Tania would sit in the moonlight, smoke an after-dinner cigarette, and watch the breakers. She wrote,

The scenery was of a divine, clean barren marine greatness, with the blue Indian Ocean before you, the deep creek of Takaungu to the South, and the long steep unbroken coast-line of pale grey and yellow coral-rock as far as the eye reached.

When the tide was out, you could walk miles away seawards, from the house, as on a tremendous somewhat unevenly paved Piazza, picking up strange long peaked shells and starfish. The Swaheli [*sic*] fishermen came wandering along here, in a loin-cloth and red or blue turbans, like Sinbad the Sailor come to life. . . . You slept with the doors open to the silver Sea; the playing warm breeze in a low whisper swept in a little loose sand, onto the stone floor. One night a row of Arab dhows came along, close to the coast, running noiselessly before the monsoon, a file of brown shadow-sails under the moon.[14]

When Denys reached Nairobi, he came straight to the farm and stayed for a very happy and long reunion. He was still living there when Mrs. Dinesen arrived in January, a fact Tanne felt obliged to explain with the old excuse that he had been "extremely ill." But the three of them lived together until Denys went home to England early in March, a period, for Tanne, of idyllic emotional security. She hoped her mother might stay with her until the fall and was disappointed when Mrs. Dinesen said she would leave in May. Thomas and Jonna were expecting their first child, and she wanted to be with them for its arrival.

The baby was born in June—a daughter, Anne. Her Aunt Tanne wished her something that she had herself valued greatly: that she might grow up "to fascinate and be fascinated."[15]

29

Lion Hunt

I

Aᶠᵗᵉʳ Mʀs. Dɪɴᴇsᴇɴ ʟᴇғᴛ there was a series of disasters on the farm. (Disasters in Africa never occurred one at a time.) Banja, Tanne's beloved deerhound, died at the age of eleven and was buried with great ceremony. The *totos* were impressed to see their Memsabu howl with grief. A few days later, still somewhat distracted, Tanne had a bad fall from Rouge. Then a little Kikuyu girl was murdered—the first of two such tragedies within several months—and a young Kavirondo was arrested and later hanged, although there was some doubt about his guilt. Thaxton, the American who managed the coffee factory and who appears as Belknap in *Out of Africa,* left to work some land of his own in Tanganyika, and Tanne vowed that in all future contracts she would specify that her employees own no land that might conflict with their loyalties to the farm. Fortunately Mr. Dickens, her general manager (Nichols, in *Out of Africa*), continued to rise in her esteem with his humor, thoroughness, and practicality.

In June Denys departed for a safari with an American client, Frederick Patterson, who had made a "hideous amount of money out of some patent penny-in-the-slot machine for correctly registering the sales of buns and ginger pop."[1] When he left, Ingrid Lindström came to stay with Tanne for a few days. Denys had arranged this visit and had often called upon Ingrid in this manner, for he was aware how terrible his departures were for his lover and how prone to despair and illness she was afterward. Tanne was always kept in ignorance of their conspiracy. Denys would arrange to "bump into" Ingrid in Nairobi and drive her back to Ngong, and this ruse invariably worked. "It was a joyful time when Ingrid came to stay with me. . . . She had all the broad bold insinuating joviality of an old Swedish peasant woman, and in her weather-beaten face, the strong white teeth of a laughing Valkyrie. Therefore does the world love the Swedes because in the midst of their woes they can draw it all to their bosom and be so gallant that they shine a long way away."[2] This passage was intended as a high and feeling compliment, for Tanne loved Ingrid and admired her—as she had admired Ellen Wanscher—for a simplicity and a rootedness she herself did not possess. But Mrs.

Lindström unfortunately misunderstood the comparison and felt mocked by her old friend for some lack of refinement or intellectuality.

When Tanne and Ingrid were together, they talked about clothes and diets like two teenage sisters. Tanne tried to get Ingrid to "play-act" with her, but Ingrid was shy of anything involving fantasy and turned her down: "You act and I'll clap." The artistic side of Tanne mystified her, and she suggested that the fantastical elements in *Seven Gothic Tales* may have occurred to her friend during bouts of malaria, "which produced strange visions in everyone."[3] But she was one of the few people not intimidated by Tanne's temper or her eccentricities and who could tease her, a quality for which Tanne was then, as later in her life, grateful.

Mrs. Lindström's sister, Henriette, was married to Tanne's neighbor Nils Fjæstad, who had been living at Ngong since 1912 and had served with Bror during the war. One Sunday morning late in August, the Fjæstads, Tanne and the Lindströms' two elder daughters went on an excursion to the top of the Ngong hills, which Tanne cheerfully described as the dry run for her funeral. In one of her grimmer moments she had made Nils promise that should she die in Africa he would bury her in the hills, and their object, that day, was to see how high the car could go.

The fog was heavy as they began the ascent and thickened as they climbed. Halfway up, the sun burst through, so strong it melted the dew and dried the grass in minutes. Up on the ridge it was clear, and there was a magnificent view west over the Rift Valley and east over the slopes of maize fields and coffee groves. There was a path much trampled by the herds of buffalo and eland who still lived in the forest, and Tanne imagined that the "big peaceful animals must have been up on the ridge at sunrise, walking in a long row," and for no other reason "than just to look, deep down on both sides, at the land below."[4]

Invigorated by this expedition, Tanne made another short safari a few days later, this time to shoot an eland for her farm workers, for whom the meat was a great delicacy. The sun was setting when they reached the Orungi plain; a herd was grazing peacefully within their range, and Tanne shot the nearest animal. By the time it was skinned and the meat shared out, it was dark, and the safari slowly made its way home, "completely in ecstasy"; hyenas howled around them, and a lion silently finished their leftovers. "I thought," Tanne reflected " . . . how much I have come to love this country; it reminded me of the safaris of my youth, with the dogs, and the happy breathless *boys* around me, and the stars coming out, and the clear night air, which after sunset goes straight through flesh and bone. . . ."[5]

Denys was out with Patterson all through the summer, and Tania, who was keeping his car, drove it into a ditch, an accident for which Farah gallantly took the blame. She intended to have it repaired before Denys came home, but he surprised her by turning up at the farm during a brief resupply layover in Nairobi. She was showing Major Taylor and his wife around the farm, and the major was, as he had so often done in the past, advising her about her coffee. The Taylors wanted to leave after tea, knowing that Tania and Denys had not seen one another for so long, but were pressed to stay for dinner to hear Denys's adventures. Errol Trzebinski interviewed Mrs. Taylor, who recalled the evening in great detail, as "like a dream. In the dark paneled room, lit by candles, Tania sat still and silent—as if a sudden move would break the spell. In the dark shadows her face looked small and white and her dark eyes huge, like a little woodland witch. . . . She hardly spoke all evening, all three sat listening to Denys."[6]

Among other things, Denys and Patterson had discovered a rare species of baboon and tamed one of them. They had also brought back magnificent photographs and some moving-picture footage of elephant and lion, and Denys was enthusiastic about game photography, an enthusiasm Tania could not share. She did not, as she wrote in *Shadows on the Grass,* "see eye to eye with the camera," and the pictures to her mind "bore less real likeness to their object than the chalk portraits drawn up on the kitchen door by our Native porters."[7] Her resentment belongs to the same philosophical category as the old painter's, in "Carnival," against modern love. Game photography was "a pleasant, platonic affair," at the end of which the parties "blow one another a kiss and part like civilized beings."[8] It was not a matter of life or death, and therefore it held no interest for her.

2

Bess Westenholz celebrated her seventieth birthday that August among the roses at Folehave, surrounded by her siblings and their children. She was a handsome, upright, silver-haired old woman who appeared to carry her age with grace, although, in fact, this was not so. Bess reached this jubilee in a state of doubt and crisis, believing herself a failure, lamenting her nothingness to all those within hearing, depressed by her solitude and creating a little tempest of anxiety within the family, whose wake inevitably reached Ngong. Aunt Bess's "case" and Tanne's involvement in it dominated her correspondence with Denmark for the next year.

Bess had always believed in the importance of living for others, but as she aged she had come to believe that marriage was the most desirable arrangement for doing so. A woman who could "live for" her husband and her children was a happy woman, a rich woman, a perfected woman, while a spinster had missed life's highest calling. Tanne, as a divorcée and the only unmarried female in the family besides Bess herself, naturally came in for the worst dose of her aunt's sympathy and disapproval. She, in turn, warded them off with her old vehemence in letters of many pages, which patiently, generally lovingly, and at times violently, spelled out her disagreement.

People of *her* ilk, she repeats to Bess, prize adventure, passion, and freedom above the security of family life. "Bourgeois happiness" is not the only kind. "Living for others" is a questionable employment of one's resources, and probably a waste of them. It is well enough to live for an immanent ideal —the poor, one's country, a coffee farm, or God—but not for some Mr. Petersen.[9]

This argument had been run through so many times that it was virtually a duet and, one must conclude, music to the ears of the two opponents. Bess continued willfully to misunderstand or to distort Tanne's examples, and Tanne to provoke her aunt with her sophisticated immoralism. Bess, who loved her niece dearly, saw it as her mission to bring her back into the fold; and Tanne, who loved her aunt just as dearly, defined her identity in revolt against Bess's orthodoxy.

Their bond was such that Tanne saw her aunt's predicament better than the others, with more compassion and less sentimentality. When Elle invited her to commiserate with, to pity Bess, she refused. For one thing, Bess had given them all the example of a certain toughness—the inspiration to become the kind of person "one didn't mess with." For another, Bess's unhappiness was nothing new. Satisfaction had always been problematic, if not actually repulsive to her. She herself had reinforced the narrow confines of the world built by her mother and had made no effort to rebel. Tanne wrote:

> It is difficult to estimate a human life, it is quite impossible to do so according to definite rules, and as time goes by one grows very cautious about it. . . . In the end there is probably *something* for every individual that he cannot renounce . . . and that which they pay for it with, is "life." That which I have achieved, and which is costing and will cost me life, is not in detail what I would have imagined for myself when I was seventeen—it is probably not so for you either, or for any one we know, with the exception of such steady and orthodox characters as Else . . . it has cost Aunt Bess her life to be an old maiden aunt at Folehave, and that seems a wretched fate for such a highly gifted person. But then it would be a very superficial view to regard my existence as that of a poor coffee farmer with a load of worries . . . her life has been, in accordance with her nature, spent in loving and exerting influence on the people with whom she has been concerned. . . . If it were not that, in her old age, in a moment of weakness, as it were, she had come to take account of the yardstick of other people, which in reality is alien to her nature, I think that she would see it this way herself. . . . [10]

In 1927, as so often and so tiresomely in the past, the brilliant flowering of the coffee trees came to little. A summer drought withered the cherries, and most of the harvest was lost. Tanne struggled to save the trees that bore fruit and calculated her diminished profits. She had lived in Africa long enough to take, at least partially, the Kikuyu view of her own misfortunes

—that they were humorous—and in a letter to her brother Anders she welcomed him to some of her dry weather. He was farming the estate of his Uncle George and Aunt Lidda in Jutland, and his grain was suffering from too much rain. "We clodhoppers understand each other and must stick together,"[11] she told him. Anders was something of a misfit in his militantly articulate family, and the others tended to condescend to him. He had become, by his early thirties, a bachelor of solitary habits and laconic speech; and his sister, who appreciated his rustic side, tended to take his own wry manner with him. She promised him that in twenty years she would come home and keep his house—if he hadn't found himself a wife—but in the meantime he must come and visit her in Africa. Anders, rooted to his patch of Jutland, never left it.

3

When Patterson went home to his cash registers, Denys made a trip alone to Eritrea, returning to Ngong, as he had promised, in time for Christmas. He brought Tania a present, a souvenir of his journey, a ring of soft Abyssinian gold that could be adjusted to fit any finger. She wore it until several weeks before his death, when, after a quarrel, he took it back from her.

On New Year's Eve they had a festive dinner *tête à tête* and went to bed well before midnight, for Denys was worried about a rifle he had given to a friend the same day and intended to set out before dawn the next morning to explain the hair trigger. The friend had gone to Narok, sixty miles away, and was traveling with a large, slow train of trucks and servants over the old road. There was a newer road under construction, a shortcut, which Tania and Denys proposed to take, although they did not know how far it went. In *Out of Africa* Karen Blixen describes that morning ride. The air was so fresh and cold that it gave her the feeling of moving through "deep dark waters" with the smells rushing past—"fresh rank smells of the olive-bushes, the brine scent of burnt grass, the sudden quelling smell of decay."[12]

Fifteen miles from the farm, as the sun was rising, Kanuthia, Denys's servant, spotted a dead giraffe by the roadside and a lean golden lion feeding upon it. Denys stopped the car and, after courteously asking his friend's permission if he might shoot—it was still her land—raised his gun and fired.

Six miles farther along, the road ended, and they were forced to return home without having accomplished their mission. When they reached the spot where they had killed the lion, Tanne saw, in the now clear dawn, a second lion, black-maned and magnificent, who paused in his meal to stare at them. They could not at first make up their minds to shoot him but decided finally that they "had to have it."[13] Denys shot—and the lion sprang into the air at the discharge of the gun and fell with an enormous thud into the dust. Kanuthia and Denys skinned both beasts, and when they had finished they sat on the grass and ate their New Year's breakfast of claret, raisins, and almonds, while overhead the vultures gathered. Tanne felt that her own heart "was as light as if I had been flying it, up there, on a string."[14]

Isak Dinesen turns this lion hunt into a love scene in *Out of Africa,* giving it more symmetry than the real event possessed. She makes the first beast into a lioness and the *"femme fatale"* of the tragedy, and in the retelling it is she and not Denys who shoots the male lion, at her lover's urging: "Here the shot was a declaration of love."[15]

Many years after she had written the passage, when she was embroidering the austere canvas of *Out of Africa* with *Shadows on the Grass,* Dinesen added: "I knew then, without reflecting, that I was up at a great height, upon the roof of the world, a small figure in the tremendous retort of earth and air, yet one with it; I did not know that I was at the height and upon the roof of my own life."[16]

30

Visitors to the Farm

I

FOR CHRISTMAS, Elle Dahl had sent her sister a small porcelain Harlequin to make a pair with the Columbine she already possessed, and Tanne had put the two figures on the stone mantel in her sitting room. They reminded her of a world which with time and distance "I have come to hold so dear"[1] —the Copenhagen of her childhood: the pantomimes and marionette comedies in the Tivoli Gardens, the ballet, the Sunday strolls through the Deer Park with her sisters. That New Year's Eve, Tanne lit a row of candles behind the Harlequin, and she and Denys noted that it would be lovely to see him do a pirouette—only one.

Their wish was gratified a week later in a dramatic fashion when three tremors shook the highlands. Denys was sleeping in his truck on the Masai Reserve and thought at the first tremor that a rhino had got under it. Tanne was in her bath and thought at the first tremor that there was a leopard on her roof. At the second she thought she was about to die, and at the third she had "an overwhelming feeling of joy." The pleasure lay in the revelation that "the dull globe, the dead mass, the Earth itself . . . something which you believed to be immovable, has got it in it to move on its own."[2]

About this time the local police advised her that a band of dangerous and brazen robbers, suspected of having killed an Indian shopkeeper in Limuru, was operating in the neighborhood and probably had their hideout on her farm. They asked if she would lay out twenty shillings as a reward for information leading to their capture, but she declined. Her sympathies were actually with the outlaws. Their leader, Muangi, was a local bravo and renowned dancer, who did indeed risk capture to attend an *ngoma* on the farm. Tanne confessed that if she could be sure he wouldn't kill her, she would like to meet him. "There is always something fascinating about people who are absolutely desperate."[3]

Another desperado found a cordial welcome on the farm. She was the young Countess de Janzé, convicted in Paris of shooting her English lover, Raymond de Trafford, in the compartment of a Calais train. The Count de Janzé owned a farm in Kenya, and the countess, a pretty American heiress to the Armour fortune, had met de Trafford at the Muthaiga Club. She had intended to kill him first and then herself, and had, in fact, hovered close to death for several weeks. After her trial and her divorce, de Trafford married her.[4]

That spring Alice de Janzé was back in Kenya to settle some business. She was in need of a little friendly cheer, and "Josh" Erroll* introduced her to Tania Blixen, who invited both of them to visit her and told the countess she could live quietly at Ngong while she prepared for her deportation.

That same afternoon Lady Macmillan and Mr. Bulpett appeared unexpectedly with two elderly American ladies in tow, passengers on a cruise ship who were spending the day in Nairobi and had driven out to Ngong, hoping to see a lion. Lady Macmillan obviously considered the Baroness a kind of lion, a picturesque attraction worth a side trip, and Tania invited them to stay for tea. The conversation turned to the shameless immorality of Kenyan society, and the two ladies, rather unpatriotically, named Alice de Janzé as the worst of the sinners and debauchees. At that moment Lord Erroll's car drove up; he and the countess were announced, and Tania noted with great satisfaction that the Devil himself could not have caused greater consternation. The scene amused her so much that she sat up in her bed that night, still laughing over it.

The robber band continued to provide conversation for the highlands, and there was some concern that it might spark a general native uprising. Tanne took up the subject one afternoon with her Norwegian friend, Gustav Mohr, who brought Kierkegaard's *The Concept of Dread* into the discussion. They both agreed that in relation to the robbers there was nothing to be afraid of, and this was true, generally, if one was honest about the real nature of fear. Life had risks and mortal dangers, but they befell you whether or not you were previously "horror-stricken" at the idea of them. Tanne suggested that perhaps only those who lived in terror of the Devil had something to fear. She made a distinction, however, between *her* devil—the dapper entrepreneur who bartered worldly triumphs for souls—and that other, more depressing Germanic personage, who promoted evil. If he did exist, though, she would be as curious to meet him as to meet Muangi.

Mohr, who was only thirty, had originally been Thomas's friend. Too young for the war, he had emigrated to America, where, like Wilhelm Dinesen, he worked at odd jobs and saw the West. From California he took a steamer to Australia, arrived in Kenya in the early twenties, and found work managing a farm. He was responsible for eleven thousand acres near Rongai and had four European managers under him. It was, Tanne noted, "a very interesting post for such a young man."[5]

---

*The Earl of Erroll, who was then married to Lady Idina Sackville, was a rather notorious figure, one of the "fast," extravagant types who gave Kenya its reputation. He was found dead of a gunshot wound in his car in 1941, and the husband of a woman known to be his mistress was arrested for the crime, although he was later acquitted.

Mohr, however, was anything but a "clodhopper." In *Out of Africa* Isak Dinesen describes him as a large-nosed, ardent, and poetic soul who would descend upon her drawing room "like a stone out of a volcano," throw himself down before her fire, declare that he was "going mad . . . in a country which expected man to keep alive on talk of oxen and sisal."[6] He would then discourse on "love, communism, prostitution, Hamsun, the Bible" and so forth until dawn, smoking cheap cigars and rejecting dinner. He loved Tanne with the same austere intensity and perhaps had inherited some of Thomas's protective feelings for her. They had a standing appointment every week for a glass of vermouth on the terrace of The New Stanley, when they loaned one another books and discussed literature. Mohr filled some of the vacuum Denys's wanderings created in Tanne's life, and when her loneliness was most raw he provided some essential human kindness and sympathy.[7] He was the first to reach her after Denys died and he stayed with her to arrange the funeral. It was Mohr who drove her to the station on the morning she left Africa. "Unlike most of the men she knew," Thomas remembered, "Gustav loved Tanne without awe, and she respected him because he was not her slave."[8]

2

Nineteen twenty-eight was an extremely busy and profitable year for Denys as a hunter, and he was in and out of Tania's house and life. That February he showed up briefly on his way to Tanganyika, to get a spare part for his truck. They ate dinner and he went straight to bed, planning to start on his safari at one in the morning. Tania sat up for a while, playing records for him, and she arose at midnight to see him off. They walked as far as the fish pond together, she dressed in a nightgown and shawl, and from there she waved good-bye. Venus was setting, the air was chill, and perhaps she then felt "that love and gratitude which the people who stay home have . . . for the wayfarers and wanderers of the world."[9]

The following Sunday another wayfarer and wanderer appeared on her doorstep. He was a Swede by the name of Otto Casparsson, who had worked briefly as maitre d'hôtel at The Norfolk and had stood behind Karen Blixen's chair when she lunched there, entertaining her in an unctuous voice with his philosophy of life. Ingrid Lindström remembered him as a plump, ruddy-faced homosexual from a "rather good" Swedish family. But he had abandoned them and wandered from city to city in Europe, working as a waiter when he could not get a better job. Now he was in some sort of trouble with the police, and the Swedish community, to whom he might have looked for help, would have nothing to do with him. It was, he complained, hard for a white man like himself to find a job, with so much native competition. He could not do manual labor, he wasn't "handy," he couldn't drive, and standing in the dust outside Mbogani House he cut a "hopeless and lonely" figure. Tanne, returning from a ride, was at first not inclined to invite him in. But he spoke about his troubles in such a hearty voice, and took such care to save her face should she reject him, that she changed her mind. "This was courtesy in a hunted animal."[10]

Casparsson told the Baroness his life story over a good dinner. He had been an actor in his better days. His greatest roles were Armand in the *Dame aux Camélias* and Osvald in Ibsen's *Ghosts*. They spoke about plays and play-wrights and the way they felt the great roles ought to be done, and Caspars-son did, in fact, suggest they read Ibsen together. Tanne was willing, but her copy was in English and he wasn't fluent in it. There is certainly an echo of their talk in "Deluge at Norderney," where Casparsson is cast as Kasparson, the imposter, and Tanne as Malin Nat-og-Dag; and it is there one may see what they had in common.

> "And why," Miss Malin asks him, "did you want this role so much?"
> "I will confide in you," said Kasparson, speaking slowly. "Not by the face shall the man be known, but by the mask."[11]

Toward the end of the evening Casparsson confided to the Baroness that he was setting out to seek his fortune in Tanganyika. When she questioned him about this journey, he confessed that he planned to walk there. When she pointed out that it was 230 miles through waterless country, filled with lions, he replied that it was only fair to his family that the lions should have a go at him, on their behalf. If he survived he could then, in perfect conscience, turn his back on them forever.

Karen Blixen wanted to see him on his way, and the following morning she drove him as far as Farah's *dukka*, gave him a bottle of ale, some sandwiches, twenty-five shillings in cash, and her blessing.[12] He was dressed in a strange black overcoat and departed, in the midst of his misery, in good humor. She did not hear of him again until some months later, when a friend informed her that he had reached Tanganyika safely after many adventures with lion and Masai. Later, he sent back the money with elaborate praises for her help and inspiration. From Cairo he wrote two articles for a Swedish newspaper, in which he recounted his adventures "Tramping Through East Africa." The Baroness figures in them—a picturesque and chivalrous figure —much as he figures in her own African memoir.

Mbogani House was something of a magnet for outcasts and a tourist attraction for important personages, who were often driven out there to be shown around. Choleim Hussein, a rich Indian timber merchant with whom Tanne had many dealings in the years when she was cutting down her forests, asked her, knowing of her imaginative hospitality, to receive an Indian high priest then making an inspection tour of the country. He offered to provide the fruit, cakes, and cash gift that were customary, and Tanne agreed, although she was alarmed, on the appointed day, to see not one but seventeen old men in fine cashmere robes descend from a motorcade of cars.

The high priest himself was a very small person with a delicate face and a fine voice, although he did not speak either English or Swahili. He and the Baroness had, as she writes, to "express our great mutual respect by pantomime."[13] After the repast, for which all of her silver was laid out, they sat together on the lawn in a strangely congenial silence. Karen Blixen was struck by his calm but lively expression, which was that of a very young baby or a very old woman of the world, incapable of surprise but interested in everything. He particularly admired her deerhounds, which were of a species he had never seen before. At the end of the visit she handed him the hundred rupees with much ceremony, and he gave her a pearl ring. But by now this sham disturbed her and she felt the need to make him a real gift, so she sent Farah to fetch the skin of a lion Denys had shot some months before. "The old man took hold of one of the big claws, and with a clear attentive eye tried the sharpness of it on his cheek."[14]

The hunt for that lion is one of the central episodes in *Out of Africa* and came to seem, even at the time, an event of great symbolic importance. On the twenty-third of April, which was the eve of Denys's forty-second birthday, Dickens brought Karen Blixen the news that two lions had been marauding the oxen in their *boma* and had carried off two young bulls. He asked her permission to lay strychnine for them, but she refused. It was not sporting, she said, and luckily Mr. Finch Hatton was in the house and the two of them would go out and shoot the lions. Dickens considered this to be a piece of folly and "bitterly" went away.[15] For Denys it came at a good moment. He had complained that his life thus far had not lived up to his expectations, and to cheer him up, Tania told him that something interesting might yet occur before his birthday.

That afternoon they dragged one of the dead oxen to a spot on a little hill near a stand of coffee trees, where they would have a good shot at the lions if they came to feed upon the animal. After nightfall they returned with Farah. He carried a large electric torch; Tania carried another, and Denys had a flashlight on his belt. The night was moonless, and Tania was trembling as she made a slow circle with her torch. The first object it lit up was a jackal, but a little to the left it fell upon "his Majesty Simba . . . twenty-five yards away, lying on the ground with his head on his paws and his eyes fixed upon us."[16]

They did not have much time. If the lion moved deeper into the trees the light would not be strong enough to follow him. So Denys fired. Farah now swung his torch around the *shamba,* and nearby, behind a coffee bush, was the second lion. Denys quickly fired a second time. This was an incredibly risky business, for either shot might have missed and, surrounded by coffee trees on a hill, there was nowhere to flee. But both thieves were dead, and the hunters returned home, tired but elated, to a bottle of champagne.

It was not long after this lion hunt that Karen Blixen received a letter from a former gun bearer, written in the flowery script of a public scribe and addressed to the "Lioness von Blixen." "Dear Lioness . . ." it began. Members of her household began to call her Lioness, which she thought was a rather dashing title. Perhaps it pleased her more than she cared to say, for the birthday lion hunt confirmed, in an almost sacramental way, a choice she felt she had made, an identity she had achieved, a triumph over the conflict which had obscured that identity in her younger years. The choice was, as she told Aunt Bess, between "lions or family life."[17] Dickens, who was a brave man but a father and a husband, had been rightfully unwilling to stalk the lions and sensible to suggest laying strychnine for them. But she and Denys were also right—and not "frivolous" or "egotistical," as Bess suggested—to defend a different sense of responsibility: "Come now," she had told her lover, "and let us go and risk our entirely worthless lives."[18] She would add, in *Out of Africa: "frei lebt wer sterben kann,"** her final answer to Aunt Bess.[19]

The epistolary debate between niece and aunt continued, each defending her ground with a great expense of passion and prose. Tanne's letters gave Bess such pleasure that she wanted to have them published. Tanne assured her aunt there was more that united than divided them, and that she was deeply grateful for "the enthusiasm, light and warmth" which Bess had represented.[20] "When something . . . happens to change my view of the various problems of life, I constantly find myself thinking: 'I would like to talk to Aunt Bess about that. . . .' "[21]

3

Despite the fact that it was such a busy year for Denys, it was a remarkably happy one in his life with Tania. She had made a truce with her feelings of abandonment, and perhaps that encouraged him to show her more affection. Her happiness saturates her letters, in the form of humor and vivacity. When a Westenholz cousin asked her to account for this, she quoted an English author whom she was reading, a critic named Philip Wicksteed. In his book of essays on Henrik Ibsen he had raised the question that dominates Ibsen's plays: " 'What is it to be oneself? God meant something when he made each of us. For a man to embody that meaning of God in his words and deeds . . . is to be himself.' "[22] Isak Dinesen would put it with greater poetic economy in *Out of Africa,* where she writes: "Pride is faith in the idea that God had, when he made us. A proud man is conscious of the idea, and aspires to realize it . . . the proud man finds his happiness in the fulfillment of his

---

*"He lives free who can face death."

fate."[23] In her friendship with Denys, in her relations with the Africans, in her life as a farmer she had understood what "God meant her to be." And once again she took the opportunity to repeat what God had *not* meant her to be: a safe and comfortable Danish matron.

That certainty of a divine intention was extremely precious to Karen Blixen, and when she lost it, as sometimes happened, she felt helpless. In her work she would, like God, create a scheme of things so orderly and beautiful that even the losses have their place, like the spaces in a great colonnade.

There was an atmosphere of romance on the farm, stimulated in part by Denys and Tania themselves. Farah's second wife, Fathima, had arrived, and they were married with great splendor. Ali also got married that year, and his wife, Maura, gave Fathima lessons in Swahili. They were such a happy couple that Kamante's heart was inflamed, too, and he decided to marry a tall and voluptuous Kikuyu maiden by the name of Wamboi. Karen Blixen helped him accumulate the cows and goats he needed for her purchase price, and at the time I did the research for this book Kamante and Wamboi, both nearly eighty, still lived together at Ngong and vividly recalled the generosity of "Mrs. Karen," which had made it possible for them to marry.

It was unseasonably hot in the month before the short rains. One afternoon, as recreation for the *totos,* Tanne drove them to Mbagathi to see an air show. Here she ran into Mrs. Bursell, the wife of her former manager, who was living in Tanganyika and who gave her news of Casparsson. She had seen him recently near Moshi, healthy, drunk, and singing at the top of his voice from the back of an open truck.

The show was exciting for the *totos* and their mistress alike. There were four small planes that did tricks and flew races. One of these was piloted by the famous Maia Carbery, a well-known local aviatrix. She was to crash, not far from Ngong, a month later, leaving Lord Carbery and a small daughter. Tanne held her up to Aunt Bess as someone who ought never to have married and who had tried, with tragic results, to combine "the lion hunt" and "family life."

In March the governor's wife, Lady Grigg, drove out to the farm for tea, bringing her parents, Lord and Lady Islington. While Lady Grigg showed her mother around the garden, Tania entertained the old lord, who had been the governor of New Zealand and in 1920 a warm supporter of Indian rights, and who still took an active role in colonial affairs. They discussed politics, the disenfranchisement of the Indians and the Africans,* the oppressive taxes

---

*The Legislative Council was composed of civil servants representing the Foreign Office and members elected by the white, Indian, and Arab communities respectively in separate elections. The whites still held an unofficial majority. The Indians still desperately wanted a "common roll," which would ensure them fairer representation. The Africans were still considered incompetent to vote or to decide upon their own destinies, and councillors (white) were appointed on their behalf.

that had been levied in recent years—at the same time that money was lavishly spent on unnecessary luxuries for the settlers. Lord Islington shared her concerns, promised to put them before the House of Lords, and invited her to London to hear him do so. When the ladies returned they teased him about his "fascination" for the Baroness, which he admitted, and she declared that "gentlemen only become really charming when they reach seventy."[24]

The Griggs had already begun their preparations for the official visit of the Prince of Wales, which was to take place that October. Sir Edward was refurbishing the ballroom at Government House, at a cost of seven thousand pounds, and had ordered the streets repaved. Denys was informed that he had been chosen to take His Royal Highness out on safari, which was not welcome news. When Tania laughed at him, he told her bitterly that she could not imagine what a "fuss" was made over English royalty.

It was a vintage year for fusses. In May there was a reception for the German Princess Marie Louise of Schleswig-Holstein, followed by Lord Delamere's second marriage, to Gladys Markham. Tania was invited to both affairs. She was enjoying this diet of aristocrats, brigands, murderesses, vagabond actors, and high prists, and she was grateful that it was still possible to find people who figured as "representatives" in the world, who stood for some higher or lower power. Democracy had its virtues, but she also thought that civilized modern men had lost much valuable symbolism from their lives. "The consciousness of being: a German, a Reventlow, of the honest guild of tinkers, an *honnête femme* has no doubt kept many people up to scratch, and filled them with a proper pride, in contrast to that of modern youth, 'who have nought but their bare humanity to rely on . . .' "[25]

Karen Blixen wrote these words at a moment when her own status as a representative of higher powers was in jeopardy. That summer she had a letter from Bror, who was in Sweden. It was the kind of letter he had always written—trivial and exhaustive in its details and bearishly affectionate in its tone—the eternal older brother writing to his little sister from the great world. But sandwiched casually between the anecdotes was a piece of hard information: "On the seventh of August I shall marry Cockie . . . I am coming out to live in Tanganyika, and so will be as little in the way as possible. This above all: I hope always to be your own true Bror."[26]

Tanne duly reported this announcement to her family, making little of it, and in an offhanded way wishing Bror better luck the second time. But to close friends she threw a fit, railing against Cockie as a usurper and accusing Bror of a gross betrayal. This was strange talk in their view, since the divorce had been final for four years and Bror's romance with Cockie was ten years old. But Tanne would not be consoled. She took this marriage as a personal and fresh insult. If she had been able to forgive Bror's infidelities when they were married, she was not able to forgive this blow to her prestige, the compromise to her social standing, the devaluation of her title; and perhaps some of the anger for old transgressions, long postponed, was now discharged.

Her friends were bewildered because none of them understood how she reckoned the importance of her title. It was not just, as Parmenia Migel writes, that she "liked to hear herself addressed as Baroness,"[27] although, of course, she did. Her ennoblement formalized her relations with the world of Frijsenborg and all it stood for. This was not just boundless wealth and grandeur and one's own maid, but also freedom and "lightness of heart." Her title also gave Karen Blixen a kind of ballast, the nature of which she describes beautifully in "Copenhagen Season": "To a nobleman his name was the essence of his being, that immortal part of him which was to live after the other lower elements had faded away. Individual talents and characteristics were supposed to be concerns of human beings outside his sphere. A young man with an old name, but with no illusions whatever as to his personal appearance or talent, would offer himself in marriage to a brilliant beauty . . . confident in the soundness of this, his real self. . . . Within this world of names and families, individual fortune or misfortune, as long as they did not touch the name, was staunchly borne. . . ."[28] And it was in that spirit she had borne her own misfortunes and had taken Bror "without illusions" as to his character or compatibility.

There was also a practical side to this dilemma, which Tanne confided to Lady Colville, with whom she stayed at Naivasha sometime in August. She was, she said, in a "quandary" about what to call herself. There would now be two Baronesses Blixen, and Cockie was the incumbent. Did she have a right to keep her title, or must she now become plain Mrs. Blixen? Lady Colville, an elderly and rather dotty noblewoman, the niece of the Duke of Marlborough, told Tania not to worry: "My dear, you shall soon be the Honourable Mrs. Denys Finch Hatton."[29] She had no inside information for this prophecy except her own good-natured wish that it come true, but Tania was desperate enough to take some comfort from it. Ingrid Lindström suggests that "perhaps she confronted Denys with it," for they had some kind of quarrel that left a reserve of bitterness in both of them, to be tapped later.

4

The Prince of Wales arrived in East Africa in the middle of October, intending to stay about eight weeks. Lady Grigg invited Tania to live at Government House during the Nairobi lap of the visit and still has a charming photograph of the royal party, posed on the veranda after a luncheon. HRH has his eyes closed, the other gentlemen seem to be digesting an excellent meal, and Baroness Blixen, the only lady present, is impishly sticking out her tongue at the camera.

Tania met the Prince for the first time at a small official dinner and declared afterward that she was "smitten" with him. He then invited her to a lively and unofficial dinner party in his private railroad car. There were sixteen guests in all, seated at four small tables, and Tania sat beside the Prince. She took this opportunity to plead the cause of the Africans "in the matter of their taxation," having decided beforehand that the appeal would have to be made in a "pleasant manner."[30] Apparently she succeeded in arousing his interest in the natives to some degree, because he invited himself to dinner at her farm and asked to see one of their *ngomas*. It was then Tuesday, and this party was to take place on Friday.

Arranging an *ngoma* in November was not a simple matter, and Karen Blixen has described her predicament in *Shadows on the Grass*. She sent Farah out to beg the chiefs to bring their people and wasn't sure until the last moment that they would come. On Thursday she drove into town to buy provisions and to "find some ladies" for the party. Only three other gentlemen had been invited: Denys; the Prince's adjutant, Piers Legh; and his secretary, Sir Alan Lascelles. Ultimately, she invited only two other women, leaving HRH the option of bringing his own guest.

One of the ladies was Vivienne de Watteville, an old friend of Denys and the daughter of a Swiss naturalist who had written a great deal about Africa. She was a beauty, an amusing talker, and she would write her own book on Africa, a memoir about her father and their adventures together, filled with poetic ecstacy, and called *Out in the Blue*. Beryl Markham, the other lady, had a harder-edged sort of charm. She was the daughter of Captain Charles Clutterbuck, who trained Lord Delamere's racehorses. After separating from his wife, Clutterbuck had emigrated to East Africa with Beryl, who was then five, leaving a son behind in England with his wife. Beryl had run barefoot through the hills around Njoro with her Nandi playmates, learning to hunt warthogs with a spear. Contemporaries describe her as a creature totally without fear and rather arrogant toward her own mortality. Her father left Kenya in 1920, and she took over the horses in his stable. About that time she married her first husband, a rugby player named Jock Purves. In the late twenties she began taking flying lessons and would become the first woman mail pilot, the first woman to attempt a solo east-to-west crossing of the Atlantic, and one of the first pilots to use a plane for scouting game. In this capacity she worked with both Bror and Denys, who figure prominently and affectionately in *her* African memoir, *West with the Night*.

Beryl Markham was then twenty-four and had recently married her second husband, Mansfield Markham, a noted sportsman and member of the Jockey Club. She was tall, broad-shouldered, and fair, resembling Greta Garbo both in her features and in a restless, pantherine grace of movement. Her private life was a subject of endless gossip and speculation, and to the common imagination Beryl was a sort of Circe. Denys was then, or had just or would soon—depending upon one's informant—have a "little walk-out" with her. Tania could not have been blind to her allure, and it speaks highly for her dedication as a hostess—and her sense of fair play generally—that she still invited her to dinner, placed her beside Denys, and later reported to her mother that Beryl had "looked ravishing."[31]

It was the evening of Kamante's greatest triumph, with a meal that began with his famous clear soup and was followed by Mombasa turbot served with hollandaise, ham poached in champagne, partridges with peas—the birds brought by the Masai—a pasta with cream and truffles, greens, pearl onions and tomato salad, wild mushroom *croustades,* a savarin, strawberries, and grenadines from the garden. Denys provided the wines and the cigars. Afterward, the guests went out to watch the *ngoma.* The chiefs had not let her down, and there was a crowd of enthusiastic dancers around the bonfires. The driveway was illuminated with several smaller fires, and Tania had hung a pair of old ship's lanterns—brought back from Denmark for Berkeley Cole —outside the house. The Prince personally thanked the chiefs, speaking to them in Swahili. Tania was "very satisfied with my Party."[32]

The royal safari finally left Nairobi under heavy rain and made its way west, toward Tanganyika, looking for elephant and lion. Denys had decided that they needed another guide, someone experienced in lion, and after calling his old friend, J. A. Hunter, who was engaged, he looked up Bror, who had returned from his honeymoon and was living with Cockie in a small farmhouse at Arusha, near the foot of Mount Babati. Bror was thrilled by the invitation and plunged into the hunt with enormous confidence, swearing the Prince would have his trophy. This, as Errol Trzebinski points out, was in marked contrast to Denys's more reserved approach. Finch Hatton warned the prince, with his typically fearless candor, that he could not produce a lion or an elephant on demand and that "Africa does not wear her heart on her sleeve . . . not even for a King's son."[33]

During the time they were in Arusha, the prince was introduced to Cockie Blixen, was immensely charmed by her, and invited her to join the safari. Cockie was a terrible shot but a good sport. When Bror, Denys, and the Prince turned up at her cottage unexpectedly one morning and asked for breakfast, she cheerfully scrambled her last few eggs for them. "There are interesting and intrinsic differences here, both between Denys and Bror, and between Cockie and Tania," writes Ms. Trzebinski. "Bror is anxious not to fall short of his reputation with lions before the Prince, whereas Denys, while wishing to please his royal client, has forewarned him that he may be unlucky. Cockie is also quite relaxed in the company of the noble guest, and not in the least perturbed either about her simple home or the fact that she has nothing up to epicurean standards to offer him for a meal, whereas Tania would have been mortified under similar circumstances."[34]

The Prince did, in fact, take Bror aside and chide him about Cockie's quarters. "I say, Blixen, you really oughtn't to let your wife live in a tumbledown place like this." "I shall never forget," Bror wrote, "the tone

of his voice. Naturally I felt ashamed, though my wife hadn't complained
—and inwardly promised to put things right."[35]

The royal safari was cut short abruptly by the cable that King George was
ill, perhaps dying, and the Prince hurriedly embarked for England. Denys
was invited to sail home with them, but he had promised Tania to be back
at Ngong with her for Christmas and had a French couple arriving for a safari
early in January, Baron and Baroness Napoléon Gourgaud. "Good luck with
your frogs," the Prince's adjutant had written him.[36] When Denys reached
the farm he retold the entire story, not omitting Cockie's potshots at pheasant
or her scrambled eggs, thinking, no doubt, that Tania would be amused. But
she flew into a jealous rage and on a postcard accused Denys of flouting the
laws of nature. How could he possibly have befriended Bror, considering the
way he had treated her? This reproach, so ferocious and so unlikely, must
have frightened Denys, for he put up his guard.

31

Spirits of the Air

I

IN MARCH OF 1929 Thomas cabled his sister that Mrs. Dinesen was gravely ill and that the doctors were not hopeful for her recovery. Tanne took the first passage to Europe that she could get, leaving the farm in the care of Mr. Dickens. But by the time she reached Denmark, her mother had improved remarkably. She stayed at Rungstedlund for the next six months while her own health deteriorated, as usual growing more and more depressed. "She was weak, self-absorbed, futureless," Thomas wrote, "emptier than I had ever seen her. I couldn't imagine what was going to happen."[1]

She met with the directors of Karen Coffee while she was home and tried to persuade them that there was still promise in the farm. The rains had begun before she left, Dickens sent rousing bulletins, and everything was "swimming in water." But then came a July frost, and a tremendous infestation of locusts. It was impossible to borrow money for operating expenses against the collateral of the harvest, and the board flatly refused another cent for a bail-out.

At this juncture Tanne turned to Denys for financial help. He agreed to "do something," but only as a stopgap until the harvest could be brought in. His solicitors wrote to her at Rungstedlund in a severe and even rather impertinent tone, to make clear that she understood both the munificence and the limitations of Mr. Finch Hatton's offer. Karen Coffee, they added, must be responsible for their legal fees. "Mr. Finch Hatton would not thank me for having put him to expense which turned out useless as far as he was concerned. . . . I would further mention that Mr. Finch Hatton himself would not be prepared to bind himself to lend the money beyond the extended date, because he cannot keep his money lying idle for any indefinite period, and it is therefore very important to him that the business should be carried out at the earliest date possible."[2]

Denys had also returned to Europe for the summer. He took flying lessons, passed his pilot's licence and "rushed around inspecting various flying machines."[3] At the beginning of October, Tania accepted his invitation to visit England and meet his brother. His parents were both dead, Toby was now Lord Winchilsea, their childhood home had been sold and the family lived at Buckfield House, Sherfield, which was near Basingstoke. Denys and Tania arrived on October 3.

Karen Blixen writes about a visit to the Winchilseas in *Shadows on the Grass,* setting it a little later in the thirties and saying very little, except that her hostess was "very lovely." The week she spent there was, in fact, somewhat strained. Tania "put herself out to be charming" but did not totally succeed. Errol Trzebinski speculates that Toby, who adored his younger brother and was possessive of him, may have felt a particularly intense jealousy toward Tania. Perhaps she was a symbol of the exotic attractions that had lured Denys away from England, or perhaps he resented their obvious complicity. One elderly relation remarked of the Baroness, "I don't like that woman. She is trying to take possession of Denys. It won't work."[4] In his diary Lord Winchilsea referred to Tania simply as "Blixen," a discourtesy which, even though private, was "unlike him."

Denys, however, was oblivious to what people thought about him and probably also to their animosity toward his mistress. He took Tania to see his childhood home while they were in the country. Haverholme was a gloomy mansion built on the ruins of an old priory in the midst of a marshy flatland. In the twelfth century there had been a great flood there, recorded by the monks and part of local lore. Errol Trzebinski believes that Denys told Tania about it and that it may have inspired the setting for "Deluge at Norderney."

He had promised the family to remain in England until late November, and Toby even offered to pay the airfare if that would persuade him to stay longer. But he changed his plans abruptly and sailed for Africa on October 28, the day before Black Tuesday in America. Tania spent Christmas in Denmark, leaving for Africa, as had become her custom, on Christmas morning. "None of us," wrote Thomas, "tried to stop her; we understood each other so well, even if Tanne still appeared to hope and perhaps was also able to work up her faith in her mind. We knew that she could not, unless it was absolutely necessary, and without a soul-shaking farewell, leave her beloved home, Farah, and the other people who were so close to her, and perhaps, for always, Denys."[5]

On the boat Tanne's ancient anglophobia was aroused by the usual glib talk about the natives. But throughout the journey she was really thinking of one thing only: the harvest which was taking place. "I was weighing the problem in my mind," she wrote in *Out of Africa.* "When I was well and life was looking friendly, I reckoned that we would have got seventy-five [tons] but when I was unwell or nervous, I thought: we are bound to get sixty tons in any case." Sixty tons at contemporary prices would have meant about four thousand pounds.

Farah was waiting at Mombasa. So was Lady Colville, who put Tania up at her hotel for the night. At first she could not bring herself to ask Farah about the harvest, and they spoke of other things: his *shauries* with Dickens, the collection of the hut tax, the recovery of a mad boy named Kairobi. But when she could not postpone the question any longer, Farah "half closed his eyes and laid back his head, swallowing his sorrow, when he said: 'Forty tons, Memsahib.' At that I knew that we could not carry on."*

2

From the time she returned to the farm at the beginning of 1930, Karen Blixen's letters to her family were few and sparse, and her voice cool, as if to ward off the feverish misery of the truth. She still spoke of her life's "uncertainty," although this had become a euphemism, for there was no uncertainty about the farm.

The usual agenda of *shauries* awaited her. A great *ngoma* was held the week she arrived, at which a man was murdered. This brought the police upon them, threatening to stop *ngomas* permanently. It also aroused the ire of Mr. and Mrs. Dickens, who considered the dances "heathen savagery." Mr. Dickens even murmured about quitting. Farah, in the meantime, was embroiled in a tribal dispute with Hassan, the former cook, who was now trying to kill him. And Denys had once again invited Bror to be his second on the Prince of Wales's next safari, which began that February.

This time Cockie and Bror stayed at Government House, and Tania was excluded, by the rigors of protocol, from all the official celebrations. Denys tried to console her by bringing the Prince out to dine at the farm, but this only emphasized her social quarantine. She felt abandoned and rejected and blamed Denys openly. To her mother she confessed that she had "made him a scene of the first water"—and had laughed at herself afterward. But she could no longer take "anything concerning him really seriously," and compared to her love for the Africans, Denys "carrie[d] no weight."[6] When she next wrote of her lover it was without rancor. But her description of him —one of the finest passages in her letters—has all the calm detachment, the leisurely precision, the almost sublimely negligent objectivity of *Out of Africa:*

> It suits Denys so well to fly. I have always felt that he had so much of the air's element in him . . . and was a kind of Ariel. But there is always a good measure of heartlessness in such a temperament . . . and Ariel was also in fact rather heartless, as you shall see if you reread *The Tempest,* but so pure, compared to the earthly beings on the island, clear, honest, without reserve, transparent— like the air, in brief. I also believe that what I loved most in Denys from the beginning was this: that he moved, spiritually, in three dimensions.[7]

---

*Isak Dinesen, *Out of Africa,* p. 324. By contrast, a good harvest for that era, without modern scientific farming aids, would have been half a ton per acre, or three hundred tons for Karen Coffee's six hundred acres. They were operating on an extremely marginal basis.

The Prince's visit renewed Tanne's animosity toward the English, a feeling that generally coincides with her own sense of estrangement. She writes continually about their mediocrity and lack of feeling, and of their wanton exploitation of the native world. She hated to see the colony develop and a "new class" of settler fill up the highlands. These were the bureaucrats and shopkeepers who drove out into the hills on Sundays to shoot the game from their cars, who despised the Somalis for their insolence and their pride, and who were buying the land around Nairobi to build bungalows with little gardens. Tania and Denys called them the "enemy," and it was her fear that the farm would, after she left, fall into "their" clutches. Denys promised that he would do what he could to prevent this, and as another stopgap measure he loaned her four hundred pounds to pay the salaries of her workers, accepting her silver and furniture as collateral.[8] That spring, while he flew back to England with the Prince, she made an inventory of the pieces.

Karen Blixen still did not believe that her farm was lost, although every letter from Denmark confirmed it. She drew up her bridges, buried herself in the day-to-day running of the farm, and lived almost exclusively, as she had at the beginning, among the Africans. Her fate, she repeated, was bound to theirs, and their welfare was her central passion. On Sundays she set her gramophone on the porch and played music for the *totos*. She carried Farah's little daughter around like her papoose, and when she began having bad nightmares that winter, she took little Saufe, then a year old, to bed with her like a doll. There was something of a lonely child playing with a doll in all her relations with the Africans: the extreme tenderness, the maternal solicitude, the sense of power and responsibility that distracted her from her own feelings of helplessness and despair.

That May, Denys wrote to Tania from England, where he was playing a great deal of golf and investigating planes that might be able to land on her lawn, the Ngong side of the house. He gave an amusing picture of "Depression" life among the leisure classes. "Everyone says they are more broke than ever this year but there seems to be just as much money being spent on inane amusements as ever . . . Rolls Royces, new fashions, extravagant parties, and everyone who has money placing it abroad in concealed concerns to avoid income tax. . . . No rats abandoning the sinking ship. The trouble is that the land, which cannot escape, is taxed to death and English agriculture is at its last gasp. Australia is bankrupt, Germany full of unemployed, America run by gangs of gunmen; France seems to be the one country which is doing well. . . . I hope," he concluded, "that you have paid a visit to my coast property. I feel it would do you a lot of good to get away from Ngong for a little. I have no news of you and am wondering how the Dickens affair has worked out. Send me a line sometime. . . ."[9]

She did not, apparently, accept his offer of Takaungu. Her health was frail, and she was constantly losing weight. Mohr was extremely concerned about her, and strangers who met her in this period found her withdrawn and *kali*. This Swahili word has a very broad range of feeling and is usually applied to wild animals, especially cats, to describe their ferocity and caprice. One young man who quarreled with Karen Blixen over his rights to shoot buffalo on part of her land was rebuked in a "very official and high-handed manner."[10] Beryl Markham came out from time to time to ride with Tania in the hills and described her as skittish and unpredictable.

Her increasing thinness and nervousness gave her a somewhat frightening aspect to the very young; one settler, then a child, thought she was a witch. There is a photograph of her from this time, fishing from some rocks, her face shadowed by a large hat, looking very much as she would in twenty years. And there is another photograph, standing with two Africans in the forest, wearing pantaloons and a smock, of which Clara Svendsen writes: "While early pictures show a well-fed European, compared to the lean Africans, at this stage illness and worry had brought about a noticeable assimilation."[11]

Denys returned in September with his new plane, a Gypsy Moth, which was painted bright yellow and named Nzige—the Swahili word for locust. (Nzige Road in Karen was named after the plane and runs along the old site of its landing strip.) For their first trip together they flew over the Ngong hills, sometimes very low, so that they could stampede the herds of zebra and impala on the hilltops. They skimmed the native *shambas,* the coffee fields and the house, and the next morning a delegation of old Kikuyus came to "interview" the Baroness on her experience. Had she seen God? No, she replied. "Then you were not up high enough," said one old man.

Sometimes they went up for fifteen minutes, so that when they came home the teapot on the millstone table was still hot. Sometimes they flew over Lake Natron or to Naivasha, or as far as Takaungu to spend a weekend there. Denys told Tania he had bought the plane solely to show her Africa from the air, and she in turn called it her "most transporting pleasure. . . . There, where there are few or no roads and where you can land on the plains, flying becomes a thing of real and vital importance in your life, it opens up a world. . . . In the air you are taken into the full freedom of the three dimensions, after long ages of exile and dreams the homesick heart throws itself into the arms of space. . . . Every time that I have gone up in an aeroplane and looking down have realized that I was free of the ground, I have had the consciousness of a great and new discovery. 'I see,' I have thought. 'This was the idea. And now I understand everything.' "[12]

The view from *Out of Africa* is itself the farm and her life there seen from the air, at such a distance that even the disasters have the beauty of a pattern. That sweep of vision which a plane flying over open country vouchsafes is the most privileged of vantage points: nothing can hide. This is the superior perspective of the artist and the aristocrat in the tales of Isak Dinesen. They are the observers of the life below them, although they in turn are smiled upon by the gods, still higher up than they are.

The experience of flying also helped Karen Blixen "make terms with fate." "Till then," she wrote, "I had been part of [the landscape], and the drought had been to me like a fever, and the flowering of the plain like a new frock. Now the country disengaged itself from me and stood back a little, in order that I should see it clearly as a whole."[13]

Not long after her first flight, the farm was sold.

32

Closing the Parentheses

*What you need now to round off all these sad details of fourteen years, is one
great and deadly defeat, brought on by no fault of your own. That is going to
make a unity of the disintegrating elements.*
—Pipistrello to Lord Byron[1]

I

THAT NOVEMBER, Denys left on a safari with Marshall Field, the American
millionaire, and his wife. Tania was still trying desperately to negotiate
a settlement that would keep her in Africa. At the last minute she made
another appeal to Denys; her letter reached him at a bush camp, and his reply
went back by runner. He agreed to some more short-term help but tried to
clarify the exact nature of it and to dispel any notion that he could save the
farm:

> . . . I should not be *buying the farm,* merely a first mortgage. If I wanted to
> buy the house and grounds, I should have to come in for it at the sale as would
> any other buyer. . . . I have not the necessary sum available to buy the mortgage.
> But I am prepared to buy the first mortgage for two thousand on behalf of
> Kiptigit, as I cannot see that K. will stand to lose anything when the sale comes.
> . . . But I am unwilling to put up the further five hundred for manning the
> place another three months. Surely the company can do that in their own
> interests. . . . I am sorry.
>   I cannot do more to help. I have not the money myself. . . . I am sorry to
> hear you are so seedy. . . . I will do anything I can to prevent your house and
> grounds going to the enemy. You are having a bad time poor thing, I wish
> I could help more. Denys.[2]

The auction took place that December. The interest on the mortgage had
not been paid for two years, and the stockholders lost more than 150,000
pounds. The buyer was a young Nairobi real estate developer named Remy
Martin. He intended to turn the farm into a suburb of expensive homes with

a large golf and country club as its main attraction, and he planned to call both the district and the club "Karen" in Karen Blixen's honor. He also made the Baroness what he believed was a chivalrous and handsome offer. She could remain in her house indefinitely while the land was sold for building plots. "I would," she replied with a disdainful smile, "prefer to live in the middle of the Sahara desert, than on twenty acres in the suburb of 'Karen.' "[3]

The final harvest belonged to the company, and as the berries would not be ripe until May, Karen Blixen was to remain on the farm and run it for the next five months. "And during this time, I thought, something would happen to change it all back, since the world, after all, was not a regular or calculable place."[4]

Kinanjui, the chief of the Kikuyus whose friendship Karen Blixen had won early in her life in Africa, died during these five months. In *Out of Africa* she makes her own part in this event—her own cowardice toward the dying chief's last request of her—the symbol both of a loss of power and of a death of her own. It stood for the end of that resistance which had given her the momentum to survive the failure of her crops, the struggles with the shareholders and with the bank, the skepticism of her family, and all the vicissitudes of her emotional life. But now, she wrote, "I had not got it in me any longer to stand up against the authorities of the world. I did not have it in me now to brave them all, not all of them."[5]

Kinanjui simply asked her to let him die on her farm instead of at the mission hospital, which he dreaded. She gave it some thought, visited him in his *manyatta,* sat by his bed in the rancid, suffocating, deathly air—and decided finally that she would have to turn him down. Making no excuse, as there was none, she told him no and left.

It is nowhere clearer than in the last chapters of *Out of Africa* that Denys Finch Hatton's detachment was absolute. He was to Tania as she was to Kinanjui. When he was not out with clients or attending to the business of his companies, he took her flying, and once or twice they spoke as if her departure were serious and imminent. He grieved over the loss, although he laughed at her distress at abandoning the Africans. But he would make no exception to the rule he had long ago established in their relationship:

> You must turn your mournful ditty
> To a merry measure
> I will never come for pity
> I will come for pleasure.[6]

In March she began her negotiations with the government on behalf of the squatters. Her goal was to see them settled on a single piece of land with all their stock. No one believed she could possibly succeed, and at first the government denied that such a tract existed.

In the meantime she made her will, leaving presents to each of her servants and providing, as best she could, for their future. Farah had his *dukka* at Ngong, which he was to keep. For Juma she found land on the Masai Reserve. His father was Somali but his mother was a Masai, and Tanne had had the foresight to register him as such. She also promised to help him build a house there. Juma, full of great dreams, laid foundations for a strange and monstrous palace, sixty-five feet square, which could not possibly be roofed in the traditional way—either thatch or tin. When Tanne saw it she sat down and wept.

Ali wanted to become a chauffeur, and Tanne gave him lessons in her own car. Before she left he passed his license, so his livelihood was more or less assured. Kamante's fate was a somewhat touchier matter. He was a genius in the kitchen and he had made some sharp deals trading cattle, but he was also a little mad, and Tanne was not certain he would be hired by another European. But he did find another job and worked for settlers until the war, when he retired to the Kikuyu Reserve. During the early 1950s he took the Mau Mau oath and was briefly sent to prison. The American photographer Peter Beard, who lives in Kenya, sought him out, and he now shares Mr. Beard's camp in Karen. Kamante has become a majestic old patriarch who walks with a cane, wears Scottish sweaters against the damp and still knows how to cook. He can tell a story with great glances and epic pauses, and he is still a figure "half of fun and half of diabolism,"[7] filled with mocking laughter. Sometimes I had the feeling he was really impersonating himself for me—playing the outcast, the *destiné,* the jester, the muse, and servant of a great artist.

In April, Karen Blixen began the work of dismembering her house. She had decided to sell most of her furniture and china, which was laid out on the dining table for viewing. It was, said Remy Martin, "the thing" in Nairobi at the time to drive out to the farm and buy something, or at least to look. People came at strange hours to finger her possessions and to haggle. Lady Macmillan bought most of the furniture for the Macmillan Library, where a few pieces are still gathering dust. But Karen Blixen finally decided to keep her books, her silver, and her table glass: "The fingers and lips of many friends had touched it."[8] She also brought home the painted screen that had stood next to her fireplace.

The effort to settle the squatters took most of her patience and energy, and there was not much time to think of her own resettlement. She tried to preclude the obvious concern of her family that she might take some drastic action against herself, but no one trusted her bright disclaimers. Friends drove out to the farm, partly to help and partly to stand guard over her. Rose Cartwright came from Naivasha, Ingrid from Njoro, Mohr from Rongai; Hugh Martin used his influence at the Land Office, and the Griggs wielded theirs with the new administration. Denys came for a few days in April, but he was preparing for a new safari, and now that the furniture was in crates and the house in disorder he moved in with Hugh, in Nairobi. It was so convenient, he explained, to have a phone and to be near a dentist. But he asked if he might drive out later, "and let me know anytime you would like me to run out if you have anything to arrange in your own plans in which I could help. I have a book here I want you to read. I will bring it out. Best love. Denys."[9]

When he did visit her he found her in a strange, ominously exalted mood. She spoke of wanting to shoot her dogs and horses, and of her own desire to disappear along with them. She assured him that this was not despair, but an even richer and deeper appreciation for life's complexity and meaning. Denys was not taken in. "Dear Tania," he wrote the next day, "your talk disturbed me very much last night. Do not think that I do not see your point of view. I do absolutely. But I feel that just now you are looking at the very darkest side of things. I would like to see you before you go and shall try to get out later. I'm sending Kanuthia to collect a box of papers and a Jaeger dressing gown from the other farm. Denys."[10]

Both Mohr and Denys begged her to write to Thomas and ask his help in making a new life for herself in Europe—a year or two of subsidy for study or travel. "For their sake," she agreed. The letter was begun in the same spirit of noble resignation and was equally violent and disturbed beneath its surface. She repeated that she was not depressed and, in fact, had achieved that "overview" which had eluded her for so long. But she also repeated that she could never come home to Rungstedlund like the prodigal daughter after so much freedom and experience. She was also "no more good-natured than before, on the contrary . . . it is still true of me that death is preferable to bourgeois life, and in death I shall declare my faith in freedom."[11]

After delivering this not so subtle threat, Tanne went on to suggest how her death might be avoided. Thomas could agree to subsidize her while she learned a trade, as a chef, perhaps, or as a journalist. The subsidy could not be too modest, for she was, "as is well known, not cheap." She spoke of Italy and Paris, or else London, as places she might live and stressed that she would have to know the precise sum Thomas was prepared to spend. But she also spoke of a project that gave him some genuine hope on her behalf. She had "undertaken what we as a family always do when we don't know what else to do. I've begun to write a book." It was written in English, for practical reasons. But as she was afraid that she might not be a good judge of her own style in a foreign language, she had sent several chapters to a friend of Mohr's—Christopher Morley—who had been encouraging: "The leisurely style and language are exceedingly attractive." Now she wanted time to finish the book—"two years to educate myself. Everyone knows that I know nothing."[12]

2

While this letter was on its way to Denmark, Tania took her leave of Denys, who was going on a long safari. Before he left he wanted to fly down to Takaungu for a few days and put his house in order. She asked to come —a last trip—but he was afraid the homeward lap of the journey would be too strenuous for her, saying that he wanted to pass over Voi and scout for elephants and would be landing and sleeping in the bush. So he said good-bye.

This, at least, is the account Karen Blixen gives in *Out of Africa*. But there seems to have been a much sadder final scene between the two lovers. Their closest surviving friends told Errol Trzebinski, and later repeated to me, that at just about this time Tania and Denys quarreled violently and that, in fact, they broke with one another.* The explosion, they suggested, had been gathering for some time, and Denys had moved out of Ngong and in with Hugh Martin not because it was inconvenient to live among packing crates, but because he felt his freedom threatened by Tania's increasingly open possessiveness and despair.

These old friends either could not or did not wish to divulge the precise substance of the "row." Some hinted that Denys had begun seeing another and younger woman, and that Tania probably flew into a jealous rage. Others thought that she had "cracked" under the strain of losing the farm, had clung to him, had perhaps asked him outright to marry her or reproached him furiously with his disloyalty and indifference. It is easy to imagine what a tide of feelings overwhelmed Tania under the circumstances, and it is also easy to imagine how Denys responded. He had an almost morbid aversion to emotional demands.

According to Thomas Dinesen, Tanne's despair at this point was so great that she tried to kill herself. The attempt took place in the house of friends, and a suicide note was found among her papers, but subsequently misplaced,† in which she apologized to those friends. Mr. Dinesen told Frans Lasson that his sister had "wounded herself,"[13] apparently by slashing her wrists, although he could not remember when this took place. She lost a great deal of blood, he said, but staunched the flow before it was too late.

After Denys left the farm, he did not take off immediately for the coast but spent the next two days in Nairobi. During this period he invited two

---

*In *Out of Africa*, Karen Blixen mentions the fact that Denys asked for his gold Abyssinian ring back, the ring he brought her from Eritrea at Christmas in 1928. He was afraid, she claimed, that she intended to give the ring as a farewell present to her miller, Pooran Singh. Errol Trzebinski analyzes this gesture differently. It would be unlikely, she thinks, for Tania to give such a precious belonging to a servant, and unlike Denys to worry about it under any circumstances unless passionate feelings were involved.
†Viggo Kjær Petersen, the young Dane authorized by Karen Blixen in 1962 to write her biography, mentioned such a note to several people, including Ms. Trzebinski. But the note vanished from the Blixen archives.

other women to make the trip with him. The first invitation was apparently not very serious. He was dining with a married couple, both his good friends, and when the wife expressed curiosity about his house he offered to show it to her.

He next asked Beryl Markham to go along. She writes in her memoir that she had flown with Denys "often" before. . . . "He had taken up flying too recently to be an expert but the competency which he applied so casually to everything was as evident in the air as it was on one of his safaris, or in the recitations of Walt Whitman which he performed during his more sombre or perhaps lighter moments. He asked me to fly down to Voi with him and of course I said I would."[14]

Beryl was dissuaded at the last moment by Tom Black, director of the East Africa Airways. He had some kind of premonition about the flight, and she capitulated to it. Instead, Denys took off with his servant, Kamau. While landing at Xipingo, he clipped his wooden propeller and wired Nairobi for a replacement, which Black dispatched. He spent the evening of May 13 dining with old friends at Voi: the District Commissioner and his wife; a Mr. and Mrs. Layzell, sisal planters; and J. A. Hunter, who was setting out with his own safari early the next morning.

The Layzells lived near the airstrip, so Denys was to stay with them, and Margaret Layzell to drive him to the plane early the next morning. Her two daughters begged to come—they wanted to see the plane. At the last moment, with the propeller already revving, Denys invited Mrs. Layzell up for a little "spin," but her youngest child became hysterical and so she reluctantly declined.[15]

Hunter and his client, Lee Hudson, were getting into their trucks when Denys taxied and took off. Hunter was the first to see the "clouds of black smoke arising from the nearby aerodrome." He rushed to the scene, in time to see the plane burst into flames and three blackened oranges roll from the wreckage. It was impossible to get near, for the heat was intense. "Denys opened up the Masai with me," said Mr. Hunter. "He was fearless and fair, and it was fitting that his remains should be buried in the land in which he had taken such delight."[16]

News of the crash reached Nairobi before it reached Ngong. Still innocent, Tania drove into town to visit some officials on the business of her squatters, and to lunch, later on, with Lady Macmillan. People turned away from her in the streets, with expressions of "mortal sadness"; they barely returned her greetings. Old Mr. Duncan, her Scottish grocer, fled from his shop, apparently in fear, when she walked in. "I began to feel as lonely in Nairobi as on a desert island."[17]

It was Lady Macmillan who, after what must have been an excruciatingly strained luncheon party, took Tania into a little study and broke the news. "It was then as I had thought: at the sound of Denys's name, even, truth was revealed, and I knew and understood everything."[18] This phrase, "I understood everything," or, "I suddenly understood everything," occurs almost liturgically in the writing of Karen Blixen. It stands for the recognition of a great mystery about oneself, long buried and suddenly come upon again by surprise. It describes a moment when it is possible to see the obscure but decisive moments of joy or loss that are the scaffolding of identity.

Gustav Mohr drove immediately to the farm, and Ingrid came a few days later. As an old woman, Mrs. Lindström reflected on the irony of Denys's death, perhaps drawing on her conversations with Tanne from those days. If she had left him behind in Africa, she would have been the one to "die" and he the survivor—he had already withdrawn from her. But his death "gave him back to her again."[19] She could not have helped but feel, even in the midst of her grief, that "the Great Powers had laughed," that "they had said among the trumpets, among the cocks and Chameleons, Ha, ha!"[20]

Denys was buried in the Ngong hills, near the spot he and Tania had chosen for their graves, and in the succeeding weeks she was treated by everyone as his widow. Her friends did not try to console her, only to give her love. "Dear Tania," wrote Lady Northey, "with Denys's tragic death the great love of your life has gone and with it all your happiness. He was so all absorbing. The loss is quite irreparable. But my dear, do you realize your own great charm and the affection of your old friends? . . . I would that I could persuade you that life still holds much for you."[21]

Bror wrote from Tanganyika to express sympathy which was, as usual, tinged with ambivalence and injured pride:

Dearest Tanne. It is terrible for all of us with Denys's death but worse for you who always had such a great support in him. It was a great loss for Kenya . . . and a sorrow to all his friends. . . . When I got the news I thought I would fly to Nairobi to see if I could do something for you—but when one has no money one is so helpless. Can I do something for your boys or your dogs? I'm leaving today for a safari of six weeks. Your devoted Bror.[22]

3

The harvest was brought in. Tania gave her surviving deerhound, Dinah, to a friend at Gil-Gil. She found a home for Rouge, rode him into Nairobi for the last time and saw him loaded, with some resistance, into the horse van of the Naivasha train. The Africans came every day and sat outside the house, unwilling to believe that she was really leaving and waiting for news about their own land and fate. The old women, she speculated, would be the ones to miss her most.

She finished her census of the squatters, their cows and children, and handed it in triplicate to the district commissioner. She finished her negotiations in Nairobi, followed everywhere by Farah in his most splendid clothes. Many people believed that after Denys's death the new governor, Sir Joseph Byrne, took pity on her, for there was otherwise no way to explain her "feat" —securing a piece of territory in the Kikuyu Reserve where all two hundred families and all three thousand head of cattle could be accommodated. Mrs. Lindström compared this concession to Queen Victoria offering Mount Kilimanjaro to Kaiser Wilhelm.

Toward the end of July, a small party of settlers and Africans gathered at the Nairobi railroad station to see Karen Blixen off. Most of the Somalis were there, and Denys's servant, Bilea. Hugh Martin had come; Lord and Lady Delamere; Major Taylor, the coffee expert, and his wife. Mohr arrived early in the morning to drive her to the train, and at the last moment he shook her hand. "He wished so strongly to impart courage to me that he blushed deeply; his face was flaming and his light eyes shining at me."[23]

Farah and Tumbo were to travel as far as Mombasa with her. Tumbo had chosen this journey as his parting gift, instead of a heifer. A friend had arranged for Tania to spend her last night at Ali bin Salim's house, and for his launch to take her out to the ship the next morning. His guest pavilion was a little open-air *banda* where she could lie in bed and look straight up at the stars—Aldebaran, Sirius, the Southern Cross—with the sound of the wind in the palm trees, and of the sea below.

Book Three

ISAK DINESEN

Left: Isak Dinesen and her mother in 1935, at a party celebrating the Danish edition of *Seven Gothic Tales. Below left:* Isak Dinesen greeting a visitor at Rungstedlund, *c.* 1943. *Below right:* Isak Dinesen and her secretary, Clara Svendsen, in the late 1950s.

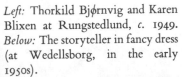

Left: Thorkild Bjørnvig and Karen Blixen at Rungstedlund, *c.* 1949. *Below:* The storyteller in fancy dress (at Wedellsborg, in the early 1950s).

. . . a certain love of greatness,
which could not be quelled, has kept
a hold on me, has been "my daimon."
—Isak Dinesen
Letters from Africa

33

Amor Fati

I

LIKE ALL THOSE SOULS who pay their obol to the boatman and are ferried to another shore, Karen Blixen was naturally a little loath to disembark. She leaned against the guardrail of the S.S. *Mantola,* an emaciated woman in a stylish hat, smoking a cigarette and letting the crowd thin out a little. Her brother Thomas was shocked when he caught sight of her from the quay, for she had lost thirty-five pounds, and she "seemed like a shadow of the woman I had once known."[1] That shadowiness was to be typical of Isak Dinesen.

A small indignity, but significant of much to her that morning, was the fact that when she disembarked her stockings were coming down—"hanging in eels," in the graphic Danish phrase. Thomas whisked her straight to a corsetière and bought her a new pair of garters. This simple transaction— which could have taken hours or days in Nairobi—miraculously cheered her up and made her optimistic about life in Europe. She told the story to Clara Svendsen many years later,[2] and it offers a glimpse of that delicate system of symbolic weights and counterweights that governed her moods.

Her terrible thinness and frailty that August were due, she believed, to a case of amoebic dysentery, which was a chronic problem for many of the settlers. Lady Grigg had urged Tania to go "straight to my Swiss clinic at Montreux" (The Clinique Valmont), which was "the only place they really *get rid of it.*"[3] Thomas had made an appointment for her there and had also taken rooms for them at a nearby hotel. They were able to make brief trips into the mountains, to discuss her prospects, and generally to decompress on what was, psychologically, an extremely painful ascent northward. It was at Montreux one evening that Tanne announced she would like to read her brother "a couple of the finished stories"[4] from her book, the book she mentions in her April letter from the farm. They were two of the *Seven Gothic Tales,* * and as he listened, Thomas "felt it growing in me. Now Tanne

---

*In all probability the two tales were "The Dreamers" and "The Old Chevalier." In *Out of Africa* she mentions working on "The Old Chevalier," and she told Thorkild Bjørnvig that "The Dreamers" was the first story she wrote after the loss of the farm. "It was like a scream, a lion's roar . . ." (Bjørnvig, *Pagten,* p. 35).

has come into the right course; now she has found her future; she will be admired and loved the world over; she will see 'the Stork.' "⁵

She herself probably wanted to see "art triumph over suffering," as Thomas put it, and "victory snatched from defeat,"⁶ for she had her own share of the Westenholz family's moral cheerfulness. But she was also more inclined to perceive what lay ahead of her as an afterlife rather than a future, and she approached "writing" in the same spirit she had proposed to run a hotel for "colored people" in Djibouti or Marseilles, or to become the matron of an insane asylum: in exile, among other exotic marginals, she looked forward to cutting a wise, inscrutable, and ruined figure.*

2

Karen Blixen's ruin was, in fact, complete, as she would shortly learn. She still had syphilis. It had not been cured in 1925, as her doctors had hoped, and it was probably causing some of the symptoms she thought were dysentery.⁷ It was also now completely beyond arrest or treatment, even by the most modern drugs.

Various critics, friends, and even relatives of Karen Blixen have supposed a relationship between her eccentricities and the disease, implying that to some degree because of it she must have been a little "mad." But the form of syphilis she suffered from does *not* generally lead to general paresis of the insane or to any cerebral symptoms. She had *tabes dorsalis:* syphilis of the spine.† For the rest of her life she would have difficulty in walking, unpredictable seizures of vomiting, an impaired sense of balance, crippling abdomi-

---

*When the Company had first threatened to sell the farm in the early twenties, Karen Blixen had compared her own fate to that of Robert Louis Stevenson's Prince Florizel of Bohemia, hero of the *New Arabian Nights,* a book that Sjögren had left behind at Mbogani House and which was one of her favorites. The prince loses his kingdom and ends his career of intrigue and adventure selling cigars in Piccadilly Circus—an enlightened and serene if not happy man. The moral of the tale, as she understood it, was that one might lose a kingdom, a leg, a child, an African farm, or any other essential and beloved part of oneself, and yet survive to find an unexpected satisfaction—or an even greater happiness than one had previously known. But one could also not "leap directly to that perception." (Karen Blixen, *Breve fra Africa: 1914–1931,* vol. 2, p. 64; Isak Dinesen, *Letters from Africa,* p. 277.)

†The phrase *tabes dorsalis* means dorsal wasting, and Dr. Mogens Fog has explained, in his essay on Karen Blixen's medical history, that the syphilitic degeneration of her spinal cord was localized in those nerves that controlled the stomach and bowels, accounting for her agonizing cramps, her gastric crises, her extreme thinness, and, at least in part, for her anorexia. (Patients with *tabes* typically are emaciated and find it difficult to gain weight, even when eating rich food. Karen Blixen, who loved being the "thinnest person in the world," had less incentive to eat properly, and her lack of interest in food seems to have aggravated the preexisting condition.)

Symptoms of *tabes* typically appear between the ages of thirty-five and fifty, which fits Karen Blixen's profile; she began to suffer the "lightning pains" associated with *tabes* in about 1921. Ataxia (unsteadiness of gait), generally occurs later in the disease, and for Karen Blixen this symptom became increasingly severe as she aged. An ashen pallor and extreme facial wrinkling—"the tabetic facies"—are also associated with this form of syphilis, as are perforating ulcers. While Karen Blixen developed ulcers, her doctors never associated them with syphilis, but rather with "mental overwork." The pains caused by the ulcers and by the syphilis were, Dr. Fog has written, almost impossible to tell apart.

nal pains and anorexia later complicated by ulcers. She often wore loose trousers so that she could lie on the floor and draw up her knees, which was the one position that brought her some relief. There would also be occasions when, despite her great physical bravery and her disdain for showing weakness, her agony was such that she would slip from the chair she sat in and lie on the floor, "howling like an animal."[8] It was not idly that she ranked the "cessation of pain" as one of life's three paramount joys.[9]

Many remedies were tried, without success. In the 1940s her doctors experimented with "fever treatments,"* which in some cases had been effective. In 1946 and in 1955 they performed operations to sever some of the pain tracks in the spinal cord, but even these drastic resorts brought incomplete relief. The pains and vomiting continued until the year before her death, when she could no longer walk or stand without assistance.

The disease was a capricious persecutor. In her late forties and early fifties, the bad days alternated with relatively long periods of good health and vigor, when she could visit her neighbors on an old bicycle and swim in the Sound before sitting down to write in the morning. But as she aged, it sapped her ability to work, to eat, to concentrate, even to sit upright, and she would dictate much of her later work to Clara Svendsen lying on the floor or confined to bed. This was a cruel irony to a woman who set such high—indeed, supreme—store in vitality; who, even in old age, still craved "experience" and had immodest standards for it. She wanted to make a pilgrimage to Mecca and to ride a motor scooter through the streets of Paris; to build a hospital for the Masai and visit the ruins of ancient Greece; to find Wilhelm's cabin in Wisconsin, and to attract, enchant, command, receive, and actively dispense her life's wisdom to a full court of admirers. She would also later have the audacity to pretend that she could fuel all this on a diet of oysters and champagne, that she needed nothing more than ambrosia. *Navigare necesse est vivere non necesse* was her motto, which literally came to mean that it was more important to keep going than to live. Unfortunately, it was not ambrosia but amphetamines that would give her the overdrive she required, and late in her life she took them recklessly, whenever strength was needed at an important moment.[10] From her doctors' point of view, or from that of any prudent person, she was running herself into the ground. But by then the conventional solicitude of the "self" toward the body had been undermined. Refusing food, denying her physical limitations, and taking pills to transcend them was, in fact, her ideal of *"savoir-mourir,"* a form of the "lion hunt," the risking of her "entirely worthless" life and the affirmation that *"frei lebt wer sterben kann."*

Her disease was, as she herself said, a "terrible thing."[11] But its reappear-

---

*The patient was closed inside a steam box and her body temperature raised to 40 degrees centigrade. But Karen Blixen became claustrophobic in this contraption, and the cure had to be abandoned.

ance, timed to coincide with her return to Denmark, was also propitious. I use the word uneasily, without any desire to mystify or exalt venereal disease, and only in an effort to assess the meanings Dinesen attached to it. Millions of unfortunates contracted syphilis, but among them were her father, Nietzsche, Baudelaire, the demonic heroes and fallen angels of Romanticism— many of the artists who, like the young Tanne Dinesen, aspired to be like Lucifer. She could accept it with a certain pride and as proof of the Devil's continuing solidarity with her, particularly as she now faced the prospect of going home, a chastened Alkmene, to the parsonage. "I promised the Devil my soul, and in return he promised me that everything I was going to experience hereafter would be turned into tales,"[12] she told her friend Bjørnvig, albeit with the privilege of hindsight. She also could have affirmed with Nietzsche, her fellow sufferer, that:

> As my inmost nature teaches me, whatever is necessary, as seen from the heights and in the sense of a *great* economy—is also the useful *par excellence:* one should not only bear it, one should *love* it. *Amor fati:* that is my inmost nature. And as for my long sickness, do I not owe it indescribably more than I owe to my health?[13]

3

Karen Blixen was not, upon her return to Rungstedlund, spared the obvious comparisons to the prodigal daughter. Certain members of the family, who had always thought her willful and proud, actually gloated. The crates with her possessions from Africa arrived after her and, except for a few special mementos, were stored away, unopened for thirteen years. Winter came and darkness fell at three. The wind that blew from the Sound rattled through the old, uncentrally heated house, but Tanne left the doors open behind her, letting the warmth go out. When her mother reproached her she retorted that "of course" she left the doors open; in Africa she had always had her *boys* to close them after her.[14] She complained that Ingeborg begrudged her the money to buy cigarettes, that she did not realize her child was no longer seventeen and that this illusion was shared even by the chauffeur, Alfred Pedersen, who wouldn't let her drive. At forty-six she was reliving her adolescence, with all its petulence and defiance, and fighting a second battle with her family for the ground she had won in Africa: the recognition that she was other, unique, a *destineé* misplaced among them.

In *Shadows on the Grass,* Isak Dinesen wrote that she had trouble "seeing anything at all as reality" during her first months at home. It was a confusion of the senses like that which a bad shock or a stroke brings to an organism's habits of feeling. Even when she was at home for visits, in the 1920s, she had counted upon the light and air of Africa, its tempo, grandeur and eventful-ness. "The landscapes, the beasts and the human beings of that existence could not possibly mean more to my surroundings in Denmark than did the landscapes, beasts and human beings of my dreams at night."[15] There was no one at home who could gauge her loss.

Denys was not dead yet a year, other African friends were dead or were about to die,* and she later felt not a little jealousy for them, "nine thousand feet up, safe in the mould of Africa," while she was "listening to the waves of the Øresund [the Sound]."[16] The numbed, bewildered figure of Barabbas in "Deluge at Norderney" may well be her own at Rungstedlund in those first few months. He comes to see the Apostle Peter a day after the Crucifixion, asking for counsel in his dilemma: his life has lost its savor; he cannot taste or feel anything at all since the death of the friend with whom he has shared all his exploits. The friend, also a thief of Jerusalem, was crucified with Jesus, while he, Barabbas, was spared—only to discover that sometimes survival is an anticlimax. He is even afraid now that the marvelous wine of the tetrarch, which he and his friend had stolen together and buried, and for which they were both condemned, will have no taste when he digs it up. Peter is sympathetic and polite, but uncomprehending. He is too ascetic by nature and too distracted by his own ambition for martyrdom to grasp what it means for a man to take no pleasure in drink or in sex. Receiving no advice from the saint, the thief eventually counsels himself that he had "better go and dig up that wine . . . and sleep with this girl. . . . I may as well try."[17]

Karen Blixen began to organize her work life. Ingeborg gave her Wilhelm's old office on the ground floor, and the paneled attic room Thomas had used as a study. She also subordinated the entire household to her daughter's need for absolute silence and privacy, a need Tanne seems to have exploited; she begrudged her mother the visits of her friends and grandchildren, and few visitors were entertained at Rungstedlund. She was described as having been bad-tempered, selfish, hypersensitive to intrusion during this time.[18] But some of it was an effort to dramatize the urgency and seriousness of her work, to resist the family's well-meaning attempts to repossess her, and to assert what had been a uniquely masculine privilege in that household: asociability, exemption from the duty to be emotionally accountable at all times to others. If "Isak" Dinesen took a man's name, it was at least partly to get a man's freedom. But she was also always ambivalent about this sexual crossing-over, as she perceived it. Twenty years later, in a speech to a feminist congress, she spoke of woman's business as "charm" and confessed that if she were a man, "it would be out of the question for me to fall in love with a woman writer."[19]

---

*Erik Otter of blackwater fever in 1923; Berkeley Cole and Sir Northrup Macmillan of heart disease in 1925; Lord Delamere and Hugh Martin in 1931; Gustav Mohr in a ferry accident in 1936; "Uncle Charles" Bulpett in 1939.

4

As a young woman starting out in life, Tanne Dinesen had been caught in a typically Romantic predicament. She was estranged from the values and milieu of her family; her inner life was at odds with her reality, and she felt cheated of that intensity which comes when one's desire and experience are not in conflict. Her struggle for a passionate life between the ages of ten and seventeen—a struggle to "become herself"—bears a close resemblance to the struggle of a whole generation of poets and artists who had grown up at the close of the eighteenth century, entered adolescence with Napoleon, believed his promises and in his example, and were left stranded in the 1820s feeling rootless, powerless, and betrayed. They took refuge from their disappointment in nostalgia for the past, in dreams of adventure and rebellion, in eccentricity and fantastic stories, in opium, in the cult of the personality or in the forests of America, and they created what Georg Brandes called an émigré literature. Some of them were actually émigrés from the *ancien régime,* and some were spiritual émigrés from their own disillusionment.

Their sense that society did not offer adequate scope for their desire and potential—for their humanity—split them and their work, and set the pattern for an entire century. Each successive generation of artists, from Lamartine to Ibsen, took a course it believed was necessary or virtuous or noble or inevitable, and also lamented: the sacrifice of "life" for "art." Tanne Dinesen toyed with this sacrifice but then sidestepped the issue altogether when she married a nobleman and embarked for a Paradise Lost, having first made practical inquiries as to its whereabouts. This was a voyage back—if not in time, in feeling—to a place where the conditions of life were "that of the eighteenth century at home," where "God and the Devil were one" and where the puritanical strictures of her childhood did not paralyze her. Now, however, the original predicament was revived—and much more dramatically than before—not only in relation to her family, but in relation to the Denmark of her youth, the class in which she had sought refuge, and the material conditions that had supported that class and its way of life and that, in 1931, were as remote as Ngong and as definitively lost. "The World of the Name" no longer existed in Denmark as she had known it. The great *battus,* the balls, the immense staffs of servants and the "unlimited hospitality" of the old castles were all finished. The aristocracy—which, as Karen Blixen understood it, depended not upon its own members for survival but upon a network of "slaves"—had declined. In the eighteen years she had spent in Africa, it had lost its land to taxes and to the new laws against the entailment of estates; its servants to the factories and the cities; and, most significantly, it had lost its political power to the rising lower and middle classes, which had been organizing since 1871 and which had finally succeeded, long after actually achieving a majority in Parliament, in forcing the king to appoint a prime minister from the Venstre Party. In 1915, while she was camping on the Masai Reserve, the old constitution was reformed, and the franchise given to women and servants. In 1919, while she was out on her first safari with Denys, the entailment law was passed. In the twenties class struggle intensified, and the Social Democrats emerged as the ruling party.

"Some of my friends are so fearful of the very word 'socialist,' " Karen Blixen told Hudson Strode in 1939. "To me, being socialist is hardly more than fulfilling one's responsibility to his fellow man."[20] But she also did not conceal her dislike for democracy. It was not so much that the common people were unworthy to rule but that the system encouraged mediocrity, "blurred distinctions," renounced "all ideals that are higher than those that can be reached,"[21] and diminished the richenss of experience that came, in her view, from a stratified society.* The *embourgeoisement* of the working class dismayed her—it was losing touch with its peasant and artisan roots—but so did that of the aristocracy, which was getting jobs and learning how to cook. "How depressing it is," she once remarked, "to go and have tea with an old lady who has no maid to make it for her."[22]

There is a good deal of irony in this position, and some perverseness, and unlike many of her admirers Karen Blixen was not naive about her own absurd position as the self-appointed representative of the age and class that had declined. She saw lucidly, and was able to translate into other historical eras, the tension between the aristocratic idealism of her own world view and the materialism that had triumphed over it, and this became the subject of her writing. The romantic heroes and heroines of *Seven Gothic Tales*—eighteenth-century figures adrift in the nineteenth—are fragile anachronisms like Karen Blixen herself, returning to the Denmark of the 1930s from a country whose political system was, practically speaking, feudalism. "The Old Chevalier," Baron von Brackel, is their epitome. Despite his travels, culture, and sensibility, "he had shown very little skill in managing his own affairs . . ." and, "Probably from a sense of failure in this respect he carefully kept from discussing practical matters with an efficient younger generation, keen on their careers and success in life. But on theology, the opera, moral right and wrong, and other unprofitable pursuits, he was a pleasant talker."[23]

That is both a brilliant self-parody and a self-appreciation of the author's own predicament in 1931, and its irony comes from the mixture of mockery and deep feeling. In this respect it evokes another author's ambivalence

---

*Karen Blixen's political philosophy comes very close, I think, to Thomas Mann's formulation in *Dr. Faustus* (p. 39): "Precisely because from the very first medieval man had received a closed intellectual frame from the Church as something absolute and taken for granted, he had been far more imaginative than the burgher of the individualistic age; he had been able to surrender himself far more freely and sure-footedly to his personal fantasy."

toward an old chevalier: Cervantes for Don Quixote:* Quixote, like Karen Blixen, cuts an absurd figure in an age of subjective materialism. But, as Arnold Hauser points out, he is at the same time a noble, even an heroic holdout—a figure whose very existence is a "critique of the disenchanted and matter-of-fact reality which has triumphed, and in which there is nothing left for an idealist to do but dig himself in behind his *idée fixe.*"[24] It was Karen Blixen's project to create such an example both in her tales and in her own persona.

This historical background would not perhaps have meant so much to her, or have penetrated so deeply, if it had not also contained an analogy to something extremely personal. That conflict of values between the old regime and the new one was the trauma of her own childhood. The little princess who had felt herself unique was forced, after her father's death, to wake from the dream, return to her family as an equal, accept a reality in which her own worth was not absolute but was relative to others' and in which "experience had fallen"—irredeemably—"in value."[25]

---

*Another of Karen Blixen's alter egos, Pellegrina Leoni of "The Dreamers," is called "Donna Quixotta." She also called her secretary, Clara Svendsen, "my Sancho Panza."

34

Seven Gothic Tales

*Reality had met me, such a short time ago, in such an ugly shape, that I have
no wish to come into contact with it again. Somewhere in me a dark fear was
still crouching and I took refuge within the fantastic like a distressed child in
his book of fairy tales. I did not want to look ahead, and not at all to look back.*
— Isak Dinesen[1]

I

K AREN BLIXEN turned for the original material of *Seven Gothic Tales* to
stories she had been outlining, sketching, and abandoning periodically for
a decade. In one of her black notebooks from the twenties she listed the titles
for a proposed volume of "Nine Tales," also called "Tales of Nozdrev's
Chef,"* which were: "The Dreamer," "Nocturne," "Carnival," "The Monkey," "Glass," "The Roads Around Pisa," "The Caryatids," "Supper at
Elsinore" and "The Poet." Five of these were developed for her first book,
two were saved for a later volume, one—"Glass"—was dropped and "Nocturne" became "The Old Chevalier." It is possible to see, from the passages
of dialogue and description, how she refined her style, building up the texture
of the tales draft by draft, layer by layer, recopying a page to change perhaps
one word. Her ideal of the finished work was like that of the tailoring that
produced the costume of Zamor, Madame de Pompadour's Negro page,
"made, a hundred and fifty years ago, regardless of cost"[2] and which the old
painter, ogling its rose-diamond buttons, judges to be "beyond reproach."
Reproach for Isak Dinesen meant Berkeley Cole's sadness to discover she had
packed her ordinary wineglasses in the picnic basket rather than her finest
Baccarat. It was an admission of fatigue, of concern for loss or of bourgeois
frugality in regard to expense or sacrifice, and it was the same ideal she
brought to her entertaining and her conversation. The pride of craftsmanship
behind the tales connects them and their author to the court poets and artists

---

*Nozdrev or Nozdref is a character in Gogol's *Dead Souls*.

of another era, who were themselves spiritually still artisans—those "perfect artisans" whom Benjamin calls "the incarnation of the devout."[3]

Unfortunately, there are no complete drafts in the notebooks, and so it is not possible to see how Dinesen evolved her form. In later years she described her method as a process of slow accretion. A tale might begin with the image of a place, a house, a landscape, and then she might begin to dream about its inhabitants.[4] Or it might begin with a "real, lived event. But that is only the grain of dust around which the pearl grows. It's not important, one doesn't finally even see it."[5] She would carry the tale around with her for a long time, sometimes for years, telling and retelling it to herself, and it was invariably complete by the time she sat down to write. It was also by then as familiar as a memory. "Storytelling," Benjamin reminds us, ". . . sinks the thing into the life of the storyteller, in order to bring it out of him again. Thus traces of the storyteller cling to the story the way handprints of the potter cling to the clay vessel."[6]

The "Gothic" of the title refers, Dinesen would explain, to the imitation of the Gothic, the Romantic Age of Byron,* and she defined her period as basically that which began with Ewald's death in 1781 and ended with the Second Empire in 1871, the "last great phase of aristocratic culture." When she was asked, in 1934, why she had chosen to set her tales a hundred years in the past, she replied simply: "Because . . . only in that way did I become perfectly free."[7] At the end of her life she would explain the formal aspect of that freedom: "With the past I find myself before a finished world, complete in all its elements, and I can thus more easily recompound it in my imagination. Here, no temptation for me to fall back into realism, nor for my readers to look for it."[8] But it was also freedom from the self-consciousness or the social consciousness of the modern writer. The voice which narrates *Seven Gothic Tales* is a generation older than the characters themselves. It is the voice of the writer of the classical age, speaking to his aristocratic audience. His wish is to entertain them—to stir their blood, perhaps, or to make them tremble in their beds, or to feed them sweets from the *bonbonnière* of his imagination—but all the while to carry on a lofty and leisurely discourse with them about Life. These are the "only two courses of thought which Mira Jama [in "The Dreamers"] deems at all seemly to a person of any intelligence. The one is: what am I to do this next moment? . . . And the other: what did God mean by creating the world, the sea, and the desert, the horse, the winds, romance, amber, fishes, wine?" Could not Mira Jama make "a terrible tale about poverty and unpopularity? 'No,' said

---

*"I am much closer to the English Gothic than the German Romantic," she told Bent Mohn in a letter of January 26, 1948, "even though there are works [of the latter school] which have meant much to me." These included Hoffmann and Chamisso (from the archives of Mr. Mohn).

the storyteller proudly, 'that is not the sort of story which Mira Jama tells.' "[9]
Dinesen herself was frequently accosted with the same order of question. "I
am periodically accused of being 'decadent' " she told Daniel Gillès the
summer before she died. "That is no doubt true, as I am not interested in
social questions, nor in Freudian psychology. But the narrator of the *Thousand and One Nights* also neglected social questions, and it is also no doubt
for that reason that today the Arabs still gather in their public squares to hear
her stories. As for me I have one ambition only: to invent stories, very
beautiful stories."[10]

There is an interesting refrain of modesty or reticence in Isak Dinesen's
public declarations about her art. She disclaimed that very complex erudition,
the understanding of her own literary history and tradition, which both
Robert Langbaum and Aage Henrikson have established for her. She liked
to remind interviewers how erratically she was educated, and if someone
mentioned Kierkegaard or the *bildungsroman* or Existentialism, she denied
any careful study of the subject. She would admit to being a passionate reader
and gave lists of the books she loved to reread,* but they generally omitted
anything that could tie her to a school, set her within a category, associate
her with a predecessor†—except, perhaps, Scheherazade. She spoke of herself
as belonging to the oral tradition and of her tales as having an almost physical
or instinctual source, like the dance. Perhaps this was just good aristocratic
manners, for intellectuality was not something one made much of in the
Frijsenborg set. Perhaps it was a respect for the "magic," the incantatory
aspect of storytelling, and the virtuoso's considerate desire to make her skill
look easy. Perhaps too, it was her old unwillingness to resemble anyone.

2

One hallmark of the tale, which sets it apart from the realistic forms of
fiction, is the absence of gratuitous detail, of *"petits faits vrais,"* of atmosphere

---

*Shakespeare, Turgenev, Stendhal—who was also a favorite of her father—Barbey d'Aurevilly, Thomas
Mann (in particular the Joseph novels), Conrad, Hans Christian Andersen, Voltaire, Chekhov, Katherine
Mansfield, Giraudoux, Aldous Huxley, Hemingway. A list of poets would have included Heine, Shelley,
Wergeland, Oehlenschläger, Baudelaire, Sophus Claussen, and Nietzsche, whom, she told Robert
Langbaum, she considered more a poet than a philosopher.
†She never mentioned certain works that, earlier in life, she had claimed as her "inspirations." She certainly
knew Brandes's *Main Currents in Nineteenth Century Literature,* which gives a splendid overview of
Romanticism and a great deal of social as well as literary history. She also told her mother, in an African
letter, that James Branch Cabell was someone from whom she had taken many of her ideas "on life and
death and art, etc." It was his approach to the past, his discontent with "things as they are," which most
appealed to her and made her hope that "perhaps a new trend in literature is ready to arise, founded
upon fantasy." (Karen Blixen, *Breve fra Africa: 1914–1931,* vol. 1, p. 209; Isak Dinesen, *Letters from Africa,*
p. 164.) And while she spoke to Bjørnvig about her childhood love of Zarathustra and in response to
Langbaum's question expressed her great admiration for Nietzsche, she never refers to the obviously
important influence he had on her philosophy.

and psychologizing. The truth of tales—or myths or dreams—is arrived at by a different process, and to that process Isak Dinesen gave the name Nemesis. "Nemesis," she told the critic Johannes Rosendahl, "is the thread in the course of events which is determined by the psychic assumptions of a person. All my tales treat Nemesis."[11] The thread, one might say, is desire, and the needle that draws it is necessity, and thus does a tale—or a myth or a dream—get its many folds.

Nemesis is an idea any observant person with a sense of humor, however agnostic, may accept, and which is also in harmony with modern theories of psychology. It is a perception that at every important moment in life (though many of these moments may seem fleeting, minor, trivial, and are missed at first glance) the "forces which have created us" exert their influence and authority, and at times oppress us in ways that are astoundingly coherent— if we can see them with enough distance. We repeat our own earliest "psychic assumptions," and those of our parents and our tribe, and this is the way our mythic past underlies our civilized present.

One of Robert Langbaum's great achievements as a critic is to have shown us how Dinesen, like Thomas Mann in his Joseph period, is working with myth in an innovative way. "Her stories show us . . . the point at which psychology makes contact with literature, and they thus make us realize that the old literary forms—tragedy, comedy, romance, pastoral—are names for clusters of concepts that we would nowadays call psychological insights. By revivifying the old forms as cultural externalizations of psychic life, Isak Dinesen is able to talk at once about psychology and culture."[12] The key to her ability to carry off this feat is her grasp of the relationship between psychology and culture in her own life, the way, particularly in *Seven Gothic Tales,* she externalized her own "psychic assumptions." This ability was in part courage and intuition; it was who she was, "the mysterious ground of the being," as Nietzsche called it, which defies analysis. It was also partly due to the stroke of fate that sealed off her youth from her maturity, her life from her art, and gave her the precious "overview." And it was partly the fact that the thread—her Nemesis—was particularly tense and strong, and so it gave her life more shape than most lives, more convolutions.

Dinesen acknowledges Nemesis in the very name she took to sign her work. Isak means, in Hebrew, "the one who laughs," and he was the child of Abraham and Sarah's extreme old age, a postmenopausal miracle, a divine joke. When she delivered him Sarah said: "God hath made me to laugh, so that all who hear will laugh with me."[13] As for choosing to write under a pseudonym, or a half-pseudonym, Isak Dinesen told an interviewer in 1934 that she had done so "on the same ground my father hid behind the pseudonym Boganis . . . [so that] he could, in *Letters from the Hunt,* express himself freely, give his imagination a free rein. He didn't want people to ask, 'Do you really mean that?' Or, 'Have you, yourself, experienced that?' "

"You keep speaking of your book as completely imaginative," the interviewer said. "But nothing is completely imaginative . . . one can only write
of what has roots in experience, hidden or open."

"That is correct," she replied.[14]

Robert Langbaum, who met Dinesen in 1959 while he was preparing *The
Gayety of Vision,* reported that she spoke of *Seven Gothic Tales* with embarrassment, as "too elaborate" and as having "too much of the author in it.' "
He believed it was "the 'decadence,' if you like . . . especially its treatment
of sexual perversion, that embarrassed her—that and her own awareness of
how deeply personal the book is."[15]

It is difficult to use the word "perversion" without implying a negative
judgment on the character of the "pervert," and I think *desire* rather than
perversion—which is only the means to the desire—is the more important
concept. Desire is, in some form and often in some very curious form, the
subject of *Seven Gothic Tales,* and I think what Dinesen writes of Malin
Nat-og-Dag is, in fact, a witty caricature of her own authorship:

> She was the catoptric image of the great repenting sinner whose sins are made
> white as wool, and was here taking a genuine pleasure in dyeing the pretty
> lamb's-wool of her life in sundry fierce dyes. Jealousy, deceit, seduction, rape,
> infanticide, and senile cruelty with all the perversities of the human world of
> passion, even to the *maladies galantes,* of which she exhibited a surprising
> knowledge, were to her little sweetmeats which she could pick, one by one,
> out of the *bonbonnière* of her mind, and crunch with true gourmandise. In all
> her fantasies she was her own heroine, and she ran through the sphere of the
> seven deadly sins with the ecstasy of a little boy who gallops through the great
> races of the world upon his rocking-horse. No danger could possibly put fear
> into her, nor any anguish of conscience spoil her peace. If there was one person
> of whom she spoke with contempt it was the Mary Magdalene of the Gospel,
> who could no better carry the burden of her sweet sins than to retire to the
> desert of Libya in the company of a skull. She herself carried the weight of
> hers with the skill of an athlete, and was up to playing a graceful game of
> bilboquet with it.[16]

To understand the glee that animates this passage, it is important to
remember that Isak Dinesen grew up in a fanatically puritanical household.
Desire did not mean to her that wholesome urge modern youth is encouraged
to explore; it was transgression. Here it would be useful to quote something
of Freud as a sort of footnote to Miss Malin's "case." "It is always possible,"
he wrote, "for the ego to avoid a rupture in any of its relations by deforming
itself, submitting to forfeit something of its unity, or even in the long run
to being gashed and rent. Thus the illogicalities, eccentricities and follies of
mankind would fall into a similar category as the sexual perversions, for by
accepting them, *human beings spare themselves repression.*"[17]

Isak Dinesen perceived the attempt to spare oneself repression, at whatever price, as heroic and ennobling; this was the lion hunt, the great gesture, the daring fantasy, the mortal sin. This also produced the note one hears throughout her work of scorn for those without the courage to take the risk. In psychological terms the characters in *Seven Gothic Tales* may well be perverts, megalomaniacs, or transvestites; they may well have Oedipal fixations or compulsions. But in Dinesen's terms they are dreamers. The dreamer is someone, Mira Jama tells us, who has been planted in the soil of life like a coffee tree with a bent taproot. That tree "will never thrive, nor bear fruit, but it will flower more richly than the others,"[18] and that same deformed root may produce a great and perhaps excessive flowering of character in the "dreamer"—eccentricity, wit, imagination, impudence, folly—at the expense of wholeness. "To act out" is the psychiatrist's description of the way certain individuals spare themselves repression; "to act," to fulfill one's destiny, is the storyteller's description. The adversity of the hero is external, that of the neurotic within himself, but they both assume a role and act it through with the greatest possible precision and fidelity and in this way are finally able to manifest their desire.

The erotic heroes and demonic daredevils of Romantic literature—including her own father—gave Tanne Dinesen her earliest notions of emotional freedom, just as the example set by the women in her life was of repression and self-surrender: accepting guilt, repudiating desire, "living for others." She also clearly understood, from her father and the others and later on from her own life, what the price was. "Those fine roots are the dreams of the tree," Mira goes on. "As it puts them out, it need no longer think of its bent taproot. It keeps alive by them—a little, not very long. Or you can say that it dies by them, if you like. For really, dreaming is the well-mannered people's way of committing suicide."[19]

Here, perhaps, is the real note of "decadence" in the voice of Isak Dinesen, a plaintive note, and what she had in common with the Symbolists, like Baudelaire, whom she and Denys had both loved, and with the later fin-de-siècle decadents like Huysmans and Villiers de l'Isle-Adam. The affinity has less to do with the way her characters cross-dress, or abuse the pleasures of the flesh, then with their and her own sense of being trapped and alienated by civilized (bourgeois) life. *"Ce pays nous ennuie/ O Mort Appareillons!"*[20] writes Baudelaire. And his *voyageur,* who departs *"seul pour partir,"* who seeks an exotic refuge for his stifled rage and lust, is her dreamer and suicide.

Arnold Hauser brilliantly draws together the older Romantic impulse and the "neo-Romantic" one that, after the 1890s, was called "decadence," and in the process he suggests the context in which *Seven Gothic Tales* should be read. Decadence, he writes, "is the consciousness of standing at the end of a vital process and in the presence of the dissolution of a civilization. The sympathy with the old, exhausted, over-refined cultures, with Hellenism, the later years of the Roman Empire, the rococo and the mature, 'impressionistic' style of the great masters, is part of the essence of . . . decadence. The awareness of being witnesses of a turning-point in the history of civilization was nothing new . . . but the idea of intellectual nobility is now connected with the concept of old age and fatigue, of over-cultivation and degeneration. . . . The analogies with Rousseauism, the Byronic weariness of life and the romantic passion for death are obvious. It is the same abyss that attracts both the romantic and the decadent, the same delight in destruction, self-destruction, that intoxicates them. But for the decadent 'everything is an abyss.' "21

But here Isak Dinesen goes her own anomalous—and wholesome—way. She had often and would often go to the edge of the abyss and even peer down into it—but the exercise never failed to cheer her up. In one of her notebooks there is the outline for a story that she never wrote, about a young man in great despair who decides to commit suicide. But having, with the greatest relish and relief, imagined what it will be like to forsake everything that has caused him such chagrin, he feels no actual need to do it.

"The awareness of how deeply personal the book is," obviously could not have occurred to Isak Dinesen as an afterthought. But the "embarrassment" did come later, as a reaction to the Danish reception of the book and to one particular review, written by a young critic named Frederick Schyberg and published in *Berlingske Tidende*. For the rest of her life Karen Blixen kept a copy of it and brought it out, much tattered and yellowed as the years passed, to show her friends, whom she asked to respond. After accusing her of coquetry and shallowness, caprice, mystification and false effects, snobbery, name dropping, and pastiche, he went on to say: "But what about the perversity? The word is ugly, but there is nothing else . . . to describe the basic fact *that there are no normal human beings in Seven Gothic Tales.* The erotic life which unfolds in the tales is of the most highly peculiar kind. Men love their sisters, aunts their nieces, various characters are enamored of themselves, and young women *cannot* or *will not* bear children. A French countess throws it up to her lover that he is not in love with her, but with her husband, and he has nothing to reply, because he 'realizes' she is right. . . . Augustus von Schimmelmann is separated from his wife because he is in love with her diamonds! Later an Italian smelling-bottle solves his complex. Morten de Coninck is in love with his ship, *Fortuna,* Baron von Brackel and Count Boris harbour feelings for a skull and an entire skeleton, respectively. There is nothing, the reviewer finds . . . behind [the author's] veil, once it is lifted."22

The barbs went deep, not just because they were so sharp but because they distorted in such a clever, vicious, and personal way the real spirit and enterprise of *Seven Gothic Tales*. Isak Dinesen was one of our most pure-hearted—not to say one of our greatest—immoralists. But no reassurance from her friends, and no amount of praise from her best critics, were sufficient to salve the pain of Schyberg's words.

3

The manuscript of *Seven Gothic Tales* was ready by the spring of 1933, but Isak Dinesen, the unknown author of a book of "stories," could not at first find a publisher. She hoped that Gustav Mohr's friendship with Christopher Morley and his interest in her book might open the doors to her at Faber & Faber, but this was not the case. Thomas remembers that she sent the book to an "American publisher, who rejected it," but this was probably the Boston-born Constant Huntington, at (the British) Putnam's. After two rejections, Karen Blixen decided that having written the book as a "man" she ought to peddle it as a "woman," to fall back upon the resources of her charm. Lady Islington, the mother of Joan Grigg, offered her a personal introduction to Mr. Huntington and arranged a luncheon party that took place that spring in London. According to Ms. Migel, Karen Blixen gave Mr. Huntington an audition of her narrative abilities, telling anecdote after anecdote from her life in Africa. He listened politely until she mentioned her new book of tales, and then he refused point-blank to read it, saying, "That way you will not be persuaded that I secretly dislike it,"[23] and he told her instead to write a novel.

She returned to Rungstedlund so enraged that she was, as Thomas put it, "close to giving up and disappearing from the world."[24] But then she remembered that her brother knew an American writer who might be in a position to help her, Dorothy Canfield Fisher. Thomas had met Mrs. Fisher at Kastrup Airport in Copenhagen and had driven her out to Folehave to meet Aunt Bess, and they all still corresponded. The manuscript was duly posted to Vermont; Mrs. Fisher read it and was deeply impressed, and in turn urged it upon her neighbor, Robert Haas, the publisher of Harrison Smith and Robert Haas, a firm that subsequently merged with Random House. Haas felt it was too good not to publish, although he didn't anticipate making money. He declined to pay an advance until a few thousand copies had been sold and stipulated that the book appear with a foreword by Mrs. Fisher. These conditions were met, the order of the tales was changed slightly,* and by September the author was reading proof. Haas was both right and wrong in his assessment of the book. *Seven Gothic Tales,* published in January of 1934, was an immediate critical success, but a commercial success as well. It

---

*In the British edition "The Roads Around Pisa" comes first, and "Deluge at Norderney" comes fourth. In the American edition this order is reversed. Isak Dinesen preferred the British arrangement, which was her own in the original manuscript.

was chosen by the Book-of-the-Month Club as its February selection, with a print run of fifty thousand copies.

This news elated Isak Dinesen, and she invited Thomas and Jonna to an "unusual" family dinner to announce it to them. Ms. Migel spotlights this scene importantly in *Titania* and continues to stress, even to flaunt, the subsequent book-club selections, five in all, as if they were the proofs positive of her friend's greatness. The naive and triumphant pride seems, in the book, to be shared by Dinesen. Hannah Arendt, in her review of *Titania,* pointed out how incongruous it is with her real stature and talent; she called it a "close to comic spectacle"—like Pellegrina Leoni embracing her insipid lovers with the force of a python. But the point needs some adjustment. Dinesen had, at the beginning of her career, no idea what the book club really was or how it made its choices, and she believed it was a literary *aerestitel*—title of honor —based entirely upon quality.[25] This misconception becomes apparent in her letters to Robert Haas at the time *The Angelic Avengers* was published, the second-rate Gothic mystery novel she wrote during the war to have a little "fun." When it, too, was selected by the book club she was vehement in declining, on the grounds that it would cheapen the "honor" bestowed upon her "legitimate" works.

By the spring of 1934 the Danish press was on the trail of "Isak Dinesen," their mysterious compatriot who wrote in English and who had made such an impression in America. Following a hint from Mark van Doren that the author was a "Danish lady," the newspaper *Politiken* tracked Karen Blixen down to Rungstedlund. On April 30 the poet and novelist Tom Kristensen published an admiring review, and the next day the paper ran an interview. There was competition among Danish publishers for the rights to a translation, which Karen Blixen finally sold to Reitzel's, a firm owned by her brother-in-law, Knud Dahl—a decision that would embroil her in a bitter quarrel and lead to an estrangement from both Knud and Elle.

The efforts of several Danish translators so disappointed Karen Blixen that she undertook the work herself. In a disparaging letter to one of the unsuccessful candidates she thanked him for his offer to correct her own version, when it was ready, but expressed the opinion that she knew Danish not only as well as she knew English, "but, I will almost permit myself to say: as well as any Danish writer. I don't mean that I can therefore write just as good a book as any Danish writer, but that [ability] comes from other sources than knowledge of the language."[26] This set a precedent, and henceforth she would always do her own Danish translations, in later years relying greatly upon the help of Clara Svendsen. But it is really misleading to speak of "translations" at all; the Danish editions of Karen Blixen's works are really original texts. She explained the process of the rewriting in her own introduction to *Syv Fantastiske Fortællinger:*

When, for my own amusement, I wrote this book in English I didn't think it would have any interest for Danish readers. Now it has been its destiny to be translated into other languages, and it was therefore natural that it should also be published in my own country. I have very much wanted it to be published in Danish as an original Danish book, and not in any—no matter how good—translation. Throughout the text the Danish names and place-names, facts of Danish history and quotes from Danish poets have been used very freely. A great deal of *Seven Gothic Tales* was thought out and some of it written in Africa, and the places in my book which touch on Denmark must be taken as a Danish emigrant's fantasies on Danish themes, rather than as some attempt to give a picture of reality. . . .[27]

Her work was delayed by ill health and other commitments, and *Syv Fantastiske Fortællinger* was not published in Copenhagen until September 1935. In the meantime, Putnam's had published the English edition and Bonniers in Stockholm a Swedish one. The English reviews were mixed, but Desmond MacCarthy hailed it as a work of genius and Anthony Eden accorded Isak Dinesen a place "on the Anglo-Saxon Parnassus." She went to London that December to enjoy "the sweetness of fame";[28] visited the Winchilseas; met Margot Asquith and the Duff Coopers; was entertained by Mr. Huntington at his house on Hyde Park, where she met Aldous Huxley, whose novels had meant so much to her in Africa, Stephan Zweig, Harold Nicolson, H. G. Wells,* Moura Budberg, Desmond MacCarthy—whose famous wit she must have enjoyed—George Bernard Shaw, and others equally illustrious.[29] Her comings and goings were faithfully reported in the Danish press, for which she was to provide a source of glamorous and controversial copy for the next thirty years. When she returned to Rungsted-lund she was "exhausted," and a stone thinner, and wrote to Lady Daphne Finch Hatton that she was "slaving" over her translation and working on a new play.†

It is such a waste of time to be an invalid, and there is such a bridge to build out to the Masai Reserve. Alas, alas, as Julian Huxley writes to me . . . I was asked to a ball at the English Legation tonight and I should have liked to go, to speak English again, but I feel that I am not at all up to dancing with one foot in the grave and the other, according to Anthony Eden, on the Anglo-Saxon Parnassus.[30]

---

*Karen Blixen was reading H. G. Wells in 1924 and told her brother at that time how much she admired his writing and philosophy, and particularly the belief, stated in *The Dream,* that the great and revolutionary idea of the modern age was to educate human beings for happiness (Isak Dinesen, *Letters from Africa,* p. 212).

†Among Karen Blixen's miscellaneous manuscripts is a cast list, but no text, for a comedy called "Perdiccas and Sibylla," signed Isak Dinesen, which leads me to believe that it is the play she mentions (KBA 110, "Andre Fortællinger," IIIa 2c; 3).

The "bridge to the Masai Reserve" refers to a project she had secretly been cherishing and that she hoped would permit her to return to Africa. It was to use her royalties to establish a hospital for Masai children, and while she was in London she had arranged to meet Albert Schweitzer and to ask his advice about it. Dr. Schweitzer was alarmed by her frailty and discouraged her. In any event she had greatly underestimated the cost of such an undertaking, and when the first American check arrived at Christmas, for eight thousand dollars, she quietly shelved the project. But she never completely abandoned the hope of going "home." In 1936 she would try to get there as a journalist covering the war in Abyssinia. In the early 1950s she solicited an assignment from *Life* to visit Mecca with Farah and his mother. And in 1962, the year she died, she tried to make a last "private mission" to see those of her old people who were still alive and still remembered her.

35

In a Dark Wood

I

IN APRIL OF 1935 Karen Blixen celebrated her fiftieth birthday. The year before, Kehlet had photographed her, full-length, in a white chiffon evening dress, and this was the first image of "Isak Dinesen" published in America when her identity became known. It is the picture of an aloof, slender, and graceful woman of the world, poised between youth and age. Her hair is pulled back simply, her head turned slightly more than her body toward the camera, her hips lightly thrust forward like a tango dancer, her dark eyes barely open under their shadowed lids, her mouth twisted into an ambiguous expression that could be irony or *hauteur* or simply contemplation —and which, like the look of kings in their official portraits, does not acknowledge an obligation to please the viewer.

For the first four years after her return to Denmark, Karen Blixen had been absorbed by the writing and publishing of her work and in the attention generated by her sudden fame. But when she finished her Danish translation of *Seven Gothic Tales* she was, for the first time, free to think about her life and her immediate future, and she keenly felt the pressure to begin "living again." It is clear from her letters to her brother that she also felt a profound anxiety about her ability to do so. That autumn an interviewer asked her if she would settle down permanently in Denmark, and she replied, "Out there I longed for Denmark, now I suffer homesickness for Africa, and think how can I ever sink roots here? One cannot possibly live on the basis that one has written a talked about book, one becomes a kind of museum-piece, a strange thing that is contemplated but not a person, with relations to the world. If I shall live here it can only be if I establish my life so that I come into relation with the people in their daily life, as I did in Kenya. One must grow if one shall live, one cannot float free in the air."[1]

At this juncture Karen Blixen experienced a crisis that had certain familiar hallmarks. I cannot say that she experienced it as familiar, although the language she used to describe it was. She felt the same melancholy, the same numbness, fatigue, and detachment she had written about at twenty-five, en route to Paris. Once again she had lost faith in herself, and she left on a visit to London in a state of conflict, hoping to find a little cheer, a little brilliance, some "meaning" for her life, but with no confidence that she could.

This crisis may have been the result of several severe pressures converging on the same vulnerable point. Many writers feel bereft or overwhelmed when they finish a book and do not have another one on the loom. Isak Dinesen describes such a predicament in *Winter's Tales:* Charlie Despard "felt in his heart that he would never again write a great book. . . . The idea of his fame augmented and intensified his despair."[2] But she had also just turned fifty, and fifty was the age at which her father committed suicide. He had begun to feel his powers waning, his political idealism frustrated, and he was disappointed in his second book. He had also just discovered that he had syphilis and felt that he would only continue to degenerate until he was a helpless invalid and "wreck," completely dependent upon his family. Such dependence was intolerable to him, as it was to his daughter, and in her case the physical degeneration had already begun. She might well have believed, like her father, that she had both fulfilled her destiny and begun to outlive it.

If this were not enough, fifty was also the age at which Miss Nat-og-Dag in "Deluge at Norderney," Karen Blixen's alter ego on so many counts, began menopause, and she had responded to it by "throwing herself into imaginative excesses." Friends thought it was an unexpected inheritance that had gone to her head, but the narrator tells us that "what changed her was what changes all women at fifty: the transfer from the active service of life—with a pension or the honours of war, as the case may be—to the mere passive state of a looker-on. A weight fell away from her; she flew up to a higher perch and cackled a little."[3] Having nothing more to gain or lose from love, Miss Malin's erotic fantasy life is set free. All the "witches" in Dinesen's tales, whether or not they are actually named so, are similarly infertile and capricious females who have more than made up in power what they have lost in sex appeal, but it is important to note that for Dinesen herself the size of the consolation was proportional to the loss. Two years later, making some notes for an address to the Danish Women's Society on the subject of African women, she would write: "All old women had the consolation of witchcraft; their relations with witchcraft were comparable to their relations with the art of seduction. One cannot understand how we, who will have nothing to do with witchcraft, can bear to grow old."[4]

Mrs. Dinesen saw her daughter's anguish and was afraid that she had played some part in it. On the day Tanne left for England Ingeborg wrote her a letter that was really a declaration of unconditional love and acceptance, setting Tanne free from any responsibility she might feel to live at Rungstedlund and play the dutiful unmarried daughter. "You can't imagine how empty it grew yesterday, after you left, nor is there a moment when I don't miss you. . . . I am only afraid that you will feel an obligation to 'please' me in my last years, and that is so far from the case.

. . . You not only have the right, you have the duty to follow your own way. . . . It would be a fine thing for a parent, having nurtured a child, to demand that she give up her future to live with a more or less dried up wreck. When I can know that you are well and happy, I . . . will be made happy: *so sits the while at home the mother well content.* Your two rooms stand as if you had just left them, ready to be used at whatever time, and you know that my arms will be around you at the same instant you appear, and with the same warmth that they held you yesterday, my beloved."[5] Some months later, writing to her daughter in Geneva with family news and general reflections on the sad state of the world, Ingeborg concluded: "I love you and know you love me. I think once in a while the relationship between us two has something in it of Father's and my feelings for each other—that must be because you are to such a great degree his daughter."[6]

Thomas Dinesen took a blunter course with his sister. "You ask me to help you free your soul, to find meaning in existence, to lay a life's plan, and I am perhaps the worst person you could come to. It is just what I have striven after my whole life, without the least luck. You write that 'morality' has made it difficult for you to live—that you are continuously plagued by the old habit of weighing everything on morality's scale . . . and I told you that day in Hellebæk that the solution, for me, lay in the view: it doesn't mean anything—and I think you understand me. . . . To speak of freeing one's soul, or finding God, or serving or resisting absolute ideas or principles is the remains of a superstition, a fear of the dark . . . it is our own desires or disappointments that we make ourselves believe have interest for the whole universe, which we project upon the firmament, and thereafter worship, or are afraid of. Obviously these subjects do not have anything to do with a life's plan. . . . What I have achieved is only . . . to free myself of the fear and the resentment, from the last remnant of the metaphysical religious nightmare. . . .

"If you completely disagree with me, if you are completely sure you have a soul, that there is an up and down on the scale of ethical meaning, a divine world, or however shall I now signify the unsignifiable, so Tanne, I would in complete seriousness advise you to seek your freedom through religion. I don't think you are naive enough to become an 'Oxford man' or affected enough to become a Christian Scientist or a Buddhist, and I confess that it would turn my stomach if you became a Protestant holywoman. But I think you could become a Catholic without great difficulty. . . ."[7]

Thomas concluded with two suggestions. One was for his sister to find a wise Catholic priest and to lay her "difficulties and complaints" before him, and the other was to hire herself a secretary and put everything else aside and begin her planned book "on the Masai." This was, under the circumstances, prescient advice. For in urging her to write the work that would become

Out of Africa, he was pointing to the way she would give her past a finality and resolve her doubts about its meaning.

2

Throughout the spring and summer of 1935 Mussolini was preparing for his invasion of Ethiopia. Britain and France both opposed his designs, partly for strategic reasons and partly out of concern for the prestige of the League of Nations, whose covenant had condemned agression. "If the League does fail," said the British Foreign Secretary, "the world at large and Europe in particular will be faced with a period of almost unrelieved danger and gloom."[8] Several compromises were offered Mussolini, including the partial dismemberment of Ethiopia—the English idea—and its transformation into an Italian protectorate with the emperor as a figurehead, which was the French plan. But Mussolini rejected them on the grounds that "they would rob him of the prestige of a military victory" and announced he had some "old and new accounts to settle."[9] He invaded on October 3.

Karen Blixen had followed the military and diplomatic maneuvers from London, and when the invasion began she felt a passionate need to become involved on Ethiopia's behalf and a deep frustration that she could not. She made the rounds of the British newspapers, trying to secure an assignment as a correspondent, citing her long experience in Africa. When she had no success there she made the rounds of the offices of the War Department, trying to get dispensation to leave for the war zone, which was denied on the grounds that she was a woman. At this point a London friend, Baroness Moura Budberg, suggested that "as a consolation" she and Tania travel to Geneva together and attend the session of the League that had been convened to condemn the invasion and to discuss sanctions. Erik Scavenius, the Danish foreign minister, who was married to a relative of Karen Blixen, was able to get them press passes.

Moura, or Marie, Budberg was one of Karen Blixen's closest friends in England before the Second World War when she spent her summers there, although there is no correspondence between them that survives and nothing to suggest that after the war they resumed contact. The baroness was a Russian woman of striking energy and charm, tall and broad-shouldered, about Tania's age and with an even more colorful and eventful past. She had been raised in great luxury in St. Petersburg where her father was a senator, and on the family's estate in the Ukraine, and before she was twenty had married her brother's friend, a young Count von Benckendorff. He was stationed at the Russian embassy in London, and during the year of their engagement she had lived in Cambridge to study English. H. G. Wells remembered meeting her for the first time in Petersburg in 1914, a lively young beauty in jewels and a chic Paris gown. Their next meeting took place in 1920, in Petrograd, by which time her circumstances had changed radically.

The count had been killed during the revolution, she had managed to smuggle their children to a family property in Estonia, had been imprisoned by the Bolsheviks and then rescued by an old friend—Maxim Gorki. On this second occasion she acted as Gorki's interpreter and impressed Wells both with her intelligence and the fact that she looked no less lovely in a "drab" post-revolutionary dress than she had in her former splendor. A year later Gorki arranged for her escape to Estonia, where she married Baron Budberg —a brief and unhappy match—for in 1922 she rejoined Gorki in Berlin to live with him. This relationship lasted until 1933, when Gorki returned to the Soviet Union and Baroness Budberg moved to England with her children. She worked as a translator of French and Russian and as a script consultant, and knew "everyone of importance in the milieu of books and the theatre."[10] By this time she was "closely associated"[11] with H. G. Wells, whose friend she remained until his death.

Moura Budberg, Ms. Migel tells us, "felt a profound attraction for Tania's 'being,'" which apparently was reciprocated. Both women described the Geneva trip to Ms. Migel in glowing terms, and Moura Budberg recalled that despite Tania's despair over the invasion, she was still "avid to see and do everything. We listened to speeches all day and got intoxicated with dance music"—at the hotel's cabaret—"all evening."[12]

The League Council condemned Italy on the day following the invasion, and all the member nations except Austria and Hungary endorsed economic sanctions, which were not, since they excluded oil, compelling enough to make Mussolini withdraw. Karen Blixen was particularly moved by the eloquence of Sir Samuel Hoare, Salvador de Madariaga, and Geneviève Tabouis, and by the dignity of the Ethiopian delegate, Wolde-Marian. "We have no tanks, no airplanes," he told her, "but Madame, we trust in God."[13]

The session was adjourned early in November, and Karen Blixen briefly went back to London, where she stayed with Moura Budberg and with friends in Richmond. But her restlessness and depression followed her. "In Geneva, at the League of Nations," she told Hudson Strode, "surrounded by all those brilliant minds, you felt it was the center of the world. You were excited, stimulated, inspired every moment. And then when you took the train to leave, it was suddenly as if you had come out of the mountains— as in the old tales of enchantment—and you realized that in the *world* Geneva and those brilliant minds had no importance at all."[14] If she hoped to make a life in England, to settle there, she changed her mind and went home to Denmark, where she "wept over every . . . mile of lost [Ethiopian] ground."[15]

3

While she was abroad the Danish edition of *Seven Gothic Tales* was published. Several influential critics attacked it, more on moral and political grounds than as a work of literature. It was the middle of the Depression, two hundred thousand people were unemployed at one point—40 percent of the Danish work force—and many were living in the streets. The predominating literary mode was social realism, the realistic novel describing the experience of working people. There was also a radical avant-garde, experimenting with modern theater, art, and film. The women's movement and the movement for sexual freedom were newly militant, the country was filling with refugees from Germany and the Spanish Civil War, and among intellectuals there was a general spirit of austerity and of sympathy for the political struggles of the working class. Many readers were offended by Karen Blixen's frank nostalgia for the *ancien régime* and by her flight from the grim realities of Danish life. There was also some resentment of the fact that she had written originally in English and had had her first success in America. Karen Blixen was never able to forgive "Denmark" for its coolness and skepticism toward her first book, and even in the 1950s, by which time she was regarded as one of her country's greatest living authors, she would still feel misunderstood and disliked.

The contrast between the American and Danish response to *Seven Gothic Tales* was so striking that she blamed it in part upon Knud Dahl's reluctance to promote the book, and when she got home she wrote him a formal letter of protest. She had no "technical complaints," but she felt he had gone back on his promises to her, promises for particular reviews, for radio publicity, for "personal work" among the Danish critics and journalists. She was particularly angry at his arrangements for a Norwegian edition. To his complaint that she herself had been abroad when the book was published, she replied that she had done more than usual for an author and that, in any case, selling herself would not be "in good taste." Henceforth he was to address all future correspondence to her lawyer.[16]

Dahl could be even more high-handed and *kali* than Tanne herself, and he told her she was "driving me a little mad" with her endless caviling and accusations, her "faulty information" and her "obsession with *bagatelles,* which all sensible people settle, should they arise, with a few words."[17] The acrimony and estrangement lasted for the next ten years and was refreshed in 1936, when Reitzel's bought the rights to Bror Blixen's memoir, *The African Hunter*—an act that seems to have been pure vindictiveness. Thomas had asked Knud to forego the book as a personal favor and was outraged when he refused—"especially in the light of your knowledge of the whole relation between Tanne and Blixen, and all his behavior to her."[18] Tanne swallowed her pride to make a "highly emotional" appeal of her own, to which her brother-in-law retorted that she had asked for a businesslike relationship, had relegated all correspondence to her lawyer, and must, therefore, "reckon that where the institutions that I am connected with are concerned, I can have no regards for your conjugal entanglements, or other personal relations."[19]

There may have been another source of fuel for this quarrel that the correspondence doesn't touch upon. In *The Life and Destiny of Karen Blixen,* Clara Svendsen notes that at the time *Seven Gothic Tales* was published, Tanne got the message from her family that "rightly or wrongly . . . she had to play down her success in order not to hurt the feelings of her sister."[20] Thomas also told me that Tanne believed Dahl had neglected her book in part to diminish, on Elle's behalf, the impact of its success. Elle had published two small books of her own, the first in 1929, the second in 1932, both under the pseudonym Paracelsus. They were urbane but slight collections of anecdote and philosophy, and neither received any serious notice. It is possible that the family was protective of Elle, or loyal, on the principle of that same scrupulous equality which had prevailed in the nursery. But there is no evidence that Elle herself begrudged Tanne her success. She wrote warmly and with insight about her sister's work and was, in later years, one of the first people Tanne turned to for honest criticism.

Shortly after the New Year, Karen Blixen received a letter from her former husband. It was scrawled in pencil and had been written somewhere in the bush of Tanganyika, where he was hunting elephant. It sent news and regards from Farah, who was still working for him, and from Rose Cartwright, Flo Martin, and other of their friends. It was signed, "Your old Bror."[21]

There is no evidence that Karen Blixen had heard from her old Bror in the five years she had lived in Denmark. He had, in the meantime, been divorced by Cockie and had married his third wife, Eva Dixon, a beautiful Swedish woman to whom many of the letters he would publish in his memoir were written. Bror had already begun to work on the book (with the help of a ghostwriter), so it was perhaps natural for him to think of Tanne and wish to renew contact with her. But it would also have been like him to try, through a friendly letter, to disarm her hostility toward any incursion into her territory—literature. At first she was incredulous that he was doing a book at all, and then anxious. She was afraid that he had "recognized the unflattering portrait of himself as Baron Guildenstern" in "The Dreamers"[22] and would write something vindictive about her. But she was even more afraid that his story would contradict her own, or detract from its sales, or influence its critical reputation. It is rather touching that she was so innocent about publishing, or so uncertain of her own worth as to believe that it could stand or fall on trifles. But it also suggests the image she had of her audience: not an anonymous and dispersed mass, but a small community, a "people," a family, with pride invested in their idea of her and susceptible to disillusion. Perhaps this was natural, given her own extremely nosy and reactive family and the tight-knit social worlds of Copenhagen and Nairobi, where every bit of gossip was propagated like milkweed.

Tanne, however, misjudged Bror Blixen. His only critical remark about her book, which was made in private, was that "we could have done with four Gothic tales instead of seven."[23] And he mentions Tanne only once in his own memoir, with affection, at the beginning when he writes of their engagement and their emigration.

Her own book on Africa had slowly been taking shape. In 1934 an interviewer had asked her if it "wouldn't have been more natural for you to write your first book about Africa?" and she replied that she might just as easily have turned immediately to that subject as to have written "about a child the day one buried it. One must have things at a distance. In my tales I have put a whole century between me and the events."[24]

When she began to plan the new book, she did not envision anything so personal or so intense in feeling as *Seven Gothic Tales*. In 1926 a Danish newspaper had asked her for some short "travel pieces" about the Africans and the landscape, which had not then come to life for her, but she had kept her notes. In March of 1934 she mentioned to Haas that she had a "few, short, quite truthful recounts [*sic*] of my life on the African farm, particularly about my relations with the Natives" and that she would like to get them published in a *good* magazine. "I suppose," she said, "that this can not in any way interfere with our contract, since the stories can not in any way be classed as a book."[25]

But a year later Thomas refers to "your book on the Masai," and on January 29, 1935, in the *Møns Folkeblad*, Karen Blixen told an interviewer that she was going to "write a book in which all things are true, where everything that is told truly happened. It shall be the truth about the Blacks. . . ."

What began as a collection of dinner-party anecdotes, of "short, quite truthful" autobiographical sketches, of travel writing, of perceptive but romantic amateur anthropology, became *Out of Africa*.

36

Out of Africa

I

By NOW it will be clear, I think, that *Out of Africa* does not describe Karen Blixen's life on her African farm as it was, in a documentary sense, lived. The serene perfection of the style, the spareness of detail, the attendance of the gods all signal that we have escaped from the gravity of practical questions and have gotten up into a purer element, one that offers less resistance to the ideal. The point of view in *Out of Africa* is that "overview" which Karen Blixen called "the one thing of vital importance to achieve in life."[1] What we see is a landscape from the air; time and action have been tremendously compressed and telescoped. So when she writes: "We grew coffee on my farm. The land itself was a little too high for coffee and it was hard work to keep it going; we were never rich on the farm,"[2] we are, in effect, taking in eighteen years of drought, mismanagement, and struggle, the endless petty quarrels with the shareholders and intrigues with bankers, the terrible fluctuations of international coffee prices, and the vagaries of the weather. And to describe how she was driven to write by these misfortunes she begins simply: "When times were dull on the farm. . . ."[3] This phrase is like a seed. It contains a complete lifetime of boredom and loneliness, and of the brief visits and precipitous departures of her lover.

Out of Africa rearranges the events of Karen Blixen's life on the farm so that there is no psychological or narrative ambivalence to them—this by contrast to the rich, novelistic ambivalence of the letters. The most dramatic alteration is the holding back of all the suffering and tragedy until the end, so that they consummate an idyll—rounding it off, delivering that bold and fatal stroke which makes a "unity" of the "disintegrating elements." From the notes on her original manuscript we can catch a glimpse of that process of selectivity and compression. She begins, for example, to write a section about her mother but deletes it—the idea that the sovereign narrator is someone's little girl is somehow incongruous. She eliminates a reference to the casual conversation on "trains and trams" in Europe—the industrialized world is not permitted to intrude. She also crosses out: "There is a limit to what the human mind can take in without breaking." There is no limit. Writing of her friend Berkeley Cole, she changes his *humanity* to his *gal-*

lantry, and she decides that the atmosphere in her clinic on the verandah should be *gay* rather than *happy.*[4] Gallantry and gaiety are the storyteller's words; they are fixed, chivalric attitudes toward life, rather than states of mind—the province of the novelist. If the feudal world of *Out of Africa* works so well, is so harmonious and beautiful, it is precisely because of its fixity. Love of fate is its central principle or, as Dinesen puts it, "pride . . . in the idea God had, when he made us."[5] Its inhabitants take their places in the hierarchy according to the degree of pride they manifest, with the Africans—mystically forebearing and amused—at the top. The European aristocrats—the great atavisms like Denys, Berkeley, and the narrator—defer to them, but just slightly and in the same spirit a gentleman feels himself to be morally inferior to a lady. Their fatalism is assertive; it is expressed as *honor,* and through it they have the privilege to understand tragedy. "If a man has a steadfast idea of honor," Dinesen told Curtis Cate, "he is absolutely safe as to what can happen to him."[6] The fact that he may lose everything he holds dear—his farm, perhaps his life—will not, under this circumstance, affect the value of the one thing that has the greatest importance: experience itself.

All books take place at the moment they are written, and *Out of Africa* was written at a moment when its author keenly felt her life lacked the dignity of a meaning. The parable of the stork, which was a favorite of the Dinesen children and which Isak Dinesen retells in the fourth section of the book, is a miniature version of her project as a whole. In the little inset story a man sets out from his house in pursuit of an obscure calamity, gets lost, stumbles into a ditch, climbs out, falls into another ditch, finds a leak in his dam, repairs it, goes back to bed. The next morning, looking out of his tower window over the course he has taken and the tracks he has left behind, he sees, to his amazement, the "shape of the Stork." "The tight place," Dinesen reflects—and it is the anguished reflection of the year 1935—"the dark pit in which I am now lying, of what bird is it the talon? When the design of my life is completed shall I, shall other people see a stork?"[7]

Karen Blixen's letters from Africa give us insight into the nature of the not so obscure calamity in her own life, of which *Out of Africa* is in part a sublime repair job. She confessed to Thomas that what most frightened her was not the fact of loving an elusive man, or having too little money or not enough confidence from the Company, but a much more basic and pathological sense of fragility, and one that went much further back for her. It was the "real terror" *(rædsel)* of "abandoning one's life and soul to something one can lose again."[8] And she explained that every moment of happiness she had known in ten years on the farm had been attended and compromised by the terror of its ending; that mourning the passing moment had become a kind of "habit, an *idée fixe* with me . . . to the point of calculating how much more time was left of something, even if it was only a trip to Nairobi."[9] At that point in her life she could not understand where the dread came from, and it seemed both "strange and unreasonable" to her. Why, she asked, could she not get used to accepting endings without anguish when she knew that everything must have one, and when she herself "had sense enough not to wish it otherwise."[10]

The place that loss occupies in her narrative is indicated in the first sentence: "I had a farm in Africa, at the foot of the Ngong Hills." Loss dominates the great calm beauty of the description that follows, the way the landscape of the farm is itself dominated by the hills rising up two thousand feet about it. It is the psychic reference point; everything that is said hereafter about Africa is also said about the loss of Africa, and at the same time the original loss, which we know to be her father's death. Robert Langbaum steps back even further and compares Dinesen's Kenya to the Paradise Lost of Romantic myth, a past in which alienated artists of the nineteenth century saw nature and civilization in harmony with one another. "It is because Africa figures as a paradise lost—both in Isak Dinesen's life and in the life of Europe—that *Out of Africa* is an authentic pastoral, perhaps the best prose pastoral of our time."[11] His analysis is suggestive and convincing, although it is worth asking why, in a secular and post-romantic age, a myth of the Fall should have such validity. It is also worth asking, in light of the African letters, why we should be so moved by this memoir of a Paradise Lost which was not, in fact, a paradise at all. One answer, I think, is that the experience of being abandoned, of losing an unconditional love, and thereby of forfeiting the simple confidence and wholeness which it sanctions, is a common childhood tragedy. It does not always take such a dramatic form as it did for Isak Dinesen, but it is still a fall, the end of a personal "golden age"— and a shock that may diminish the value of all subsequent experience. If Dinesen's voice has such authority, it is partly because she reassures us, as much by her absolute self-possession as by her explicit counsel, that the most traumatic losses can be survived, and more, transcended. There is none of that terror in *Out of Africa* that Dinesen describes in her letters, and there is no nostalgia, either. Langbaum sums up the achievement by saying that she has been able to "recover in the imagination what she has lost in the external world"—or to round out the myth of the Fall with her own redemption.[12]

Dinesen adopts a divine perspective, even a divine persona, in *Out of Africa*. She is, indeed, the redeemer who suffers an exemplary "death" so that she can hold out, to the rest of us, the promise of spiritual freedom. This may be ironic or even bitter at first glance; it is the freedom which Scheherazade shows the Sultan, and which the gods suggest to Isak Dinesen when they answer her sentimental call for a sign with the terrible scene between the cock and the chameleon. It has nothing to do with freedom from pain or with finding happiness, but simply with the richer sense of things that comes to those who learn to tolerate contradiction.

Many years later, Isak Dinesen wrote contemptuously about the "humanistic" art of the novel that, for the sake of its characters' well-being, "will be ready to sacrifice the story itself." To this she opposed the "divine" art of the story, which will sacrifice everything *but* itself. The story has no compassion for its characters; it does not "slacken its speed to occupy itself with [their] mien or bearing. . . . It makes the one faithful partisan of the old mad hero cry out in awe: 'Is this the promised end?'—goes on, and in a while calmly informs us: 'This is the promised end.' "

The art of the story may well seem "hard and cruel" and yet, she asserts, for its human characters "there is salvation in nothing else in the universe. For within the whole universe the story only has the authority to answer that one cry of the heart . . . 'Who am I?' "*

Out of Africa is the "story" of Isak Dinesen's life told according to her own rigorous laws of storytelling and faithful to her own understanding of what a tale is and must be. It was motivated by an anguished "human" cry—the "Who am I?" of the year 1935—and it settles that question definitively, complexly, in the divine fashion. In some ways, Isak Dinesen's real life ends here. Her autobiography is a crucible, like that fire in "The Cardinal's First Tale" that confounds the identities of the two twins, Dionysio and Athanasio, and in it the woman and the storyteller are confounded. One of them survives, but which one?

All artists claim a certain omnipotence in relation to their material, and as Dinesen puts it herself, "a poet's mission in life is to make others confound fiction and reality in order to render them, for an hour, mysteriously happy. But he himself must . . . hold the two apart."[13] From the time she finished *Out of Africa,* this would be increasingly difficult for her. Her readers took it, on her word of honor, so to speak, that "she"—literally the woman in the story—had really survived an experience "outside the range of imagination."[14] However much a sense of humor she would maintain in the face of the persistent reverence and mystification of her admirers, it was not enough to prevent her taking some of that heady stuff to heart. From the time she finished *Out of Africa,* a subtle change is noticeable in her relationships and her self-presentation. "Slowly the center of gravity of her being would be shifted from individual to symbol."[15]

2

Karen Blixen spent all of 1936 writing, interrupted twice by brief stays in the hospital. One, she told Robert Haas, was for an inflamed jawbone, and the other for a gallstone operation, although these seem to have been covers for her real malady, the "gruesome old pains"[16] of tertiary syphilis.

---

*Cardinal Salviati and his lady penitent compare the novel and the story in "The Cardinal's First Tale," *Last Tales,* p. 23.

She had other, more pleasant distractions, too. In late March, *The Revenge of Truth* was performed at the Royal Theater in Copenhagen, by actors rather than marionettes. It was an event she had longed for since the early twenties and in which she took an active role, attending rehearsals and making suggestions for the staging and costumes. As soon as it was over, she left for England to attend the wedding of Denys's niece, Lady Diana Finch Hatton, to Mr. Peter Tiarks. Diana and her sister Daphne had been teenagers when their uncle died; they had idolized him, and his mistress Tania was a highly romantic figure to them. They had both confided in her about their own first loves, and Tania had responded with great warmth and a girlish complicity. She was included as one of the family at the rehearsal dinner, and if there had been a strain between her and Lord Winchilsea, the wedding healed it. The following year Diana gave birth to a daughter whom she named Tania and who was referred to as "little Tania." When the original Tania came home to Denmark and climbed Ewald's Hill again, she was able to think of Denys for the first time without a "bitter sense of loss."[17]

Robert Haas inquired politely from time to time about her new book, and Karen Blixen replied somewhat defensively that he must not hurry her, that she was doing her best. Ingeborg was ill, and conditions at Rungstedlund were not as conducive to concentration as they had been in 1931 and 1932. In the autumn she packed her books and papers into the car she had bought her mother as an eightieth birthday present and drove to Skagen, a peninsula at the northernmost tip of Jutland, where the North Sea meets the Baltic. Here she lived until the book was finished. At one point she felt she could not go on without a second opinion and begged her brother to come and read the fourth section of the manuscript, "From an Immigrant's Notebook," of which she was unsure. Thomas obliged her and stayed to spend Christmas, which understandably upset his family.

As soon as the English text was finished, she launched into the Danish version, which her new publisher, Gyldendal, was anxious to receive. There was some difficulty and disagreement between the author and her various publishers about her title. Her choice for the English edition was *Ex Africa,* but Haas persuaded her that *Out of Africa* was less formidable. In Sweden the book was called *The African Pastoral,* which she didn't like and called affected. *Den afrikanske Farm (The African Farm)* was her choice for the Danish version. There was also a minor conflict between Dinesen and Haas toward the end of the summer of 1937, when the manuscript was ready to be published. She insisted that the book appear on the same day in America as it did in England and Scandinavia, although the proofs had been delayed and this meant it would be an almost impossible feat of timing. He explained patiently that simultaneity was not important and that to push it through would be detrimental both to its sales and its reception. But she was adamant, and only after an urgent exchange of telegrams did she explain herself in full:

> America took me in when I could not even make the publishers in Europe have a look at my book, and the American reading public received me with such generosity and open-mindedness as I shall never forget. I was delighted with the reviews of the American Critics. I feel the deepest gratitude toward you all. It was a great disappointment to me that I was not at the time well enough to go over and see the country and to meet the people who had been so kind to me. . . . With all this perhaps you will understand that it has given me real pain to think that through the negligence of my agents (who delayed the return of the proofs) here I might somehow lose touch with the public in America —that it might look as if I had lost interest in the public, and that through that, the public might lose interest in me. I have, somehow, taken this very much to heart, it is very difficult to me to get over. It is possible that you will think this rather ridiculous, for the American public may not notice at all that a book of mine is being published in Denmark and England before it appears in America, but I myself have been feeling it as a very cruel trick of fate, in which I am myself completely innocent.[18]

Out of Africa was not published simultaneously in all three countries. It was, however, extremely well received when it did appear in America, and it consolidated Isak Dinesen's reputation. It was once again sold to the Book-of-the-Month Club. Danish critics were also extremely cordial and admiring, and as Langbaum notes, "It was . . . in Denmark that *Out of Africa* made the most difference, for it reassured the Danes, who had not liked the decadent, fantastic, cynical and perverse quality of *Seven Gothic Tales* that Isak Dinesen had, after all, a regard for and knowledge of reality and humanity."[19] Constant Huntington reported that the "intellectual circles" in England liked it but that the "great governing class" did not—"they think that there is a lion in the streets."[20] This seemed to please the author as much as unqualified praise, for it made her feel properly dangerous.

Karen Blixen was ill again that spring but managed to recover sufficiently to leave on the trip to London, which had by now become an annual event. She hoped to make an even longer voyage in the fall to America, about which she had a long correspondence with Robert Haas. She wanted primarily to meet the American people and to express her gratitude to them; she also wanted to receive those "fresh impressions and impulses which I believe America would give me more than any other country. But," she hesitated, "I will come only if people will like me to, I do not want to force myself upon your country!"[21]

The American trip did not materialize, and Isak Dinesen would have to wait another twenty-one years for it; she was almost immediately recalled from England by a telegram that her mother was ill. Mrs. Dinesen rallied miraculously almost as soon as Tanne reached her, and for a while she suspected that, consciously or not, her mother was clinging to her, forcing her to renounce her freedom at a time of life when it meant more than anything to her. She expressed some of this resentment to her Aunt Lidda, who replied that Tanne oughtn't to "feel sorry for us old ones . . . and another thing . . . I don't think you should feel tied down at Rungstedlund. . . . *Mohder* will be the first one to wish your freedom. . . . Anders thinks—you too, maybe—that your father suffered from being tied down, but he's wrong. I'm convinced if Wilhelm wanted to go away for a year or two, to go to war or around the world three times, your mother would have given him leave with a peaceful and glad heart."[22]

Ingeborg Dinesen died on January 27 at the age of eighty-five. To a family member who expressed a rather maudlin concern for Tanne's solitude in the house, she replied coldly and proudly that, on the contrary, her mother's presence was so tangible that she felt no need to grieve—the house was filled with her. But to Parmenia Migel she confessed that she was, in fact, tormented not only by her sorrow but by a retroactive guilt for all that she had taken and demanded of Ingeborg over the years and for having thrown back her "inadequacies" at her. "She had groaned . . . over the Sunday lunches at 'Mama's'; she had derided her mother's political activities and lack of social ambition. She had drawn unfavorable comparisons between the simple pleasures her mother had enjoyed, and the aristocratic *train de vie* at Katholm and Frijsenborg. She had taken all her mother's sacrifices for granted."[23] At fifty-four, Tanne Blixen experienced her mother's death much as she might have at nineteen—with the full force of ambivalence fanning her grief, the ambivalence of a young rebel who is also a loving, fearful, and deeply attached child.

As usual she turned for comfort to her brother and unburdened her feelings to him, but he, for once, rejected her, reminding her bitterly of all her ingratitude and selfishness toward their mother. Perhaps he wanted to nurse his own grief without having to worry first about his sister's; or perhaps he, too, felt some kind of guilt, which he appeased by figuring to himself Tanne's greater shortcomings. It was a terrible time for them both. They fought about the past, the farm, the fortune Tanne had squandered. And this even brought them to quarrel over the inheritance of Rungstedlund, which had been left in equal parts to Anders, Thomas, and Tanne. (Elle was so well provided for by her husband that she was not considered to have an interest.) Anders, Tanne pointed out, lived on the estate at Leerbæk that he would inherit from Aunt Lidda, and Thomas had inherited Folehave from their grandmother. She felt she ought to have Rungstedlund for herself and wanted to live on there alone.

The immediate bitterness subsided and they became friends again, although the problem of the inheritance would be revived in the 1950s. But it was not until Karen Blixen got a little distance from her mother's death that she was able to see what the experience meant, what, in the tumult of the moment, had eluded her. "When I am dead," she told a young friend, who was struggling with his own filial dependence and who was unable to see *her* completely as a human being, "it will be easier. It will be then for you as it was for me, when my mother died, and I sat vigil through the night at her bedside. I saw then not only the old woman, but the lovely young wife, and the girl, and I grasped much I had not understood before."[24]

3

For the first time in her life Karen Blixen had financial independence, no immediate obligations of any kind, and a lull in her physical suffering. That spring she applied for and received a travel grant, the Tagea Brandt traveling fellowship, which had been established by a rich man in memory of his wife and was awarded to women "of liberal persuasion with a slightly conservative tendency."[25] Her plan was to "fulfill an old dream," hatched with Farah in the hard times on the farm, which was to make a pilgrimage to Mecca.

But the fellowship was somewhat modest for an undertaking Karen Blixen admitted would be "silly . . . unless you could carry it through in style," so she proposed to an editor of *The Saturday Evening Post* that in exchange for "a good deal of money" she do a series of letters for them from Arabia. "I am not out for adventure," she stressed. "For one thing I will in no way try to do what I am not allowed to do—it will not be, in any way, a case of 'society woman sneaking into Mekka disguised as a Dervish,' or anything of the sort. I want to travel with the pilgrims, and to talk with them. If I shall not be allowed to enter Mekka, which is very likely, they probably will not have foreign women there—I shall get as near as they will let me, and camp there, and let my servants go in. I shall like to travel in Arabia, to see the horse-market, and to study the ways of the Arabs as much as possible. What I write will be a *document humain* and nothing sensational . . . it is the real everyday life of the Arabs which I want to know—although I do hope, of course, that I may have the opportunity of meeting with unusual happenings and people as well—I have generally been lucky in this way."[26]

That summer, while she waited for a reply, she went to London and made contact with the Arabian legation there. Her hope was to obtain a letter of introduction to King Ibn Saud and an escort from him. While this was pending, she returned to Denmark to attend a performance of *Hamlet* at Kronborg Castle, which starred John Gielgud and which she was to remember as the definitive experience of the play for her. Ole Wivel, who was then a young poet and who did not yet know her personally, watched her mingling with the players before the performance, "sharing her gayety and wisdom with them," and he later caught sight of her in the front row, "a dark-eyed lady in a hat . . . whose lips could form every speech in *Hamlet* as perfectly as the prompter in his box. . . ."[27]

On September 1, the Third Reich invaded Poland, and England and France declared war. On September 3, Karen Blixen drove into Copenhagen and went to see the editor of *Politiken,* a Mr. Hasager. "Give me," she asked, "some work as a journalist, of whatever sort at all, so long as it's outside Denmark." She stressed to him, as she had to the editors of the *Post,* that she was not interested in adventure or sensationalism and, in fact, had "no insight into politics nor any flair for it," which proved to be an accurate self-assessment. But she thought that perhaps "a layman's viewpoint of the war in Europe would be of interest as a *document humain.*"[28] To her utter amazement, the editor agreed. He proposed that she visit the capitals of the three warring powers, Berlin, Paris, and London, and write four articles from each city, which *Politiken* would publish in conjunction with a Swedish and a Norwegian paper. She decided to do her German report first. "I had friends and acquaintances in the government in London, and the expedition would therefore, I thought, be plain-sailing there. I also had good prospects for being able to carry it out in Paris. But I couldn't speak German and had no connections in the Third Reich. After some reflection, I therefore decided to go first to Berlin."[29]

She was, in fact, not quite so resourceless as she claimed; she left for Germany with a letter of introduction to Herman Göring. The young Swedish relation who provided it assured her that Herr Göring was a charming person and a humanist.[30] She also urged Tanne, whose sympathies, she knew, were not with the Nazis, to be fair to Hitler and to National Socialism.

The Third Reich welcomed Baroness Blixen as an important and influential visitor. She was assigned a car, guide, and translator, and she discovered that the Ministry of Propaganda had already planned her itinerary, which included the Reich's "great achievements." This was disappointing, as she had hoped to range somewhat freely through the city. But she began to understand why the government's hospitality was so comprehensive when her guide reminded her, at every stop, to "tell them about this in England."[31]

Many of the Reich's "great personalities" also invited her to meet them. With one exception she declined—aware, however, that this was not being a good reporter. The exception was Hitler, who had personally asked for an introduction. But when she was informed that the Führer would be pleased to accept autographed copies of her books, she "caught a cold and couldn't go. . . . Something in the thought must have been distasteful to me."[32]

In many ways, however, Karen Blixen did follow her Swedish relative's admonition to be "fair." The four essays she wrote from Berlin are critical of National Socialism, but politely so. They take the poetic, disengaged view of the nineteenth-century traveler who is keeping a diary of the strange customs and barbaric notions of an exotic kingdom, and not the view of a woman who did not live far from the German border and whose brother, father, and grandfather had fought Germany in three successive wars. It was, perhaps, an effort to bend over backward, and when she first published the letters, in *Heretica* in 1948, she wondered if her readers would "think that I expressed myself with unreasonable indirection, when I could have been straightforward. They must bear in mind that the letters were written before the Occupation. Denmark was then still neutral and there were matters to be taken into account which later disappeared."[33] Her disclaimer notwithstanding, that serene detachment which was fitting and beautiful in *Out of Africa* seems inappropriate and even negligent in the Berlin of 1940. Of Hitler she observes, "It is strange to think that the being of a single man, like a magnet which passes over a collection of metal fragments, can rearrange and transform a society,"[34] and parts of *Mein Kampf* remind her of the Koran. She draws a parallel between the Nazi bureaucracy and the priesthood during the Catholic Church's period of greatest power—they are filled with the same righteous ardor. She makes a fine discrimination during a concert of Beethoven's Fifth Symphony between the superman and the god and remarks that holiness is absent from this version. She spends the first section of her report describing a visit to her old friend, General von Lettow, in Bremen, in which she reminisces about Africa, deplores colonialism, and identifies the difference between the belligerence of Imperial Germany and that of the Nazis as one of class. She also visits the young Princess Louise of Schaumburg-Lippe, in a villa filled with Meissen and old lace, and goes to the UFA studios to see two films being made: *Jüd Suss,* and a drama about Mary Stuart. What most impresses her is the vulgarity of the costumes and the irony that Zara Leander, who is playing Queen Mary, must take the scene of her capture again and again. Perhaps such delicate insights will have more resonance in a hundred years. But there are some facts of history that simply cannot be assimilated into a *commedia divina,* even as its chapters in Hell. Karen Blixen's viewpoint in her "Letters from a Land at War" is simply too lofty, too personally exempt, too privileged and cautious to give the sinister facts any of their real gravity or importance.

With this in mind it is possible to backtrack a little and to put the Danish criticism of *Seven Gothic Tales* into its contemporary context. The people who were honestly offended by the book (as opposed to the prigs) felt then that the tasks and the suffering of the present were so urgent that it was cavalier to ignore them, to escape from them or to defend the system that had perpetuated them. They felt about the tales as I did about "Letters from a Land at War" when I first read them: that a certain style is inadequate to a certain subject, at a critical point in history.*

Karen Blixen ended her visit to Berlin on April 2 and returned to Copenhagen. She was to fly from there to London, the next lap of her assignment, on April 10. But on the ninth Hitler invaded Denmark.

---

*One may well object that Karen Blixen was innocent of Hitler's plans to exterminate twelve million people. But she was well aware of the violence already perpetrated against the Jews; it was talked about in the family, and soon after Kristallnacht, Mrs. Dinesen, who, like her daughter, had great sympathy and admiration for the Jews, abhors it in a letter. Denmark also had its Nazi speeches and demonstrations in the late thirties and its own homegrown little Führer. What is surprising, in a way, is that with her fine nose for spiritual vulgarity, Karen Blixen was not more offended in Berlin, by its stench.

37

Winter's Tales

G ERMANY SLIPPED a black hood over Denmark, and at first the country
sat calm, but bewildered and furious, on its captor's wrist. Cut off from
the rest of Europe, largely confined to Rungstedlund and its environs by the
lack of gasoline, beset by her usual pains and disinclined to entertain with
no help in her old house, Karen Blixen lived quietly and worked on her third
book, *Winter's Tales,* which she had begun almost as soon as *Out of Africa*
was finished. She took the title from Shakespeare, and a working epigram
as well: "a sad tale's best for winter."

In some ways Karen Blixen's existence during the Occupation resembled
her life on the African farm. She was poor—or, more precisely, strapped. Her
royalties from abroad were, of course, not coming through. She lived alone,
in relative solitude, but said she didn't mind it. A friend who accompanied
her home from a dinner party at which she had been ill watched her disappear
into the vast, blacked-out house and tried to offer his sympathy or assistance,
but she repulsed him. "To be lonely is a state of mind, something completely
other than physical solitude; when modern authors rant about the soul's
intolerable loneliness, it is only proof of their own intolerable emptiness."[1]

The first two winters of the war were exceptionally cold, and in 1940 the
Sound froze over, an event that occurred only a few times in a century. Karen
Blixen shut down the large, drafty reception rooms at Rungstedlund and
moved into the old west wing, where the ceilings were low. Her bedroom
was in a garret, where it was not only warmer but where, on the days when
her pains and cramps kept her in bed, she could see over the low windowsill
across the lawn to the Strandvej and the Sound beyond, and on clear days
to the coast of Sweden. The same friend describes how she would descend
from the garret by a narrow stair to light the fires in the old ceramic and
wrought-iron stoves, stoking them with wood from her own grove as the
servants used to do when the family had lived there and before, when the
house was an inn. Despite its hardship she enjoyed the ritual because she felt
it connected her to the past.

In winter her study was a small room on the ground floor, painted the
color of a fading banknote and called "The Green Room." In summer she

worked in "Ewald's Room," so named by Wilhelm, where he had written *Letters from the Hunt.* The old French wooden screen from Mbogani House was here, and the chests with her things from Africa. In one corner there stood a collection of Masai spears and the tusk of a narwhal. Her desk was placed at right angles to the window, which looked east toward the stony beach, and on it there stood a photograph of Denys from his Eton days in a green leather frame. In summer, when she was feeling strong, she took a bath in the Sound before sitting down to write, and then she would begin by revising and polishing the pages of the preceding day. Throughout her life she worked on the ancient Corona machine she had had in Africa and on which she had typed all her letters. "She could never get used to any other."[2]

Winter's Tales is the most Danish of Karen Blixen's books, the most somber and introspective, the most luminous, and her own favorite. The tales are filled with a poetic feeling—reminiscent of Wilhelm's in *Letters from the Hunt**—for the Danish landscape, its particular stillness and light; for the tempos and speech of rural Danish life and its mythology. Langbaum and other critics have suggested that it was written, at least in part, to secure the good opinion of her countrymen, and perhaps it was. But it was not only a defensive strategy, a desire to repair her past estrangement; it grew out of a feeling of Danish solidarity. These were the fruits that, with care and passion, she could grow in her own garden, and the monotony and scarcity of life under the Occupation are here transmuted into a chasteness of prose. Seven of the tales are set in Scandinavia, and they reflect the determination Karen Blixen felt, in common with her country, not to be colonized or stifled. "Honour thy father and thy mother: that thy days may be long upon the land which the Lord thy God giveth thee." This, she said, was one of the truths the Occupation taught her.†

A great sigh ripples through *Winter's Tales,* and if one theme unifies the eleven stories it is the theme of longing. "The essence of his nature was longing," Isak Dinesen writes of Jens, the dreaming child. But it is also the essence of Peter and Rosa, of Lady Helena, of Charlie Despard. It is the essence of King Erik and of Alkmene. For them desire and experience are at odds—"the two caskets of which each contains the key to the other."

In most of the tales death is the reconciler, and this gives the book its "darkness." But it would be wrong to think of death as a tragedy here— or anywhere—in the work of Isak Dinesen. It is a moment of surrender,

---

*"The Sailor Boy's Tale," which comes first in the British and Danish editions of *Winter's Tales,* was taken from an old folktale that Wilhelm retells in his book *Jagtbreve og Nye Jagtbreve,* on p. 101.

†Annamarie Cleeman, "Karen Blixen Fortæller," *Samleren,* p. 35. The allusive nature of this statement is explained by the fact that it was made during the Occupation, when the media were carefully screened for any explicit anti-German statements. It is a call to patriotism and a reminder of the Danes' hereditary struggles with Germans over Danish soil.

revelation, fulfillment, even ecstasy, and she generally reserves the privilege for those who, like Anne-Marie in "Sorrow Acre," courageously embrace their fates. The real tragedy is to be stranded in some insipid paradise, in some limbo with no charge, to lead an existence like Alkmene's middle age, about which a tale could not be made.

The austere landscape of *Winter's Tales* is the landscape of Isak Dinesen's own childhood: the parsonage where she studied for her communion; the kitchen at Rungstedlund, which was a refuge from the sadness of its salons; the beech woods around the house; the sea; the wild and barren moors of Jutland, which were the moors of Katholm. It is also filled with dreaming children and young people who, like Tanne as a girl, feel themselves to be, in the midst of others, completely alone. They have no equals and are unrecognized by those they live among; their spouses or suitors or foster parents don't understand them, or else they are slavishly adored for the wrong reasons. They feel *forsaken*—but at the same time sense that they have been *chosen*. God is their real parent—a princely, omnipotent lost father—and they must somehow reconnect with him, repossess their birthright. "If he were not a great artist," Charlie Despard asks himself, "who was he that God should love him?"[3] Anyone who has been a precocious misfit as a child will understand this question. Feelings of grandeur and worthlessness vie for his soul.

Isak Dinesen never slaked the longing of her childhood, a fact of which she was proud. She told her friend Bjørnvig that she counted her longing a precious thing, the instinct of some wild, migratory bird, which kept her imagination mobile. She also never really overcame her loneliness. Sometimes she could laugh at it, sometimes even welcome it. But this, too, was a question of "feeling an excess of strength"[4] or none at all. In the periods when, like Charlie Despard, she was neither working nor in love, the sense of worthlessness won out. One could say that she was either passionately connected to her father and to what he stood for in her life, or she was lost—it was another aspect of the either/or. And she would struggle with depression for much of her old age.

Robert Langbaum speaks, in relation to *Winter's Tales,* of Isak Dinesen's "bottomless wisdom." It is a choice expression, especially as there is so much sea imagery in the book. One image in particular keeps recurring: an enveloping blueness, in which the horizon dissolves and the sea and the sky seem to be the same element. This is the vision King Erik has when he clears the hill and looks down upon the shore where Granze is fishing, and it is what Lady Helena remembers about her nine days with the young sailor: "There is no up and down in the sea." She cannot rest until she finds the same blue: "For then everything will be as it was then. All shall be blue around me, and in the midst of the blue world my heart will be innocent and free . . . "[5] The heart can be innocent and free, Dinesen is saying here and throughout

Winter's Tales, only when it is not artificially divided against itself—when heaven and earth, body and spirit can be one. In the case of Lady Helena it is convention which does the dividing: her father's assumption that nine days with a common sailor must be embarrassing for his daughter. In "Alkmene" it is fear of the senses, Puritan morality, smallness. In "The Fish" it is Christianity seen from a more sweeping perspective. " 'Tell me, Sune,' " says the medieval Danish King Erik to his childhood friend, " 'is it by the will of the Lord that mankind cannot be happy, but must ever be longing for the things which they have not, and which, maybe are nowhere to be found? . . . Might not man be in such understanding with the Lord as to say: "I have solved the riddle of this our life. I have made the earth my own, and I am happy with her?" ' "[6]

Sune answers the only way he can, as a Christian priest. Christ, he says, has shown man that the solution to the riddle is acceptance of his earthly misery in exchange for Paradise. But the pagan thrall, Granze, the old wizard, has a different answer. He offers the king a fish that he has caught. In its entrails is a ring. The ring belongs to a lady whom the king will love. Her husband will avenge their adultery by murdering the king. " 'Now the fish has swum, and has been caught. . . . It remains but for you to eat it; your meal is here for you,' "[7] Granze says. At first this seems ominous and even tragic, for by accepting the fish and the ring, the king also seals his fate. But at the same time he enters upon the vital path to his desire.

The pagan Granze understands that "the riddle of this our life"—the nature of experience—is neither good nor evil, neither sacred nor profane, but ironic. The pagan Africans understood this irony, and that is why in *Out of Africa* they seem so much worldlier than their Christian masters and are so inscrutable to them. The natives are amused at life; they tolerate contradiction; they are "in their element," as the more civilized but anxious and rigid Europeans—who must always justify themselves to their own consciences—never can be.

The heroes in the tales of Isak Dinesen all share this ironic vision, which reconciles contradiction. It permits Heloïse, the exotic dancer, to bravely feign chaste indignation. It permits Kasparson, the pervert and murderer, to play the saintly cardinal. It permits Cardinal Salviati to be both Dionysio and Athanasio. This irony was Dinesen's own hard-won attitude to life. She could never "heal" the split in her own nature, but she could transcend it in her tales, where she was free to explore her own limits and paradoxes. Hence the emphasis on metamorphosis, the sexual crossings-over, the harsh laughter and self-mockery—and the blitheness.

Isak Dinesen loved the fact that her old aunts, who were so repelled by sexuality, were also so enthralled with the subject of sexual misconduct, and the same irony operates in her own case. The obsession of her own decadent and fantastic heart is morality. Where she is reticent about psychological analysis, she is fearless about moralizing, although, of course, she does this, like Scheherazade, in the most entertaining way. But the very fact that Isak Dinesen became a storyteller rather than, say, a novelist was a moral choice. She was taking sides with the "heroic" past, and with the fabulists of an older age, against her own contemporaries. The old tales have a common ground with hers, which Walter Benjamin suggests with his usual felicity: "The wisest thing—so the fairy tale taught mankind in olden times, and teaches children to this day—is to meet the forces of the mythical world with cunning and high spirits. (This is how the fairy tale polarizes *Mut,* courage, dividing it dialectically into *Untermut,* that is, cunning, and *Übermut,* high spirits.)"[8]

Dinesen's tales make the same point—in a dialectic manner. They contrast Christian morality with its guilt and humility—which make it passive—to what could be called an heroic morality that is based on honor: trial by ordeal, incurring risk and taking its consequences. The motto of the Finch Hatton family sums up this aristocratic principle most succinctly: *Je responderay.* There is a certain machismo to all this; Dinesen's moral choices are stark and elemental, and they exclude a whole range of mature behavior based on compromise; nor do they preclude unhappiness, error, megalomania, villainy —even death. But they leave the individual free to *act,* to fulfill his destiny, to become "himself." This is the moral of "The Heroine," where it is delivered with wonderful lightness. It is also the great bass note of "Sorrow Acre." There is cruelty, even barbarism in the old lord's sentence upon Anne-Marie, but it leaves her a scope for spiritual grandeur which his nephew's more enlightened philosophy will do away with. The sequel to "Sorrow Acre," which will be the story of young Adam's romantic wanderings, his philanthropy to the peasants, his struggles of conscience, his love for his uncle's wife, is the realm of the novelist.

Thomas often bicycled over from Hillerød to have supper, to read the manuscript and to offer criticism. They sat and talked late into the night as they had in Africa, close in feeling, distant in outlook. The war revived some of their old complicity: "Tanne showed me," her brother wrote " . . . a world above space and time and this absurd war. We certainly did not always agree in our opinions, but after every talk with her I rode back . . . to our strange war duties with fresh inspiration."[9] When the manuscript was finished, early in 1942, she submitted the Danish version to Gyldendal and took the English version to Stockholm. By invoking the names of "mighty" friends in London —Eden, Duff Cooper, even Churchill*—she was able to persuade the British embassy there to forward it in the diplomatic pouch to Putnam's, and

---

*Eden and Duff Cooper were close friends of Lord and Lady Winchilsea; I am not sure how the connection with Churchill was made, but perhaps through the same channels.

Constant Huntington sent it on to Random House in New York. "I can sign no contract and I can read no proofs," she told her publishers. "I leave the fate of my book in your hands."[10]

2

In the spring of 1939 Isak Dinesen had taken Hudson Strode, an American writer from Alabama, on a walk through her woods and gardens, kicking off her shoes at the back door and slipping on a pair of wooden clogs. He had met her only the week before, when they had lunched together at the Yacht Club on the Langelinie—she dressed in a smart suit with a fox boa and a Paris hat—and he had not at first recognized her in her country incarnation. Her hair was tied in a pigtail with a grosgrain ribbon; she wore a pair of old flannel trousers and two black sweaters, with a black woolen "fascinator" around her neck. Her face was scrubbed of rouge and kohl, and Clara Svendsen remarked upon her resemblance, in this garb, to the poet Ewald.

The Baroness and Mr. Strode walked down gravel paths lined with marigolds, tansy, and delphiniums and overgrown with wild flowers. They crossed the small white-painted wooden bridge that spanned a pond and led to Ewald's Hill. Here the forest began. There were ancient beech, ash, maple, and alder trees, and by May it would be like a great vault under the foliage, filled with watery green light. Birds of all kinds nested here, and nightingales lived among the nettles. But the leaves had not yet unfolded, and wild anemones bloomed beneath them. Coming back, she proudly pointed out her kitchen garden. During the war it supplemented the strictly rationed foods available in the grocery, and when Karen Blixen entertained, which was rarely, it was of necessity in a homely, kitchen-garden style. One friend remembers a lamplit winter supper of goose and pancakes that was "so *hyggelig* and Danish"[11]—and so untypical. In the same spirit she looked around to see what diversions and friendships lay within close range. She often set off on her bicycle, dressed in tweeds and a tricorne, riding abreast with the other cyclists on the Strandvej and enjoying their conversation. "There is a snobbish class distinction among motorcars," she told Strode, "but with bicycles the model counts for nothing, nor the age, nor even the sex."[12]

Dr. Vibeke Funch remembered Karen Blixen pedaling her bicycle up the steep hill to Hillerød, dressed in her "curious old clothes," and once arriving on it for a garden party in a long black skirt hitched up with clothespins. Dr. Funch still treats many of the same families her father attended in the days when he was the Dinesens' physician. She reminisced about Rungsted before it was suburban, when the old wooden hotel and its bathing pavilion still stood on the long beach and when the steamer plied the Sound to Copenhagen. She also recalled making house calls to Rungstedlund to give Karen Blixen injections when her pains were particularly bad. "It was the strangest thing about her disease. She could be prostrate one day, barely able to breathe, and the next have the energy of a young girl."[13]

Hartvig Frisch, a classical scholar and socialist, one of the leaders of the Social Democrats, was another neighbor and good friend, who always addressed Tanne as "Mrs. Blixen." He introduced her to the literary critic Aage Marcus and to the great Danish writer Johannes V. Jensen, who would win the Nobel Prize in 1944. Karen Blixen wrote about this meeting to Christian Elling: "On the first occasion we spoke about the sagas . . . and we were immediately united in a great common enthusiasm. J.V.J. was always friendly and amiable to me, and Hartvig Frisch once said, 'I have seldom seen J.V.J.'s rare smile come so spontaneously forth as in talk with you.' "[14]

According to Clara Svendsen, Karen Blixen's conversations with Frisch were of great significance to her. Was there really, she had asked him skeptically in 1941, a true working-class culture, an *arbejderkultur?* She herself had written that "the people's own art is or will be satiric—a kind of tragic satire which preempts all of life's misery and horror as its domain, and laughs at it . . . caustically."[15] But she also felt that the proletariat in contemporary Denmark was no longer distinct from the middle class.

"And the lord of the manor's culture, the *herregaardskultur,* what's that then?" Frisch had asked her in return. She took some pains to reply and did so in a tale. That spring, at the castle of her cousin, Count Bernstorff-Gyldensteen,* she wrote "Sorrow Acre."† It contains her majestic view of the relations between the classes in a pre-Industrial society, when their shared assumptions bound them together in mutual dependence, just as the stark differences between their fates set them apart. She believed that these clear, formal, immutable roles gave each member of the society his dignity and ballast—a role to play in a divine scheme of things. "Sorrow Acre" is also the tale that most clearly expresses her idea that comedy is the privilege of the god and of the aristocrat in his godlike capacity, while tragedy is the privilege of the common man. Unfortunately, we do not know what Hartvig Frisch thought or said about the tale.

Steen Eiler Rasmussen, a noted Danish architect, lived with his family in Rungsted and first met Karen Blixen in 1939. After a formal introduction, they would see each other in a more neighborly fashion. She might, once a week, appear at teatime, "dressed in old rags like a storyteller," announcing that she would "only sit for five minutes." These visits, which might well last through the evening, were as "unaffected and spontaneous as her talk." Conversation skirted the war, and instead they liked to gossip or to play parlor games, of which Karen Blixen was very fond. One of these was a version of the old Victorian game of Preferences, which had been the passion

---

*The count had married Countess Sophie Frijs, sister of Daisy.
†The story is based on a medieval fable, retold by the Danish writer Paul la Cour.

of Aunt Bess. "Who," their modern version went, "would you most like to spend the night with?" "Stalin," said Karen Blixen. "You would never know what he was capable of."[16]

Professor Rasmussen also remembered her making certain good-neighborly rounds. She paid regular visits to a blind man, sitting in the gloom of his parlor, telling him stories or reading him the news. He was literate and opinionated, and liked to discuss the Danish classics with her. She also frequently saw her Aunt Bess. Bess was then in her eighties, still cranky and vigorous, and Tanne's books—of which she was a fan—had greatly enriched the scope of their debates. Bess was probably not at all insulted by her resemblance to Aunt Maren in "The Pearls." This tale develops Tanne's side of an old quarrel—over Sigrid Undset's *Kristin Lavransdatter*. Undset takes the part of the oppressed, virtuous, and hard-working wife against the careless noble husband, and this was how Bess had insisted on seeing her niece's marriage to Bror Blixen. Karen Blixen interprets the conflict as one of attitude, rather than simple oppression. Jensine, in the tale, is the daughter of rich and prudent burghers, who becomes engaged to a young nobleman and guards officer. Aunt Maren, the self-appointed "conscience" of the family, warns her that aristocrats are another and incompatible species, but Jensine won't hear it. On her honeymoon in Norway, however, she discovers that her aunt was right. Alexander, her husband, is a creature totally without fear, and it seems to Jensine also totally without attachments or moral scruples of any kind. She tries to inspire some sense of loss in him—which is to say, some anxiety—by standing on the edge of cliffs and going boating in an electric storm, but this only increases his admiration for her. The only thing that makes him nervous is the way she twists the pearl necklace he has given her, an heirloom that has been in his family for generations. Jensine finally does break the string and takes it to an old shoemaker in the mountains, carefully counting out the pearls as she hands them over. This amuses the old man. We subsequently learn that the shoemaker is a great folklorist and might have been a poet, and the tales he collects are compared to pearls. When he gives Jensine her necklace back, she thinks it feels lighter than before, but as a gesture of defiance to her husband she doesn't count the pearls. When they return to Copenhagen, the Dano-Prussian War is imminent. Alexander is blithely confident of Denmark's invincibility; Jensine has a more realistic sense of the danger and is indignant at her husband's arrogance in the matter. She decides at this moment to count the pearls, after all, perhaps as a way of asking for some sympathy from the heavens. There is, however, one extra, rather than one less, on the strand—and that worth more than the whole necklace. She writes to the old shoemaker, and he explains in a charming letter that he has had a little fun with her, that the pearl belonged to an English lady whose necklace he had once restrung and who had never come back for it. She sees then that she will "never conquer these people"[17]: not her noble husband, nor the old shoemaker—who, as an artisan and a poet, has more affinity with the aristocratic attitude to life than with her own—nor the English lady, whose pearls were of such great price and who had never bothered to recount them. "The carefree people," Langbaum explains gracefully, "are those who live by symbols. It is as a symbol of continuity that the pearls matter to Alexander. And it was in the spirit of artistic play that the old shoemaker added the pearl and so created the story that would be handed down with the necklace." But as in "The Old Chevalier," "Deluge at Norderney" and "Sorrow Acre," Dinesen ends the tale with the "ironic recognition that the aristocratic point of view she is defending had in any case been defeated."[18]

3

Nineteen forty-three was the bicentennial year of Johannes Ewald, Denmark's great lyric poet, who had lived and worked at Rungstedlund, supposedly in the room that was Karen Blixen's study. A group of his devotees wanted to organize a festival and she became involved, offering to open her house and grounds and to give a talk on the occasion. It took place on June 11. A large crowd climbed Ewald's Hill, where a podium had been set up in the clearing, and listened to the speeches and readings. Afterward, there was a reception with light refreshments at the house. The old plank floors of the drawing room were bare and polished and smelled faintly of beeswax. The summer curtains had been hung, long panels of antique lace that swept the ground. The walls were painted a pale blue and hung with family portraits in round gilt frames. A tub of roses, spectacularly arranged, stood on a brass-studded campaign chest and another great bouquet, filled with wild flowers, on a chiffonier. There were some armchairs in the style of Louis XVI, a chintz-covered sofa, and a collection of snuffboxes on a console. The French doors stood open to the garden so the guests could wander out, perhaps reflecting, as Ewald had, on "Rungsted's Beatitudes" ("Rungsteds Lyksaligheder").

At such moments it was almost possible to forget the presence of the Germans, who had been, until then, relatively unobtrusive. When Hitler delivered his ultimatum in 1940, the Danes understood it was pointless to resist and had acted to preserve as many lives and as much of their freedom as possible, while letting the world know that they were not pro-Nazi. From the beginning, German policy was to let Danish life continue "normally," so as to encourage the production of vital food supplies—beef and butter. They also wanted to establish Denmark as a showcase for their administrative benevolence. Schools remained open; the government was permitted to function, albeit with the foreign minister Erik Scavenius, willing to cooperate with the Nazis. The courts and police retained some of their jurisdiction, and the press, while officially censored, was free to publish what it liked about internal matters—a freedom it made use of to attack the Danish Nazi Party. When Scavenius signed the anti–Comintern Pact in 1940, there were demonstrations in the streets of Copenhagen, and angry citizens also broke up a rally of the Danish Nazis—with no interference from the Gestapo. The king refused to accept any Nazis in the government, and in 1943 there was a parliamentary election, much vaunted by the Germans, but in which the Nazis won less than 3 percent of the vote. A Resistance movement existed, abetted by the English, and the opposition to the Germans was widespread and deep. But for the first two years most of it was expressed as *den kolde skulder*—the cold shoulder. King Christian had asked his subjects to remain dignified and calm, and to set an example he rode his horse through the streets of Copenhagen every morning without an escort, a gesture very moving to the Danes and "symbolizing the old days of peace and democracy."*

By 1942 there was an active underground press in Denmark. Three newspapers were published daily, and courageous printers ran off large numbers of anti-German books before their presses were destroyed. A small Communist-led commando group began to carry out acts of sabotage, and other fighters trained privately all over the country, including one troop of Jutland boy scouts. The BBC "V" campaign was seized upon with great enthusiasm by the Danes. "The letter began appearing wherever there was a blank space on an open wall . . . and Beethoven's Fifth Symphony became a favorite selection on the radio . . . for the opening bars duplicated in musical terms the Morse code for the letter *V*—dot, dot, dash."[19] When Hitler sent the king an effusive birthday greeting in 1942, he replied with a terse cable that said, "My utmost thanks, Christian Rex." This outraged the Führer so much that he recalled his ambassador, demanded that Denmark provide thirty thousand soldiers for the German army, called for the ousting of the Danish government and its replacement with Danish Nazis or pro-Germans, and assigned a plenipotentiary, Werner Best, who was instructed to "rule with an iron hand." Tensions and acts of sabotage continued to increase, but Best actually proved to be a moderate who sought a "policy of understanding" with the Danes.

This was how things stood by the summer of 1943. The Germans were in retreat on all fronts, and on September 8, Italy surrendered to the Allies. The Danish underground was now receiving considerable help from England, and a series of strikes and demonstrations had disrupted the production of war matériel. Best was instructed to clamp down severely on Danish freedoms. He presented the Cabinet, now headed by Scavenius, with a series of demands that included the death penalty for sabotage, the surrender of all weapons, and a ban on strikes. But Scavenius refused to comply. The Danish

---

*Richard Petrow, *The Bitter Years: The Invasion and Occupation of Denmark and Norway, April 1940–May 1945*, p. 178. He did not, however, ever put on or promise to put on a yellow armband.

army was immediately disbanded and its officers jailed; the navy's ships were seized, although a few captains managed to scuttle their vessels at the last moment; and a number of prominent citizens were thrown into jail, including two leaders of the Danish Jewish community. Hitler had, in fact, decided to round up and deport the Danish Jews to the Terezin concentration camp, although a few days later the Chief Rabbi was assured that they would not be molested. In the meantime, the leaders of the Resistance organized a Freedom Council to coordinate the efforts and communications of the many groups. It came into being just in time to execute one of the most extraordinary and heroic rescue operations of the war: warning, hiding, and transporting to safety eight thousand Danish Jews.

The roundup was to take place on October 1, and two German troopships had already secretly dropped anchor in Copenhagen harbor. But on September 27, an anti-Nazi employee of the German embassy, G. F. Duckwitz, the shipping attaché, leaked the plans to the leaders of the Social Democratic Party.* They immediately called the two Jewish leaders whom the Nazis had just released, the banker C. B. Henriques and Chief Rabbi Feiniger. Both men refused, point-blank, to believe the warning, saying that not only Werner Best but the Bishop of Copenhagen had assured them there was nothing to fear. Desperate, the socialist leaders turned to other Jewish friends, and it took two days before Henriques and Feiniger were convinced. They made the announcement to their congregations at pre-Rosh Hashonah services, asking everyone present to pass the alarm. "Relative warned relative, friend warned friend, Jew warned Jew; non-Jewish Danes warned their Jewish acquaintances."[20] Local Resistance leaders were given rosters of names to call. Many people acted privately. One ambulance driver read through the Copenhagen phone book looking for people with Jewish names, drove to their homes in his ambulance and offered to take them into hiding. He transported many of them to Bispebjerg Hospital, where the doctors and nurses dispersed them with false charts through the wards. Eight hundred were eventually hidden and saved by this route. Members of the Resistance stopped Jews on the street —they tended to stand out "like ravens," as someone put it—and offered them keys to their apartments. The conductor of a suburban train saw one of his regular passengers, a factory worker, returning from work at midday and immediately offered to hide him and his family. The Chief Rabbi, the rebbetzin, and their five children were given sanctuary by a Lutheran pastor, who refused to see them separated. "So widespread was the willingness of the average Dane to help that by the evening of October first most Jews found safety somewhere. One Dane wrote of his feelings: "In the midst of

---

*A number of historians believe that Best "permitted" the leak. He was resentful of his treatment by the Nazi high command. Petrow speculates that the rescue operation could never have been so successful had the Nazis tried harder to catch the Jews and prosecute those who helped them.

all this tragedy we underwent a great experience, for we saw how that same population which had hitherto said to itself, in awe of German power, 'what can we do?' this same population suddenly rose as one man against the Germans and rendered active help to their innocent brethren."[21]

When the raid began, the Germans shut down all Danish telecommunications and fanned out with the names of eight thousand Danish Jews. They found only some two hundred of them. The poorest Jews—the indigent, those without family or contacts—had not been reached. An Orthodox old-age home had been overlooked, and the patients, all between seventy and ninety, were taken to the synagogue, savagely beaten, and forced to watch its desecration by the Gestapo. A few families had refused to believe "the silly rumors," and they were captured. But more than seven thousand Jews had gone into hiding. That Sunday, October 3, the Bishop of Copenhagen and every Lutheran pastor in the country simultaneously read a proclamation from their pulpits, abhorring the persecution of the Jews and affirming their duty as Christians to oppose it. Labor unions, teachers, lawyers, the police, the Danish Supreme Court, and many social groups vehemently protested to the Germans, and the universities shut down for a week. The Freedom Council denounced the "pogroms" and proclaimed that any Dane who helped the Nazis would be considered a traitor when Germany was defeated. The fate of the Jews was linked with the fate of Denmark, and it galvanized the Resistance and the morale of the entire nation.

Karen Blixen was scheduled to address a meeting of librarians in Hørsholm that Sunday, October 3. One of the librarians was a young woman named Birthe Andrup, who would visit and correspond with Karen Blixen for the rest of her life. The planned literary agenda was immediately scrapped, and instead the meeting turned into a war council. "For Tania," Miss Andrup wrote, "it had an added dimension, which concerned her father and the battle he had fought at eighteen, against the Germans at Dybbøl. The same fight was now ours."[22]

The strategy they discussed, and which was being coordinated all over Denmark by the Resistance, was how to transport the Jews from their various hiding places across the Sound to neutral Sweden, which had agreed, under considerable pressure, to let them in. The distance was about fifteen miles, but the water was well patrolled by German gunboats, and the captains of the fishing fleet who agreed to transport the Jews knew they might be executed or deported along with them if they were caught. The action was carried out in stages, with enormous heroism and daring. Many of the houses along the Strandvej were used as stations on the escape route, and Karen Blixen had given the keys to her kitchen door to two friends in the Resistance, Johannes Rosendahl and Mogens Fog, her doctor, who was a member of the Freedom Council. "There were Jews in the kitchen and Nazis in the garden," she told Ms. Migel. At night she went to bed in her clothes, and looked out her garret window and prayed for dark. When the Germans arrived to inspect the house she held them at the door, "assailing them with sarcasm and rude taunts. . . . It was a pleasure and satisfaction to insult them and there was, if anything, too little risk in doing so."[23]

One group of Jews was betrayed by a fisherman and another by a pro-Nazi Danish woman, and in addition to the 200 arrested on the first night, another 275 were captured and deported. But by the beginning of November, 7,200 Danish Jews had been transported safely to Sweden. The rescue could not have been so successful if many Germans had not looked the other way. One Resistance worker, stopped at a roadblock with a car full of Jewish children, looked the German soldier in the eye and said simply, "Be human."[24] The soldier let them pass. But there was also some bitterness about the money that changed hands; certain captains demanded enormous sums, and certain Jews refused to pay for their poorer brethren. For the Jews, certainly, it was a "period of darkest despair." But for the non-Jewish Danes it was a moment of triumph—and the turning point of the Occupation. "October of 1943 marked a rebirth of hope and dignity through action. . . . Its efforts to rescue the Danish Jews gave the Danish underground an impetus that continued until final victory."[25]

It is worth remarking that the Danish people acted, when they mobilized to save the Jews, in accordance with one of Karen Blixen's most dearly held and most often reiterated principles. Reading accounts of the Occupation, you have the feeling that their courage did not come simply from their deep humanitarian commitment, their sympathy for the persecuted, or even their hatred for the Germans—although this was part of it. It was an idea of honor, a pride shared by an entire people in their own humanity. They would not stand aside and see it violated.

38

Life in a Cage

I

W HEN *Winter's Tales* appeared in Denmark in 1942, Karen Blixen gave an interview to Annamarie Cleeman that was published in *Samleren*. "I don't believe I will ever come to write a novel," she said, "—although one should not forswear anything—for it is not the length that determines the question. . . . It is a qualitative difference between a novel and a short story, a tale."*

But finding herself extremely bored and "life in a cage" too tame, she did begin to write a novel, a kind of thriller, which she called *The Angelic Avengers*. Gyldendal gave her an advance and a stenographer, and, as she freely admitted, she made up the story as she went along. It was never intended to be a work of literature, but just to give its author "a little fun." Nor did she sign any of her established names to it. It was published in 1944 under the pseudonym of a Frenchman, Pierre Andrézel.† The press, however, had no trouble unmasking her, and when *Politiken* asked her to admit her authorship she refused, on the grounds that Andrézel might not want to avow it.

The story of *The Angelic Avengers* is refreshingly silly. Two beautiful and pure young girls become, through a series of disasters, the wards of a puritanical Scottish pastor and his wife, who take them to a villa in the south of France for an "education." The girls discover that the Penhallows are, in fact, white slavers, and that if they are treated well it is only to throw the authorities off the scent of the couple's other abominations. They try to keep their guardians from finding out they know the truth but don't succeed, and Penhallow tries to do away with them. But in the end he hangs himself and the girls marry handsome noblemen. The book was very popular and sold briskly, which was as the author hoped. Several critics did

---

*Annamarie Cleeman, "Karen Blixen Fortæller," *Samleren*, p. 33. A novel, she said, sketches and describes, gives psychological motivation, and may well employ forms of speech one does not hear spoken. But a tale "treats what happens, and the *way* it happens. The tale is the original form of literature . . . tales are written the way one speaks. I also hope that my tales can be told, for thus they have been conceived, and such is my natural form of expression, when I write."
†"Translations" from the English were forbidden.

her the honor of discerning a political allegory in it—the two innocent virgins were Denmark and Penhallow was Hitler—and this added to the sales and the cachet, as it was daring to mock the Nazis. But the book also raised an outcry among some of Karen Blixen's devotees, the vestals of her authorship, and also a number of reviewers, who thought that she had sullied her reputation by writing "trash." Birthe Andrup, the Hørsholm librarian, was originally among them. "No, you will not get my Berlin chronicles or anything else," Karen Blixen scolded her, "until you have changed your Germanic attitude toward Pierre Andrézel, or at least desist from serving it up to me."[1] Later, Karen Blixen confessed her chagrin over the affair to Ms. Andrup: "There is something in the Danish mentality I can't 'take,' and I have felt myself lonely since I came home from Africa. The Danes speak all the time of their sense of humor, 'det danske Lune,' but . . . they have so many times <u>insisted</u> upon taking me seriously, they have not been able or willing to 'play' with me. . . . It is a terribly disconcerting feeling to be the only intoxicated one at a party of very sober people, one feels oppressed. . . . Nor is it one's own fault, for one should have the right to get a little high ('the best of life is but intoxication'). And one can always be very comfortable if one just has a little glass of bubbly along with one's predicament."[2]

The most conciliatory and intelligent word on the matter came from Christian Elling, the cultural critic. In an essay in *Politiken* he alluded to the eighteenth-century Venetian custom of pinning a small mask to one's lapel when one wished to go about incognito without the bother of a disguise, and observed that this symbol was respected. A pseudonym gives an author the same privilege. *"The Angelic Avengers* must be written by Pierre Andrézel," he concluded. "His name stands on the title page."[3]

2

Also on the title page was the name of the purported translator of *The Angelic Avengers:* Clara Svendsen. It was a name that would for the next twenty years be intimately associated with that of Karen Blixen. At first she was her maid and cook; later she became her secretary and companion, her nurse and translator, and finally her literary executor.

Clara Svendsen* has kept a discreet profile through the years, as she did when she worked for the Baroness. Her own memoirs of that service are called simply *Notater om Karen Blixen (Notes on Karen Blixen),* although "notater" could also be translated "minutes," and they are just that: an unembellished and scrupulously factual accounting of daily life, with its small pleasures and chagrins. Parmenia Migel describes Clara's plainness, her

---

*In 1980, Clara Svendsen changed her name to Clara Selborn, but to avoid confusion I use the name by which she is best known in connection with her service to Karen Blixen.

simplicity, her youth—all blushes and lowered eyelids—when she came to work at Rungstedlund. But the fact is she was then twenty-eight, she had had a promising academic career, she spoke several languages well enough to translate from them (including Latin), and was an accomplished pianist. Her letters from the time reveal a style, a forceful and developed sense of irony, and a great lucid spiritual ambition—similar to, although a negative version of Karen Blixen's own. Where Tania aspired to be a priest, Clara aspired to be a follower and communicant. Her model was Saint Adauctus, the martyr's martyr, the "extra" one, who saw Saint Felix and a group of Christians going to their deaths, got the idea that he would go along with them, did so, died, and was blessed. "I think," wrote Clara to Karen Blixen, "that if I shall really hope to exist . . . so must it be as an Adaucta. Should I have the opportunity to do *you* a service once or twice . . . I should certainly comport myself less conspicuously than the good Adauctus."[4]

When Clara was getting to know Karen Blixen but had not yet come to live with her—this was in the second half of 1943—she sat by the fire at Rungstedlund and described the events and stages in her life that had led her, as she believed Karen Blixen could plainly see, to become a person for whom "existence was, in a literal sense, a question of life or death."[5] Her mother had died when she was five. When she was seven or eight her father had taken her to the museum in Copenhagen, where she had seen a portrait of Christ among the dead. It made an overwhelming impression on her, an impression perhaps like that which the eighteenth-century erotic pastoral made upon Calypso in "Deluge at Norderney," or upon Frederick Lamond in "The Heroine": suggesting to a lonely and bereft young person that there was a vital potentiality she had not suspected, a world of love, of friends and recognition. Clara decided that she would become a Catholic, despite great opposition from her father and his second wife. She studied theology and Church history on her own, and in the meantime earned a scholarship to the university, moved to a small apartment so as to be more independent, took several summer jobs, and went on with her plans for conversion.

At seventeen, the age at which Tanne Dinesen felt herself to be "perfect" and at which the highborn virgins in her tales emerge from their convents and are taken to wed, Clara discovered that her life had room for another passion, although of a different sort. She fell in love with Byron and confessed to Karen Blixen that this man, who "had died a hundred years ago, fascinated me more than any living person."[6]

The Baroness was not one to let herself be eclipsed by Byron, or even God. While she was certainly moved by Clara's eloquent confidence to reciprocate with her own, she was also perhaps egged on a little by a spark of competition. Looking Clara in the eye, she told her what had been a strictly kept secret until then, except within the family: that she had been smitten with syphilis by her husband in her first year in Africa. Clara had never before seen a living person with such a "crucified expression."[7]

The die was cast, and Clara knew it. She had met, outside the Church, "a secret martyr."[8] Writing to the Baroness from Risskov in November of 1943, where she had a teaching job, she explained how the tales had revealed the meaning of true religious faith to her and changed her experience of the Communion. She told the story of Saint Adauctus and offered to be of whatever service, however minor, that she could be. She also pointed out to Karen Blixen that she had created a figure very like the martyr's martyr in Marcus Cocoza, who looked forward to introducing himself at the gate of paradise as the "friend of Pellegrina Leoni." That was, she hinted, akin to her own ambition.

Clara Svendsen served Karen Blixen with remarkable unselfishness until she died and devoted much of her own later life to administering the Blixen archives and literary estate. In all true faith there is some doubt and denial, without which it would not be true. And perhaps despite the humility Clara showed and the humiliation that at times she endured, she, like Karen Blixen, saw her existence in the simple, grand, and absolute terms of a parable.

3

After their first few meetings—at a church bazaar where Karen Blixen spoke, over tea at Rungstedlund, and on a summer afternoon, when Clara was invited to gather strawberries and peonies from the garden—Karen Blixen drew her into the elaborate scheme for protecting the identity of Pierre Andrézel. She proposed, and Clara, of course, accepted, that the title page bear her name as the "translator."

In 1944 Clara had the opportunity to render the Baroness another service. There had, for a while, been an excellent if eccentric maid at Rungstedlund, Karen Hansen, who had grown up in an orphanage, loved classical music, and was not intimidated by her employer. But she discovered that she had asthma, which was aggravated by the damp sea air, and the doctor advised her to move inland. Clara was now enlisted to help find a replacement, and when there was no response to their inquiries and advertisements, she decided to "take an unconventional step down on the career ladder"[9] and offered herself as a cook and housemaid. The Baroness, wrote Clara, had some misgivings about someone "sacrificing herself"; she also, wrote Ms. Migel, suspected that while Clara "might become a convenience, she was much more likely to become a nuisance."[10] But she was not one to stand in the path of another's destiny, and she had, around this time, a dream in which Denys, Farah, and Clara all appeared together. So Clara was provided with a uniform and shortly thereafter was asked to address

Karen Blixen in the third person, as *Baronessen,** the Baroness, rather than simply with the polite "you" *(De)*. This did not offend Clara, who, on the contrary, found it quite normal.

Clara made a good sorcerer's apprentice. She had no idea how to cook; Karen Blixen would blithely drop plunkets of wild mushrooms on the table and ask for them to be served on toast at tea, or in *croustades* for dinner as Kamante used to do them, or would refer her to some simple recipe in Mrs. Beeton's cookbook for a poached turbot with hollandaise. Clara would regard the peculiar fungus or the dead fish with an un-Catholic despair and generally do them to death. As Karen Blixen later retold the story to Truman Capote—using considerable poetic license—"After three wretched meals I accused her, 'My dear, you are an imposter. Speak the truth!' She wept and told me she was a schoolteacher from the north of Denmark who loved my books. . . . Since she couldn't cook we arranged she would be secretary. I regret the decision exceedingly, Clara is an appalling tyrant."[11]

But Clara did not immediately become Karen Blixen's secretary. When it was apparent that she lacked any future as a cook, she decided that she could best justify her future employment at Rungstedlund by seeking some experience as a housemaid, and she applied to work as an apprentice with a rich family in the country where she had once tutored the daughter in English. "I understand," she told them, "that my position cannot be the same as before. . . ."[12] In November of 1944 she returned to Rungstedlund and became a maid there.

Clara Svendsen was and has remained an extremely youthful-looking woman with a girlish air, even in her sixties. She has a broad face, soft cheeks and eyes, and a wide mouth. Her hair is worn simply, and her clothes are invariably modest. Clara is not particularly large, but she seemed so beside the frail and tiny Karen Blixen. They cut, as a couple, a rather piquant figure

---

*In the mid-fifties Karen Blixen asked Clara to call her *Tania,* and in 1961, the year before her death, she asked her to use *Tanne.* As for the construction *Baronessen,* it is possible, in Danish, to speak with someone face to face in the third person, using his or her title repetitively in place of the pronoun *you.* "Will the Professor have another pastry?" "Yes, thank you. The Baroness is so kind." It is a very formal usage.

Within a small circle of childhood friends, Karen Blixen was on *du* (the familiar you) terms, but to the rest of Denmark she was the Baroness. The formality was not, of course, one-sided. Where possible, she addressed people by their titles. The young poet Thorkild Bjørnvig was always the Magister; Steen Eiler Rasmussen, her neighbor, was the Professor. And there was always an element of playfulness, of irony in the strict formality, much as in aristocratic South American families the youngest child is often addressed as *usted* by all the others. But people laughed at her for it. She defended herself rather lamely by claiming that it was the old Swedish custom, that it was appropriate to her Swedish title, and that in any case she was used to it. Some people, even family members, questioned the right and the propriety of a divorced woman using her former husband's title, and when she returned from Africa she had briefly considered calling herself "Mrs. Dinesen." But this was awkward for many reasons, and she finally decided against any change, on the grounds that her former servants would never then be able to reach her.

—Sancho Panza and Don Quixote, as they themselves said. There was, as the years passed, every kind of cynical and fantastic speculation about the nature of this relationship, as there had been in the case of the Baroness and Farah Aden. Karen Blixen's family was appalled by the manner in which she could "abuse" Clara, and the manner in which Clara accepted to be treated. But Tanne had once reminded them that intimacy is mysterious, that no outsider should presume to judge a marriage, and the same suspension of disbelief is owed to other intimate covenants. Because of her violent temper and her caustic wit, people generally misjudged or misread Karen Blixen's depth of feeling in a given relationship. Most of her abuse was superficial, and she lamented it later. It was an intense experience to be her friend, and the greater part of that intensity was the extraordinary vigor of her love. Clara gives us a glimpse of what the relationship really contained in a sentence from a letter in 1944: "I have never," she told Karen Blixen, "felt so overwhelmed, annihilated and blessed as with you the other day."[13]

4

Other young people began to gravitate toward Karen Blixen during the war. Erling Schroeder, a theater director, came to discuss the possibility of dramatizing one of her tales and remained her friend for life. He had the looks and charm of the matinée idol he had been, a silvery voice, a gallant manner, and, as Ms. Migel writes, "Tania was as vulnerable as anyone, but it was Schroeder, in the end, who succumbed."[14] He became her confidant, infinitely indulgent with her dark moods, and when she needed to be told that she was beautiful, she called him and he responded. He was also someone she could "play" with: fantasize, gossip, flirt, behave with a confident and shameless coquetry.

Johannes Rosendahl also met Karen Blixen in 1943. He was a literary critic and writer who was then teaching high school and had written an essay on Karen Blixen that she had liked. They met; she was struck, as Ole Wivel was, by the heroic proportions of his character, and with her "typical instinct" for her friends' real potential, she sent him a little thank-you present for the essay. It was simply an empty matchbox with the picture of "Tordenskjold"* on the cover and a note that read: "There ought to be many men like him!"[15] Rosendahl at the time was a pacifist, but he subsequently became active in the Resistance, one of the most daring saboteurs in south Jutland. He was hated by the Nazis, who finally caught him, tortured him, and condemned him to death. But he survived and after the war credited Karen Blixen with having inspired him to act.

Ole Wivel, who tells the story of Rosendahl's heroism in his memoirs,

---

*"Tordenskjold," whose head appears on Danish matchboxes, was the nom de guerre of Admiral Wessel (1690–1720), a great Danish naval hero.

also met Karen Blixen in 1943. He was a slight, elegant, and very fair young man from a family of rich merchants who had an estate on the coast a little south of Rungstedlund. He was still in his early twenties, studying business but writing poetry, filled with great literary and spiritual ambitions, but also with "pangs of conscience and self-contempt."[16] *Seven Gothic Tales* had not meant much to him, but he and his best friend, Knud W. Jensen, had read *Winter's Tales* aloud, so moved and filled with turbulent admiration that they couldn't get to sleep afterward. He had then written to Karen Blixen, sending her his manuscript of poems, and she had replied with an invitation to come and see her.

"Karen Blixen stood in the sitting room and received me with a sweetness and a calm that immediately felt liberating. There was a fire in the hearth, we sat drinking tea, she smoked cigarette after cigarette and spoke without interruption, slowly and with her peculiar diction, which was at the same time bred of old culture and solemnity and . . . warmed by a wealth of nuance."[17] They spoke about the neighborhood, the stretch of the Strandvej so familiar to them both, and all the while Wivel was taking in her presence, her "great, dark, brilliant eyes, and the long hair tied in a pigtail. . . . There was a grey streak in her hair, but she seemed youthful when she rose and opened the verandah doors to the garden, and spoke about her father's and mother's love for the place. It was one of the mildest winters I can remember, January had the air of Spring, and the Sound lay free of ice and was turning blue in the sunshine."[18]

From then on they visited and corresponded. Wivel sent her his own essay on her authorship, which she praised as "original and rich in thought." He was proud to be told that this was "just how I would have my authorship understood." But when he sent her a piece of fiction, she was honest with him. "I think that you have talent, but that to a certain degree you lack courage . . . it takes terrible courage to create! A French officer who rode in the *concours hippique* once told me that one had to *jeter le coeur* over the fence first, and then it was easy to make the horse follow. Writing is the same."[19]

39

Heretics

T HE GERMANS WERE naturally frustrated and enraged by the disappearance from under their noses of seven thousand Jews, and there were reprisals. The homes of suspected leaders of the Resistance were raided and suspects dragged off to be tortured and killed. The Resistance then stepped up its acts of sabotage, blowing up supply dumps and even factories, and began to execute any Dane known to be betraying his fellow workers. The Germans countered with the murder of Kaj Munk, the writer, and other selected culture heroes. They also burned the Tivoli Gardens and organized bands of criminals to commit acts of terror—rape, assault, and the random murder of passersby—in the streets of Copenhagen. Tension in the capital was so high that early in the summer of 1944 a curfew was imposed, and assemblies of more than five people were forbidden. A day later the workers walked off their jobs at the country's two largest shipyards; other workers followed suit, and their action led to a spontaneous general strike in Copenhagen, during which the citizens took to the streets, demonstrating against the Gestapo terror. Commandant Best responded by imposing martial law and cutting off the city's electricity, gas, and water, but the tactic didn't work; the demonstrations only intensified.

That September, having established that the police were working with the Resistance, the Germans decided to round them up and send them off to concentration camps. Before the raid, the officers went into hiding as the Jews had done, but two thousand were caught and deported. From then until the end of the war Denmark was without a police force, and the population organized patrols of unarmed volunteers to deal with the problem of common crime as best they could. In the final months of the Occupation, violence and bloodshed increased dramatically: railroad lines were blown up; the Gestapo headquarters in Jutland, Copenhagen, and Funen were bombed and their archives destroyed; and "reprisals were made in a crescendo of violence and brutality."[1]

On April 17, Karen Blixen quietly celebrated her sixtieth birthday with a hot-chocolate party for her household. This now included Clara as the secretary and housemaid; Helene Lundgren, the gardener's widow, who was serving temporarily as the housekeeper; Alfred Pedersen, the family's old chauffeur and former coachman; and Mr. Nielsen, the new gardener, who gave Karen Blixen a newborn Alsatian puppy. She called him Pasop, after the peasants' dog in "Deluge at Norderney" who spends the night in the hayloft with the aristocrats. Of all her dogs—even Dusk and Banja, the Scottish deerhounds—he became her most beloved. The birthday, however, was a particularly painful landmark. She "loathed the idea of growing old."[2]

Two weeks later, the Allies conquered Berlin. Ole Wivel was alone that evening in his house at Vedbæk, and he cycled to Rungstedlund, embraced Karen Blixen, and drank a glass of wine with her. "She was like a young girl who was finally going to the ball she had, for so long, looked forward to," he remembered. She told Wivel a touching story. Earlier in the day she had phoned her brother Thomas to exult over the victory with him. He had invited a group of friends to the house, had poured champagne for them and made a speech—raising his glass at the end of it and saying, "To our conquered foe." It was the expression, in Wivel's words, of his "youth's barbarous chivalry." The room fell silent. No one would join him, and Thomas emptied the glass alone.[3]

That summer Karen Blixen entered the hospital. She had been suffering from severe stomach cramps, a new twist to her more familiar pains. The doctors diagnosed a duodenal ulcer and told her that it came from "mental overwork." They decided not to operate on the ulcer, but they enforced bed rest and idleness. When she had gained some weight and recovered a little strength, they wanted to perform surgery on her spine, which, if it worked, would relieve some of the syphilitic pain. In the meantime Karen Blixen was confined to bed, and during this period she worked on the English translation of *The Angelic Avengers,* dictating to Clara, who worked overtime with no additional pay, retyping and revising. The operation to sever some "vegetable nerves"[4] was performed in the middle of February 1946, and it brought her immediate relief from the worst of the pain. But she wouldn't give her body enough time to heal and instead began taking long rides on her bicycle, working in the garden, and—despite the fact that the doctors had sawed through a rib—carrying heavy buckets of water on an old yoke from the well to the espalier. She had to be recommitted to the hospital for some supervised convalescence.

While she was there, Thomas brought Tanne a sad and ironic piece of news: Bror Blixen had died in Sweden, of injuries sustained in a car crash. Divorced from his third wife, Eva Dixon, he had left Africa in the late thirties and gone briefly to work for the millionaire sportsman Winston Guest as a sort of master of the hunt on his Long Island estate. Mr. Guest found it difficult to believe that "Blicky" suffered from tertiary syphilis and described him, at fifty, as a man of undiminished appetite, stamina, and extravagance.[5] On a Gardiner's Island pheasant shoot Bror had tried to break the record bag of thirty-two hundred birds—and had come close. The arrangement did not ultimately work out, and Bror returned to Sweden, settling down in Borringe Kloster, a small family dependency owned by his cousin, Count Bech-Friis, the driver of the car in which he died. It was exactly the kind of small farm and life he had fled when he married Tanne.

Elle Dahl wrote to her sister at the time of Bror's death, and her letter also struck a note of melancholy irony. Tanne had been reconciled with the Dahls the preceding Christmas at her own request, and Knud had died a short time later. Now Elle felt herself utterly destitute. Commiserating with her sister on her operation, she reminded Tanne that "you yourself always say that you are at your best when you don't move." But as for herself, she saw no consolation in the future. "You always had the happiness," she told Tanne, "that in the midst of your unhappiness you could rage at Fate—wail and complain—but I cannot. Unlike you I can also not live in the continuation of a bygone happiness, because a door has been shut between me and it. Knud was my life, and with him I have not only lost my rudder, but my sail and my ballast, and a ship that no longer has any of its parts is badly fixed, especially because *navigare necesse est.*"[6]

2

As soon as the mails were open to America, Robert Haas wrote to tell Isak Dinesen that *Winter's Tales* had been a great critical and financial success, that it had been sold to the Book-of-the-Month-Club, and that she had more than thirty thousand dollars in royalties on account. He also enclosed the Armed Services edition of *Winter's Tales,* a book sized to fit the pocket of combat fatigues and printed on onionskin. "Few things," Dinesen replied, "during these last years have given me such pleasure. I consider it a great honor to be published in this way, and to feel that my book may have entertained and pleased a few of our gallant allies! . . . I had tea with our Queen yesterday, and presented her with one of the copies you sent me, and she was extremely pleased with it. I also had the great joy of receiving a letter from an American soldier who told me that he and his comrades have been reading my book in Germany and the Philippines."[7]

Haas was naturally not pleased to hear that Isak Dinesen would under no circumstances consent to having her name appear as the author of *The Angelic Avengers.* "I think," he flattered her, "that the way you have created an authentic Jane Austen atmosphere is a real *tour de force,*"[8] and he also cajoled her with the prospect of enormous royalties. But as susceptible as Karen Blixen the woman was to compliments and Karen Blixen the scrooge was to money, Isak Dinesen the author was unmovable on what she considered a point of honor: this bastard of no literary value must not be treated as a legitimate offspring. Writing from her sickbed, filled with regret that she lacked the force to be persuasive, she explained to Haas "what great delight it gives me to be told that my name has become one almost to conjure with on the American market. But the more it is so, the greater care I will take of that name, the more I shall feel my artistic responsibility and the call of *noblesse oblige.* You tell me that as far as you know I am the only author who until now has written just three books, all of which were B.O.M. selections. I do not now want to give my name as an author to a book which cannot possibly come into consideration for such a selection. (Or even, if *par impossible,* the B.O.M. should consider this book, I should refuse to have it selected and would rather withdraw the manuscript altogether, than have it placed in this category with my other books.")[9]

The B.O.M. did select *The Angelic Avengers;* Isak Dinesen reacted as she had promised; Haas patiently brought her around, by which time she understood how the selection worked and felt some embarrassment at her prior elation and pride.

For the next two years, with ghoulish regularity, Karen Blixen was in and out of the hospital for more operations and periods of convalescence. In 1947 she told an old friend (her former stenographer, Ulla Pedersen) that she was so thoroughly "sliced through on all my flanks and edges"[10] that it really ought to suffice. It was very difficult for her to gain weight, especially as tempting foodstuffs were scarce after the war,* and she was generally so weak that she began taking "something to get her going in the morning,"[11] a medication that contained amphetamines, which became a force of habit, undermining her even further. But what was most distressing was the fact that she had aged so drastically since the war began. Ole Wivel had described her "girlish" air in 1943, and Hudson Strode had admired her "boyishly" slender figure. But now her face seemed to have collapsed; the fine lines became deep furrows.

Under these conditions it was tremendously hard work for her to write, and she fought to reach—and kept falling short of—her standards for the first three books. Although she would not publish a new book for the next ten years, she did have two full-scale projects that she worked on when her strength permitted: an immense and intricate "novel" composed of self-contained but interwoven tales, rather like the *Thousand and One Nights,* which she called *Albondocani,*† and a volume of *New Winter's Tales,* with primarily Danish settings. But she was also firmly convinced that she should

---

*Haas and other American admirers sent her care packages of rice, olives, bananas, coffee, dried fruit and nuts, white flour, and Virginia cigarettes, but some of this was embezzled by dishonest servants. "It is always so tiresome to be disappointed in one's belief in people, but without being too materialistic may I say it is doubly tiresome when one's confidence is disappointed to the tune of 12 lbs. of coffee and a sack of rice, which one hoped to have in store for festive occasions." (KB to Ulla Pedersen, 20 November 1947, KBA 67.)

†*See* below, p. (363). She also mentions the "riches of Albondocani" in her *Letters from Africa,* p. 357.

keep up the "lighter" side of her authorship, which had brought her such unexpected wealth. She told Haas she would write tales that would "not be without literary interest" but that could not be compared to her "real" work, and for the purposes of their correspondence she referred to them as *Anecdotes of Destiny.* [12] She did eventually write a handful of magazine pieces that were published in *The Ladies' Home Journal* and recited on the Danish radio. But the title *Anecdotes of Destiny* was redeemed for the final volume of tales published in her lifetime, which contains some of her greatest work.

At the time of her operations in 1946, Karen Blixen spoke to Birthe Andrup about the three forms of perfect joy in life. The first was the cessation of pain; the second, to feel an excess of strength; and the third, to be convinced one was fulfilling one's destiny. [13] She would never again have an excess of strength, but almost as soon as she had anything above the subsistence level she made some travel plans. She told Haas that she was coming to America, and twice that she would be going to Paris or Rome—and could he slip her a little spending money from her royalties, a few hundred dollars under the table, so to speak, by sending them to her *poste restante* at the Danish embassy? [14] But the American trip was canceled when her health deteriorated, and the Italian journey by the sudden death, on May 8, 1947, of Bess Westenholz at the age of eighty-nine. Tanne had sat vigil at her aunt's deathbed and had genuinely mourned her, but the death was not premature. After the funeral it was "too late to go South," and she consoled herself with "three splendid weeks in London." [15]

Her ambitious travel plans were made possible by her postwar royalties, which, at least before they were taxed, were considerable; *The Angelic Avengers* alone sold ninety thousand copies in America. She could now afford some first-rate help, and after Mrs. Lundgren retired she hired a professional cook and a proper maid. Clara was put on a reduced salary, and she left to find translation work, coming back to Rungstedlund on the weekends to help Karen Blixen with her correspondence.

Much of this correspondence, at least with Robert Haas, was devoted to financial problems, and in particular to taxation. Until a new international agreement was signed, authors' royalties were doubly taxed, once in their own country and once in the country where their books were sold. Karen Blixen claimed that she lost 90 percent of her profits this way, although it is difficult to understand what she then could have lived on. But the problem was compounded by the fact that enormous sums had been credited to her account in a single year, after five years without income. It was also compounded by the fact that her business was managed by a series of agents and lawyers who seem to have been as incompetent and quixotic in such matters as Karen Blixen herself. Either they did not respond to cables, made outlandish demands and then lapsed into silence, or they had only the vaguest notions about the American tax laws. It is also possible that their advice, distilled through Karen Blixen's harassed understanding of it, was distorted, or that her own inaction rendered their work void. But in the end she blamed Denmark and democracy for trying to ruin her; she complained to Ole Wivel that she would have to sell Rungstedlund and emigrate; her outrage at the supertax coalesced with her outrage at the way the Danish critics misunderstood her work.

3

During the war Karen Blixen often visited Ole and Kil Wivel at their villa in Vedbæk. She motored down the Strandvej in her little two-seater, in her baggy trousers and an old sweater, and generally barged in on them unexpected. She would, of course, politely swear that she could stay only for five minutes, but then she would sit for hours, drinking tea and refusing food, smoking fiendishly, "speaking in her dark voice on everything that was bright and wonderful in the world, on her own expectations and hope, and her belief that a new art of poetry would rise like a phoenix from the war's smoldering embers." There were many occasions when the young couple crouched on the floor under the windowsill when they saw her car. Sometimes Ole's friend, Knud W. Jensen, was with them, and the three of them would have to hold their breaths so they wouldn't laugh. Thirty years later Wivel spoke of it with a smile, but also a certain shame. "She was lonely," he said. "She let herself have a good time with us. Now it's too late."[16]

After the war Wivel began bringing a new generation of Danish writers and poets to meet Karen Blixen, serving up the handsome young men in shirt-sleeves to her as he served up the ravaged old genius in black to them. Many of them were Wivel's authors, for he and Jensen had started a small publishing venture. Jensen, like Wivel, was the scion of rich Copenhagen merchants, but unlike Wivel he had been pressured by his family to forsake an academic career in art history and run the business. He was an aggressive entrepreneur and very rich, but he also wanted to preserve his contact with the world of art. Eventually he would build, furnish, and endow the splendid Danish museum of modern art, Louisiana.

In the beginning Wivels Forlag was hardly a publishing "house"; the whole operation was lodged in and conducted from Jensen's Copenhagen pied-à-terre, with Wivel and another friend, Helge Bertram, a socialist painter, doing the editorial work and Jensen paying the bills. Their first list had four books, all in translation, all dealing with the theory and problems of modern art. Esthetics was to be their specialty as publishers, and they especially wanted to find books that explored, as Wivel put it, "the problems of modernism vs. tradition." They were searching for new ideas and new examples of literature and painting that would liberate them and Denmark from what they perceived as a sterile impasse for "the human spirit." Specifically, they wanted works that eschewed both Marxist and orthodox Christian morality. They hated what they saw as a vast ideological "mobilization" on both the left and right, which threatened to trample the individual's "right to a free self-understanding." Art, they believed, was not only the purest and noblest expression of that self-understanding but might also be the means to it, if the public's consciousness could be heightened. That was to be their mission in the coming decade.[17]

They were joined by other like-minded young idealists. Among the first of these was Bjørn Poulsen, who had translated T. S. Eliot's essays into Danish. Poulsen was something of a foil for the small and courtly Wivel. He was a Jutlander, a man both "hearty and sarcastic," with a mixture of "rustic originality and intellectual precision" in his speech.[18] Poulsen in turn drew Thorkild Bjørnvig into the group. Bjørnvig, now one of Denmark's leading poets, was then finishing his master's degree at Aarhus University and writing a dissertation on Rilke, whose sensibility and eroticism had a great influence on his own work. He had collected his manuscript of poems but not yet published it, and in the next few years he was torn between his overwhelming desire to do nothing but write and other demands: an academic career; marriage and a child; editing the literary review *Heretica;* * and what was to be the most consuming distraction of all, his relationship with Karen Blixen.

Bjørnvig, like Poulsen, was a curious mixture of ferocity and nuance, although in his case there was more nuance. Physically he was rather compact, a small bear, with a bear's stubbornness, greed for life, and charm. He was forthright in his warmth and a little indecisive in his movements, which could make him seem rather vulnerable in contrast to his sturdiness. His eyes were an astonishing blue, and his dark hair was thick and tousled. Today it is snow white.

Much later, defining himself (ironically) by one of Karen Blixen's check-lists for him, Bjørnvig would write: "I was not humble and uncomplicated like Rosa, not unambivalently faithful, like Pasop, did not possess Farah's stability and *grandezza,* but was, despite periods of ecstatic and inspired certainty, of a passionate and awkward, irresolute and contradictory nature, one who came easily to hybris and to depression and reposed best in humor and submission."[19] Ole Wivel, more reserved than Bjørnvig, more existentially cautious, found him "as mysterious as a sorcerer."[20]

The group, this "Vedbæk Parnassus," thus consolidated. To its members it had the glamour of a cenacle. The young men felt themselves to be part of a revolutionary avant-garde, and the works of art and criticism they would create or publish would be the "tools," the "weapons" of this revolution. Wivel envisaged rousing "the emotional and intellectual forces" in Denmark to a "cultural crisis." The language and the mood were apocalyptic.

---

*Bjørnvig edited *Heretica* from 1947 to 1949.

There were certain striking features about this little group, which made its headquarters in the Jensen and Wivel villas at Vedbæk. It was exclusively young and male, and eager to make something happen. Its members were the products of the Danish university system, and even though they came from very different social worlds they formed a class, almost a tribe of "students" in the traditional European sense. Their intimacies took place through the medium of intellectual debate, late nights spent arguing the details of language and the meaning of symbols. Criticism was to them as wrestling to friends of another class and world: a form of almost physical contact and understanding. Naturally there were extraordinary rivalries and conflicts in that closed circle, under the pressure of all that ambition. But these, too, took intellectual forms; they were worked through in reference to art and ideology, to *Weltanschauung* and God. "What a stupid husband I have," Bjørn Poulsen's wife joked. "All he ever lives for is to write letters."[21]

Poulsen and Wivel had been discussing a literary journal, a "manifesto" that would embody the editorial ideals of the publishing house and the Vedbæk Parnassus. They saw it as a forum for radical works and theories of "any persuasion," so long as they were not tainted by or subservient to an ideology. They did not immediately perceive the hidden reactionary bias of this idea, although it was not unperceived by others. As the journal began to take shape, Helge Bertram left Wivels Forlag. He could not reconcile his socialist principles with the estheticism that was becoming more militant by the day.

Wivel and Poulsen were clear about one thing: that if their journal was to have any influence, it needed two kinds of support—the prestige of quality and the prestige of greatness. They were confident that their roster of young critics and poets would provide the quality. They also intended to approach certain of Denmark's older distinguished authors, whom they felt would share their outlook. If they could not persuade them to join the editorial board, they hoped at least to persuade them to contribute works. The first writer they approached was Martin A. Hansen. The second was Vilhelm Grønbech.* The third—although naturally they did not say what the order was—was Karen Blixen.

4

Karen Blixen's place in contemporary Danish literature and the influence of other Danish writers on her work do not, unfortunately, fall within the

---

*Vilhelm Grønbech (1873–1948). A Danish philosopher and historian, professor of the history of religion, and "the great synthesist of twentieth century Denmark, as Grundtvig and Kierkegaard had been the synthesists, seers and prophets of nineteenth century Denmark. His first great work was a study of the pagan beliefs of the Germanic peoples. He called for a return to metaphysics; modern man, he repeated, was desperately in need of a new myth. Wivel, in particular, took up this challenge in his own poetry and believed that only through myth could the experience of war be understood." (P. M. Mitchell, *A History of Danish Literature*, p. 290.)

scope of this biography or of my own competence as a critic. The subject is complex and rich, but one about which I cannot do more than generalize —and thus risk doing less than thorough justice to Karen Blixen's Danishness.

In some ways, though, her relationship with Martin A. Hansen is a little mirror (with dark glass) that reflects the larger picture. He is generally regarded as the greatest writer of his generation and one of the greatest Danish writers of this century. Thorkild Bjørnvig wrote a book on Hansen's authorship; Ole Wivel, who was Hansen's friend, was profoundly influenced by his religious thought; and, indeed, it would be hard to find a poet or a novelist in postwar Denmark who was not, in some way, touched by him. He was important not only to the intellectuals; his work was demanding, but despite this fact it sold in large numbers and continues to do so. This is because he speaks so directly to the Danes about the conditions of their life and about their common spiritual predicaments. It is also because, as H. Wayne Schow, his English translator, has written, "Only a few writers are gifted with an instinct for finding symbols . . . and charging them with meaning. The words 'gifted' and 'instinct' are used deliberately, for it is doubtful that mythic vision of this kind is acquired with intent."[22] Hansen has this and certain other things in common with Karen Blixen. But she acknowledged her relationship to him only obliquely and ironically, in the anagram she made of his name: *Han Er Min Satan.* *

Hansen was born in 1909, the son of a small farmer in Stevns, a peninsula to the south of Copenhagen, and from his childhood he was "exposed to the last phase of the dying *almue kultur,* i.e., the culture of the rural commoners derived from the old peasant tradition,"[23] with which his work is deeply imbued. Like Karen Blixen and Thomas Mann, he perceived his parents as a duality. His father was the stable, prudent, "blue-eyed" one, from a family much respected in its neighborhood. But his mother, the daughter of a poor woodcutter, was of a passionate and unsteady people, their lives "marked by excess, irrationality and tragedy. 'Two kinds of blood course in my veins,' " Hansen said.[24]

At seventeen he left the farm to study at a seminary and then became a schoolteacher in Copenhagen. During the thirties he rebelled against the deeply ingrained religiousness of his childhood and became a Communist sympathizer. His first two novels describe the desperate straits of small farmers like his father during the Depression. They are grim and eloquent portraits of rural life, vivid in their feel for Danish nature and very much in the literary mainstream of that decade. He attributed his social conscience to his father, but from his mother he felt he had got what Schow calls his

---

*"He is my Satan" (Bjørnvig, *Pagten,* p. 36). Making anagrams was one of her favorite pastimes, a parlor game she sometimes played with her friends. She worked them out on grids, often on the backs of tales that she was working on.

"dedication—both reluctant and willing—to the poet's calling, including its asocial and demonic dimensions." The Second World War and the Occupation shook his faith in the rational, materialistic, and essentially hopeful philosophy he had adopted, and "into the resulting intellectual vacuum flowed nihilism with all of its terrible enticements."[25] His two major novels of the forties are fantastic folkloric allegories. *Jonatans Rejse* (1941) is the tale of a smithy who captures the Devil in a bottle and, as he doesn't know what to do with him, decides to bring him to the king. *Lykkelige Kristoffer* (1945) is a "quest" novel set in the Denmark of the Reformation. An impoverished young nobleman searches for something "to live and die for, when everything seems in the process of dissolution."[26] Hansen also published two volumes of short fiction during this period and wrote prolifically for the underground press. He had a "demonic" impulse to work, coming home after his day of teaching to write through the night, suffering from migraines and insomnia, and becoming dependent upon stimulants to keep his strength up. He was both convinced and terrified he would die young, which he did—at forty-six.

After the war Hansen began to make peace with his anguish, his sense of life's absurdity, and, as Schow puts it, "made a Kierkegaardian" leap to faith.[27] In the late forties and early fifties he began to define a philosophy he called "ethical pessimism." It argued that human beings must first despair before they can find meaning, that there is a price to pay for a moral life, that whosoever would be honest toward reality cannot avoid unhappiness. But it also argues that one may recover one's spirituality—"return to the metaphysical by way of reason."[28] Hansen himself turned back to the Christian tradition that had been so great a part of his early life, although not to the established Church. He preached an ironic, an existential Christianity. With Ole Wivel he would make a tour of Denmark's Romanesque churches and study its pre-Gothic Christianity, and from this work came *Orm og Tyr,* a remarkable history of Scandinavian religious literature and of the relations between pagan and Christian cultures.

Karen Blixen would have strong objections to and a certain jealousy toward Hansen's influence on her young friends. To her, his religiosity was insincere, a sham. And when a critic, writing in *Heretica,* compared Hansen's lyrical nature poetry to the magical nature poetry of primitive peoples, she got angry. It "astonished" her, she told Bjørnvig, that Martin A. Hansen and his disciples believed they could "work magic . . . by the rules of an esthetic textbook or a catechism," and she went on to say that she was in harmony with God and nature as Hansen and his friends could never hope to be. "I can forget . . . as [they] certainly cannot—what day of the week it is, but not where the four corners of the world are, or from which direction the wind is blowing, or what phase the moon is in. . . . These modern poetic spirits—Martin A. Hansen, Paul la Cour, Ole Wivel—they talk so much about the mystical, but are without belief, and in my own opinion, without honor."[29]

Ole Wivel describes his first meeting with Martin A. Hansen in the summer of 1947. Hansen and his wife, Vera, had come to visit the Wivels at Vedbæk, and the two couples sat in the lush garden by the Sound throughout a long June afternoon. The sun was hot and steady, and Hansen "gave off warmth from his being like a great stone. . . . I felt his magnetic power not—as often among other artists—as a feeling of intoxication or of seduction, but as peace."[30] About that time, Wivel must have discussed Blixen and Hansen with each other, for he writes about their mutual reservations. "Perhaps," he speculates, "they esteemed one another so highly that they could only express their judgment in the form of criticism. In any case Martin remarked that in Karen Blixen's tales there was the scent of moldy winter apples in a peasant's hayloft. She in turn found it hard to breathe in his plebian air." But they both were fascinated by each other's eyes. "Karen Blixen spoke of Martin's strong and clear blue eyes, while he admired the fact that she didn't blink at all with her great dark ones, when flashbulbs went off at them."[31] Their wariness finally reminded Wivel of an old cartoon that hung in his grandmother's bedroom. It showed King Christian IV meeting a peasant on the bridge outside the Frederiksborg Palace. "The King stops, leans on his walking stick and asks the peasant: 'Who do you think is king here in this country?' The peasant replies, 'Well it must be either you or me.' "[32]

5

Ole Wivel, Bjørn Poulsen, and Thorkild Bjørnvig had all driven to Rungstedlund on a lovely June morning in 1947 to engage Karen Blixen's lance on their great crusade, but she wasn't home; she had gone to visit the Bernstorff-Gyldensteens in the country. Her absence gave them time to conceive certain misgivings about approaching her. They knew she would not like sharing the role of banneret with Martin Hansen. Perhaps they also suspected that certain of their humanitarian and religious objectives would be alien to her. So they let the summer pass.

When Karen Blixen came home from her visit, she called Wivel and asked him to drop in on her. Wivel now consulted Poulsen on the best tactic to employ, and Poulsen counseled brazen flattery. Tell her, he said, that we "honor her life's wisdom as the noblest brew we've got. . . ."[33] This Wivel did. He prefaced it with a long exposition of how different conditions were for his generation, what tasks they faced, and then asserted their enormous spiritual debt to her. "The metaphysical exists in our time only abstractly, but in you . . . it has physical life. Style, one used to say, is the spirit's manifestation, and style in life is precisely that. It is to be found, supremely, where your being works its magic."[34]

This speech came in the nick of time to rescue Karen Blixen from a bout of depression. She was weak, unable to work or to connect with her work; she felt herself a complete "stranger" in the Danish literary milieu, misunderstood by her countrymen; and her taxes were oppressing her so that she couldn't "make ends meet" at Rungstedlund—she had again thought of emigrating. Now Wivel put his case so strongly—and her needy ears so slanted what he said—that she believed this journal was being created as a tribute to her art and values, and promised it her protection.

After a long search, during which such names as Orpheus, Phoenix, Thermopylae, and Atlantis were suggested—the latter three "warmly disadvised"[35] by Karen Blixen on the grounds that they were too mystical—the editors decided to call their manifesto *Heretica*. They were—in an age of orthodoxies—heretics, transgressors. It was a name that suggests the intensity of their convictions and also the view they took—and that it was possible to take in the hothouse atmosphere of Danish intellectual life—of their importance. The first issue of *Heretica* appeared in January of 1948, edited by Poulsen and Bjørnvig.*

Knud W. Jensen bought a house in Hørsholm, which was not far from Vedbæk and close to Rungsted; he built a guest cottage on the property where Thorkild Bjørnvig and Bjørn Poulsen, who both lived in Aarhus, could stay with their families when they came to Copenhagen. It also meant that all the core members of *Heretica* would be within a few miles of one another. Isak Dinesen had set her tale "The Poet" in this charming little town. It was in Hørsholm that Councillor Matthieson and his friend, Count von Schimmelman, took their walks, recalled Weimar, and spoke of Destiny; and it was here, too, that the councillor met the young poet of peasant origins, Anders Kube, for whom he would plan a tragic destiny—throwing him together with his own young wife. Suffering and unrequited passion, he thought, would make Anders into a great artist and a credit to his creator.

Bjørnvig met Karen Blixen at Jensen's house in Hørsholm, although he claims not to remember their first meeting. It took place late in the winter of 1948, in March. Karen Blixen had come home from the Jensens' party and told Clara that she had met a young poet there "about whom there was

---

*Heretica was published until 1953. It had a surprisingly large number of subscribers, which, as P. M. Mitchell notes, "evidences the timeliness of the theses which were expounded and the questions which were debated in the periodical . . . the writers who originally contributed to *Heretica* . . . represented the first concentrated efforts of an identifiable literary school in Denmark since the days of Johan Ludvig Heiberg a century before. And, like the Heiberg school, the *Heretica* group stressed the aesthetic nature of literature. Literature was again to be art and not propaganda.

"In answer to the criticism that *Heretica* inclined too much to the metaphysical, Martin A. Hansen wrote that the periodical had arrived at the metaphysical through the use of reason, therewith implying that the new school was progressive and transcendental rather than reactionary" (Mitchell, *A History of Danish Literature*, p. 293).

something special."[36] On March 9, Bjørnvig wrote a short note to the Baroness: "I like so much to hear you talk . . . I can plainly conjure back your patient-impatient expression when the conversation begins to run down, where there is no more fertile soil. When you begin to speak there is no reality in the room."[37]

She gave him a standing invitation to come and see her, with more than her usual casual generosity, and he accepted. At first they talked mostly about her work, and she inevitably showed him Schyberg's review of *Seven Gothic Tales,* a ritual she performed with all the young writers who came to see her. She asked Bjørnvig to respond to it, which he did, gracefully—but also gracefully declined to write the rebuttal she desired, or the book on her authorship she urged him to undertake, immediately, in time to anticipate a critical study by the critic Hans Brix. Bjørnvig was not, he made it clear, to be her literary page boy.

Almost as soon as this was settled, their relationship began to deepen. Karen Blixen told Bjørnvig that she saw it had "another meaning" and that "one day soon" she would tell him what it was.[38]

40

Death of a Centaur

I

THROUGHOUT THE FORTIES Rungstedlund saw a procession of servants come and go. There was no bathroom in the house until 1960, and the maids had to carry the hot water for Karen Blixen's bath up a narrow flight of stairs and empty it into the old tub in her dressing room. The vessel they used was called the "quitting bucket," for the obvious reasons. In the kitchen cooks and housekeepers struggled with the old wood-burning stove, and under the quaint tyranny of Mrs. Beeton's book on household management. Some of them made off with bags of rice or coffee, others with tales of mistreatment or penury. There were certain spiritual privileges in working for Karen Blixen, and a great many practical disadvantages. She gave her employees the freedom of the demesne, invited them and their friends to gather her strawberries and her peonies, celebrated their birthdays, "took a deep interest in their lives."[1] She also tended to niggle about their actual wages.

In the spring of 1949 a new housekeeper, Caroline Carlsen, joined the staff, which then included a parlormaid and a chambermaid, a gardener, Clara, and Alfred Pedersen. Mrs. Carlsen had a son, Nils, who was then four, tow-headed and cherubic, and who was to play a minor but important and characteristic role in Karen Blixen's domestic life: he became her *toto*.

Nils Carlsen had quite naturally been afraid of the Baroness when they were first introduced. Skinny, wrinkled, odd, with a deep voice and a piercing gaze, she could not have seemed quite human to a four-year-old, particularly as his own mother was a plump and fair young woman in her thirties. But gradually he was disarmed. The Baroness got down on the carpet with him and played safari, bringing out her collection of beautiful old wooden animals, or made him toys from raw potatoes. She patiently let his curiosity overcome his shyness and invited him to come and visit her when-ever he liked—to sniff her out. In the evenings, after his mother had put him to bed and gone out with her own friends, Karen Blixen would go to his bedroom and tell him stories. Once she forgot, and then he came howling into the drawing room, saying he had had bad dreams. "A real friendship sprang up between them," Mrs. Carlsen wrote in her memoir of Karen

Blixen, "and he felt a boundless confidence and faith in her, a faith which she never disappointed. He could always go to her, whether or not she had guests or was working, the door was never locked."[2]

Karen Blixen tried to teach Nils Carlsen "fearlessness" and other aristocratic virtues, and when he had lived with her for a year she had a little military uniform tailored for him, with braids and epaulets, and he was initiated as her page into the ancient rites of the drawing room. If she won his trust completely by never failing to respond to him, perhaps she also gave him a sense of the high value of what he had got by making demands on him in turn: for an imaginative response to *her* being. There was an element in their relationship of Titania and her changeling boy, who was a slave-child and a god-child at the same time, plaything and idol, revered but possessed, spoiled but also exploited for her own pleasure. Karen Blixen's interest in Nils, as in the children of her brother or her old friends, the Reventlows, was passionate but not conventionally maternal. She was not one of those people who "loves children" or who takes a kind, mentorly interest in young people. She looked them over more like a gypsy, with an eye for what might, with a little trouble, be made of them. Many of her young friends rebelled when she tried to treat them as human dolls and dress them up from her great steamer trunk of destinies, even if they often went along a little way for the fun of it. Her adolescent nieces would rebel, as would Thorkild Bjørnvig. But Nils did not have to, partly because there was less pressure on him and partly because he was so much younger. It is a child's dream to be "exploited" in this fashion—skillfully, attentively—to be "made something of" by an imaginative adult. Young children were, in general, an appreciative audience for Karen Blixen's special human qualities and needs: her playfulness and her caprice, her love of ritual and belief in magic, her resourcefulness with words and things. She recovered, among them, a sense of the identity she had enjoyed among the Africans. Bjørnvig uses the word *urmoder* to describe her: primeval mother.

Mrs. Carlsen had come to Rungstedlund not completely aware of "whose house I was in." When she began to take stock, "it shocked me a little." She knew vaguely who Karen Blixen was and had read *The Angelic Avengers,* but she now bought a copy of *Out of Africa.* After the honeymoon period of her service, she also began to assess its difficulties. There were the archaic procedures by which the house was kept in working order, and there were its stubborn and at times conflicting personalities, who challenged her patience and agility to much the same degree. The Baroness had a bad temper, particularly when she was ill. If things went wrong she took them personally, as she had in Africa. In the beginning there was a subtle power struggle over Nils, and when Mrs. Carlsen explained that there were certain things she had to deal with on her own, that he was *her* son, Karen Blixen replied a little plaintively: "Yes, but he is also now a little mine."[3] Yet Mrs. Carlsen was also strong enough to set limits, both as a mother and an employee; she had a good Danish sense of humor, and she came to perceive the charm both of Rungstedlund and its mistress. "I have never thought that she was sweet and nice all the time, or that it was always pleasant to live under her roof. She was, though, a person with stronger feelings than so many others. Therefore there were things which pained her, and when something pains you, it can well make you unreasonable. You can't blame someone for that. I know that some people criticized her for being aristocratically remote and unapproachable, but she was in so many respects much more human than ordinary people could ever dream of being."[4]

2

After the war Karen Blixen began to entertain much more frequently. She writes with pride about a visit from Queen Alexandrine and another from Niels Bohr. Ole Wivel continued to feed her his new discoveries, like the gifted young "Adonis," Frank Jæger.* Her door was open to anyone who wanted to discuss her work seriously, and Bent Mohn, a literary critic at *Politiken,* met her in this way. He in turn introduced her to his friend Eugene Haynes, a black American pianist whom Karen Blixen welcomed with particular warmth and who returned often as her houseguest. Bent and Eugene were in their early twenties: Bent lanky and fair, Eugene round-cheeked and mahogany, both of them tender, civilized, and responsive.

Karen Blixen's dinners and luncheon parties were always small, never more than six or eight, so that she could speak with and appreciate each guest. She had a great gift as a hostess; she could turn her attention upon a guest with such radiance that he felt he had never before been so articulate or so well understood. The refinement of the setting played its part, as did the food. The Baroness herself ate frugally and shunned "artful [culinary] refinements," but it was a great pleasure for her, as it had been in Africa, to spoil her guests. Turbot from the Sound, asparagus and strawberries from the garden, oysters, wild mushrooms gathered in her woods, soufflés, the perfect consommé— these were all specialties of the house. Everything was "made from scratch," and neither she nor Mrs. Carlsen would have dreamed of offering a guest bakery tea cakes. At lunch and dinner there were always three courses, and they were served with well-chosen wines.

This, of course, did not come cheap. Nor did the maintenance of Rungstedlund, which was eternally in need of some repair. Nor did the salaries, however sketchy, of her large staff. Money continued to be a vital issue for Karen Blixen, just as feeling herself on the brink of bankruptcy was a habit

---

*Frank Jæger (1926–1977). A lyric poet who is, however, better known for his witty prose, particularly *The Sufferings of the Young Jæger,* 1953.

she never could outgrow. There were moments when she treated her publishers and agents with the same high-handed shrewdness she had shown the shareholders of Karen Coffee, and despite a good working relationship with Robert Haas, for example, and the fact that she received a 20 percent royalty, she threatned periodically to take her books elsewhere. Her family and close associates, particularly Clara, were asked to make "sacrifices" as in the old days. Clara had been promised a percentage of the royalties for her work on *The Angelic Avengers,* but when the time came to hand over the money, Karen Blixen pleaded poverty.

Early in the summer of 1949 she went to Venice for a brief holiday, accompanied by one of her oldest friends, Count Julius Wedell, the husband of Inger Frijs, who would serve as a *cavalier servente* on several future trips abroad. He was a large, suave, and handsome man in his late sixties, a connoisseur of art and antiques, and his taste was so definitive that Tanne had nicknamed him "Petronius," after Petronius Arbiter. They visited noble friends, dined at the Cipriani, gambled at the Lido, rode in gondolas, listened to music, and, of course, looked at art. Karen Blixen came home exhilarated but broke and decided she would try her hand at writing for the lucrative American magazine market. "Sorrow Acre" had originally appeared in *The Ladies' Home Journal,* and in August a visiting English friend, Geoffrey Gorer, made her a bet she couldn't write something acceptable to *The Saturday Evening Post.* She took the bet, but not Gorer's advice to do it with "tongue in cheek," which was beneath her dignity. But she would try to keep the requirements of the "market" in mind. And what were they? "Write about food," Gorer told her. "Americans are obsessed with food."[5]

The result of this wager was "Babette's Feast," one of Isak Dinesen's most deft and exquisite comedies. Like certain feats in the kitchen, the lightness of the finished work belies the heaviness of its ingredients, for the tale takes issue with the notion of an either/or, an irreconcilable duality of experience, and shows how, in the work of a great artist, "bliss" and "righteousness" may be reconciled. That epiphany, that mystical high which the guests achieve at Babette's table, seems also to be the echo of Tania's own suppers with Denys at Ngong. General Galliflet sums up the experience in terms she herself had used with Thomas when he tells the young Lorens Loewenhielm: "This woman is turning a dinner at the Café Anglais into a kind of love affair—into a love affair of the noble and romantic category in which one no longer distinguishes between bodily and spiritual appetite or satiety."[6]

Isak Dinesen was never more like Pellegrina Leoni than when she set out to conquer the American magazine market arrayed in all the splendor of her talent, and found out that she had been "invited to a homely gathering in honour of the police magistrate, at which everyday clothes are worn."[7] *The*

Saturday Evening Post rejected "Babette's Feast," although they did take a much inferior story, which Dinesen herself called "idiotic."* Next, she sent Babette to *Good Housekeeping,* still hopeful that its subject—food—would be up their alley. They wrote to say how great a stir the manuscript had caused in their offices, but that, alas, the story could be of interest only to "those in the upper income brackets," and they had to turn it down. Growing more and more discouraged, she posted it to *The Ladies' Home Journal* and for a long interval heard nothing. But they did eventually accept it and took another tale. They were published in 1950 and 1951 respectively.†

The return from Venice to Rungstedlund, the intense work of the summer and its meager rewards, all depressed Karen Blixen. Her deep depression took a familiar form—an almost paranoid sense of estrangement and alienation from the Danes. This was how she had felt toward her family at the most unhappy moments of her childhood and how, in the darkest periods on the farm, she had felt toward the English. One day at the end of October she motored down the Strandvej in her little car and paid an uninvited visit to Ole and Kil Wivel, who did not, on this occasion, crouch under the window-sill. She told them straightaway that she could not "continue," that indeed she was dying and that they must promise—as they had once spoken of making a trip with her to Nairobi—to fly to Africa with her ashes and scatter them in the Ngong hills. Aghast, all they could think to say was yes.

3

By 1949 Karen Blixen had been back in Denmark a year longer than she had lived in Africa. She had lost touch with her friends from that era and with her servants. When, after the war, she wrote to her former solicitors in Nairobi to inquire about her people, Messrs. W. C. Hunter & Co. told her that Farah had died and that without him it was impossible to contact the others. It was rare now that she spoke English. Denmark had closed around her the way the polite aristocratic world had swallowed up Lady Helena (in "The Young Man with the Carnation") after her "ordeal" with

---

*"Uncle Seneca," retitled "The Uncertain Heiress," which was published in December 1949. The heroine of the tale is the daughter of a poor but proud and rather vainglorious Shakespearean actor who goes to visit her rich relations in the country with the object of making them feel ashamed of how they have treated her father and of their own philistine way of life. The young man of the family, her cousin Albert, falls in love with her and promises to give her the money for her father's monument. But she repulses his advance. "Uncle Seneca," a kindly old relation who lives with the rich cousins, is the only member of the household who appeals to her, and the attraction is mutual. Before she leaves, he confesses that he is Jack the Ripper. Shortly thereafter he dies, leaving her his large fortune but obliging her, when she does raise the monument to her father's genius, to carve an inscription at its base. The inscription is: "In memoriam, J.T.R."
†"Ghost Horses." Along with "Uncle Seneca" and other uncollected or unpublished minor work, this was published by the University of Chicago Press in *Carnival, Entertainments and Posthumous Tales* (1975).

the young sailor, and she was out of touch with the forces which in Africa had given her spiritual strength.

She had tried to maintain a sense of connection by becoming, in postwar Denmark, her own "brass serpent."* She took it upon herself to represent the values of the lost aristocratic world to the modern one with exemplary clarity—the clarity of a parable or a myth. And she had begun to chisel a public figure in which those values were dramatically embodied and stylized: the grande dame, the sibyl, the storyteller who was "three thousand years old and had dined with Socrates."† But there were also times—when her work went badly, when her health failed, when a critic misunderstood her or an inferior book was highly praised—that she looked down from her pinnacle with the bitterness of Lear. She, too, had lived to see the power that had once been centered in her person (her class, her ideals) dissipated into warring factions. She had no sympathy for the Left, with its "despair and *ressentiment,*" and less for the metaphysical right, which, under the guidance of Martin Hansen, was turning back to a modern version of Grundtvig's Christian idealism. Ole Wivel and many of his friends were influenced by this trend, and it was reflected in the contents of *Heretica*. This was all the more disillusioning for Karen Blixen, who had hoped that the journal would be the manifesto of her own outlook. They had *no honor,* she would repeat to Bjørnvig. The Christ they talked and wrote about redeemed his followers "under anesthesia." They were unwilling to "stand in a direct relation to God." What made religion interesting in the old days, she told him, was the risk one took with one's soul. Then the drama wasn't belittled, as she believed it to be by liberal modern religions with their "symbolic" Christs and their salvation "under anesthesia." Honor, she went on—by which she meant the courage to take a risk wasn't challenged by experience anymore, and modern life also tended to obscure what was still a truth: that the danger (of perdition) was real. She urged Bjørnvig not to write for "*Heretica* or any movement or culture camp . . . but to write because you owe God an answer."[8]

Like Nietzsche, Karen Blixen liked to sneer at the healthy-mindedness of her contemporaries, and they always seemed to rise to it. Wivel described how she would "alienate" people with her reactionary pronouncements. "I am willing to accept democracy," she liked to say, "when all women are beautiful and intelligent. But if I am more interesting than seven others, they should be grateful to have so high a standard to live up to."[9] This was a calculated provocation; she had, after all, been provoking the outrage of

---

*See *Out of Africa*, p. 106. The Africans turn Karen Blixen into a symbol, and she uses the term "brass-serpenting" to describe it.
†The young men on *Heretica* so described her. See Thorkild Bjørnvig, *Pagten,* p. 131; Isak Dinesen, *Daguerreotypes*, p. 18.

liberals since she was ten and knew the trick. But she also complained to Wivel, Birthe Andrup, and others that she was "always taken so *seriously,*" when she had just wanted to play, wanted a little sport, a little fun—a puppy growling at a metaphysical bone in the hope that someone would throw it far enough to provide some exercise in the retrieval. *She* was alienated, she sighed, by all their solemn pronouncements about God, magic, and poetry, in which they really had no belief. She listened to their talk about the political and social consequences of art, and laughed at the way a poem full of obscure religious dogma was greeted as an historical event comparable to the bombing of Hiroshima, or how a provincial academic theologian was made into an intellectual hero.

In the winter of 1949 a novel appeared that crystalized all her disgruntlement and hurt. This novel, *Rytteren (The Riding Master),* was consumed with almost universal delight by the Danish public and achieved, almost immediately, the status of a modern classic. Karen Blixen took the story very personally and identified with the fate of its central character, a centaur. She also sat down to write a critique of it, addressed in a sincere and personal voice to the author himself, Hans Christian Branner. Briefly, the story concerns four characters who have all known and in different ways fallen under the spell of a riding master named Hubert. He is dead, trampled by a horse, and this was either an accident or a murder, for several of the characters claim to have killed him. But none of them can forget him, and, indeed, the novel is a series of conversations in which they argue, lament, execrate, revere, and struggle with his memory.

The two central characters are the centaur's mistress, Suzanne, and her current lover, a physician named Clemens. He is a small, ungainly man in a shiny suit, prone to fat and sweating, who lives in an apartment cluttered with French furniture. Despite the rather pathetic light in which he is first portrayed, he becomes a heroic figure in the story, identified with Christ himself. He lays the centaur's ghost; he wrests Suzanne's soul from its bondage to Hubert's memory—and here Karen Blixen points out that Branner had followed the plot of an old Danish ballad, in which a knight redeems his beloved from the body of a falcon. But she takes him to task for his "dishonesty" with the story, first because he violates its internal logic, manipulates events and feelings for the sake of effect and without regard for their actuality: "Where there is a long and careful spiritual accounting, conscientiously carried out, it is not permissiable to withhold a single cipher from the first column of numbers or to keep it secret."[10] But her most serious complaint is that Clemens is so repulsive as a redeemer. "In the new gospel of *The Riding Master* Clemens is the Savior, the personification of the good, and he saves through charity. As long as he practices this automatic salvation in the book, without cooperation from those he saves, he redeems them less than he demeans them. We ask ourselves and the author, 'How could Suzanne permit this disgrace? She has loved Hubert. She has lain with him in the stall among the horses—and there was no bed, only an outspread horse-blanket and, about them, the large sleeping horses. She has dreamed about a time before time, and about vast foggy plains where the horses wandered freely. She has desired to bear her lover a horse-child, a horse-god. How did she arrive in Clemens's bed, amidst his heirloom furniture?"[11]

The essay concludes with a passionate cry or outcry, which is also the throwing down of the demon's gauntlet: "Danish poets of the year of Our Lord 1949! Press the grape of myth or adventure into the empty goblet of the thirsting people! Do not give them bread when they ask for stones—a rune stone or the old black stone from the Kaaba; don't give them a fish, or five small fish, or anything in the sign of the fish, when they ask for a serpent."*

---

*Karen Blixen, *Daguerreotypes,* p. 191. Here Karen Blixen is taking a swipe at Ole Wivel, who had published a long theological poem called "In the Sign of the Fish," 1948.

41

Folie à Deux

I

IN THE SPRING OF 1949 Thorkild Bjørnvig, his wife Grete, and their son Bo
moved to Knud W. Jensen's guest cottage in Hørsholm to be near the other
members of *Heretica,* of which Bjørnvig was, with Bjørn Poulsen, the
co-editor. He was now able to visit Karen Blixen often. Sometimes he came
with Wivel and Jensen, and one afternoon Jensen took photographs of the
Baroness and the Magister together in the garden, with a little puppy. She
was wearing a pair of loose velvet trousers and a strange peaked hood, like
that of a witch in an old book of fairy tales; her eyes were darkly made up
and shining, and her smile was not ambiguously twisted, as it is in almost
all her other pictures, but unchecked by irony. She looked radiantly beautiful.
Bjørnvig, by comparison, seemed somewhat bemused and faraway. Until he
joined *Heretica* he had thought Karen Blixen was dead, and he had not
completely recovered from his surprise to find her still alive. He saw her as
"a person of the kind I had only heard of in myths and stories." That
afternoon in particular she looked and acted the part, and he wrote to her
afterward: "Your presence makes me very nervous and very pure. I feel as
if there is a great stirring in the air, a power, and can one long for more?"[1]
Notes like this were exchanged between them in the months which followed.
No man had ever responded to Karen Blixen with such powerful, articulate,
and reckless self-surrender, and she is not to be blamed if she got a little drunk
on it.

The Baroness had invited Bjørnvig to come and see her whenever he liked,
and had done so in such a way that it was clear she was not simply being
polite. They dined together in the Green Room, and at first their conversations turned upon the politics and personalities of *Heretica.* But gradually
they discovered "greater and more common themes, like Eros and Christen-
dom, animals and the cosmos, war and vivisection, and the often unexpected
and spontaneous agreement didn't stop the flow of talk, as may happen, but
led it on . . . into a kind of blissful productive dimension."[2] When Bjørnvig
went home to his cottage he was filled with "a more powerful expectation
of life"[3] than he had ever known.

This was a period of great slackness in Karen Blixen's own life. It was the period of her sterile and frustrating attempt to make money writing for magazines, of having her inferior stories accepted and her good ones turned down, of receiving letters from Haas inquiring with patient insistence if she did not have any new tales and of having to reply that her "lighter" work was not fit to be offered for the same consideration as her serious writing. The more a "blissful productive dimension" eluded her in her own work, the more she looked upon Bjørnvig, on his great but unpolished talent, as an alternative project: she would take him under her protection and tutelage and turn him into the major poet he was capable of becoming. Imperfect and incomplete alone, together they would be a unity.

In the months that followed Karen Blixen expressed to Bjørnvig, in an increasingly explicit and solemn manner, the extraordinary faith and confidence she felt in him. He confessed that he did not actually understand what she meant, but he also let her know that whatever it was, he reciprocated it without reservation. This was what she needed to hear. In a letter written in January of 1950 she told him: "It is very good to know that there is a person I can count upon as I counted upon Farah. Therefore I will now lay my cape over you, as Elias did with Elisha, as a sign that I will let three-quarters of my spirit rest with you."[4]

This letter was the first formal document of what they called their "pact" and which Karen Blixen considered to be a mystical union, a vow of eternal love, a covenant similar to the covenants she had felt between herself and Wilhelm, Farah, and the Africans. But there was a rather more disturbing, grandiose dimension to it: Bjørnvig was, as Karen Blixen saw it, entrusting his soul to her, in exchange for her eternal vigilance and protection. As she claimed she had once promised her own soul to the devil in exchange for the gift of telling tales, she now took over the demonic role and promised the same gift of genius to someone else.

2

Karen Blixen's relationship with Thorkild Bjørnvig lasted for four years. One could also say it "ran," as a play runs; or that it raged, as a fury rages. It was one of the great dramas of her life, dramatic in many senses, not the least of which was that she herself staged its scenes punctiliously. She spoke and acted throughout as from an archaic manuscript she had long ago learned by heart, one like *The Revenge of Truth,* which she had written as a girl and carried with her from Denmark to Africa and back again, all the while revising. From time to time she had tried out a little scene with one friend or another: with Eduard Reventlow in Paris, who had been bewildered; with Denys, who had trouble keeping a straight face; with Casparsson or Erling Schroeder, gallant professionals, but not more than that. She had, of course, taken some of the best parts for her tales, and the scenario had been pillaged thoroughly by 1949, when Bjørnvig came on the scene. But she had never until then been able to see it played precisely as it was written.

What made the production possible, finally, was the fact that Bjørnvig—who naturally did not have a copy of the script—nevertheless threw himself into it as if he had known the speeches all along, from another life, and had been gifted with the ability to speak and improvise in the same riddling, archaic poetry. He fumbled in places and let her down; he laughed self-consciously, almost giggled, which she couldn't stand; his timing was too slow, his movements too hesitant and awkward; he was "too soft." But these, Karen Blixen felt, were the traces of his rustic origins and provincial education, and here she excelled as a coach. Taking great pleasure in the effort, she set out to perfect him, to make him—as she herself phrased it—"hard."

Isak Dinesen tells the story of her passion for Bjørnvig in "Echoes," written after the pact was broken, and which we shall look at in its proper place. It is Thorkild Bjørnvig's account that admits us to their intimacy. It is called *Pagten (The Pact),* and it is generous with details, conversations, letters, and eloquent about his own feelings. The decision to write this memoir, twenty-five years later, was difficult for him. He finally did so, partly at the urging of Frans Lasson* and partly because he had promised the Baroness that he would write about her after her death. *Pagten* is a masterful work of self-revelation, in part because Bjørnvig does not attempt to censor or to mitigate with irony his own state of mind at the time the events took place or to revise the figure cut by the young Thorkild Bjørnvig. This he renders in all its innocence and pride, pathos and absurdity; in all its torment, craziness, and poetry.

There is an aphorism Bjørnvig quotes that came to stand for him as the expression of that strange pact. One day, reading Franz Werfel's *Theologumena,* he came across a passage that he read aloud to the Baroness. "God speaks only to the oldest souls," it began, "the ones most experienced in living and suffering: 'You shall belong to no one and to nothing, to no party, to no majority, to no minority, to no society except in that it serves me at my altar. You shall not belong to your parents, not to your wife nor children, nor to your brothers and sisters, nor to them who speak your language, nor those who speak any other—and least of all to thine own self. You shall belong only to *me* in this world.' " Karen Blixen took the book away from him at that point and, in a strong hand, crossed out the word "God" where it appeared on the page and wrote the word "I" over it. Under the passage she signed her name. "This became a formula for our pact," wrote Bjørnvig, "and . . . the expression for an extreme case of *folie à deux.*"[5]

One afternoon, shortly after the pact had been made, Karen Blixen drove

*Editor of her *Letters from Africa* and of *The Life and Destiny of Karen Blixen,* and president of the Karen Blixen Society.

down to Vedbæk, where the Bjørnvigs had found a little house. Standing in their parlor, she suddenly embraced and kissed their son, Bo, who was then two. Thorkild was perplexed by so "uncharacteristic a fit of tenderness" and not less so when, the next evening, he was summoned to Rungstedlund. Karen Blixen received him in the drawing room and with great dignity proceeded to relieve him of an anxiety he had never dreamed of feeling: that Bo would catch syphilis. She had, she said, assumed that he knew her "life's bitter secret," and she went on to explain that it had not only cut her off "from life, not only from the Erotic, but had made any physical contact taboo."⁶ It was no longer contagious, she assured him, and could only still hurt herself. She then asked Bjørnvig to imagine what a terrible sacrifice it was for a young woman to forego all the pleasures of the flesh. At that moment she had promised the Devil her soul, in exchange for the power of telling tales.

The significance of this little scene is manifold. It dramatized the demonic source of her authority and talent; it aired her own anxiety about contagion, an anxiety, according to Dr. Fog, she continued to feel, irrationally, despite his reassurances.⁷ But it also permitted her to air—and to seek reassurance for—an anxiety of a different kind. Their talk turned, in conjunction with syphilis, to Nietzsche, and Karen Blixen told Bjørnvig that she had loved Zarathustra since her youth. Then she said to him: "But since you understand Nietzsche so well, you must also be able to tell me, if you see, if you have seen, any sign of the same kind of megalomania in me. And if you do, you must warn me immediately—you truly owe that to me, for it is part of our pact: you shall protect my honor."⁸

That April, Bjørnvig and his family went to Paris on a fellowship. Karen Blixen had encouraged him to make the trip and to study French, which she considered would be an "experience" for him, a step in the direction of refinement. When he described his difficulties with the language, she wrote a long, exhortatory letter taking him to task. If it had not been for his wife, she told him, she would have given him the advice her father had shared with the readers of *Letters from the Hunt*: *"Il faut coucher avec sa dictionnaire."** Thorkild took this to mean something like "putting the dictionary under your pillow," and he didn't understand why it would annoy his wife.

She had already begun her program to strengthen his spirit through adventure and suffering, to refine his manners and his style through pleasure and travel, and to make him a man of the world in the mold of Wilhelm or Denys. And he had already begun to put up a kind of subliminal resistance to her. His first letters from Paris were filled with a mixture of "dementia praecox and hybris." Back at Rungstedlund, Karen Blixen lost her patience

---

*"One should sleep with one's dictionary" (Thorkild Bjørnvig, *Pagten*, p. 17; cf. Wilhelm Dinesen, *Jagtbreve og Nye Jagtbreve*, p. 50).

and pounded on her writing table: "I wish this blow might hit the Magister in the head." As it happened, Bjørnvig tells us, on the same day, at the same hour, he struck his head on the sharp corner of a table and had a concussion, which he ignored against the advice of his doctors until a month later, when he finally collapsed. The Baroness wrote a sweet letter of condolence to his wife. Privately she reproached herself for "having hit too hard."[9]

3

The seventeenth of April, 1950, was Karen Blixen's sixty-fifth birthday, and she invited Ole Wivel alone to dinner in the Green Room. The table had been decorated for a party, and they toasted one another, talking playfully as they had so many times before. But while dessert was being served, the hostess excused herself and came back with two volumes. One was the latest issue of *Heretica,* and she had marked a page in it from which she now, in a solemn and dry voice, began to read. It was Ole's own editorial, commemorating the end of the Bjørnvig-Poulsen regime and announcing a change in editorial policy. The new editors, Wivel and Martin A. Hansen, thanked their predecessors for having created a journal whose high standards had been based on the principle of artistic "responsibility. . . . It is our conviction that this responsibility is not only an esthetic, but also a moral one," it continued.

Karen Blixen put down the book and looked around with "distant, shining eyes, but not shining with enthusiasm, on the contrary, with anger or contempt." She opened the other book she had gone to fetch. "Beauty, Phaedros," she began, "mark it well . . . only beauty is divine and sensuous at the same time."

When she had finished with Socrates's speech, she took a sip of wine and then told Wivel a story from her own youth, the story of how Aunt Bess had taken her to hear a famous moralist speak at the folk high school and how she had been "repelled." Without understanding it at the time, she said, she had been torn between the ethical philosophy of her mother's family and the senuous esthetic of her father's. It had been a source of immense joy to discover that in Africa the conflict between the two had been resolved. "Heavenly and earthly love were not in opposition out there, as among Christian Europeans, and as is apparently the case with Martin A. Hansen and now *Heretica*—a disease caught from the tradition of dualism," and a disease she thought they had, with courage, engaged themselves to fight. "I warn you," she told her old friend sternly, "with your choice of the Moral and your inclination toward the Ethical. Has not precisely this choice in our Protestant cultures led us straight against our own will into the abyss? Has not Christianity excluded ecstasy, with its gifts and mysteries, denied and driven out our sensuality? And has it not also barred the way to the world of the spirit, through the means, the basic circumstances of existence which are the only ones we have? . . . I think," she concluded, "that you and Martin A. Hansen are following in dangerous footsteps."

When Wivel rose to leave, Karen Blixen said that she wanted to bless him before she let him go, and her blessing was a little verse written by the moralist Johannes Jørgensen to the symbolist poet Sophus Claussen, whose work had long been her own "Bible":

> *I forgot my Greek for Latin,*
> *To Homer you stayed true.*
> *I tell you God is CHARITY,*
> *EROS! Answer you.**

4

At the end of June, Karen Blixen herself made a trip to Paris. She stayed at a great old hotel, the St. James and Albany, on the Rue de Rivoli, where she had often come on her way back from or out to Africa in the twenties. One of its attractions was the Danish hall porter who had once been the butler "to an old uncle of mine."[10]

She was entertained in Paris by a rich, cultivated American admirer named Parmenia Migel whom she had met two years before. Ms. Migel owned a house on the Île St. Louis; her husband, Arne Ekstrom, was in the diplomatic service, and the couple had the means to provide a very pleasant program of entertainments for the Baroness. It included dinners prepared by their chef and served by their butler, parties with titled ladies and young painters, shopping trips, the best seats at the Comédie Francaise, and something for "every hour of the day." Karen Blixen was also looking for an artist to paint her portrait for the Danish Hall of Fame, and Ms. Migel introduced her to Pavel Tchelitchew. It was a meeting full of poignance for both of them. Tchelitchew was dying. He had come back to Paris after an absence of many years, during which time he had made his reputation in America, and now he was demoralized by his lack of recognition in France. He had loved Isak Dinesen's books, and she was one of the people he had most wanted to meet, although without any real expectation that he would. Although he declined to do her portrait—"I am finished forever with all that"—he talked "excitedly and uninterruptedly for three hours. . . . Tania, who was used to

---

**Jeg glemte mit Græsk for Latin*
du blev hos Homeros
jeg nævner dig CARITAS Gud
saa svarer du EROS.

From Ole Wivel, *Romance for Valdhorn*, pp. 213–215.

doing all the talking, had hardly said a word all afternoon, and Tchelitchew felt that he had found the perfect listener. . . . At first Tania had been rather shocked by his categoric refusal to paint her portrait, but when she learned how anxious he had been to know her she was mollified."[11]

Her main object in coming to Paris, however, had been to see Bjørnvig there. He and his wife came to her hotel, and she took them out to dinner in a restaurant where they would never "have dared to set foot."[12] The next day she visited them in their room at the Cité Universitaire, surveyed the charming view and drank tea. When Grete Bjørnvig tactfully withdrew, she showed Thorkild a poem that she said her nephew Tore Dinesen had written and of which she asked his opinion. "Conventional pastiche," he told her. "She took it well, the more so as it later turned out she had written it herself."[13]

In return, Bjørnvig read her his lyrical erotic work, "The Raven." She listened quietly and then, visibly proud and moved, told him he had obeyed the poem's explicit as well as unwritten laws and had achieved "high and powerful art, not just pornography." She repeated to him what she had told him earlier, in connection with *Heretica,* that he must not write for any single human being, or on behalf of any movement or cultural party, but because he owed God an answer: *Je responderay.* [14]

For their last meeting Karen Blixen rented an open touring car and took Bjørnvig, alone, on a drive through the Bois de Boulogne. The woods were in bloom, and the air was sweet and heavy. The Baroness told story after story with a deadpan expression and a masterly, grotesque comic delivery. Bjørnvig was euphoric.

But when she returned to Denmark he went to Brittany, to a hotel by the sea. And there, after a series of frustrations and disasters aggravated by his concussion, he had a kind of nervous breakdown. Part of this breakdown was a "telepathic" experience with Karen Blixen, who, unknown to him, had been taken to the hospital for a new and very painful treatment. Lying in his bed, listening to the sea, he had dreamed of his wife and child, and then dreamed that he heard Karen Blixen calling to him, as if she were in need of him and wanted him to come. When he did return to Denmark he discovered that on the night of his dream she had, indeed, been thinking "very hard" about him. Their pact had then seemed to be "a burden for her and a danger for me, for which she did not dare take responsibility," and she had tried "with all her power to cast me away, out of the pact and out of her life." But then she saw that Bjørnvig "had, so to speak, ricocheted, and that instead of irrevocably casting you away I had . . . dragged you to me. I decided that if the pact . . . were to be renounced, it had to be you, yourself, who does it."[15]

Here was an emotional arrangement much like the little scene with two-year-old Bo in Vedbæk. Karen Blixen saw the danger of the situation, but she could not grapple with it herself and so made Bjørnvig responsible. At the same time she could surrender to it with no further inhibitions.

When Bjørnvig emerged from the hospital, Karen Blixen invited him to convalesce in total peace and comfort at Rungstedlund, and he accepted gratefully. She installed him in the Green Room and imposed a strict regime of seclusion and rest. His "bedtime" was fixed at nine o'clock, and she herself came to enforce it. She strictly limited the visits of his friends, even his wife, and they were shooed away early. In the beginning she let him eat alone and appeared in his doorway at eight to begin the ritual of tucking him in. She told him stories until the clock struck nine, when she rose and bade him good night. On one of the first evenings, as she was leaving, she put the "Adagio" from Tchaikovsky's First String Quartet on her old gramophone, which stood in the adjoining room. So had she done with Denys when he had retired early on the night before a hunt. The music, she said, would "rock your heart to peace, so that later in your life you will never forget these evenings . . . and the first time you heard it."[16]

Bjørnvig was a guest at Rungstedlund until Christmas, the lost traveler ripe for a mystic romance who enters the enchanted castle and falls under the spell of its lonely chatelaine. Alternating between discipline and indulgence, Karen Blixen set out to make him a knight of the imagination, hard and pure in spirit and pledged faithful to an ideal that was embodied in her own person and art. "Much of what Karen Blixen said to me," wrote Bjørnvig, "on every possible subject, had more or less hidden intention for me. She . . . did not conceal that she expected the extraordinary from me, both in human and poetic terms."[17] There was, of course, a cutting edge of tyranny to that expectation. She sometimes ridiculed him, telling him he was a fool or a coward; or that he had been saturated by his milieu like a ladyfinger in a cup of coffee; or else she flew into sudden and inexplicable rages over trifles, behavior all her closest friends had observed and no one liked to talk about. Intoxicated by her own influence over Bjørnvig, she forgot the complex truth she had set forth in "The Old Chevalier": that the representative of the old order, riding full tilt into the modern age, is doomed to cut a comic and compromised—however noble—figure. She also forgot the rather more sinister lesson she had expounded in "The Poet": that it is presumptuous and unhealthy to tamper with someone else's destiny.

Bjørnvig's own yearnings and fantasies corresponded with Karen Blixen's in such a way that any resistance she might have opposed at the beginning became impossible for her, and she simply let go and gave in to the ecstasy of requited love which had for so long been denied her. Bjørnvig held up a mirror in which she saw herself not only as the old storyteller with the wisdom of three thousand years, but as the young girl of seventeen ("How beautiful the Baroness can look, how infinitely young when she speaks of these things"),[18] and with the erotic vitality of an experienced woman in her prime. It was a hermetic relationship, complete except for actual touch; they metamorphosed before each other, played all the roles in their respective psychic repertoires. The more intense it grew, the more it seemed—at least from the outside—that some kind of tragedy was inevitable. Karen Blixen told a friend—probably Ole Wivel, for it made its way back to Grete Bjørnvig—that unless Thorkild came to live with her at Rungstedlund permanently, she would leave Denmark forever, or she would die.

5

Among the other denizens of Rungstedlund, Bjørnvig was looked upon with not a little jealousy and skepticism. Mrs. Carlsen declared that she thought he would "never amount to much." Alfred Pedersen's disgust had left him speechless, and he would not even refer to Bjørnvig by his name but simply pointed, grimaced, and snarled: *"Ham derinde";* him, the one inside. Bjørnvig recalled Pedersen's "intense suspicion" on the day he found him carving the initials "T.B. and K.B." in an old tree behind the house. He simply stood there and "glowered" while Bjørnvig worked, and Thorkild, who felt just as ludicrous as Pedersen thought he looked, was too gallant to explain that the Baroness had made him do it.[19]

With Clara, however, Bjørnvig became friends. They were close to the same age, and despite the fact that Karen Blixen called him the Magister and always addressed him with the formal *De,* he and Clara were on *du* terms. If she had envious feelings, they were transformed into a protective yet deferential complicity and affection. Thus she might have felt toward a son of Karen Blixen's or, had she been lady-in-waiting to the elderly Elizabeth I, toward the young doomed Essex. When Bjørnvig went abroad again and Karen Blixen let a long time elapse between her letters, Clara took up the slack, writing to assure Thorkild that the "Baroness thinks of you all the time. I don't know why she hasn't written."[20]

That October was extremely mild. Bjørnvig felt that he was "healing." He took long walks in the autumn light, through the woods or along the beach, and he had begun to work in secret on a long poem he eventually called "The House of Childhood," which was the expression of that state of grace and joy he had known at Rungstedlund. Karen Blixen left him working and went to visit Wedellsborg, on Funen, the estate of Inger and Julius Wedell. She was, of course, always a welcome guest at the castles and manors of her old friends. They had taken her fame in their stride, as they also took her eccentricities and were neither overly impressed by her "aura," as was Bjørnvig, nor repelled by it like certain members of the family and the critical establishment. One has the feeling that their response to Tanne had not changed much since the days when she returned from Paris as a *"raffiné, sharp-tongued young lady"* who had a talent, rare in their circle, for fantasy. They were proud of her achievements and she was proud of them, simply for existing and continuing to carry on a way of life. Her own view of that way of life was, as it had always been, more exalted than their own, and she told both Bjørnvig and Ole Wivel that only in the country, on the great estates, could she feel truly at ease in Denmark, for only there could she still find people who understood what it meant to be "honorable" in the same sense she did.[21]

But there was also something simpler between her and these childhood friends, an essential human connection based on continuity with the past. "We wear masks when we get old," she told Bjørnvig, "the masks of our old age, but the young people don't know it, or don't think that they are masks. . . . Therefore it is often a great relief and liberation for me to be together with my contemporaries and enjoy myself and laugh with them . . . for we know we are wearing masks, and can forget them."[22] The Wedells, the Bernstorffs, the Reventlows, the Folsachs—these were the people among whom Karen Blixen was, and always had been, *du*. "They are," she wrote to Clara that October, "almost like natives."[23]

Bjørnvig tells a charming story that puts his own relationship to that *herregaardskultur*—and through it Karen Blixen's—into relief. While he was staying at Rungstedlund she sent him to fetch a luncheon guest, the young Countess Caritas Bernstorff-Gyldensteen, daughter of the Count Erich and the Countess Sophie. As he was setting out in her little car she entwined a bunch of freesias in his thick dark hair and ordered him, on pain of displeasure, not to remove them. He felt idiotic, and even more so when he got lost and had to stop, roll down the window, thrust forth his Caravaggiesque head, and ask directions from a stranger.

Neither Caritas nor her mother made any reference at all to Bjørnvig's appearance as they politely showed him their villa and gardens. But finally he could no longer stand the suspense, and he alluded to the curious fact that there were freesias in his hair. Then they laughed; they had taken it for granted, they said, that it was "one of Tanne's pranks."[24]

6

Karen Blixen's relations with her own family, and in particular with Thomas, had grown somewhat strained after the war. She continued to send both him and Elle her works in progress and regarded their opinions highly. But her brother would not give her the uncritical admiration she got from the young men of *Heretica*, or the serene acceptance she found at Wedellsborg, where, as she told Clara, she was "not exposed to criticism, and not on guard against being deceived."[25] Thomas knew her too well, for one thing, and had lived with her for too long. If he had smiled at the way she "distorted things" on the pleasant side in her writing, he was frankly put off by her evolving mythological persona. "Sometimes," Jonna Dinesen recalled, "we would visit her at Rungstedlund, and be sitting there talking, and a guest would enter. Tanne suddenly perked up and began speaking in a completely different way, in an unrecognizable voice. She only became a 'private person' again at the very end."[26]

As they aged, Tanne's old competitiveness with Thomas grew more acute, and their arguments on art, religion, Wilhelm, politics, and the family became more embattled. "You said yesterday as you have said before," he wrote to her in June of 1950, "that you and I are so at odds with each other about practically everything."[27] They were disagreeing about esthetic judgment, which Thomas maintained was a matter of taste, while Tanne argued that there were absolute standards of beauty. And then he went on to write, with restrained but perceptible anger, about her interference in his children's lives.

Thomas and Jonna had two sons and two daughters, all of whom had beauty and vitality in abundance. Their Aunt Tanne felt possessive toward them. "Although I have no children of my own, and cannot have any contact with the future, I would like to *do things* for you,"[28] she said. But she did not have in mind the usual line of old-auntish excursions, bequests or advice. She thought, for example, that it might be really nice to get her nephew, Tore, tattooed and to enroll him in a course in tattooing, so that when he made a proposed trip around the world by steamer, he would have some means of earning a living and of striking up a rapport with the other sailors. Once she arranged with a man from the circus to come to Rungstedlund and teach the children how to wield a lasso. They remembered this with great delight.

For her nieces she had more conventional ambitions: a tragic romance or a brilliant marriage or both simultaneously. As she had a large selection of eligible young men at her disposal, *"die Töchtern,"* as she called them, were sent out riding with Ole Wivel and Knud W. Jensen, or to dinner with Bjørnvig, or taken on trips to the castles of her old friends, where Karen Blixen energetically threw them together with the noble sons of the men to whom she herself had perhaps once aspired.

Thomas did not object to this except when his children did, and Anne had balked at being dragged to Wedellsborg and paraded about there like a young heifer. It was Ingeborg, her younger sister, who finally went. She remembered that every evening a half hour before dinner she had to present herself for inspection. If Aunt Tanne did not approve of her toilette, she had to redo it. "Her rituals were wonderful but annoying."[29]

The children were torn by fascination, gratitude, love, and horror of their aunt. She gave them wonderful presents—a fur hat, a piece of jewelry, or a costume—and then called up months, even years later, to take them back. Her egotism was inexplicable to them. But like all the young people whom she attracted, she challenged them in a way they found irresistible; she listened to them in a manner that made them feel extraordinary and unique. "If she loved to talk, and could do so almost incessantly, she was also the most wonderful of listeners. Your own experience became something shining and admirable in the retelling. When she listened, she made you feel *bright,* and you believed that she had enjoyed it so much. Because she set such a high store in pleasure, you felt doubly rewarded. You could talk to someone else for hours, even years, and never have the feeling you had revealed yourself in such a true and clear light."[30]

Part of the tension in her relationships with these adolescent children came from jealousy. She teased them about their love and loyalty for their parents, and as much as she tried, she could not "seduce" them to her side. "Can't you ever say anything *bad* about them?" she would tease. Or: "Family life, yech! How can you bear it?" Just as she reproached Bjørnvig for his "softness," she reproached them for their refusal to rebel against the "harmlessness" of their home life. "We had a warm and natural childhood," her niece Ingeborg recalled. "She wanted us to surrender to her, to fall under her spell. If we did so at times we could not do it the way she wanted. That disappointed her, and eventually she simply gave up trying to change our personalities."[31]

Karen Blixen had a third niece, Ea's daughter Karen—Mitten—who was then divorced and in her early thirties. She had two daughters and she worked at the immunization hospital in Copenhagen. That November, as a result of her work, she contracted meningitis. Karen Blixen went almost daily to visit her in the hospital and returned to describe her misery and suffering to Bjørnvig, implying that he might write a poem about her. "I tried," he said, "but as I had never seen the girl, it was abstract for me."[32]

Karen de Neergaard Sveinbjørnsson died on November 26, and her aunt dressed the coffin herself and arranged the flowers for the funeral. That evening Clara, Bjørnvig, and the grieving Baroness sat in the Green Room and listened to Schubert's "Death and the Maiden."

7

Bjørnvig had been writing prodigiously, but in secret, throughout the autumn. In November he could finally read Karen Blixen the long poem that was the fruit of her efforts as a muse, nurse, and hostess. She told him it was all that she had hoped, kissed him, and sank into a reverie. A little later she made a few critical comments. One thing shocked her: Bjørnvig had confused a new moon with a morning moon, and she lectured him at great length on his responsibility to nature, which no degree of fantasy could abridge. Finally she paid him a "roguish" compliment, in which the essence of their affair of the preceding months was perfectly rendered: "You have been fooling me. It is as in *Hansel and Gretel.* Here I've been keeping you in a cage, and every time I come to see if you are fat enough for a feast you, like Hansel, stick

ISAK DINESEN

out a bone instead of a finger. Now for the first time can I see how ripe with flesh and delicious you have become."[33]

Christmas was approaching, but the ripe and fleshy Bjørnvig was determined not to be Karen Blixen's holiday bird—he wanted to see his wife and son. So he took his leave of her on Christmas Day.

42

Goddess and Barfly

I

A S EARLY AS 1945 Karen Blixen had spoken on the Danish radio, to give a talk in honor of her father's centennial. In the early fifties her radio talks became more frequent and were very popular. Her lighter works were read aloud by prominent Danish actors and actresses, and she herself spoke out on subjects of deep personal significance to her. The first of these talks, broadcast from Rungstedlund on two successive January evenings in 1951, were called "Daguerreotypes." In them Karen Blixen attempted to convey to the younger generation a sense of the ideals and values she herself had grown up with and prized, and which democracy had largely rejected: the meaning of class differences within the ordered, hierarchic cosmos of the manor; the importance of woman's honor and mystery; and the concept of prestige, which set glory and beauty above comfort and necessity. As she had done in *Seven Gothic Tales,* she acknowledged how quaint and perhaps even sinister these ideals must seem to her modern audience. She was not restating them as their apologist or as their champion, but as their interpreter. It was, she believed, important to preserve a sense of continuity with the past—not just objectively as history, but through touch, speech and remembrance—the passing down of something alive. She could help to do so in two ways: as a woman of sixty-six, who had a personal, verbal connection to the last century through the old people in her family; and as a storyteller. "A group of my young friends has determined that I am three thousand years old,"[1] she said. In this capacity she had access to and could point the way to the mythic past.

In 1952 Karen Blixen delivered a cogent and moving talk against vivisection, and in particular the use of dogs for painful laboratory experiments. She did not make her appeal on humanitarian grounds or as a liberal, but on the grounds of honor: the needless infliction of pain on a helpless and trusting animal dishonored the human race. The next year she spoke at a seminary for teachers, delivering a speech she had been asked to make but had never given for a women's rights congress fourteen years before. This belated "oration at a Bonfire"* developed her own views on feminism, on the role

---

*A *baaltale,* a bonfire speech—i.e., a ceremonial speech at a rally, funeral, execution, victory, etc.

of women in society and on the nature of femininity. These views had grown considerably more conservative since her letters on the subject to Aunt Bess, when she had called feminism the most revolutionary issue of the nineteenth century and had defined manliness as a desirable and noble *human* rather than exclusively male cluster of qualities. But now she spoke of man and woman as an "expedient" union of opposites, greater than but similar to the master and the servant, the old and young. She located woman's substance, her center of gravity, in "what she is," her being; and man's in "what he has achieved," his actions. She was not "against feminism" or opposed to women as surgeons and lawyers, and she was grateful to the first generation of "just, courageous, loyal and sly" feminists—the contemporaries of her aunt and mother—who had stormed the citadel of the professions undercover, "in a costume which intellectually or psychologically represented a male" but at the expense of their "female dignity" and nature. Now she encouraged the young women in her audience to repossess their femininity and "confidently open their visors."[2]

In 1954 Karen Blixen spoke out against a plan to simplify and modernize Danish spelling, and the following year, on April 17, she gave a seventieth birthday speech in which she told her audience what an immense pleasure it was "to be a voice and not a piece of printed matter." Her public speaking fulfilled a need she had expressed as far back as 1935: "to stand in relation to a people," as she had done in Africa. She was famous in literary circles and well known among educated Danes, but the radio brought her a public as opposed to a readership and confirmed her identity as a *storyteller:* the member of an "ancient, idle, wild and useless tribe," with her roots in the oral tradition and her power from a charged complicity with those who listened.*

2

It was as a storyteller, a vivid presence, that she also most enjoyed holding forth in her own salon. She had an exceptionally low and dusky speaking voice, which Glenway Wescott describes as "spooky, strong, but insubstantial."[3] Her accent in Danish was almost archaic, with the broad, drawled

---

*Merete Klenow With, "Om Karen Blixen og hendes Forfatterskab," *Karen Blixen: Et Udvalg,* p. 216.

In this context it is worth quoting an observation that John Berger makes in his "The Primitive and the Professional" (collected in *About Looking,* New York: Pantheon Books, 1980): "The category of the professional artist, as distinct from the master craftsman, was not clear until the 17th century. (And in some places . . . not until the 19th century.) . . . The craftsman survives so long as the standards for judging his work are shared by different classes. The professional appears when it is necessary for the craftsman to leave his class and emigrate to the ruling class, whose standards of judgement are different." Isak Dinesen's sense of her role as an artist fit a pre-nineteenth-century mold. She hoped that her work was accessible to the "different classes," and to some extent—perhaps more in Denmark than in America —it was.

vowels of "Old Copenhagen." It was an accent not heard much, even among
old aristocrats, and it had something of a dialect that an accident of history
or geography has preserved from the linguistic mainland. She emphasized the
same quaintness in her appearance, and by her late sixties Karen Blixen had
become a picturesque old figure who was relentlessly interviewed and photographed.

"She had," said her friend Professor Rasmussen, "a fixed idea of what an
Isak Dinesen tale should be, and an Isak Dinesen conversation, interview,
pronouncement, etc. It became a brand name in a funny way, a standard form
which she simply filled in, according to a rigid formula."⁴ She was, in the
role of Isak Dinesen or the role of *Baronessen,* extremely consistent and,
indeed, professional, as the mass of interviews and the reports of those who
met her late in life attest. It is astonishing how, almost verbatim, they reiterate
the same anecdotes and *bon mots.* The coherence, of course, enhanced her
legend, for it made it easier to disseminate. But it also grossly simplified her
humanity.

Ole Wivel remarked that in a small circle of admirers Karen Blixen
became the Ancient Mariner and that one of her requirements for a close
friend was the "willingness to put a coin into her meter and listen."⁵ Bent
Mohn, who was often invited to Rungstedlund to "give her the cues,"
spoke of her "grande dame repertoire" and observed that she was capable
of "going on and on without a pause, and speaking over the heads of
people."⁶ Bjørnvig also describes a mode of talk to which she resorted
when strangers were present, when she had a partially fresh audience. It was
a "circus act of proven witticisms and paradoxes, anecdotes and old stories.
. . . People had to put up with it if she were to put up with them," and
she exhibited a "total contempt" for the fact that some of them might have
heard things "hundreds of times" before.⁷ How could a woman with such
great sensibility behave so rudely? The answer may be that Karen Blixen's
compulsive talking was a kind of heightened, dreamlike and perhaps erotic
state, virtually a trance, and that she was not fully conscious when she fell
into it.* Nancy Wilson Ross describes it very well: "In her eyes I saw a
concentration so total as to be almost frightening: the abstracted, trancelike
stare of a soothsayer, who is living wholly in another space and time."⁸
Karen Blixen did not recognize the voice of her own compulsion; she
found it disconcerting, even ugly. And she gives the best description of
it herself, in a letter to a Swedish journalist who interviewed her after
the publication of *Anecdotes of Destiny.* He submitted his transcript for
her approval, which she withheld, saying: "I think the whole interview
gives an extremely disagreeable picture of a twisted and self-absorbed—in

---

*The stimulants she took for energy may well have intensified this state.

reality senile—person who with relish delivers herself of pretentious banalities. . . ."⁹

The fact that so many of her friends were willing to put up with this behavior, even to abet it, is a tribute to the other rewards of friendship with Karen Blixen, to the pleasures of "her other kinds of discourse." One of these was as Bjørnvig described it, based on Plato's symposium, his ideal of talk as adventure. She had, on occasion, arranged symposia at Rungstedlund, inviting guests with the widest and most different experience in life to discuss a given theme: socialism, for example, or Christianity. She tried to create, with food, wine, and her own stewardship, that same "heightened, erotically-charged atmosphere"¹⁰ in which she imagined that the first symposia had taken place, and to lead her friends into a dimension of inspired talk. She was invariably disappointed in her attempts, and so she fell back on evenings with imaginary guests—Shelley, Stalin, the Empress of China, or St. Francis. "We won't have any prophets," she told Bjørnvig one evening as they were drawing up a guest list, "for they can't be talked to, they only want to speak."¹¹

If, on public occasions and among strangers, she herself insisted upon speaking, there were the private times when she turned an almost beatific attention upon a guest, the complete gravity of her being. "When she was present in spirit," wrote Aage Henriksen, the critic, "then she was a tireless, ubiquitous, imaginative providence. She was then as realistic, self-sacrificing and resourceful as Kuan-Yin, the Chinese goddess of mercy and female cunning. There can be no doubt that it was approximately in this guise that she was perceived by her servants. 'This faithful mother of ours,' Mohammed Juma calls her."¹² Bjørnvig, alluding to the same incarnation, described Karen Blixen on these occasions as "wiser than anything she had written—and she also spoke as if she had never written anything."¹³

The friends who did feed coins into her meter acquiesced because they could also count upon this other form of intimacy with her. They could depend upon her to give perspective to their sorrows, and sanction their instincts and their transgressions. It was not necessarily that they judged her more competent in human relations than they; Aage Henriksen once accused her of naiveté, and she agreed with him. But the moment they tried to squeeze a little pity out of her, a little cheap commiseration—a painless placebo—she laughed at them. "There are three solutions for an unhappiness such as yours," she once told the lovesick Bent Mohn. "Suicide, America, or the Foreign Legion."¹⁴ Ultimately the young Danes brought her their problems the way the Africans brought her their stomachaches—in hopes of an imaginative, rather than a sensible, cure. Thus there gathered around Karen Blixen, in the early fifties, a circle of young men who humored her like a very powerful, cranky, and capricious old queen. They did so because she rewarded them with glimpses of their own potentiality. She exploited their loyalty at times, but she also held them to a high standard of self-respect and discipline in their work and their private lives. Her capacity to love was a power to command that the best in them pay homage to the princely trust she showed in it.

If Bjørnvig was the favorite at this court and Erling Schroeder its master of revels, Karen Blixen found a chamberlain in Erik Kopp, the man who married her niece Anne in 1950. Erik was handsome, rugged, blunt, and opinionated. He had demonic eyebrows over fierce blue eyes, and he immediately made a good impression on the Baroness by declaring that he hated Shakespeare and had not read any of her books. He had, she later confessed, many of the qualities that had attracted her to the young Bror Blixen; he was "the same kind of fine man."[15] Among other things, he had Bror's appeal to women and his racism, which his aunt tolerated to a point. But when he was insulting to Eugene Haynes she put her foot down. "You go too far, Erik," she told him frigidly. And after that the word "nigger" was never pronounced in her house again.[16]

In the late fifties Karen Blixen hired Kopp to supervise the care of Rungstedlund and its grounds. "A man should have proper work," she told him, meaning contact with the land and animals. He was frequently invited without his wife to host her parties—and was even asked to "flirt" with her female guests. "You should have a girl on your left-hand," she said, "and bring her to tea at Rungstedlund to meet me." Erik Kopp was one of the few people who understood that Karen Blixen's provocations were a form of testing, that she was really hoping someone would set limits and would laugh at her, as Denys had done. "She wanted to be told off," he put it simply.[17] And he was also one of the few able, in a modest way, to do so.

3

In the winter of 1951 Thorkild Bjørnvig lived in Sletten with his family, working there under circumstances his wife had struggled to make as ideal as possible. His intimacy with Karen Blixen and his long "convalescence" at Rungstedlund had made Grete Bjørnvig as jealous and unhappy as if her husband and the great old writer had been lovers, which, indeed, in all respects except the most technical, they were. Karen Blixen had also made it clear, though not directly to the young woman, that a conventional domestic life—wife and child—could only be fetters on Bjørnvig's genius. Perhaps Mrs. Bjørnvig was susceptible to that idea; in any event, she suffered, she attempted valiantly to give her husband the space and the tranquility he had at Rungstedlund and to make her own home competitive with it. Of course, this was, with her modest means, a small child to care for, and against the immense undertow of fascination Karen Blixen exerted on Thorkild

Bjørnvig, impossible. He began going back to Rungstedlund once a week for dinner and to spend the night.

Writing about those dinners of the late winter and early spring, Bjørnvig repeats the word *rus:* intoxicated, ecstatic. They were spent drinking wine, quoting poetry to each other, playing Schubert (they had a mania for the "Winterreise"), making imaginary voyages and taking imaginary lovers. Karen Blixen partook very little of the refreshments but refilled Bjørnvig's glass and miraculously kept pace with his own increasing high, laughing, pulling his hair, "throwing herself" into fantasies. They were "shocking things"; he does not tell us why.* But it would seem that Karen Blixen became the fearless young Scheherazade who had entertained her lover in another small candlelit sitting room thirty years before. Then she had also played Schubert over and over on the gramophone, and she told Bjørnvig that it was "like an echo of that time, slighter but the same, the same."[18]

At the end of April he came to stay for several days. In May, at the end of a long argument in which Karen Blixen had her way, he left to spend the summer in Bonn. He did not, in fact, want to go. But when the University of Copenhagen invited him to compete for a travel stipend Karen Blixen urged it. And when he won she insisted it was a matter in which his honor and integrity were involved, "God's will" for him. When the money finally came through he wavered again; it was still possible to turn it down. But now Karen Blixen drew up a peculiar document for him to sign, which she called "The Ritual of Choice." In it she made him renounce any further doubt or regret concerning his decision, and to accept it of his own free will, "So help me Goethe, Rilke, and Hölderlin."[19] It was not enough that he go to Bonn to please *her,* he had to *want* to go. This was the curious stipulation she had attached to her mother's second trip to Africa—and it is also a very clear echo of Kierkegaard's Seducer, who insists that the young girl he had manipulated and deceived come to accept his love *of her own free will:*

> She must owe me nothing, for she must be free; love exists only in freedom, only in freedom is there enjoyment and everlasting delight. Although I am aiming at her falling into my arms, as it were, by a natural necessity, yet I am striving to bring it about so that as she gravitates toward me it will not be like the falling of a heavy body, but as a spirit seeking spirit.[20]

---

*But one game she often played with friends was to take turns confessing one's "worst sin." Hers, she claimed, was to have seduced a cabin boy on the ship home to Denmark in 1915, when she knew that she had syphilis. He was too beautiful to resist, she liked to say—although she also claimed that she arranged for his treatment in Paris. Weighing this "confession" with everything one knows about her state of mind at that moment, her physical suffering, her character, and her attitude toward sex, it is almost certainly pure invention: the fantastic reminiscence of Miss Malin Nat-og-Dag. (From interviews with Suzanne Brøgger, Copenhagen, 1976, and New York, 1978.)

Bjørnvig uses almost the same words:

Once more she touched the ideal nerve in our relation: I must *myself* spontaneously wish what she wished. . . . "Do what your spirit leads you to do." I was in no dobut that the spirit was Karen Blixen's.[21]

Bjørnvig departed for Aarhus and shortly afterwards for Bonn. Karen Blixen, who had been ill, recovered some of her strength and left on May 3 for a trip to Greece as the guest of Knud W. Jensen and his lovely wife, Benedicte. Mrs. Jensen had met Karen Blixen the year before and fallen under her spell. She had a not uncommon response to her: a feeling of deep gratitude that she existed, and a desire to do something wonderful for her in turn.

The Jensens' invitation was perhaps meant to be that something. Karen Blixen fantasized constantly about traveling, which she considered one of life's greatest joys. She had never been to Greece, and the Jensens arranged to spend an extremely charming and luxurious few weeks there. From Athens they flew to Rome, staying at the Hassler, above the Spanish Steps. Karen Blixen had an audience with Pope Pius XII, who made "a great impression" on her. Clara Svendsen reports on their interview in her memoir. The Pope, she writes, told the Baroness that "all great art is in God's honor." Karen Blixen had brought with her an old medal with a picture of the Virgin that her mother had acquired in Rome "under his predecessor," who had spoken to her on the dogma of the Immaculate Conception. "And now," Karen Blixen said, "if His Holiness, who has recently explained the dogma of Maria's ascension to Heaven would add his blessing, the medallion would acquire even greater value for its possessor."[22]

4

Before he left for Bonn, Bjørnvig had introduced Karen Blixen to a young man he thought would amuse her, perhaps in a way act as his surrogate: Jørgen Gustava Brandt. Brandt was then nineteen, a poet himself and a connoisseur of the old Danish authors whom Karen Blixen loved. He had even written a little essay comparing her to Goldschmidt. In dress he was a dandy in the English manner, perhaps somewhat reminiscent—though a swarthy version—of Berkeley Cole. In speech he was a cynic of the darkest hue, a jester and a desperado. But he was something even more congenial to the Baroness: an incorrigible gossip. They discovered each other's "shamelessness" and ranged unsparingly over the flaws and follies of their friends. Brandt had begun to publish his work in *Heretica,* but its new editorial good intentions, its "ethical pessimism" disgusted him, and this was a great subject for them to teethe on. Nothing was safe from Brandt's mockery—not Karen Blixen herself. "Can't you see it?" he once asked Bjørnvig. "She's a barfly from the twenties!" Bjørnvig laughed uneasily. He was also a little shocked at the liberty taken with the sacred person. "For me," he thought, "she was always Pellegrina."[23]

But Brandt was not a successful surrogate for his friend. Having sent Bjørnvig to Bonn against his will, Karen Blixen was now restless, miserable, and cranky with missing him. He, too, was completely miserable, living in a small room with other foreign students and giving himself up to beer drinking and self-pity. Periodically he begged for permission to come home, but instead of jumping at the opportunity she held him off. Her letters were those a general might send to a battle-weary lieutenant or a bishop to a young priest wavering in his vocation: retreat if you must, but I thought you had the courage to hold out! She invoked God, Saint Francis, good manners, her faith in him, the stigmata and the regents of the university. Even Clara threw in her weight, to let Thorkild know how much praying was going on over his soul, how many wishes had been made on four-leaf clovers and candles lit to the Virgin. In the end he did come home to Denmark to spend the autumn at Rungstedlund. But not before a dramatic and, in the context, revolutionary act had been committed: he fell in love. Years before, Karen Blixen had playfully and somewhat perversely urged him to do so, to find a snake charmer or a sword swallower and to give his "body" to her. She had also made him promise to tell her all about it. But this was not quite what happened. Bjørnvig's love was guilty and romantic. Its object was a young Danish woman whom Karen Blixen knew well, the lovely wife of a close mutual friend. And for a while, at least, neither of them said anything about it.

5

That summer Clara Svendsen was faced with a crucial decision. She had been working for Karen Blixen only part-time and had been taking courses in library science. Now she was eligible for a job as a librarian if she wanted to apply for one. Her family and friends pressured her to pursue her own career; she was, they pointed out, thirty-five, and she had already made considerable scarifices of time and momentum, not to mention money. Since the beginning of her service with Karen Blixen her father had been contemptuous of it: "It isn't your name on the books."[24] But the Baroness had recently begun to write again; she was too weak for long hours at the typewriter and had begun to dictate her tales to Clara, whom she now declared to be indispensable. As Clara writes in her memoir,

> "My calling triumphed. I had once and for all decided to be at Karen Blixen's disposition. There was, however, a difficult little discussion between us. I was, I said, completely convinced that it would be correct to drop my library career if there was going to be some work on a new book, but not if there were only

to be stories written . . . for publication in magazines. Karen Blixen did not believe I had the right to permit myself to say this.[25]

Thus Clara proves herself as true a Legitimist as any in Karen Blixen's tales. She was less faithful to the person of the monarch than to the idea of majesty which it represented.

43

"The Immortal Story"

I

T HE TALE Isak Dinesen dictated to Clara that summer was "The Immortal Story." It was one of three Dinesen tales concerned with the cosmic meddler, one who, innocent or deluded about his omnipotence, tries to usurp the role of the gods in another person's life, to introduce his own plan for its development and outcome, to graft his own desire onto its fate-in-progress. The first of these tales was "The Poet," written in the early thirties, which anticipated with an uncanny coincidence of detail Karen Blixen's friendship with Thorkild Bjørnvig. The third tale, "Echoes," written in the late fifties, was the epitaph of that friendship.

"The Immortal Story" was written at a moment when Dinesen's own meddling had backfired; she was suffering from it, and her consciousness of its absurdity and perhaps its danger could never have been more vivid to her. She was able to channel that consciousness into a special kind of loneliness. In its structure, its organization of irony and detail, it ranks with the best tales she has written and is perhaps the most exemplary. Among the later work it was her own favorite.

In "The Immortal Story" a rich old man sets out to "manifest his omnipotence" over two young lives. He does this with the help of a young clerk in his employ, a Jew named Elishama. In the relationship between those two we may glimpse something of the friendship that had sprung up at Rungstedlund between Karen Blixen and the poet Brandt. They also shared a negative recognition, a complicity in their proud but hurtful detachment from humanity. The clerk, like Brandt, is someone prematurely old and worldly, and from whom all desire has been washed away and buried. Karen Blixen began to call her friend Elishama, and he bore the name proudly. He, too, "did not want friends" even as she, surrounded by her retinue, did not really want them. For friends were "people who suffered and perished—the word itself meant separation and loss."[1]

The "immortal story" of the title is one that all sailors know. It tells how a rich old gentleman approaches a young seaman near the port, invites him home for a splendid meal, and offers him five gold guineas to make love to and impregnate his beautiful young wife. It is immortal precisely because, as Elishama explains to Mr. Clay, it cannot possibly come true. The real world, the world outside the story, is a place where desire and experience are forever at odds and which is governed by the laws of "supply and demand." In the world of the story—and that is its raison d'être—desire and experience may be briefly reunited. In this sense the story is a substitute for and a recollection of Eden.

Mr. Clay, the old meddler, has become immensely rich because he understands the laws of supply and demand with a single-minded obsessiveness and has never been distracted by any other kind of need, desire, or understanding. He has dealt in facts and commodities all his life, read only account books, wanted only money, and through money has achieved supreme power over many others. He has nothing but contempt for the world of the story when, through his clerk Elishama and at the age of seventy, he comes to realize that it exists.

Elishama has been reading account books to the old man to keep him company through his sleepless nights (he too is an insomniac), but in time they run through them all. Mr. Clay suspects—and this reveals he has a spark of yearning, of desire, still unextinguished—that there must be "other kinds of books," but he does not know precisely what he means by that. Elishama is not sure either. But he himself possesses an example of the other kind of writing: a talisman, given to him as a child by an old Jew, which he has kept throughout all his wanderings. He now reads it to Mr. Clay: it is part of Elijah's prophecy of the coming of the Messiah. Even though Clay is outraged that someone would speak about and set down something that was not supposed to happen for a thousand years, he is reminded that he, too, once heard a story, on the boat out to China when he was a young man. It is the story of an old gentleman who approaches a young sailor near the port . . . Elishama interrupts him, supplying the ending and revealing that it is not, as Mr. Clay believed, a factual recital, but merely the formulation of a desire all sailors feel and none realize. Mr. Clay decides that he will make the tale come true, at least for one sailor in the world. But he does this not as a generous or a playful gesture; on the contrary—because he has such deep contempt for fiction and because he cannot help wanting to take possession of it; to buy it, so to speak. He will pay a young woman to lie in his bed and find a sailor to make love to her there. He will do this not just to own their sexual vitality vicariously, but so they will dance like "jumping jacks" when he pulls their strings. This is, in fact, an analogy to the way he has made his fortune, and to capitalism itself, which is the opposite and the counterpart of storytelling.

The old capitalist tells us:

> It was not my limbs that ached in the tea-fields, in the mist of morning and the burning heat of midday. It was not my hand that was scorched on the hot

iron-plates upon which the tea leaves are dried. Not my hands that were torn in hauling taut the braces of the clipper, pressing her to her utmost speed. The starving coolies in the tea-fields, the dog-tired seaman on the middle watch, never knew that they were contributing to the making of a million pounds. To them the minutes only, the pain in their hands, the hail-showers in their faces, and the poor copper coins of their wages had real existence. It was in my brain and by my will that this multitude of little things were combined and set to co-operate to make up one single thing: a million pounds. Have I not, then, legally begotten it?[2]

The capitalist exploits the "real existence" of other human beings and the feelings and sensations that go into it, and turns this into an abstraction, "a million pounds," which he keeps for himself. The storyteller, who also has an idea, exploits the "real existence" of other human beings but returns it to them in the form of something repeatable, accessible, which belongs to no one. In Dinesen's tale these two forces are pitted against each other. Mr. Clay confidently believes he can buy the immortal story, corrupt it, "materialize" it, although he also realizes he will have to pay very dearly for it. But the immortal story proves more powerful than the mortal Mr. Clay—and is much dearer than he is capable of imagining. He himself will be transformed by it, will fall into the hands of a Higher Power, will become a character, which is to say an instrument rather than a maker of destiny. The gods outwit him with a richer and far more complex irony than he ever could have wrought.

Mr. Clay, the miser who has never told a story in his life and has heard but one, whose element is the dull and infertile "clay," is not an obvious self-portrait of Isak Dinesen, whose element was the air and who had lived with the deepest contempt for the laws of supply and demand. But Dinesen and Clay are counterparts in transgression. He takes to meddling with fiction. She takes to meddling with real life.

Long ago she had learned that in her own case, at least, desire and experience were irreconcilable, except within the very strict limits of a tale. That, perhaps, was the true meaning of the little scene she had staged for Bjørnvig in the early days of their pact, when she told him how syphilis had cut her off from erotic life but made it possible to tell stories. It was an untruth in its context—Africa—but it was the real truth of her experience in Denmark, of her middle and old age there. Illness had cut her off from erotic life, and "in exchange" she had been able to turn everything into tales. The trade-off was satisfactory or acceptable until she fell in love. This is the turning point for Mr. Clay as well—his desire is awakened. She discovered then that she could not live with her old bargain and that she could not reconcile human longing and a need for intimacy with the storyteller's priestly distance. Her attempt to invade Bjørnvig's life, to make him into her ideal, was analagous to Mr. Clay's attempt to enter and possess the immortal story. He fails, or rather he succeeds beyond his intentions, and his attempt turns into something else.

When Isak Dinesen wrote "The Immortal Story" she had not yet failed with Bjørnvig, but she would. Like "The Poet," it was prophetic. A few years later he would reject her with great bitterness and resentment. After that, her loneliness again became absolute, even if she led a more and more frantic life, full of people. There were to be subsequent flirtations, a series of young male "hopes," but Bjørnvig was her last love. And when, shortly after they had parted, a new young writer had come to sit at her feet, someone quite as brilliant as Thorkild and equally prepared—perhaps more so—to dedicate a soul to her service, she told him that he had come too late. "I cannot give you a place in my existence now. It is a shame for you, but you should have come before . . . for me there is nothing left but to bring my destiny to its end."[3]

2

Bjørnvig came to spend the autumn at Rungstedlund, much to the dismay of his wife. He did not have the excuse of a concussion, nor of needing a quiet place to work, which he had at home. But both he and Karen Blixen had their passionate motives for wishing him there. She was ill and wanted him nearby. She also hoped to convince him to move permanently to Rungstedlund, and spoke of leaving the house to him in her will, which shocked him. He, on the other hand, wanted to be away from his family and to be able to meet his lover. Absorbed in his poetry and his affair, he was more withdrawn than Karen Blixen had ever known him. For the first time he had a secret from her. And though she could not know they were "not alone together as they had once been," she sensed it. It was the beginning of a descent into an old maelstrom for her, and she would respond as she had done with Denys: grasping desperately at him, "increasing her interference in my life." Henceforth, she decided, they would meet the public as a literary "couple" and go down in literary history together.[4] She would lead him out of his provincial milieu and show him *den store verden* (the great world). They would visit England together, dine with Huxley and Gielgud.[5] Her antipathy to his marriage now became pronounced, and if she had once teased him that he was, in relation to his more delicate and refined wife, "like someone who used a violin to hammer nails,"[6] she now declared that the marriage was an embarrassment.

When Karen Blixen urged Bjørnvig to have adventures and fall in love, when she had played what he called "procuress" for him, she had also played false to her own feelings. She did not reckon with her own capacity for jealous rage and suffering. Bjørnvig and his lover had not reckoned with it either. Shortly after the new year they both, separately, confided their secret to Karen Blixen. The young woman did so believing that the baroness knew, or half knew. She had invited both of them to Rungstedlund several times without their spouses, to give them, it almost seemed, the opportunity to meet and the blessing to do so under her roof. But if, indeed, she had suspected something, it was not what she was given to understand the affair had become. Confronted with its seriousness she felt doubly betrayed: as God and Woman. To the young woman she was "terrifying" in her disapproval, lecturing her, of all things, on the moral outrage of adultery. To Bjørnvig she was "mellower," and mixed with her hurt and fury was a strange compassion for his suffering. "Can you see," she told him, "that it is as if claws had been dug into your heart, as if you had been pummeled by a wild beast? Oh how I remember it, how I know it well. It is the greatest pain that there is in the world. No, no I am not sorry for you. I envy you for it. No, I wish it for you with all my heart."[7]

3

Isak Dinesen's work during the long and intense relationship with Bjørn-vig was naturally much influenced by it and by him, and a dozen private jokes and intimate details are commemorated in her later tales. That autumn she was working on a tale in Danish that she called "Converse at Night in Copenhagen," dictating it to Clara from her bed. Bjørnvig lived at the other end of the house, writing poetry, and in the late afternoon, with the heavy light streaming through the windows, they exchanged notes and manuscripts. He saw that her tale contained, beautifully transmuted into historical fantasy, a portrait of their *rus* dinners of the winter before.

"Converse" takes place at the end of the eighteenth century, on a dark night in the back alleys of the capital. The mad young king Christian VII is out on one of his infamous rampages, pursued by his councillors and warders. But he manages to elude them and pushes open an unexpected door to a pleasant, firelit room where the poet Ewald, roaring drunk, is spending the evening with his mistress Lise, a prostitute of the town.*

Without missing a beat, Ewald enters into the adventure of the conversation. He addresses his unexpected guest as "King Orosmane" and introduces himself as "Yorick." The dialogue which then takes place corresponds to Karen Blixen's ideal of the symposium—a musical, indeed choreographed, formal interplay.† This is the speech her characters rise to at the moments

---

*Lise does not say anything in the tale, but she plays an important role. She is the hostess who creates the "heightened, erotically accentuated atmosphere" that makes the converse possible. Both the king and the poet agree upon her innocence, and upon the holiness of the erotic life.
†In Karen Blixen's working notes for "Converse at Night in Copenhagen" the tale is outlined like a sonata, with four movements.

of greatest drama and feeling in her tales, the moments when they slip from their individual into their mythic roles.

It is easy to see that the young *rus* Ewald of the tale is Thorkild Bjørnvig, and it is also easy to see how the "amorous exchange between souls," as Langbaum calls it,[8] is the mode of his "converse" with Karen Blixen. But it is less obvious that King Christian embodies and fulfills one of her own oldest yearnings: to escape from the clutches of the pedants who had kept her from "raging," to push open an unexpected door, to find herself in an atmosphere that is charged both erotically and poetically: "Yes he was among friends—such as he had read about and looked for but had never found, such as would understand who he really was."[9]

4

Bjørnvig's love affair shook Karen Blixen more than she was able to realize at the time, even if they enjoyed a brief season of work and harmony. In November Bjørnvig left for a trip to Norway, where he was to lecture, and then returned to his family in Sletten. At the end of a few weeks the Baroness called him there and asked for a rendezvous, intimating that she had something urgent to discuss. They met at an old inn and had tea. She quickly confronted Bjørnvig with a letter which she had found in the Green Room. It was not from his mistress but from a friend of Grete Bjørnvig's, and its contents seemed relatively innocuous. The friend had found a copy of the picture that hung over Bjørnvig's bed at Rungstedlund and offered it to Grete, so that she might hang it over his bed in Sletten. It was a kind of joke, and Thorkild explained that he and his wife had enjoyed it together.

But for some reason, the semblance of a plot between Mrs. Bjørnvig and her friend outraged the Baroness, and she accused all three of the crassest ignobility in the affair. Thorkild had the presence to point out that it was not a very noble thing to read someone else's correspondence, but Karen Blixen was unimpressed by his logic. Not only was she unrepentant about the invasion of his privacy, Bjørnvig believed that had she lived in another era, she would have been unrepentant about doing away with Grete Bjørnvig altogether.

Considering that the letter betrays a rather touching sense of inferiority on Mrs. Bjørnvig's part, it is difficult to take Karen Blixen's outrage as anything else than a mask, conscious or not, for what she really felt was Bjørnvig's betrayal and lack of honor: the affair he had not confided to her, his excluding her, not from the "enjoyment" of the letter with his wife, but his enjoyment with his mistress of a guilty passion under her own roof. It may well have been that she was rummaging through the trunk in the first place to look for love letters, and that finding none she had seized upon something, however harmless, in order to make her point and her feelings clear.

The Baroness spoke with such bitterness and contempt for this offense of Bjørnvig and Grete's—and their lack of honor—that she even suggested it would not be possible for them to meet again. But when Bjørnvig began to fold the letter she snatched it away from him and, with an expression of "infinite fury," said she would keep it. They started back to Sletten in silence, and he felt the worst was over. But then Karen Blixen stopped the car in a lonely spot and, bringing her face close to his, whispered plaintively, "Set me free, set me free."[10]

44

The Pact Is Broken

I

K AREN BLIXEN spent Christmas, as had become her custom, at Wedells-borg after a trip to Leerbæk in Jutland, where her brother Anders had been gravely ill. She settled down after the new year to a quiet period of work on "The Cardinal's Third Tale," which would be published later in the year as a luxurious coffee table book with illustrations by the artist Erik Clemmesen. The tale was the first chapter in what Karen Blixen intended as an extremely long novel called *Albondocani,* * something in the style, she told Robert Haas, of Jules Romain's *Les Hommes de Bonne Volonté.* It was to contain as many as a thousand and one separate but connected tales, all taking place in the kingdom of Naples in the 1830s.† As her health declined in the late fifties, she still spoke of finishing it before her death, "but just before."[1] Several of the chapters were ultimately included in *Last Tales.*

"The Cardinal's Third Tale" introduces Cardinal Salviati, who will make his appearance in her work several times again. Salviati is Dinesen's most exemplary artist-priest. We will learn in his "first" tale, which was written later, that he is one of two noble twins named Dionysio and Athanasio. When

---

*An Italian Prince Albondocani was to wander through the tales. Langbaum suggests that Dinesen took the name for such a character from Sultan Al-Bundukdari, in *Supplemental Nights* (to the *Thousand and One Nights*). She may also have been thinking of Stevenson's Prince Florizel in *New Arabian Nights,* which she had had in Africa and admired highly.

†Some of Isak Dinesen's working notes for *Albondocani* survive among her unedited papers, and they provide a rare glimpse of the method by which she assembled and organized the wealth of incident and detail that went into one of her tales. Using sheets of dated, legal-sized paper, she made lists of quotes, references, memories, and dramatic situations, generally ironic, which might be turned into tales. For example: "The old lord who has the happiness to live in Seville thirty years after Don Juan has seduced its women. The unhappy girl who was not seduced by Don Juan." Or: "Judas, who proudly pointed out that he was the only one of the disciples who *didn't* fall asleep in the Garden of Gesthemene." Or: "The girl (in Aunt Bess's story about Dories) who was the last of nine sisters, all born (Henriette Danneskjold) because the family wanted a son and heir, and who felt that a great injustice had been done her from the beginning, and that she had the power to exist in her own right."

Some of the entries, which were generally numbered, were simply a quote, or a stanza of poetry, or the note of some incident from the work of another writer. For example: "The distinguished family which calls a conference when its son has smitten his wife with a disease (Fru Gyllemborg)."

Similar thematic lists exist for *Shadows on the Grass,* "Converse at Night in Copenhagen," and Karen Blixen's essays (KBA 146).

they were infants one perished in a fire, which also confounded their identities. Who has survived? Their mother believes it is Dionysio and their father that it is Athanasio, but we are given to understand that the survivor has both the sensuous and the godly aspects within him, which is the source of his wisdom and of the "salvation" he is able to offer. As a character, the cardinal radiates a seductive combination of worldly and spiritual authority.

In the person of Cardinal Salviati and in the tale he narrates, Dinesen was speaking directly to her young friends on *Heretica,* who had so dangerously, in her view, embraced the "poisonous" tradition of dualism. Mogens Fog, her friend and doctor, told me that she intended "The Cardinal's Third Tale" in part as a kind of warning to and a friendly mockery of them, that she saw their renewed belief in an ethical Christian salvation as a "flight from reality."[2]

The heroine of the tale, Lady Flora Gordon, is an enormously rich Scottish noblewoman, descended from kings, who is traveling through Italy in the 1830s. She is another of Dinesen's great *solitaires,* who has grown up to mistrust her instincts and all human contact and is consequently in flight from the reality of her needs and feelings. She is an atheist who says of salvation: "What I have neither ordered nor paid for will I not receive."[3] And she is a giantess, enormous, statuesque in scale, who feels the same kind of disgust for her body that Gulliver felt toward the Brobdignagians. Dean Swift, we are told, is one of her favorite authors, and she makes use of his book "to deride in toto the Almighty's work of creation."[4]

In Italy she meets a Catholic priest of humble origins named Father Jacopo, who tries to convert her and at whose behest she makes generous contributions to worthy charities. He fulfills one aspect of the priestly role, which is to breach Lady Flora's inhuman solitude. They have a rather touching and incongruous friendship, and their conversations on theology are, as Langbaum puts it, full of "profundity and sweetness."[5] I would hazard the guess that Father Jacopo stands, in part, for Martin A. Hansen. He has some of Hansen's spiritual charms and—as Dinesen saw them—his spiritual limitations. Like Hansen, he is in touch with nature and is able to feel awe toward Creation. But in his ethical certainty there is nothing of the demonic, of the Dionysian aspect of experience she believed was so essential. Father Jacopo is a plebeian, the son of peasants (as was Hansen). He cannot recognize, as the aristocratic Cardinal Salviati does, that Lady Flora "is a noblewoman, and it is she who will transform the things which strike or touch her—not the outside things that will ever transform her."[6] Jacopo's submissiveness and humility are an inadequate solution for her.

The final remedy for Lady Flora's frigidity, her loneliness, her too high idealism is not theology but syphilis, and here Dinesen is making a rather daring and completely serious advertisement for her own "way." She catches it by kissing St. Peter's bronze foot in the Vatican immediately after a young worker has pressed his moist lips to the same spot. But it is not until she has left Italy and gone to Greece—to Missolonghi—that she discovers the small red sore, which is both like a "rose" and like a "seal" on her lip.

Syphilis is the "seal" of that vitality which is expressed as desire. Desire, Karen Blixen believed, unites all human beings, and the denial of desire cuts them off from that "true humanity which will ever remain a gift, and which is to be accepted by one human being as it is given to him by a fellow human. The one who gives has himself been the receiver. In this way, link by link, a chain is made from land to land and from generation to generation. Rank, wealth, and nationality in this matter all go for nothing. The poor and downtrodden can hand over the gift to kings and kings will pass it on to their favorites at Court, or to an itinerant dancer in their city. The Negro slave may give it to the slave-owner or the slave-owner to the slave. Strange and wonderful it is to consider how in such community we are bound to foreigners whom we have never seen and to dead men and women whose names we have never heard and shall never hear, more closely than if we were all holding hands."[7]

At the end of the tale Cardinal Salviati meets Lady Flora at a mountain spa, where distinguished ladies and gentlemen are treated discreetly for their infections. She is, psychologically, almost unrecognizable: an amiable and charming woman of the world, who is greeted with much affection by the other patients. She has, in the terms of the Jørgensen poem, forgotten her Latin for Greek, her Charity for Eros, and in the process has recovered her humanity.

2

That May a small domestic crisis took place at Rungstedlund as a result of which Clara was sent—not for the last time that year—into temporary exile. Karen Blixen had been working on a new tale, an early version of "Ehrengard," which she classed with a group of stories very different in tone, scope, and intention from the chapters of *Albondocani*. These were her *Anecdotes of Destiny*, which were meant to represent the lightest side of her authorship.* To Clara, "Ehrengard" seemed too light, and she said so. It was, perhaps, her one small luxury to be stubborn on certain points of what she considered honor and to take the consequences for doing so. The Baroness flew into a rage, and Clara went to live in Copenhagen.

Bjørnvig, in the meantime, was back with his wife. She had discovered

---

*In early letters to Robert Haas she calls them "in a literary sense, jokes" and includes in this category the stories written for the American mass-circulation magazines. But in the course of the fifties the contents of the volume changed; the original and rather trivial pieces were dropped from it, and three of Dinesen's finest mature tales took their place: "Tempests," "The Immortal Story," and "Babette's Feast."

the affair and became so depressed that she threatened to commit suicide, a threat that hung over their marriage for many years. His lover was also guilt-stricken, left her husband and went to live abroad. The more Bjørnvig thought about his situation, the more it seemed to him that the origin of his tragedy was—and the blame for it lay with—Karen Blixen. He had, at her behest, transferred his will to her, in exchange for her promise of divine protection. She had encouraged him to transgress, to set passion and spontaneity before duty, and he had done so. When he then demanded the protection she had promised—the sanction that would have expiated his guilt—she denied it to him. She had, in fact, promised much more than she could deliver. He asked her to act like a god, transcend her own loneliness and need for love, and she responded like a jilted mistress. He was now more than angry or disappointed; the same excess which had characterized his self-surrender charged his rejection of her. He wrote a letter dissolving the pact and giving her her "freedom."

But Thorkild should have known Karen Blixen better than that; it was not so easy to get rid of her. She wrote back reaffirming her faith in him and telling him that he did her an "injustice" with his letter. Too much was still unsaid; he must come to Rungstedlund to talk. And so he did. She then explained to him that when she had asked him to "set her free" she was terribly upset and had not meant it. She wanted now to renew the pact and, as a sign of its indissolubility, to sign it in blood. "Blood is thicker than words," she said.[8] Bjørnvig listened, secretly disheartened and feeling his resistance to her failing. He could not tell her that he didn't want any more pacts, that he wanted to leave the satanic madness behind them. But he also could not agree to something so deranged as mixing blood with her. He was caught in a bind of dependence on her love, fear of her wrath, rebellion against her authority—like an adolescent trying to free himself from a parent but unwilling to leave the safety of childhood behind. So he said nothing. Karen Blixen sensed his confusion and changed the subject. Her yearnings and fantasies rose up like her rages and then subsided, without her being able to do much about them or to correct the impression which they left on others, and she knew this.

After the turning point with Bjørnvig, Karen Blixen fell into a black depression. Brandt was there to try to lighten it and to console her. He wrote her an impetuous love letter, addressing her as *du;* sent her a live heifer garlanded with flowers; and cheerfully tried to bad-mouth his old friend, advising the Baroness not to rise to Bjørnvig's provocations, not to resume contact with him. Throughout the summer, however, she got sadder and more disoriented, and her state of mind undermined her health. "I am so unhappy," she said to Clara, who had returned from exile. Clara prided herself on her lack of curiosity and did not probe any further. But when the Baroness fell down a flight of stairs and was badly hurt, she understood that the fall "was due to a kind of general debilitation caused by her sorrows."[9]

Earlier on, Karen Blixen had gossiped casually with Brandt about Bjørn-vig's affair, and Brandt had let slip maliciously to Bjørnvig how much he knew, treating the whole thing as a joke. Now the Baroness confided some personal details of the situation to Clara, who was alarmed on Thorkild's behalf and felt that his despair was serious enough to justify her friendly intervention. But when she approached him to offer comfort, she also be-trayed the fact that the Baroness had confided in her to begin with. Bjørnvig chose to construe this as yet another theft, another sacrilege. He lashed out at Karen Blixen; she struck out at Clara, who was sent away from Rungsted-lund again for several months, without pay, although she did get the "job" of translating "The Immortal Story" into Danish. While Clara did not protest, she temporarily lost her enthusiasm for "helpful interventions."[10]

3

Bjørnvig describes the breaking of the pact as a "very long swan song, or one of Beethoven's eternal finales."[11] While Clara was in exile Karen Blixen wrote to him, pleading loneliness, and invited him to dinner. He came. She embraced him and, with "an exceptional and understated emotion in her voice," recited the first lines of a Schubert lied: *Sei mir gegrüsst, sei mir geküsst.* They dined in the Green Room, the Baroness refilling the Magister's glass, and they gave themselves up to their old bliss. Their "sorrows were ancient, and my most recent one as remote as her oldest." Bjørnvig got drunk, and we may speculate that Karen Blixen did, too, as in the old days, by osmosis. By the end of the evening he felt absolutely indifferent as to what might happen. She left the room for a moment and came back with a revolver, braced herself with one hand, took aim with the other. Bjørnvig didn't care; "there was nothing that could disturb my perfect happiness. I thought every-thing was insoluble . . . so why not now rather than later?" They looked at each other with "mutual demented understanding," and she dropped her arm. Later, Bjørnvig slept in his old bed, and Karen Blixen played him the Tchaikovsky String Quartet.[12]

But this, too, was a false ending. Karen Blixen proceeded from it as if a new understanding had been achieved. Bjørnvig once again withdrew. That Christmas she sent Alfred Pedersen up to Sletten with presents for him and Bo, and he sent back an insipid and formal thank-you note, next to which, in pencil, she scrawled the word "Idiot." A year passed with very little contact. Bjørnvig was working on a series of Hölderlin translations, and Karen Blixen was writing a "trilogy" of tales for the novel *Albondocani,* based on their relationship. She sent him the manuscripts as they were finished. Then in January of 1954, on the feast of the Epiphany, he came to Rungsted-lund again. She was not dressed in her usual evening clothes to receive him but wore an old satin Pierrot costume, with a tulle ruff. It had been made for one of the Dinesen childhood theatricals, and she had found it in a trunk in the attic. She had already worn it on two occasions: once on an excursion into Copenhagen with Knud W. Jensen, to be photographed by Rie Nissen; and once at a party for *Heretica,* where it had, as she complained to Schroeder, fallen flat.[13] Now she received Bjørnvig in this earliest of her dramatic personae.

The visit to Rungstedlund, which was to be his last for many years, began cheerfully enough. The Baroness told Bjørnvig that she had called his former mistress in Jutland but that the young woman, who had recently come back from abroad, did not want to see her and had written later that all she desired was to be left in peace. Then suddenly it seemed as if a demon got into Karen Blixen. She began to mock the girl to Bjørnvig and to make fun of the couple they had made, distorting their expressions and their speech with her great gift of mimicry until they became two pathetic and absurd figures. "Can't you see that her soul isn't any bigger than a lentil?" she asked Bjørnvig. "And you next to her, you with your stupid spite and cowardice, you who don't dare to mix your blood with mine, simply because you are afraid to see blood."[14]

Bjørnvig laughed with her. He laughed because he felt paralyzed by her irony. He laughed at himself, his beloved, and his own experience, feeling all the while that she was cursing him. The more trivial his experience seemed, the more fury he felt toward Karen Blixen, who had first sabotaged his love and then robbed him of his tragic perception of it. When he stopped laughing he pronounced a curse on her of his own and walked out.

They met again. On Ewald's Hill. On a bench, in the fresh air. Karen Blixen was waiting for him with Pasop in the still, bright autumn sunlight. But they could not speak without recriminations and pettiness, and after a while they both fell silent. Bjørnvig thought it was their final meeting. But Karen Blixen could not let him go without at least trying to give him a blessing and to get one from him. Some months later he had gone to a remote spot in the north of Jutland by the sea, to write and be alone. One morning he looked up from his work and saw Karen Blixen standing outside the window. When he opened the door she offered him her hand and explained that she had come to see where he lived and how he was.

He made her tea, and she reminisced about the time she had lived in Skagen, writing *Out of Africa.* Their talk ranged over literary matters, among them the difference between the lyric poet and the storyteller. Karen Blixen could not resist a little dig: she suggested that it corresponded to the difference between the superman and the god. But for her it was a meeting full of joy and promise: "I think we have so much to speak of," she told him, "and there is so much I would like to ask you and to say to you. I miss you."[15]

Toward midday she rose to leave, saying she had an appointment for lunch, and she asked Bjørnvig to walk back to town with her. They took a path that went along the beach, he walking a little ahead as it was narrow, and on the sand bank he saw a snake lying in the sun, curled up, sunning itself, which did not move at their approach.

When they got to the town he borrowed a car to drive her to her luncheon and went as far as her friend's door. There they said good-bye.

Karen Blixen returned to Rungstedlund and almost immediately wrote the Magister a happy letter, telling him that their meeting had resolved the terrible feelings of loss which their previous encounter had created. The snake, she told him, had been a sign to her—a sign given to her by that old landscape. She felt it would protect their friendship from harm or evil.[16]

In the meantime, Bjørnvig had written to *her*. After she had left he had been unable to work. Feelings of rage overwhelmed him. Just when, after so much turmoil and crisis, he had found peace again, she appeared to destroy it. There was nowhere "safe" from her, and this threat acquired such proportions in his agitated imagination that at that moment he believed she would pursue him beyond the grave. The snake on the path had been a symbol for him, too, but not a benevolent nod from the Jutish landscape. It was a terrible intimation of Karen Blixen's immortal and satanic power over him.

The letter he sent her, once and for all renouncing any hope of reconciliation, was not cruel or hysterical. It was full of explosive feelings, carefully phrased, but also full of gratitude. He asked her not to take back that gift of "inner freedom" she had once given him. He also said that while he had once felt he would founder if he had to give her up, he now felt he would founder if he had to go back to her. "What use is it, that I should want to resume our friendship and return to Rungstedlund once again, when the pure mighty wilderness around me sings, with all its voices, no, no, no. . . . It is not a conventional conscience which rebels, but my daemon, . . ."[17]

When it arrived Karen Blixen cabled him: "Have received your letter burn mine." The pact was broken.

4

Karen Blixen's fear, early in her friendship with Bjørnvig, that she might succumb to megalomania was, as we have seen, well founded. But asking him to intervene and warn her was like asking a mystic not to have visions. He had too much stake in her divinity to deny himself the spiritual benefits of it. When the Devil grinned at him he had not had the presence, or the experience, or the desire to grin back.

She took the responsibility for the debacle, for having pushed Bjørnvig too far, expected too much, used bad judgment. But she was also contemptuous of Bjørnvig's passivity. Telling Ole Wivel the story of the afternoon when she had strewn freesias in her disciple's hair and sent him to fetch the *Komtesse* Caritas, she lamented: "The fool did what I asked him to do. It made me look ridiculous."[18]

Ole Wivel, who had remained good friends with Bjørnvig throughout this period, listened with the ironic detachment he had learned to adopt in relation to Karen Blixen. He was one of the people best able to appreciate the insoluble contradictions of her character, the way in which the sharpest insight into human nature coexisted with the blindest vanity toward the paradoxes of her own. Years before, he had made the decision to keep his own safe distance from her without, however, sacrificing their mutual respect. He could at times ridicule what he felt were her cruelties or her absurdities, but he never lost sight of her greatness, and he was therefore not compelled, as was Bjørnvig, and later Aage Henriksen, to feel disillusioned or to reject her.

"I love and admire your well-ordered cosmos, but I cannot live in it," he had told her at the time when they had quarreled over the moral redirection of *Heretica*. And on the same occasion, admitting to himself how profoundly just her feelings were and how much love she had showed in her remonstrance, he had thought:

> She knows everything about the sublimation of loss, about suffering as the nourishment of genius, about pain's resonance as harmony in a work of art— and all the same she yielded to the most banal human moods and impulses: pettiness, impatience, caprice, stinginess. She suffered from a craving for power in spite of her generosity; she toyed with human fates in spite of her contempt for such toying; yes, she suffered from self-contempt in spite of her mighty, legitimate self-confidence and pride. She was a paradox, outside of any moral category—and also, a bad judge.[19]

Many of her close friends felt that behind her provocations and displays of egotism she was testing them and reality, trying to find someone who would stop her, set limits, laugh. But this was not, as Wivel suggests, because she felt she was outside any moral category, and it was not the result of fame or illness or old age. Tanne Dinesen had felt this way at twenty and expressed that same proud desperation in her tale, "The Ploughman."

A few people did come to her rescue in this way. One of them was Erik Kopp. Another was her distant relation, Tove Hvass, a corpulent, earthy woman her own age, who made fun of Tanne's pretensions, and even her appearance, with impunity. Tanne liked both of them the better for it. The belief in her own omnipotence was a sad thing for her and a meager consolation for the absence of anyone to be her "equal." It confirmed her in her loneliness that she was, by her own doing, taken so seriously, listened to with such naiveté, held in so much awe.

Bjørnvig was aware of this paradox in her nature, the way in which its greatness would appear unexpectedly, "like a rare wild animal," and then vanish again. Suddenly she was present, completely, and suddenly she was gone. What she said, he understood many years later, sounded like wisdom, but it was missing "that which characterizes wisdom—invulnerability and consistence. . . ."[20] She could crave a responsible and steady realtionship "with all her heart," but she found it practically impossible to achieve, "except with her servants and her animals."

The last word on this subject should be hers. "If only," she would complain, "people would treat me like a lunatic. It would be such a relief."[21]

45

Betrayals

If I were you, I would let no man be my equal.
—Osceola[1]

I

Clara Svendsen returned from her second exile in November of 1952, somewhat warier, perhaps, but no less dedicated or enthusiastic about her "calling." The first reconciliation with Bjørnvig had also taken place, and Karen Blixen was able to embark upon a long period of productive work. She began to write a trilogy of tales intended as chapters in *Albondocani*. "The Cardinal's Third Tale," published earlier that year, set the tone for the new work, which, as she told a friend, "was to be more concise and less elaborate of style than *Seven Gothic Tales* or *Winter's Tales*."[2] Robert Langbaum would refer to them as Dinesen's "diagrams of spirit." "Her plots have become more diagrammatic, with even less disparity than before between the mechanics of the story and symbolic meaning . . . the best stories come closest to being perfect fables or myths or parables. Certain other virtues have been sacrificed to this effect, but it is the effect toward which she worked all through her career."[3]

They were in essence religious parables, concerned with the relations between divinities and mortals. We know from Clara Svendsen's *Notater* that, quite apart from her "pact," theological questions interested Karen Blixen enormously at this time. She organized two "theological dinners," one in 1952, the other early in 1953, ostensibly to "provide her brother Thomas with the opportunity for religious discussion with people of different outlooks,"[4] but also, naturally, as a forum for her own views on the subject. The guests included a Lutheran pastor, a Catholic priest, Count Wedell, the critic Aage Henriksen, Thomas, Johannes Rosendahl, Clara, and several others. Karen Blixen had also hoped to provide "a common Christian," but such a person proved difficult to procure. "I went from house to house," Clara relates, "and asked, 'Is there a Christian here? Do you know a Christian?' "[5]

Karen Blixen and Johannes Rosendahl had been friends since the war, from which he emerged as a hero of the Resistance. In 1947 he had asked the Baroness to contribute a verse to be inscribed on a Resistance monument, a bell, telling her that she had been an inspiration for him during the war, and that was why he was writing to her. But the commission made her nervous; she wasn't confident about her ability to write poetry. And one day that autumn she asked Ole Wivel to come and hear what she had come up with.

"One night a dream had come to her assistance," Wivel wrote. "She had dreamt that a little elf had come into her bedroom and had stood by her bed. Standing there the elf had recited a verse, which she thereafter understood was meant as a suggestion for the bell's inscription. It went:

> *I am an echo from that time*
> *When, in their deeds, Skræp rang.**

When she asked Wivel his opinion of these lines he lit a cigarette, "putting on the same poker face that she had," and told her that "it was a clever elf, and that his suggestion was a good one. There was a beat and movement in the lines like that of a clapper against a bell. Karen Blixen subsequently disavowed responsibility for the elf's poem, but sent it on to Johannes Rosendahl. I have never forgiven him for dissociating himself from it, and I stressed many times later on that we had become good friends despite my first impression of him—before we met—as an unmusical idiot."[6]

Karen Blixen also remained friends with Rosendahl, and they continued to have a polite and formal but intellectually lively correspondence. Much of it concerned religion,† and in a letter of January 1952 Karen Blixen explained her disappointment with one of their "theological dinners." The guests had not given her an answer to the question she had put before them, which was: "Why [in the world] do you believe this?" Throughout the evening the word "faith" had been used to signify Christian faith exclusively, and this, she felt, was a great shortsightedness. "If I were to clarify my own point of view, which is that of the detached spectator, I would come to say something like the following:

---

*Jeg er Genlyd her fra dengang
Da i deres Faerd Skræp klang.

(Skræp is a mythical sword.)
†Johannes Rosendahl published an interesting study of the influence of Unitarianism on Karen Blixen's work, *Karen Blixen: Fire Foredrag* (Copenhagen: Gyldendal, 1957).

[373]

"Christianity is the belief that, in an historically given year, one of three persons in a triune Divinity became a human being; that he completely absorbed human nature into his divine nature, and that he thereby in a mystical way, united a fallen or apostate humanity with his destiny. That he, in an historically given period, in a geographically given earthly region, shared humanity's conditions, gave lessons and performed miracles and finally was crucified by an unsympathetic human race, and truly suffered a human death. That he rose up from the grave, still in his human body, but in a uniquely transfigured form, and thereby gave each human being hope of a resurrection. That he, after a given time in this human and transfigured shape went up to Heaven. And that God Himself, through this series of historical events, became reconciled with humanity's offense toward God. All human beings can, from a given day, count upon being completely forgiven and completely reconciled with their divine beginnings, provided that they are imbued with conviction on the aforenamed events' historical incontrovertibility, and that in their lives on Earth they make use of particular means of deliverance, which God, in his human expedition on Earth has taught them, and which he has put at their disposal—baptism and communion and in the original Christian Church other so-called sacraments— and that they also follow, to the best of their abilities, the ethical teachings which he has at the same period communicated to them.

"Now I ask the Christian, also from my position outside of Christianity, why do you believe this?

"I have asked before and have often gotten the answer, 'Because it says so in the Bible.' Here I have also had to ask, 'Why do you choose, in a very high degree, to set your faith in a little foreign and to us remote people's collection of mythological notions and tales? There have been, in the world and through the ages, many such written down, without your giving them any meaning or credence as the illumination of the whole universe's prevailing truth. . . .' "

She did not consider herself a Christian, explaining, "I myself was . . . raised by Unitarians and got my strongest impression of religious faith from Mohammedans. That means I must approach Christianity as an outsider. I think that I have really honestly sought to understand what it was . . . but any real understanding in a connected sense I have never achieved."[7]

2

At the end of 1952 Karen Blixen had been honored by a Danish booksellers' organization for the two books she had published that year: the splendid edition of "The Cardinal's Third Tale"; and an extremely inexpensive, pocket-size edition of "Babette's Feast," which she had hoped people would buy and send as a sort of Christmas card. The booksellers presented her with a laurel wreath, and she was photographed wearing it, dressed in a Grecian robe. The image caught her imagination, and she sent a copy of the picture to Robert Haas. She also took the name "Allori"—laurel leaves—for the hero of her trilogy.

These three tales—"The Cloak," "Night Walk," and "Of Secret Thoughts and Of Heaven"—describe the relationship between Leonidas Allori, a great old sculptor called "The Lion of the Mountains," and his young disciple and chosen heir, Angelo Santasilia. Angelo reveres the old man like a father and a god, but also loves his beautiful young wife, Lucrezia. Leonidas is not entirely innocent in the construction of this triangle; he has made his wife pose naked for his disciple and has praised her beauty enthusiastically.

Leonidas is also the leader of and inspiration to a group of revolutionaries. His activities are discovered; he is arrested by the authorities and condemned to death. Cardinal Salviati intervenes, and because of the old man's great prestige as an artist he is granted one night of freedom to take leave of his wife—on condition that his disciple Angelo act as his hostage. Meanwhile Angelo has, after great struggles of conscience, made a rendezvous with Lucrezia for the same night. He has told her he will throw stones at her window, and that she may recognize him in the dark by a splendid cape he will be wearing. At the time they make this arrangement she is ignorant of her husband's arrest, and Angelo of the plan for him to act as hostage—to which, however, he readily agrees. Before setting out for his last night with Lucrezia, Leonidas asks Angelo to lend him the cloak. We are left in suspense as to what takes place between husband and wife; the old sculptor's expression the next morning is enigmatic, and he is put to death.

"The Cloak" may naturally be read without any knowledge of the events behind it, and Robert Langbaum sums up its moral with his usual delicacy and intelligence: "Leonidas's creed is not only appropriate to the artist; it also sets forth the paradox of the moral life, which is lived between opposite imperatives. We must be faithful to others and to ourselves. The son must obey and revere the father, yet he must psychologically overthrow him and biologically replace him. It is God's scheme that we rebel even against Him in the course of our moral development. In the enigma for Angelo of the intention behind Leonidas's words and actions, we see the enigma of the moral life, which must be lived without certain knowledge of God's intention and judgment."[8]

But Thorkild Bjørnvig explains in *Pagten* that the tale, and the entire trilogy, were intended as a commentary on his "infidelity" to Karen Blixen.* In this respect it is a rather self-idealizing portrait, for the serene old master does not admit to or acknowledge any jealousy in the affair. The burden of feeling is left entirely upon the young disciple, who in the next tale of the trilogy, "Night Walk," begins a period of wandering and insomnia that ends when he meets Judas obsessively counting and recounting the thirty pieces of silver. (During the time Karen Blixen was writing the tale, Bjørnvig himself, torn by his various guilts, also suffered from insomnia.)

---

*The "cloak" alludes to the cape Elijah lays upon Elisha as the emblem of the pact.

Bjørnvig describes the third tale of the trilogy, "Of Secret Thoughts and Of Heaven," as an *åndrigt efterspil,* an unexpected happy ending. Angelo is a great sculptor; he has married Lucrezia; they have three children, and she is expecting their fourth. The symbolism of "three" and "four" that has recurred throughout the trilogy is finally explained as referring to the proportions of the golden section. The first three figures mark the corners of a rectangle, in which the width is to the length as the length is to the sum of the two. They also stand for Angelo as he appears in each of the three tales of the trilogy. The young disciple of the first tale, he tells his friend Pino Pizzuti, will not go to heaven—his soul has not been tested. The successful, happy Angelo of the third tale will also not go to heaven—he doesn't want to. But the bereft, tormented Angelo of "Night Walk" will go to heaven. He has not been saved by "anesthesia," but by the only means one can, in Dinesen's view, be saved: by transgression, the risk of one's immortal soul for one's desire.

The ending of the trilogy, Bjørnvig writes, was "an earth-motherly gesture, characteristic of [Karen Blixen's] generous, zealous, grandiose and passionate nature." It contains elements of the megalomania that had motivated the pact to start with; it also contains evidence of the very deep love Karen Blixen felt for Bjørnvig. She gave him the tales to read as they were finished and let him understand that he should perceive the ending of the trilogy as a "prophecy. . . . What she wished my story to become."[9]

3

Karen Blixen had a spell of fair wind that carried her into the spring of 1953. Her work was going well, and she was feeling relatively strong. In April she made plans for a trip to Paris and asked Robert Haas, as usual when she went abroad, to send her a little mad money in care of the Danish embassy. But at the last moment "an absurd disaster"[10] befell her; she caught whooping cough from Nils Carlsen. The illness rapidly exhausted her little reserve of energy—mental and physical—and the large doses of penicillin she received contributed to a depression that would outlast the symptoms. Bjørnvig had lately begun seeing a new other woman, and learning of it in this vulnerable condition brought Karen Blixen almost to despair. Touchingly she asked Brandt to tell her about Bjørnvig's new lover, and Brandt, trying to offer some consolation, told her that Bjørnvig had no talent for romance, took a tragic view of love generally, and, that if his girlfriend suited him it was simply because she had played hard to get.[11]

In her diary Clara Svendsen records the efforts Karen Blixen made to shake off her "coal black" moods. She liked to weed a patch of garden, to bake pancakes, to knit and sew; and this was, Clara writes, "a kind of therapy, though she would not have used that expression."[12]

One such practical task was to prune her literary garden. She made a list of the tales she had finished and had in progress, and wrote a long letter to Haas for the purpose, it seems, of making sense, both for herself and him, out of a confusing multiplicity of literary plans.

There was the novel *Albondocani*. It was to run between six and nine hundred pages and to have a hundred characters. It would be written so that "each chapter may be read as an independent story . . . the different groups of characters disappearing and reappearing as the story goes on."

She was also working on a volume of *New Winter's Tales*. These, she told Haas, were to be "much in the nature of the first *Winter's Tales*—possibly a bit sadder, possibly also on a somewhat greater scale." She hoped to have the first of these, "A Country Tale," ready to send him at the end of October.*

Next, there were the *Anecdotes of Destiny*, the "lighter" works she had been writing for American magazines. "They are the stories," she told Haas, "of which Mr. Huntington thought so very little! I myself look upon them as pieces of music played on different instruments from my other stories—say, clarinets and bassoons—and in the manner of such compositions, they are not to be taken too seriously. But this definition does not, to my mind, necessarily affect the question of their *quality* as works of art. Even a very serious composer may be free to give himself up, from time to time, to lighter games!" They would not be a separate volume, but the best of them might be included in *Last Tales*, which was to be an umbrella volume in which she would collect her works-in-progress from the other books. Karen Blixen recognized—and anticipated that Haas would, too—that it would be better to finish one book at a time rather than to collect fragments from two of them into a third volume. But she had, she told him, been "struggling with these two books for a couple of years, and it has been a most absurd and worrying dilemma to me that the moment I was trying to concentrate upon one of them, the other would inevitably assert itself, the effect of this being a complete misery and paralysis in the author. . . . It has," she concluded, "become a matter of vital importance to me to get a book out in the not too remote future, not only from a financial point of view, but in order to get my mental circulation of blood functioning once more."[13]

As it happened, the publication of *Last Tales* was postponed for four years. An event took place, shortly after Karen Blixen sent the letter off to Haas, which she blamed for her subsequent inability to write and for a new bout of depression. It was a sorry little act of opportunism that Karen Blixen took deeply to heart and would refer to for the rest of her life with great bitterness.

---

*It was not finished until 1956.

4

Early that November Danish booksellers received a publicity kit for a new novel, written by a pseudonymous author called "Alexis Hareng." The novel was titled *An Evening in the Cholera-Year,* and the material strongly insinuated that Hareng was yet another nom de plume for Karen Blixen. Her own local bookseller in Rungsted called her for confirmation of the fact, which she denied in the most strenuous and indignant terms. But then she had also denied her authorship of *The Angelic Avengers.* Even among her close friends there was speculation that she had, in fact, published a new book.

An Evening in the Cholera-Year subsequently appeared and, despite her continued denials, was reviewed in several papers as a work by Karen Blixen. She herself judged it to be "an extraordinarily brazen imitation of my books,"[14] but she was furious with the critics for being unable to discriminate synthetic Karen Blixen from the real stuff—and her rage was so consuming that it poisoned her against the entire Danish reading public. *Heretica* was about to publish one of her tales, "Converse at Night in Copenhagen," and she demanded to have it back, saying that "henceforth not a single word of hers would ever appear in Danish."[15] The editors asked Bjørnvig to intercede, and he went to Rungstedlund braced for an argument. Mozart, he began, had once been asked how he would refute his detractors and had replied: "I will refute them with new works."[16] Oughtn't she to do the same? No, she answered sulkily. His cheerful, patient needling eventually pried the tale out of her, but it didn't substantially change her feelings.

When the author of the book was finally unmasked, he turned out to be a young man named Kelvin Lindemann who had been a frequent guest at Rungstedlund. In one of his flattering letters to the Baroness he had written, apropos of the Cloak trilogy: ". . . One gets the impression from the novels of Henry James that there are two kinds of people in the world, those who betray and those who are betrayed."[17] Karen Blixen later underlined this in red. She naturally felt that he had abused her friendship and her hospitality, but curiously enough she also never took the hapless imposter himself that seriously. To Bjørnvig she described him as "a big friendly dog, who liked to spring up and put his paws on your shoulders."[18] It was the critics whom she held responsible—and, of course, the publishers. She brought suit and pursued the case in Sweden and Norway. The following year she asked Robert Haas to use his influence to have an American edition stopped. The suit dragged on for several years, and Karen Blixen eventually lost it. But she never really got over the "Lindemann affair." It was filed away, with Schyberg's review of *Seven Gothic Tales,* in the compartment where she stored her deepest resentment against Denmark and the Danish "mentality."

Even Karen Blixen's most uncritical admirers found it hard to understand the "absurd matter" of *An Evening in the Cholera-Year.** Parmenia Migel wonders "how it could have caused such distress to Tania, who had weathered so many real tragedies with calm and courage."[19] But one of Clara Svendsen's notes suggests what its real significance may have been. "Karen Blixen told me," she writes, "how it had become almost impossible to work. 'When I throw myself into the "Cardinal's First Tale," I see a caricature of myself. If I come into a group of people and meet someone who is dressed up and masquerading as me, how can I, myself, be there?' "[20] There is a note of hysteria in this question, and it seems that Isak Dinesen saw Kelvin Lindemann not simply as an impudent upstart or a literary opportunist, but as a kind of *doppelgänger.*

---

*Translated into English as *The Red Umbrellas* (New York: Appleton-Century-Croft, 1955).

46

Should Not My Mind
Keep the Knots?

I

A T THE BEGINNING of the Lindemann affair, Bjørnvig had bluffly told
Karen Blixen that he saw no reason she could not have written *An
Evening in the Cholera-Year* as a kind of literary joke, the way she had written
The Angelic Avengers. Aage Henriksen had also initially believed in her
authorship, and he developed a theory about it that was as ingenious and
poetic as it was distorted. Karen Blixen, he boldly suggested to her, had seen
herself reflected in him, had been amused, looked closely at the discrepancies,
made a parody of them; and this became the Hareng book. Neither she nor
he but the mirror image was the real author. He read the initials A.H. as his
own.[1]

Henriksen was an intense young man with heavy features set in a pale
complexion. He was then thirty, a lecturer at the University of Lund, a
specialist in Kierkegaard, and was considered by his contemporaries to have
enormous intellectual promise. In 1951 he had chosen "The Contemporary
Danish Short Story" as a theme for his course, had subsequently discovered
Karen Blixen and found her work "enormously exciting."[2] Ole Wivel, who
had been at school with Henriksen, published the exquisitely reasoned and
written lectures as a small book, *Karen Blixen and the Marionettes (Karen
Blixen og Marionetterne)*. "Karen Blixen," it begins,

> is the great aristocrat and the sibyl in our literature, the great anachronism in
> whom the old culture and the ancient *ukultur* come together. But this portrait
> contains only the half truth, and it is not exempt from being a little banal. There
> is much spirit in Karen Blixen's art, but not as much witchcraft as one has
> wished to attribute to it; she charms, but she doesn't hex. And her loftiness is
> not as great as her religiosity."[3]

Henriksen goes on to identify a central myth and a central symbol in Karen
Blixen's work. The myth is the Bible's account of the Fall, and the symbol
is the marionette. To illustrate how they come together he recalls an anecdote

from Heinrich von Kleist's "On Marionettes," in which a ballet master compares a human dancer unfavorably to a puppet. The puppet, he tells the narrator, can teach the dancer about divine grace precisely because it lacks a soul. The narrator asks how the puppet master manages to control the multitude of strings, to which he replies that it is only necessary to have a well-made puppet and to control its torso. The limbs are then absolutely obedient to the laws of gravity and fall as they should. But the human dancer's center of gravity is his soul, and since the Fall it has not coincided with his center of intention. Will and desire were in complete harmony in Eden, both with one another and with the will of God. The self-conscious human being strives for, but cannot regain, that total mastery, which was indistinguishable from total surrender. Only the marionette, which is soulless matter, or God who is pure spirit, can achieve divine Grace.

Henriksen followed this essay with three others on Karen Blixen as a woman and an artist, and with a related discussion of "Thomas Mann's *Amor Fati.*" He, like Langbaum and independently of him, perceived many parallels between her work and Mann's. In "Portrait" he tells us that she compared herself to Adrian Leverkuhn, the composer in Mann's novel *Doctor Faustus,* * (who was in turn modeled at least in part on Nietzsche). The Joseph novels were among her favorite works of fiction, and her copies of them were, according to Clara, thumbed almost to tatters. Henriksen compared Karen Blixen's intentions as an artist to Mann's at that late stage of his career when he had moved away from a depiction of the individual and his psychology —the province of the bourgeois novel—and toward a representation of the "mythical-typical." Mann's beautiful description of this process, in his essay "Freud and the Future," compares to Dinesen's much sketchier allusion to it in her letter to Rosendahl on Nemesis. ("Nemesis is that thread in the course of events which is determined by the psychic assumptions of a person. All my tales treat Nemesis."[4]) Psychoanalysis had suggested to Mann that not only the individual but also the culture carries within itself, and is compelled to repeat, its oldest and most primitive patterns of experience; that in myth, as in dreams, will and desire act without our knowledge, that we step into ancient roles and by repeating them express our inmost natures. Myths, he believed—and it is the same belief incorporated into the tales of Isak Dinesen —provide an answer to "the mystery of the unity of the ego and the world."[5]

Her own most succinct expression of this mystery comes in "The Fish" and is given by Granze, King Erik's Wendish thrall. The pagan thrall, like the storyteller herself, has access to the collective unconscious. His memory reaches back to the harmonious fatalism of a primitive age and of a people who did not distinguish between themselves and the rest of nature—which

---

*He was also born in 1885, in the (linden) "blossom time," contracted syphilis, and, of course, bartered his soul to the Devil in exchange for his art.

is also the innocence of early childhood. It is just this innocence of which Christianity, the "poisonous tradition of dualism," has, in her view, deprived us. In the landscape Granze inhabits, sea and sky, heaven and earth, conscious and unconscious, past and present are one, undifferentiated. This is also the sum of the storyteller's power of vision: " '. . . with us Wends it is a different thing,' " Granze tells the Christian king. " 'What has happened to our father's father, and to those old men who were mould when he was suckled . . . we still keep in our mind; we recall it whenever we want. You, too, have the lusts and fears of your fathers in your blood, but their knowledge you have not. . . . That is why each of you has to begin anew from the beginning, like a newborn mouse fumbling in the dark. . . . My two hands here did not do the work [of the past, of the dead generations] and still they are knotted with it; should not my mind keep the knots as well?' "[6]

The "fish" of the title is one of Isak Dinesen's most rich and allusive images. It is a symbol of the continuity between the Christian, pagan, and animalistic mysteries, and it reminds us that when she writes of "God" it is always as a pantheist. The tale was, fittingly, one of her own oldest pieces. Early drafts date from her adolescence.

Another and very brief essay, "The Messenger" ("Budbringersken"), upset some of Karen Blixen's more uncritical admirers when it appeared in 1962 as Henriksen's contribution to the Danish memorial anthology. It particularly disturbed Parmenia Migel, who, in *Titania,* accused Henriksen of an "abnormal" attachment to the Baroness and of having unjustly "claimed that she repudiated normal adult relationships . . . casually dismissing the whole rich pattern of her life of affection received and bestowed."[7] This was in turn a distortion of Henriksen's careful words and a dismissal of his own very deep and complex feeling for Karen Blixen, at least part of it reciprocated. He was the first to write publicly about her aloofness, her artifice, her extreme moodiness, which were the private observations of so many others; he described her as a woman whose greatness could not be extricated from her strangeness and who "permitted herself the impermissible" in the realm of fantasy. In her presence, he wrote, the boundary between "the inner and outer" dissolved, and she "butted in" from both directions.[8] His "Portrait" (1965) gives a brilliant description of how the same incest between "inner and outer" operates in her tales:

> . . . Karen Blixen clears away the fortuitous happenings of the external world, by reducing them to triggers of latent forces in the persons whom they affect. . . . She used a special projection technique which she had learnt from Goethe and Shakespeare, but which in its simplest form is a part of everyday psychology. "Show me your friends," as the saying goes," and I will tell you who you are." . . . By this rule [she] reduces the number of active characters in a story to correspond with the number of forces which contend on the psychological

level, and the characters are formed in the likeness of the passions which they arouse.*

2

Aage Henriksen first came to Rungstedlund in the summer of 1952 while Clara was in exile, for she does not remember meeting him until much later. Early in their relationship Karen Blixen seems to have tested his potential as a playmate: she asked him to have "adventures" with her, which presumably meant to enter into her fantasies, and he accepted. Subsequent events, and his own oblique references, suggest that these adventures were not a complete success. They were ambivalent to each other. She attracted him but also frightened him. He regarded her with awe but also a psychological shrewdness to which she was not accustomed. His insights into her work were penetrating and subtle, but also slightly overwrought. She admired his intellect and talent, but found certain of his attitudes—such as his fantasy that he was her *semblable*—presumptuous. The erotic undertone of the "adventures" may have disconcerted him, although he would also admit wryly that she never trapped people in *her* games, she trapped them in their own.[9] But perhaps the greatest impediment to their intimacy was timing. Henriksen had arrived at Rungstedlund, like Viola at the court of Orsino, at the height of Karen Blixen's lovesickness for Bjørnvig. The deep spiritual recognition that he wanted she could not give. There were moments when she seemed to encourage him, to give him proofs of favor and even love, but they would be followed by inexplicable withdrawals, brusque rejections, the resumption of a frigid and condescending formality. Consciously or not, Karen Blixen tantalized Henriksen, and he observed of her that where "illusions are concerned . . . the seducer and the redeemer are hard to tell apart. . . ."[10] He also confessed that "in the years I visited Rungstedlund I had more than one opportunity to send fraternal thoughts to Shakespeare's Malvolio."[11]

From Karen Blixen's point of view, Henriksen lacked an earthiness that she perhaps prized more than intellectual compatibility. There is an echo in this late friendship of a much earlier one—with Mario Krohn. He, too, was a brilliant man with impeccable artistic taste, who was better prepared than anyone in her circle to give her recognition. But he also seemed too yielding, too ethereal. Her own inhibitions apparently made her demand fearlessness in a partner, and Tanne Dinesen rejected Krohn on much the same (paradoxical) grounds Karen Blixen would finally reject Aage Henriksen. She wanted to be loved as a woman and not as an artist, or as a priest of art. "For her young male friends," Henriksen wrote, "who were invariably two genera-

---

*Aage Henriksen, "Portræt," p. 97. These essays were collected in *The Divine Child and Other Essays on Karen Blixen (Det Guddomelige Barn og Andre Essays om Karen Blixen)* (Copenhagen: Gyldendal, 1965), one of the finest and most evocative critical studies of Karen Blixen.

tions younger than herself, the reverse would have at first been easier, but eventually they learnt that the world of sex is more comprehensive than one is apt to suppose."[12]

Her other "young male friends" observed Henriksen's struggles, some with sympathy, some with amusement. They recalled him as a fastidious and aloof young man, who did not want to be part of her coterie and who often gave others the impression that he was standing in judgment of them. Clara found him formidable, and he himself had once asked the Baroness, in an agonized way, to help him understand why he distanced people. Some believed that his possessiveness frightened Karen Blixen, that and his "spiritual virginity."[13]

Despite the rigor of his mind and prose, there was an anguished, mystic vein in Aage Henriksen, and their correspondence suggests that Dinesen was impatient with it; she took a somewhat malicious pleasure in bringing him down to earth. When he compared her to Kierkegaard, for example, saying that their ways met in the demonic and then parted again, each going in the opposite direction "to follow very different arts of religiosity,"[14] she retorted that the problem with Kierkegaard was that he had an unpleasant (ubehagelig) body, and that he was both conscious and unconscious of it.

Nevertheless, Aage Henriksen played an increasingly important role in Karen Blixen's life during 1954, precisely when she was losing Bjørnvig. They had a voluminous correspondence; he sometimes stayed at Rungstedlund. He was well aware that he could not supplant or replace Bjørnvig in her affection, that she was not passionately involved with him. But he consoled himself with the role of confidant, intellectual chamberlain, and puckishly declared that she had asked for a snake but had got a fish. During the summer, Karen Blixen invited him to spend a week, and they discussed his projected book on her authorship. In her anguish and depression she was also frequently cross with him but would then be flooded with insecurity and remorse. He was touched, took it in stride, assured her that an evening of bad temper could not shake his love or change his literary plans. He also dared to poke gentle fun at her. That September, when Bjørnvig made his break, Henriksen compared Karen Blixen's predicament with Titania's.

3

The Nobel Prize for Literature was awarded that November to Ernest Hemingway. Accepting the honor, Hemingway deferred to three others whom he felt should have been considered before him. One was "that beautiful writer Isak Dinesen."* Hemingway had been a good friend of Bror,

---

*The other two were Carl Sandburg and Bernard Berenson. Later Hemingway explained to his friend General Charles T. (Buck) Lanham: ". . . Between us I was thinking like this: Sandburg is an old man and he will appreciate it. [He did.] Blickie's wife [Dinesen] is a damn sight better than any Swede they ever gave it to and Blickie [Baron Bror von Blixen-Finecke] is in hell and he would be pleased if I spoke well of his wife. Berenson I thought deserved it (no more than me) but I would have been happy

who was the model for the white hunter Robert Wilson in "The Short, Happy Life of Francis Macomber."[15] Thanking him for his "kind words," Karen Blixen told him that they gave her "as much heavenly pleasure—even if not as much earthly benefit—as would have done the Nobel Prize itself. ... It is a sad thing we have never met in the flesh. I have sometimes imagined what it would have been like to be on safari with you on the plains of Africa."[16]

Karen Blixen's health deteriorated rapidly with the new year 1955, and by the beginning of April she was more ill and weak than she had been in years. Earlier that month she recorded a speech and a tale for the Danish radio, which were to be broadcast on her seventieth birthday, April 17. The speech was a greeting to her listeners and an expression of gratitude to them, and the tale was "The Cloak"—a story, fittingly, about the death of an old master.

On her birthday afternoon there was the traditional hot-chocolate party at Rungstedlund for the present and former servants of the house and their friends. But Karen Blixen was too ill to preside, and she sent Anne and Erik Kopp in her place while she retired to the quiet of Elle's apartment on Sølvgade. That evening a group of her friends gathered at Ole Wivel's house to celebrate the occasion and to toast the Baroness in her absence. Each guest had prepared a greeting for her, and there may have been a feeling at the dinner—competitive and incestuous at the same time—like that among the young men in "The Dreamers," sharing their reminiscences of Olalla. Besides the Wivels there was Knud W. Jensen, whom the Baroness called "my Captain"; Bjørn Poulsen, whom she had found "so forthright and amusing" and who was completely unable to understand his friends' infatuation with her; Jørgen Gustava (Elishama) Brandt; Johannes Rosendahl, "who Karen Blixen was grateful was not a poet"; Tage Skou-Hansen, the last editor of *Heretica*, with whom she had corresponded about dualism; Thorkild Bjørnvig; and finally Aage Henriksen, who, Bjørnvig remarked, "yet had his tale of woe to live through." They ate dinner, listened to the broadcast, and then each read his homage.[17]

That July, Karen Blixen was taken to the hospital for observation. She was to spend the better part of her seventieth year in a hospital bed, fighting for her life. Her old pains had recurred, more intolerable than they had been even before her first operation, and she was in far worse physical condition to withstand them. The doctors decided to do a chordotomy, a delicate and potentially dangerous operation to sever some of the nerves in her spinal chord. They did not minimize the risks to her, and at the last moment Dr. Busch asked her if she would prefer to forget about the whole thing and live with

---

to see him get it. Or any of the three. That's the way your brain is working." (Ernest Hemingway, *Selected Letters, 1917–1961*, ed. Carlos Baker [New York: Charles Scribner, 1980], p. 839.)

the pain. But her decision had been made, and she would not abandon it.

The operation was performed in August, and it did not immediately bring her much relief. She came home at the end of the month, and her condition continued to deteriorate. Mrs. Carlsen, who had trained as a nurse, believed that she would die, and her brothers and sister Elle were summoned to attend her deathbed. But in the meantime the doctors diagnosed a secondary problem, a bleeding ulcer. This cheered everyone enormously, as it could be treated. Clara vividly remembers the afternoon that the family arrived. Despite her agony Karen Blixen was able to help Mrs. Carlsen mix the batter for some tea cakes.

· She was readmitted to the hospital for a preoperative stay to take nourishment and gain weight, and Clara came to take dictation. On the twentieth of December she sent a letter to her girlhood friend, Count Eduard Reventlow:

> I lie here like a goose that must be fattened up for the slaughter, and the doctor thinks that he will do another operation, but that I am too thin and wretched for him to do it for the time being. This past eight months have been more horrible than I can really describe to others—such continuous, insufferable pains, under which I howled like a wolf, are something one cannot fully comprehend. I feel that I have been in an Underworld. Can you remember the lovely place in Gluck's Orpheus where he comes to Hades, and the dreadful dark spirits bay at him . . . then comes Orpheus's lovely motif: "Ah, have pity, have pity on me! / Furies! Monsters! Shadows so fearful, / oh hear my song so tearful, / And your heart may heed my plea. Chorus: No! No! No! No!" So I have felt once before in my life, when I saw I couldn't keep my farm, and Denys crashed—it was as if it were precisely no longer decent to be "still alive." . . . And yet it is still a kind of privilege or grace that existence's most frightful abysses are after all interpreted in music. The problem for me now is how I shall manage to come back into the world of human beings. It sometimes feels practically insoluble, though I believe that if I find something to look forward to, it could be possible. Will you travel with me to Madrid and Granada in April? Have a good time at Amalienborg. Could you find an opportunity to express my deepest regret to their Majesties that I had lost my Ingenio et Arti* on the way from the vestibule of the Angleterre out to your car? That isn't true, I completely forgot that I had it, but that would certainly cause a scandal to admit. I think, however, that I saw both of them, with some apprehension, staring at my chest, but couldn't figure out why, as I am not, by any means, Lollobrigida.

---

*This is a reference to a party at the Royal Palace and to a decoration Karen Blixen had received and forgot to wear. Clara Svendsen elucidates the circumstances in *Notater*, p. 101. "She loved parties and not least in the grand style, and the evening would normally have been a great pleasure, but she was so miserably sick that it was a problem to get through it. . . . In the fine new off-white gown, the bodice embroidered with pearls, and a long pleated skirt of heavy satin, she was racked with pain and anxiety about causing a scandal."

This will be the only Christmas letter I shall write, or rather dictate to Clara, for I cannot do anything else but lie flat on my back. Hug the whole family for me. I hope we shall see each other if I survive this new round. And so we shall for once really speak about the old days. Your Tanne.[18]

On Christmas Eve a young men's choir made the rounds of the wards, singing hymns and carols for the patients. For Karen Blixen they sang "When the fjords turn blue," and she began to weep. Clara had never seen her cry before. It upset her terribly, the more so as she could not stay—she had to "desert" Karen Blixen to keep a long-standing engagement in Copenhagen with her stepmother.[19]

In the middle of January a good part of Karen Blixen's stomach was removed, along with her ulcers. She would never again eat normally or in normal quantities, and she would never again weigh more than eighty-five pounds. Her sufferings, and particularly her emaciation, aged her drastically. The flesh of her face hung down from her bones like Grecian drapery, pleated, held up by the muscles of her expression. It gave her an antique, noble beauty, the beauty of a relic. She did not, in fact, like looking so old, even though she often referred to it herself. But exhibiting that heroism she called *chic,* she made the best of it, turning it into a joke, swathing herself in bearskins and her head in turbans, accentuating her ghostly pallor with white powder and her enormous limpid eyes with kohl. She enjoyed the shock her appearance gave to people and the contrast she provided to the robust and round-cheeked Clara. She also enjoyed the prestige of sweeping into a drawing room like a black figure out of Boccaccio, evocative of the abyss. She was gratified finally to have become the "thinnest person in the world" and to have achieved, in her seventies, a quality that was recognized as great beauty.* If a woman had to age, the most dignified way to do it was—as she has a fat, aging woman put it in *Last Tales*—to " 'become a skeleton, a skull, a memento mori. . . . Then I should still be an inspiring figure. . . . I should still inspire them with horror.' "[20]

In the last seven years of her life Isak Dinesen seemed really too slight, too fragile to be alive; and it was that fragility, in contrast to her voracity for experience, which most impressed the people who met her for the first time. The visual effect of her suffering was to dramatize, particularly for

---

*Photographers found Isak Dinesen irresistible as an old woman. Cecil Beaton, an old friend, did several portraits of her, including the famous one: in profile, sitting on a chair, in a black cloche. Richard Avedon photographed her for his book *Observations,* for which Truman Capote wrote the text. He emphasized the strength but also the twistedness in her knotted hands and the ghostly pallor of her wrinkled face, with her dark eyes opened unnaturally wide. She thought the pictures were malicious and cruel and was much hurt by them. Peter Beard was one of the last to photograph her, smoking, pensive in an old sweater, and he caught a depth and a sadness she rarely showed, except in prose. She was photographed in New York with Marilyn Monroe, and that image was more "typical" of the old Isak Dinesen: twisted smile, elegant gray suit, head swathed in a turban, body muffled in a fur.

strangers, the sense of an unbridgeable gap between her and them—the impression of her age, her wisdom, her courage, her very being as a mystery. And so the physical degeneration completed that imaginative process by which, practically since Africa, Isak Dinesen had been defining herself as a symbol, as one who had "been through death—a passage outside the range of imagination, but within the range of experience."[21]

Book Four

PELLEGRINA

Left: Isak Dinesen and her brother, Anders, in front of Oregaarde, their great-grandfather Hansen's summer house. *Below:* Nyack, 1959. Isak Dinesen (guest of honor) with Arthur Miller, Marilyn Monroe, and Carson McCullers (hostess). *Right:* Isak Dinesen and Clara Svendsen en route to America. *Opposite page, below:* The storyteller visits the great flowering hawthorns of the Deer Park.

*It is the work of the artist . . . that invents
the man who has created it, who is supposed
to have created it. "Great men" as they are
venerated are subsequent pieces of minor
fiction.*

—NIETZSCHE
Nietzsche Contra Wagner

*So your own self, your personality and existence
are reflected within the mind of each of the
people whom you meet and live with, into a likeness, a caricature of yourself, which still lives
on and pretends to be, in some way, the truth
about you. Even a flattering picture is a
caricature and a lie.*

—ISAK DINESEN
"The Roads Around Pisa"

47

Baksheesh

I SAK DINESEN perceived what was left of her life as borrowed time—
baksheesh *—and she felt it was an urgent matter to crowd it with new
experiences and sensations. The old sorrow she had felt in Africa, the sense
that the moment was slipping away even as she lived it, was heightened by
the real and constant reminder of her mortality: her wasting body, the
dramatic change in her appearance, her difficulty walking and standing, a new
invalidism to which she had to defer but which—*frei lebt wer sterben kann*
—she never deigned to.

She had "planned to die" in 1955, she told a friend, and had made
preparations. She revised her will and wanted to give a last radio speech about
"how easy it was to die. Not a morbid message . . . but a message of well,
cheer . . . that it is a great and lovely experience to die."[1] After the operations
it took a while before she was convinced that she was, in fact, alive, describing
her state as "hovering like a sea gull" above life's surface.[2] Her friends
responded with gallantry and imagination. Early in the spring while she was
still in bed, Birthe Andrup came to visit, bringing a troupe of marionettes
she had made herself: the cast for *The Revenge of Truth*. "Amiane naturally
looked like Karen Blixen."[3] Aage Henriksen also came. He spoke about his
desire to write something on Wilhelm Dinesen. This pleased her enormously,
and she looked through her father's works herself and sent him notes she
thought might be useful.

As she had written to Count Reventlow, she also thought that "something
to look forward to" might make it easier to rejoin the world. Her Danish
publisher offered her a trip abroad, and she decided to go to Rome. The
choice, Parmenia Migel noted, was inspired by the sight of two men fishing
from a small boat. This seascape, framed by her bedroom window, reminded
her of a painting by Guardi.

The Roman holiday was scheduled for May, three months after her
operation and following almost a year of debility and illness. It did not matter
to her that she had not completely regained her strength, although she was

---

*Swahili for a gift, a surprise, a gratuity.

no longer confident enough to travel alone. Clara, who was invited to come with her, was tremendously excited at the prospect and with solemnity recorded in her diary that she "bought the world's best watch" and "a new pair of eyeglasses" so as to better discharge her responsibilities "for the practical."⁴

As the trip was taking shape they received a letter from Eugene Walter, a young American writer living in Rome, who was the editor of Princess Caetani's literary review, *Botteghe Oscure.* He had written to ask Isak Dinesen for a tale and was informed that she herself would be coming to Rome to "try to get into the world again."⁵ Walter, a Southern gentleman, immediately offered his services as cicerone, and she accepted them. He proved to be a blond, plump, courtly, irreverent person, and Isak Dinesen fell in with him as if they had known each other for many years. She was also impressed by his clairvoyance; he served up just the kind of treats she had hoped for: poetry, theater, interesting little dinners, and a retinue of Roman *bels esprits* to pay her homage. Walter had arranged to interview Isak Dinesen for *The Paris Review*'s series of "Writers on their Work." Sitting at a table in the Piazza Navona in the rosy afternoon, she talked more willingly and candidly about her authorship than she had in many years.

The trip was such a success that she would return again, and from Denmark she wrote to tell Walter what it had meant to her:

> I need your arm for up and down stairs, your shoulder to rest my head upon, your charming gift of imagination to fall in with my own fantasies. I shall not forget you, and I beg you, too, to remember that altogether we have salted sweet hours, made the years rewind, eaten all the ripened heart of life, and made a luscious pickle of the rind.⁶

2

The old homecoming depression was waiting for her at Rungstedlund. She described it in a letter to her cousin Philip Ingerslev, observing that in Rome she had forgotten all about her problems, discovered a resource of "miraculous" vitality, and had more than kept up with Clara. But as soon as she came home her strength deserted her, and she was overwhelmed with pain, sickness, and anxiety.

This anxiety took the old form of the fear that taxes would impoverish her and that she would lose Rungstedlund. The previous summer, when she had made her will, her lawyer Jonas Bruun had reviewed all her contracts and had been disturbed by the potential illegality, under Danish law, of her private agreement with Random House to limit any year's royalties to $10,000. Mr. Bruun wanted some kind of statement from Random House that this was a legal arrangement in the United States, and Karen Blixen was suddenly panic-stricken at the prospect that all her earnings from *The Angelic*

Avengers would be retroactively assessed by the Danish tax comptroller for the fiscal year in which they were earned, depriving her of the comfortable income she was still receiving from the delayed royalties. Although Haas gave her what personal reassurance he could, he could not make any promises having to do with Danish tax laws. Subsequent correspondence did not allay her fears, and although no action was taken in Denmark, the specter of bankruptcy acquired disturbing proportions. She went to Wedellsborg for a short vacation in July and wrote to Clara, in considerable anguish, that the subject of taxes weighed terribly on her mind, was driving away her tranquillity, and "how, how" would she be able to write?[7] It is not clear that any of this worry was grounded in reality. Clara observes in *Notater* that the subject of money inevitably stirred up the trauma of losing the farm, and Karen Blixen herself admitted that the problem was in part "psychosomatic."[8]

3

On August 1, 1956, Karen Blixen received a letter from her Paris friend, Parmenia Migel. She wrote in order to discuss a project that had been on her mind for several months—a biography. Perhaps Tania had considered writing a memoir of her own, but there were bound to be things which modesty would prevent her from saying. These were precisely the sort of things Ms. Migel could and wanted to say. She asked her friend to think about it and to let her know.

Karen Blixen did think about it and three weeks later asked Aage Henriksen to undertake the project. He had come to dine alone with her in the Green Room, and they had been speaking about the difficulties—indeed, the impossibilities—of writing about a life whose most important circumstances and events were of the kind one could not discuss. She told Henriksen that she had saved the letters she had written to her mother from Africa but now thought of burning them. The talk stopped there, but as he was leaving, tired, not completely with his wits about him—he had a cold—he realized that she had asked him, nevertheless, to write her life.

This was a major policy reversal, for Karen Blixen had always been extremely shy of any biographical inquiries. In the late 1940s she had deep misgivings about Hans Brix, the Danish literary critic, pursuing his study of her work precisely because of his customary interest in the author's life. When Aage Kabell asked her biographical questions while doing research for *Karen Blixen debuterer,* she responded playfully that she felt he was a hunter "following her spoor"[9] and that it made her nervous. But apparently her failing health and her brush with death had also made her concerned to assure that her reputation—her "mythos," as she would call it—would outlive her. She had already asked Bjørnvig to write about their relationship when she was dead, when things would be clearer and he would be free of the obligation to please her. Perhaps she also felt it was time to encourage a full-length study and to leave her imprint on it. She showed great astuteness in choosing Henriksen, although later he came to feel he could not oblige her. Parmenia Migel, in the meantime, heard nothing for a year and wrote again, with as much pique as her deference permitted, to remind Tania about her offer. In the autumn of 1957 the Baroness agreed to cooperate and received, in exchange, a statement of her biographer's proposed methodology. Tania was to tell her as much as she wanted to when they next met. In the meantime she was to set down her reminiscences or dictate them to Clara. The book was to be obedient to Karen Blixen's own instructions, and Ms. Migel compared herself to a pianist studying the composer's fingering.[10]

In the course of the next five years Karen Blixen met several times with Ms. Migel, who took notes, although she seems not to have used a tape recorder. After Karen Blixen's death Ms. Migel interviewed a number of friends and family members, visited Katholm and Frijsenborg, and stayed with Count and Countess Wedell. Although she had access to all of Karen Blixen's personal papers and her African letters, she did not care to have them translated. She also did not, at Karen Blixen's wish, travel to Africa, explaining that it had changed too much and that Tania wanted her to imagine it for herself. She did choose to give the greatest emphasis to that part of her subject's life she knew best: the last years, the 1950s and early 1960s; to Isak Dinesen's honors and awards; and to Isak Dinesen's socializing with famous, talented, and titled people. She defended the image of the great aristocrat and Sibyl, often with what Hannah Arendt, in her review of *Titania,* called a "naive impudence." Unfortunately this also led Ms. Migel to exaggerate, unwittingly, the vanity and snobbism that were certainly elements of Dinesen's character, but also certainly not such prominent or un-self-conscious ones. "It would be better to pass over *Titania* in silence," Hannah Arendt wrote, "were it not for the unhappy fact that it was Isak Dinesen herself (or was it the Baroness Karen Blixen?) who had commissioned it, as it were . . . had spent hours and days with Ms. Migel to instruct her, and who, shortly before her death, reminded her once more of 'my book,' exacting a promise it would be finished 'as soon as I die.' "[11]

W. Jackson Bate, in his splendid biography of Dr. Johnson, offers an insight that may help to put Isak Dinesen's "cooperation" into better focus. "The temptation to act a role," he says, "and in the process to shock the complacent, is partly the simple willingness of most people to live up to the picture others have of us, provided it does not demand too much effort, and even at times, if our spirits are high, to offer them a self-caricature."[12]

Isak Dinesen was apparently flattered by Parmenia Migel's adoration, and she lived up to her expectations, offering just such a spirited self-caricature as Dr. Bate describes. Ms. Migel, all innocently and with the additional distortion of a second-generation image, transmitted it into *Titania.*

48

Echoes

DESPITE THE RESOUNDING FINALITY with which the pact was broken, Karen Blixen and Thorkild Bjørnvig gingerly resumed some contact. He made the overture, sending her the sonnet he had composed for her seventieth birthday. She replied:

> You have made it difficult for me to thank you, for I must feel every word I address to you, orally or in writing, as a break with a word I have given you —now almost half a year ago—and honestly meant to keep. However, I would like to say thank you, and if you can receive a thank you I would like us to see each other. Not to speak much, it hasn't worked out very well these last few times—but I would like to have you give me your hand. What shall I otherwise, in the long run, do with an homage to a friendship which was . . . struck down by a curse?[1]

Bjørnvig accepted her invitation. Karen Blixen rejoiced over the prospect of his homecoming, describing it to Clara as the "prodigal son's return." She must have been nervous about it, though, for she pressed Clara to have tea with them, Clara tactfully declining on the grounds that she had her own work to do.* The Baroness grumbled about her being no better than the "eldest son." But instead of saying "eldest son," it came out "fatted calf"; she was no better than the "fatted calf." This delighted both of them, and *Fedekalven* became Clara's nickname.[2]

Throughout the summer and into the autumn of 1956, Karen Blixen worked on the tale that was her version of an epitaph for the pact, and as Bjørnvig put it, "her answer to me." "Echoes" is a postscript of sorts, or really a literary caret to an earlier tale, "The Dreamers," and it fills in the story of Pellegrina Leoni during the period when she runs away from Lincoln Forsner, afraid he will learn her true identity. In the course of her flight she comes to a small village in the mountains and stops in its church, where she

---

*Clara supplemented her wages with translations from the Italian (Lampedusa, Alberto Denti di Pirajno); from the English (Graham Greene, Rosamund Lehmann, and Paul Bowles); with work for the Copenhagen library; and she also contributed short articles and reviews to a variety of periodicals.

hears a young boy singing the Magnificat. He has an unearthly pure and sublime soprano she recognizes as the voice of the young Pellegrina Leoni. She also realizes that she has three years at most before the boy's voice will change, but she is determined that within this time she will make a great singer out of him, so that the voice of Pellegrina, which has been lost in the fire at the Milan Opera House, will be resurrected, however briefly.

Taking lodgings in the village, Pellegrina lets it be known that she is the widow of a famous opera teacher, and she offers to train this boy, Emmanuele, who is the son of peasants and an orphan but who is being raised by the village squire. His guardian agrees, and he becomes her pupil. Their relationship is mysteriously charged from the beginning, and she also tells herself that at the three years' end he will be her lover. One day Emmanuele confirms that they were destined to meet. He tells her that he knows who she really is—not "signora Oreste, from Rome," but the great diva Pellegrina Leoni. He is the only other living person besides Marcus Cocoza, her old friend, to know this secret, as the world believes she is dead.*

Such was the mystical recognition Karen Blixen felt Bjørnvig had given her. But like Bjørnvig, Emmanuele has several shortcomings which disturb his teacher. They are his softness, his vulnerability, and his cowardice. She repeatedly tells him "only a hard metal can make a ring." And to make him hardy, to teach him to endure pain, she pricks his finger three times with a needle, wiping the blood off with her handkerchief and then putting it to her lips.

The day after this alarming demonstration Emmanuele does not appear at the usual hour. Pellegrina goes in search of him and realizes that he has run away from her. The boy seems to have grasped what is unstated in the text but implicit in her fixation on his exquisite voice—that she might castrate him to keep it. When she does catch up with him he hurls a stone at her, accusing her of black magic. She is a witch, a vampire; she wants to suck his blood; he has seen her do it. "Peasant," she shouts back. And she rubs the stone into the wound it has made in her forehead, smearing it with her own blood before she throws it back. Later, she reflects upon his naiveté. He had no way of knowing that the mingling of blood is not the drinking of blood. "Oh, my dear child, dear Brother and Lover," she thinks. "Be not unhappy and fear not. It is all over between you and me. I . . . have been too bold, venturing to play with human hands on an Aeolian harp."³

At the end of the tale, Pellegrina goes back to the church where she first heard Emmanuele sing. A mass is in progress; an old woman who has just taken communion returns to her seat; Pellegrina watches her munching on

---

*Emmanuele's cousin, Luigi, had been Pellegrina's servant, knew she was still alive, had an intuition Emmanuele would get to meet her, and described her looks and saintly qualities so that he might know her.

the host and thinks that one may "allow oneself many things toward Him which one cannot allow oneself toward man. And because He is God, in doing so one will even be honoring Him."[4] In other words, one may eat the flesh of the Lord and drink His blood, and this is the mode of adoring Him. But to devour the flesh and drink the blood of a human being, even symbolically—that is cannibalism.

Robert Langbaum, who had other reservations about "Echoes," nevertheless believed that "in her soul-searching Isak Dinesen pointed the finger of accusation against herself."[5] Bjørnvig, however, believed that she wanted the world to know how deep her disappointment was and how deep, too, was her solitude. Dinesen herself explained to Viggo Kjær Petersen that the tale was based on a concept of the Eucharist as a mutual sacrifice and a mutual homage, and she clearly felt that Bjørnvig was not prepared to make the sacrifice or to understand how unselfish was her homage. To a different critic, Aage Kabell, she observed that in any intimate relationship there is always a mutual consumption of flesh and blood, "and it is not always possible to determine who is eating who."[6]

Pellegrina does not directly blame Emmanuele for his desertion, although she has contempt for the provinciality of the milieu that has so stunted him. This was the essence of Karen Blixen's own contempt for Denmark, *Heretica*, and the limitations of Bjørnvig's outlook, which she had tried so hard to sophisticate. It is difficult, however, to see where she really "points the finger . . . at herself." She forgives Emmanuele for disappointing her and even rewards him with a blessing. But she also implies that the relationship between master and pupil fails because Pellegrina has too much greatness of spirit.

This is not the Pellegrina Leoni of "The Dreamers," a woman whose experience of loss has convinced her that it is unsafe to be "one woman again, to suffer so much." This Pellegrina is a worldly saint, speaking in parables and uplifting souls with her generosity and her wisdom. Her solitude is divine: it is that of one whose "element is joy" among the suffering. Her fearlessness is divine: she has not been afraid to give away her soul. Karen Blixen seems to have answered Thorkild Bjørnvig with divine forgiveness for his human frailty—and by writing a tale that perpetuates the same delusion of grandeur whose folly it describes, which was the undoing of their relationship.

Bjørnvig attempts to explain Karen Blixen's grandiosity in his own summing up of the tale and of the pact. He attributes it to her personal communion with nature, which was "magnificent and deep . . . intense and strange . . . wise . . . unromantic . . . precise." This rootedness made her "relations with God so personal, so anthropomorphic that again and again they had to slip into self-worship, and lead seductively to a show of force—with divine insignia of battle. Confronted by this brilliant madness one could well feel struck by awe, but also by horror. One had to capitulate, to submit, or go away. Hence, in spite of friends and family, in spite of publicity and fame, [Karen Blixen's] inhuman solitude."[7]

"Echoes" is a tale, a metaphor, and even if Isak Dinesen did closely identify with Pellegrina, the question must still be asked: did she actually believe she had magic or divine powers? The evidence suggests that she wasn't sure. Two years later, in the course of a long discussion on religion with her brother Thomas, she asked him if *he* didn't believe that the faithful got their power from God, the way witches got their powers from Satan. He answered her, as he always had, reasonably: "That religious people can develop their powers by unusual and remarkable means I cannot deny. But the question is: do they get their help and power from something outside themselves?"[8]

2

Karen Blixen's relationship with Thomas had cooled over the years. They still saw each other, but they disapproved of one another's way of life. He laughed at her public persona, her sibylline airs, the manner in which she held forth seductively to a circle of boys young enough to be her grandsons. Although he was devoted to her, he was not prepared to give her the lavish and uncritical admiration she craved, which in any case was alien to his candid nature. She, in turn, berated him for having "betrayed" his class, for having "drummed himself out of the gentry." She teased his children about their "disgusting" love for their parents, and she also made fun of Jonna Dinesen, with some malice, to Jonna's son-in-law, Erik Kopp.

Their rivalry focused in the middle fifties on an issue of real substance and great importance to Karen Blixen: the disposition of Rungstedlund. In her panic over the "supertax" she had sought advice about how best to assure herself a place to live until her death and was told that she ought to deed the estate to a charity, or share it with an institution, reserving a lifetime interest in it. But to do this she needed to be its sole owner, and so she asked her brothers either to give or to sell her their shares. Anders was willing, and so was Thomas, but he wanted cash. She offered 46,000 kroner, but he did not want to sell for less than 100,000; he had to keep his children's inheritance in mind. Apparently Tanne could have met his price but didn't want to. She felt she was owed a consideration from her brother for the fact that he and his family had no financial worries, that they lived in "great ease and luxury," and that she had managed to earn a living only with very hard work "in the course of many years."[9] She could not, she told another family member, get beyond this view of the unfairness of the situation, even though she had tried.

The tug-of-war over Rungstedlund seems to have been the echo of a much older and more painful twofold struggle in Karen Blixen's life. There was her sense as a child of her special talent and uniqueness, which she couldn't prove and which was refuted by the family's insistence on scrupulous equality among the siblings. Later, there was her sense of her special tragedy and loss in regard to Wilhelm, which had made things so much harder for her and which her family also had never sympathized with or understood. When she speaks of her brother's "luxury" and his "ease" she must have been feeling deprived, not only in regard to his financial security but to his emotional security, too—his happy marriage and loving children—which she took such unnatural pains to mock. She had suffered, she was alone and she deserved compensation. The depth of those feelings perhaps explains why she could not "get beyond" them.

The quarrel dragged on for several years, causing hurt and bitterness on both sides. It was ultimately resolved when Elle Dahl offered to buy Thomas's share and turn it over to the Rungstedlund Foundation.

3

After spending Christmas at Wedellsborg, Karen Blixen returned to a period of concentrated work on *Last Tales,* which was to be published the following November. She had conceived the title while she was convalescing from her operations, and it had cheered her up greatly. *Anecdotes of Destiny* was now also ready, and she had originally expressed the wish to Haas that both books be published simultaneously—"hand in hand." She was afraid, after a hiatus of fifteen years, that neither was great enough on its own to live up to her readers' expectations, and that "her reappearance . . . would have to be something of a sensation if it was not to be an anti-climax."[10] Haas did not agree, and *Anecdotes* was published the following year. Originally he assumed that the order of the two books would be reversed, but Dinesen wrote to insist that *Last Tales* must come first: *Anecdotes,* she felt, was not of lesser quality but did "carry less weight."[11]

There was now one outstanding *Last Tale*—"Copenhagen Season"—that she had promised Haas, which she very much wanted to include. But she had unusual trouble getting any work done. There were new severe pains in her back, which made it difficult for her to sit up, and periods of extreme weakness. Her doctors recommended a series of blood transfusions for which she entered the hospital in March. In the meantime she continued to dictate, sometimes supine on the floor. The necessity to speak her prose was tremendously discouraging, but as she would tell Marianne Moore a few years later, "It also taught me a lesson. When you have a great and difficult task, something perhaps almost impossible, if you only work a little at a time, every day a little, *without faith and without hope* . . . suddenly the work will find itself."[12]

Since the thirties, Isak Dinesen had wanted to try her hand at writing about her father's love for Agnes Frijs and the milieu he had lived in before his marriage to Ingeborg, which she renders in "Copenhagen Season" with much tender detail. "It has amused me," she explained to Haas, "to write down what I myself have been told as a child about conditions, individuals and happenings of my father's generation, before knowledge of these things has been altogether lost. To write, too, somehow, in the way of that past age itself."[13]

The tale takes place early in 1870 in the drawing rooms of Copenhagen as the great winter season is in full swing. Ladies and sofas are elaborately upholstered, and it is a moment exemplary for Dinesen, which she calls "the eleventh hour of the Danish aristocracy." A great historical transition is taking place that affects all the ideals and meanings people live by, but which is still invisible to them. It is the same revolution taking place in the France of the Second Empire: wealth and power are shifting from the land and the old ruling class to the cities, the banks, and the bourgeoisie. The aristocracy may be enjoying unprecedented prosperity, but the same economic conditions that have made this possible have also sealed its fate—and that of the whole rural world. An age of science and money—a mobile, parvenu age—has dawned, and to Dinesen this means, as the old painter Professor Sivertsen tells a group of elderly grande dames, that honor—fidelity to a system of fixed values and relations—has become obsolete. Their grandchildren will travel to the moon, but they will fight no duels and commit no hara-kiri. They will also be incapable of understanding tragedy.

In the classical sense, an individual has the possibility for tragedy only when his fidelity to an ideal—his honor—is so fundamental to his being that he will renounce what is most precious to him before he betrays it. In most tragedies it is some form of passion that tempts or compels the hero to waver from his ideal. In the tales of Isak Dinesen the ideal is often passion itself. Dinesen lectured her young friends on this subject, complained about the shallowness of their affairs and about the moral flimsiness of the age, and declared that only on the great estates, the *herregaardene,* could she still find people who understood the concept of honor as she herself did "to a mystical degree."[14]

By the time of "Copenhagen Season" even the Counts von Galen, who are the greatest lords of Denmark (and based on the Frijs family), have been insidiously compromised and softened up. Leopold (Mogens) proves to have the soul of a common bounder, and Adelaide (Agnes) values the coronet on her hanky higher than her passion. From now on, the tale implies, the old ideals will be carried on by figures like the Angels (the Dinesens) who are not necessarily aristocrats. They may be artists like Professor Sivertsen, who would not "exchange the idea of honor for a flying ticket to the moon"; or they may be actors, like Heloise and Kasparson from other tales, who have no honor of their own but who assume an heroic role and in it call forth the heroism of others. They may also be noble atavisms like Miss Malin or Baron von Brackel or the narrator of *Out of Africa*—classical figures in a factual age and, like the Angels, "marked down for ruin."[15] What they are able to do best is to sit their horses like a tribe of centaurs and to discuss theology and the opera; they have their twisted roots "deep in the mold" and are in harmony with the elements and the instincts. Above all, they keep alive the "honor in their hearts." The honor of the Angels in "Copenhagen Season" has a double edge: passion and rigor, and these were Isak Dinesen's ideals in a friend or lover or a work of art, and her greatest lessons as a teacher. They are also the qualities she felt were most lacking in the modern Danes.

That May, a week after the deadline Dinesen had set for finishing the story, she was able to send it to Haas. "At last!" she wrote triumphant. "It is different from my other tales, and I do not know if you will like it."[16] Actually, it was the story in *Last Tales* of which she was "proudest," for "here she felt she had finally done the novel."[17] The "novelistic" elements of the tale are the leisurely descriptive prose which sets its scene without advancing the plot and its subtle understanding of the *embourgeoisement* that was transforming all relations in society. But she did not really "do" her characters like a novelist. They are treated, as in her other tales, as symmetrically poised and motivated contrapuntal forces. Nor are the Angels a "novelistic" family; they are figures from a fairy tale or a saga. Every possible perfection of soul and body has been heaped together in them: perfect bowels and noses, exquisite dreams and senses, unflagging gallantry, humor and lust—all glossed with doom. They also rather bring to mind those strange, dreamy rococo paintings in which the nymphs and satyrs are composed entirely of pieces of fruit. Dinesen, however, seems to have meant the portrait seriously, even naturalistically, and elsewhere she laid claim to many of the same qualities.* One could cavil over them with her or at least point to the portrait as another instance of her vainglory. But it also offers an important clue to her charisma. "Inspired by some hidden source of energy in life," she writes about the Angels/Dinesens, "they did in turn inspire their surroundings. To ... their more obtuse friends it was a pleasant thing to have existence proved to be a privilege."[18]

When "Copenhagen Season" was finished she sent it to her brother Thomas for his opinion. She might have expected it to touch a nerve which had always been sensitive in their relationship: her possessiveness toward their father. "To such a degree as Ib represents my father," Thomas told her, "I can hardly agree that [his] conduct in a situation like this would have been so completely based on class-consciousness, and so tradition-bound—his whole life contradicts this, I believe."[19] He also laughed at his sister's auda-

---

*In an "interview" with Bent Mohn, published in the *New York Times*, November 3, 1957 (49:1), Isak Dinesen declared that "at times I have been so happy that it has struck me as overwhelming, almost supernatural. . . . I have been exceptionally equipped for this. I have had exceptionally fine and keen senses. . . . I have never met anyone who could see as well as I could." Mr. Mohn told me in 1975 that he actually had had no part in the "interview"—Isak Dinesen had written both the questions and the responses herself.

cious self-idealization and tried to point out, in a tactful manner, that an "inspired" version of reality might well be very beautiful, but that once one knew the truth, it wouldn't do. He gave her an analogy. Suppose, he wrote, one flew over the North Pole in an airplane. Seen through the window, the ice seems to be brilliantly colored. Suppose one wrote a poem about that brilliance. And then suppose, he said, that it was pointed out that the glass was tinted. Tanne would argue that it didn't matter; he would answer that while he might admire the poem, he wouldn't get excited about the ice cap on the next trip.[20]

Their differences on the subject of Wilhelm's character became a sore point to them both in the next few years. After one particularly bitter argument at which Anders was present, Thomas solicited his opinion. "Have you any sense of your father's character and nature?" Anders thought awhile. *"Ja,* I have—wait a minute—big farmer."[21]

4

Roger Lubbock, who had succeeded Constant Huntington as publisher at (the British) Putnam's, paid Karen Blixen a visit in June, before the publication of *Last Tales.* He barely concealed his reservations about the book and about the reception it could expect in England. It would, he said, "seem too frivolous" to be chosen by the English Book Society, and "even his own staff had been shocked at certain pages in it."[22] The most shocking pages were those in "The Cardinal's Third Tale" that describe how Lady Flora Gordon, a proud and fanatic virgin, catches syphilis by kissing the foot of Saint Peter's statue in the Vatican after a young Roman worker has kissed it before her, leaving the bronze still moist with his saliva. Karen Blixen had intended the moment to be ironic but also moving, and she told Lubbock with some hurt that she was "innocent" of frivolity. Of course, she did not explain that she herself suffered from syphilis, a fact that considerably affects one's reading of the tale, and it continued to be criticized and misjudged, particularly in Denmark. But it also may have influenced the American judges of the Book-of-the-Month Club, for that August Haas informed her that the club had rejected *Last Tales,* the first of her works it had passed over. No reason was given, but Dinesen was alarmed and afraid that she might have "estranged" her American readers "towards whom I have always felt a special gratitude." This—and the blow to Random House—were much more important considerations to her than the money or the honor. "I feel it will have been a great disappointment to you," she told Haas, "and indeed, after we have taken this fine obstacle four times together, it would have been fun to have done it the fifth time! As for myself, I have been through the last twelve months working on *Last Tales* with a leg and a half in the grave. Most of the time I have thought that I should never get the work finished. I can at this moment feel little more than deep gratitude at the miraculous fact I have succeeded in completing the task, and a firm trust that the fate of the book now rests in stronger hands than mine. We shall still have a great deal of fun out of this book!"[23] And with typical courtliness she described to Haas how fine the roses in her garden had been that summer and how she wished she might have sent him some.

But the general feeling that *Last Tales* was weaker than Isak Dinesen's first three books has, I think, some merit. Part of this was not the author's fault. Her earlier work was written in sustained bursts of creative energy, while *Last Tales* was labored on for many years and interrupted by much ill-health and depression. It is, however, also the most frankly didactic of her books, the furthest from her own ideal of storytelling as "entertainment." She instructs her readers, as she had instructed Bjørnvig and the "heretics," with more than a little moral superiority. And in assuming the master's "cloak," in speaking with the master's stately, mystifying, and exalted voice, she loses touch with one important source of her own power: the humility of the storyteller as artisan.

Throughout the summer and early autumn Karen Blixen was busy with guests. Mikhail Sholokov, the Russian novelist, came out to visit her at the end of June; the Kopps, the Wivels, the Reventlows, and Bent Mohn helped her entertain Roger Lubbock and his wife; Eugene Haynes was preparing a European concert tour, using Denmark as his home base, and his music, cheerful company, personal beauty, and unstinting adoration brought Karen Blixen much delight. When he gave his first major concert in Copenhagen that October he claimed that its success was due entirely to her presence, and she in turn proclaimed October 1 "Eugene's Day, made a charming speech, recited a poem to me, and kissed me. It was a magical moment."[24]

About the same time a well-known Swedish journalist named Anders Lundebeck arrived at Rungstedlund for an interview and slipped Karen Blixen an interesting piece of news: the Swedish Academy had nominated her for the Nobel Prize, and he "knew positively" that she was the favorite. No one was more excited to hear this than Clara, who felt that at last her own years of patience and sacrifice stood to be vindicated, publicly and grandly, to those who had always reproached her for abandoning her own career. She looked forward to the financial security the prize money would bring her employer, but especially to the new works that could then, in tranquillity, be undertaken. Karen Blixen herself did not speak about the prize "but had about her some of that air of radiant expectancy which at times was apparent in her even until the very last days of her life."[25] On the morning of October 17, when the decision was to be announced, Clara bicycled to Mikkelborg to hear mass and say a prayer, but the day passed with no phone call from Stockholm. At six-thirty they listened to the radio newscast in the Green Room, learning that Camus had won the prize.

Positive assurances of her nomination, inquiries from reporters, the stirring up of hopes and then the bleak disappointment were to be repeated the next year. She was, Robert Langbaum writes, "a leading contender"[26] for the prize until her death.

5

Karen Blixen wished to avoid the publicity and also the tension that attended the appearance of a new book, and she planned to spend November 4, the Danish publication day of *Last Tales,* in Rome. She had been in touch with Eugene Walter, her "monkey prime minister," and sent him a little sketch of the sort of treats she hoped he might provide. Would there, she wondered, "be people in Rome prepared to make those three or four days really sweet to me, so that I should think of them later on with tears of joy in my eyes? . . . Would anybody ask me for supper in the darkest den of Trastevere, haunt of thieves and murderers? Or could you possibly arrange a rendezvous with a Cardinal for me in the moonlight in Piazza Navona?"[27] Walter did serve up the cardinal—in a marionette comedy, written in her honor and performed at the house of the American writer John Becker. There was also a dinner in the medieval palace of Countess Mitti Risi, which overlooked the Tiber; and an evening of music in the apartment of Princess Brianna Carafa, which overlooked Piazza del Popolo. But Walter delivered his greatest coup in the taxi from the airport when he produced the manuscript of Kelvin Lindemann's detested novel and proposed to dump it into the Tiber. They stopped their car on one of the narrow, crowded bridges which lead into the city and descended—Karen Blixen dressed in a bearskin coat and turban. The traffic was backed up for at least two blocks behind them, and the other drivers were out on the pavement, furiously shouting insults. "It's always a pleasure to hold up the business of the world," Walter noted, "and the more impatient and irritated that world is, the greater the pleasure." He had written a little curse which they pronounced while heaving the book ceremoniously upon the slime-encrusted waters:

> *Rat shit*
> *Bat shit*
> *Three-toed sloth shit*
> *Tiber and Oblivion*
> *Receive this book and its author.*[28]

Isak Dinesen and Clara Svendsen spent a month travelling abroad. From Rome they went to Paris, and then to London. They toured with much of the pomp and baggage of a royal progress, for part of the fun of such a trip was the dressing up. The Baroness kept track of her clothes the way the Queen of England does, by giving them each a descriptive title—in her case

[406]

whimsical.* Entertainments in Paris had again been arranged by Parmenia Migel, who used the opportunity to take notes for her biography. The time was parceled out virtually to the hour, and Karen Blixen moved from one event to another, insatiable for fun, talking incessantly, barely eating, wreathed in smoke and, in the words of an observer, "visibly growing more transparent by the day, like a dying narcissus."[29] It was as if she had scrawled across the pages of her diary, in the italics of her frailty, *Navigare necesse est vivere non necesse.* It was now more important for her to keep going than to live.

She collapsed more than once, and Ms. Migel describes how Tania arrived for a session on their book one afternoon, having walked to her house from a luncheon in her honor at the Vert Galant. It was "a tiring and tiresome task, this dredging up of memories from the past, trying to be accurate, attempting to situate a hundred details of facts and dates. Sad events and humiliations put out of mind long ago, were once more dragged into view, elusive faces and places were lured into focus . . ."[30] After a while Karen Blixen could not continue. She had an attack of nausea, fainting, and vomiting, and spent the rest of the afternoon lying in a "semi-coma" on a daybed. But, typically, she went out again that evening to another "dazzling soirée."

Among her Paris friends, Ms. Migel writes, Karen Blixen counted the Princess de Polignac, Violet Trefusis, Edmée de la Rochefoucauld, Princess Dolly Radziwill (who was married to a Danish painter), and the urbane and literary Philippe de Rothschild. There were others of the same caliber: people with musical old names who could still afford to keep their family houses, patronize the arts and entertain "regardless of expense"—a little phrase Dinesen loved and which gave her a pleasant *frisson* to use. She explains this idea in "Copenhagen Season," where Ib Angel reflects upon his attraction to the milieu of the von Galens. "We have been drawn to the world of splendor, irresistibly, like moths to the flame—not because it was rich, but because its riches were boundless. The quality of boundlessness in any sphere would have drawn us in the same manner."[31]

Implied in the boundlessness he speaks of is an emotional freedom, too—the means to give free play to one's heart's desires. The aristocratic world had always held out this promise to Karen Blixen; this was its real charm for her, something many of her friends, who didn't understand her "idiotic snobbery," could not see. It also helps to explain a curious fact. Abroad, she claimed that she could draw upon an almost "boundless" reserve of energy, which vanished the minute she came home to Denmark. It was as if the

---

*The following list has been preserved in the Karen Blixen archives (158, III B 5b):
  Evening gowns: Bergère brune, Sappho, Tate Gallery, Eminence Grise, Libelle, Hortense.
  Lunch-Cocktail: Beau Brummel, Petit Diable, Claudine, Poilue, Bôhème.
  Suits: Petit Favori, Tschui, Black Grouse, Sober Truth, Atta Troll.

gravity of home was heavier than that of France or Italy—and in a psycho-logical sense it was. The "wanderer" as described in fiction and by psychologists is frequently someone who flees from an external situation that is apparently intolerable, but reflects an inner state of tension, an internal danger. The vitality bound up at Rungstedlund with depression, resentment, and anxiety was set free when she got away. This was the miraculous "lightness of heart" that she had experienced in the highlands, and now she told her friend Professor Rasmussen, in almost the same words: "The real European air is liberating to breathe, one feels that here one is where one ought to be. . . . Lately, I have had the feeling in Denmark of being under suspicion, almost as if I were on parole. But here everyone has shown me a magnificent indulgence."[32]

It is a measure of how much that indulgence meant to Isak Dinesen that so many of her new friends were, on relatively brief acquaintance, invited to contribute to her Memorial Anthology. Their remembrances are some-times delicate and bright, sometimes trivial or sentimental, depending upon the writer, but they are strikingly uniform in their details—as uniform as the interviews Dinesen gave in the last decade of her life, when she had perfected her persona and almost never set it aside. Mme. de la Rochefoucauld captures the spirit in which this world rose up to greet Isak Dinesen when she writes of her as: *celle qui a tué un lion, et dont on parle pour le Prix Nobel.* *

6

One afternoon on the Rue St. Honoré, Isak Dinesen and Clara Svendsen heard a resonant English voice shout, "Tania," and turned to find John Gielgud, who threw his arms around her. He was in Paris to give a reading of Shakespeare at the Théâtre des Ambassadeurs, to which he invited them. He also invited them to come to Stratford in ten days' time to see him play Prospero in a production of *The Tempest,* which he had also directed. They spent a week in London first, staying at the Connaught. Tania visited with Denys's two nieces, Lady Daphne Straight and Lady Diana Tiarks, although she was feeling extremely fragile and also spent a good deal of the time in her hotel room. Clara went off to Bond Street to look for a cameo Tania had promised her as a reward for all the extra work the trip had created. She found an old and very beautiful one, with the head of a man who looked like Byron and who, the saleslady believed, probably was.

By the day they were to see *The Tempest* Tania had revived. They took the train to Stratford and lunched with Gielgud and some friends, and afterward, Clara remembers, Tania stood on the bridge over the Avon for a very long while, looking down into the water "with an expression of a

---

*"She who has killed a lion and who is spoken of for the Noble Prize." Edmée de la Rochefoucauld, "Karen Blixen," in *Isak Dinesen: A Memorial,* p. 83.

happiness I had rarely seen."[33] It seems likely that this play, which she had never seen performed and which was so intimately linked with Denys, had powerfully re-evoked his memory. She had always thought of him as a character of Shakespeare's, in the early days as a kind of Hamlet, and in *Out of Africa* she describes him so. But at the end of her life in Africa, when he had begun withdrawing from her, he had come to seem like Ariel.

Karen Blixen returned to Denmark to write a tale that she wanted to send to Gielgud in thanks for his play, which was itself to be called "Tempests." It, too, was to be its author's last great work, and her summing up.

49

"Tempests"

I N FEBRUARY OF 1958 a great snowstorm blanketed the Sound and stalled
traffic on the Strandvej. Karen Blixen lay immobile in her attic bedroom,
dictating to Clara. She had come home from England and, after a curtailed
Christmas at Wedellsborg, had taken to her bed with symptoms of malnutrition and exhaustion as severe as those her doctors had seen in concentration
camp prisoners. Since then she had been struggling to write "Tempests," not
only in the face of her own weakness but also against an "overwhelming
anxiety" about her finances and her future, which was part of that predictable
depression that always ambushed her at Rungstedlund when she came home
from her travels. The drastic contrast between the vitality she could muster
abroad and her physical collapse in Denmark dramatized to her, perhaps
really for the first time, the degree to which, as she put it to her cousin Philip
Ingerslev, "my illness is what could be called psychosomatic."[1] But there was
little that she could do except stay in bed and try to get her weight above
seventy pounds. She was terrified, she told an English friend, Hugh Pooley,
whom she asked to read a draft of "Tempests," "that my weakness will come
out in my work."[2] It is a measure of her vigilance and of the power she still
possessed that it did not.

"Tempests" was one of the few tales Isak Dinesen wrote originally in
Danish. It is set in Norway, against the background of the fjords and in the
little fishing villages along the coast—romantic scenery that Denys Finch
Hatton's mother had taken him to visit every summer of his childhood. Herr
Soerensen, the old actor of the tale, had also been taken to stay with his
mother's relations in Norway, and he had "kept a deep, undying passion for
the land of fells," which he associated with Shakespeare, Ossian, the sagas,
and the heroic in art generally.

Herr Soerensen has abandoned a prominent and comfortable career at the
Royal Theater in Copenhagen to tour the Norwegian seacoast towns with
his small repertory company. His friends cannot understand this "sad come-
down," but he himself "delighted in his freedom." These sophisticates, along
with the townspeople of the heroine's village, will be a bourgeois chorus in

the story, coming forward at the moments of loss, passion, and risk-taking to interject their skepticism and disapproval.

But if Herr Soerensen is a visionary, he is also a man of the world, and he illustrates one of Dinesen's favorite but little-practiced maxims: that you cannot neglect reality while surrendering to your dreams. He keeps a careful account of his profits and at the same time expounds a theory that "we should express our feelings and communicate with one another in blank verse." This is the heightened speech that Dinesen's noblest characters use at their moments of true feeling, and that he and Malli fall back upon at the tale's end.

The "life-old dream" of this actor has been to produce *The Tempest,* with himself playing the role of Prospero. As the tale begins he has been able to cast all the parts in the play except for Ariel. Finally "his eye fell on a young girl" who had recently joined the troupe and who did not have much experience in the theatre. She seems, to the uninitiated, an unlikely choice, not only because of her sex, but because she is large and slow in her movements. But this does not daunt Herr Soerensen—on the contrary. He explains that a more obvious Ariel would not need poetry to suggest that he was capable of flying. The real homage to Shakespeare will be, precisely, to let his poetry and not realistic casting inspire the audience to believe Ariel's magic powers.

This Ariel is a girl named Malli Ross, the daughter of a milliner from a small Norwegian fishing village. As a young woman, her mother, Madam Ross, had been wooed and wed by a Scottish sea captain whose ship had put into the little port for repairs. He was a "big, handsome man, who had sailed round the world" and who married her "in haste and with a will, such as he did everything." He is an elemental figure, an irresistible force, the force of nature itself. "It's the sea that brought me, little heart of mine," he tells his wife, and at the end of the summer he sails off, leaving her pregnant and with a pile of "pure gold"—the "pure gold" of the fairy tale, which is also a clue to his mythical nature.

Captain Ross has promised to return at Christmas, but Christmas passes, and then many Christmases. His wife chooses to believe that he has gone down with his ship, but the gossipy townspeople, the bourgeois chorus, insist that he has deceived her, that he probably had another wife elsewhere, that he had never meant to return at all. Madam Ross behaves very much like Ingeborg Dinesen in a similar predicament. She defies them quietly, saying little but keeping her own faith. And she gives birth to a daughter, Malli, "who would, she thought, in the years to come, help her in the task."

Malli and Madam Ross, like Tanne and Ingeborg, are united in a passionate but tacit conspiracy to protect their vision, even their obsession with the Captain. The daughter defends her mother "against the whole world" but is also secretly proprietary toward her father. She nurtures a sense of her own connection to him—a patrimony she does not completely understand, but which sets her apart and makes her proud: "beneath her quiet manner there lay a vital, concealed gaiety and arrogance." She studies English, "her father's tongue," with an old governess in the town and discovers Shakespeare. When Herr Soerensen and his troupe give a performance in the little theater, she is in the audience, and the experience of the poetry releases "all the vigor and longing in her, which for years had been forcibly mastered." This vigor and longing, we infer, have been for a scope of feeling and desire, for a heroic dimension to life, such as her father and Shakespeare symbolize.

Malli decides impulsively to become an actress, goes to see Herr Soerensen, and begs him to take her into his troupe. He is impressed enough to accept her as an apprentice. But when she tells her mother of her decision, Madam Ross "became as if deranged with horror and grief." Although it is not stated, the tale suggests that Madam Ross realizes she will lose her daughter to the same powers that have reclaimed her husband. (The sea, in Isak Dinesen's iconography, is a Luciferian life force.) In their struggle over Malli's decision, her mother "inexplicably lived her short marriage over again. It was from day to day the same surprises and emotions: a foreign, rich and enrapturing power, that had once taken her by storm. . . . She fell in love with her daughter as she had once fallen in love with the father."[3]

In discovering her destiny, Malli discovers that same erotic power her father had, which seduced her mother—but it is a masculine eroticism. She is able to spare herself the futile, passive longing for a father by transforming that longing into an active identification with him. This sexual crossing-over will have two effects: it will deprive her of a normal emotional life, the fairy tale's happy ending: a man's true love. But it will also make her into an artist: the epicene spirit Ariel, neither male nor female, but, as Tania had once said of Denys, able to move in three dimensions. Indeed, as the tale progresses, Malli "grows more Ariel" and more spiritlike by growing visibly more male, until Herr Soerensen, who has been rehearsing her with Prospero's own loving harshness, claps his hands and exclaims: "And I meant to have a girl like that trip about in a pair of French silk slippers! Fool, fool, that I was! Who did not know that it was a pair of seven-league boots that fitted those legs."[4]

On their way to the premiere of *The Tempest* in the town of Christian-sand, the company is caught at sea in a terrible snowstorm and gale. They and some crew members take to the lifeboats, but Malli chooses to remain on board. It is by her courage and through her inspiration that the crew, and in particular a young sailor named Ferdinand, are able to save the ship. Un-self-consciously, even arrogantly, she has stepped into the role of Ariel.

The next morning the town receives her as a heroine; the owner of the ship, old Jochum Hosewinckel, brings her into his own house; his handsome son Arndt carries her from the port in his arms and, while the crowd cheers, gives her a kiss. He is the fairy tale prince, and this is the fairy tale first kiss that awakens the heroine to her desire. She and Arndt subsequently become engaged; she warms to family life; even her body begins to change. Herr Soerensen is amazed to see how suddenly her "bosom has become rounded."

Arndt Hosewinckel is an amalgam of all the Nordic demigods whom Tanne Dinesen had adored, and Malli discovers the pleasures of male company in the old shipowner's house much as Tanne must have discovered them at Katholm and Frijsenborg. "It was, she thought, because for such a long time she had been longing for a father that she liked being with men, and herself felt that in glance, posture and voice she had much to give them."[5] Watching this process taking place, Herr Soerensen realizes that he has lost his Ariel—who has chosen instead to play Miranda. In his imagination he pursues her into married life and even sketches a sequel to *The Tempest*, in which he, as Prospero, makes a "father-in-law visit" to the young king and queen of Naples. Yet even as he invents the scene he realizes it is absurd: what will follow where *The Tempest* ends—the domestic life of the young couple —cannot possibly be turned into art. "The project of lifting daily life onto the stage was paradoxical and in its essence blasphemous. For it was more likely that daily life would drag down the stage to its own level." When he does attempt to play the paternal role, that of the father giving the bride away, he cannot do it. As he is leaving Malli, having said farewell, he begins to behave strangely, blows her a kiss, and recites a sexually aggressive and even menacing little verse:

> *My Pegasus is slack,*
> *Plays truant when he can!*
> *But wait, thou ancient hack,*
> *I am thy master man.*
> *(I'll show thee who's the man.)*[6]

The magician father thus vows to reclaim his daughter from her bridegroom and to keep her with him on the magic island.

Both psychologically and dramatically, the moral crisis that brings Malli back to the arms of Herr Soerensen is somewhat contrived. She learns that Ferdinand, the young sailor who kept vigil with her throughout the night of the tempest, has died of internal injuries. She has never once thought of him since they were both carried ashore triumphantly on the shoulders of the villagers, but now she is overwhelmed with grief and guilty despair. As Robert Langbaum explains it, Malli thinks that she has willed the tempest herself, for it "fulfilled her desire—it enabled her to play Ariel, to become her father, a male and a spirit, and she feels responsible for the storm as people do for their subconscious desires that come true."[7] Believing that she has killed a man, that she is fatal to those who love her, that she is indeed Ariel and not Miranda (able to love and be loved), she renounces Arndt and goes back to Herr Soerensen. The role of Ariel is to reconcile desire and experience —that is the role of all magicians—but he can do so only within the boundaries of a dream, a play, a magic island. What draws people to him —his magic—is useless to them in real life and, in fact, cannot be possessed. Denys had the same allure and was in the same way untouchable, as was Isak Dinesen herself as an old woman. But what this explanation may conceal, and what the drift of the tale really suggests, is that Malli makes a calculated choice. She is not forced morally to give up Arndt, to give up her mythical father and her magic powers for her mortal lover. She is *unwilling* to remain Miranda. She shrinks from real human love because she is afraid of it, afraid of being trapped in it. To be loved, to love, to be a woman means to be someone like her mother, someone who has been abandoned.

After the death of Ferdinand, Malli falls into a black melancholy. She does not want to hear news of the "real world" and instead asks for "accounts of old times, even . . . plain nursery tales." She now also grows close to old shipowner Hosewinckel, who, with the onset of a mild and lovely form of senility, "can no longer distinguish between past and present." He tells Malli legends of the North, imagines himself running with her "into a darkness of their own," and this ancient world of fairy tales offers them both a "refuge from life, to which a bad conscience was not admitted."

But one evening the old man tells Malli a different kind of story, one that is, precisely, about bad (and good) conscience. It is the story of his own ancestor, Jens Aabel, an upright burgher, who, when his house was threatened by fire, called upon the elements themselves to reward his righteousness. They did: the winds changed, and his house was spared. It is, he tells her, a tradition in the family to consult Jens Aabel's Bible for moral advice, and it has never failed him when he has put to it a question of right or wrong. Malli now decides to consult this oracle about her own moral dilemma. She approaches the old book with some trepidation, lets it fall open at random, and when she reads the judgment faints dead away. It is the twenty-ninth chapter of Isaiah, which begins: "Woe to Ariel, to Ariel! . . . And thou shalt be brought down, and thou shalt speak out of the ground . . . and thy voice shall be as of one that hath a familiar spirit, out of the ground, and thy speech shall whisper out of the dust!" But it is not until she gets to the eighth verse that she understands its meaning for her: "It shall even be as when an hungry man dreameth, and behold, he eateth; but he awaketh, and his soul is empty; or as when a thirsty man dreameth, and behold, he drinketh; but when he awaketh, and behold, he is faint, and his soul hath appetite."[8] This is the revelation about desire and experience that, the tale implies, Captain Ross had when he left his wife and never returned: that he, as a mythical being, a familiar spirit, could never give his mortal lover what she would need or want in reality. His power was an ideal and a vision. And in the same spirit, Malli will write to Arndt:

I have made you poor, my sweetheart dear,
I am far from you when I am near.
I have made you rich, my dearest heart.
I am near when we are far apart.

And so Malli goes back to Herr Soerensen and tells him she has betrayed Arndt and Ferdinand, and that "I betray them all, as Father betrayed Mother." He understands, for he was married once himself to a "good, lovable woman." He left her, as Captain Ross left his wife, in secret and saying nothing. On their last evening she told him: "Everything that you do in life, Valdemar, you do to make me happy. That is so sweet of you." "Oh, yes," Malli cries. "That is how they talk to us, that is what they believe about us."[9]

Prospero can now release Ariel from bondage, and Herr Soerensen arranges that he and Malli will quietly slip out of Christiansand and go away. But at the last moment, which is one of the saddest in all of Dinesen's tales, the girl protests, cries out in the voice of a young human child: "But why must things go with us like that?" And the old man answers her with her own old storyteller's voice and tells her what Isak Dinesen had learned about the priestly sacrifice of life for art, and of its price:

"And in return we get the world's distrust—and our dire loneliness. And nothing else."[10]

2

This is Isak Dinesen's miraculously rich and compressed retelling of her own life and of the stages that led her to become an artist—someone who, as she had written of Jens, the dreaming child, enables other people "to see themselves with the eye of the dreamer" and who impels them to "live up to an ideal."[11] In this tale she explores her likeness to and longing for the demonic father who unlocked the secret of her vitality and talent—her "magic powers"—and the incestuous and guilty nature of the relationship with him, which cut her off from a real human love and ultimately stranded her alone. Here her conviction about the sexual sacrifice exacted for art— her feeling, often repeated, that she was a great transgressor—come into sharper focus. She had promised the Devil* her soul, and he had promised her that her life would be turned into tales, and so, literally, it was.

"Tempests" is as layered and as dense in psychological detail as a dream, and it reveals the remarkable clarity with which Isak Dinesen understood

---

*Søren, or Soeren, is a Danish nickname for the Devil; thus Herr Soerensen.

herself. Speaking of Freud and of his importance to modern literature, she had once remarked that "it is not necessary to dig up the roots, to know that they are there."* Her own power as a storyteller comes from keeping those roots buried, but the channels down to them unobstructed.

---

*New York Times, 3 November 1957, 49:1. The image of the buried roots is suggested by an anecdote in Wilhelm's Letters from the Hunt on p. 99. An anthropologist once asked his permission to dig up some burial mounds on his property, which he, in the most vehement terms, refused. "And so," he wrote, "my mounds lie there today, and hide what they preserve."

50

Isak Dinesen in America

I

PASOP, Karen Blixen's beloved German shepherd, also called Rommy, was thirteen years old on the twenty-fifth of March, and as usual the day was celebrated with a party. The "birthday boy" sat at the table surrounded by his presents, and the "two-footed" guests, as Clara delicately put it, drank hot chocolate. A few weeks later Pasop, Clara, and the Baroness went for a walk around the dam, which was as far as the old dog could go.[1] He died at the month's end of heart disease and old age. When there was nothing more the veterinarian could do for him, Karen Blixen clipped a lock of his hair, had him put to sleep, and buried him on Ewald's Hill, near the site of her own grave. He was, she once said, the most lovable and faithful creature she had ever owned.

She continued to rally after a winter of almost complete immobility, and in May she wrote to Eugene Walter that since she was on her feet again she needed a pair of the smartest Roman sandals to put them into. He was to watch the sidewalks and see to it that she should "not be any less well *chaussée* than the smartest drug fiends and Black Swans."[2] She then immediately seized upon this slight margin of vitality and spent it. Accompanied by Thomas, she made a trip to Germany to visit General von Lettow Vorbeck, who was eighty-seven and living quietly near a married daughter in Altona. They had last met in Bremen, a week before the Nazis invaded Denmark, and before then at Mombasa, on the day of her marriage to Bror Blixen. The young lieutenant-colonel's erect figure, bending over slightly to speak with her on the deck of the *Admiral,* and the old general's, bowing over her hand at the door of his apartment, were the two brackets of a parenthesis which contained Karen Blixen's adult life.

There are echoes of von Lettow throughout the tales in the courtesy, belligerence and honor of various old soldiers, and one feels even more strongly that Isak Dinesen's proud Teutonic virgins, like Ehrengard and Athena, must be his aunts. He himself was an avuncular figure to her: Parmenia Migel remarks that Tania had looked forward to this visit with a "childish anticipation," and that in the general's presence she forgot her own age, gazing at his wrinkled face and hoping hers would not come to resemble it. They spoke of Africa and the war, which to both Thomas and von Lettow meant the first war, and when they left, Tanne reminded him of the kiss she had been too modest to bestow on the quay at Mombasa. Two years later, when he was ninety and she seventy-five, he would write gallantly that he might yet come "and collect it for himself."[3]

There were very few people left alive who remembered the young Tanne and with whom she might speak of Africa. Ingrid Lindström was one. She still lived in the highlands with her old servant Kemosa. Her hair was white, her children grown, and she was several times a grandmother. Ingrid had not seen or kept in touch with Tanne, and when *Out of Africa* was published she had been hurt by her portrait. But that May she wrote with the news that her husband Gillis had died. "Dearest Friend Ingrid," Tanne replied immediately. "So many memories from the time of youth, joyous and solemn, flooded me when I received your letter. . . ."

I had to look around the room to make myself understand that I was so far from my beautiful and unforgettable old domain. I had to laugh aloud again at the memories of some of my visits to Njoro . . . once, when we wandered home from Birkbeck's farm, all in very high spirits after strong drink, Gillis explaining how he could always find the way through the fields in the dark because he lifted his legs so high. . . . And so many conversations about our adventures up in the heights, at six thousand feet, where I shall perhaps never again set foot, nor sit drinking around a fire.

I myself feel it as a personal, an unexpectedly painful loss and . . . I understand your great sorrow and the deep emptiness you must feel. Gillis stands in my memory as an able and admirable and to an extraordinary degree unselfish person, but with an unusual ability to meet life's phenomena. I also believe . . . he has been an unusually happy person, and that it is in large measure due to you. For whatever else you gave him, you above all made life festive for him. . . .

I would so much love to have real news about you all. It is practically impossible to think that Calle is now almost an older woman! How many grandchildren do you have, and in how many parts of the world? I can not very well believe that you still have Kemosa, whose figure is as inseparable to me, from your own, as the children's. I myself hear from and about some of my old people, Kamante, Tumbo, Abdullai. I have also sometimes thought of visiting Kenya, but it has certainly changed too much for me, and I would come to feel like a ghost there.

Unfortunately I have, for the last four years, been laid up in a hospital bed or in bed at home, and I don't think that I shall improve very much. I cannot get my weight over thirty-five kilos, and I have a kind of paralysis of the legs so that I can't really stand up or walk. However it has been a great happiness that, through a superhuman work of slavery, which would have been criminal if one had imposed it on another, I published a book last year and am having a book published next autumn. . . .

How I would love to be able to sit for an hour together with you and speak of old days, and of Gillis. My thoughts have, since I got your letter, been constantly with you. You are so luminous Ingrid, that there is a shining around you even when one thinks of you in sorrow. There was also a light around Gillis's face and form, of a different kind, but which is impossible to forget. . . . Now you must greet everyone who yet remembers me, and the landscape itself around you, the woods behind the house where the Ndorobos lived, and the white-flowering old crooked trees on the plain. And if you should see any of the old animals who, in my time, one still met up there, who really possessed the country, salute them too.

So dearest Ingrid, I send you a deep and a heartfelt embrace. Thank you for all the good in life. God bless you.

Your Tanne.[4]

2

By the time Karen Blixen and her brother went to Germany they had settled their quarrel over the disposition of Rungstedlund. She had worked out a plan with her lawyers and advisers that would enable her to live in the house until her death, and afterward to preserve it and the grounds from the fate of the African farm: sale to real estate developers. Elle Dahl bought out Thomas for one hundred thousand kroner, and she, Anders, and Tanne then deeded the property to the nonprofit Rungstedlund Foundation, which was pledged to maintain the house "for cultural and scientific purposes"[5] and the grounds as a bird sanctuary, accessible to the public. Karen Blixen donated the royalties of her books in perpetuity to the maintenance of the sanctuary, and, anticipating the day when the copyright would expire, she made an appeal to the Danish people for a "reserve fund" that would continue when her own endowment ended. That July she went on the radio to tell the history of the house and of the wildlife and birdlife in its woods, and to ask any Dane who had ever had any pleasure from her books to send one krone for the fund. She did not want anyone to send more than a krone because she hoped to be able to count precisely how many friendly readers she had.[6] More than eighty thousand Danes responded. People stopped her on the streets of Copenhagen, in elevators, and hotel lobbies, so that the coins jingled in her pockets as she walked. Waiters, doormen, and cabdrivers returned a krone with her change or tips; and one day at the Rungsted Inn a butcher and his family, who were having a rowdy party at the next table, presented her with an envelope containing five hundred kroner—over the limit but accepted gratefully. A few minutes earlier the Baroness had been complaining about their "vulgarity," and she was chastened: "See how wrong you can be about people," she told her nephew.[7]

Her speech was broadcast on July 6, and for once she made an exception to the rule of never listening to her own voice. Afterward she remarked to Erik Kopp that it was "the best job of begging I ever heard."[8]

3

Anecdotes of Destiny was published in October to acclaim on both sides of the Atlantic. Despite its brevity and Karen Blixen's feeling that it was "lighter" than *Last Tales,* it contains three of her finest stories, and it is in no sense the anticlimax she had feared. This fear—of going soft or dull, of ignobly winding down—continued to harass her, and she continued to defy it with the reckless courage of a seventeen-year-old girl or the optimism of a gambler with a fresh letter of credit. She laid ambitious plans for work: drafting new tales, revising older ones, hoping to finish her novel of a hundred characters, *Albondocani.* And at the beginning of the new year she embarked upon a project that was even more strenuous than the "superhuman slave work" of writing *Anecdotes.* She made a trip of three and a half months to America.

Isak Dinesen had looked forward to this journey since 1934, when her mother's illness had first forced her to postpone it. Then her health began to deteriorate, the war intervened, and afterward the expense daunted her. But after her operation in 1955 she realized she could not afford to wait much longer, and in 1957 she began making serious preparations. Her original idea was for a rather quiet private visit. She would come sailing into New York harbor; visit her American friends; go to the opera and hear jazz; and find Frydenlund, her father's cabin in Wisconsin, which she thought she had located on an old map. But this was not how it came to pass. Her trip was the tumultuous curtain call of her authorship.

In May of 1958, while she was finishing the English draft of "Tempests," Isak Dinesen received a letter from Dr. Alvin Eurich of the Ford Foundation's Fund for the Advancement of Knowledge, asking her to read and discuss her work on film as part of a series on the world's "greatest living writers." "The filming could be done in Denmark," Dr. Eurich wrote, "or if you prefer, we would be pleased to make the necessary arrangements to have you visit this country. We would, of course, cover all expenses in connection with such a trip."[9] Next to this passage Isak Dinesen made a very thick black exclamation point.

Reservations were made, and Clara was invited to come along. Karen Blixen's large, earthy, and irreverent relative, Tove Hvass, expressed a desire to see America and "tag along," and so she did. The retinue left by plane in foul weather on January 2, despite the fact that Karen Blixen needed some emergency dental work and had a temporary bridge glued in by a "not dentally trained assistant."[10] This struck Clara as particularly ominous, for in addition to her other frailties the Baroness now had to wonder if her teeth were going to fall out.

Considering her age and health, Isak Dinesen did, indeed, face a formidable agenda of commitments. To make the visit pay she had sought other work, and the Institute of Contemporary Arts, her cosponsor, had arranged for her to appear in Boston, New York, and Washington. The American Academy of Arts and Letters, which had made her an honorary member in February of 1957, invited her to be the guest of honor at its annual dinner and to give the keynote speech. Random House had set up press conferences and a number of interviews. Once she arrived, she was besieged by other invitations, and she accepted the most interesting or profitable of them. They included a talk show with Alex King, lectures at Radcliffe College and Brandeis University, a Shakespeare symposium at the Folger Library, and the making of a film for the Encyclopedia Britannica. She would also sit for her portrait by René Bouché and pose for photographs by Richard Avedon, Eduardo Brofferio, Carl van Vechten, and Cecil Beaton. She performed at the Cosmopolitan Club, where she was staying, and at several parties in her honor, and received a stream of visitors—authors, agents, film producers, and scholars (including Robert Langbaum)—at her hotel. Clara noted with some bitterness that Isak Dinesen was expected to "earn her bread by hard work,"[11] although Dinesen herself did not seem to mind. She fell in with the tempo of New York—with its "demon," as she called it—and was overwhelmed by America's openness and "generosity" toward her.* In such a way, with such reckless curiosity and infatuation, had the Africans welcomed her to the farm.

The most famous of Isak Dinesen's American appearances were the three evenings she spoke at the Y.M.H.A. Poetry Center on Ninety-third Street in New York. After her first performance there was such a wild clamor for an encore that she was called back two more times. *The New York Times Book Review* caught the city's mood in a cartoon set in a Village coffeehouse, in which one beatnik asks another, "Did you catch Isak Dinesen at the Y?"[12] There was an astonishing current between Dinesen and her audience. To those who were seeing her for the first time, which was practically everyone, the contrast between her extreme frailty and her remarkable presence confirmed the impression that they had of her from her books. This was the wise, noble, and heroic survivor of the past—the master—they had been expecting. It also dramatized the distance between her and them. Later, when people reminisced

---

*As opposed to the ambivalence and wariness of the Danes. While she was in New York she was interviewed by a Danish reporter to whom she explained: "I did not come to America for the purpose of running down my own country [some of her remarks had been so interpreted] . . . but when I compare the American and Danish reviews of my first book I cannot help but think how much better I have been understood and accepted in America than in Denmark. Yes, finally I have also got a name in Denmark, but for a long time my name was always spoken of and written about in parenthesis when one considered Danish writers. In Denmark one is not now, as in America, interested in fantastic stories, there is more enthusiasm for the realistic school. In my last book, *Anecdotes of Destiny,* there was a story which a Danish critic stamped as pornography. In America one apparently has a more liberated attitude to literature" (*Berlingske Tidende* [Copenhagen], 1 February 1959).

about her, it was about someone incalculably old, and they were surprised to learn that she had been only seventy-four.

When Dr. Eurich had first asked Isak Dinesen to read a tale she replied that she was not a reader nor even really a writer, but a storyteller, and that if he were agreeable she would tell one of her tales from memory. She came to America with three different programs: "Barua a Soldani," "The Blue Eyes" and "The Wine of the Tetrarch."* Those who heard a tale for the second or third time realized with astonishment that it had been told verbatim. Her memory was prodigious,† and Glenway Wescott noted that her performances at the Y, which lasted almost an hour, were as grueling as the major roles in Wagner. "She has an ideal voice," he went on, "strong, though with a kind of wraithlike transparency, which she is able to imbue with emotions, but only narrative emotions. She rarely indulges in mellifluousness in the way of poets, neither does she do much Thespian mimicking. . . . What especially colors Isak Dinesen's voice, what gives it overtone and urgency, is remembrance or reminiscence. With soft strong tone seeming to feel its way, sometimes almost faltering, shifting its direction as power of evocation sways, not perturbed by her listeners, perhaps helped by them, she seems to be re-experiencing what she has to tell, or if it is fable or fantasy, redreaming it."[13]

4

The annual dinner of the American Academy took place in a snowstorm on the twenty-eighth of January. Isak Dinesen had given much time and thought to her address, and it was one of the rare occasions on which Clara had seen her become "really nervous."[14] Glenway Wescott, who was then president of the academy, escorted her to the podium, assisted by e.e. cummings, one of the writers she had specifically asked to meet. The audience rose to its feet and acclaimed her, as it did everywhere she appeared.

The subject of her speech was "On Mottoes of My Life," and like the American trip itself it was a vantage point from which, with deep gratitude and some amazement, she surveyed her life. She could now look back over it virtually in its entirety, and she divided it into five ages. The first was the age of the "little girl in her mother's house": casting about for the form, the direction her life should take, and poring through a treasury of the world's mottoes with a sense of awe at the rich possibilities there were. She finally

---

*"Barua a Soldani" had originally been written for the Danish radio and would be published in *Shadows on the Grass;* "The Blue Eyes" was an inset tale from "Peter and Rosa"; and "The Wine of the Tetrarch" was an inset tale from "Deluge at Norderney."

†Not only for her own work. She could recite long passages from all the great poets whom she loved —Shakespeare or Oehlenschläger, Sophus Claussen or Heine—and it was a grace she particularly prized in other people.

settled, at twelve, for one with a pretty sound whose meaning she was not entirely sure of: *Sicut aquila juvenescam.* *

The second age was that of the young art student: the Romantic in revolt against bourgeois life, in love with heroism and masculinity, with personal bravery and greatness. Her new motto, and her first real one, was taken from Pompey: *Navigare necesse est vivere non necesse.* Under this motto she rode by train to the Danish Academy and threw her lunch out the window, and also under its protection she had sailed to Africa "into my *Vita Nuova,* what became my real life."

The third age was that of the farmer, the colonist, the wife, and woman in love who took her lover's motto, *Je responderay.* In Africa, she explained simply, she finally found that answer to her own cry which had eluded her for so long. "My daily life out there was filled with answering voices; I never spoke without getting a response; I spoke freely and without restraint, even when I was silent." She also liked the Finch Hatton motto "for its ethical content. I will answer *for* what I say or do; I will answer *to* the impression I make. I will be responsible."[15]

The fourth age was that of the desolate and bereft woman who, no longer young, returned to her native country where nothing and no one answered her, and who began to write "in great uncertainty about the whole undertaking, but nevertheless, in the hands of both a powerful and happy spirit." And for this age she took the motto, *Pourquoi pas? Pourquoi,* she explained, was a wail or a complaint or a cry from the heart, but when one added the negative—*pas*—it transformed a pathetic question into an answer, a directive and a signal which expressed a wild hope. Under that motto she had written all of her books.†

The fifth age, she concluded, was the present: the age of a woman "fully aware of the eternity behind and before her." And her fifth motto, under whose auspices she had come to America, was taken from the inscription over the three gates of an English city. *Be Bold* stood over the first gate. *Be Bold* stood over the second gate. *Be Not Too Bold* stood over the third gate. This motto did not contradict *Pourquoi pas?* but was its natural consequence, just as the age of caution and reflection was the natural consequence to the age of action and courage. The former laid the groundwork for the latter, as Nietzsche had so well understood when he wrote: "I am a yea-sayer and a warrior I have been, so that one fine day I could have my arms free to bless."[16]

At the dinner that followed, Isak Dinesen sat next to one of her most distinguished fans, Carson McCullers. It was something of an epiphany for

---

*Like the eagle I shall grow up.
†*Pourquoi-Pas* was the name of the ship on board which the polar explorer Dr. Jean Baptiste Charcot (1867–1936) was shipwrecked near Iceland during a hurricane in the winter of 1936. At this time, Karen Blixen was writing *Out of Africa* in Skagen.

both women, for Dinesen had admired *The Heart Is a Lonely Hunter* and had reread it many times, while McCullers had "fallen in love with Isak Dinesen twenty years before, after reading *Out of Africa.*" Despite her own extreme frailty, she had come to the dinner hoping to wangle an introduction to her "African heroine."*

When McCullers learned that Isak Dinesen longed to meet Marilyn Monroe, she eagerly volunteered to arrange it. Arthur Miller, an old friend, was sitting at the next table; he came over, and the party—a luncheon—was set for February 5. The Millers were to call for the Baroness and Clara in their car, and they arrived with the unpunctuality Marilyn was famous for. She had just finished *Some Like It Hot* and her beauty was at its ripest. Dressed in a black sheath with a deep décolletage and a fur collar, incredibly fair, radiant, and rather shy, she looked—Clara thought— "fifteen years old."[17] Isak Dinesen, wearing the gray ensemble she called "Sober Truth," had a different kind of radiance; "her face was lit like a candle in an old church."[18]

A meal that included oysters, white grapes, champagne, and a soufflé was laid on Carson McCullers's black marble table. Marilyn told the party an amusing story about her own culinary adventures. She had tried to make pasta for her husband and some guests, using her mother-in-law's recipe. But it got a little late, the company was arriving, and the pasta wasn't ready, so she had tried to finish it off with a hair dryer. Everyone laughed, but Clara was a little shocked.[19] She found it odd that a goddess would spend her time cooking macaroni. Arthur Miller, in the meantime, questioned the Baroness about her eating habits. Was it wise, he asked, for someone so frail to eat nothing but grapes, oysters, and champagne? She brushed him off by saying: "I am an old woman and I eat what agrees with me."[20]

"Carson," writes her biographer, "always performed best in small groups in which she could be assured control as the center of attention. Yet this day [she] happily relinquished the stage to her guest."[21] Isak Dinesen told "Barua a Soldani" and went on talking about her life "with such warmth that her listeners didn't have to try to interrupt her marvelous conversation."[22] Later, she sought out her hostess's black housekeeper, Ida Reeder,

---

*"As early as 1937," writes Margaret McDowell, Carson McCullers "had recognized a kinship with Karen Blixen. . . . All the rest of her life she ritualistically reread Dinesen each year, and Dinesen's fiction provided her with her strongest influence for experimentation in the Gothic mode." Clara Svendsen has pointed out that Carson and Tania had their suffering and debility in common, and were both able to transcend them with uncommon courage. McCullers suffered from rheumatic fever as a young girl, and a series of strokes in her early thirties paralyzed her left side and left her (temporarily) blind and speechless. From 1958 she had a series of "severe illnesses and operations" and was in the care of a psychiatrist for a "depressive illness." See Margaret B. McDowell, *Carson McCullers* (Boston: Twayne, 1980), p. 51 and unpaginated chronology.

and had a long talk with her, explaining that she "missed her black friends." Toward the end of the afternoon, so the story goes, McCullers put a record on the phonograph and invited Marilyn and the Baroness to dance with her on the marble table, and they took a few steps in each other's arms. Other members of the party (including Miller) "doubt" that this took place, but the hostess loved to retell it. This was "the best" and most "frivolous" party she had ever given, and she expressed "childlike pleasure and wonderment at the love which her guests seemed to express . . . for each other."[23]

Whether or not they danced together, it is difficult to picture a more poignant or fantastic couple than Dinesen and Monroe. They died the same year, and Glenway Wescott imagined that "the same boat carried them across the Styx."[24] Dinesen "loved" Carson McCullers and enjoyed meeting Arthur Miller, but it was Marilyn who made the real impression. "It is not that she is pretty," she told Fleur Cowles, "although of course she is almost incredibly pretty—but that she radiates at the same time unbounded vitality and a kind of unbelievable innocence. I have met the same in a lion cub that my native servants in Africa brought me. I would not keep her."[25]

5

Isak Dinesen was the most sought-after dinner guest in New York, and many famous hostesses entertained her. Barbara Paley gave a luncheon in her honor at the St. Regis, at which Truman Capote and Cecil Beaton were also guests. Gloria Vanderbilt and Sidney Lumet had her to dinner in their penthouse, and Mr. Lumet carried her around the terrace in his arms to see the lights while Ms. Vanderbilt gave her a suit by Mainbocher. Ruth Ford and Zachary Scott threw a great party for Isak Dinesen at the Dakota that was later cited proudly by the historian of that building as one of its brightest social moments. Leo Lerman escorted her to the Met; she heard Maria Callas sing Il Pirata and was mobbed by fans on Fifty-seventh Street. Callas "enraptured" Dinesen, and of that night she said: "It is not always possible to see over the shadow of one's own invention, and here is someone so closely related to [Pellegrina]."[26]

She had many distinguished cavaliers. Carl Van Vechten took her to hear (Verdi's) Macbeth, and Samuel Barber invited her to the premiere of his opera, Vanessa, bringing Gian Carlo Menotti as a date for Tove Hvass. John Steinbeck threw her a cocktail party, and the Danish ambassador a reception. She was feted by Robert Haas, whom she was meeting for the first time after a correspondence of twenty years, and by Bruce and Beatrice Gould, who had published her work in The Ladies' Home Journal. Count Rasponi took her to lunch, as did Gian Giacomo Feltrinelli, her Italian publisher, in town from Turin. Isak Dinesen was exhibited, scrutinized, spotlit, and passed from hand to hand like some extraordinary and precious relic recovered from a tomb and on loan to America for the first and last time. Clara had begun calling her *Khamar*. This was a nickname that came from a private joke and referred to an Arabian battle horse in an old Danish ballad. Thoroughbreds, Dinesen liked to say, kept on running until they dropped, and "that," Clara affirmed, "was her own practice."[27]

But to Clara, on call twenty-four hours a day, fell the bitter role of Madam Knudsen: she had to become the nay-sayer. She was appalled at the way people exploited Tania and frightened at how she drove herself. This was a familiar syndrome: manic overactivity, the refusal to eat or rest sufficiently, and a state of exaltation that encouraged more manic overactivity. Sometimes Isak Dinesen actually talked herself into a trance. This struck the young writer Nancy Wilson Ross, a friend of the Finch Hatton family, who came to see her at the Cosmopolitan Club in February. The Baroness had agreed to tell a story to the clubwomen, and, spurred on by their delight, she told a second one. When a reception was called off to spare her strength she became upset and called for a fresh audience, which was hastily assembled. The day wore on; the second sitting of ladies left, but the storyteller went on as if possessed. "She did not want the magic to slip away, to find herself suddenly alone, charged with all this creative force, but without attendant ears. She begged me to stay and dine with her . . . and I left with the uneasy feeling that I had somehow failed her."[28]

Parmenia Migel recounts an even more alarming incident. She and her husband Arne Ekström had moved back to New York from Paris, were living in a house they had built in the east eighties, and had been extremely solicitous of both Tania and Clara throughout their visit. Tania had asked to meet Pearl Buck, and Ms. Migel, who had known her for some years, managed to arrange a luncheon on rather short notice. Pearl Buck came in from the country, and there was another guest, the poet Arthur Gregor. Isak Dinesen arrived late, dressed to the teeth, wearing more dark eye makeup than usual, "and diffusing her most calculating charm." She proceeded to talk through the entire meal, not touching her grapes or oysters, not even smoking the chain of cigarettes she had lit, and paying no attention to Pearl Buck, her hosts, or their other guest. When she finally left for her next appointment there was a shocked and painful silence.[29]

On the day after her performance for the Cosmopolitan Club, Isak Dinesen was admitted to the Harkness Pavilion on the brink of death. Her doctors now discovered that to make up the deficit between the energy she had and that which she needed she had been taking amphetamines.[30] Her condition had been aggravated by her anorexia, and the doctors warned her that if she intended to live she would have to take sensible nourishment and remain immobile for a while. This she did, meekly letting them drip blood and glucose into her veins. But when she was discharged a few weeks later she resumed her fatal pace. Clara—distraught, exhausted, and also probably rather angry—now lost her Byron cameo. On the seventeenth of April, Karen Blixen's seventy-fourth birthday, the battle horse "Khamar" was dragged, almost forcibly, home to Denmark.

51

Homeless

I

SINCE HER OPERATION OF 1955 Karen Blixen had come to depend increasingly upon Clara Svendsen. She now dictated all of her tales and correspondence to Clara, who also worked on the Danish translations. They were alone together for a good part of every day, and in the evenings they often played bezique or listened to music. When Karen Blixen traveled Clara not only acted as secretary and companion, but as purser, nurse, and mistress of the wardrobe; Parmenia Migel describes her arriving for a photographic session with her cheeks flushed and her arms laden with hatboxes. At the lowest point of the American tour Isak Dinesen was too weak to dress herself, and Clara had to carry her the short distances she could not walk.

No one knew Isak Dinesen more intimately than Clara Svendsen or spent more time with her over a prolonged period, and there is also no doubt that Dinesen's love and respect for her secretary were very deep; she made Clara the literary executor of her estate. But Dinesen was not good-natured when she was in pain, physical or mental. She could be sarcastic and even vulgar in her choice of insults, and while she often made unreasonable demands on Clara's time (breaking up her day "into pieces of tinder"[1]), she could also complain to others contemptuously about her secretary's "constant and unwanted presence."[2] Long ago Clara had learned to shrug off such pronouncements. "I gradually learned something about certain irrational reactions that Karen Blixen had, a kind of anxiety about being bound in a human relation."[3] The insult she did feel keenly was to be treated as a child. The Baroness liked to pretend that Clara could not hold a serious opinion, or she mocked her when she expressed one. And to someone so studious and dedicated about her calling, this was hard to bear.

Their close friends tended to ascribe the friction between the two women to their very different temperaments, which was certainly a factor. But Clara was astute enough not to take much of the abuse personally. Physical helplessness enraged Karen Blixen, and she spent that rage upon the nearest object, who was also the person likeliest to accept and forgive it. The rage at needing help and at being beholden was also a fundamental part of her character; she had stormed against her family in the same spirit and at precisely those moments when she made the greatest demands upon them. The frailty and invalidism of her old age recreated the dependence of her adolescence, and Clara, with her orthodox moral nature and her willingness to live for others, reminded her of Aunt Bess. ("You are just as bad [*slem*] as Aunt Bess," she had once told her.[4]) In a better mood she had also compared her secretary to Farah. But Farah had followed her in the African night with a shawl and a loaded rifle; he had never circumscribed her with concern, and he had never discouraged her from taking risks. Clara, for obvious reasons and with a different bias, tried to tone down Karen Blixen's excesses and the mortal danger she courted with them. And this, too, could not easily be forgiven.

The trip to America, three and a half months of being inescapably "bound in a human relation," had increased the strains on them. The summer after they returned, Karen Blixen made a round of country house visits, attended by the young niece of Mrs. Carlsen, while Clara lived on her own, translating Lampedusa's *Il Gattopardo* into Danish. She relished this productive time alone, and when Tania returned, cranky and demanding, Clara found it hard to continue slaving for her as before. By the end of the year they had a quarrel that pushed Karen Blixen to a shocking step: despite Clara's thirteen years of devoted service, she brusquely dismissed her. Clara left the way open for a reconciliation, as she had done before, but she also told Philip Ingerslev, Karen Blixen's cousin, that if in the meanwhile she took another job, she would not resign it to come back.

2

Two weeks after her homecoming from New York, Karen Blixen was suffering from her usual lethargy and depression, and she phoned her devoted *cavaliere*, Erling Schroeder. As Ms. Migel recounts their conversation, Tania lamented that Denmark was so dull, that New York was so exciting. "In New York everyone loved me. Tell me you love me. I need to hear that. I need it."[5] Erling reassured her of his love, and he also arranged to have a single perfect rose delivered to her. It would come every day for the rest of her life, and when she left Rungstedlund it followed her abroad or to the houses of her friends. The sender remained anonymous, and Karen Blixen never tried to unmask him.

Erling Schroeder was one of the last of Karen Blixen's old *boys,* as Ms. Migel aptly called them; for in many ways they had filled the place in her affections vacated by Tumbo, Abdullai, Juma, and Kamante. *Heretica* had ceased to publish, and the young writers had gone their separate ways. "They have all left me," the Baroness complained to several visiting friends. Aage Henriksen was among the last to leave. It is not clear what happened, but while Karen Blixen was working on "Copenhagen Season" she had somehow let him know that he was not one of her "kind," and this had hurt him deeply. When she sent him "Echoes" for a critique he had replied with a tale of his own, taking the events an imaginary step further, and this had also struck her as presumptuous. A tale, she told him sternly, always ended where it had to end, and to take it on was a sacrilege. He, in turn, had refused to play along with a staged tea party arranged for the photographers of *Life* in December of 1958, or to attend a lecture with her in 1959—this on the grounds that there was too much tension between them and that he would not be comfortable meeting her so formally. Toward the end of 1958 his letters began to grow more curt and brief; not perfunctory, but incredibly wary. Finally he announced that their relationship had reached an impasse, and that rather than letting it go on with increasing bitterness, they should part as friends. He blessed her and let her go. In the 1967 interview for *Politiken,* Henriksen summed up his understanding of Karen Blixen with the spiritual economy he and his mentor had in common. "Her writing," he said, "rests upon a knowledge of the way human beings hang together, and of how they can be split apart."[6]

In the spring of 1959, after her homecoming from America, Karen Blixen received a visit from a young Danish graduate student named Viggo Kjær Petersen. Petersen had defied the policy of his department to write his thesis on Karen Blixen; the faculty maintained that it was inappropriate to work on a living author, and he that their "Marxist leanings" had prejudiced them against her.[7] But the finished thesis, written in three weeks in a "white heat," won the university's highest marks, and Petersen, who had not wanted to meet Karen Blixen while he was writing it, sent her a copy.

After their first encounter Karen Blixen encouraged Petersen to return, and he did, filled with the reverent ardor of a young priest and the same willingness to serve. He could not ever replace Bjørnvig, but he was apparently able to console Karen Blixen, to pay her outrageous compliments, to rally her from her depressions and to call forth her sense of fun and coquetry. She could also talk to him in depth about her work, and according to Parmenia Migel she believed that he had a "grasp of certain elements [in it] . . . of which she herself had only been subconsciously cognizant."[8] On the strength of this deepening affection and confidence she would, before she died, ask Petersen to undertake an official critical biography, a work she hoped would appear after Ms. Migel's, and which would bring her life and work into focus as an organic unity.* It made her decline easier to bear, she told him, to know that her "mythos" was in such good hands.[9]

Through the mediation of Philip Ingerslev, Clara Svendsen eventually returned to Rungstedlund. She and Tania reached an understanding about her free time: she would have Sundays to herself, "like the oxen on the farm";[10]

---

*The biography is, apparently, still in progress.

and for the rest of the week she would be at Karen Blixen's disposition. At the beginning of 1960 they embarked upon a new project, collecting and shaping the chapters of *Shadows on the Grass,* which was the epilogue of *Out of Africa.* * Three of the four chapters had been written earlier in the fifties. "Farah" was first delivered as a radio talk in 1950, then published as a booklet by Ole Wivel. "Barua a Soldani" had been written originally for the Danish radio and was one of the tales Isak Dinesen had told in America. A shorter version of "The Great Gesture" was published in 1957 in the Danish woman's magazine *Alt for Damerne.* Some of the anecdotes and images in these three sections had originally been written for—but left out of—*Out of Africa.* Only "Echoes from the Hills" was entirely new. It brings the reader up-to-date with the fates of Karen Blixen's former servants, but it also violates one of her sternest dicta about storytelling: that the threads of a story, once knotted, should not be untied and drawn out further. Robert Langbaum found this the weakest chapter in the book, because its facts "are somehow just facts, such as they might be in any memoir or article. They lack the extra reverberations that make literature of *Out of Africa* and the rest of *Shadows.*"[11] Karen Blixen was herself sensitive to the weaknesses of this part of the book, which she ascribed to her own continually failing health, to the pain she had suffered while she was writing it and to the conditions of chaos—Rungsted-lund was being renovated—under which the book was finished. She told Haas that she hoped the other parts of the book, written when she was not so feeble, would "carry it along."[12]

3

Ellen Dahl had died in February 1959, while Tanne was in America. A letter from Thomas preparing her for the news had not been sent up to her hotel in Cambridge, and when she returned to New York the telegram was waiting.

Elle and Tanne had disagreed passionately on many subjects. Elle had been a socialist as a young woman, although after her marriage she had tended to defend her husband's ultraconservative politics, which the rest of the family abhorred. Her marriage and her patriotism were perhaps her two strongest passions. There was little lightness in Elle, although there was great dignity, fairness, and generosity. She became, as she aged, an imposing woman with

---

*Shadows on the Grass was undertaken in part because Isak Dinesen wanted to maintain her feeling of connectedness to her American audience. "I have," she told Robert Haas, "been feeling myself that the opportunity of publishing some kind of work of mine, while I am still so to say in personal contact with my American audience, should not be lost." She originally conceived of *Shadows* as a picture book, which was in keeping with its light, anecdotal tone, and she also very urgently wanted it to be cheap. In this context she explained how Fremad, in Copenhagen, had brought out a popular-library edition of "Babette's Feast" at so low a price that people were able to send the little book as a "Christmas card," and it sold one hundred thousand copies.

a square frame and jaw and a handsome, rather equine face. Her great wealth enabled her to become a patroness, not of the arts or literature but of social scientists and historians; and like her sister, she, too, had a "court." Her niece Ingeborg described her as austere in her tastes and habits, and rather prim; she did not like to be touched and explained this to her niece by saying: "Men like you on a pedestal."[13]

Elle was also one of Tanne's most faithful and discriminating critics. For all their differences, they loved to argue and did so without anger. "They really earnestly, energetically tried to *convince* the other one, even if they were both fairly inflexible. But they listened. They gave the viewpoints of the other one great credit and respect. They were," said their niece, "artists at disagreement, and would, like artists, turn over and play with the shape of their materials."[14]

Among the Dahl properties was an apartment in Copenhagen on Sølvgade, where Tanne had often stayed when she wished to escape from Rungstedlund. Elle also owned the tiny, narrow, eighteenth-century wooden house next door, which was said to be the smallest building in the capital and which she had promised to her sister as "winter quarters." Tanne was enchanted with it and began to write to her friends about *ma maison à moi*—"a little house which I have been given"—and Professor Rasmussen had drawn up plans for its renovation. But after Elle's death and in the absence of any formal provision in her will, her heirs revoked the gift.

Karen Blixen now decided that if she were to survive another winter at Rungstedlund she would have to put in central heating and a modern bath. Again Professor Rasmussen was appealed to, and he worked out a blueprint that would modernize the old house without any radical alteration of its appearance. This meant, however, that for a while it would become uninhabitable. Work began that autumn, and by the winter Karen Blixen had to move. She and Clara checked into the Bellevue Strand Hotel in Klampenborg, and later into the Angleterre. They expected their sojourn to be brief, but the renovations were going more slowly than anticipated, and the tedium and expense of hotel life became prohibitive. The invalid faced the prospect of spending her seventy-fifth birthday "on the road," with her work pressing and her strength and morale declining steadily. At this point Clara suggested they take a trip to Dragør, where she had, in the early fifties, bought a small cottage. Dragør is a little fishing village south of Copenhagen and near the airport. The streets are cobbled, the cottages are thatched, and the hollyhocks grow almost to the rooftops. Clara's house had two small rooms on the ground floor and two tiny attic bedrooms. Karen Blixen was given one with a view of the sea, and she was grateful to be "in a real home."[15] Her friends, as usual, were solicitous. Ole Wivel sent his secretary to help with the Danish translation of *Shadows on the Grass.* Erling Schroeder dropped by with caviar and *gelée royale,* and Clara, who hated to cook, found that she could order her own dinners from a local caterer. As for Karen Blixen's, "it was . . . an unpleasantly simple matter . . . as she couldn't eat anything."[16]

To offset the lack of space, Karen Blixen and Clara took walks along the port and brief excursions. They visited the linden trees at Store Magleby, a substitute for the traditional yearly excursion to the great flowering hawthorns in the Deer Park. Another morning they embarked in the small boat of Clara's house painter, accompanied by Nils Carlsen and the Kopps, to visit Saltholm Island, which lay in the channel beyond the harbor and was uninhabited except for great flocks of seabirds and Dragør geese. It was a tradition in the village to send one's goose to Saltholm to be fattened up for Christmas, and every spring a boat departed with the village flock. No cars were permitted on the island; the only vehicle was the gooseherd's tractor, and in it Karen Blixen rode across the flat, shimmering, golden landscape, full of ecstasy.

About this time she had a mystic experience—she received some kind of sign—although the nature of it remains a mystery. But one day in May she copied down a line of poetry from a psalm: *"Gud skal alting mage,"** and underneath it she wrote, "In this house did I experience, in May 1960, a great happiness." Without a word she handed it to Clara, who did not ask for an explanation. "But," Clara wrote, "a little later [Tania] added the confident observation that she believed she had now recovered, and that she could write again."[17]

This moment of happy assurance was short-lived. The renovations dragged on throughout the summer, and in May and June, Karen Blixen and Clara became active in the local celebration of the International Year of the Refugee. Karen Blixen loaned one of her African portraits to an exhibition and told "The Wine of the Tetrarch" on television, donating her honorarium to the fund which had been established. Although her doctor warned her against taking part in a rally at the port, she insisted. A special stamp had been minted for the occasion, and Karen Blixen addressed the first three letters that would carry it. She made a speech and told another tale—appropriate to the occasion—"The Blue Eyes." These were, as Clara noted, "two small

---

*Karen Blixen had recited this psalm to Bjørnvig when he was about to enter the hospital after his nervous collapse-concussion in Brittany. She recited it with "a dark fervour, in her old Copenhagen dialect" (Bjørnvig, *Pagten*, p. 30):

Gud skal alting mage	God shall put all things to right
Dig ved Haanden tage	take you by the hand
naar du synke skal.	when you begin to fall.
Naar du vil fortvivle,	When you are in despair,
finder ingen Hvile,	find no rest anywhere,
udi Modgangs Dal.	in Adversity's vale,
Gud da vil	then shall God's help
selv træde til.	prevail.

acts, small in relation to the problems but large in relation to her powers," and considering the circumstances, she was rewarded with an insult and an injustice. Replying to a letter from the Hørsholm committee on the refugees, she happened to write that at the moment she herself was "a kind of refugee." A Copenhagen newspaper got hold of the letter, and, despite the fact that it was informal and private, printed it. The paper subsequently received a number of outraged letters, which pointed out that someone who moved from one first-class hotel to another could scarcely consider herself a refugee. Late that same night a crowd gathered under the windows of Clara's cottage, chanting, "Karen Blixen, Karen Blixen, go home to Rungsted." She was, the next morning, "astounded and begrieved."[18]

Throughout July, Karen Blixen's physical condition deteriorated. Tove Hvass drove her and Clara over to inspect the work at Rungstedlund, and when they stopped at Store Magleby to smell the linden blossoms Karen Blixen could not stand up alone. In the bright sunlight Clara suddenly realized how deathly frail she had become.

By the beginning of August the work on *Shadows on the Grass* was finished, but Clara told Robert Haas that Tania's strength had been failing almost daily. On the sixth, an ambulance was called. While they were waiting for it Karen Blixen suddenly exclaimed, "And this was my last, friendly, flower bedecked refuge. Now it's a hospital!"[19] The melodrama of the outburst frightened Clara: It was so untypical. She took it as a sign that Karen Blixen believed she was about to die.

52

Wings

IN OCTOBER OF 1960, after a year in rented or borrowed lodgings and three months in a hospital bed, Isak Dinesen returned home. It was a home of which she was finally in secure possession, whose rooms were heated and insulated, and which now counted several bathrooms with hot running water. She had resisted the corruptions of *le confort moderne* for seventy-five years, long enough to have no spiritual, financial, or esthetic scruple about enjoying it.

Isak Dinesen's financial house was now also in order. Her lawyers had succeeded in simplifying and rationalizing her arrangements with publishers, and she was assured that her royalties would no longer be doubly taxed. She looked forward in the autumn, with her last two books still selling vigorously and the news that *Shadows on the Grass* had been chosen by the Book-of-the-Month Club, to a period of living "regardless of expense." This favorite English phrase, the invocation of boundlessness, cheered her simply to speak it. In practical terms there was no orgy of extravagance. She began to serve her guests truffles, ordered some new clothes from a first-class Danish couturier, hired a household manager (whom the staff resented and who didn't stay long), and planned a trip to Paris for the next spring.

The Revenge of Truth was performed that October on the Danish television. It was the third production of the little play since the Dinesen children had first staged it at Rungstedlund in 1904. Isak Dinesen had never wavered from the fatalism she had advocated as a nineteen-year-old girl with such precocious confidence. "When we first began no one knew what his role was like," Sabine, the ingenue, says at the end; "indeed we ourselves didn't know, for who can know what a character will look like on the stage? But now we have said those lines we had in us, we haven't kept a single one back, and when the curtain falls, no one can have any doubt about what we really were."[1] The speech now had all of an old storyteller's authority and all of her long life behind it.

Isak Dinesen knew that the years that were left "could be counted on one hand," and she felt it was an urgent matter that she "close the parenthesis" of her existence with some bold, unifying stroke. She also perceived that the story demanded that she return to Africa. She had wanted to go back since the thirties and had planned to on two occasions: just after the publication of *Seven Gothic Tales,* and just before the second war. Now *Life* was willing to send her.* But she hesitated, afraid that after so many years it might be an anticlimax. To gauge this danger better she wrote to her nephew, Gustaf Blixen-Finecke, who was farming outside Nairobi:

> Kenya and my relations with the Natives have meant so much to me that I think it would round out my whole existence beautifully and harmoniously if I could, again, if only for a short time, stand face to face with it altogether. But the truly *great* element in the experience depends upon the Natives remembering me. It is a lot to expect after thirty years of separation. As happy as it would make me for the Africans to come, of their own desire to greet me, I feel it would be just so pretentious and meaningless to sit crestfallen in Nairobi, with no real connection to the earth around it, or the life within it.[2]

She asked her nephew to keep this feeler confidential until she made up her mind. But *Life* was not interested in a more personal piece, and her horrified physician swore to her that she would die en route. The African parenthesis was never closed.

2

While a trip to Paris was not a substitute for a trip to Kenya, it was still something. Karen Blixen gave the poet Charles Henri Ford a list of people she would like to meet and wrote to Philippe de Rothschild, anticipating the pleasure of reading *Le Faux Jour* with him "and of myself taking the part of the Countess Rosmarine."[3] This set the tone for the visit, which was to be given over to high society and an orgy of theatergoing.

But Karen Blixen was so depleted and ill throughout the winter that it was not certain she would make it to Paris at all. After she returned from her Christmas at Wedellsborg, she fell in the bath and broke a rib—"from sheer exhaustion," Clara believed. As the spring approached, the prospect of the trip revived her; she ordered a suit and several dresses, and on the day of her appointment with the tailor Clara followed her around with awe. After climbing the steep flight of stairs to his studio, she visited her dress-

---

*The editors of the magazine wanted Isak Dinesen to report on the Kenya Colony's struggle for independence, and for a moment she was tremendously excited by the idea. But she also saw quickly that the commission was beyond her physical or reportorial scope—it would be too demanding. She wanted a more private homecoming.

maker on the Gammelstrand, walked to the Thorvaldsen Museum to see the bust of Byron, went on to have a hairdo, and then to the Royal Academy to see an exhibition of Danish landscape paintings. After dinner at Rungstedlund she opened her house to a party of "literary pilgrims" and arranged flowers before she went to bed.[4]

Eugene Haynes was expected in Denmark in the middle of June, just before Karen Blixen and Clara were to leave for France, and Clara offered him the use of her cottage in Dragør, which had an excellent piano, and where he had stayed before. But Tania invited him to come along to Paris with them; and Erling Schroeder, who had a "premonition" that the trip would be her last, decided that he had to come, too. (Tania made him promise to take her around the Left Bank on a motor scooter.)* The staff at their hotel could not figure out this party of foreigners, although indubitably they made a picturesque cluster of humanity. There was Eugene, with his dark cultivated face and his boyish accent; the distinguished, craggy, Nordic Erling; Clara, solid and modest; and the old Baroness in a red turban that she called "Prince Calendar," the "thinnest person in the the world," talking incessantly, gesturing with her cigarette holder, and shining. At three o'clock on a spring morning, outside a restaurant near Les Halles, the waiters put up the chairs but did not ask them to leave. "Perhaps," wrote Clara, "it was clear for everyone to see that this visitor, who was so happy to be in Paris . . . was here for the last time."[5]

Karen Blixen visited many of her old friends and made several new ones, including two women who had venerated her for years, Monica Stirling and Solita Solano. She was interviewed for French television and entertained by her publisher, Gallimard; she also went to a play or a ballet every night. On one occasion she saw Nureyev, who had just defected; and on another she saw Jack Gelber's *The Connection,* which contained a boast that she had once innocently made to *Life:* "I am the only white person the Natives really loved."† It was delivered sarcastically by a black man.

The trip was to have ended with a little coda in Madrid, but after four weeks she was too tired to go on and returned to Denmark. On July 26 she wanted to be at Wedellsborg, to help Julius and Inger Wedell celebrate the count's eightieth birthday. Ms. Migel describes her radiance and extraordinary happiness that evening, which was also one of her last with her old friend; he died in an accident the same month. After the dinner she rose to make a speech. It concluded:

---

*Actually, Erling Schroeder was one of two friends who called her "Karen." The other was Ingeborg Andersen at Gyldendal.

†It was apparently Hugh Martin who first made this comment: "Tania Blixen was the only white person the natives really loved." The quote, attributed to Hugh, is among her notes for *Out of Africa.*

Il faut dans ce bas monde aimer beaucoup de choses
Pour savoir après tout, ce qu'on aime le mieux. . . . . *

The remainder of the summer was crowded with visits. Robert Langbaum came to discuss his book; René Bouché, the artist, came to present his portrait of Karen Blixen to a Danish collection; John Gielgud came, and at their luncheon Karen Blixen told him that of all Shakespeare's characters she would most like to have played Horatio, "the perfect friend, who is so silent and understands so well." "You are my Horatio," he replied.[6]

In August Aldous Huxley arrived in Denmark and drove out to Rungstedlund with a friend, Timothy Leary, who was still teaching at Harvard and had come to attend a conference. Dinesen had met Huxley in the 1930s, through friends in London, and told him then that his novels were among those which had meant the most to her in Africa. The two men discussed their experiments with mind-altering drugs, speaking with great enthusiasm; and Huxley, whose eyesight was failing, described the joy that the visions brought him. Dinesen had herself chewed *miraa* in Africa with Denys and had enjoyed its mild hallucinogenic effect. She had perhaps also smoked opium. Now she listened to them with interest and accepted a rose Leary had been given at a séance and which he said "came from the world of the spirits." But she declined their invitation to try peyote on the grounds, Ms. Migel asserts, "that she was filled with enough fantasies . . . without any external stimulus."[7]

That September Karen Blixen bought a new dog, a Dandie Dinmont. After Pasop's death neither Tanne nor Clara had even wanted to think of a replacement, and as Karen Blixen put it, they had "sat *shivva* over Pasop for a while." But after the return to Rungstedlund from the hospital she began to complain about "the misery of a dogless life,"[8] and while she was at Wedellsborg that July she visited the estate of some old friends who bred Dandie Dinmonts. It was a dog that had always appealed to her; they appeared in the novels of Walter Scott, where they were inevitably called Mustard or Pepper. Her old friends, Baron and Baroness Bille Brahe Selby, made her the present of an "irresistible grey puppy" and delivered him in person two months later. He was promptly christened Pepper, and "his health was toasted in champagne."[9]

---

*One must, in this lower world, love many things
To know finally what one loves the best. . . .

See KBA 150.

3

When she was in New York Isak Dinesen had told Nancy Wilson Ross that she felt she was "so full of untold stories that if you prick me they will flow out." When the summer tourist season was over she returned to her writing. She had not renounced her ambition to finish *Albondocani* before her death, and she had an outline of new chapters for the novel waiting to be developed: a tale about the cardinal, and one about Byron. But she had also continued to fantasize about the Angel and von Galen families and envisaged a sequel to "Copenhagen Season," written in the "novelistic" vein of the original. It would follow the life of Drude Angel and was provisionally entitled "Thirty Years After," in homage to Dumas.

There was a certain frantic edge to her working life that autumn, for she was afraid that she might yet live on for a long period unable to write and unable to generate new royalties to support her household. The Rungsted-lund Foundation had borrowed money several months before to offset its operating expenses, and the familiar specter of the banks foreclosing on her property—while the risk was certainly minimal—still haunted her. Clara recognized an old dilemma: too many conflicting projects competing for her energy and detracting from one another; and a mounting sense of helplessness and desperation, which made it hard to write. But when she shared these observations with Karen Blixen she was rebuked: "I was only supposed to be a human dictaphone, and to sit still and write, and not meddle in the work in any other way than by showing interest in it."[10]

As a way of "warming up" for her new work, Karen Blixen began to revise some of the tales she had excluded from the earlier collections. She took up "Carnival" again and "The Last Day." This had been intended for *Winter's Tales,* and while she never perfected it, in its structure it is almost a paradigm of a Dinesen story: symmetrical couples, an erotic event concealed and exalted by myth and poetry. "The Bear and the Kiss," written in 1958 but not finished in time for *Anecdotes of Destiny,* was also never rewritten to her satisfaction; but she did eventually revise "Ehrengard," which appeared as a separate volume in 1962 after her death. Originally published in *The Ladies' Home Journal* as "The Secret of Rosenbad," it is an elegant but, by Dinesen standards, thin romantic comedy, which Robert Langbaum generously interprets as Dinesen's answer to Kierkegaard's "Diary of a Seducer."

"Thirty Years After" was never written, but the last chapter of *Albondocani,* "The Second Meeting," is a beautifully turned story that develops the theme of her desire to "round off my existence harmoniously," to "close the parenthesis with a flourish." It is the tale of a second meeting between Pino Pizzuti (Pipistrello), the director of a famous marionette theater whom we meet in "The Cloak Trilogy," and Lord Byron; and it takes place during the poet's last days in Italy before he sails to his death at Missolonghi. Pizzuti is Byron's double, and he has had the fortune and the honor (for so he reckons it) to have saved Byron's life fourteen years before. He has now come to the Casa Saluzzo to see what that fourteen years and his own act have vouchsafed to his double, and he also now tells Byron the real story of his rescue. At the time, when the poet was at the height of his powers and his fame, he had lived briefly on Malta. Pizzuti, the son of an extremely poor but pious widow of the island, had learned that three brothers—ruffians or pirates— intended to kidnap the poet and kill him for seducing their sister. He reasoned that someone so sublimely favored by God deserved to live and that he might really be serving God's plan by dying in his stead. So he borrowed the poet's horse and clothing from his valet and rode to the place of the poet's rendez- vous with the maiden, to be ambushed by her brothers. They were not fooled but they thought it a fine joke and asked Byron to ransom the life of this imposter at whatever price he might deem it worth. Byron had sent them a golden sovereign through his servant, and the robbers had given it to Pizzuti. He used the money to establish the marionette theater that had brought him fame and wealth, but at the same time he realized that by taking the money he had "forfeited my claim to a real human life." Everything that happened to him thereafter he "turned into tales."

Now, he tells Byron, he has come to make an inventory, to round off the poet's stock and "collect it into a unity . . . I am going to turn it into a story." He also declares candidly that the only stroke that can unify the "disintegrat- ing elements" of Byron's life—the petty, self-inflicted defeats—is "a great deadly defeat, which will redeem them." This makes the poet angry; he reckons it a bad enough omen to meet his double, much less to have that double prophesy his downfall, and he tells Pizzuti that he really ought to throw him out. To this Pizzuti replies that the defeat will bring him great rewards in the future—although not, as Byron first imagines, that it will make his works immortal, for in a hundred years "they will no longer be taken off the shelves." But there will be one book, he assures him, "that will be rewritten and reread, and will each year in a new edition be set upon the shelf . . . *The Life of Lord Byron.*"[11]

Pizzuti and Byron may be considered—like so many of the couples, twins, and *semblables* in Dinesen's tales—one character split into two, each embody- ing the missing attributes of the other and together "like a hook and an eye" making up a unity. Byron keeps faith with passion and the life force, Pizzuti with the imagination. Byron dies an heroic death so that his life will be immortal, and Pizzuti "forfeits" his claim to a real life so that his art will be immortal. They may also be considered together as the two phases of Isak Dinesen's own life: the Byronic phase, her *"Vita Nuova,"* her "real life" in Africa; and the period that followed, which was ransomed so that she might live to write about it. Pizzuti's boast and lament, that he has turned all his experience into tales, was her own. And one afternoon in 1961, while Clara was straightening Tanne's writing desk, she found a pad with a single sentence written on it in the familiar spidery script: *"forfeited my claim to a real human life."*[12]

4

Isak Dinesen continued literally to waste away. Advanced syphilis of the spine made it increasingly difficult and painful for her to walk, even to stand, and it took courage to mount the narrow stair to her bedroom every evening. She was also now so emaciated that her skin bruised to the touch; when a young gardener, who had come across her on a path struggling to make the distance back to the house, lifted her in his arms, she was as black and blue as if she had been beaten.

She did not want to live on in such weakness. To Monica Stirling, the English writer she had recently met in Paris, she wrote: "I wish I could die, I wish to die, it's like Shakespeare, do you remember: 'Thou thy worldly task hast done'?"[13] When Eugene Haynes came to visit her in the summer of 1962 and reminded her that she would not let her life go until it had blessed her, she replied, "It has blessed me."

Her family understood that she was going to die soon, and most of her friends also accepted it, although Clara stubbornly hoped that she would get a "new lease on life," as in the past; and Viggo Kjær Petersen, with the greedy love of someone who has come too late, railed that she was "too hard on herself . . ." "too hard on Pellegrina." His energetic adoration sparked little bursts of vigor in her, but they could not be sustained.

Isak Dinesen was in no way intimidated by her death. She went to smell the linden blossoms and to hear the nightingales, knowing it was for the last time, but this sense of finality was not morbid: it heightened the moment for her, and for those who shared it. Nor did she give up seeking and instigating "fun." When Daniel Gillès interviewed her for Belgian television she gave one of her most sumptuously camp performances. *"Je déteste la littérature,"* she claimed, *"et en particulier celle d'aujourd'hui."* And in the same breath, *"Je lis avec un appétit de jeune fille, qui croit qu'elle va trouver le Prince Charmant dans les livres."* And in the next, apropos of Giraudoux whose *Ondine* she admired, *"Je crois qu'il est un décadent, n'est-ce pas? Tout comme moi!"**

That spring and summer she held court, sitting on her verandah in an armchair, wrapped in old sweaters, mugging for the camera, making Clara take each new visitor up the hill to see the spot she had chosen for her grave. Many old friends came to see her: Bent, Eugene, Erling, Else and Eduard

---

*"I detest literature, and particularly modern literature. . . . I read with the appetite of a young girl, who thinks she is going to meet Prince Charming in a book. . . . I think he is a decadent, no? Just like me!" From Gillès, "La Pharoanne de Rungstedhend," in *Isak Dinesen: A Memorial,* p. 177.

Reventlow, Ellen Wanscher, and many friends from her most recent trips abroad. In May she received a visit from two young Kikuyu students on scholarship to Denmark; and the young woman, Emma Wamboi, brought greetings from her father, a nephew of Kinanjui. Karen Blixen had been following the struggle of the Kenyans for their independence throughout the year, and she had remarked to Clara how sad it was that she could not be with them now "of all times."[14]

In a letter to Parmenia Migel of that spring Isak Dinesen warned her friend that she would find her so much weaker than she had been, even at the darkest point of her American trip, and completely an invalid. To Violet Trefusis, whom she had visited in the splendor of her villa outside Paris, she wrote that she would have loved to stay with her in Florence, where she also had a home, and "once more to realize how much beauty there is in the world. But alas my dear, it is out of the question for me at the time being. I am so much weaker than when we met in Paris . . . I cannot walk two steps without support, nor stand and keep my equilibrium . . . and I cannot eat, so I cannot get my weight above seventy pounds. I may have to go into the hospital for some blood transfusions. The doctor tells me that I have all the symptoms of a concentration camp prisoner, one of them being that my legs swell so that they look like thick poles and feel like cannon balls. This last thing is terribly unbecoming and for some reason very vulgar. Altogether I look like the most horrid old witch, a real Memento Mori. If this is not going to be a continued decline, I shall have to try to get some of my strength back during the summer months."[15]

But the photographs taken by Peter Beard, who met Isak Dinesen in June of 1962, capture the strange radiance of her last months, which Thomas and Jonna Dinesen also remarked upon. She let down her guard, she relaxed her crooked smile, and her eyes—which she still carefully made up with kohl —seemed to stream with light. There was something almost inhuman about her fragility, or transitional: she seemed half-metamorphosed into a bird.

She was, in fact, dying of malnutrition. After the asparagus season was over she lived exclusively on glasses of fruit and vegetable juice, ampules of *gelée royale,* oysters and dry biscuits. On the evening of September 5 she played bezique with Clara and listened to music on a new phonograph, the gift of Solita Solano. They played excerpts from *The Marriage of Figaro* and an aria of Handel that Denys used to sing. "The idea never entered my mind," Clara told Robert Langbaum, "that when I had supported her upstairs to her bedroom she would never come down alive. But that is how it was."

On September 6, Isak Dinesen seemed very sleepy. When Clara came to see her in the early afternoon she had difficulty speaking. Clara thought she was simply tired, but Mrs. Carlsen, who brought some consommé and lemon juice, recognized that it was the end. Thomas and Jonna Dinesen were summoned and "arrived in time for her to recognize them."[16]

When her doctor came he gave her an injection, and after a while she lapsed into a coma from which she did not awake. She died the following evening, Friday, September 7—the cause of death, emaciation.[17]

"And by the time I had nothing left, I myself was the lightest thing of all, for fate to get rid of."[18]

Citations

See the note on citations on page xiii for an explanation of the abbreviations used in this section.

1. *EITHER/OR*

1. Attributed to Matthew Arnold, but actually a paraphrase of similar statements in Matthew Arnold, *Literature and Dogma*, pp. 16–18.
2. Interview with TD, Leerbæk, Vejle, July 1975.
3. Isak Dinesen, *Last Tales*, p. 253 (hereafter cited as *LT*).
4. Ibid., p. 260.
5. Robert Langbaum, *The Gayety of Vision*, p. 39 (hereafter cited as *Gayety*).
6. *LT*, p. 253.
7. Mary Bess Westenholz, "Erindringer om Mama og hendes Slægt" [Memoirs of Mama and her family], *Blixeniana 1979*, p. 82 (hereafter cited as "Om Mama").
8. Thomas Dinesen, *My Sister, Isak Dinesen*, trans. Joan Tate, p. 15 (hereafter cited as *My Sister*).
9. Westenholz, "Om Mama," p. 200.
10. I. Dinesen, *Letters from Africa: 1914–1931*, trans. Anne Born, p. 380 (hereafter cited as *Letters*).
11. Interview with CS, Dragør, July 1976.
12. "Autobiography of Ingeborg Dinesen," written for her children, KBA 99/D.
13. Westenholz, "Om Mama," p. 117.
14. T. Dinesen, *Boganis: Min Fader, Hans Slægt, Hans Liv og Hans Tid*, p. 96 (hereafter cited as *Boganis*).
15. Ibid., p. 97.
16. T. Dinesen, *My Sister*, p. 12.
17. T. Dinesen, *Boganis*, p. 17.
18. Frans Lasson and Clara Svendsen, eds., *The Life and Destiny of Karen Blixen*, p. 18 (hereafter cited as *Life and Destiny*).
19. T. Dinesen, *Boganis*, p. 18.
20. Ibid.
21. I. Dinesen, *Letters*, p. 381.
22. I. Dinesen, *Daguerreotypes and Other Essays*, trans. P. M. Mitchell and W. D. Paden, p. 23 (hereafter cited as *Daguerreotypes*).
23. I. Dinesen, *Shadows on the Grass*, p. 30 (hereafter cited as *SG*).
24. KB to Aage Henriksen, 1 April 1956, KBA 66.

2. THE CAPTAIN

1. Friedrich Wilhelm Nietzsche, "Nietzsche Contra Wagner," *The Portable Nietzsche*, ed. and trans. Walter Kaufmann, p. 680.
2. Georg Brandes, "Wilhelm Dinesen," *Samlede Skrifter*, p. 196.
3. Ibid., p. 195.
4. Ibid., p. 189.

5. Wilhelm Dinesen (Boganis), *Jagtbreve og Nye Jagtbreve* [Letters from the Hunt and New Letters from the Hunt], p. 48 (hereafter cited as *Jagtbreve*).
6. T. Dinesen, *Boganis*, pp. 47–48.
7. Bent Rying, ed., *Denmark: An Official Handbook*, trans. Reginald Spink, p. 92 (hereafter cited as *Denmark*).
8. Brandes, "Wilhelm Dinesen," p. 197.
9. Ibid., p. 196.
10. T. Dinesen, *Boganis*, p. 50.
11. I. Dinesen, *Seven Gothic Tales*, p. 125 (hereafter cited as *SGT*).
12. W. Dinesen, "Fra et Ophold i de Forenede Stater" [From a sojourn in the United States], *Tilskueren*, p. 779 (hereafter crited as "Fra et Ophold")
13. T. Dinesen, *Boganis*, p. 70.
14. Brandes, *Main Currents in Nineteenth Century Literature*, vol. 1, p. 31 (hereafter cited as *Main Currents*).
15. Arnold Hauser, *The Social History of Art*, vol. 3, p. 75.
16. Richard B. Vowles, "Boganis, Father of Osceola; or Wilhelm Dinesen in America, 1872–1874," *Scandinavian Studies*, vol. 48, Autumn 1976, p. 370.
17. W. Dinesen, "Fra et Ophold," p. 783.
18. Thomas Dinesen gives *hasselnød* as the translation. Richard B. Vowles cites Donald Watkins as saying that in southwestern Chippewa the name translated "little nut" (Vowles, p. 381).
19. W. Dinesen, "Fra et Ophold," p. 785.
20. Parmenia Migel, *Titania: The Biography of Isak Dinesen*, p. 10 (hereafter cited as *Titania*).
21. *Morgenbladet* (Copenhagen), 24 January 1887.
22. T. Dinesen, *Boganis*, p. 113.
23. W. Dinesen, *Jagtbreve*, p. 280.
24. Ibid., p. 90.
25. Brandes, "Wilhelm Dinesen," p. 187.
26. T. Dinesen, *Boganis*, p. 113.
27. Hauser, *The Social History of Art*, vol. 4, p. 35.
28. W. Dinesen, *Jagtbreve*, p. 136.
29. *SGT*, p. 96.
30. I. Dinesen, *Letters*, p. 427.
31. "Autobiography of Ingeborg Dinesen," KBA 99/D.
32. Ibid.
33. MrsD to WD, 5 August 1880, KBA 61/D.
34. Ibid.
35. T. Dinesen, *Boganis*, p. 100.
36. MrsW to WD, 4 May 1880, KBA 61.
37. WD to MrsD, 3 April 1880, KBA 61.
38. MrsW to WD, 4 May 1880, KBA 61.
39. WD to MrsD, 3 April 1880, KBA 61.
40. MrsD to WD, 5 August 1880, KBA 61.
41. MrsW to WD, 3 April 1880, KBA 61.
42. MrsD to WD, 5 August 1880, KBA 61.
43. "Autobiography of Ingeborg Dinesen," KBA 99/D.
44. MrsD to WD, 31 July 1880, KBA 61.
45. T. Dinesen, *Boganis*, p. 101.
46. I. Dinesen, *Letters*, p. 427.
47. W. Dinesen, *Jagtbreve*, p. 112.

3. A FAMILY ROMANCE

1. From the manuscript notes for *Out of Africa*, KBA 159.
2. Westenholz, "Om Mama," p. 204.

3. Ibid., p. 201.
4. Ibid., p. 201.
5. Ibid., p. 198.
6. I. Dinesen, *Winter's Tales,* p. 108 (hereafter cited as *WT*).
7. Westenholz, "Om Mama," p. 207.
8. Migel, *Titania,* p. 8.
9. MrsD to her children, "House Rules," recopied by Tanne Dinesen, unedited early manuscripts, KBA 105, IIIa, 3–4.
10. Lasson and Svendsen, *Life and Destiny,* p. 144.
11. I. Dinesen, *Letters,* P. 111.
12. *WT,* p. 209.
13. Ibid., p. 202.
14. Langbaum, *Gayety,* p. 39.
15. Steen Eiler Rasmussen, "Karen Blixens Rungstedlund," *Det Danske Akademi, 1960–1967,* p. 251.
16. Langbaum, *Gayety,* p. 45.
17. *SGT,* p. 193.
18. Nietzsche, *The Birth of Tragedy and the Case of Wagner,* trans. Walter Kaufmann, p. 22 (hereafter cited as *Birth of Tragedy*).
19. T. Dinesen, *Boganis,* p. 120.
20. Migel, *Titania,* p. 13.
21. Lasson and Svendsen, *Life and Destiny,* p. 40.
22. T. Dinesen, *Boganis,* p. 135.
23. Ibid., p. 136.
24. KB to Aage Henriksen, 1 April 1956, KBA 66.

4. "ALKMENE"

1. I. Dinesen, *Letters,* p. 428.
2. Lasson and Svendsen, *Life and Destiny,* p. 43.
3. Migel, *Titania,* p. 14.
4. I. Dinesen, *Letters,* p. 271.
5. Lasson and Svendsen, *Life and Destiny,* p. 43.
6. KB to Aage Henriksen, 1 April 1966, KBA 66.
7. T. Dinesen, *My Sister,* passim.
8. I. Dinesen, *Anecdotes of Destiny,* p. 81 (hereafter cited as *AD*).
9. *WT,* p. 194.
10. Ibid., p. 195.
11. Ibid., p. 200.
12. Ibid., p. 202.
13. Ibid., p. 205.
14. Ibid., p. 218.
15. Ibid., p. 220.
16. I. Dinesen, *Letters,* p. 380.
17. I. Dinesen, *Out of Africa,* p. 20 (hereafter cited as *OA*).

5. THREE SISTERS

1. T. Dinesen, *My Sister,* p. 30.
2. Interview with TD, Leerbæk, Vejle, July 1975.
3. T. Dinesen, *My Sister,* p. 30.
4. I. Dinesen, *Letters,* p. 350.
5. Interview, Copenhagen, July 1975.
6. I. Dinesen, *Letters,* p. 211.
7. Ibid., p. 129.
8. Interview with CS, Dragør, July 1976.
9. ED to KB, May 1946, KBA 57.
10. I. Dinesen, *Letters,* p. 409.

11. Georg Brandes, *An Essay on Aristocratic Radicalism* (trans. not credited), p. 10 (hereafter cited as *On Aristocratic Radicalism*).
12. Brandes to Nietzsche, January 1888, appended to *On Aristocratic Radicalism*, p. 144.
13. I. Dinesen, *Daguerreotypes*, p. 4.
14. I. Dinesen, *Letters*, p. 315.
15. Ibid., p. 67.
16. Interview with TD, Leerbæk, Vejle, July 1975.
17. Karen Blixen's unedited early manuscripts, KBA 106, IIIa, 3–4.
18. Ibid.
19. Ibid.
20. Ibid.
21. MrsD to her children, "House Rules," recopied by Tanne Dinesen, unedited early manuscripts, KBA 105, IIIa, 3–4.
22. Ibid.
23. My account is drawn primarily from Alfred Gnudtzmann, "Tivoli," *Copenhagen, The Capital of Denmark* (Copenhagen: Danish Tourist Society, 1898), pp. 88–94.
24. *OA*, p. 16.
25. Karen Blixen's unedited early dramatic works, KBA 107 III.
26. Ibid., A$_2$ a$_1$.
27. Clara Svendsen, *Notater om Karen Blixen*, p. 188 (hereafter cited as *Notater*). Ms. Svendsen also notes that they mistook "Arabella" for "Annabella."
28. Hauser, *The Social History of Art*, vol. 3, p. 212.
29. T. Dinesen, *My Sister*, p. 32.
30. *WT*, pp. 251–285.

6.   THE ROAD TO KATHOLM

1. *WT*, p. 176.
2. Ibid., p. 255.
3. Ibid., p. 251.
4. Brandes, *Main Currents*, vol. 1.
5. *WT*, p. 254.
6. T. Dinesen, *Tanne, Min Søster Karen Blixen*, p. 19; cf. *My Sister*, p. 22.
7. KB to Birthe Andrup, undated, from Ms. Andrup's private archives.
8. *WT*, p. 254.
9. *OA*, p. 72.
10. I. Dinesen, *Letters*, p. 209.
11. Thorkild Bjørnvig, *Pagten*, p. 15.
12. Brandes, *On Aristocratic Radicalism*, p. 49.
13. Migel, *Titania*, p. 16.
14. Nietzsche, "Ecce Homo," *The Portable Nietzsche*, p. 660.
15. From a series of Tanne Dinesen's blue notebooks, containing her love poems, serenades, ballads, sonnets, cradle songs, harvest songs, Midsummer night's dream songs, and miscellaneous apostrophes to the elements and planets, KBA 106, III A$_1$.
16. I. Dinesen, *Letters*, p. 393.
17. Laurie Magnus, *A Dictionary of European Literature* (London: George Routledge & Sons, 1927), p. 203.
18. Ibid.
19. Rying, *Denmark*, p. 677.
20. I. Dinesen, *Letters*, p. 395.
21. I. Dinesen, *Carnival: Entertainments and Posthumous Tales*, p. 338 (hereafter cited as *Carnival*).
22. Lasson and Svendsen, *Life and Destiny*, p. 32.
23. KBA 106, III A$_1$.
24. Migel, *Titania*, p. 18.
25. Ibid., p. 21.

26. Interview with TD, Leerbæk, Vejle, July 1976.
27. I. Dinesen, *Daguerreotypes*, p. 23.
28. *SGT*, p. 81.
29. From Karen Blixen's notes for a speech to the Danish Women Citizen's Society *(Dansk Kvindesamfund)* on the subject of African women, 9 November 1938, KBA 152, III B₄; cf. *Daguerreotypes*, p. 72; *OA*, p. 16.
30. Migel, *Titania*, p. 28.
31. Ibid., p. 21.
32. I. Dinesen, *Letters*, pp. 202–210.

7. AUNT BESS

1. Nietzsche to Brandes, appended to *On Aristocratic Radicalism*, p. 65.
2. Interview with CS, Dragør, July 1976.
3. Migel, *Titania*, p. 16.
4. I. Dinesen, *Letters*, p. 199.
5. Ibid., p. 265.
6. *SG*, p. 4.
7. Interview with TD, Leerbæk, Vejle, July 1976.
8. *SGT*, p. 277.
9. T. Dinesen, *My Sister*, p. 10.
10. Brandes, *On Aristocratic Radicalism*, p. 6.
11. Ibid., p. 65.
12. Meyer, *Ibsen*, p. 357.
13. Henning Fenger, *Georg Brandes et la France* (Paris: Presses Universitaires de France, 1963), p. 39.
14. Meyer, *Ibsen*, p. 346.
15. Rying, *Denmark*, p. 220.
16. Elias Bredsdorff, *Den Store Nordiske Krig om Sexualmoralen: En dokumentarisk fremstilling af sædelighedsdebatten in nordisk literattur i 1880'erne* [The great Scandinavian war over sexual morality], p. 7.
17. Ibid., p. 41.
18. Ibid., p. 73.
19. Brandes to Nietzsche, January 1880, appended to *On Aristocratic Radicalism*, p. 123.
20. I. Dinesen, *Letters*, p. 299.
21. Ole Wivel, *Romance for Valdhorn*, p. 215 (hereafter cited as *Romance*).
22. I. Dinesen, *Letters*, p. 163.
23. Ibid., p. 382.

8. ART AND LIFE

1. Interview with TD, Leerbæk, Vejle, July 1975.
2. Ibid.
3. I. Dinesen, *Letters*, p. 381.
4. Ibid., p. 246.
5. Frans Lasson, ed., *Karen Blixens Tegninger, Med to Essays of Karen Blixen* (Karen Blixen's drawings, and two of her essays), p. 20 (hereafter cited as *Tegninger*).
6. Ibid.
7. Ibid., p. 19.
8. Interview with Ida Palludan, New York, 1980.
9. Lasson, *Tegninger*, p. 23.
10. Ibid.
11. Ibid.
12. Unedited early work, KBA 113, III A 3, 1.
13. Lasson, *Tegninger*, p. 23.
14. Ibid.
15. Ibid., pp. 27–28.
16. *WT*, p. 71.

17. *SGT,* p. 46.
18. Ibid., p. 47.
19. Ibid., p. 48.
20. Ibid.
21. Ibid., p. 46.
22. I. Dinesen, *Letters,* p. 209.
23. T. Dinesen, *My Sister,* p. 43.
24. Langbaum, *Gayety,* p. 2.

9.   COUNTESS DAISY

1. I. Dinesen, *Letters,* p. 246.
2. All quotations in section 1 are from Karen Blixen's unedited early manuscripts, KBA 111, III A 3a, 1.
3. All quotations in section 2 are from Karen Blixen's diary of February 11–March 17, 1906 (Dagbog, København, Sct. Annæ Plads 15) KBA 118.
4. Ibid.
5. Svendsen and Lasson, *Life and Destiny,* p. 64.
6. KBA 111, III A 3.
7. Ibid.
8. Interview with CS, Rungstedlund, July 1975.
9. *SGT,* p. 219.
10. T. Dinesen, *My Sister,* p. 23.
11. Migel, *Titania,* p. 209.
12. Interview, Copenhagen, 1975.
13. Migel, *Titania,* p. 210.
14. *SG,* p. 39.
15. I. Dinesen, *Letters,* pp. 346, 204.
16. Ibid., p. 380.
17. See below, p. 92; "Paris Diary," KBA 118.
18. KBA 113, III A 3, 1.
19. Ibid.
20. T. Dinesen, *My Sister,* p. 23 (emphasis added).

10.   FIRST TALES

1. *AD,* p. 13.
2. T. Dinesen, *My Sister,* p. 37.
3. Lasson, *Tegninger,* p. 22.
4. KBA 111, III a, 3a 1.
5. KBA 112, III A 3 1.
6. Ibid., p. 159.
7. Lasson, *Tegninger,* p. 23.
8. Valdemar Vedel to KB, 17 October 1906, KBA 52.
9. Karen Blixen, *Osceola,* ed. Clara Svendsen.
10. *Politiken* (Copenhagen), 1 May 1934, p. 12.
11. K. Blixen, *Osceola,* p. 37.
12. Langbaum, *Gayety,* p. 2.
13. Walter Benjamin, "The Storyteller: Reflections on the Works of Nicolai Leskov," *Illuminations,* trans. Harry Zohn, ed. Hannah Arendt, p. 104 (hereafter cited as "The Storyteller").
14. K. Blixen, *Osceola,* p. 82.
15. Ibid., pp. 90–91.
16. Ibid., p. 51.
17. Ibid., p. 52.
18. Ibid., p. 46.
19. Ibid., p. 57.
20. Migel, *Titania,* p. 13.

11. LOVE, HUMBLE AND AUDACIOUS

1. *WT,* p. 277.
2. T. Dinesen, *My Sister,* p. 48.
3. Undated diary, KBA 115, III a 3e, notebooks 7–10.
4. Interview with TD, Leerbæk, Vejle, July 1976.
5. T. Dinesen, *My Sister,* p. 24.
6. Errol Trzebinski, *Silence Will Speak,* p. 16.
7. T. Dinesen, *My Sister,* p. 40.
8. Migel, *Titania,* p. 23.
9. Lasson and Svendsen, *Life and Destiny,* p. 54.
10. W. Dinesen, *Jagtbreve,* p. 308.
11. Unpublished memoir of Bror and Hans Blixen, with the kind permission of Christopher Aschan.
12. Ibid.
13. Ibid.
14. Interview with IL, London, June 1976.
15. Lasson and Svendsen, *Life and Destiny,* p. 65.
16. *SGT,* pp. 82–83.
17. I. Dinesen, *Letters,* p. 281.
18. "Paris Diary," KBA 118, III A 4, March 24–May 22, 1910.
19. KBA 116, III A; a 7 1.

12. RUE BOCCADOR

1. "Paris Diary" (Dagbog), March 24–May 22, 1910, KBA 118, III a 4. All subsequent quotations in this chapter are from the above, unless otherwise credited.
2. Aage Kabell, *Karen Blixen debuterer* [Karen Blixen makes her debut], p. 29.
3. Ibid.
4. Ibid.
5. KBA 112, III A 3 6.
6. Migel, *Titania,* p. 31.
7. Count Eduard Reventlow to Karen Blixen, 1955. From the archives of, and by kind permission of, Count Christian Reventlow.

13. "LA VALSE MAUVE"

1. KBA 116, III B f 9, "Kærlighedsklokkerne."
2. Ibid.
3. KBA 116, III B f 11, "Rosa."
4. KBA 112, III A_3 7, "La Valse Mauve."
5. Interview, Copenhagen, 1975.
6. Nietzsche, *Thus Spake Zarathustra, The Portable Nietzsche,* p. 78.
7. "Paris Diary," KBA 118.
8. KBA 116, III A_2 9.
9. T. Dinesen, *My Sister,* p, 49.
10. KBA 116, A III f, "Susanna."
11. KBA 113, III A_3 2.
12. Eugene Walter, "Isak Dinesen," *Paris Review,* Autumn 1956, pp. 43–59.
13. Migel, *Titania,* p. 38.
14. I. Dinesen, *Letters,* p. 42.
15. Interview with CS, Dragør, July 1976.
16. Ibid.
17. I. Dinesen, *Letters,* p. 42.
18. Kabell, *Karen Blixen debuterer,* p. 30.
19. Ibid.
20. Ibid.

14. NOBLE PROSPECTS

1. T. Dinesen, *My Sister*, p. 50.
2. KBA 114, A III.
3. KB to Christian Elling, undated, KBA 66.
4. Trzebinski, *Silence Will Speak*, p. 92.
5. Interview with CS, Rungstedlund, 1975.
6. T. Dinesen, *My Sister*, p. 53.
7. I. Dinesen, *Letters*, p. 287.
8. Migel, *Titania*, p. 39.
9. T. Dinesen, *My Sister*, p. 53.
10. *AD*, p. 85.
11. Lasson and Svendsen, *Life and Destiny*, p. 66.
12. I. Dinesen, *Letters*, pp. 192, 263.
13. Ibid., p. 191.
14. Bror von Blixen-Finecke, *The African Hunter*, p. 10.
15. T. Dinesen, *My Sister*, p. 52.
16. B. Blixen, *The African Hunter*, pp. 9–10.
17. T. Dinesen, *My Sister*, p. 52.
18. B. Blixen, *The African Hunter*, p. 12.
19. KB to Christian Elling, undated, KBA 66.
20. I. Dinesen, *Letters*, p. 123.
21. T. Dinesen, *My Sister*, p. 53.
22. B. Blixen, *The African Hunter*, p. 12.
23. Ibid.
24. Interview with Remy Martin, Nairobi, September 1975.
25. Count Gustaf Lewenhaupt to KB, 17 March 1938, KBA 31.
26. Migel, *Titania*, p. 42.

15. SEA CHANGE

1. KBA 119, III A 5, 5–8.
2. Charles Miller, *Battle for the Bundu*, p. 38.
3. I. Dinesen, *Letters*, p. 2.
4. Karen Blixen, "Breve fra et Land i Krig," *Essays*, p. 122; cf. *Daguerreotypes*, p. 92.
5. I. Dinesen, *Letters*, p. 1.
6. I. Dinesen, *Daguerreotypes*, p. 6.
7. *SG*, p. 17.
8. Ibid., pp. 3–5.
9. *OA*, p. 297.
10. I. Dinesen, *Letters*, p. 2.
11. Wilhelm, Prince of Sweden, "Afrikanskt Intermezzo," *Episoder*, pp. 150–151.
12. Ibid., pp. 152–153.

16. A STILL COUNTRY

1. *OA*, p. 3.
2. Carl Jung, *Memories, Dreams and Reflections*, trans. Richard and Clara Winston, p. 284.
3. *OA*, p. 98.
4. Miller, *Battle for the Bundu*, p. 26.
5. Basil Davidson, *Let Freedom Come: Africa in Modern History*, p. 118.
6. Neal Acheson, "Longing for Darkness," *The New York Review of Books*, 18 September 1975.
7. *OA*, p. 135.
8. Basil Davidson, *A History of East and Central Africa: To the Late Nineteenth Century*, p. 168.
9. Ibid., p. 294.

17. THE CLEAR DARKNESS

1. Trzebinski, *Silence Will Speak,* p. 84.
2. *OA,* p. 12.
3. Interview with Rose Cartwright, Nairobi, September 1975.
4. Trzebinski, *Silence Will Speak,* p. 99.
5. I. Dinesen, *Letters,* p. 3.
6. *OA,* p. 4.
7. Ibid., p. 17.
8. I. Dinesen, *Daguerreotypes,* p. 8.
9. Bjørnvig, *Pagten,* p. 21.
10. Bror Blixen to MrsD, undated, KBA 61.
11. I. Dinesen, *Letters,* p. 2.
12. Ibid., p. 4.
13. KB to Ea, unpublished excerpt, KBA 65.
14. Interview with Sir Charles Markham, Nairobi, September 1975.
15. Interview with Beryl Markham, Nairobi, September 1975.
16. I. Dinesen, *Letters,* p. 10.
17. Interview with Nathaniel Kivoi, Karen, September 1975.
18. Interview with Kamau, Karen, September 1975.
19. *OA,* p. 253.
20. Ibid., p. 9.
21. I. Dinesen, *Letters,* p. 16.
22. *OA,* p. 4.
23. I. Dinesen, *Letters,* p. 6.

18. SAFARI LIFE

1. *OA,* p. 70.
2. I. Dinesen, *My Sister,* p. 55.
3. Ibid., pp. 56–57.
4. *OA,* p. 231.
5. K. Blixen, "Ex Africa," *Osceola,* p. 157.
6. Interview with SER, Rungsted, August 1975.
7. B. Blixen, *The African Hunter,* p. 231.
8. Miller, *Battle for the Bundu,* p. 51.
9. *OA,* p. 272.
10. Ibid., p. 20.
11. I. Dinesen, *Letters,* p. 23.
12. Miller, *Battle for the Bundu,* p. 322.
13. I. Dinesen, *Letters,* p. 17.
14. Ibid., p. 26.

19. LUCIFER'S CHILD

1. Bror Blixen to MrsD, 3 March 1915, KBA 61.
2. I. Dinesen, *Letters,* p. 29.
3. Interview with CS, Dragør, July 1976.
4. Migel, *Titania,* p. 55.
5. Interview with Dr. Mogens Fog, Copenhagen, August 1976.
6. Interviews, OW, Copenhagen and Sir Charles Markham, Nairobi, August–September 1975.
7. Bjørnvig, *Pagten,* p. 104.
8. Interview with CS, Dragør, July 1976.
9. I. Dinesen, *Letters,* pp. 281–283.
10. Ibid., p. 17.
11. Ibid., p. 30.
12. Migel, *Titania,* p. 55.
13. R. D. Catterall, *A Short Textbook of Venereology: The Sexually Transmitted Diseases,* p. 153.

14. Mogens Fog, "Karen Blixens Sygdomshistorie," *Blixeniana 1978*, p. 142.
15. Westenholz, "Om Mama," p. 215.
16. T. Dinesen, *My Sister*, p. 58.
17. I. Dinesen, *Letters*, p. 281.
18. Bjørnvig, *Pagten*, p. 50.
19. K. Blixen, *Osceola*, p. 8.
20. Ibid., p. 157.
21. T. Dinesen, *My Sister*, p. 22.
22. Interview with TD, Leerbæk, Vejle, July 1976.
23. T. Dinesen, *My Sister*, p. 60.
24. I. Dinesen, *Letters*, p. 33.
25. Ibid., p. 35.
26. Ibid.
27. Ibid., p. 36.
28. Ibid., p. 37.
29. Ibid., p. 39.

20. THE WING OF DEATH

1. I. Dinesen, *Letters*, p. 41, and interview with IL, London, June 1976.
2. I. Dinesen, *Letters*, pp. 41–42.
3. Ibid., p. 41.
4. Svendsen, *Notater*, p. 206.
5. I. Dinesen, *Letters*, p. 44.
6. Ibid., p. 54.
7. Ibid., p. 51.
8. Interview with IL, Philadelphia, December 1976.
9. *OA*, p. 349.
10. I. Dinesen, *Letters*, p. 51.
11. Ibid., p. 46.
12. Ibid., p. 76.
13. "Sang til Harpe," KBA 118, III A 1 12.
14. I. Dinesen, *Letters*, p. 55.

21. DRAMATIS PERSONAE

1. *OA*, p. 210.
2. *SGT*, p. 81.
3. Noel Anthony Scawen Lytton (4th Earl), *The Stolen Desert*, p. 162.
4. Ibid., p. 116.
5. I. Dinesen, *Letters*, p. 62.
6. Ibid., p. 59.
7. Lytton, *The Stolen Desert*, p. 167.
8. Migel, *Titania*, p. 61.
9. I. Dinesen, *Letters*, p. 347.
10. Ibid., p. 62.
11. K. Blixen, *Breve fra Africa: 1914–1931* (hereafter cited as *Breve*), vol. 1, p. 99; cf. *Letters*, p. 65.
12. KB to ED, December 10, 1918, KBA 62.
13. I. Dinesen, *Letters*, p. 67.
14. *OA*, p. 368.
15. Interview with Rose Cartwright, Limuru, September 1975.
16. Trzebinski, *Silence Will Speak*, p. 37.
17. Interview with Cockie Hoogterp (Jacqueline Alexander Birkbeck Blixen Hoogterp), Bror Blixen's second wife, England, June 1975.
18. *SGT*, p. 355.
19. T. Dinesen, *My Sister*, p. 62.
20. *SG*, p. 57.

21. I. Dinesen, *Letters,* p. 77.
22. *OA,* p. 214.
23. Trzebinski, *Silence Will Speak,* p. 73.
24. *OA,* p. 206.
25. Miller, *Battle for the Bundu,* p. 29.
26. Trzebinski, *Silence Will Speak,* p. 112.
27. Ibid., p. 114.
28. Ibid., p. 121.
29. *OA,* p. 237.
30. Interviews, Cockie Hoogterp, England, 1975, and IL, Philadelphia, 1977.
31. I. Dinesen, *Letters,* p. 321.
32. Interview with TD, Leerbæk, Vejle, July 1975.
33. Interview with Ulf Aschan, Nairobi, 1975.
34. Nietzsche, *Birth of Tragedy,* p. 21.
35. *OA,* p. 43.
36. I. Dinesen, *Letters,* p. 73.
37. Interview with Rose Cartwright, Limuru, September 1975.
38. I. Dinesen, *Letters,* p. 69.
39. Ibid., p. 70.
40. Ibid., p. 80.
41. Ibid., p. 82.
42. Ibid., p. 86.
43. T. Dinesen, *My Sister,* p. 61.
44. Trzebinski, *Silence Will Speak,* p. 146.
45. I. Dinesen, *Letters,* p. 91.
46. Ibid., p. 98.
47. Among her notes for *Out of Africa* there was, in Karen Blixen's handwriting, a very sketchy chronology of her life in Kenya, from which this is an excerpt. The chronology was no longer in the archives when I consulted them, but Ms. Trzebinski had been shown a copy, which she graciously shared with me.

22. INTERMEZZO

1. Bjørnvig, *Pagten,* p. 63.
2. Trzebinski, *Silence Will Speak,* p. 130.
3. Interview with Cockie Hoogterp, England, June 1975.
4. *OA,* p. 23.
5. I. Dinesen, *Letters,* p. 100.
6. Interview with Sir Charles Markham, Nairobi, 1975.
7. Interview with Kamante Gatura, Karen, September 1975.
8. K. Blixen, *Breve,* vol. 2, p. 178; I. Dinesen, *Letters,* p. 377.
9. Trzebinski, *Silence Will Speak,* pp. 179–180.
10. Interview with Cockie Hoogterp, England, June 1975.

23. THOMAS

1. Interview with Cockie Hoogterp, England, June 1975.
2. Interview with Lady Altrincham (the former Joan Grigg), England, 1976.
3. T. Dinesen, *My Sister,* p. 92.
4. *OA,* p. 223.
5. Interview with TD, Leerbæk, July 1975.
6. Ibid.
7. T. Dinesen, *My Sister,* p. 64.
8. Interview with TD, Leerbæk, July 1975.
9. Interview with IM, Copenhagen, July 1975.
10. T. Dinesen, *My Sister,* p. 72.
11. Interview with Beryl Markham, Nairobi, September 1975.
12. KBA 75.

13. I. Dinesen, *Letters*, P. 111.
14. Ibid.
15. I. Dinesen, *Letters*, p. 116.
16. Migel, *Titania*, pp. 75–76.

24. KAMANTE AND LULU

1. I. Dinesen, *Letters*, p. 123.
2. Ibid., p. 135.
3. Huxley, *Lord Delamere and the Making of Kenya*, vol. 2, p. 62.
4. Ibid., p. 67.
5. I. Dinesen, *Letters*, p. 283.
6. Bjørnvig, *Pagten*, p. 66.
7. Cf. *OA*, p. 312.
8. K. Blixen, *Breve*, vol. 1, p. 279; I. Dinesen, *Letters*, p. 225.
9. I. Dinesen, *Letters*, p. 171.
10. Ibid., p. 139.
11. Ibid., p. 54.
12. Hudson Strode, "Isak Dinesen at Home," *Isak Dinesen: A Memorial*, ed. Clara Svendsen, p. 102.
13. "On Nationality," KBA 113, III A 3, 3.
14. I. Dinesen, *Letters*, p. 99.
15. Ibid., p. 259.
16. I. Dinesen, *Daguerreotypes*, p. 65.
17. I. Dinesen, *Letters*, p. 5.
18. Wivel, *Romance*, p. 215.
19. Bjørnvig, *Pagten*, p. 25.
20. Interview with OW, Copenhagen, 1975.
21. I. Dinesen, *Letters*, p. 137.
22. Peter Beard, ed., *Longing for Darkness: Kamante's Tales from Out of Africa*, unpaginated.
23. *OA*, p. 22.
24. Beard, *Longing for Darkness*.
25. *OA*, p. 30.
26. Beard, *Longing for Darkness*.
27. *OA*, p. 35.
28. Beard, *Longing for Darkness*.
29. *OA*, p. 36.
30. I. Dinesen, *Letters*, p. 40.
31. Ibid.
32. Beard, *Longing for Darkness*.
33. I. Dinesen, *Letters*, p. 140.
34. K. Blixen, *Breve*, vol. 1, p. 183; I. Dinesen, *Letters*, p. 141.
35. *OA*, p. 33.
36. *SGT*, p. 277.
37. Interview, Copenhagen, July 1975.
38. Interview with IL, London, 1976.
39. Interview with Remy Martin, Nairobi, 1975.
40. *OA*, p. 67.
41. Ibid., p. 72.
42. I. Dinesen, *Letters*, p. 362.
43. *SG*, p. 122.
44. *SG*, p. 129.
45. Trzebinski, *Silence Will Speak*, p. 58.
46. K. Blixen, *Breve*, vol. 1, p. 195; I. Dinesen, *Letters*, p. 152.
47. Huxley, *Lord Delamere and the Making of Kenya*, vol. 2, p. 282.
48. *OA*, pp. 159–169.
49. Ibid., p. 207.

50. Ibid., p. 359.
51. *See* I. Dinesen, *Letters*, p. 221. My information on syphilis, and on Karen Blixen's case, has come primarily from interviews with Dr. Mogens Fog in Copenhagen, Dr. Duncan MacDonald in London, from Dr. Fog's essay on Karen Blixen's medical history ("Karen Blixens Sygdomshistorie," *Blixeniana 1978; see* ch. XIX, n. 12), and from R. D. Catterall's *A Short Textbook of Venereology* (*see* ch. XIX, n. 13) pp. 87–153.
52. I. Dinesen, *Letters*, p. 160.

25.   A LOVE OF PARALLELS

1. *OA*, p. 225.
2. *SGT*, p. 387.
3. Otto Fenichel, *The Psychoanalytic Theory of Neurosis*, p. 44.
4. *OA*, p. 157.
5. Interview with IL, London, 1975.
6. T. Dinesen, *My Sister*, p. 102.
7. *Tales from the Thousand and One Nights*, trans. N. J. Dawood, p. 21.
8. I. Dinesen, *Letters*, p. 216.
9. K. Blixen, *Breve*, vol. 1, p. 193; I. Dinesen, *Letters*, p. 150.
10. K. Blixen, *Breve*, vol. 1, p. 218; I. Dinesen, *Letters*, pp. 180–181.

26.   NATURE AND THE IDEAL

1. T. Dinesen, *My Sister*, p. 84.
2. Ibid., p. 85.
3. K. Blixen, *Breve*, vol. 1, p. 221; I. Dinesen, *Letters*, p. 174.
4. Interview with Rose Cartwright, Limuru, 1975.
5. *OA*, p. 214.
6. I. Dinesen, *Letters*, p. 214.
7. Karen Blizen, "Om Natur og Ideal." I discovered this essay in the *dubia* file of Karen Blixen's archives, and supplied the evidence necessary to attribute it positively. It has been published as "Moderne Ægteskab og Andre Betragtninger" [Modern marriage and other observations] in *Blixeniana 1977*.
8. T. Dinesen, *My Sister*, p. 86.
9. *SG*, p. 147.
10. *OA*, p. 135.
11. K. Blixen, *Breve*, vol. 1, p. 252; I. Dinesen, *Letters*, p. 202.
12. I. Dinesen, *Letters*, pp. 187–191.
13. Ibid., p. 194.
14. Interview with Rose Cartwright, Limuru, 1975.
15. Interviews with Ulf Aschan, Sir Charles Markham, and Beryl Markham, Nairobi, 1975.
16. *SGT*, p. 81.
17. I. Dinesen, *Letters*, p. 193.
18. I. Dinesen, *Carnival*, p. 62.
19. *SGT*, p. 63.
20. Interview with IL, Philadelphia, 1976.
21. Interview with IL, England, 1976.
22. Interview with Sir Charles Markham, Nairobi, 1975.
23. Interview with IL, England, 1976.
24. K. Blixen, *Breve*, vol. 2, p. 60; I. Dinesen, *Letters*, p. 274.
25. DFH to KB, 19 March (1924?), KBA 15/F.
26. I. Dinesen, *Letters*, p. 218.
27. "Udenfor Tiden," KBA 117 III A 5, notebooks 1–4, 5–8. It includes a brief outline for chapters on: Masai history, Masai morality, relations with the whites, and "Epos."
28. KBA 121, III B 2 a.
29. Benjamin, "The Storyteller," p. 94.
30. I. Dinesen, *Letters*, p. 212.
31. Ibid., p. 428.

32. Ibid., pp. 202–210.
33. Migel, *Titania*, p. 77.
34. KBA 117, III A 3g, 15.

27. HOLDING OUT

1. *SGT*, p. 101.
2. Interview with TD, Leerbæk, Vejle, 1976.
3. I. Dinesen, *Letters*, p. 279.
4. K. Blixen, *Breve*, vol. 2, p. 67; I. Dinesen, *Letters*, p. 280.
5. Kabell, *Karen Blixen debuterer*, p. 86.
6. Sven Møller Kristensen, "Karen Blixen og Georg Brandes," *Politiken* (Copenhagen), 17 June 1981.
7. Kabell, p. 87.
8. Karen Blixen, *The Revenge of Truth*, trans. Donald Hannah, appendix to: Donald Hannah, *"Isak Dinesen" and Karen Blixen: The Mask and the Reality*, p. 201.
9. T. Dinesen, *My Sister*, p. 92.
10. Ibid., p. 93.
11. I. Dinesen, *Letters*, p. 242.
12. Ibid., pp. 240–241.
13. Ibid., p. 255.
14. *OA*, p. 225.
15. I. Dinesen, *Letters*, p. 223.
16. Ibid., p. 249.
17. T. Dinesen, *My Sister*, p. 98.
18. DFH to KB, 21 May 1926, KBA 15/F.
19. KB to DFH (in her handwriting, on the back of his telegram), KBA 15/F.
20. DFH to KB, 15 June 1926.
21. DFH to KB, 12 September 1926.
22. I. Dinesen, *Letters*, p. 286.
23. Ibid., pp. 259–265.
24. T. Dinesen, *My Sister*, p. 104.

28. A RELEASE FROM SELF

1. T. Dinesen, *My Sister*, p. 108.
2. Benjamin, "The Storyteller," p. 108.
3. I. Dinesen, *Carnival*, pp. 67–68.
4. Ibid., p. 67.
5. Ibid., p. 65.
6. Ibid., p. 95.
7. Ibid., p. 77.
8. Ibid., p. 60.
9. I. Dinesen, *Letters*, p. 382.
10. Ibid., p. 294.
11. *OA*, p. 63.
12. KB to MBW, KBA 67.
13. DFH to KB, 12 September 1926, KBA 15/F.
14. *OA*, pp. 345–346.
15. T. Dinesen, *My Sister*, p. 111.

29. LION HUNT

1. Trzebinski, *Silence Will Speak*, p. 230.
2. *OA*, p. 209.
3. Interview with IL, England, 1976.
4. *OA*, p. 7.
5. K. Blixen, *Breve*, vol. 2, p. 104; I. Dinesen, *Letters*, p. 312.

6. Trzebinski, *Silence Will Speak*, p. 248.
7. *SG*, p. 58.
8. Ibid.
9. I. Dinesen, *Letters*, pp. 304–309.
10. Ibid., p. 351.
11. Ibid., p. 326.
12. *OA*, p. 229.
13. I. Dinesen, *Letters*, p. 333.
14. *OA*, p. 231.
15. Ibid., p. 230.
16. *SG*, p. 60.

30. VISITORS TO THE FARM

1. I. Dinesen, *Letters*, p. 334.
2. *OA*, p. 295.
3. I. Dinesen, *Letters*, p. 334.
4. Account of the de Janzé–de Trafford case from the *New York Times*, March 26–30, 1927; April 5, 9, 19, 20, 1927; June 19, 1927; December 15, 1927.
5. I. Dinesen, *Letters*, p. 339.
6. *OA*, p. 208.
7. I. Dinesen, *Letters*, p. 276.
8. Interview with TD, Leerbæk, Vejle, 1975.
9. *OA*, p. 377.
10. Ibid., p. 198.
11. *SGT*, p. 75.
12. I. Dinesen, *Letters*, p. 341.
13. *OA*, p. 172.
14. Ibid., p. 174.
15. I. Dinesen, *Letters*, p. 359.
16. Ibid., p. 360.
17. Ibid., p. 365.
18. Ibid.
19. *OA*, p. 233.
20. I. Dinesen, *Letters*, p. 368.
21. K. Blixen, *Breve*, vol. 2, p. 153; I. Dinesen, *Letters*, p. 356.
22. Ibid., p. 375.
23. *OA*, p. 261.
24. I. Dinesen, *Letters*, p. 343.
25. Ibid., p. 337.
26. Bror Blixen to KB, July 5, 1928, KBA 57/B.
27. Migel, *Titania*, p. 40.
28. *LT*, p. 253.
29. Trzebinski, *Silence Will Speak*, p. 182.
30. *SG*, p. 38.
31. I. Dinesen, *Letters*, p. 387.
32. Ibid.
33. Trzebinski, *Silence Will Speak*, p. 262.
34. Ibid., p. 266.
35. B. Blixen, *The African Hunter*, p. 160.
36. Trzebinski, *Silence Will Speak*, p. 270.

31. SPIRITS OF THE AIR

1. T. Dinesen, *My Sister*, p. 117.
2. KBA 76, C/149, Letter dated 21 October 1929.
3. Trzebinski, *Silence Will Speak*, p. 280.
4. Ibid., p. 281.

5. T. Dinesen, *My Sister,* p. 120.
6. I. Dinesen, *Letters,* p. 407.
7. Ibid., p. 413.
8. DFH to KB, undated, KBA 15/F.
9. DFH to KB, 11 May 1980, Trent, New Barnet, KBA 15/F.
10. Interview with Merwyn Cowie, Nairobi, September 1975.
11. Svendsen and Lasson, *Life and Destiny,* p. 130.
12. *OA,* pp. 238–239.
13. Ibid., p. 330.

32. CLOSING THE PARENTHESES
1. I. Dinesen, *Carnival,* p. 337.
2. DFH to KB, undated, KBA 15/F.
3. Interview with Remy Martin, Nairobi, 1975.
4. *OA,* p. 329.
5. Ibid., p. 338.
6. Percy Bysshe Shelley, from "Song": "Rarely, rarely comest thou, spirit of delight" (stanza 4).
7. *OA,* p. 32.
8. Ibid., p. 362.
9. DFH to KB, undated, KBA 15/F.
10. DFH to KB, undated.
11. T. Dinesen, *My Sister,* 122.
12. Ibid., p. 123.
13. I. Dinesen, *Letters,* xx.
14. Beryl Markham, *West with the Night,* p. 165.
15. Trzebinski, *Silence Will Speak,* p. 309.
16. Ibid., p. 310.
17. *OA,* p. 350.
18. Ibid., p. 351.
19. Interview with IL, England, 1976.
20. *OA,* p. 370.
21. Evangeline, Lady Northey, to KB, undated, KBA 37.
22. Bror Blixen to KB, undated, KBA 57.
23. *OA,* p. 388.

33. *AMOR FATI*
1. T. Dinesen, *My Sister,* p. 125.
2. Lasson and Svendsen, *Life and Destiny,* p. 138.
3. Joan, Lady Grigg, to KB, undated, 1931 (by kind permission of Lady Altrincham).
4. T. Dinesen, *My Sister,* p. 126.
5. Ibid., p. 126.
6. Ibid., passim.
7. Interview with Dr. Mogens Fog, Copenhagen, July 1976.
8. Interview with IM, Copenhagen, August 1976.
9. Migel, *Titania,* p. 137.
10. KBA 71 (Karen Blixen's medical records).
11. Bjørnvig, *Pagten,* p. 50.
12. Ibid.
13. Nietzsche, "Nietzsche Contra Wagner," *The Portable Nietzsche,* p. 680.
14. Migel, *Titania,* p. 91.
15. *SG,* p. 113.
16. Ibid.
17. *SGT,* p. 69.
18. Interviews with TD, Leerbæk, Vejle 1975–1976.
19. I. Dinesen, *Daguerreotypes,* p. 77.

20. Strode, "Isak Dinesen at Home," *Isak Dinesen: A Memorial,* ed. C. Svendsen, p. 103.
21. Ibid., p. 102.
22. Interview with IM, Copenhagen, 1975.
23. *SGT,* p. 52.
24. Hauser, *The Social History of Art,* vol. 2, p. 146.
25. Ibid.

34. *SEVEN GOTHIC TALES*

1. *SGT,* p. 98.
2. I. Dinesen, *Carnival,* p. 103.
3. Benjamin, "The Storyteller," p. 107.
4. Annamarie Cleeman, "Karen Blixen Fortæller," *Samleren,* Aargang 19, Nr. 2, October 1942, pp. 33–35.
5. Daniel Gillès, "La Pharoanne de Rungstedlund," *Isak Dinesen: A Memorial,* ed. C. Svendsen, p. 179.
6. Benjamin, "The Storyteller," p. 92.
7. *Politiken* (Copenhagen), 1 May 1934, p. 11.
8. Gillès, "La Pharoanne de Rungstedlund," p. 179.
9. *SGT,* pp. 278, 275.
10. Gillès, "La Pharoanne de Rungstedlund," p. 178.
11. KB to Johannes Rosendahl, 11 October 1944, KBA 43.
12. Langbaum, *Gayety,* p. 3.
13. Genesis, 21:6.
14. *Politiken* (Copenhagen), 1 May 1934, p. 12.
15. Langbaum, *Gayety,* p. 44.
16. *SGT,* p. 22.
17. Fenichel, *Psychoanalytic Theory of Neurosis,* p. 465 (emphasis added).
18. *SGT,* p. 277.
19. Ibid.
20. Charles Baudelaire, "Le Voyage," stanzas I and VIII, *Les Fleurs du Mal.*
21. Hauser, *The Social History of Art,* vol. 4, pp. 185–186.
22. Frederik Schyberg, "Syv Fantastiske Fortællinger," *Berlingske Tidende,* 25 September 1935, pp. 11–12.
23. Interview with Lady Altrincham, England, June 1976.
24. T. Dinesen, *My Sister,* p. 127.
25. Christian Elling, "Karen Blixen," *Danske Digtere i den Tyvende Aarhundrede* p. 527. "The Book-of-the-Month," writes Dr. Elling, is "America's literary *aerestitel* (title of honor)." His article about Karen Blixen was based on correspondence and a personal acquaintance with the author, as well as on his literary studies. She apparently supplied this bit of information.
26. KB to Jesper Ewald, 22 February 1935, KBA 66.
27. Karen Blixen, *Syv Fantastiske Fortællinger.*
28. Kabell, *Karen Blixen debuterer,* p. 95.
29. Ibid., p. 95.
30. KB to Lady Daphne Finch Hatton, 14 January 1935, KBA 67.

35. IN A DARK WOOD

1. *Politiken* (Copenhagen), 10 September 1934.
2. *WT,* p. 2.
3. *SGT,* pp. 20–21.
4. Notes for a speech to the Danish Women's Citizen's Society *(Dansk Kvindesamfund),* dated 9 November 1938, KBA 152, III B4.
5. MrsD to KB, 23 April 1935, KBA 58.
6. MrsD to KB, 24 September 1935, KBA 58.
7. TD to KB, 16 May 1935, KBA 58.
8. Alexander Rudhart, *Twentieth Century Europe,* p. 506.

9. Ibid., p. 508.
10. Migel, *Titania*, p. 103.
11. My material on Moura Budberg comes primarily from Lovat Dickson, *H. G. Wells: His Turbulent Life and Times*, pp. 283–304.
12. Migel, *Titania*, p. 104.
13. Ibid.
14. Strode, "A Visit with Isak Dinesen," *Isak Dinesen: A Memorial*, ed. C. Svendsen, p. 106.
15. Migel, *Titania*, p. 105.
16. KB to Knud Dahl, 1 December 1935, KBA 70.
17. Knud Dahl to KB, 22 December 1935, KBA 70.
18. TD to Knud Dahl, 26 April 1937, KBA 70.
19. Knud Dahl to KB, 3 May 1937, KBA 70.
20. Lasson and Svendsen, *Life and Destiny*, p. 144.
21. Bror Blixen to KB, 23 January 1936, KBA 57.
22. Migel, *Titania*, p. 107.
23. Interview with Cockie Hoogterp, England, June 1975.
24. *Politiken* (Copenhagen), 10 September 1934.
25. Langbaum, *Gayety*, p. 120.

36. *OUT OF AFRICA*

1. K. Blixen, *Breve*, vol. 2, p. 223; I. Dinesen, *Letters*, p. 417. (See also *Breve*, vol. 2, pp. 56, 96; *Letters*, pp. 267, 305.)
2. *OA*, p. 7.
3. Ibid., p. 15.
4. Manuscript notes for *Out of Africa*, KBA 171.
5. *OA*, p. 261.
6. Curtis Cate, "A Talk with Isak Dinesen," *Isak Dinesen: A Memorial*, ed. C. Svendsen, p. 144.
7. *OA*, p. 235.
8. K. Blixen, *Breve*, vol 2, p. 57; I. Dinesen, *Letters*, p. 271.
9. K. Blixen, *Breve*, vol. 2, p. 67; I. Dinesen, *Letters*, p. 280.
10. K. Blixen, *Breve*, vol. 2, p. 22; I. Dinesen, *Letters*, p. 242.
11. Langbaum, *Gayety*, p. 119.
12. Ibid., p. 125.
13. I. Dinesen, *Carnival*, p. 175.
14. *OA*, p. 386.
15. *SGT*, p. 64.
16. KB to Fru Ulla Pedersen (her stenographer), 2 April 1938, KBA 67.
17. Migel, *Titania*, p. 113.
18. KB to RH, 23 August 1937.
19. Langbaum, *Gayety*, p. 155.
20. KB to RH, 6 February 1938.
21. Ibid.
22. Karen Sass (Aunt Lidda) to KB, 14 June 1938, KBA 59.
23. Migel, *Titania*, p. 115.
24. Aage Henriksen, *Det Guddommelige Barn og Andre Essays om Karen Blixen*, p. 104.
25. I. Dinesen, *Daguerreotypes*, p. 223.
26. KB to Mr. Bryan, 21 July 39, from the Robert Haas Correspondence.
27. Wivel, *Romance*, p. 75.
28. K. Blixen, *Essays*, p. 119; I. Dinesen, *Daguerreotypes*, p. 89.
29. Ibid.
30. Lilian von Rosen to KB, 20 September 1938, KBA 59.
31. I. Dinesen, *Daguerreotypes*, p. 90.
32. Ibid., p. 91.
33. Ibid., p. 92.
34. K. Blixen, *Essays*, p. 134; I. Dinesen, *Daguerreotypes*, p. 105.

37. *WINTER'S TALES*

1. Steen Eiler Rasmussen, "Karen Blixens Rungstedlund," *Det Danske Akademi,* p. 83.
2. Lasson and Svendsen, *Life and Destiny,* p. 124.
3. *WT,* p. 5.
4. See below, p. 312.
5. *WT,* p. 20.
6. Ibid., p. 235.
7. Ibid., p. 247.
8. Benjamin, "The Storyteller," p. 102.
9. Migel, *Titania,* p. 122.
10. *SG,* p. 132.
11. Interview with SER, Rungsted, July 1975.
12. Strode, "Isak Dinesen at Home," *Isak Dinesen: A Memorial,* ed. C. Svendsen, p. 110.
13. Interview with Dr. Vibeke Funch, Rungsted, August 1976.
14. KB to Christian Elling, undated, KBA 66.
15. I. Dinesen, *Essays,* p. 254; *Daguerreotypes,* p. 125.
16. Interview with SER, Rungsted, July 1975.
17. *WT,* p. 123.
18. Langbaum, *Gayety,* p. 163.
19. Richard Petrow, *The Bitter Years: The Invasion and Occupation of Denmark and Norway, April 1940–May 1945* (hereafter cited as *The Bitter Years*), p. 170. My account of the Occupation comes primarily, although not exclusively, from this source.
20. Ibid., p. 208.
21. Ibid., p. 212.
22. Migel, *Titania,* p. 129.
23. Ibid., p. 130.
24. Petrow, *The Bitter Years,* p. 178.
25. Ibid., p. 220.

38. LIFE IN A CAGE

1. Migel, *Titania,* p. 132.
2. KB to Birthe Andrup, 31 November 1944. From the archives of Ms. Andrup, and by her kind permission.
3. Migel, *Titania,* p. 132.
4. CS to KB, 1 November 1943, KBA 48.
5. Svendsen, *Notater,* p. 18.
6. Ibid., p. 19.
7. Ibid.
8. Ibid., p. 20.
9. Ibid., p. 23.
10. Migel, *Titania,* p. 136.
11. Truman Capote, *Observations,* p. 143.
12. Svendsen, *Notater,* p. 25.
13. CS to KB, 18 December 1944, KBA 48.
14. Migel, *Titania,* p. 140.
15. Wivel, *Romance,* p. 194.
16. Ibid., p. 117.
17. Ibid.
18. Ibid., p. 118.
19. Ibid., p. 119.

39. HERETICS

1. W. Glynn Jones, *Denmark,* p. 180.
2. Migel, *Titania,* p. 141.
3. Wivel, *Romance,* p. 143.
4. Fog, "Karen Blixens Sygdomshistorie," *Blixeniana 1978,* p. 145.

5. Interview with Winston Guest, New York City, 1975.
6. ED to KB, May 1946, KBA 57.
7. KB to RH, 16 February 1946.
8. RH to KB, 20 February 1946.
9. KB to RH, 9 March 1946.
10. KB to Ulla Pedersen, 20 November 1947, KBA 67.
11. Interview with Dr. Vibeke Funch, Rungsted, August 1976.
12. KB to RH, 23 July 1947.
13. Migel, *Titania,* p. 137.
14. KB to RH, 23 July 1947.
15. Wivel, *Romance,* p. 143.
16. Interview with OW, Copenhagen, August 1975.
17. Wivel, *Romance,* pp. 153–154.
18. Ibid., p. 154.
19. Bjørnvig, *Pagten,* p. 89.
20. Wivel, *Romance,* p. 155.
21. Ibid., p. 157.
22. Martin A. Hansen, "Introduction," *Against the Wind,* trans. and ed. H. Wayne Schow,
    p. 1.
23. Ibid., p. 3.
24. Ibid., p. 5.
25. Ibid.
26. Jørgen Claudi, *Contemporary Danish Authors,* trans. Jørgen Andersen and Aubrey Rush,
    p. 138.
27. Hansen, "Introduction," *Against the Wind,* p. 7.
28. See footnote, p. 320.
29. Bjørnvig, *Pagten,* pp. 77–78.
30. Wivel, *Romance,* p. 165.
31. Ibid., p. 164.
32. Ibid.
33. Ibid., p. 163.
34. OW to KB, November 1947, KBA 60.
35. Wivel, *Romance,* p. 170.
36. Svendsen, *Notater,* p. 39.
37. TB to KB, 9 March 1948, KBA 61.
38. Bjørnvig, *Pagten,* p. 12.

40. DEATH OF A CENTAUR

1. Interview with CS, Dragør July 1976.
2. Caroline Carlsen, "Erindringer om Karen Blixen, fortalt til Frans Lasson," *Blixeniana 1976,* eds. Hans Andersen and Frans Lasson, p. 15.
3. Ibid., p. 16.
4. Ibid., p. 33.
5. Svendsen, *Notater,* p. 45.
6. *AD,* p. 58.
7. *SGT,* p. 292.
8. Bjørnvig, *Pagten,* p. 25.
9. Interview with OW, Copenhagen, August 1975.
10. I. Dinesen, *Daguerreotypes,* p. 188.
11. Ibid., p. 177.

41. *FOLIE À DEUX*

1. TB to KB, 2 March 1949.
2. Bjørnvig, *Pagten,* p. 12.
3. Ibid., p. 13.
4. Ibid.

5. Ibid., p. 94.
6. Ibid., p. 14.
7. Interview with Dr. Fog, Copenhagen, July 1976.
8. Bjørnvig, *Pagten,* p. 15.
9. Ibid., p. 19.
10. Migel, *Titania,* p. 198.
11. Ibid., pp. 185–186.
12. Bjørnvig, *Pagten,* p. 24.
13. Ibid.
14. Ibid., p. 25.
15. Ibid., p. 29.
16. Ibid., p. 32.
17. Ibid., p. 36.
18. Ibid., p. 39.
19. Ibid., p. 40.
20. Ibid., p. 86.
21. Interview with OW, Copenhagen, August 1975; Bjørnvig, *Pagten,* p. 78.
22. Bjørnvig, *Pagten,* p. 114.
23. KB to CS, 25 October 1950, KBA 67.
24. Bjørnvig, *Pagten,* pp. 100–101.
25. Svendsen, *Notater,* p. 70.
26. Interview with Jonna Dinesen (Mrs. Thomas Dinesen), Leerbæk, July 1976.
27. TD to KB, 18 June 1950, KBA 61.
28. Interview with IM, Copenhagen, 1976.
29. Ibid.
30. Ibid.
31. Ibid.
32. Bjørnvig, *Pagten,* p. 46.
33. Ibid., p. 47.

42. GODDESS AND BARFLY

1. I. Dinesen, *Daguerreotypes,* p. 18.
2. Ibid., p. 80.
3. Glenway Wescott, "Isak Dinesen, the Storyteller," *Images of Truth,* p. 162.
4. Interview with SER, Copenhagen, 1975.
5. Interview with OW, Copenhagen, 1975.
6. Interview with Bent Mohn, Copenhagen, July 1975.
7. Bjørnvig, *Pagten,* p. 52.
8. Nancy Wilson Ross, "A Remembrance of Karen Blixen," *Isak Dinesen: A Memorial,* ed. C. Svendsen, p. 42.
9. KB to Christian Banck, 12 September 1958, KBA 66.
10. Bjørnvig, *Pagten,* p. 59.
11. Ibid., p. 56.
12. Aage Henriksen, "Portræt," *Guddommelige Barn,* p. 79.
13. Bjørnvig, *Pagten,* p. 54.
14. Interview with Bent Mohn, 1975.
15. Interview with Erik Kopp, Copenhagen, July 1975.
16. Ibid.
17. Ibid.
18. Bjørnvig, *Pagten,* p. 66.
19. Ibid, p. 67.
20. Søren Kierkegaard, "The Seducer's Diary," *Either/Or,* vol. 1, trans. David F. Swensen and Lillian Marvin Swenson, p. 356.
21. Bjørnvig, *Pagten,* p. 71.
22. Svendsen, *Notater,* p. 65.
23. Bjørnvig, *Pagten,* p. 124.

24. Svendsen, *Notater*, p. 96.
25. Ibid., p. 61.

43.   "THE IMMORTAL STORY"

1. *AD*, p. 165.
2. Ibid., pp. 202–203.
3. Henriksen, "Portræt," *Guddommelige Barn*, p. 72.
4. Bjørnvig, *Pagten*, p. 94.
5. Ibid., p. 97.
6. Ibid., p. 90.
7. Ibid., pp. 104–105.
8. Langbaum, *Gayety*, p. 215.
9. *LT*, p. 325.
10. Bjørnvig, *Pagten*, p. 109.

44.   THE PACT IS BROKEN

1. Gillès, "La Pharoanne de Rungstedlund," *Isak Dinesen: A Memorial*, ed. C. Svendsen, p. 180.
2. Interview with Dr. Fog, 1976.
3. *LT*, p. 87.
4. Ibid., p. 78.
5. Langbaum, *Gayety*, p. 215.
6. *LT*, p. 93.
7. Ibid., pp. 87–88.
8. Bjørnvig, *Pagten*, p. 122.
9. Svendsen, *Notater*, p. 79.
10. Ibid., p. 80.
11. Bjørnvig, *Pagten*, p. 127.
12. Ibid., pp. 128–129.
13. Migel, *Titania*, p. 155.
14. Bjørnvig, *Pagten*, p. 135.
15. Ibid., p. 141.
16. Ibid., p. 147.
17. Ibid., p. 146.
18. Interview with OW, 1975.
19. Wivel, *Romance*, p. 216.
20. Bjørnvig, *Pagten*, p. 52.
21. Ibid.

45.   BETRAYALS

1. K. Blixen, *Osceola*, p. 22.
2. KB to John Gosning, 8 May 1954.
3. Langbaum, *Gayety*, p. 210.
4. Svendsen, *Notater*, p. 88.
5. Ibid., p. 89.
6. Wivel, *Romance*, p. 93.
7. KB to Johannes Rosendahl, 15 January 1952, KBA 67.
8. Langbaum, *Gayety*, p. 208.
9. Bjørnvig, *Pagten*, p. 134.
10. KB to RH, 29 May 1953.
11. Correspondence of Jørgen Gustava Brandt and KB, May through July 1953, KBA 160.
12. Svendsen, *Notater*, p. 90.
13. KB to RH, 25 October 1953.
14. KB to RH, 9 November 1953.
15. Bjørnvig, *Pagten*, p. 62.

16. Ibid., p. 61.
17. Kelvin Lindemann to KB, undated, KBA 31.
18. Bjørnvig, *Pagten,* p. 61.
19. Migel, *Titania,* p. 176.
20. Svendsen, *Notater,* p. 91.

46.   SHOULD NOT MY MIND KEEP THE KNOTS?

1. Correspondence of Aage Henriksen and KB, July through October 1954, KBA 22.
2. *Politiken* (Copenhagen), 24 September 1967, p. 41.
3. Henriksen, "Karen Blixen og Marionetterne," *Guddommelige Barn,* p. 9.
4. KB to Johannes Rosendahl, 10 November 1944, KBA 43.
5. Thomas Mann, "Freud and the Future," *Essays of Three Decades,* trans. H. T. Lowe-Porter, p. 197.
6. *WT,* pp. 240–241.
7. Migel, *Titania,* p. 174.
8. Henriksen, "Budbringersken," *Guddommelige Barn,* p. 66.
9. *Politiken* (Copenhagen), 24 September 1967.
10. Henriksen, "Budbringersken," *Guddommelige Barn,* p. 69.
11. Ibid., p. 67.
12. Henriksen, "Portræt," *Guddommelige Barn,* pp. 101–102.
13. Interview with OW, Copenhagen, 1975.
14. Henriksen, "Karen Blixen og Marionetterne," *Guddommelige Barn,* p. 32.
15. Gillès, "La Pharoanne de Rungstedlund," *Isak Dinesen: A Memorial,* ed. C. Svendsen, p. 174.
16. KB to Ernest Hemingway, 1 November 1954, KBA 66.
17. Bjørnvig, *Pagten,* p. 149.
18. KB to Count Eduard Reventlow, 20 December 1955, from the archives of Count Christian Reventlow, and by his kind permission.
19. Ibid., p. 107.
20. *LT,* p. 214.
21. *OA,* p. 386.

47.   *BAKSHEESH*

1. Migel, *Titania,* p. 192.
2. Ibid.
3. Svendsen, *Notater,* p. 110.
4. Ibid., p. 111.
5. Migel, *Titania,* p. 192.
6. KB to Eugene Walter, 8 June 1956, KBA 67.
7. Svendsen, *Notater,* p. 114.
8. KB to Philip Ingerslev, 13 January 1958, KBA 66.
9. KB to Aage Kabell, 29 April 1958, KBA 66.
10. Correspondence of KB and Parmenia Migel, August 1956 through October 1957, KBA 14, 66.
11. Hannah Arendt, "Isak Dinesen, 1885–1962," *Men in Dark Times,* p. 99.
12. W. Jackson Bate, *Samuel Johnson* (New York: Harcourt Brace Jovanovich, 1975), p. 198.

48.   ECHOES

1. KB to TB, 7 June 1955, KBA 66.
2. Svendsen, *Notater,* p. 116.
3. *LT,* p. 189.
4. Ibid., p. 190.
5. Langbaum, *Gayety,* p. 225.
6. KB to Aage Kabell, 9 April 1958, KBA 66.
7. Bjørnvig, *Pagten,* p. 160.

8. TD to KB, 28 November 1959, KBA 61.
9. KB to Philip Ingerslev, 5 January 1958, KBA 66.
10. Langbaum, *Gayety*, p. 202.
11. KB to RH, 25 September 1956.
12. Wescott, *Images of Truth*, p. 162.
13. KB to RH, 8 May 1957.
14. Bjørnvig, *Pagten*, p. 78.
15. *LT*, p. 263.
16. KB to RH, 8 May 1957.
17. Langbaum, *Gayety*, p. 236.
18. *LT*, p. 261.
19. TD to KB, 30 June 1957, KBA 61.
20. TD to KB, 21 March 1957, KBA 61.
21. TD to KB, 29 June 1960, KBA 61.
22. KB to RH, 23 August 1957.
23. Ibid.
24. Migel, *Titania*, p. 199.
25. Svendsen, *Notater*, p. 125.
26. Langbaum, *Gayety*, p. 203.
27. Migel, *Titania*, p. 197.
28. Ibid., p. 179.
29. Interview with Nieves de Madariaga, Cortona, 1978.
30. Migel, *Titania*, p. 200.
31. *LT*, p. 297.
32. Rasmussen, *Det Danske Akademi*, p. 254.
33. Svendsen, *Notater*, p. 128.

49. "TEMPESTS"

1. KB to Philip Ingerslev, 13 January 1958, KBA 66.
2. KB to Hugh Pooley, KBA 67.
3. *AD*, p. 85.
4. Ibid., p. 88.
5. Ibid., p. 99.
6. Ibid., p. 109.
7. Langbaum, *Gayety*, p. 258.
8. *AD*, pp. 147–148.
9. Ibid., p. 140.
10. Ibid., p. 146.
11. *WT*, p. 172.

50. ISAK DINESEN IN AMERICA

1. Svendsen, *Notater*, p. 130.
2. KB to Eugene Walter, 22 March 1958, KBA 67.
3. Paul von Lettow Vorbeck to KB, 27 November 1960, KBA 31.
4. KB to IL, 18 June 1958, from the archives of Mrs. Lindström and with her kind permission.
5. Lasson and Svendsen, *Life and Destiny*, p. 195.
6. Migel, *Titania*, p. 215.
7. Interview with Erik Kopp, Copenhagen 1975.
8. Ibid.
9. Dr. Alvin C. Eurich to KB, 2 May 1958, from the Haas correspondence.
10. Svendsen, *Notater*, p. 143.
11. Ibid., p. 145.
12. Langbaum, *Gayety*, p. 203.
13. Wescott, *Images of Truth*, p. 151.
14. Svendsen, *Notater*, p. 150.

15. I. Dinesen, *Daguerreotypes,* pp. 4–9.
16. Ibid., pp. 9–12.
17. Svendsen, *Notater,* p. 153.
18. Carson McCullers, "Isak Dinesen: In Praise of Radiance," *Isak Dinesen: A Memorial,* ed. C. Svendsen, p. 36.
19. Svendsen, *Notater,* p. 153.
20. Carson McCullers, "In Praise of Radiance," p. 37.
21. Virginia Spencer Carr, *The Lonely Hunter: A Biography of Carson McCullers,* (Garden City, N.Y.: Doubleday, 1975), p. 479.
22. Ibid.
23. Ibid., p. 480.
24. Svendsen, *Notater,* p. 154.
25. KB to Fleur Cowles, 21 February 1961, KBA 66.
26. Leo Lerman, "A Little Album, Tania," *Isak Dinesen: A Memorial,* ed. C. Svendsen, p. 50.
27. Svendsen, *Notater,* p. 131.
28. Nancy Wilson Ross, "A Remembrance of Karen Blixen," *Isak Dinsen: A Memorial,* ed. C. Svendsen, p. 40.
29. Migel, *Titania,* p. 231.
30. Correspondence of Dr. Henry Aranow and Dr. Samuel Standard, KBA 71.

51. HOMELESS

1. Svendsen, *Notater,* pp. 81–82.
2. Ibid.
3. Ibid.
4. Ibid., p. 83.
5. Migel, *Titania,* p. 233.
6. *Politiken* (Copenhagen), 24 September 1967, p. 41.
7. Migel, *Titania,* p. 261.
8. Ibid., p. 263.
9. Correspondence of KB and Viggo Kjær Petersen, January 1961–August 1962.
10. Svendsen, *Notater,* p. 166.
11. Langbaum, *Gayety,* p. 154.
12. KB to RH, 2 August 1960.
13. Interview with IM, Copenhagen, 1976.
14. Ibid.
15. Svendsen, *Notater,* p. 168.
16. Ibid., p. 173.
17. Ibid., p. 171.
18. Ibid., p. 173.
19. Ibid., p. 174.

52. WINGS

1. Karen Blixen, *The Revenge of Truth,* appendix to Donald Hannah, *"Isak Dinesen" and Karen Blixen,* p. 201.
2. KB to Gustaf Blixen-Finecke, 3 March 1961, KBA 57.
3. KB to Baron Philippe de Rothschild, 17 November 1960, KBA 67.
4. Migel, *Titania,* p. 269.
5. Svendsen, *Notater,* p. 183.
6. John Gielgud, "Karen Blixen," *Isak Dinsen: A Memorial,* ed. C. Svendsen, p. 23.
7. Migel, *Titania,* p. 256.
8. Svendsen, *Notater,* p. 185.
9. Ibid.
10. Ibid., p. 191.
11. I. Dinesen, *Carnival,* p. 338.
12. Svendsen, *Notater,* p. 191.

13. Monica Stirling, "Lions and Hearts," *Isak Dinesen: A Memorial,* ed. C. Svendsen, p. 190.
14. Svendsen, *Notater,* p. 194.
15. KB to Violet Trefusis, KBA 67/T.
16. Langbaum, *Gayety,* p. 204.
17. Interview with Dr. Mogens Fog, Copenhagen, July 1976.
18. *OA,* p. 379.

Works by Isak Dinesen

This list is limited to works in English and Danish. For all foreign editions consult the catalogue of the Royal Library in Copenhagen.

BOOKS

Dinesen, Isak. *Seven Gothic Tales.* New York: Harrison Smith and Robert Haas, 1934. London: Putnam, 1934.

Dinesen, Isak. *Syv fantastiske Fortællinger.* Copenhagen: Reitzels, 1935.

Dinesen, Isak. *Out of Africa.* London: Putnam, 1937; New York: Random House, 1938.

Blixen, Karen. *Den afrikanske Farm.* Copenhagen: Gyldendal, 1937.

Dinesen, Isak. *Winter's Tales.* New York: Random House; London: Putnam, 1942.

Blixen, Karen. *Vinter Eventyr.* Copenhagen: Gyldendal, 1942.

Blixen, Karen, [Pierre Andrézel] *Gengældelsens Veje.* Translated into Danish by Clara Svendsen [sic]. Copenhagen: Gyldendal, 1944.

Dinesen, Isak. *Last Tales.* New York: Random House; London: Putnam, 1957.

Blixen, Karen. *Sidste Fortællinger.* Copenhagen: Gyldendal, 1957.

Dinesen, Isak. *Anecdotes of Destiny.* New York: Random House; London: Michael Joseph, 1958.

Blixen, Karen. *Skæbne Anekdoter.* Copenhagen: Gyldendal, 1958.

Blixen, Karen. *Skygger paa Græsset.* Copenhagen: Gyldendal, 1960.

Dinesen, Isak. *Shadows on the Grass.* New York: Random House; London: Michael Joseph, 1961.

Blixen, Karen [Osceola]. *Osceola.* Edited by Clara Svendsen. Copenhagen: Gyldendal, Julebog ed., 1962.

Dinesen, Isak. *Ehrengard.* New York: Random House; London: Michael Joseph, 1963.

Blixen, Karen. *Ehrengard.* Translated into Danish by Clara Svendsen. Copenhagen: Gyldendal, 1963.

Blixen, Karen. *Essays.* Copenhagen: Gyldendal, 1965.

Blixen, Karen. *Karen Blixens Tegninger: Med to Essays af Karen Blixen.* Edited by Frans Lasson. Copenhagen: Forening for Boghaandværk, 1969.

Blixen, Karen. *Efterladte Fortællinger.* Edited by Frans Lasson. Copenhagen: Gyldendal, 1975.

Dinesen, Isak. *Carnival: Entertainments and Posthumous Tales.* Chicago: University of Chicago Press, 1977.

Blixen, Karen. *Breve fra Africa: 1914–1931.* Edited by Frans Lasson. Copenhagen: Gyldendal, 1978.

Dinesen, Isak. *Daguerreotypes and Other Essays.* Translated by P. M. Mitchell and W. D. Paden. Chicago: University of Chicago Press, 1979.

Dinesen, Isak. *Letters from Africa: 1914–1931.* Edited by Frans Lasson. Translated by Anne Born. Chicago: University of Chicago Press, 1981.

ESSAYS, BOOKLETS, MAGAZINE PUBLICATIONS

Blixen, Karen, [Osceola]. "Eneboerne." *Tilskueren,* August 1907, pp. 609–35.

[Osceola]. "Pløjeren." *Gads Danske Magasin,* October 1907, pp. 50–59.

[Osceola]. "Familien de Cats." *Tilskueren,* January 1909, pp. 1–19.

Blixen-Finecke, Karen. "Ex Africa" [poem]. *Tilskueren,* April 1925, pp. 244–46. *Berlingske Sondags Magasin,* 6 December 1942 pp. 1–2.

Blixen-Finecke, Karen. "Sandhedens Hævn: En Marionetkomedie." *Tilskueren,* May 1926, pp. 329–44; published as a booklet, Copenhagen: Gyldendal, 1960.

Blixen-Finecke, Karen. *The Revenge of Truth.* Translated by Donald Hannah in the appendix to his book, *"Isak Dinesen" and Karen Blixen: The Mask and the Reality.* New York: Random House, 1971.

Dinesen, Isak. "Karyatiderne: En ufuldendt fantastisk Fortælling." *Tilskueren,* April 1938; "The Caryatids: An Unfinished Gothic Tale." *Ladies' Home Journal,* November 1957.

Blixen, Karen. "Om Retskrivning." Copenhagen: *Politiken,* March 23–24, 1938; published as a booklet, Copenhagen: Gyldendal, 1949.

Dinesen, Isak. "Sorrow Acre." *Ladies' Home Journal,* May 1943.

Blixen, Karen. "Breve fra et Land i Krig." *Heretica* 1 (1948): 264–87; 332–55.

Dinesen, Isak. "The Uncertain Heiress." *Saturday Evening Post,* 10 December 1949.

Blixen, Karen. *Farah.* Copenhagen: Wivel, 1950.

Dinesen, Isak. "Babette's Feast." *Ladies' Home Journal,* June 1950.

Dinesen, Isak. "The Ring." *Ladies' Home Journal,* July 1950; *Harper's Bazaar,* October 1958.

Blixen, Karen. "Hartvig Frisch som Nabo." *Hartvig Frisch.* Copenhagen: Fremad, 1950.

Blixen, Karen. *Daguerreotypier.* Copenhagen: Gyldendal, 1951.

Dinesen, Isak. "The Ghost Horses." *Ladies' Home Journal,* October 1951.

Blixen, Karen. *Kardinalens Tredie Historie.* Illustrated by Erik Clemmesen. Copenhagen: Gyldendal, 1952.

Blixen, Karen. "Omkring den nye Lov om Dyreforsøg." Copenhagen: *Politiken,* 1952.

Blixen, Karen. "Samtale om Natten i København." *Heretica* 6 (1953): 465–94.

Dinesen, Isak. "The Immortal Story." *Ladies' Home Journal,* February 1953.

Blixen, Karen. "En Baaltale med 14 Aars Forsinkelse." Copenhagen: Berlingske Forlag, 1953; *Det danske Magasin* 1 (1953): 65–82.

Blixen, Karen. "Dykkeren." *Vindrosen* 1 (1954): 400–414.

Dinesen, Isak. "The Cloak." *Ladies' Home Journal,* May 1955.

Blixen, Karen. *Spøgelseshestene.* Copenhagen: Fremad, 1955.

Blixen, Karen. *Babettes Gæstebud.* Copenhagen: Fremad, 1955.

Blixen, Karen. Review of *Denmark,* by Sacheverell Sitwell. *Sunday Times* of London, 6 May 1956.

Dinesen, Isak. "A Country Tale." *Botteghe Oscure* 19 (1957): 367–417; *Ladies' Home Journal,* March 1960.

Dinesen, Isak. "Echoes." *Atlantic Monthly,* November 1957.

Dinesen, Isak. "The Nobleman's Wife." *Harper's Bazaar,* November 1957.

Blixen, Karen. "Den store Gestus." *Alt for Damerne,* no. 51 (1957), pp. 10–14.

Blixen, Karen. "H.C. Branner: Rytteren." *Bazar,* April 1958: 50–63; May: 71–94.

Dinesen, Isak. "The Wine of the Tetrarch." *Atlantic Monthly,* December 1959.

Dinesen, Isak. "The Blue Eyes." *Ladies' Home Journal,* January 1960.

Dinesen, Isak. "Alexander and the Sybil" in "Isak Dinesen Tells a Tale," by Glenway Wescott. *Harper's,* March 1960.

Dinesen, Isak. "On Mottoes of My Life." *Proceedings of the American Academy of Arts and Letters and the National Institute of Arts and Letters,* Second Series, no. 10 (1960) New York.

Blixen, Karen. Introduction to *Holly,* by Truman Capote. Copenhagen: Gyldendal, 1960.

Dinesen, Isak. Introduction to *The Story of an African Farm,* by Olive Schreiner. New York: Limited Editions Club, 1961.

Blixen, Karen. Introduction to *Det genfundne Afrika,* by Basil Davidson. Copenhagen: Gyldendal, 1962.

Dinesen, Isak. Introduction to *Thumbelina and Other Fairy Tales,* by Hans Christian Andersen. New York and London: Macmillan, 1962.

Blixen, Karen. "Rungstedlund: En radiotale." *Hilsen til Otto Gelsted.* Aarhus: Sirius, 1958; "Tale of Rungstedlund." *Vogue,* November 1962.

Dinesen, Isak. "The Secret of Rosenbad." *Ladies' Home Journal,* December 1962.

Blixen, Karen; Salomonsen, Finn; and Larsen, Carl Syrach. *Karen Blixen og Fuglene.* Copenhagen: Rhodos, 1964.

Blixen, Karen. "Rungstedlunds Lyksalighed." *Det Danske Akademi 1960–67.* Copenhagen: Gads, 1967.

Blixen, Karen. "Det sidste Dag." Copenhagen: *Politiken,* March 26 and 30; 2 April 1972.

Blixen, Karen. "Moderne Ægteskab og Andre Betragtninger." *Blixeniana 1977.* Edited by Hans Andersen and Frans Lasson. Copenhagen: Karen Blixen Selskabet, 1977.

Blixen, Karen. "Sorte og Hvide i Africa," and "Foredrag ved den katolske Bazar i Moltkes Palae." 8 November 1942. *Blixeniana 1979,* Edited by Hans Andersen and Frans Lasson. Copenhagen: Karen Blixen Selskabet, 1979.

Selected Bibliography

For a complete, annotated bibliography of works by and about Isak Dinesen, see *Isak Dinesen: A Bibliography,* by Liselotte Henriksen. Chicago: University of Chicago Press, 1977.

Andersen, Hans. "Om Mama og Moster Bess." *Blixeniana 1979.* Edited by Hans Andersen and Frans Lasson, pp. 59–69. Copenhagen: Karen Blixen Selskabet, 1979.

Arendt, Hannah. "Isak Dinesen, 1885–1962." *Men in Dark Times.* New York: Harcourt Brace Jovanovich. 1968.

Arnold, Matthew. *Literature and Dogma.* New York: Macmillan Co., 1873.

Beard, Peter, ed. *Longing for Darkness: Kamante's Tales from Out of Africa.* New York: Harcourt Brace Jovanovich, 1975.

Benjamin, Walter. "The Storyteller: Reflections on the Works of Nicolai Leskov." *Illuminations.* Translated by Harry Zohn. Edited by Hannah Arendt. New York: Schocken Books, 1969.

Bjørnvig, Thorkild. *Pagten.* Copenhagen: Gyldendal, 1974.

———. *Udvalgte digte.* Copenhagen: Gyldendal, 1970.

Blixen-Finecke, Bror von. *The African Hunter.* London: Cassell & Co., 1937.

Bogan, Louise. "Isak Dinesen." *Selected Criticism.* New York: Noonday, 1955.

Brandes, Georg. *An Essay on Aristocratic Radicalism.* London, Macmillan, 1914.

———. *Main Currents in Nineteenth Century Literature.* Translated by Diana White and Mary Morison. London: William Heinemann, 1901.

———. "Wilhelm Dinesen." *Samlede Skrifter,* vol. 3 (1919), pp. 189–196.

———. *Uimodstaaelige Attende Aarhundrede i Frankrig.* Copenhagen: Gyldendal, 1924.

Brandt, Jørgen Gustava. "Et Essay om Karen Blixen". *Heretica* 6 (1953): 300–20.

Bredsdorff, Elias. *Den Store Nordisk Krig om Sexualmoralen.* Copenhagen: Gyldendal, 1973.

Brix, Hans. *Karen Blixens Eventyr.* Copenhagen: Gyldendal, 1949.

———. "Sandhedens Hævn Til Isak Dinesen: 'Vejene Omkring Pisa,' " "Et Eventyr af Karen Blixen." *Analyser og Problemer* 6, pp. 286–306. Copenhagen: Gyldendal, 1950.

Capote, Truman. *Observations.* New York: Simon & Schuster, 1959.

Carlsen, Caroline. "Erindringer om Karen Blixen, fortalt til Frans Lasson," *Blixeniana 1976.* Edited by Hans Andersen and Frans Lasson. Copenhagen: Karen Blixen Selskabet, 1976.

Cate, Curtis. "Isak Dinesen: The Scheherezade of Our Times." *Cornhill,* Winter 1959–60, pp. 120–37.

———. "Isak Dinesen." *Atlantic Monthly,* December 1959, pp. 151–155.

Catterall, R.D. *A Short Textbook of Venereology: The Sexually Transmitted Diseases.* London: English Universities Press, 1974.

Claudi, Jørgen. *Contemporary Danish Authors.* Translated by Jørgen Andersen and Aubrey Rush. Copenhagen: Det Danske Selskab, 1952.

Claussen, Sophus. *Udvalgte digte.* Copenhagen: Gyldendal, 1952.

Cleeman, Annamarie. "Karen Blixen Fortæller." *Samleren* 19 (1942): 33–35.

Dahl, Ellen [Paracelsus]. *Introductioner.* Copenhagen: Reitzels, 1932

———. *Parabler.* Copenhagen: Gyldendal, 1929.

Davenport, John. "A Noble Pride: The Art of Karen Blixen." *The Twentieth Century,* March 1956, pp. 264–74.

Davidson, Basil. *A History of East and Central Africa: To the Late Nineteenth Century.* Garden City, N.Y.: Doubleday, Anchor Books, rev. ed., 1969.

———. *Let Freedom Come: Africa in Modern History.* Boston: Little Brown, 1978.

Dickson, Lovat. *H.G. Wells: His Turbulent Life and Times.* New York: Atheneum, 1969.

Dinesen, Thomas. *Boganis: Min Fader, Hans Slægt, Hans Liv og Hans Tid.* Copenhagen: Gyldendal, 1972.

———. *My Sister, Isak Dinesen.* Translated by Joan Tate. London: Michael Joseph, 1975.

———. *Tanne, Min Søster Karen Blixen.* Copenhagen: Gyldendal, 1974.

Denesen, Wilhelm. "Fra et Ophold i de Forenede Stater." *Tilskueren* (1887): 778–796.

Dinesen, Wilhelm [Boganis]. *Jagtbreve og Nye Jagtbreve.* Copenhagen: P.G. Philipsens, 1889; Spektrum, 1966.

Elling, Christian. "Karen Blixen." *Danske Digtere i det Tyvende Aarhundrede.* Edited by Ernst Frandsen and Niels Kaas Johansen, pp. 521–559. Copenhagen: Gads, 1951.

Fenichel, Otto. *The Psychoanalytic Theory of Neurosis.* New York: W.W. Norton, 1945.

Fog, Mogens. "Karen Blixens Sygdomshistorie." *Blixeniana 1978.* Edited by Hans Andersen and Frans Lasson. Copenhagen: Karen Blixen Selskabet, 1978.

Freud, Sigmund. *On Creativity and the Unconscious.* Translated by Alix Strachey. Edited by Benjamin Nelson. New York: Harper & Row, Harper Torchbook, 1958.

Hannah, Donald. *"Isak Dinesen" and Karen Blixen: The Mask and the Reality.* New York: Random House, 1971.

Hansen, Martin A. *Against the Wind.* Translated and edited by H. Wayne Schow. New York: Frederich Unger, 1979.

Hauser, Arnold. *The Social History of Art.* vols. 2–4. Translated by Stanley Godman. New York: Random House, Vintage Books, undated.

Heine, Heinrich. *Selected Works.* Translated by Helen M. Mustard, Max Knight, and Joseph Fabry. Edited by Helen M. Mustard. New York: Random House, Vintage Books, 1973.

Hemingway, Ernest. *The Snows of Kilimanjaro and Other Stories.* New York: Charles Scribner & Sons, Scribner Library, 1955.

Henriksen, Aage. *Det Guddomelige Barn og Andre Essays om Karen Blixen.* Copenhagen: Gyldendal, 1965.

Henriksen, Liselotte. *Isak Dinesen: A Bibliography.* Chicago: University of Chicago Press, 1977.

———. *Karen Blixen: en bibliografi.* Copenhagen: Gyldendal, 1975.

———. "Supplement 1978." *Blixeniana 1979,* pp. 220–230. Edited by Hans Andersen and Frans Lasson. Copenhagen: Karen Blixen Selskabet, 1979.

Huxley, Elspeth. *White Man's Country: Lord Delamere and the Making of Kenya.* 2 vols. New York: Praeger, 1968.

Jaspers, Karl. *Spinoza.* Translated by Ralph Manheim. Edited by Hannah Arendt. New York: Harcourt Brace Jovanovich, Harvest Book, 1974.

Johannesson, Eric O. *The World of Isak Dinesen.* Seattle: University of Washington Press, 1961.

Jones, W. Glynn. *Denmark.* New York: Praeger, 1970.

Juhl, Marianne, and Jørgensen, Bo Hakon. *Dianas Hævn.* Odense: Odense Universitetsforlag, 1981

Jung, Carl. *Memories, Dreams and Reflections.* Translated by Richard and Clara Winston. New York: Random House, 1963.

Kabell, Aage. *Karen Blixen debuterer.* Munich: Wilhelm Fink, 1968.

Kierkegaard, Søren. *Either/Or.* Translated by David F. Swensen and Lillian Marvin Swensen. Princeton: Princeton University Press, 1959.

Kleist, Heinrich von. "Les Marionettes." ["Uber das Marionettentheater"] Translated by Flora Klee-Palyi and Fernand Marc. Paris: Gallimard, 1947.

Kristensen, Sven Møller. "Karen Blixen og Georg Brandes." Copenhagen: *Politiken,* 17 June 1981.

Langbaum, Robert. *The Gayety of Vision: Isak Dinesen's Art.* New York: Random House, 1965.

Lasson, Frans, ed. *Karen Blixens Tegninger: Med To Essays af Karen Blixen.* Copenhagen: Forening for Boghaandværk, 1969.

Lasson, Frans, and Svendsen, Clara, eds. *The Life and Destiny of Isak Dinesen.* London: Michael Joseph, 1970.

Lindemann, Kelvin. *The Red Umbrellas.* New York: Appleton-Century-Croft, 1955.

Lytton, Noel Anthony Scawen (4th Earl). *The Stolen Desert.* London: Macdonald, 1966.

Mann, Thomas. *Dr. Faustus.* Translated by H.T. Lowe-Porter. New York: Random House, Vintage Books, 1971.

―――. *Essays of Three Decades.* Translated by H.T. Lowe-Porter. New York: Alfred A. Knopf, 1947.

Markham, Beryl. *West with the Night.* London: George Harrap, 1943.

Meyer, Michael. *Ibsen.* New York: Doubleday, 1971.

Migel, Parmenia. *Titania: The Biography of Isak Dinesen.* New York: Random House, 1967.

Miller, Charles. *Battle for the Bundu.* New York: Macmillan, 1974.

Mitchell, P.M. *A History of Danish Literature.* Copenhagen: Gyldendal, 1957.

Nietzsche, Friedrich Wilhelm. *The Birth of Tragedy and the Case of Wagner.* Translated by Walter Kaufmann. New York: Random House, Vintage Books, 1967.

―――. *On the Genealogy of Morals and Ecce Homo.* Translated by Walter Kaufmann and R.J. Hollingdale. Edited by Walter Kaufmann. New York: Random House, Vintage Books, 1969.

―――. *The Portable Nietzsche.* Edited and translated by Walter Kaufmann. New York: Random House, Vintage Books, 1954.

Petersen, Viggo Kjær. "Karen Blixen." *Danske Digtere i det Tyvende Aarhundrede.* Edited by Frederik Nielsen and Ole Restrup. vol. 2, pp. 699–734. Copenhagen: Gads, 1966.

Petrow, Richard. *The Bitter Years: The Invasion and Occupation of Denmark and Norway, April 1940–May 1945.* New York: William Morrow, 1974.

Propp, V. *Morphology of the Folktale.* 2d rev. ed. Translated by Laurence Scott. Edited by Louis A. Wagner. Austin and London: University of Texas Press, 1968.

Rasmussen, Steen Eiler. "Karen Blixens Rungstedlund." *Det Danske Akademi 1960–1967.* Copenhagen: Gads, 1967.

Rosendahl, Johannes. *Karen Blixen: Fire Foredrag.* Copenhagen: Gyldendal, 1957.

Rudhart, Alexander. *Twentieth Century Europe.* Philadelphia: J.B. Lippincott, 1975.

Rying, Bent, ed. *Denmark: An Official Handbook.* Translated by Reginald Spink. Copenhagen: Ministry of Foreign Affairs, 1974.

Schyberg, Frederik. "Syv Fantastiske Fortællinger." Copenhagen: *Berlingske Tidende.* 25 September 1935, pp. 11–12.

Stafford, Jean. "Isak Dinesen: Master Teller of Tales." *Horizon,* September 1959, pp. 111–112.

Svendsen, Clara, ed. *Isak Dinesen: A Memorial.* New York: Random House, 1965.

―――, ed. and trans. *Karen Blixen* [memorial anthology]. Copenhagen: Gyldendal, 1962.

―――. *Notater om Karen Blixen.* Copenhagen: Gyldendal, 1974.

Tales from the Thousand and One Nights, Translated by N.J. Dawood. Harmondsworth: Penguin Classics, 1955.

Trzebinski, Errol. *Silence Will Speak.* London: Heinemann, 1977.

Vowles, Richard B. "Boganis, Father of Osceola; or Wilhelm Dinesen in America, 1872–1874." *Scandinavian Studies* 48 (1976): 369–383.

Walter, Eugene. "Isak Dinesen." *Paris Review,* Autumn 1956, pp. 43–59.

Wescott, Glenway. "Isak Dinesen, the Storyteller." *Images of Truth.* New York: Harper & Row, 1962.

Westenholz, Mary Bess. "Erindringer om Mama og hendes Slægt". *Blixeniana 1979.* Edited by Hans Andersen and Frans Lasson, pp. 71–217. Copenhagen: Karen Blixen Selskabet, 1979.

Wilhelm, Prince of Sweden. "Afrikanskt Intermezzo." *Episoder.* Stockholm: Norstedt, 1951.

With, Merete Klenow. *Karen Blixen: Et Udvalg.* Copenhagen: Gyldendal, 1964.

Wivel, Ole. *Romance for Valdhorn.* Copenhagen: Gyldendal, 1972.

Index